THE NEW
AMERICAN
COMMENTARY

An Exegetical and Theological
Exposition of Holy Scripture

THE NEW AMERICAN COMMENTARY

Volume
4

DEUTERONOMY

Eugene H. Merrill

BROADMAN
& HOLMAN
PUBLISHERS

A Tribute to Donald K. Campbell

It is a pleasure, on the occasion of his retirement from long and faithful service to Dallas Theological Seminary, to honor Donald Campbell with this contribution dealing with Deuteronomy. One of the themes of the book is transition of leadership from Moses to Joshua (Deut 3:28; 31:14,23; 34:9) so it is appropriate that one who is about to pass on the mantle to his successor be recognized for his many significant achievements. It is hoped that this study will to some extent reflect the esteem and appreciation due its recipient.

Eugene H. Merrill

Editors' Preface

God's Word does not change. God's world, however, changes in every generation. These changes, in addition to new findings by scholars and a new variety of challenges to the gospel message, call for the church in each generation to interpret and apply God's Word for God's people. Thus, THE NEW AMERICAN COMMENTARY is introduced to bridge the twentieth and twenty-first centuries. This new series has been designed primarily to enable pastors, teachers, and students to read the Bible with clarity and proclaim it with power.

In one sense THE NEW AMERICAN COMMENTARY is not new, for it represents the continuation of a heritage rich in biblical and theological exposition. The title of this forty-volume set points to the continuity of this series with an important commentary project published at the end of the nineteenth century called AN AMERICAN COMMENTARY, edited by Alvah Hovey. The older series included, among other significant contributions, the outstanding volume on Matthew by John A. Broadus, from whom the publisher of the new series, Broadman Press, partly derives its name. The former series was authored and edited by scholars committed to the infallibility of Scripture, making it a solid foundation for the present project. In line with this heritage, all NAC authors affirm the divine inspiration, inerrancy, complete truthfulness, and full authority of the Bible. The perspective of the NAC is unapologetically confessional and rooted in the evangelical tradition.

Since a commentary is a fundamental tool for the expositor or teacher who seeks to interpret and apply Scripture in the church or classroom, the NAC focuses on communicating the theological structure and content of each biblical book. The writers seek to illuminate both the historical meaning and contemporary significance of Holy Scripture.

In its attempt to make a unique contribution to the Christian community, the NAC focuses on two concerns. First, the commentary emphasizes how each section of a book fits together so that the reader becomes aware of the theological unity of each book and of Scripture as a whole. The writers, however, remain aware of the Bible's inherently rich variety. Second, the NAC is produced with the conviction that the Bible primarily belongs to the church. We believe that scholarship and the academy provide an indispensable foundation for biblical understanding and the service of Christ, but the editors and authors of this series have attempted to communicate the findings of their research in a manner that will build up the whole body of Christ. Thus, the commentary concentrates on theological exegesis while providing practical, applicable exposition.

THE NEW AMERICAN COMMENTARY's theological focus enables the reader to see the parts as well as the whole of Scripture. The biblical books vary in content, context, literary type, and style. In addition to this rich variety, the editors and authors recognize that the doctrinal emphasis and use of the biblical books differs in various places, contexts, and cultures among God's people. These factors, as well as other concerns, have led the editors to give freedom to the writers to wrestle with the issues raised by the scholarly community surrounding each book and to determine the appropriate shape and length of the introductory materials. Moreover, each writer has developed the structure of the commentary in a way best suited for expounding the basic structure and the meaning of the biblical books for our day. Generally, discussions relating to contemporary scholarship and technical points of grammar and syntax appear in the footnotes and not in the text of the commentary. This format allows pastors and interested laypersons, scholars and teachers, and serious college and seminary students to profit from the commentary at various levels. This approach has been employed because we believe that all Christians have the privilege and responsibility to read and seek to understand the Bible for themselves.

Consistent with the desire to produce a readable, up-to-date commentary, the editors selected the *New International Version* as the standard translation for the commentary series. The selection was made primarily because of the NIV's faithfulness to the original languages and its beautiful and readable style. The authors, however, have been given the liberty to differ at places from the NIV as they develop their own translations from the Greek and Hebrew texts.

The NAC reflects the vision and leadership of those who provide oversight for Broadman Press, who in 1987 called for a new commentary series that would evidence a commitment to the inerrancy of Scripture and a faithfulness to the classic Christian tradition. While the commentary adopts an "American" name, it should be noted some writers represent countries outside the United States, giving the commentary an international perspective. The diverse group of writers includes scholars, teachers, and administrators from almost twenty different colleges and seminaries, as well as pastors, missionaries, and a layperson.

The editors and writers hope that THE NEW AMERICAN COMMEN-

TARY will be helpful and instructive for pastors and teachers, scholars and students, for men and women in the churches who study and teach God's Word in various settings. We trust that for editors, authors, and readers alike, the commentary will be used to build up the church, encourage obedience, and bring renewal to God's people. Above all, we pray that the NAC will bring glory and honor to our Lord who has graciously redeemed us and faithfully revealed himself to us in his Holy Word.

SOLI DEO GLORIA
The Editors

Author's Preface

Many Bible scholars consider Deuteronomy to be at the heart of the Old Testament theological witness, an opinion clearly supported by our Lord Jesus Christ himself, who quoted its texts on many occasions. Though I have often suspected this judgment to be true through many years of teaching the book, the reality of the matter has been driven home in a fresh and altogether convincing manner by the opportunity to dig deep into the truth of Deuteronomy and to marvel at its riches. How rewarding the experience has been and how much incumbent it is upon me to offer my gratitude to individuals whom God has used to provide me the wherewithal to begin, pursue, and complete this wonderful adventure.

First, I stand in great debt to Broadman & Holman Publishers for the invitation to come on board in the first place. The particular persons involved are too numerous to name, but long years of friendship and mutual counsel compel me to single out Ray Clendenen, the General Editor of the NAC.

No one is more responsible for the success of the project than my secretary, Mrs. Chris Wakitsch. She did all the word processing, learning en route how to decipher the lines and arrows and abbreviations which are an aggravating characteristic of my computer-illiterate approach to writing. Her patience and humor never flagged, and her constant encouragement kept things going when they might otherwise have ground to a halt.

Finally, I must again, as always, thank my wife, Janet, who, as a scholar herself, is uniquely able to empathize and provide advice and counsel when things seem most impossible.

Eugene H. Merrill
Dallas, Texas

Abbreviations

Bible Books

Gen	Isa	Luke
Exod	Jer	John
Lev	Lam	Acts
Num	Ezek	Rom
Deut	Dan	1,2 Cor
Josh	Hos	Gal
Judg	Joel	Eph
Ruth	Amos	Phil
1,2 Sam	Obad	Col
1,2 Kgs	Jonah	1,2 Thess
1,2 Chr	Mic	1,2 Tim
Ezra	Nah	Titus
Neh	Hab	Phlm
Esth	Zeph	Heb
Job	Hag	Jas
Ps (pl. Pss)	Zech	1,2, Pet
Prov	Mal	1,2,3 John
Eccl	Matt	Jude
Song	Mark	Rev

Commonly Used Sources

AASOR	Annual of the American Schools of Oriental Research
AB	Anchor Bible
ABD	*Anchor Bible Dictionary*
ABW	*Archaeology and the Biblical World*
AC	An American Commentary, ed. A. Hovey
AcOr	*Acta orientalia*
AEL	M. Lichtheim, *Ancient Egyptian Literature*
AJSL	*American Journal of Semitic Languages and Literature*
Akk	Akkadian
AnBib	Analecta Biblica
ANET	J. B. Pritchard, ed., *Ancient Near Eastern Texts*
AOAT	Alter Orient und Altes Testament

AOTS	*Archaeology and Old Testament Study,* ed. D. W. Thomas
ArOr	Archiv orientální
ATD	Das Alte Testament Deutsch
ATR	*Anglican Theological Review*
AusBR	*Australian Biblical Review*
BA	*Biblical Archaeologist*
BAGD	W. Bauer, W. F. Arndt, F. W. Gingrich, and F. W. Danker, *Greek-English Lexicon of the New Testament*
BARev	*Biblical Archaeology Review*
BASOR	*Bulletin of the American Schools of Oriental Research*
BDB	F. Brown, S. R. Driver, and C. A. Briggs, *Hebrew and English Lexicon of the Old Testament*
BETL	Bibliotheca ephemeridum theologicarum lovaniensium
BFT	Biblical Foundations in Theology
BHS	*Biblia hebraica stuttgartensia*
Bib	*Biblica*
BKAT	Biblischer Kommentar: Altes Testament
BO	*Bibliotheca orientalis*
BSac	*Bibliotheca Sacra*
BSC	Bible Study Commentary
BT	*Bible Translator*
BurH	*Buried History*
BZ	*Biblische Zeitschrift*
BZAW	Beihefte zur ZAW
CAD	*The Assyrian Dictionary of the Oriental Institute of the University of Chicago*
CAH	*Cambridge Ancient History*
CBSC	Cambridge Bible for Schools and Colleges
CBC	Cambridge Bible Commentary
CBQ	*Catholic Biblical Quarterly*
CHAL	*Concise Hebrew and Aramaic Lexicon,* ed. W. L. Holladay
CTR	*Criswell Theological Review*
DOTT	*Documents from Old Testament Times,* ed. D. W. Thomas
DSS	Dead Sea Scrolls
EBC	Expositor's Bible Commentary
Ebib	Etudes bibliques
ETL	*Ephermerides theologicae lovanienses*
FB	Forschung zur Bibel
FOTL	Forms of Old Testament Literature

GKC	Gesenius' Hebrew Grammar, ed. E. Kautzsch, tr. A. E. Cowley
GTJ	*Grace Theological Journal*
HAR	Hebrew Annual Review
HAT	Handbuch zum Alten Testament
HBT	*Horizons in Biblical Theology*
HDR	Harvard Dissertations in Religion
Her	Hermeneia
HKAT	Handkommentar zum Alten Testament
HSM	Harvard Semitic Monographs
HT	Helps for Translators
HTR	*Harvard Theological Review*
HUCA	*Hebrew Union College Annual*
IB	*Interpreter's Bible*
IBC	Interpretation: A Bible Commentary for Teaching and Preaching
ICC	International Critical Commentary
IDB	*Interpreter's Dictionary of the Bible,* ed. G. A. Buttrick, et al.
IDBSup	IDB Supplementary Volume
IBHS	B. K. Waltke and M. O'Connor, *Introduction to Biblical Hebrew Syntax*
IEJ	*Israel Exploration Journal*
IES	Israel Exploration Society
Int	*Interpretation*
ITC	International Theological Commentary
IOS	*Israel Oriental Society*
ISBE	*International Standard Bible Encyclopedia,* rev. ed. G. W. Bromiley
IJT	*Indian Journal of Theology*
ITC	International Theological Commentary
JANES	*Journal of Ancient Near Eastern Society*
JAOS	*Journal of the American Oriental Society*
JBL	*Journal of Biblical Literature*
JBR	*Journal of Bible and Religion*
JCS	*Journal of Cuneiform Studies*
JEA	*Journal of Egyptian Archaeology*
JETS	*Journal of the Evangelical Theological Society*
JJS	*Journal of Jewish Studies*
JNES	*Journal of Near Eastern Studies*
JNSL	*Journal of Northwest Semitic Languages*
JPOS	*Journal of Palestine Oriental Society*

JSJ	*Journal for the Study of Judaism in the Persian, Hellenistic, and Roman Period*
JSOR	*Journal of the Society for Oriental Research*
JSOT	*Journal for the Study of the Old Testament*
JSOTSup	JSOT—Supplement Series
JSS	*Journal of Semitic Studies*
JTS	*Journal of Theological Studies*
JTSNS	*Journal of Theological Studies, New Series*
KAT	Kommentar zum Alten Testament
KB	Koehler and W. Baumgartner, *Lexicon in Veteris Testamenti libros*
LCC	Library of Christian Classics
LLAVT	*Lexicon Linguae Aramaicae Veteris Testamenti*
LTQ	*Lexington Theological Quarterly*
MT	Masoretic Text
NAC	New American Commentary
NCBC	New Century Bible Commentary
NICOT	New International Commentary on the Old Testament
NJPS	New Jewish Publication Society Version
NKZ	*Neue kirchliche Zeitschrift*
NovT	*Novum Testamentum*
NTS	*New Testament Studies*
Or	*Orientalia*
OTL	Old Testament Library
OTS	*Oudtestamentische Studiën*
OTWSA	*Ou-Testamentiese Werkgemeenskap in Suid-Afrika*
PCB	*Peake's Commentary on the Bible*, ed. M. Black and H. H. Rowley
PEQ	*Palestine Exploration Quarterly*
POTT	*Peoples of Old Testament Times*, ed. D. J. Wiseman
RA	Revue d'assyriologie et d'archéologie orientale
RB	*Revue biblique*
ResQ	*Restoration Quarterly*
RevExp	*Review and Expositor*
RSR	Recherches de science religieuse
SANE	Sources from the Ancient Near East
SBLDS	Society of Biblical Literature Dissertation Series
SBT	Studies in Biblical Theology
SJT	*Scottish Journal of Theology*
SP	Samaritan Pentateuch
SR	Studies in Religion/Sciences religieuses
ST	*Studia theologica*

STJD	Studies on the Texts of the Desert of Judah
Syr	Syriac
TDOT	*Theological Dictionary of the Old Testament,* ed. G. J. Botterweck and H. Ringgren
Tg	Targum
TrinJ	*Trinity Journal*
TLZ	*Theologische Literaturzeitung*
TOTC	Tyndale Old Testament Commentaries
TS	*Theological Studies*
TWAT	Theologisches Wörterbuch zum Alten Testament, ed. G. J. Botterweck and H. Ringgren
TWOT	Theological Workbook of the Old Testament
TynBul	*Tyndale Bulletin*
UF	*Ugarit-Forschungen*
Vg	Vulgate
VT	*Vetus Testamentum*
VTSup	Vetus Testamentum, Supplements
WBC	Word Biblical Commentaries
WEC	Wycliffe Exegetical Commentary
WTJ	*Westminster Theological Journal*
WMANT	Wissenschaftliche Monographien zum Alten und Neuen Testament
ZAW	*Zeitschrift für die alttestamentliche Wissenschaft*
ZDMG	*Zeitschrift der deutschen morgenländischen Gesellschaft*
ZDPV	*Zeitschrift des deutschen Palätina-Vereing*
ZTK	*Zeitschrift für katholische Theologie*

Contents

Deuteronomy

INTRODUCTION

1. Title of the Book

In line with ancient and well-attested practice with respect to the other books of the Pentateuch, the title of the Book of Deuteronomy in the Hebrew canon derives from the first word or two of the composition itself, in this case *ʾēlleh haddĕbārîm*, "these are the words" (Deut 1:1).[1] The term "Deuteronomy" in the English versions (and its equivalents in the various modern languages) thus has nothing to do with the Hebrew title. Rather, it is based on the Latin Vulgate *Deuteronomium,* which in turn reflects the Septuagint (LXX) *Deuteronomion,* "second law." This ancient version, which understood the book as essentially a repetition of Exodus, drew

---

[1] S. R. Driver, *A Critical and Exegetical Commentary on Deuteronomy*, ICC (Edinburgh: T & T Clark, 1902), i.

upon Deut 17:18 (*mišneh hattôrâ hazzôt,* "a copy of this instruction") as an expression of the real essence or nature of the document.[2] Unfortunately this notion of Deuteronomy as merely a copy or restatement of Exodus has led to a failure in many circles to appreciate the singular uniqueness and importance of the book. Deuteronomy, as will be demonstrated hereafter, is not a second law but an amplification and advancement of the covenant text first articulated to Moses and Israel at Sinai nearly forty years earlier.

2. Date and Authorship of the Book

Precritical Jewish and Christian tradition nearly unanimously attributed Deuteronomy to Moses, at least in its basic substance, though there were always dissenters who argued for post-Mosaic interpolations and additions such as the account of the great lawgiver's own death (Deut 34:5-12).[3] These issues will all be addressed at the appropriate place in the commentary. The Mosaic authorship tradition finds its initial articulation in Deuteronomy itself, for after the "title" the text goes on to say *ʾašer dibber mōšeh,* literally, "which Moses spoke," a statement that attributes the immediately following passage and, by implication, the entire work to Moses. Beginning with Joshua (Josh 1:7-8), the attribution to Moses continues throughout the Old Testament (e.g., Judg 1:20; 3:4; 1 Kgs 2:3; 2 Kgs 14:6; 2 Chr 25:4; Ezra 3:2) and also the New Testament (Matt 19:7; Mark 12:19; Luke 20:28; Acts 3:22; Rom 10:19; 1 Cor 9:9). There can be no doubt that the prophets, Jesus, and the apostles concurred with the witness of Deuteronomy about its authorship. Departures from this tradition will receive attention in due course.[4]

Authorship by Moses presupposes certain chronological parameters that must also be addressed. First, Deuteronomy itself claims to have originated in the "land of Moab" (Deut 1:5) at the end of the wilderness journey and on the eve of the conquest of Canaan (Deut 4:44-49; 34:1-4). Second, this completion of the itinerary occurred precisely forty years after the exodus according to the biblical witness (Deut 2:7,14; Josh 5:6; cf. Num 14:33-34). This reduces the matter of the date of Deuteronomy to a consideration of the date of the exodus itself, a problem that can be addressed only briefly at this point.[5]

---

[2] R. K. Harrison, *Introduction to the Old Testament* (Grand Rapids: Eerdmans, 1969), 635.

[3] See, e.g., the reservations of Baruch (Benedict) de Spinoza at this point in his *Tractatus Theologico-Politicus,* trans. R. H. M. Elwes (London: George Routledge & Sons, n.d.), 121-24, 128-32.

[4] See D. L. Christensen and M. Narucki, "The Mosaic Authorship of the Pentateuch," *JETS* 32 (1989): 465-71.

[5] For a full discussion see E. H. Merrill, *Kingdom of Priests: A History of Old Testament Israel* (Grand Rapids: Baker, 1987), 66-75.

As is well known, the Masoretic tradition dates the founding of Solomon's temple to his fourth year (1 Kgs 6:1), that year being, according to the best chronological reconstruction, 967/966 B.C. The fixed date with which this achievement is associated is the exodus, which the historian located 480 years earlier. The exodus then must be assigned to the year 1447/1446. It follows that the wilderness era ended in 1407/1406 and that the Book of Deuteronomy must have taken shape at the same time. The communiqué of Jephthah the judge to the Ammonites bolsters this view of events, for according to it the Israelites of the Transjordan had been there for three hundred years, that is, from the time of the beginning of the conquest until Jephthah's own day (Judg 11:26). Since the judgeship of Jephthah can be determined with reasonably good precision as having fallen in the last decade of the twelfth century (ca. 1106–1100), Jephthah's data clearly agree with those of 1 Kings. In short, the only biblical texts that directly attest to the dates of the exodus and conquest converge on 1447/ 1446 and 1407/1406 respectively, thus offering prima facie evidence for the date 1400 or so for the composition of Deuteronomy. Even if one were to grant the dates of a "late" exodus and conquest (ca. 1275–1235), Mosaic authorship is unaffected, for the Mosaic chronology could itself, of course, be lowered accordingly. In fact, as will be demonstrated below, a thirteenth-century background would be all the more compatible with the comparison of Deuteronomy to Hittite suzerain-vassal treaty texts (a matter of supreme importance in understanding Deuteronomy's full implications), for these secular texts find their florescence in a period slightly later than 1400. Despite this, the traditional early date will be followed here and will prove to be consistent with all other aspects of the problem.

3. Historical Background

On the assumption of Mosaic authorship of Deuteronomy and in support of the "early" (that is, 1400 B.C.) date of its composition, it is important to give careful attention to the Late Bronze Age (ca. 1550–1200 B.C.) Eastern Mediterranean world that provided the milieu presupposed in the book.[6] Egypt especially is central to the discussion inasmuch as the bibli-

---

[6] See for an overview T. G. H. James, "Egypt: From the Expulsion of the Hyksos to Amenophis I," *CAH,* ed. I. E. S. Edwards et al. (Cambridge: Cambridge University Press, 1973), II/1, 289-312; W. C. Hayes, "Egypt: Internal Affairs from Tuthmosis I to the Death of Amenophis III," *CAH* II/1, 313-416; K. Kenyon, "Palestine in the Time of the Eighteenth Dynasty," *CAH* II/1, 526-56; R. de Vaux, *The Early History of Israel* (Philadelphia: Westminster, 1978), 82-123, 321-472.

cal tradition links Deuteronomy to Israel's sojourn in and emergence from Egypt under the leadership of Moses.

According to Exod 12:40 Israel had resided in Egypt for a period of 430 years, a sojourn that had commenced with the descent of Jacob and his family (Gen 46). Given a 1446 date for the exodus, the beginning of the sojourn would have been approximately 1776 B.C. After a period of favorable treatment by the rulers of the Twelfth Egyptian Dynasty, a time in which Joseph was elevated to a position high in Egyptian government, the Israelites fell under the control of the Semitic Hyksos invaders who occupied all of Lower Egypt, especially the eastern delta region, from ca. 1730 to 1580 B.C. The Old Testament is silent about this era, but Hyksos-Hebrew relationships likely remained peaceful and mutually advantageous particularly in light of their common Semitic culture.[7]

All this changed abruptly with the expulsion of the Hyksos from Egypt by Amosis, founder of the Southern Dynasty Eighteen, under the leadership of his commander Ahmose. The hatred for the Hyksos by this new native Egyptian regime probably impacted the Hebrews as well, for though there is no indication they collaborated with the Hyksos in their domination of Egypt, their ethnic affinity would have been sufficient to bring them into the disfavor of the resurgent Egyptians, a condition hinted at in the cryptic statement that "a new king, who did not know Joseph, came to power in Egypt" (Exod 1:8). This possibly was Amosis himself, who ruled from 1570 to 1546, though it could also have been his son and successor Amenhotep I (1546–1526).

There can be little doubt that Amenhotep I was responsible for the edict authorizing the death of all Hebrew male newborns since it apparently did not apply to Aaron, Moses' elder brother, but was in effect by the time Moses was born three years later. A consistent reconstruction of the biblical chronology places Moses' birth at 1526 B.C., just about the same year as the commonly accepted accession date of Amenhotep.[8] Thus Moses appeared at precisely the time when the need for divine deliverance first became most apparent.

When at age forty Moses was forced to flee Egypt and find refuge in Midian, the throne of Egypt was occupied by Thutmose III (1504–1450), the mightiest of the rulers of Dynasty Eighteen. Leader of at least seventeen major military campaigns into Palestine alone, Thutmose greatly enlarged Egypt's sphere of influence. He also continued and even intensi-

---

[7] For the Hyksos see J. Van Seters, *The Hyksos: A New Investigation* (New Haven: Yale University Press, 1966).

[8] See Merrill, *Kingdom of Priests,* 59.

fied Egyptian oppression of the Hebrews who, under his administration, were reduced to slaves laboring under onerous and inescapable bondage (Exod 2:23-24).

At last Thutmose died, allowing Moses, who had fled from him in the first place (Exod 4:19), to return to Egypt in order to begin the process of exodus deliverance. Amenhotep II, who had coreigned with his father Thutmose for about six years,[9] was now Pharaoh and, indeed, was the ruler who experienced the plagues, including the death of his own firstborn son (Exod 11:5; 12:29), and who witnessed the miraculous escape of the Hebrew slaves from his kingdom.

Amenhotep, presumably weakened and demoralized by this turn of events, made no attempt to pursue the Israelite hosts after they had crossed the Red Sea and, in fact, never again conducted a major incursion into the Sinai or central Palestine. His son and successor Thutmose IV (1425–1417) also attested no significant penetration to the north and east nor did even Amenhotep III (1417–1379), under whom Egypt rose again to strength and prominence on the international scene. Clearly it was this lack of Egyptian involvement in Palestinian affairs, particularly in central Palestine, that allowed Joshua and the Israelites to enter, conquer, and largely occupy the Palestinian hill country by the end of the reign of Amenhotep III's son Amenhotep IV (or Ikhnaton, 1379–1362).[10]

According to a face-value chronology, the composition of Deuteronomy forty years after the exodus locates it during the reign of Amenhotep III. As just noted, Egypt under this powerful ruler was strangely absent from Palestine and the Transjordan, thus allowing Moses and Israel relief from any threat from that quarter. The Bible does attest to Edomite, Moabite, and Ammonite opposition, however, but is unequivocal in its testimony to Israel's complete conquest and domination of these peoples who, presumably, still existed primarily in a nomadic or seminomadic manner of life. Archaeological evidence thus far seems to suggest this, and the Old Testament narrative does not demand otherwise.[11]

As for other foes or potential foes, only the Canaanites, Amorites, and related peoples of Palestine posed any problem to Israel. The Assyrians had not yet become an international force; the Kassites, who had overcome and replaced the Babylonians in central and lower Mesopotamia, appar-

---

[9] W. J. Murnane, "Once Again the Dates for Tuthmosis III and Amenhotep II," *JANES* 3/1 (1970-71): 5.

[10] B. G. Wood, "Did the Israelites Conquer Jericho? A New Look at the Archaeological Evidence," *BAR* 16:2 (1990): 51.

[11] G. L. Mattingly, "The Exodus-Conquest and the Archaeology of Transjordan: New Light on an Old Problem," *GTJ* 4/2 (1983): 245-62.

ently had little interest in the west; and the Hittites and Mitanni were stalemated by each other and by a newly emerging and increasingly powerful Egypt. Thus the indigenous populations of Palestine alone remained to threaten Israel and stand in the way of conquest and, as it turned out, were not up to the task.

The picture that emerges, then, is that of a liberated slave people poised in the plains of Moab to launch an attack across the Jordan River in response to the purpose and command of the Lord their God to enter and occupy the land of promise. God, Creator of all things and Sovereign of history, had prepared the way in every respect for this transition. The great nations were stymied, thus creating a power vacuum in Palestine that the tiny city states that lived there could not hope to fill.

4. Occasion of the Book

The historical situation just described contributes to the question of the occasion for the Book of Deuteronomy. It (and most likely much of the rest of the Pentateuch as well) was written by Moses on the eve of the conquest of Canaan as a means of addressing a number of questions and concerns. First, it was important that the people understand who they were, where they originated, and what their God intended for them in the years to come. Genesis enabled them to trace their roots back to the patriarchs and to the patriarchal covenant that promised a people and a land. Exodus rehearsed the story of the growth of that people, their redemption from cruel and despotic bondage, and their covenant affiliation with the Lord who called and equipped them to be a kingdom of priests and a holy nation (Exod 19:4-6). That book together with Leviticus outlined the means by which the nation might have access to a holy God and how it must function as a holy people in fulfilling the covenant requirements. Numbers provides instruction for the people in movement from covenant to conquest. Finally, Deuteronomy reiterates the covenant, but it does so in a greatly expanded form and in terms appropriate to a new generation, one about to enter a new life experience and to engage in a new realm of responsibility. The Sinai generation of thirty-eight years earlier was largely off the scene; and the new generation, about to embark on conquest, stood in need of covenant reiteration and reaffirmation, a procedure in line with covenant relationships attested to throughout the ancient Near Eastern world.[12] A covenant made between

---

[12] K. A. Kitchen, "Ancient Orient, 'Deuteronomism,' and the Old Testament," in *New Perspectives on the Old Testament,* ed. J. B. Payne (Waco: Word, 1970), 3-13.

a great king (a term used in Hittite treaties) and a vassal people had to be renewed by his and their successors with the passing of the generations.

Second, Moses was about to die, so it was essential that he commit to writing the whole collection of tradition and truth that he understood to be the very revelation of God. This was especially urgent in the case of Deuteronomy, for that composition would serve as the corpus of law and practice for the covenant community from that day forward.[13] For Moses to hand on to Joshua the mediatorship of the covenant necessitated the transmission of the covenant text itself. That this was precisely how both Moses and Joshua understood the matter is clear from Moses' injunctions to the Levitical priests concerning the reading of the law (i.e., Deuteronomy) in years to come (Deut 31:9-13) and his insistence that they carry it with the ark into the land of promise (Deut 31:24-26). Joshua was confirmed in his mediatorial role by direct revelation and was told explicitly that he personally must be "careful to obey all the law my servant Moses gave you" (Josh 1:7), an indisputable reference to Moses' writings and most likely to Deuteronomy especially. In other words, covenant leadership must presuppose and be accompanied by covenant transmission, hence the need for a full and final statement of covenant requirement prior to Moses' death and Joshua's succession.

5. Structure, Literary Forms, and Literary Characteristics of the Book

Traditional analyses of Deuteronomy tend to view it as an address or collection of addresses delivered by Moses to a representative gathering of his Israelite compatriots, the whole of which was then put to pen and ink. Thus the book is viewed as more or less homiletical in style with a strong hortatory or parenetic flavor.

---

[13] The matter of the relationship of law and covenant will not be addressed here except to say that the law code(s) of Deuteronomy are, in effect, the stipulation sections of the covenant document. As such they will receive attention as they appear in the exposition of the book. For now see W. Eichrodt, "Covenant and Law," *Int* 20 (1966): 302-21; cf. A. Alt, "The Origins of Israelite Law," in *Essays on Old Testament History and Religion* (Garden City: Doubleday, 1968), 101-71; G. Braulik, *Die deuteronomischen Gesetz und der Dekalog* (Stuttgart: Katholisches Bibelwerk, 1991); C. C. Carmichael, *Law and Narrative in the Bible* (Ithaca, N.Y.: Cornell University, 1985); A. Cholewinski, *Heiligkeitsgesetz und Deuteronomium*, AnBib 66 (Rome: Biblical Institute Press, 1976); H. W. Gilmer, *The If-You Form in Israelite Law* (Missoula, Mont.: Scholars Press, 1975); R. P. Merendino, *Das deuteronomische Gesetz* (Bonn: P. Hanstein, 1969); G. J. Wenham, "Legal Forms in the Book of the Covenant," *TynBul* 22 (1971): 95-102.

A typical earlier approach to the nature and structure of Deuteronomy is that of S. R. Driver, who in the 1902 edition of his *International Critical Commentary* states that "the book consists chiefly of three discourses, purporting to have been delivered by Moses in the 'Steppes' (34:1) of Moab, setting forth the laws which the Israelites are to obey and the spirit in which they are to obey them, when they are settled in the land of promise."[14] These discourses he identifies as (1) the introductory discourse (1:6–4:40), (2) the exposition of the law (5:1–26:19; 27; 28), and (3) the third discourse, which serves as a supplement (29:1–30:20). The remainder of the book consists of various introductions (1:1-5; 4:44-49), conclusions (31:1-8; 32:48–34:12), and other matters, many of which appear not to be integral to the overall structure.

It is remarkable perhaps that Driver's analysis anticipates and largely conforms to the organizational pattern of Deuteronomy that more recent study of ancient Near Eastern suzerain-vassal treaty texts reveals. For example, he observes that chaps. 5–26 and 28 must be subdivided into chaps. 5–11 and 12–26; 28. He even refers to the respective sections as (1) a development of the first commandment of the Decalogue and a set of general theocratic principles and (2) the code of special laws "which it is the object of the legislator to 'expound' and encourage Israel to obey."[15] This distinction between general and specific stipulations is very much in line with modern analyses based on covenant comparisons.

These comparisons were first set forth in a detailed and comprehensive way by G. E. Mendenhall.[16] Building on the publication and study of Late Bronze Age treaty documents found at *Hattušaš* (or Boghazkeüi, its modern name), the capital of the New Hittite Empire, Mendenhall demonstrated that Deuteronomy (and Exod 20–23, the so-called "Book of the Covenant") contained all the essential elements of these Hittite treaty texts and in precisely the same order. He therefore concluded that the author(s) or redactor(s) of Deuteronomy must have patterned their work after the Hittite model. With this judgment a whole host of scholars have concurred, especially those of a conservative persuasion,[17] though obviously others

---

[14] Driver, *Deuteronomy,* i.

[15] Ibid., ii.

[16] G. E. Mendenhall, "Covenant Forms in Israelite Tradition," *BA* 17 (1954): 50-76; now reprinted in *Law and Covenant in Israel and the Ancient Near East* (Pittsburgh: Biblical Colloquium, 1955), 24-50. His work was based on the earlier studies of V. Korošec, *Hethitische Staatsverträge* (Leipzig: J. C. Hinrichs'sche, 1931).

[17] See especially K. A. Kitchen, *Ancient Orient and Old Testament* (London: Tyndale, 1966), 90-102; id., *The Bible in Its World* (Downers Grove: InterVarsity, 1978), 79-85; M. G.

challenged the comparisons from the beginning and continue to do so.[18] The current state of the debate will receive attention below.

The implications of these comparative studies are, of course, extremely profound. For example, if one can show that Deuteronomy is patterned after late Hittite exemplars, its date presumptively must be early (no later than 1300 or so) and its Mosaic authorship more assured. But for now it is important to see how the very literary structure and form of the book, in light of these clearly attestable similarities, yields insight into its function, purpose, and meaning.

Granting the remarkable parallels suggested thus far, it is still important to point out that Deuteronomy is more than a mere formal covenant text. For one thing it is much longer than any extant documents of that kind. For another it still presents itself as a farewell address by Moses, the covenant mediator, one filled with nonlegal passages such as itineraries, pareneses, and hymns and other poetic material.[19] In other words, Deuteronomy is of mixed and varied genre. But all this does not invalidate understanding the essential core of the composition as being covenant in style and purpose. It is covenant expressed in narrative and exhortation, the whole thing together comprising a farewell address.

More than forty years of scholarship has reached a near consensus about

---

Kline, *Treaty of the Great King* (Grand Rapids: Eerdmans, 1963); id., *The Structure of Biblical Authority* (Grand Rapids: Eerdmans, 1972); J. A. Thompson, *The Ancient Near Eastern Treaties and the Old Testament* (London: Tyndale, 1964); G. J. Wenham, *The Structure and Date of Deuteronomy* (Ph.D. diss., University of London, 1969), 182-216.

[18] K. Baltzer, *The Covenant Formulary in Old Testament, Jewish, and Early Christian Writings* (Philadelphia: Fortress, 1970); R. Frankena, "The Vassal-Treaties of Esarhaddon and the Dating of Deuteronomy," *OTS* 14 (1965): 122-54; D. R. Hillers, *Covenant: The History of a Biblical Idea* (Baltimore: Johns Hopkins, 1969); D. J. McCarthy, *Treaty and Covenant*, AnBib 21 (Rome: Pontifical Biblical Institute, 1963); ibid., *Old Testament Covenant* (Atlanta: John Knox, 1972); R. Smend, *Die Bundesformel*, TS 68 (Zürich: EVZ, 1963); M. Weinfeld, *Deuteronomy and the Deuteronomic School* (Oxford: Clarendon, 1972).

[19] For literary and form-critical analyses see the following examples of a vast literature: G. Braulik, *Die Mittel deuteronomischer Rhetorik* (Rome: Biblical Institute Press, 1978); D. L. Christensen, "Form and Structure in Deuteronomy 1–11," in *Das Deuteronomium*, ed. N. Lohfink (Leuven: University Press, 1985), 135-44; F. Garcia-Lopez, "Analyse Littéraire de Deutéronome, 5-11," *RB* 84 (1977): 481-522; *RB* 85 (1978): 5-49; J. L'Hour, "Formes littéraires, structure et unité de Deutéronome," *Bib* 45 (1964): 551-55; N. Lohfink, *Das Hauptgebot*, AnBib 20 (Roma: Pontificio Instituto Biblico, 1963); A. D. H. Mayes, "Deuteronomy 4 and the Literary Criticism of Deuteronomy," *JBL* 100 (1981): 23-51; S. Mittmann, *Deuteronomium 1:1–6:3*, BZAW 139 (Berlin: de Gruyter, 1975); B. Peckham, "The Composition of Deuteronomy 5–11," in *The Word of the Lord Shall Go Forth*, ed. C. Meyers and M. O'Connor, *BASOR* Special Volume Series 1 (Winona Lake, Ind.: Eisenbrauns, 1983), 217-40; J. Plöger, *Literarkritische, formgeschichtliche und stilkritische Untersuchungen zum Deuteronomium* (Bonn: Peter Hanstein, 1967).

the essential elements of standard Hittite treaty texts. These consist of (1) preamble, (2) historical prologue, (3) general stipulations, (4) specific stipulations, (5) blessings and curses, and (6) witnesses.[20] These are all represented to some degree or other in Deuteronomy, but Deuteronomy, as has been suggested already, expands upon these by adding unique covenant elements such as covenant recapitulation and other material of a hortatory or narrative nature. When examined from this perspective, the structure of the book may be analyzed as follows:

1. *The preamble (1:1-5).* The purpose here is to introduce matters of setting and occasion. Since it is important to show that the covenant text to follow is one originated by the Great King himself (i.e., Yahweh) and that it is being mediated by a divinely appointed mediator-spokesman (i.e., Moses), this information is carefully spelled out.

2. *The historical prologue (1:6–4:40).* The right of the Great King to assert his hegemony over his vassals is often based on their past relationships. Perhaps he or an ancestor had conquered them or had delivered them from the oppression of a third party. There may have been instances of special protection or other favor extended by the Great King, benefits that certainly ought to elicit loyalty and gratitude from his people. It might even be that the relationship had been stormy and that the present covenant was being imposed in order to prevent thought of rebellion or other insubordinate or recalcitrant behavior. The historical résumé here in Deuteronomy consists primarily of a retracing of Israel's journey from Sinai to the plains of Moab, a narrative account punctuated by instances of Israel's rebellion (1:26-28,32; 3:26) and God's retribution (1:34-40,45; 2:14-15; 4:3). The entire section is designed to show that the Lord had a claim on his people and despite their disobedience had brought them to the present time and place so that he might reaffirm his covenant commitment to them.

3. *The general stipulations (5:1–11:32).* This section spells out the principles of the relationship between the parties to the covenant. It clarifies who the Great King is, what he has done for those whom he has chosen for covenant fellowship, what he will do for the years to come, and how they are to respond. As for Deuteronomy, the essence of the relationship is intimated in the so-called Shema of 6:4-5: "Hear, O Israel: The LORD our God, the LORD is one. Love the LORD your God with all your heart and with all your soul and with all your strength." Who the Lord is is further amplified in the first four commandments of the Decalogue (Deut 5:6-15), and how the love of Israel is to be expressed is outlined in the remaining six (5:16-21). The general stipulation section as a whole focuses on these

---

[20] Mendenhall, "Covenant Forms in Israelite Tradition," 58-60.

two poles, the kingship of Yahweh and the appropriate response of his people Israel.

4. *The specific stipulations (12:1–26:15)*.   Next follows a continuing enlargement of the covenant regulations outlined in the form of apodictic laws (see discussion on p. 144). One might view the development in terms of concentricity in which the Shema forms the focal point, the Decalogue a specific categorizing of the principles of the Shema, the remainder of the general stipulation section as a narrative and parenetic comment on the Decalogue, and the specific stipulation section as the application of the principles to every aspect of life, that is, as case law rooted and grounded in the covenant relationship.

Prior to the development of recent study that links Deuteronomy with treaty form and function, scholars were at a loss to account for the structure of the book as a whole and particularly the arrangement of the laws in this very section. To most they seemed random, without internal coherence and without clear linkage to the rest of the book.[21] A number of recent scholars have argued that Deut 12:1–26:15 is a statement of specific stipulation (a point already noted by scholars such as Driver) and, moreover, that its arrangement is not haphazard but deliberate and discernible. This point has been compellingly made by S. Kaufman particularly, who has shown that the key to the order of the section lies in the Decalogue itself. That is, the specific stipulations are elaborations or applications of the Ten Commandments in order.[22] The likelihood of this approach will be argued in the commentary itself although, as will be seen and as has been pointed out by other scholars, it is not without its problems and may have to be modified here and there. Despite these disclaimers there can be little doubt about the essential correctness of the view that Deut 12:1–26:15 is a more specific and detailed exposition of the general principles of relationship and behavior addressed in 5:1–11:32.

5. *The blessings and curses (27:1–28:68)*.   Any treaty must have its statement of reward and sanctions. To the extent the vassal was true and faithful to the relationship into which he entered either willingly or by coercion, to that extent he could expect the favor of his sovereign to be displayed. Conversely, disloyalty and disobedience called forth disciplinary

---

[21] Thus R. H. Pfeiffer writes that "the disorder [of chaps. 12–26] is so extreme that one would almost call it deliberate, unless it arose as a result of successive additions of new material" (*Introduction to the Old Testament* [London: Adam & Charles Black, 1952], 232).

[22] S. A. Kaufman, "The Structure of the Deuteronomic Law," *Maarav* 1/2 (1978-79): 105-58; cf. also A. Rofé, "The Arrangement of the Laws in Deuteronomy," *ETL* 64 (1988): 265-87; J. H. Walton, "Deuteronomy: An Exposition of the Spirit of the Law," *GTJ* 8 (1987): 213-25.

wrath and judgment. It could even result in an annulling of all the benefits outlined in the list of blessings. In no respect has Deuteronomy scholarship benefited more from the recognition of its covenant nature than here. What appeared to be more or less arbitrary lists of divine response to human behavior may be seen now as standard expressions of expectation deriving from a relationship of mutual commitment.

6. *The witnesses (30:19; 31:19; 32:1-43)*.   Inasmuch as a treaty arrangement was, in the final analysis, a legal transaction, proper protocol required that it be drawn up before and certified by appropriate witnesses. In the Hittite tradition the ceremony was enacted in the presence of the gods, who presumably took careful note of all that was said and done and who would guarantee their favor to the contracting parties as they were faithful to the covenant terms but withdraw it in the event of covenant infidelity.

In the case of a covenant between the Lord and Israel such as that of Deuteronomy, it was obviously impossible for the "gods" to be invoked as witnesses since they did not exist in Israel's view. Indeed, it was inconceivable that the Lord could or would be subject to the scrutiny and judgment of any other being. That being the case, the technical nature of the legal and covenant arrangement could be fully expressed only by the formality of calling upon heaven and earth as witnesses (Deut 30:19). Whenever either the Lord or his people took note of the created world around them, they would "remember" their mutual commitment the one to the other. In addition, Moses was to compose a song the singing of which would call to mind the Lord's nature, his gracious dealings with his people, his historical acts of judgment because of their sin, and his promise of deliverance and salvation in the ages to come (31:19; 32:1-43). Thus the song would witness in its own way to the binding nature of the relationship established by the Lord with his elect servant people.

The foregoing is sufficient to show that the elements that are critical in identifying Deuteronomy as a covenant document are in place. In addition, of course, there are other components that result in the structure of the composition, all of which will appear in the analysis of contents and in the relevant discussions in the commentary itself.

6. Deuteronomy and Critical Scholarship

There is a virtual consensus among contemporary adherents of source-critical and traditio-critical approaches to the Old Testament literature that Deuteronomy as a literary composition cannot antedate the seventh century and, in fact, probably is later in its present form.[23] This assessment of the matter finds its classic expression in the view of W. M. L. De Wette that the "book of the law" referred to in the account of the reformation of Judah's religious faith under Josiah was none other than the Book of Deuteronomy.[24] The basis for this identification was the very phrase "book of the law" (2 Kgs 22:8,11; cf. Deut 31:24-26) and the nature of the reform, which, among other things, mandated that all worship sites except that at Jerusalem, the central sanctuary, be destroyed (2 Kgs 23:4-20).

This insistence on only one place of worship by the community is most clearly articulated in Deut 12:1-14. Thus it seemed to De Wette that Deuteronomy must have provided the specific impetus to Josiah's action, but inasmuch as Josiah and his colleagues seem to have had no previous knowledge of the document, it must have been of recent origin, at least in written form. Most likely, he thought, it had been composed by pious conservatives who were deeply troubled by the apostasy of Josiah's predecessors Manasseh and Amon and who placed the book in the temple with the hope that it would be found and produce the effect that, indeed, it did. To add authority to the work, it was attributed to Moses and subsequently was added to the corpus of "Mosaic" writings that had already begun to take shape as a result of the composition and integration of the Yahwistic and Elohistic traditions. Thus Deuteronomy (D) was added to the earlier Yahwistic (J) and Elohistic (E) strands of the Pentateuch. Eventually, as the so-called documentary hypothesis developed in the years following De Wette, the Priestly (P) writings were said to be added in the exilic and postexilic period, and the four sources, carefully interwoven and redacted, produced the Pentateuch as it exists in its present form.

Prior to De Wette, Deuteronomy was thought by most scholars to be part and parcel of the two-source view of analysts such as Spinoza and

---

[23] For a full review of the matter see E. W. Nicholson, *Deuteronomy and Tradition* (Philadelphia: Fortress, 1967), 1-17.

[24] M. J. Paul, "Hilkiah and the Law (2 Kings 22) in the 17th and 18th Centuries: Some Influences on W. M. L. De Wette," *Das Deuteronomium,* 9–12; O. Eissfeldt, *The Old Testament: An Introduction* (New York: Harper & Row, 1965), 171-73; H. Gressmann, "Josiah und das Deuteronomium," *ZAW* 42 (1924): 313-37; B. Halpern, "The Centralization Formula in Deuteronomy," *VT* 31 (1981): 20-38; G. Langer, *Von Gott erwahlt, Jerusalem: die Rezeption von Dtn 12 in fruhen Judentum* (Klosterneuberg: Osterreichisches Katholisches Bibelwerk, 1989); N. Lohfink, "Zur deuteronomischen Zentralisationsformel," *Bib* 65 (1984): 297-329; J. R. Lundbom, "The Lawbook of the Josianic Reform," *CBQ* 38 (1976): 293-302; E. W. Nicholson, "The Centralization of the Cult in Deuteronomy," *VT* 13 (1963): 380-89; J. Niehaus, "The Central Sanctuary: Where and When?" *TynBul* 43 (1992): 3-30; D. W. B. Robinson, *Josiah's Reform and the Book of the Law* (London: Tyndale, 1951); G. J. Wenham, "Deuteronomy and the Central Sanctuary," *TynBul* 22 (1971): 103-18.

Astruc. That is, it was maintained that the division of the material of Genesis into J and E sources could be sustained throughout the Pentateuch, including Deuteronomy.[25] The usual criteria for identifying these sources were not so clear in Deuteronomy. Therefore it was with some relief that critics came to embrace De Wette's hypothesis that Deuteronomy had nothing to do with the JE materials but was a document created independent of them and much later, albeit with certain concerns and themes in common with them.[26] These were attributed by some to an oral prehistory that may have gone back to Moses himself, a concession that was made with reference to the J and E sources as well.[27]

A major and relatively recent development in Deuteronomy scholarship has been the assertion that the book provides the springboard and rationale for the Old Testament historical Books of Joshua through 2 Kings. That is, an unknown theologian-historian, or a "school" of such individuals, reflecting back on the history of Israel and Judah from an exilic perspective, recounted and judged that history in terms of the adherence or lack of adherence of the people of Yahweh to the covenant demands of Deuteronomy. It is posited that this so-called "Deuteronomistic history" is not a mere recital of the events and movements of the post-Mosaic age but a telling of the story as Heilsgeschichte, or "sacred history."[28]

There are major implications to this approach. First, in order for Deuteronomy to serve as a touchstone against which Israel's early history is to be evaluated is tantamount to accepting its own antiquity, at least in some form. One must concede, it seems, that a document made up of whole cloth from only the seventh century could hardly serve as a guideline for historical events that antedated it by several centuries. Surely the deuteronomic

---

[25] This approach, to be known later as the "Fragment Hypothesis," was in fact a modification of the earlier documentary hypothesis, one made necessary because of the existence in Exodus through Deuteronomy of legal and other materials that could not be accommodated to the narrative literature particularly characteristic of Genesis. See Eissfeldt, *Old Testament,* 161-62.

[26] C. Cornill, *Introduction to the Canonical Books of the Old Testament* (New York: G. P. Putnam's Sons, 1907), 46-47.

[27] S. R. Driver, *An Introduction to the Literature of the Old Testament* (Cleveland: World, 1956), 90-91.

[28] The scholar most responsible for this development is M. Noth, *Uberlieferungs geschichtliche Studien* (Halle: M. Niemeyer, 1943); now in English translation, *The Deuteronomistic History,* JSOTSup 15 (Sheffield: JSOT, 1981). Cf. also R. Polzin, *Moses and the Deuteronomist: A Literary Study of the Deuteronomic History* (New York: Seabury, 1980); R. D. Nelson, *The Double Redaction of the Deuteronomistic History,* JSOTSup 18 (Sheffield: JSOT, 1981); R. P. Gordon, "Deuteronomy and the Deuteronomistic School," *TynBul* 25 (1974): 113-20.

principles must have been in place alongside and even anterior to the course of Israel's history. Otherwise, how could the nation have been expected to conform to its requirements? Thus it is common in contemporary scholarship to accord Deuteronomy a long oral prehistory, one, some would say, going back to the times suggested by the tradition itself, that is, to the founding days of the nation under Moses and Joshua.[29]

Moreover, to suggest that the deuteronomistic history can be based on Deuteronomy, can reflect the covenant expectations of that book, and yet can consist essentially of a nonfactual record of Israel's actual historical experience is to border on the absurd.[30] Even if one grants that Joshua To 2 Kings is fundamentally a theologically tendentious account of Israel's past, to deny that it is based upon genuine and documentable events is to suggest that Old Testament Israel could logically accommodate the same bifurcation of history that modern critics are comfortable with, a dichotomy that allows one to view history at two levels—one scientifically recoverable and the other the creative reconstruction of faith.[31] In short, for the deuteronomistic history to be an assessment of Israel's life in light of the teachings of Deuteronomy is to presuppose the prior existence of both Deuteronomy and subsequent historical records in some reliable form, if only oral.

The solution offered by most critics who wish to retain Deuteronomy within a seventh-century context is that Joshua to 2 Kings is a continuation of ancient, even Mosaic traditions but a continuation edited into its present form by a deuteronomistic hand.[32] Thus the essential historicity of the events is allowed, but the whole has been shaped in such a way as to conform to the deuteronomistic philosophy of history. All the comments in these books of an interpretive, evaluative nature are therefore by the collectors and redactors of the ancient traditions, namely, the deuteronomists, whose theological point of departure is the Book of Deuteronomy. This approach allows the history to be essentially authentic but also to be viewed through the prism of a deuteronomistic ideology.

---

[29] Nicholson, *Deuteronomy and Tradition*, 121-24.

[30] Such a skeptical view of the historical traditions that underlay the "deuteronomistic history" is revealed repeatedly in J. Van Seters, *In Search of History* (New Haven: Yale, 1983), 322-53. For a more moderate view see B. Halpern, *The First Historians* (San Francisco: Harper & Row, 1988).

[31] This, of course, is precisely the view of such scholars as G. von Rad. See his *Old Testament Theology,* vol. 1 (New York: Harper & Row, 1962), 105-8; cf. also his "Beginnings of Historical Writing in Ancient Israel" in *The Problem of the Hexateuch and Other Essays* (London: SCM, 1984), 166-204.

[32] Nicholson, *Deuteronomy and Tradition,* 119-24.

Commitment to the late date of Deuteronomy and its resultant deuteronomistic history continues to hold the field in critical scholarship, but the
last few decades have introduced new complications into the discussion.
These have attended the discovery of ancient Near Eastern covenant and
treaty texts, especially from Anatolia, documents that strikingly resemble
in form and ethos certain biblical texts.[33] Once these Hittite exemplars had
become known to Old Testament scholars, it became quite apparent that
the similarities between them, and especially Exod 20–23 and Deuteronomy, were more than superficial. Clearly these biblical compositions
shared much in common with the Hittite materials, so much so that it
seemed almost self-evident that the former were modeled after the latter.

Conservative scholars were particularly gratified by the implications of
the parallels being drawn, for they seemed to give new and unanticipated
support for the antiquity of Deuteronomy.[34] The most complete and important of the Hittite texts originated in the period from 1400 B.C. to the fall
of the Hittite kingdom in 1200 B.C. This, of course, was precisely at the
time of the composition and dissemination of the covenant texts of Exodus
and Deuteronomy according to the traditional chronology. In addition, the
form and substance of the respective documents were so patently of a kind
as to provide a whole new set of interpretive guidelines. Though Deuteronomy had always been recognized as having a certain covenantal aspect or
emphasis, these new comparative studies made it most evident that Deuteronomy was itself a long but self-contained covenant document. It shared
all the salient features of texts of this kind from Hittite archives and, moreover, arose from the same Late Bronze milieu.

Many critical scholars, though certainly aware of and even positively
affected by these new insights in many respects, nevertheless reject the
conclusion that Deuteronomy as a written document is old just because it
shares these archaic features. Rather, it is suggested that the form of the
book may be ancient—indeed, that it may be modeled after the Hittite
texts—but that the content is the result of a gradually developing accretion
of tradition, especially created and preserved by cultic circles.[35] Since

---

[33] For bibliography on the treaty texts and studies on them, see McCarthy, *Old Testament
Covenant*, 90-93; Weinfeld, *Deuteronomy and the Deuteronomic School*, 371-83.

[34] See especially Kline: "Now that the form-critical data compel the recognition of the
antiquity not merely of this or that element within Deuteronomy but that of the Deuteronomic treaty in its integrity, any persistent insistence on a final edition of the book around the
seventh century B.C. can be nothing more than a vestigial hypothesis, no longer performing a
significant function in Old Testament criticism" (*Treaty of the Great King*, 44).

[35] G. von Rad, *Deuteronomy: A Commentary*, OTL (Philadelphia: Westminster, 1966),
21-23.

from De Wette's day Deuteronomy has been assigned to a time no earlier than the seventh century, no amount of alleged parallels with fourteenth century Hittite documents can dislodge it from that setting. An uprooting of Deuteronomy from its place necessitates a total repudiation of source-critical and traditio-historical hypotheses that have been firmly in place since the time of Wellhausen.

Support for maintaining the late date while recognizing the covenantal literary form of the book has become possible in the view of many scholars by associating Deuteronomy not with Hittite suzerain-vassal treaties but with Neo-Assyrian models, especially from the reigns of Sennacherib and Esarhaddon, both of whom ruled in the seventh century.[36] This setting appears most conducive to parallels and to biblical dependence not only because of the time frame but also because of the greatly heightened contact between Assyria and Judah in that period. It seems quite obvious that the "Assyrian crisis" that was about to overwhelm Judah as it had Israel provides a most obvious rationale for the composition of Deuteronomy with its message of expectation and judgment and in a literary form well known by then from Assyrian sources.

Careful scrutiny of these Assyrian treaty texts reveals, however, that they lack certain elements found in the biblical covenant texts.[37] Despite recent attempts to disavow or downplay these differences or even to adduce examples that do contain some of the missing clauses,[38] there can be no doubt that the Old Testament materials much more closely exemplify the Hittite models than they do the Assyrian. At the present stage of research, then, the balance of favor must be tilted toward the early date of Deuteronomy on the basis of comparative literary-critical studies.

7. Canonicity of the Book

Earliest Jewish and Christian tradition knows nothing of a late, non-Mosaic Deuteronomy. Every arrangement of the canon from the earliest time up to the present considers the book to be part of the Torah and ascribes it to Moses.[39] Departure from that understanding of things derives

---

[36] Frankena, "Vassal-Treaties of Esarhaddon," 122-54. The principal edition of the texts is D. J. Wiseman, *The Vassal-Treaties of Esarhaddon* (London: British School of Archaeology in Iraq, 1958).

[37] See the careful comparisons of Kitchen, *Ancient Orient and Old Testament,* 95-96.

[38] Weinfeld, *Deuteronomy and the Deuteronomic School,* 59-61.

[39] R. Beckwith, *The Old Testament Canon of the New Testament Church* (Grand Rapids: Eerdmans, 1985), 181-82.

no support, then, from early canonical witnesses but only from source-critical analyses that not only separate Deuteronomy from the remainder of the Pentateuch but, as we have seen, require it to be centuries later than Moses.

Of no little importance and authority to the question of Deuteronomy's canonicity is its citation in later Old Testament and especially in New Testament passages where portions of the book are accorded full recognition as divine revelation and, specifically, revelation mediated through Moses. In fact, no Old Testament book is referred to more in the New Testament as a basis for proper belief and behavior.[40]

8. Outline of the Contents of the Book

The following outline of Deuteronomy reflects the underlying covenant nature and structure of the book but also, of course, includes narrative, parenetic, and transitional elements that usually did not appear in secular covenant texts. Thus there are many more major divisions than would occur in such documents.

─────────────── *OUTLINE OF THE BOOK* ───────────────

I.   The Covenant Setting (1:1-5)
II. The Historical Review (1:6–4:40)
     1. The Past Dealings of the Lord with Israel (1:6–3:29)
     2. The Exhortation of Moses (4:1-40)
III. The Preparation for the Covenant Text (4:41-49)
     1. The Narrative concerning Cities of Refuge (4:41-43)
     2. The Setting and Introduction (4:44-49)
IV. The Principles of the Covenant (5:1–11:32)
     1. The Opening Exhortation (5:1-5)
     2. The Ten Commandments (5:6-21)
     3. The Narrative Relating the Sinai Revelation and Israel's Response (5:22-33)

---

[40] Deuteronomy is quoted or alluded to scores of times in the NT. For an exhaustive list see W. Dittmar, *Vetus Testamentum in Novo* (Göttingen: Vandenhoeck & Ruprecht, 1903), 300-305.

     4. The Nature of the Principles (6:1-25)

     5. The Content of the Principles (7:1–11:32)

V.   The Specific Stipulations of the Covenant (12:1–26:15)

     1. The Exclusiveness of Yahweh and His Worship (12:1–16:17)

     2. Kingdom Officials (16:18–18:22)

     3. Civil Law (19:1–22:8)

     4. Laws of Purity (22:9–23:18)

     5. Laws of Interpersonal Relationships (23:19–25:19)

     6. Laws of Covenant Celebration and Confirmation (26:1-15)

VI.   Exhortation and Narrative Interlude (26:16-19)

VII. The Curses and Blessings (27:1–29:1 [28:69 HT])

     1. The Gathering at Shechem (27:1-13)

     2. The Curses That Follow Disobedience of Specific Stipulations (27:14-26)

     3. The Blessings That Follow Obedience (28:1-14)

     4. The Curses That Follow Disobedience of General Stipulations (28:15-68)

     5. Narrative Interlude (29:1 [28:69 HT])

VIII. The Epilogue: Historical Review (29:2–30:20)

     1. Exodus, Wandering, and Conquest (29:2-8)

     2. The Present Covenant Setting (29:9-15)

     3. The Results of Covenant Disobedience (29:16-29)

     4. The Results of Covenant Reaffirmation (30:1-10)

     5. The Appeal for Covenant Obedience (30:11-20)

IX.   Deposit of the Text and Provision for Its Future Implementation (31:1-29)

     1. The Succession by Joshua (31:1-8)

     2. The Deposit of the Text (31:9-13)

     3. The Commissioning of Joshua (31:14-23)

     4. The Anticipation of the Leaders' Defection (31:24-29)

X.   The Song of Moses (31:30–32:44)

     1. Introduction to the Song (31:30)

     2. Invocation of Witnesses (32:1-4)

     3. Indictment of the People (32:5-6)

     4. Review of Past Blessings (32:7-14)

     5. Israel's Rebellion (32:15-18)

     6. God's Promise of Judgment (32:19-25)

9. Analysis of the Contents of the Book

I. The Covenant Setting (1:1-5)

The setting of Deuteronomy is Moses' address to an assembly of Israel in the plains of Moab just east of the Jordan River, an address that consists of a farewell to his people that includes covenant instruction and pastoral exhortation.

II. The Historical Review (1:6–4:40)

In line with the practice in suzerain-vassal treaties of rehearsing the past relationship of the parties to the contract, Moses sketches out the highlights of national life since the Sinai convocation to the present hour. The historical review proper (1:6–3:29) is followed by an exhortation based upon its assessment (4:1-40).

III. The Preparation for the Covenant Text (4:41-49)

Following the historical review and as a logical consequence to it, Moses designated three cities in the Transjordan as places of refuge to which individuals who had committed manslaughter could flee for sanctuary (4:41-43; cf. 19:2-13). He then restated the setting of the covenant that he had at first called "words" (Deut 1:1) and designated "stipulations, decrees, and laws" (4:44-49).

IV. The Principles of the Covenant (5:1–11:32)

This central division of the book opens with an explanation for the need of covenant renewal and an exhortation to the people to take it seriously (5:1-5). Moses then states the Ten Commandments, those principles that define who God is and what he requires of Israel and, indeed, of all humankind (5:6-21). Moses then reflected once more on the Sinai revelation, where Israel encountered Yahweh in his theophanic glory and responded in appropriate fear (5:22-33). They had been introduced to the "commands, decrees, and laws" (5:31) at that time; but this was a new time and a new generation, one that must for itself experience covenant encounter.

The nature of the relationship between Yahweh and Israel consists fundamentally of the recognition that God is one (6:4-5) and that his people, if they are to enjoy the benefits of the ancient patriarchal promises, must serve him with undivided loyalty and faithfulness (6:1-25). This will express itself in many ways, including the dispossession of the inhabitants of the land of promise and a staunch refusal to undertake alliances with them (7:1-26). God's people must confess that he alone is Lord and the source of all blessing (8:1-20). All they are and have are the fruits of his grace, beneficences poured out upon them despite their unworthiness (9:1–10:11).

The oneness and exclusivity of Yahweh call for a loving response on the part of his people, one that by its very expression denotes covenant fidelity. But this cannot be limited to love of God alone, for covenant has a horizontal as well as vertical dimension. In either case love is more than mere emotion—it must be worked out in action (10:12-22). Israel had learned from history the tragic results of covenant disobedience (11:1-7), and Moses now reminded them that success in the future could be guaranteed only as they loved God and kept his commandments (11:13-25). Blessing and curse was set before them now and would be in the land of Canaan as well. It was up to them to choose the course of action that would bring the one and preclude the other (11:26-32).

V. The Specific Stipulations of the Covenant (12:1–26:15)

The broad principles of covenant relationship and responsibility having been set forth (chaps. 5–11), Moses next addressed more specific examples of their application. First of all, he dealt with the issue of the location of Israel's God among his people in a specified, central place, the single sanctuary where community worship must be carried out (12:1-14) in an appropriate manner (12:15-31).

One of the major aspects of pagan religion was its dependence on professional religious practitioners such as diviners and enchanters who served as channels of divine knowledge and power. The fact that this presupposed the existence of other gods obviously put it out of bounds for God's people. In fact, such practitioners, even if they came from within Israel (or, perhaps, especially if they did), must be put to death if they counseled God's people to forsake him and go after other gods (13:1-18).

To return to the matter of animals and their use in sacrifice and slaughter, Moses again drew distinctions between Israel as a holy people and the surrounding nations by distinguishing between clean and unclean animals (14:1-21). The heathen regularly ate and sacrificed animals Yahweh declared to be off limits and in doing so revealed their hopeless ignorance of his ways. Israel must therefore demonstrate their calling and character as a holy people by conforming to Yahweh's definitions of clean and unclean animals and making use of only those that were not forbidden.

Still another expression of homage to the sovereign God of Israel was the people's generous offer of tribute to him in the form of tithes of all their productivity (14:22-29). This could be in kind or, if the central sanctuary were too far distant, in money. Every third year the Levites would receive the tithes for themselves since this was their only means of support (14:28-29). Every seventh year was a year of release in which poor Israelites were freed of all financial encumbrances that attached to them as a result of their having obligated themselves in service to their countrymen (15:1-18). In a sense, however, all Israelites were beholden to Yahweh because he had spared the firstborn son of every Israelite household in the tenth plague (Exod 13:11-16). This being so, the faithful of Israel were to offer up the firstborn of their herds and flocks annually as an expression of devotion (15:19-23). This was done in connection with the Passover and Feast of Unleavened Bread (16:1-8). Other occasions for offering tribute to the Great King as a community of faith were the Feast of Weeks (or Pentecost), seven weeks after Passover (16:9-12), and the Feast of Tabernacles in the seventh month of the year (16:13-17).

Though Israel was a theocratic community in which, ideally at least, Yahweh was Head of State, in practical terms there must be human governance as well with all the officialdom and bureaucracy that is entailed.

These are not only tolerated but positively sanctioned. The first of these were the "judges and officials" (16:18–17:13) whose task was to administer justice in a fair and evenhanded manner (16:18-20) and without resort to heathen means (16:21–17:1). That is, justice is related to a proper understanding of Yahweh and his insistence on exclusive worship.

It was clearly understood that Israel would someday evolve from a "tribal consensus" kind of government to a monarchy (17:14-20; cf. Gen 17:6). There would also be religious officials of Israel including the priests and Levites, the responsibilities of whom also receive at least brief attention (18:1-8). Since the Lord was their inheritance, they had no private lands or properties but had to live off the gifts and offerings of God's people. The prophets, also important in shaping the course of Israel's theocratic life, received greater attention (18:9-22).

Though Israel was most basically a religious community that understood itself corporately, it was nevertheless one composed of individuals who had to live together in peace and order. This implied naturally that there was a social and civil dimension to life as a covenant people. This dictated the need for civil legislation, for rules of behavior in a social setting (Deut 19:1–22:4).

The first of these rules deals with homicide (19:1-13). The sixth commandment (Deut 5:17) had already addressed this in principle, but inasmuch as all homicide is not murder, every case had to be dealt with on its own merits. The second statute concerns the removal of boundary markers (19:14). Since land was the very essence of covenant inheritance, for one to cheat his neighbor by moving property lines was to infringe on a God-given patrimony. Fundamental to equitable civil law in ancient Israel as well as now was the presumptive innocence of the accused short of proof of guilt. This required, among other things, that one not be condemned by the testimony of one witness only but that there be at least one other for corroboration (19:15-21).

As a nation about to enter Canaan in conquest, Israel had to have guidelines regarding proper prosecution of war. This was especially important because much of the conflict would involve "holy war," that is, war fought on behalf of Yahweh and for covenant principles whereas the rest would be war of the normal, "secular" type. Related to death in war is the problem of homicide without witnesses. Israel's sense of corporate solidarity was such that the residents of the village nearest the corpse were held liable and had to offer up a heifer as an atonement for the whole community to thus absolve it of guilt (21:1-9). As a result of war, prisoners frequently would come under Israelite control. Females in such cases could become the wives of their captors after a suitable period, but if the arrangement proved not to be satisfactory, they were allowed to go free and, in any event, could not usurp the rights of existing wives (21:10-17).

Civil law, finally, dealt with rebellious sons who were ungovernable by their parents (21:18-23) and the problem of lost property (22:1-4). Any Israelite who found a possession of a fellow citizen must either return it to him or wait for him to come and claim it. If it were an animal that had fallen by the wayside, brotherliness mandated that it be lifted up and restored to its owner.

A central thrust of the Mosaic Covenant is the clarion call that Israel was a holy nation and must live a holy life before the world. Like Leviticus (cf. Lev 17–25), Deuteronomy has its "holiness code," its set of guidelines by which Israel was to achieve and maintain its purity (22:5–23:18). Though the reason for the inclusion of some of these may escape the modern reader, in their own time and circumstances they must have contributed to Israel's understanding of what it meant to be a people peculiar to Yahweh and unique among the peoples of the earth.

The laws of purity find enlargement in precepts governing interpersonal relationships in general (23:19–25:19), for there are areas of social life which, though not strictly cultic in nature, have moral and ethical implications important to covenant life and faith.

The specific stipulation section of Deuteronomy concludes with the laws of covenant confirmation and celebration (26:1-15). When Israel finally entered the land of Canaan, they were to acknowledge Yahweh's faithful provision by offering their firstfruits to him while reciting the history of his beneficent covenant dealings with them from the ancient days of the patriarchs to the present (26:1-11). This ceremony appears to have been in conjunction with the Feast of Weeks (that is, Harvest or Pentecost; cf. Exod 23:16; Lev 23:15-21). Following the offering of the first of the grain harvest the farmers of Israel were to provide the Levites and other dependent citizens the tithe of their produce (26:12-15). In this manner tribute to God and the support of the needy merge into one glorious act of worship.

VI. Exhortation and Narrative Interlude (26:16-19)

Following the presentation of the body of covenant stipulations, Moses commanded the people to obey them and not just perfunctorily—they must do so with all their hearts and souls (26:16). The very essence of the covenant, he said, was the pledge they had made to be God's people and the Lord's reciprocal promise to be their God. It was the will of God that Israel continue to be his special people, a holy community called to be an expression of praise and honor of the Lord.

VII. The Curses and Blessings (27:1–28:68)

A central element of any bilateral covenant was the section describing the rewards for faithful compliance to its terms and the punishments befitting disobedience to it. As a suzerain-vassal treaty text Deuteronomy obviously holds only Israel—and not Yahweh—accountable, though there was the promise of the Sovereign that he would respond to Israel's obedience with blessing beyond measure.

The ceremony of blessing and cursing, to take place once Canaan had been occupied, must occur at Shechem, the site of early patriarchal encounters with God (27:4; cf. Gen 12:6; 35:4; Deut 11:26-29). The order of the curses and blessings appears to take the form of an envelopment in which the curses that follow disobedience of specific stipulations (27:15-26) and those that issue from disobedience of general stipulations (28:15-68) embrace the list of blessings that attend obedience (28:1-14). As a great antiphonal chorus, tribal representatives would stand on Gerizim to shout "amen" at the listing of the blessings while others, on Ebal, would do so when the curses were sounded.

The first list of curses (27:15-26) deals with representative covenant violations without specifying the form the curses might take. The blessing section (28:1-14) promises prosperity in physical and material ways and reaffirms God's intention to make Israel an exalted and holy people. The second list of curses (28:15-68) threatens loss of prosperity (28:15-19), the ravages of disease and pestilence (28:20-24), defeat and deportation with all the misery that would entail (28:25-35), and a reversal of roles between Israel and the nations (28:36-46). Rather than being exalted among them, Israel would become their servant. All of this would result in indescribable distress and hopelessness (28:47-57). In effect, covenant violation would undo the exodus and deliver the nation back into the throes of bondage (28:58–29:1).

VIII. The Epilogue: Historical Review (29:2–30:20)

By way of summary Moses rehearsed God's dealings with Israel in the exodus and wilderness (29:2-9) and exhorted them to covenant fidelity as the new generation chosen by the Lord to represent him in the earth (29:10-21). Their commitment must be personal and sincere, for if it is not, the time of judgment would come in which the nations would question whether or not Israel was in fact the people of the Lord (29:22-29).

That this was a foregone conclusion is clear in Moses' promise that God would visit his people in their day of calamity and exile and would cause them once more to reflect on their covenant privileges. He then would exercise his grace and restore them to full covenant partnership with all its blessings (30:1-10). Their pledge to faithful adherence to the terms of the covenant could bring immediate and lasting reward (30:11-16), but disobedience would produce only judgment (30:17-20).

IX. Deposit of the Text and Provision for Its Future Implementation (31:1-29)

Though the ceremony of covenant does not explicitly appear in the narrative (but cf. 29:10-13), it did take place as is clear from Moses' selection of Joshua to succeed him as covenant mediator (31:1-8) and his delivery of the covenant text to the priests for safekeeping (31:9-13). The fact that they were designated as the ones who carried the ark (v. 9) is significant, for the ark had already been set aside as the repository of the tablets of the Decalogue (Exod 25:16; cf. Deut 31:26). Moreover, the Lord commanded Moses, who was at death's door, to compose a song that would outlast him, one whose purpose was to remind the nation of the covenant oaths they had made (31:14-23). This certainly presupposes that such pledges had already been confessed. Finally the Lord, in true covenant fashion, invoked heaven and earth as witnesses to the promises that Israel had sworn (31:24-29).

X. The Song of Moses (31:30–32:44)

This wonderful hymn of covenant commitment (32:1) extols the God of Israel for his greatness and righteousness (32:2-4) despite the wickedness of his people (32:5-6a). He had created them (32:6b) and had redeemed (32:7-9) and preserved them (32:10-14). They rebelled in turn and followed other gods (32:15-18), a course of action that provoked his judgment in the past and would do so in the future (32:19-38). At last, however, he would remember his covenant and bring his people salvation (32:39-43).

XI. Narrative Interlude (32:45-52)

Having spoken his song, Moses urged his people to subscribe to its demands as a covenant instrument (32:44-47). Then he ascended Mount Nebo to await the day of his death (32:48-52).

XII. The Blessing of Moses (33:1-29)

Before he departed, Moses presented to his fellow Israelites a will and testament similar to that by which Jacob had blessed his sons (cf. Gen 49:2-27). After praising the God of deliverance and covenant (33:2-5), he listed the tribes by name, assigning to each a prophetic blessing (33:6-25).

He concluded with a paean of praise of Israel's God (33:26-28) and a promise that his chosen ones would ultimately triumph over all their foes (33:29).

XIII. Narrative Epilogue (34:1-12)

Having ascended Mount Nebo (or Pisgah), Moses viewed all the land of promise, a land guaranteed to the patriarchal ancestors but denied to Moses himself because of his intemperate behavior at the rock in the wilderness (34:1-4). He then died and was buried by the Lord in an unknown and unmarked grave (34:5-6). With great lament the people of Israel mourned his passing, for though Joshua possessed the spirit and authority of Moses, neither he nor any man to come could compare with this giant in the earth who knew God "face to face" (34:7-12).

10. Theology of the Book[41]

In line with the general correspondence of the form of a thing to its function, it is safe to say that one cannot understand the theology of Deuteronomy without reference to its covenant form and structure, a matter elaborated already (see pp. 27-32). That is, the very fact that the book is in the shape and style of a covenant text presupposes that the covenant relationship between Yahweh and Israel is a major concern. It follows then that the theology of Deuteronomy must be sensitive to this state of affairs and that, in fact, it must be informed from beginning to end by covenant concerns. It is no exaggeration to maintain that the concept of covenant lies at

---

[41] The following is elaborated in E. H. Merrill, "Theology of the Pentateuch," in *A Biblical Theology of the Old Testament*, ed. R. B. Zuck (Chicago: Moody, 1991), 62-87. For other theological studies see G. Braulik, "Das Deuteronomium und die Geburt des Monotheismus," *Gott, der Einzige,* ed. G. Braulik and E. Haag (Freiburg: Herder, 1985), 115-59; W. Brueggemann, "The Kerygma of the Deuteronomic Historian," *Int* 22 (1968): 387-402; A. Cholewinski, "Zur Theologischen Deutung des Moabbundes," *Bib* 66 (1985): 96-111; R. E. Clements, *God's Chosen People: A Theological Interpretation of the Book of Deuteronomy* (London: SCM, 1968); E. R. Clendenen, "Life in God's Land: An Outline of the Theology of Deuteronomy," in *The Church at the Dawn of the 21st Century*, ed. P. Patterson et al. (Dallas: Criswell Publications, 1989), 159-78; J. G. McConville, *Grace in the End: A Study in Deuteronomic Theology* (Grand Rapids: Zondervan, 1993); id., *Law and Theology in Deuteronomy,* JSOTSup 33 (Sheffield: JSOT, 1984); P. D. Miller, "The Gift of God: The Deuteronomic Theology of the Land," *Int* 23 (1969): 451-65; C. Schaefer-Lichtenberger, "Göttliche und Menschliche Autorität im Deuteronomium," in *Pentateuchal and Deuteronomistic Studies,* ed. C. Brekelmans and J. Lust (Leuven: University Press, 1990), 125-42; J. D. W. Watts, "The Deuteronomic Theology," *RevExp* 74 (1977): 321-36.

the very heart of the book and may be said to be the center of its theology.[42]

Covenant by its very definition demands at least three elements—the two contracting parties and the document that describes and outlines the purpose, nature, and requirements of the relationship. Thus the three major rubrics of the theology of Deuteronomy are (1) Yahweh, the Great King and covenant initiator; (2) Israel, the vassal and covenant recipient; and (3) the book itself, the covenant organ, complete with the essentials of standard treaty documents. This means, moreover, that all the revelation of the book must be seen through the prism of covenant and not abstractly removed from the peculiar historical and ideological context in which it originated. With this in mind, the following discussion will consider (1) the character of God, (2) the nature of Israel and humanity, and (3) the nature of their relationship.

(1) The Character of God

In Deuteronomy (and, indeed, in Scripture generally) God reveals himself in acts, in theophany, and in word. The acts of God, when viewed all together and as part of a pattern, constitute history itself.[43] This obviously begins with God as Creator (an aspect lacking in Deuteronomy) and continues, in its peculiar relationship to Israel, with God's self-disclosure as Elector of his people (Deut 26:5-9), their Redeemer from Egypt and the wilderness (1:30-31; 3:34-39; 6:21-23; 8:14-16; 11:2-7; 16:1-7; 26:6-9), the Divine Warrior who fights on their behalf as well as on his own (2:21-22,30-31; 7:1-2,20-24; 31:4), Israel's Benefactor (32:15-18), and as the coming Redeemer and/or Judge (7:13-16; 11:14-15; 30:3-9; 32:19-43; 33:2-29).

As the God who transcends history, Yahweh also reveals himself in the awe-inspiring splendor of theophany.[44] In Deuteronomy this otherness of God finds expression typically in the brilliance of light, especially fire, and in its opposite, darkness. This polarity is suggestive of his immanence, his accessibility to his creation, but also of his inaccessible remoteness. He is the Great King who desires to communicate with and to receive the homage of his people but who reminds them constantly that he is above and beyond them in unapproachable glory. It is precisely at the point of his

---

[42] J. A. Thompson, *Deuteronomy,* TOTC (Downers Grove: InterVarsity, 1974), 68-69.

[43] For an excellent statement of God's acts as revelatory events, see C. Barth, *God with Us: A Theological Introduction to the Old Testament* (Grand Rapids: Eerdmans, 1991).

[44] S. Terrien, *The Elusive Presence: Toward a New Biblical Theology* (New York: Harper & Row, 1978), 199-213.

making covenant with them that the theophanic disclosure is most emphatic (4:11-12; 5:4-5,22-26; 9:10,15; 33:2; cf. Pss 50:2; 80:2; 94:1).

The most intelligible and therefore least ambiguous mode of revelation is that in prophetic word. That word of God in Deuteronomy is, of course, the book itself expressed in its uniquely covenant form. But as already pointed out, Deuteronomy is a covenant text in a broader than normal sense inasmuch as it contains not only the *sine qua non* of standard documents of that genre but also itineraries, narratives, hymns, and homilies, all designed to provide both a covenant document as well as a historical, existential, and eschatological context in which to interpret it. Thus there are the solemn and formal pronouncements of covenant initiation (1:6b-8; 2:4b-7; 4:12-13; 5:4,6-22) as well as constant enjoinders to be faithful to its stipulations (e.g., 1:37-38; 4:15-31; 6:1-4; 7:1-5).

The subject of divine self-disclosure, that is, the content of Yahweh's revelation about himself, must also be seen in terms of the covenant purposes of the Book of Deuteronomy. It is therefore not surprising that the covenant name Yahweh is by far the most commonly attested to, occurring about 221 times. By this name he encountered Moses at Sinai (Exod 3:13-16; 6:2-9; Deut 5:1-5), and it is in this name that he constantly commands his people to keep the covenant made there.[45] The rare occurrences of Elohim (twenty-three times) and other names and epithets (about eighteen times) reinforce the covenant character of the book and its almost exclusive attention to Israel. These names, especially Elohim and its byforms, occur most regularly in contexts describing God's more cosmic or universal interests in creation and history.[46]

Deuteronomy is replete with references to the name of the Lord as a surrogate for himself (12:5,11,21; 14:23-24; 16:2,6,11; 26:2), so much so that it is common to speak of a "Name theology."[47] Eichrodt traces the course of the development of this theology from the idea of God as manifested in his name, to the Name as representative of the transcendent God, to a virtual hypostatization of the Name, and finally, in late Old Testament times, to the transformation of the divine Name to divine essence. In other words, God is his Name, and the Name is God.[48] It is an easy transition into the New Testament, where the name of Christ is itself a vehicle of power and authority (Phil 2:9-11).

---

[45] G. Vos, *Biblical Theology: Old and New Testaments* (Grand Rapids: Eerdmans, 1954), 129-34.

[46] H. Ringgren, "אֱלֹהִים *ĕlōhîm*," *TDOT* 1:267-84.

[47] Terrien, *Elusive Presence*, 198-203.

[48] W. Eichrodt, *Theology of the Old Testament* (Philadelphia: Westminster, 1967), 2:40-45.

The revelation of God's person in Deuteronomy follows typical biblical patterns. In highly anthropomorphic terms he is said to possess hands (2:15; 3:24; 4:34), an arm (4:34; 5:15), a mouth (8:3), a face (5:4; 31:18; 34:10), a finger (9:10), and eyes (11:12; 12:28); and he walks (23:14), writes (10:4), and rides (33:26). He is both immanent (4:7,39; 31:8) and transcendent (4:12,35-36; 5:4,22-26), unique (3:24; 5:7; 6:4,15) and without material form (4:12,15). He is the Sovereign (10:17-18; 32:8-9) and the Eternal One (30:20; 32:40) who is nonetheless a Father (14:1; 32:5-6).

According to his character and attributes Yahweh is gracious (5:10; 7:9,12), loving (1:31; 7:7-8,13), righteous or just (4:8; 10:17-18), merciful (4:31; 13:17), powerful (4:34,37; 6:21-22), holy (5:11), glorious (5:24-26), faithful or loyal (7:9,12), and upright (32:4). But he is also an angry God (1:37; 3:26; 9:18-20), one zealous for his own honor (4:24; 13:2-10; 29:20).

The roles or functions of Yahweh in Deuteronomy must be understood in light of the multifaceted ways he reveals himself there, but they can be more finely nuanced and specified, in view of Deuteronomy's character as a covenant text, so as to reveal him most particularly as the Great Sovereign who has entered into covenant with a people through whom he desires to reign and to manifest himself to the world. Therefore his many undertakings are adjunctive and subservient to that overall task of exercising his dominion over the vassal nation.

This right to reign is, of course, predicated on Yahweh's initial work as Creator (4:32) and Redeemer (5:6,15; 6:12,21-23; 9:26,29). Having brought the heavens and earth into existence, thus declaring his lordship over them and all things in them, he chose one nation, Israel, to reveal and mediate that lordship. This elective grace resulted in his initiating promises to the patriarchal ancestors (1:8,11,21,35; 6:3,10,19), promises that found expression in the Sinai covenant (4:13,20,34; 5:2-3; 7:6-8; 9:10-11) and that included preeminently the occupation and possession of the land of Canaan (1:8,20-21,39; 11:24-25; 19:2-3; 33:49,52).

The accomplishment of all this requires that Yahweh be a Lawgiver (4:2,8,10,14,40), a Warrior (1:4,30,42; 2:15,21-22; 7:1-2,22-24), and a Benefactor (1:8,21,25; 3:28; 7:13-14; 8:3-4,7-10; 11:14-15) but also a Judge of and Rewarder for evil (1:17; 4:27; 8:19-20; 9:19-20,25-26). All of these prerogatives were inherent in his capacity as Great King, the only God before whom and to whom his people Israel were accountable.

(2) The Nature of Israel and Humanity

The second major theme of the theology of Deuteronomy—that pertaining to the recipient of the covenant initiated by Yahweh—consists primarily of references to the single nation or people Israel. Israel, however, serves a functional role in Deuteronomy, one, in line with the formal nature of the book, that portrays it as a servant of Yahweh whose mission was one of modeling the kingdom of God on earth and pressing its claims on the alienated nations so in need of God's salvation. It is necessary, therefore, that the concepts of nationhood be understood and with them those of humanity as well, including both the generic and individual aspects.

Deuteronomy has little to say about humankind in general apart from the fact that God created them (4:32) and provides for both their physical and spiritual needs (8:3). As for anthropology, the nature and character of the individual, the standard Old Testament ideas prevail. Thus "man" is *'îs, 'ĕnôs, geber,* and *zākār,* all suggesting man as opposed to other creatures or male as opposed to female. "Woman" is *'iššâ, naʿărâ, rakkâ* (Deut 28:56), and *nĕqēbâ.* The usual psychosomatic terms also appear. An individual sometimes is a *nepeš* (4:9; 10:22; 13:7), and at other times this term refers to the essential being (6:5; 12:28; 19:6), the emotional element (24:15), or to the will or desire (12:15,20-21; 14:26). An individual's intellectual and mental aspect is described as one's *lēb,* that is, heart (4:39; 6:6; 8:5), though *lēb* also refers to the emotions (15:7,9-10; 19:6). On a few occasions it is synonymous with *nepeš* and therefore connotes the person as such (2:30; 7:17; 18:21). The final major Hebrew term in biblical anthropology, *rûaḥ,* occurs only once (2:30) and then only as a parallel to *lēb* and meaning the inner disposition.

Clearly, then, Deuteronomy is little concerned with humankind apart from their constitution as nations, particularly the nation Israel. The typical terms *gôy* and *ʿam* are used, the latter with more of an ethnic and theological sense than nationalistic (thus 9:2; 28:33).[49] Both Israel and the pagan nations are called *gôy,* usually with the emphasis on Israel as a national unit called from among the others and charged with a specific mission as a nation (4:6-8,34). That Israel is an ethnic entity as well, however, constituted by covenant, is clear from Deut 27:9, where it is told, "You have now become the people [*ʿam*] of the LORD your God." There is more to Israel, then, than a national organization of tribes. Israel is an ethnic, eponymous people, a kinfolk who can trace their origins back to a common ancestor whom God promised to make a great nation (29:13; cf. 9:26,29; 21:8; 26:15; 32:9,36,43).

---

[49] G. J. Botterweck, "גוֹי *gôy*," *TDOT* 2:426-30.

(3) The Nature of the Relationship

The third (and perhaps most important) rubric of the theology of Deuteronomy is that of the covenant itself, both its form and its content. As has been noted, modern scholarship has drawn attention to the remarkable correspondences between Old Testament covenant form and pattern and that of Late Bronze Age Hittite vassal treaties. Though this has been challenged vigorously by recent scholars, who opt for parallels with much later literature, the weight of evidence still lies with the proponents of the Hittite analogies.[50]

Of greater theological importance than the structure of the book is its content. But that content is so inextricably linked to its covenant context that the theology of Deuteronomy should be viewed continually as a statement of relationship—that of Yahweh the Great King with his elect and commissioned people Israel.

More particularly, Deuteronomy is a covenant renewal document and not an initial statement of covenant establishment. This is clear from the frequent references to the original Sinai (or Horeb) covenant setting (1:6; 4:1-2,5,10,15,23,33-40; etc.) and the change in language in Deuteronomy as compared with Exodus due to the changed historical and theological circumstances surrounding the respective settings (5:12-15; cf. Exod 20:8-11; 7:1-5; cf. Exod 23:32-33; 12:5; cf. Exod 20:24; 15:12-18; cf. Exod 21:2-6). Moreover, Deuteronomy is a greatly expanded and more detailed rendition of the covenant text because of the anticipated changes that would be brought about by entrance into settlement in the land of promise.[51]

After tracing the course of events from Sinai (1:6–3:29) to the present site of covenant renewal in Moab (1:1-5), Moses, in a lengthy parenesis (4:1-40), urged the people to obedience as a precondition to blessing (4:1,6,40). He went on to point out that the document of covenant was inviolable (4:2), that it must be taught to future generations (4:9-10,40), and that its infraction would result in divine chastisement (4:26-28).

Moses next introduced the general stipulations of the covenant in a passage that clearly establishes the technical nature of the relationship (4:44-49). The following *tôrâ* ("law" or, better, "instruction"), he said, would consist of *ʿēdôt* ("stipulations"), *ḥuqqîm* ("decrees"), and *mišpāṭîm* ("laws"), terms associated with such treaties. They are picked up again in association with the very word *běrît* ("covenant") in the exhortation that immediately precedes the basic list of stipulations, the "Ten Words" (5:1-5).

---

[50] For more detailed discussion see "Deuteronomy and Critical Scholarship" (pp. 36-37).
[51] Watts, "The Deuteronomic Theology," 324-25.

The form of the Decalogue here (5:6-21) is virtually identical to its recension in Exodus, although, as noted already, there are slight differences because of the new historical and environmental circumstances awaiting this new generation of Israel. Also like its model in Exodus, the Deuteronomic Decalogue provides a platform of principles upon which the remainder of the general stipulations must rest and, indeed, of which they are a detailed interpretation and elaboration (5:22–11:32).

These stipulations, again, are described as *miṣwâ* (singular here, best rendered "commandment"), *ḥuqqîm*, and *mišpāṭîm* (6:1; cf. 5:31). They are intimated in the Shema of 6:4-5, the confessional fulcrum of Old Testament faith that defines Yahweh as the unique Sovereign and reduces Israel's obligation to him to one of exclusive love, that is, obedience. The whole purpose of the collection of stipulations is, in fact, to set forth application of the principles of the Ten Words and the Shema (6:6; cf. 5:22) as an expression of the fundamental duty of the servant people.

The basic stipulations (7:1–11:32) required the dispossession of non-vassals who were to be utterly destroyed because they would cause Israel to become disloyal. Moreover, the land belonged to Yahweh, and since Israel was the vassal of Yahweh, only they had legitimate claim to tenancy. They also insisted that Israel recognize Yahweh as the only source of blessing and life in the land. He who supplied manna in the desert could and would provide all that his people needed in Canaan. The principles of the covenant stipulations, however, went on to emphasize that all blessings, past and future, are attributable to Yahweh's grace. Possession of the land is not just an accident of history but an outworking of Yahweh's irrefragable promises to the fathers and of his sovereign pleasure.

The specific stipulations (12:1–26:15), based squarely on the principles of the foregoing section, serve at least two major theological purposes. First, they further elucidate the fundamental covenant themes of Deut 4:40–11:32. That is, they function in a real sense as a case-by-case commentary on that section. Second, they define precisely the terms of the covenant relative to cultic, ethical, and societal/interpersonal/interethnic relationships. That is, they make practical application of what was more or less theoretical propositions.

Though the rationale for the present canonical arrangement of the material in this section is elusive (see p. 31), the following is at least a possibility: (1) the exclusiveness of Yahweh and his worship (12:1–16:17); (2) the theocratic officials (16:18–18:22); (3) civil law (19:1–22:4); (4) laws of purity (22:5–23:19); (5) laws of interpersonal relationship (23:20–25:19); and (6) law concerning covenant celebration and confirmation (26:1-15). It is evident that all of these find their center in Yahweh, his people, and the covenant that binds them together.

The exclusiveness of Yahweh is underscored by the insistence that worship be centralized in one place, the place where Yahweh would choose to "put his name" (12:5,11). There and only there could tribute offered to the sovereign—especially that of the blood of sacrificed animals—be presented to him. This is in opposition to the notion of the multiplicity of pagan gods and their respective shrines, all of which were to be eradicated, including the prophets who promoted these competing (if nonexistent) deities (13:5,9-10). Another mark of the distinction between the purity of Yahwistic faith and the corruption of paganism was the line of demarcation drawn between the clean and unclean animals (14:1-3). The arbitrary definition of a clean animal suggests the sovereign election by Yahweh of a people whom he alone declared to be holy. Finally, Yahweh's exclusiveness was celebrated by the tribute paid him by his vassal people Israel. This took the form of the tithe (14:22-29); the septennial release of bondslaves who symbolized Israel as a liberated slave people; the dedication of the firstborn to Yahweh in recognition of his having spared the firstborn in the tenth plague; and annual pilgrimages to the central sanctuary, journeys whose purpose was to proclaim the lordship of Yahweh to whom his loyal subjects came in submissive presentation of tribute.

The chasm between the ineffable Lord and his theocratic citizens was bridged in part by officials appointed by him to represent him to them and them to him. Thus there were judges and "officials" (*šōṭĕrîm*, 16:18), kings, Levitical priests, and prophets, all of whom bore the awesome privilege and heavy responsibilities incumbent on those who would serve the King. For them to fail was to invite divine displeasure and judgment (e.g., Deut 18:20-22).

Israel's role as a theocratic community did not elevate them to the point of removing them from among the family of nations. They were a people of heavenly purpose, serving the only and transcendent God, but they had their feet firmly planted on the earth. As such, Israel was to operate within the framework of ordinary civil and social relationships. Therefore they had to know how to deal with all the exigencies of national life though, as the vassal people of Yahweh, in such a way as to draw attention to that unique role. This would impact the way the nation dealt with homicide (19:1-13); boundary disputes; due process; war; and the just treatment of wives, children, criminals, and moveable goods.

Purity laws, which dealt directly or indirectly with forms of separation, testify to the need for Israel to maintain covenant purity and separation. They concern such matters as clothing (22:5), mother birds (22:6-7), freedom from liability (22:8), mixed seed, animals, and cloth (22:9-11), and a variety of other cases whose significance with respect to the principle of purity is not always easy to determine. What bound them together theologically was the recognition that Yahweh himself was among his people and that his holiness demanded their best efforts at holiness (Deut 23:14).

The theological importance of proper behavior of a covenant member toward his fellow is reemphasized by another set of stipulations (23:20–25:19), similar in some respects to those already addressed (especially in 21:10–22:4) but with greater business and economic interests in view. Because all members of the theocratic community are equal before God, they must be absolutely evenhanded and scrupulously honest and fair in their dealings with one another. If the heart of covenant confession was the requirement that they love the Lord their God with all their heart, soul, and strength (Deut 6:5), the corollary, that they love their neighbor as themselves (Lev 19:18), was equally obligatory.

The sixth area of concern in the specific stipulation section is that of regular and consistent recognition by the vassal of his indebtedness to his beneficent God for all his redemptive and restorative acts of grace. This was to find expression particularly at the time of harvest festival when the worshiper, with offering in hand, recited the sacred history of his people, dedicated himself anew to the task of covenant keeping, and gave evidence of that commitment by the presentation of a special tithe to God's dependent ministers (26:1-15). It is fitting that this pledge of covenant fidelity was made at precisely the place mentioned at the beginning of the special stipulation section, that is, at "the place the LORD your God will choose as a dwelling for his Name" (26:2; cf. 12:5).

The permanency of the covenant relationship is implied by the command that Israel, once in the land of promise, should undertake covenant renewal at Mount Ebal, a ceremony centered on the very words of the covenant text being composed by Moses (Deut 27:1-7). The solemnity of what they would do there would be apparent in the curses that would result from their disobedience to the aforementioned stipulations (27:11-26; 28:15-68) and the blessings that would ensue the pursuit of obedience (28:1-14). Such curses and blessings had already attended Israel's pilgrimage to that point and were a guarantee that Yahweh's dealings with his people in the present and future would be no different. Therefore, Moses said, the present generation, as well as those to come, must commit and recommit themselves to covenant faithfulness (30:11-20).

Since the covenant was articulated in the Mosaic writings themselves, specifically in Deuteronomy (31:9), future commitment to its principles presupposed its preservation in a place both safe and accessible. The document was thus entrusted to the Levitical priests and the elders of Israel who, upon stated occasions, would release it for public reading. As a reminder of the pledge the people had undertaken to keep covenant they would also regularly sing a song whose very content was a recitation of God's redemptive work on behalf of Israel (32:1-43). Finally, in affirmation of the steadfastness of Yahweh's commitment to the nation, Moses offered a promissory blessing in which the tribes are prophetically described as recipients of divine favor (33:2-29).

The theology of Deuteronomy is best seen, then, in terms of the form and structure of the book. It is a covenant text, so one is not surprised at the centrality of covenant as the dominant theological motif. The other necessary ingredients—Yahweh, the covenant initiator, and Israel, the covenant recipient—also find their natural place in the theological interpretation of the composition.

The theological relevance and importance of Deuteronomy to the New Testament and to Christian faith is most apparent from the fact that the book is lavishly quoted and/or cited in the New Testament by Jesus and the apostles (cf. Matt 4:4,7,10; 5:21,31; Mark 7:10; 12:19; Luke 10:27; John 8:5,17; Rom 10:8). To them it was one of the foundational Old Testament writings upon which Christian doctrine and the church itself must be based. This does not suggest, of course, that there was no distinction between Deuteronomy as a covenant-legal text with special and even limited application to Old Testament Israel as a theocratic community and Deuteronomy as an expression of the character and purposes of God as manifested in the redemptive work of Jesus Christ. However, as E. R. Clendenen points out: "Life in its fullness for Israel as for the church required the recognition that it was an undeserved gift of an awesome and loving God, and consisted in gratefully living in the presence of and according to the character of that God."[52] Such a commonality of theme between the Testaments makes plain the ongoing theological importance of Deuteronomy to all believers.

11. Text of the Book

Virtually all scholars agree that the Masoretic Text of Deuteronomy is remarkably superior. The Ben Asher manuscript traditions of about A.D. 1000 as well as the Aleppo codices of a slightly earlier time reflect a homogeneous reading that is supported by the Qumran scrolls which, taken together, allow a reasonably good reconstruction of the pre-Christian Deu-

---

[52] Clendenen, "Life in God's Land," 171.

teronomy Hebrew text.[53] The variations from the MT in the ancient versions are very minor for the most part and, in any case, are seldom persuasive of changes in the Masoretic reading. Where versional and other textual witnesses do affect the meaning of the relevant passages, they will receive ad loc attention throughout the commentary.

---

[53] P. C. Craigie, *The Book of Deuteronomy,* NICOT (Grand Rapids: Eerdmans, 1976), 84-86. For texts, manuscripts, and versions see also I. Drazin, *Targum Onkelos to Deuteronomy* (New York: KTAV, 1982); B. Grossfeld, *The Targum Onqelos to Deuteronomy, The Aramaic Bible: The Targums,* vol. 9 (Wilmington: Michael Glazier, 1988); R. Le Deaut and J. Robert, *Targum du Pentateuque,* vol. 4, *Deutéronome* (Paris: Editions du Cerf, 1978-81); J. W. Wevers, "Attitudes of the Greek Translator of Deuteronomy towards His Parent Text," *Beitrage zur alttestamentlichen Theologie,* ed. H. Donner et al. (Göttingen: Vandenhoeck & Ruprecht, 1977), 498-505; id., "The Earliest Witness to the LXX Deuteronomy," *CBQ* 39 (1977): 240-44; S. A. White, "The All Souls Deuteronomy and the Decalogue," *JBL* 109 (1990): 193-206; id., "4 Q Dtn: Biblical Manuscript or Excerpted Text?" in *Of Scribes and Scrolls,* ed. H. W. Attridge et al. (Lanham, Md.: University Press of America, 1990), 13-20; id., "Three Deuteronomy Manuscripts from Cave 4, Qumran," *JBL* 112 (1993): 23-42; T. Wittstruck, "So-called Anti-anthropomorphisms in the Greek Text of Deuteronomy," *CBQ* 38 (1976): 29-34.

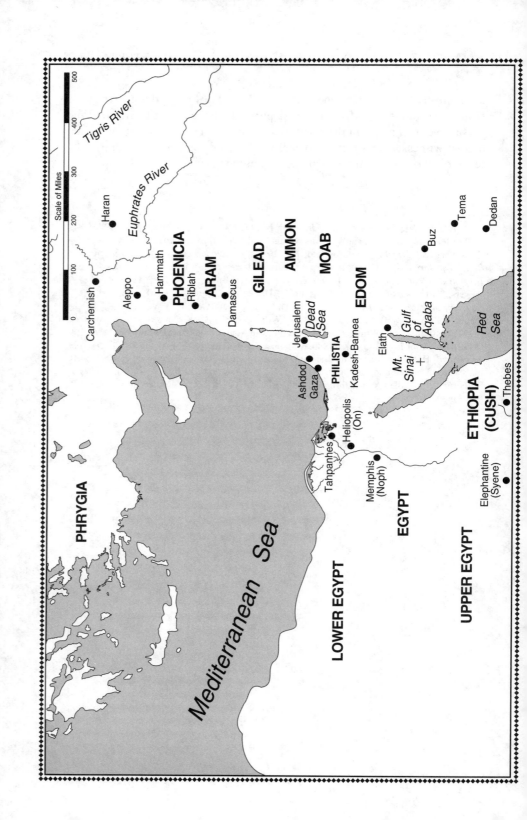

¹These are the words Moses spoke to all Israel in the desert east of the Jordan—that is, in the Arabah—opposite Suph, between Paran and Tophel, Laban, Hazeroth and Dizahab. ²(It takes eleven days to go from Horeb to Kadesh Barnea by the Mount Seir road.)

³In the fortieth year, on the first day of the eleventh month, Moses proclaimed to the Israelites all that the LORD had commanded him concerning them. ⁴This was after he had defeated Sihon king of the Amorites, who reigned in Heshbon, and at Edrei had defeated Og king of Bashan, who reigned in Ashtaroth.

⁵East of the Jordan in the territory of Moab, Moses began to expound this law, saying:

The content of this introductory section provides the geographical and historical setting for the covenant message Moses is about to deliver to the tribes of Israel. In line with form-critical analysis of the Book of Deuteronomy as a covenant renewal text of the sovereign-vassal type, however, it could be described as the *Preamble,* the term commonly applied in secular examples of this kind of covenant.[1] As such, its purpose is to introduce the occasion for the covenant, the parties involved, and any other information necessary to identify the document and the peculiarities of its composition. These are precisely the elements that appear in this section.

1:1 Moses, the covenant mediator, was the spokesman here. His role as such is clear from the fact that he spoke "to all Israel" (v. 1) "all that the LORD had commanded him" (v. 3). That is, he provided the prophetic linkage between the initiator of the covenant (i.e., Yahweh) and all its demands and the recipient of that gracious overture, Moses' own people Israel. This, of course, was much in line with his function as revealed elsewhere in Scripture (see Num 12:6-8; Deut 18:18; 34:10-12; 1 Kgs 8:53; 2 Kgs 18:6; 23:25; Luke 16:29,31; 24:27; Heb 9:19).

The covenant text itself is described here by the technical term "words" (*dĕbārîm*), a term pervasively used in Deuteronomy in this sense (1:18; 4:2; 6:6; 11:18; 30:14) as well as in a more limited way to speak of individual regulations (12:28; 15:15; 24:18,22) or of the Decalogue as a whole

---

[1] G. E. Mendenhall, *Law and Covenant in Israel and the Ancient Near East,* Part II, "Covenant Forms in Israelite Traditions" (Pittsburgh: Biblical Colloquium, 1955), 32. Christensen includes v. 6a as part of this section on the basis of a resulting concentric structure that contains דברים and דבר in line *A,* דבר in line *A',* and דבר in the hinge line *D* (D. L. Christensen, *Deuteronomy 1–11,* WBC 6A [Dallas: Word, 1991], 6). In terms of treaty form, however, the division between vv. 5 and 6 is to be preferred.

(4:10,13,36; 5:5,22; 9:10; 10:2,4).[2] That is, although Moses obviously was speaking words to the assembly, they were words that constituted the covenant document as a whole and in its parts. This does not preclude the fact, of course, that not all of Deuteronomy is a covenant text in the strict sense. There are words in addition to those that properly are part of the standard text of the covenant instrument. That Moses intended "words" in the more restricted sense is clear, however, from his own interpretive gloss in v. 5: "Moses began to expound this law" (*tôrâ*). "Law" here and "words" in v. 1 are thus synonymous terms.[3]

Moses' audience, "all Israel," is not to be taken literally as though the entire population of the nation was assembled in one place and at one time to hear his address. Given a postexodus population of over 600,000 men of twenty years and older (Num 26:51; cf. 26:4), the nation as a whole must be numbered in the several of millions. Moses therefore was speaking to representatives of "all Israel," probably the elders (cf. Num 11:16-30; Deut 27:1; 31:9,28), though obviously the message was intended for all and would become accessible to all when it finally was committed to writing.[4]

In establishing the setting, the historian focused first on the geographical arena in which the message of covenant renewal took place. It was "in the desert east of the Jordan" (v. 1)[5] in what is now the Hashemite Kingdom of Jordan. More particularly it is the Arabah, a word for desert that usually refers to the section of the Great Rift Valley between the Dead Sea and the Gulf of Elath (or Aqabah) but occasionally to the Jordan River valley itself.[6] Here the section immediately north of the Dead Sea is in view, for elsewhere the place of assembly is designated as "the plains of Moab by the Jordan across from Jericho" (Num 35:1; 36:13).[7]

The following elaboration is extremely difficult to reconstruct. The place of gathering is said to be "opposite Suph," and, moreover, "between Paran and Tophel, Laban, Hazeroth and Dizahab." Only Paran and Hazeroth can be identified with certainty, the former being the great desert between

---

[2] W. H. Schmidt דָּבַר (*dābhar*); דָּבָר (*dābhār*) *TDOT* 3:117-18.

[3] P. C. Craigie, *The Book of Deuteronomy*, NICOT (Grand Rapids: Eerdmans, 1976), 92.

[4] Cf. J. W. Flanagan, "The Deuteronomic Meaning of the Phrase 'kol yisraʾel,'" *SR* 6 (1976-77): 159-68.

[5] "East of the Jordan" translates בְּעֵבֶר הַיַּרְדֵּן, i.e., "in the Transjordan." Cf. B. Gemser, "Beʿēber Hajjardēn: In Jordan's Borderland," *VT* 2 (1952): 349-55. This was a geographical technical expression that provides no clue about the location of the author. From the Canaanite perspective the area of Moab was "in the Transjordan," and thus even persons in that area would view themselves as being "in the Transjordan" (cf. 3:8; 4:41). Gemser suggests for this passage "at the side of, in the region of the Jordan" (p. 353).

[6] Y. Aharoni, *The Land of the Bible* (Philadelphia: Westminster, 1979), 35-36.

[7] J. Ridderbos, *Deuteronomy*, BSC (Grand Rapids: Zondervan, 1984), 51-52.

Mount Sinai and Kadesh Barnea and the latter a stopping place for Israel in the southern part of Paran (Num 11:35; 12:16).[8] This being the case, they hardly could have been the place where Moses spoke the covenant address, for that clearly took place in Moab (v. 5), opposite Jericho.

The best solution might be to take the words "opposite Suph" and following as a way of describing the Arabah itself. That is, the Arabah in mind is that which extends from lower Paran northward to the plains of Moab. The identification of Suph is problematic.[9] But inasmuch as the Red Sea in general appears to have been known as *Yam Sûph* ("sea of reeds," Exod 10:19; 13:18; 15:4,22; Deut 11:4) and even its eastern branch, the Gulf of Elath, was so designated (Num 21:4; 14:25; Deut 1:40; 2:1; 1 Kgs 9:26), "opposite" (*môl*) Suph (or "in front of" or "towards") means only "adjacent to the sea."[10] That is, the Arabah extended loosely from Paran northward and parallel to the Gulf of Elath. Tophel,[11] Laban,[12] Hazeroth,[13] and Dizahab[14] would be places along the route of the Israelite itinerary from Sinai to Moab, way stations in or alongside the Arabah.

1:2 This interpretation gains strong support in the following declaration that "it takes eleven days to go from Horeb to Kadesh Barnea by the Mount Seir road" (v. 2). Rather than being merely parenthetical (as in NIV), this statement further identifies the Arabah route as none other than the "Mount Seir road" that connects Horeb with Kadesh Barnea.[15] "Horeb" is the name for Mount Sinai favored by Deuteronomy, occurring nine times as compared to a single instance of "Sinai" (Deut 33:2, a poetic section). Sinai, however, is the usual name in Exodus (thirteen times versus three for

---

[8] "Paran" (Modern Feiran) refers to the wilderness from Sinai to Kadesh Barnea generally (including the wilderness of Zin [Num 20:1; 27:14]). Hazeroth may be identified with modern 'Ain Khadra. Cf. Aharoni, *Land of the Bible*, 199-200.

[9] B. F. Batto, "The Reed Sea: *Requiescat in Pace*," *JBL* 102 (1983): 27-35. Batto does not refer to this passage but shows how complex the term *(yam) sûp* is throughout the OT.

[10] Many scholars identify Suph with some place in Moab or Edom such as Supah (Num 21:14). Thus A. D. H. Mayes, *Deuteronomy*, NCBC (Grand Rapids: Eerdmans, 1979), 114. As Weinfeld points out, however, this does not fit the itinerary (*Deuteronomy 1–11*, AB [New York: Doubleday, 1991], 126).

[11] Perhaps et-Ṭafîleh in Edom; cf. H. Cazelles, "Tophel (Deut. 1:1)," *VT* 9 (1959): 412-15. Cazelles identifies Tophel with a region known now as Dâbîlu, perhaps another name for Paran (p. 415).

[12] Perhaps Libnah (Num 33:20); cf. Craigie, *Deuteronomy*, 90, n. 8.

[13] See n. 8.

[14] Perhaps Mina-al-Dhahab on the east Sinai coast; Weinfeld, *Deuteronomy 1–11*, 127.

[15] G. I. Davies, "The Significance of Deuteronomy 1:2 for the Location of Mount Horeb," *PEQ* 111 (1979): 100; L. Perlitt, "Sinai und Horeb," in *Beiträge zur Alttestamentlichen Theologie: FS, W. Zimmerli*, ed. H. Donner et al. (Göttingen: Vandenhoeck & Ruprecht, 1977), 302-22.

Horeb) and Numbers (twelve times and none, respectively). Mount Seir is simply a way of describing the entire land of Seir or Edom.[16] The reason for pointing out that the distance from Horeb to Kadesh Barnea is an eleven-day journey (ca. 140 miles) is no doubt to give some idea of the ruggedness of that terrain and of the difficulties Israel had experienced in reaching the present place and moment of covenant renewal. On the other hand, eleven days would contrast sharply with the forty years of wandering necessitated by Israel's wilderness rebellion (Num 14:34).

1:3 The narrator turns next to the chronological aspect of the setting. It is the fortieth year (obviously with reference to the exodus; cf. Num 33:38) or about 1406 B.C. (see Introduction, p. 23). The first day of the eleventh month (Shebat in the later Hebrew calendar) would correspond to a date in January/February in the Gregorian calendar.[17] Since the conquest of Canaan under Joshua commenced at Passover (Josh 5:10) in the first month of the religious calendar, Moses' address, death, and succession all took place in two months or so.

1:4 More specifically, the conclave in Moab took place after Israel, under Moses, had successfully engaged two enemy kings in battle: Sihon of the Amorites, who ruled from Heshbon, and Og of Bashan, whose capital was Ashtaroth. Both campaigns are described more fully in Num 21 and in Deut 2:26–3:22.[18] The Amorites, whose roots are found in upper Mesopotamia and Syria (ancient Amurru), appear to have migrated to Palestine at ca. 2200–1800 B.C. and to have displaced the Canaanites in the hill country especially (cf. Num 13:29; Josh 10:6). They also had expelled the indigenous Moabites east of the Jordan (Num 21:26) and occupied Moab north of the Arnon River, making Heshbon their capital. Their king Sihon is unknown outside the Bible.

Bashan lay north of the Yarmuk River, the great tributary of the Jordan that enters it just south of the Sea of Galilee. It was ruled by Og (also unattested extrabiblically) from Ashtaroth, probably to be identified with Tel 'Ashtarah, some twenty miles due east of the Sea of Galilee. Moses and Israel defeated him at Edrei (Num 21:33), about fifteen miles southeast of Ashtaroth. The ethnic identity of the people of Bashan is unclear though Og himself is said to have been a Rephaite giant who required an iron bed (Deut 3:11; cf. 2:11,20).

---

[16] Aharoni, *Land of the Bible,* 40, 142.

[17] R. de Vaux, *Ancient Israel* (New York: McGraw-Hill, 1985), 1:185-86.

[18] For full discussion see commentary on Deut 2:26–3:22.

II. THE HISTORICAL REVIEW (1:6–4:40)
  1. The Past Dealings of the Lord with Israel (1:6–3:29)
    (1) Events at Horeb (1:6-18)
      The Command to Journey On (1:6-8)
      The Incapacity of Moses (1:9-15)
      The Instructions of Moses (1:16-18)
    (2) Instructions at Kadesh Barnea (1:19-25)
    (3) Disobedience at Kadesh Barnea (1:26-33)
    (4) Judgment at Kadesh Barnea (1:34-40)
    (5) Unsuccessful Conquest of Canaan (1:41-46)
    (6) The Journey from Kadesh Barnea to Moab (2:1-15)
      Instructions concerning Edom (2:1-8)
      Instructions concerning Moab (2:9-15)
    (7) Conflict with Transjordanian Enemies (2:16–3:11)
      Instructions concerning Ammon (2:16-25)
      Defeat of Sihon, King of Heshbon (2:26-37)
      Defeat of Og, King of Bashan (3:1-11)
    (8) Distribution of the Transjordanian Allotments (3:12-17)
    (9) Instructions to the Transjordanian Tribes (3:18-22)
    (10) Denial to Moses of the Promised Land (3:23-29)
  2. The Exhortation of Moses (4:1-40)
    (1) The Privileges of the Covenant (4:1-8)
    (2) Reminder of the Horeb Covenant (4:9-14)
    (3) The Nature of Israel's God (4:15-24)
    (4) Threat and Blessing Following Covenant Disobedience (4:25-31)
    (5) The Uniqueness of Israel's God (4:32-40)

II. THE HISTORICAL REVIEW (1:6–4:40)

In terms of standard elements of ancient Near Eastern treaty texts, particularly those of the Hittites after which the biblical examples are modeled, this section of Deuteronomy may be designated "The Historical

Prologue."[1] The purpose of such an element was to call to mind the past relationship that existed between the maker of the covenant and the subject peoples with whom it was being made or renewed. This was done particularly to emphasize the goodness of the Great King and to celebrate his watchcare over his weak and defenseless vassal. The utter dependence of the lesser partner was thus also underscored. Moreover, the historical résumé would also draw attention to the punishment that inevitably attended covenant infidelity and, conversely, the reward that followed obedience.

The portion in view here includes all of these themes and, in addition, is interspersed with parenesis, that is, with Mosaic injunctions and exhortations to the effect that Israel ought to have learned something from history.[2] Those things that had been true and beneficial ought to be continued in the present and on into the future whereas the mistakes and sins and shortcomings of the past ought, at all cost, to be avoided. Deuteronomy 4 is almost exclusively hortatory in tone and content, yet even this passage harks back to the past so that history might provide the context in and against which covenant renewal can take place.

1. The Past Dealings of the Lord with Israel (1:6–3:29)

(1) Events at Horeb (1:6-18)

[6]The LORD our God said to us at Horeb, "You have stayed long enough at this mountain. [7]Break camp and advance into the hill country of the Amorites; go to all the neighboring peoples in the Arabah, in the mountains, in the western foothills, in the Negev and along the coast, to the land of the Canaanites and to Lebanon, as far as the great river, the Euphrates. [8]See, I have given you this land. Go in and take possession of the land that the LORD swore he would give to your fathers—to Abraham, Isaac and Jacob—and to their descendants after them."

[9]At that time I said to you, "You are too heavy a burden for me to carry

---

[1] G. E. Mendenhall, *Law and Covenant in Israel and the Ancient Near East,* Part II, "Covenant Forms in Israelite Traditions" (Pittsburgh: Biblical Colloquium, 1955), 32. P. C. Craigie (*The Book of Deuteronomy,* [Grand Rapids: Eerdmans, 1976], 145) extends the prologue through 4:43 and yet equivocates on the inclusion of 4:41-43, conceding that these verses "are not a part of the address of Moses," that is, of the prologue proper. See commentary on 4:41-49.

[2] On the educative and hortatory elements of Moses' address, see S. Amsler, "La motivation de l'ethique dans la parenese du Deutéronome," in *Beiträge zur alttestamentlichen Theologie: FS W. Zimmerli,* ed. H. Donner et al. (Göttingen: Vandenhoeck & Ruprecht, 1977), 11-22.

alone. [10]The LORD your God has increased your numbers so that today you are as many as the stars in the sky. [11]May the LORD, the God of your fathers, increase you a thousand times and bless you as he has promised! [12]But how can I bear your problems and your burdens and your disputes all by myself? [13]Choose some wise, understanding and respected men from each of your tribes, and I will set them over you."

[14]You answered me, "What you propose to do is good."

[15]So I took the leading men of your tribes, wise and respected men, and appointed them to have authority over you—as commanders of thousands, of hundreds, of fifties and of tens and as tribal officials. [16]And I charged your judges at that time: Hear the disputes between your brothers and judge fairly, whether the case is between brother Israelites or between one of them and an alien. [17]Do not show partiality in judging; hear both small and great alike. Do not be afraid of any man, for judgment belongs to God. Bring me any case too hard for you, and I will hear it. [18]And at that time I told you everything you were to do.

Moses did not commence his review of history with creation or even with the call of Abraham or the exodus. The explicit purpose of Deuteronomy was to call the people Israel to covenant renewal, that is, to a reaffirmation of that arrangement between the Lord and his people that was begun at Sinai (or Horeb).[3] Thus the proper beginning place was the inaugural of the covenant and the series of events that accompanied it and proceeded from it over the forty years just past.

THE COMMAND TO JOURNEY ON (1:6-8). **1:6-8** After approximately a year at Mount Sinai (cf. Exod 19:1; Num 10:11), the Lord commanded his people to leave that region and begin the long trek to the land of promise. There is no hint that they were to take any but the shortest and straightest route, for until then the punishment of wandering the desert had not been inflicted (see vv. 34-40). The following description of the land (v. 7) is remarkably comprehensive in its scope and in its precision in marking out regional and topographical features. The "hill country of the Amorites" refers to the interior of Canaan and the Transjordan, an area inhabited by the Amorites since at least 1800 B.C. (see comment on v. 4).[4] The "neighboring peoples in the Arabah" (lit., "all its neighboring [places] in the Arabah and elsewhere") no doubt refers to settlements in the Jordan Valley and

---

[3] This is not to say that there are no references to the fathers or the exodus, but such references are interwoven throughout the discourse, showing, among other things, that the present covenant, though resting on ancient antecedents (cf. 1:8,11,21,35), is itself the center of focus. Cf. Craigie, *Deuteronomy,* 94.

[4] M. Liverani, "The Amorites," in *Peoples of Old Testament Times,* ed. D. J. Wiseman (Oxford: Clarendon, 1973), 124-26.

in the eastern deserts that adjoined the hill country. The "mountains" describes hill country outside that of Samaria and Judah, most likely that of the Galilee area and the upper Negev; the "western foothills" are the lowlands between the Mediterranean coastal plain and the hills of Judah; the Negev was the vast desert south of Judah; and the seacoast obviously the Mediterranean littoral that has always formed Israel's western border. The "land of the Canaanites" speaks of the valleys and plains, especially those of Jezreel to the north, that remained in Canaanite control well into the time of the Israelite judges (Judg 4:1-3).[5]

The great extent of the land—"as far as the great river, the Euphrates" —reflects the ideal inheritance that God had promised the patriarchal ancestors as part of the covenant pledge he had vouchsafed to them (Gen 15:18-21; 26:3; Exod 23:31). The fact that this territory was never, in its entirety, brought under Israelite control except possibly in the heyday of David and Solomon (cf. 1 Kgs 4:21) does not vitiate the promise, for its eschatological fulfillment lies yet ahead (Ezek 47:15-20). That it was theirs by right and not by might is clear from the verb "take possession" (v. 8), for in context of the covenant promise the Heb. *yāraš* ("take possession of") connotes inheritance.[6] Yahweh the Great King owns all the earth, and it is his to bestow upon his peoples as he wishes. His people, therefore, were not about to take the land of other people but to receive the land as a gift from its divine owner, coming into their own rightful claim as vassals who work the royal estate of the Lord their God (cf. 1:39; 3:20; 10:11; Josh 1:15; 21:43).[7]

THE INCAPACITY OF MOSES (1:9-15).   **1:9-10**   Again appealing to the past,[8] Moses reminded his listeners of the time, even before the Sinai covenant was made, when he expressed his inability to manage the affairs of leadership because the population of the nation had become so great (Exod 18:13-27). This burgeoning growth had come about, of course, as a direct fulfillment of promise to the fathers (Gen 15:5; 17:2; cf. Exod 1:7; Deut

---

[5] With many scholars it might be argued that "land of the Canaanites" is equivalent to "along the seacoast," thus suggesting Canaanite occupation of the Mediterranean coast as far north as Lebanon. So, e.g., J. A. Thompson, *Deuteronomy,* TOTC (Downers Grove: Inter-Varsity, 1974), 85.

[6] A. D. H. Mayes, *Deuteronomy,* NCBC (Grand Rapids: Eerdmans, 1979), 120-21.

[7] N. Lohfink, "יָרַשׁ *yāraš*," etc. *TDOT* 6:384-85.

[8] D. L. Christensen draws attention to the unity of the section (1:9-18) on the basis of the rubric "at that time" that occurs in both v. 9a and v. 18a (*Deuteronomy 1–11,* WBC 6A [Dallas: Word, 1991], 19); see also his "Prose and Poetry in the Bible: The Narrative Poetics of Deuteronomy 1:9-18," *ZAW* 97 [1985]: 179-89). While this is beyond dispute, vv. 9-18 can also be divided topically between Moses' problem (vv. 9-15) and its solution (vv. 16-18). Christensen sees such a break (p. 187).

10:22; 26:5). Moses therefore saw this state of affairs not as a problem but as a sign of the blessing of the Lord. In fact, he reported that his innermost desire was that God make them not just as numerous as the stars but a thousand times more so. The language of hyperbole —"as many as the stars" and "increase you a thousand times" (vv. 10-11)—is not, of course, to be taken literally. In fact, however, the descendants of Abraham have become many more than the stars the patriarch could have counted with the naked eye.

1:11-13 Nevertheless, the blessing of numbers brought about its practical problems of administration. Moses therefore had urged his fellow citizens to select from among them those who had the capacity for leadership.[9] The necessary attributes were that they be wise, understanding, and respected (v. 13). The first of these qualifications is expressed by the common Hebrew word *ḥokmâ*, a term suggesting capability in practical matters, here ability in civil and military affairs (cf. v. 15). The juxtaposition of this word with *nābon* ("understanding"), a synonym in many passages (Gen 41:33,39; 1 Kgs 3:12; Isa 5:21; Jer 4:22; Prov 1:5; 16:21; 17:28; 18:15),[10] might best be rendered here as a hendiadys, "very wise" or the like. The third adjective, "respected," derives from a verb meaning "to know." That is, these leaders must be well known to the community and, having passed the test of close scrutiny, end up being respected by it.[11]

1:14-15 All those men who met the criteria just listed were then selected by Moses to have authority over the nation (v. 15). There is somewhat of a problem here in the Hebrew rendition in that v. 13 says literally, "I will appoint them as your heads [i.e., leaders],"[12] whereas v. 15 reads, "So I took the heads of your tribes . . . and appointed them as heads over you." It is perhaps best to take the first occurrence of "heads" as a proleptic glance toward the actual appointment. That is, the wise and respected of v. 13 were destined to become the tribal leaders and so were already referred

---

[9] For the technical terms used to describe the following officials see H. Cazelles, "Institutions et terminologie en Deutéronome 1, 6-17," VTSup 15 (Leiden: Brill, n.d.), 97-112.

[10] H.-P. Müller, "חָכַם *chākham*," etc., *TDOT* 4:371.

[11] The passive form of the verb וִידֻעִים, from יָדַע, supports the idea of reputation here, that is, of being known. Thus S. R. Driver, *A Critical and Exegetical Commentary on Deuteronomy*, ICC (Edinburgh: T & T Clark, 1902), 16-17. So also C. F. Keil and F. Delitzsch, *Biblical Commentary on the Old Testament*, vol. III, *The Pentateuch*, trans. J. Martin (Grand Rapids: Eerdmans, n.d.), 286.

[12] On the term "head" see J. R. Bartlett, "The Use of the Word רֹאשׁ as a Title in the Old Testament," VT 19 (1969): 1-10. Bartlett views the use of the term here primarily as a reference to the judiciary (p. 4).

to as such in the first clause of v. 15.[13] The point is that leaders are not always chosen because they are wise and of good reputation, but in this case those are the only qualifications that matter.

The function of these leaders is both military and civil.[14] The first of these is clear from the common divisions of military forces—thousands, hundreds, fifties, tens—over which the new commanders would exercise authority. This may almost be described as a standard military formula in the Old Testament by which to characterize military forces (1 Sam 8:12; 22:7; 2 Sam 18:1; 1 Chr 13:1; 2 Chr 1:2; 25:5), although only here and in the original setting to which Moses was referring (Exod 18:21) do all four divisions occur. The "tribal officials" (Heb. *šōṭĕrîm*) are the civil leaders including magistrates and judges.[15] In fact, a few textual traditions (LXX, Vg.) read "judges" here (*šōpĕṭîm* for *šōṭĕrîm*) no doubt under the influence of the reference to "judges" in v. 16. The MT should be retained, however, in light of the obvious attempt at "correction" by these traditions.

THE INSTRUCTIONS OF MOSES (1:16-18). **1:16-18** The role of the judges in this early stage of Israel's history is unusually well spelled out here (vv. 16-17).[16] They were to hear cases involving fellow Israelites and even between Israelites and aliens,[17] and they must render a just verdict (v. 16). Moreover, they must not be influenced by social status. The Hebrew idiom here (*lōʾ takkîrû pānîm*) means literally "do not regard faces," that is, do not be impressed by the reputation or actual standing of parties who are subject to judgment. Indeed, such persons can be intimidating, so Moses went on to say to the judges, "Do not be afraid of the face of men" (*lōʾ tāgûrû mippĕnê ʾîs*) (v. 17). One might even render the last phrase, "Do not be afraid of human faces [that is, of men]," for the next clause

---

[13] Besides, the reference is back to Exod 18:25, as Mayes points out (*Deuteronomy,* 123), where Moses did the appointing (in line with Deut 1:18) based, perhaps, on candidates already proposed by the people.

[14] M. Weinfeld, "Judge and Officer in Ancient Israel and in the Ancient Near East," *IOS* 7 (1977): 65-88.

[15] The term שֹׁטֵר derives from the verb שָׁטַר, "to write" (BDB, 1009); thus the "officer" of this kind had to do with business affairs that concerned orders, arrangements, records, and the like. Cf. R. D. Patterson, "שׁטר (shtr)," *TWOT* 2:918-19.

[16] For the origin and function of the office of judge in early Israel see F. C. Fensham, "The Judges and Ancient Israelite Jurisprudence," *OTWSA* 2 (1959): 15-22; A. van Selms, "The Title 'Judge,'" *OTWSA* 2 (1959): 41-50; H. Reviv, "The Traditions concerning the Inception of the Legal System in Israel: Significance and Dating," *ZAW* 94 (1982): 566-75; J. Milgrom, "The Ideological and Historical Importance of the Office of the Judge in Deuteronomy," in *Essays on the Bible and the Ancient World: Isaac Leo Seeligmann Volume,* ed. A. Rofé and Y. Zakovitch (Jerusalem: Elhanan Rubinstein, 1983), 129-39.

[17] P.-E. Dion, "Israel et L'Etranger dans le Deuteronome," *L'Altérité Vivre,* ed. M. Gourges and G.-D. Mailhiot (Montréal: Bellarmin/Cerf, 1986), 211-33.

emphasizes that judgment belongs to God. Since he is absolutely sovereign and furthermore knows the true guilt or innocence of parties in judgment, he, not human litigants, is to be feared.

This suggests that fairness in judgment is a theological as well as legal matter. There may be the need for due process at the practical and human level, but the ultimate standard of righteousness and justice is that which inheres in the character of God himself. Therefore, when human capacity for equitable judgment reaches its limits, appeal must be made ultimately to God. Israel's judges were to recognize this and conduct their legal proceedings in light of their accountability to him.

If they reached a stalemate, Moses said, they could appeal to him for adjudication of difficult cases. Moses' unique role of prophetic mediator between God and the people qualified him to translate their concerns to God and to render God's every decision to them (cf. Num 12:6-8).

(2) Instructions at Kadesh Barnea (1:19-25)

[19]Then, as the LORD our God commanded us, we set out from Horeb and went toward the hill country of the Amorites through all that vast and dreadful desert that you have seen, and so we reached Kadesh Barnea. [20]Then I said to you, "You have reached the hill country of the Amorites, which the LORD our God is giving us. [21]See, the LORD your God has given you the land. Go up and take possession of it as the LORD, the God of your fathers, told you. Do not be afraid; do not be discouraged."

[22]Then all of you came to me and said, "Let us send men ahead to spy out the land for us and bring back a report about the route we are to take and the towns we will come to."

[23]The idea seemed good to me; so I selected twelve of you, one man from each tribe. [24]They left and went up into the hill country, and came to the Valley of Eshcol and explored it. [25]Taking with them some of the fruit of the land, they brought it down to us and reported, "It is a good land that the LORD our God is giving us."

1:19 Moses now turned his attention to the journey of Israel from Horeb to Kadesh Barnea (and on to Moab eventually)[18] following the route to Mount Seir he had already described (1:1-2). The destination was the "hill country of the Amorites" (v. 19), that is, the central part of

---

[18] For the itinerary through the wilderness as a whole and for the Deuteronomy version compared to that in Exodus and Numbers (esp. as in Num 33:1-49), see, among others, G. I. Davies, "The Wilderness Itineraries: A Comparative Study," *TynBul* 25 (1974): 46-81; Z. Meshel, "An Explanation of the Journeys of the Israelites in the Wilderness," *BA* 45 (1982): 19-20; J. T. Walsh, "From Egypt to Moab: A Source Critical Analysis of the Wilderness Itinerary," *CBQ* 39 (1977): 20-33.

Canaan, which formed the heart of the promised inheritance (cf. v. 7). There is no reason to doubt that Kadesh Barnea was to be only a stop along the way and that the penetration of Canaan would be from the south, precisely the route followed by the twelve explorers (cf. vv. 22-25; Num 13:21-24). The later entry from the east and by way of Jericho was undertaken only because all other options had been closed because of Israel's disobedience (cf. Deut 2:1; 40; together with Num 14:25; 21:4).

The eleven-day journey from Horeb to Kadesh Barnea (v. 2) was fraught with danger and difficulty as v. 19 makes clear. The Paran desert through which it passed was "vast and dreadful," a situation described in great detail in the long itinerary account of Num 11:1–12:16. There must have been great relief then in reaching Kadesh Barnea, a large oasis with abundant springs and pastures. Most scholars identify it with modern 'Ain Qedeis, a major crossroads for travel between the south Sinai and the central hill country of Canaan and between the Gulf of Elath and the Mediterranean Sea.[19] It was to become the principal place of residence for the twelve tribes for the next thirty-eight years.

1:20-21 Having arrived at Kadesh Barnea, Moses urged his people to move on into the Amorite hill country, the southern reaches of which lay only a few miles to the north. At last they had come to the land that the Lord was about to give them (the better translation of the participle nōtēn in v. 20). In fact, Moses asserted the possession of the land was such an absolute certainty that he could speak of it as the land "the LORD your God has given you" (v. 21). The difference is that theologically and by divine grant from ancient times (cf. Gen 13:14-17) the occupation of the land was a *fait accompli* (hence the perfect tense of v. 21), but historically and practically it was yet to be taken (hence the participle of v. 20).[20]

In any event, whether in potential or in fact, the land lay open to the people for their taking. The urgency of Moses' insistence that they do so may be seen in the double imperatives "go up, take possession" (v. 21; cf. v. 8), which in the Hebrew text (unlike the NIV) lacks any conjunction.[21] There could not be any hesitation in order that Israel might capitalize on

---

[19] R. de Vaux, *The Early History of Israel* (Philadelphia: Westminster, 1978), 423-24. Recent scholarship identifies Kadesh Barnea explicitly with Tell el-Qudeirat, an oasis that probably was part of a triangle with ʿAin Qedeis and ʿAin Muweilah, the whole making up Kadesh Barnea. See R. Cohen, "Excavations at Kadesh-barnea 1976–1978," *BA* 44 (1981): 94-95.

[20] As I. Cairns puts it, "Promises five hundred years old are at the point of fruition" (*Word and Presence: A Commentary on the Book of Deuteronomy,* ITC [Grand Rapids: Eerdmans, 1992], 35.

[21] GKC § 120h.

the element of surprise but, more importantly, because the Lord, "the God of your fathers," had thus commanded. The identification of the Lord as the God of the fathers ties the present strategy and objectives to the ancient promises to Abraham, Isaac, and Jacob that Canaan, the land just over the horizon, belonged to their descendants by covenant grant (Gen 12:1; 13:14-17; 15:18-21; 17:8; 26:3-4; 48:3). It was, moreover, a promise reinforced by the Lord's instructions since the making of the Sinaitic covenant to the effect that that covenant was not complete until the land had been entered and occupied (Exod 23:20-31; 33:1-3; 34:10-11).

In light of both the promise and the command, Moses had good reason to exhort his audience to be neither afraid nor discouraged (v. 21). These two verbs, "afraid" and "discouraged," occur commonly in parallel or are juxtaposed to create a stock expression conveying the idea, in the positive, of complete confidence in the Lord and his ability to save (Deut 31:8; Josh 8:1; 10:25; 1 Sam 17:11; 1 Chr 22:13; 28:20; 2 Chr 20:15,17; 32:7; Jer 23:4; 30:10; 46:27; Ezek 2:6; 3:9).[22]

1:22 Moses went on to remind his present audience that their fathers, the previous generation, were not wholly persuaded of the presence and power of God, for they requested of Moses that he send intelligence agents on ahead who could survey the land and bring back a report about proper approach and objectives (v. 22). The account in Num 13 suggests that it was the Lord who prompted Moses to send out the advance party (Num 13:1-2). This apparently conflicting view of events is by no means antithetical to Moses' recollection in Deuteronomy, for clearly the idea originated with the people, was sanctioned, and then ordered by the Lord and implemented by Moses (Num 13:17). Nor is v. 23 particularly problematic, for one can well imagine that the people's request was made to Moses who, convinced it was a good idea, consulted the Lord and from him received endorsement that the Numbers version construes as an idea that had originated with the Lord in the first place.[23]

Though the plan to send spies may have bespoken a lack of total trust in God and, in fact, resulted in an undermining of Israel's resolve to enter Canaan at all (vv. 26-28), one can hardly criticize it as imprudent or impractical in such circumstances. In fact, the command (or at least permission) of the Lord in the first place (Num 13:1-2) is sufficient to show that the procedure was not totally lacking of divine support.

1:23-25 Be that as it may, Moses' own reaction is clear enough: "The idea seemed good to me" (v. 23). He therefore selected a representative

---

[22] F. Maass, "חתת, ḥātat," etc., *TDOT* 5:280.
[23] Thus, Craigie, *Deuteronomy,* 101.

from each tribe, the names of whom appear in Num 13:4-15. They made their way up into the hill country of Canaan, arriving first in the valley of Eshcol (v. 24). The résumé contained here in Deuteronomy appears to limit the exploration of the spies to Eshcol, but the full account in Num 13 indicates that they traveled the length and breadth of Canaan, "from the Desert of Zin as far as Rehob, toward Lebo Hamath" (v. 21).[24] Furthermore, the "fruit of the land" (Deut 1:25) is identified in Numbers as primarily grapes, a single cluster of which was so large and heavy that it required two men to carry it (Num 13:23). In fact, the place was later called Eshcol ("cluster") precisely because of its remarkable production of grapes (Num 13:24). There is little wonder that the returning scouts reported to the camp that "it is a good land that the LORD our God is giving us" (Deut 1:25) or, in the words of the Numbers narrative, "it does flow with milk and honey" (Num 13:27).

(3) Disobedience at Kadesh Barnea (1:26-33)

[26]But you were unwilling to go up; you rebelled against the command of the LORD your God. [27]You grumbled in your tents and said, "The LORD hates us; so he brought us out of Egypt to deliver us into the hands of the Amorites to destroy us. [28]Where can we go? Our brothers have made us lose heart. They say, 'The people are stronger and taller than we are; the cities are large, with walls up to the sky. We even saw the Anakites there.'"

[29]Then I said to you, "Do not be terrified; do not be afraid of them. [30]The LORD your God, who is going before you, will fight for you, as he did for you in Egypt, before your very eyes, [31]and in the desert. There you saw how the LORD your God carried you, as a father carries his son, all the way you went until you reached this place."

[32]In spite of this, you did not trust in the LORD your God, [33]who went ahead of you on your journey, in fire by night and in a cloud by day, to search out places for you to camp and to show you the way you should go.

1:26 The favorable report of the bounty of the land notwithstanding, the people refused to press on into Canaan and, in fact, rebelled against the Lord (v. 26).[25] Again, the more complete record of events must be sought in Numbers, where the negative side of the whole episode is spelled out.

---

[24] The abbreviated version of Deuteronomy may be explained, in part, by the emphasis in v. 25 on the fruit of the land. The Numbers account agrees that that bounty was especially associated with Eshcol (Num 13:20,23-24), so there is no need here to recount the entire travels of the scouts. For a possible identification of Eshcol with Burj Haskeh, two miles north of Hebron, see R. K. Harrison, *Numbers,* WEC (Chicago: Moody, 1990), 206.

[25] G. W. Coats, *Rebellion in the Wilderness: The Murmuring Motif in the Wilderness Traditions of the Old Testament* (Nashville: Abingdon, 1968).

The land of Canaan was indeed bountiful, they said, but it was also popu-
lated by powerful people who inhabited large and impenetrable cities
(Num 13:27-29). Furthermore, the majority of the spies argued, it was
foolhardy to think that the gigantic people who lived there could be overcome by Israel. Canaan was a land, so they said, that "devours those living
in it" (Num 13:32).

For Israel to rebel against the Lord was tantamount to covenant violation, for in the nature of such arrangements complete compliance and subservience was expected of the vassal partner. In fact, the verb used here
(*mārâ*) to express rebellion, when accompanied by *ʾet pî yhwh* (lit., "rebel
against the mouth of Yahweh"), regularly expresses violation of specific
commandments of the Lord (cf. Deut 1:43; 9:23; Josh 1:18; 1 Sam
12:14).[26] Rebellion of this kind was nothing short of high treason, hence
the apparently extreme measures of judgment that ensued including and
culminating in the sentencing of that generation to die in the desert, never
to enter the land of promise (Deut 1:35-36; cf. Num 14:20-23).

1:27   The covenant context of the dialogue finds further support in the
allegation of the grumbling dissidents that "the Lord hates us" (v. 27). The
peculiar grammatical construction here (the noun *śinʾâ* plus preposition *b*
functioning as a verb) requires that the evidence of the Lord's hating be the
fact that he brought Israel out of Egypt only to destroy them. A literal rendering might be, "Because of the hatred of Yahweh for us, he brought us
from the land of Egypt."[27]

This is strong language, and it should not and cannot be mitigated or
justified as far as its sinfulness is concerned. However, it is important to
note that the verb *śānēʾ* and noun *śinʾâ* frequently are technical terms to
describe covenant rejection or, to put it in more theological language, nonelection. They are antonyms of the verb *ʾāhēb* and noun *ʾahăbâ* which,
therefore, speak of election to covenant fellowship.[28] Thus Moses pointed
out that the Lord chose Israel because he loved them in accordance with
the patriarchal covenant promises (Deut 7:8). As a result he would love
them in the land and show that by his bountiful provision, again in line
with covenant initiative (Deut 7:12-16).

The book of the prophet Hosea is especially rich in the use of *ʾāhēb/
ʾahăbâ* to express the Lord's covenant choice of Israel. The prophet was

---

[26] Driver, *Deuteronomy*, 22-23.

[27] For the use of the subjective genitive with a verbal meaning, see *IBHS* § 9.5.1.

[28] W. L. Moran, "The Ancient Near Eastern Background of the Love of God in Deuteronomy," *CBQ* 25 (1963): 77-87; cf. P. A. Verhoef, *The Books of Haggai and Malachi*, NICOT
(Grand Rapids: Eerdmans, 1987), 201-2; J. A. Thompson, "Israel's Haters," *VT* 29 (1979):
200-205.

commanded to love his wife, who had broken their marriage covenant, just "as the LORD loves the Israelites" (Hos 3:1). The contrast between the Lord's love and hate (election and rejection) is clear from Hos 9:15:

> Because of all their wickedness in Gilgal,
>   I hated them there.
> Because of their sinful deeds,
>   I will drive them out of my house.
> I will no longer love them;
>   all their leaders are rebellious.

Here the rebellion of the leaders is the direct cause of the Lord's no longer loving his people.[29]

An even clearer connection between loving and election may be seen in Hos 11:1:

> When Israel was a child, I loved him,
>   and out of Egypt I called my son.

The poetic parallelism here makes "I loved him" synonymous with "I called my son." That is, for God to call (or choose) is another way of expressing his love for the object of his elective grace.[30]

Jeremiah 31:3 also makes the connection between love and covenant election in the words of the Lord's declaration:

> I have loved you with an everlasting love;
>   I have drawn you with loving-kindness.

Here the Hebrew construction requires that the Lord's extension of loving-kindness (that is, *ḥesed*, another term freighted with covenant significance) be predicated on his love. That is, because he loved Israel he brought them into covenant fellowship with himself. This raises the verb *ᵓāhēb* to a dimension above and beyond mere emotion to that of choice. For the Lord to love means for him to choose one to salvation and service.

This is nowhere more clearly stated than in Mal 1:2-3: "I have loved you," says the Lord. "But you ask, 'How have you loved us?' "Was not Esau Jacob's brother?" the Lord says. "Yet I have loved Jacob, but Esau I have hated." The reference obviously is to the selection of Jacob over Esau to be the heir of the covenant promises. As devious as Jacob was in acquiring the rights of primogeniture, in the inscrutable purposes and plan of

---

[29] D. Stuart, *Hosea-Jonah,* WBC 31 (Waco: Word, 1987), 153.

[30] F. I. Andersen and D. N. Freedman, *Hosea,* AB 24 (Garden City: Doubleday, 1980), 576-77.

God the matter was one that resulted in Jacob's selection, both by prophecy (Gen 25:23) and by divine sanction (Gen 25:32-34; 28:13-15; 48:3-4).[31] Paul was fully aware of the predestinarian significance of the language of loving and hating, for in his classic discourse on the subject he quoted both Gen 25:23 and Mal 1:2-3 to make the point that election and nonelection are tantamount to God's loving and hating, respectively (Rom 9:10-13). Just as to love means to choose so, in covenant terminology to hate means to reject.[32]

1:28 To return to Moses' recapitulation of Israel's rebellion, it should be evident from the previous discussion that their excuse for rebellion was that the Lord had come to hate them, that is, to reject Israel as a covenant partner. Evidence of this, they said, was the Lord's determination to annihilate them at the hands of the Amorites. It is difficult to believe that this was a deep-seated conviction on the part of Israel's leaders. Rather, it appears to be the standard response of those who lack faith and courage. Israel was happy to accept covenant partnership and responsibility (cf. Exod 19:8), but when called upon to exercise that responsibility, they found it all too easy to reject God's leadership, to rebel against him, and, in fact, to attribute their own failure to God's having disowned them ("the LORD hates us") as a servant people.

The grumbling of the unbelievers finds expression also in the question "Where are we going up?" (v. 28; not as in the NIV, "Where can we go?").[33] This appears to suggest that they had not abandoned all hope of conquest but simply were in a quandary about how it could come to pass. On the other hand, the account in Numbers indicates that they knew exactly what to do—they would return to Egypt (Num 14:4). The further statement in our passage that "our brothers have made us lose heart" (v. 28) would seem to agree with the Numbers version that all hope to enter Canaan was gone. It seems best to take their question, then, as a rhetorical question, one that demands or expects the answer that there was no longer hope of claiming the land of promise.

The idiom "to lose heart" (thus NIV, v. 28) reflects the literal Hebrew "cause the heart to melt" (*hēmassû ʾet lĕbābēnû*). The phrase occurs commonly in contexts of war, especially so-called holy war (cf. Deut 20:8; Josh 2:11; 5:1; 7:5; 2 Sam 17:10; Isa 13:7; 19:1; Nah 2:11 [Eng. 2:10]; Ezek 21:12 [Eng. 21:7]), and more particularly with references to the enemies of

---

[31] E. H. Merrill, *Haggai, Zechariah, Malachi* (Chicago: Moody, 1994), 388-89.

[32] L. Morris, *The Epistle to the Romans* (Grand Rapids: Eerdmans, 1988), 356-57.

[33] The participle in עֹלִים אֲנַחְנוּ אָנָה, without further modal qualification, most naturally yields a literal,"Where are we going up?"

the Lord who are terrified at his coming.[34] Ironic indeed is that Israel, on the verge of conquest as the army of the Lord, should itself lose heart.

The reasons for despair are the strength and height of both the people and the cities of Canaan. There is obvious hyperbole in the description of the walls that go "up to the sky," but there can be no doubt that some of the people encountered by the twelve spies were gigantic indeed. The reference to "Anakites" is sufficient proof of this, for a number of other biblical texts characterize these people as being unusually tall (Num 13:33; Deut 2:10,21; 9:2). They took their name from a certain Anak whose forefather Arba was the founder of the city of Kiriath Arba, later known as Hebron (Josh 21:11; cf. 14:15).[35] Joshua and Caleb later defeated the Anakites in and around Hebron (Josh 11:21-23; 15:14) and took their lands as part of their own inheritance. This forced the Anakites to leave central Canaan and to move to the coastal plain (later Philistia), where they settled in Gaza, Gath, and Ashdod (Josh 11:22). It is very likely that Goliath and other Philistine giants were descendants of this stock (cf. 1 Chr 20:4-8).

Rather impressive walled cities are attested to archaeologically from this Late Bronze (ca. 1550–1200) period, so the majority report of the spies is not totally without foundation.[36] Moreover, Israel had had no experience in offensive warfare at this point and clearly lacked proper equipment to undertake successful siege and conquest of fortified cities. Humanly there was just cause for faintheartedness, and one can understand the reluctance and even rebellion of the people.

1:29-31 However, this was not ordinary human war but "Yahweh war." That is, it was conflict originated by Yahweh, carried out under his direction, and guaranteed of success by those who followed its prescriptions.[37] He was the Great King. Canaan was the land he had ordained as

---

[34] D. J. McCarthy, "Some Holy War Vocabulary in Joshua 2," *CBQ* 33 (1971): 228-30.

[35] R. B. Allen, "Anak (Anakim)," in *Baker Encyclopedia of the Bible*, ed. W. A. Elwell (Grand Rapids: Baker, 1988), 1:84.

[36] A. Mazar, *Archaeology of the Land of the Bible 1000–586 B.C.E.* (New York: Doubleday, 1990), 239-42. See also J. J. Bimson, *Redating the Exodus and Conquest*, JSOTSup 5 (Sheffield: University of Sheffield, 1978). He dates the destruction of the major cities of Canaan from the end of the Middle Bronze Age (ca. 1430 B.C.) to as late as 1400 (p. 192) and points out the formidable defenses of these cities (pp. 201-15). The date of the exploration by the Israelite scouts was ca. 1445 B.C.

[37] For "holy war" or (better) "Yahweh war" see P. C. Craigie, "Yahweh Is a Man of Wars," *SJT* 22 (1969): 183-88; F. M. Cross, "The Divine Warrior in Israel's Early Cult," in *Studies and Text III* (Cambridge: Harvard University, 1966), 11-30; N. K. Gottwald, "Holy War in Deuteronomy," *RevExp* 61 (1964): 296-310; G. H. Jones, "Holy War or YHWH War?" *VT* 25 (1975): 642-58; S.-M. Kang, *Divine War in the Old Testament and in the Ancient Near East*, BZAW 177 (Berlin: de Gruyter, 1989); M. Lind, *Yahweh Is a Warrior*

the dwelling place of his people (cf. Gen 12:1; 13:14-17), and now he was about to use them to overcome and dispossess its inhabitants who, after all, were merely squatters who had no legitimate claim to it.

The passage at hand has all the hallmarks of Yahweh (or holy) war in its classic expression. There is first the injunction "Do not be terrified; do not be afraid of them."[38] Their hearts had already fainted as though it were their war (v. 28), but, in fact, it was Yahweh's war; they did not need to fear at all (cf. Deut 20:3; 31:6; Josh 8:1). Second, the battle was Yahweh's, and as such he would fight for them (v. 30; cf. 3:22; 20:4; Exod 14:13-14). He had done so in the past, Moses reminded them, and the foe was none other than mighty Egypt (Exod 7:4-5; 12:29; 13:3,14-15; 14:4). Yahweh's role as warrior in the exodus deliverance is best seen in the Song of Moses (Exod 15:1-18).[39] There he is described as a warrior (v. 3) whose own right hand shattered the enemy (v. 6) and whose breath submerged them in the sea (v. 10). As a result, the hearts of all his enemies who heard of his exploits melted away (v. 15), and they became powerless before him (v. 16).

Yahweh the warrior fought for Israel also in the desert, both before he met them in covenant at Sinai (Exod 17:8-16) and afterward (Num 10:35). From beginning to end the enterprise was his, and, one could almost say, Israel was along only for the ride. Moses described the years of desert travail as a time when the Lord carried Israel along as a father carries his son (v. 31), similar to the imagery of Hos 11:1-4.

The reference to Israel as God's son is also covenantally significant, for when the Lord instructed Moses to return to Egypt from Midian to lead Israel from bondage, he referred to the slave people as his "firstborn son" (Exod 4:22). Such familial language was common in ancient Near Eastern treaty texts where the maker of the covenant would be "father" and the receiver "son."[40]

(Scottdale, Penn.: Herald, 1980); P. D. Miller, "God the Warrior," *Int* 19 (1965): 39-46; G. von Rad, *Der Heilige Krieg im alten Israel* (Göttingen: Vandenhoeck & Ruprecht, 1965); M. Weinfeld, "Divine Intervention in War in Ancient Israel and in the Ancient Near East," in *History, Historiography and Interpretation* (Jerusalem: Magnes, 1984), 121-47.

[38] The Heb. phrase לֹא־תַעַרְצוּן וְלֹא־תִירְאוּן (or, more commonly, with jussive negation אַל) occurs commonly as a word of encouragement in the face of impending threat of war. See P.-E. Dion, "The 'Fear Not' Formula and Holy War," *CBQ* 32 (1970): 565-70; H. F. Fuhs, "יָרֵא *yārēʾ*," *TDOT* 6:304-5.

[39] F. M. Cross, *Canaanite Myth and Hebrew Epic* (Cambridge: Harvard University, 1973), 121-44.

[40] D. J. McCarthy, "Notes on the Love of God in Deuteronomy and the Father-Son Relationship between Yahweh and Israel," *CBQ* 27 (1965): 144-47; H. Haag, "בֵּן *bēn*," *TDOT* 2:155.

1:32 Despite all the assurances of God's presence and, indeed, the historical evidence of his intervention on their behalf in the exodus and beyond, Moses reminded his listeners that they (that is, their fathers) refused to trust the Lord. The verb used here for trust is *ʾāman,* a term that, with the following preposition *bě,* means to "make oneself secure" in the Lord.[41] Jepsen suggests that in this context of exodus deliverance "the people of Israel were expected to rely completely on their God and his promises; if they did not manifest this kind of trust, they would be punished, their existence would be threatened."[42]

1:33 Moses viewed this lack of trust in the Lord as utterly baseless given the theophanic presence of God, who, in typical divine warrior fashion, preceded the marching tribes "in fire by night and in a cloud by day" (v. 33).[43] The fire and cloud motif finds its earliest Old Testament expression in the exodus experience, though the fire by itself had already appeared in the burning bush as a sign of divine presence (Exod 3:2). As soon as Israel had crossed the Red Sea, they had encountered the pillar of cloud that guided them by day and the pillar of fire that led them at night (Exod 13:21-22). That these phenomena represented the presence of God is clear from Exod 14:24, which notes that "the LORD looked down from the pillar of fire and cloud at the Egyptian army and threw it into confusion." This also connects the fire and cloud with the pursuit of holy war.

The double theophany continued to lead the way through the desert even after the conclave at Sinai. Thus at the outset of the journey the cloud covered the tabernacle by day and the fire by night. Whenever they remained at rest, the camp remained; but when they rose up and moved on, this was the signal for the people likewise to move (Num 9:15-23). Particularly instructive is the connection between these actions of cloud and fire and the very person of the Lord himself: "At the LORD'S command the Israelites set out, and at his command they encamped" (Num 9:18).

Even more striking in terms of Yahweh's role as warrior are the texts, especially in poetry, that suggest not only that the cloud represented him but that he, like a cavalry rider, mounted them as a charging steed.[44] Thus a psalm (Ps 18:9-10) of David says:

> He parted the heavens and came down;
>> dark clouds were under his feet.
> He mounted the cherubim and flew;
>> he soared on the wings of the wind."

---

[41] A. Jepsen, "אָמַן *ʾāman,*" etc., *TDOT* 1:298.

[42] Ibid., 304.

[43] T. W. Mann, "The Pillar of Cloud in the Reed Sea Narrative," *JBL* 90 (1971): 22-24.

[44] A. Weiser, *The Psalms,* OTL (Philadelphia: Westminster, 1962), 190-91.

In similar vein the psalmist exhorted: "Sing to God, sing praise to his name, / extol him who rides on the clouds" (Ps 68:4). Another psalm describes the clouds as a chariot upon which Yahweh rides (Ps 104:3b).

The prophet Isaiah was familiar with this imagery, and in a poetic oracle concerning Egypt he employed great irony when he depicted the Lord as a warrior not delivering his people from Egypt but coming to Egypt to inflict judgment (Isa 19:1):[45]

> See, the LORD rides on a swift cloud
>   and is coming to Egypt.
> The idols of Egypt tremble before him,
>   and the hearts of the Egyptians melt within them.

(4) Judgment at Kadesh Barnea (1:34-40)

³⁴When the LORD heard what you said, he was angry and solemnly swore: ³⁵"Not a man of this evil generation shall see the good land I swore to give your forefathers, ³⁶except Caleb son of Jephunneh. He will see it, and I will give him and his descendants the land he set his feet on, because he followed the LORD wholeheartedly."

³⁷Because of you the LORD became angry with me also and said, "You shall not enter it, either. ³⁸But your assistant, Joshua son of Nun, will enter it. Encourage him, because he will lead Israel to inherit it. ³⁹And the little ones that you said would be taken captive, your children who do not yet know good from bad—they will enter the land. I will give it to them and they will take possession of it. ⁴⁰But as for you, turn around and set out toward the desert along the route to the Red Sea."

1:34-35 The rebellion of Israel and other signs of their unfaithfulness to the covenant (vv. 26-27) prompted the Lord to respond with anger. Elsewhere the verb used here to express that anger (*qāṣap*) strongly suggests a wrath that tempts God to respond in kind, that is, to break the covenant also.[46] Later in this book Moses said that the Lord was so angry as to destroy his people (9:19). That kind of anger, in fact, had resulted in the death of Aaron's sons Nadab and Abihu following their offering with unauthorized fire (Lev 10:1-2,10) and had condemned rebellious Korah and his allies to die (Num 16:22). Later that very verb speaks of the anger of the Lord that brought about the Babylonian exile (Isa 47:6). Jeremiah was so alarmed about the divine wrath that he wondered if it implied utter and final rejection of Israel (Lam 5:22).

---

[45] O. Kaiser, *Isaiah 13–39*, OTL (Philadelphia: Westminster, 1974), 100.
[46] B. E. Baloian, *Anger in the Old Testament* (New York: Peter Lang, 1992), 72-73, 99-101; cf. G. van Groningen, "קָצַף (*qāṣap*) I," etc., *TWOT* 2:808-9.

The penalty for covenant disobedience is already spelled out in Lev 26:14-39. As a sample and foretaste of the catalog of judgments listed there, the Lord, Moses said, swore that the generation that refused to enter the land at his behest would forever forfeit it (v. 35). The account in Numbers nuances the punishment by making it clear that only the men twenty years of age and older who had rebelled in their unbelief were to be included (Num 14:22-23,29,31). Presumably women and youth under twenty years of age were not affected.

1:36 Two other notable exceptions were Caleb and Joshua, the two explorers who had brought back a favorable and confident report (vv. 36,38; cf. Num 13:6,8,16,30; 14:30,38). Caleb, a Judahite, was a descendant of Jephunneh of the clan of Kenaz (Num 13:6; 32:12; Josh 14:6).[47] Of his further ancestry nothing is known, but he does appear in later Old Testament history as the father-in-law of Othniel, the first judge of Israel (Judg 1:13). Moreover, he asked for and received a private allotment in the land following its conquest, an inheritance upon which he had already set foot as a spy among the twelve (v. 36; cf. Num 14:24). This, it turns out, consisted of Hebron, the city that ironically had been inhabited by Anakites, the giant people whom Caleb had said Israel need not fear (Josh 14:12-15; cf. Num 13:22,30,33). To prove it, the aged warrior drove them out of Hebron and vicinity all by himself (Judg 1:20; cf. vv. 9-12).[48]

1:37-38 The other exception, Joshua, is introduced here as Moses' successor, and it was by virtue of that office as well as his implied faithfulness as a spy along with Caleb that he was allowed to enter Canaan. In fact, it was partially because of Moses' own sin and consequent disqualification that Joshua found himself in this privileged position.

The wording here seems to imply that Moses blamed his predicament on the people— "Because of you the LORD became angry with me" (v. 37). This need not be the case at all, however, as other occurrences of the adverbial form *biglal* ("because of") make clear. For example, Laban was aware that the Lord had blessed him because of Jacob, that is, Jacob was the occasion of blessing and not its cause (Gen 30:27,30). Likewise, Moses attributed his punishment to none other than his own disobedience, though that act of defiance was occasioned by the people or by his desire

---

[47] "Caleb," in *Baker Encyclopedia of the Bible*, 1:399.

[48] The role of Caleb and the Calebites is a notoriously complicated one in terms of the conquest of Canaan and the distribution of the tribes and clans. For a typical traditio-historical reconstruction see J. M. Miller, "The Israelite Occupation of Canaan," in *Israelite and Judaean History,* ed. J. H. Hayes and J. M. Miller (Philadelphia: Westminster, 1977), 222-25. For an alternative model see E. H. Merrill, *Kingdom of Priests: A History of Old Testament Israel* (Grand Rapids: Baker, 1987), 132-33, 144, 147.

to address their needs.[49]

The incident in view is Moses' intemperate smiting of the rock, the story of which appears in Num 20:10-13.[50] The Lord had told him to speak to the rock so that it might yield water for the thirsty multitudes (v. 8). Moses, however, struck it with his rod twice (v. 11) and as a result was rebuked by the Lord, who said, "Because you did not trust in me enough to honor me as holy in the sight of the Israelites, you will not bring this community into the land I give them" (v. 12). Thus Moses took full responsibility; therefore "because of you" (Deut 1:37) must be construed as "in your interest" or "for your sake" or the like. The seriousness of Moses' punishment was, of course, in proportion to his role and responsibility as covenant mediator.

Joshua, son of Nun, had distinguished himself early as a heroic warrior and as an assistant to Moses. He first appears in the record as commander of Israel's forces against the Amalekites (Exod 17:8-16) and then as Moses' attendant who accompanied him up Mount Sinai to receive the law (Exod 24:13). When twelve men were chosen (one from each tribe) to spy out the promised land, it is not surprising that Joshua should be picked to represent his tribe, Ephraim (Num 13:8,16). Only he and Caleb brought back a favorable report, a true assessment of the enemy and of the God who would enable Israel to prevail. The report was delivered in the name of Caleb only (Num 13:30), Joshua's name being omitted perhaps because he was younger (but cf. 14:6, where Joshua is mentioned first) or, more likely, Caleb was simply the first one to speak up.[51]

In his retelling of the story in Deuteronomy, Moses again mentioned Caleb first (1:36) and then Joshua (v. 38). Here Joshua is called, literally, "the one who stands before" Moses (*hāʿōmēd lĕpāneykā*) rather than the usual *nāʿār*, "youth," "minister."[52] This reveals an increasing degree of intimacy between Moses and his assistant, one that paves the way for Joshua's ultimate succession to the office of covenant mediator. In fact,

---

[49] Keil and Delitzsch, *The Pentateuch*, 3:289-90.

[50] Because the smiting of the rock occurred after the sojourn at Kadesh Barnea, most scholars do not link Yahweh's anger here with that incident. So, e.g., Driver, *Deuteronomy*, 26-27. However, as Keil and Delitzsch point out (ibid., 3:289), "Moses did not intend to teach the people history and chronology, but to set before them the holiness of the judgments of the Lord." Moreover, Deut 1:37 is virtually a direct quotation of Num 20:12, suggesting that innerbiblical exegesis at least has the smiting of the rock in view.

[51] Thus, Keil and Delitzsch, *The Pentateuch*, 3:90-91.

[52] See Driver, *Deuteronomy*, 28; Weinfeld, *Deuteronomy 1–11*, 151. The phrase still connotes a position of subservience the one to the other (cf. Gen 41:46; 1 Sam 16:21-22; 1 Kgs 1:2; Jer 52:12; Dan 1:5; Zech 3:4).

the Lord here says that Joshua would enter the land of promise and would be his agent in allowing Israel to inherit it (v. 38; cf. 3:28; 31:7-8; Josh 1:6).

1:39   Along with Caleb and Joshua would go even the youngest and weakest of the people, the babies that the rebellious generation had predicted would perish as Canaanite prisoners (cf. Num 14:3,31), infants so young that they did not know the difference between good and bad (v. 39; cf. Isa 7:16; 8:4; Jonah 4:11). They would become the seed of the next generation, the foundation upon which the theocratic community would be built in the land of promise.

1:40   As for the rebels, they had to leave Kadesh Barnea and set out for the Red Sea (v. 40).[53] The destination here, however, was not to be the Red Sea just east of Egypt from whence they had come but the eastern arm of the Red Sea known also as the Gulf of Elath or Aqaba.[54] The equation is seen most clearly in 1 Kgs 9:26, where the port of Elath is located on the Red Sea. The Hebrew name for the sea, *yām sûp*, is the same whether referring to the western Gulf of Suez (Exod 10:19; 13:18; 15:4,22) or the eastern Gulf of Elath (as here and Num 21:4). That Moses had the latter in view in this account is clear from the narrative of Num 21, which specifies that the Israelites "traveled from Mount Hor along the route to the Red Sea, to go around Edom" (v. 4).

One need not conclude from this hint of an itinerary that the Israelites actually traveled all the way to the Red Sea. In fact, the plain sense is that they were to set out on the route from Kadesh Barnea to the Red Sea, traveling thus in a southeasterly direction.[55] But how far they were to take that route cannot be known. What in fact happened was that they went to Mount Hor, just northeast of Kadesh Barnea (Num 20:22) and from there bypassed Edom (Num 21:4; Deut 2:1-3). Whether they did so by going all the way to the Gulf of Elath and then east and north of Edom or by simply going on the west side of Edom up the Arabah is a matter of contention

---

[53] The identical command occurs in Num 14:25. The intent apparently was to uproot the people from the relative stability and permanence of Kadesh Barnea and consign them to the Arabah wilderness. Whether they actually set out from Kadesh Barnea at that time is not clear, though it is unlikely they did at once given the preemptive strike against Hormah recorded in Num 14:39-45. They must have done so later, at least from time to time, for they are found returning to Kadesh in Num 20:1. In any event, the command of Num 14:25 and Deut 1:40 refers to the same occasion, prior to the thirty-eight-year wandering (cf. 2:1). The command was finally obeyed in the fortieth year (Deut 2:1; cf. Num 20:22–21:4). See Thompson, *Deuteronomy*, 89; Driver, *Deuteronomy*, 31-33.

[54] Batto, "The Reed Sea: *Requiescat in Pace*," 27-28.

[55] The so-called "*hē* directive" on הַמִּדְבָּרָה suggests the rendering "set out in the direction of the Arabah by the route toward the Red Sea." See Aharoni, *Land of the Bible*, 58.

(see the discussion of Deut 2:1-8).[56]

(5) Unsuccessful Conquest of Canaan (1:41-46)

[41]Then you replied, "We have sinned against the LORD. We will go up and fight, as the LORD our God commanded us." So every one of you put on his weapons, thinking it easy to go up into the hill country. [42]But the LORD said to me, "Tell them, 'Do not go up and fight, because I will not be with you. You will be defeated by your enemies.'" [43]So I told you, but you would not listen. You rebelled against the LORD'S command and in your arrogance you marched up into the hill country. [44]The Amorites who lived in those hills came out against you; they chased you like a swarm of bees and beat you down from Seir all the way to Hormah. [45]You came back and wept before the LORD, but he paid no attention to your weeping and turned a deaf ear to you. [46]And so you stayed in Kadesh many days—all the time you spent there.

1:41-42 True to human nature, as soon as access to Canaan was denied that early rebellious generation (vv. 35,40), they decided that that precisely was what they would do. To justify their decision they donned a cloak of hypocritical repentance ("we have sinned against the LORD," v. 41; cf. Num 14:40) and announced that what they were about to do was in compliance with the perfect and explicit will of God. But they had completely misread the mind of the Lord, for he had closed that window of opportunity once and for all. The account in Numbers puts this beyond doubt, for there Moses states, "Because you have turned away from the LORD, he will not be with you" (Num 14:43). No amount of rationalizing about the ease with which they could accomplish their objective (v. 41) could outweigh the simple fact that the Lord was not with them (v. 42).[57]

This absence of the Lord from the conflict is indicative once more of the role of the Lord in Holy War though here, of course, in a negative way. For Israel to attempt war in Yahweh's name without his sanction and presence was to court inevitable disaster. Thus, Moses said that without the Lord, Israel could anticipate defeat by their enemies (v. 42).

1:43 All warning notwithstanding, the armies of Israel rebelled (lit.,

---

[56] See Z. Kallai, "The Wandering-Traditions from Kadesh-Barnea to Canaan: A Study in Biblical Historiography," *JJS* 33 (1982): 175-84; J. R. Bartlett, "The Conquest of Sihon's Kingdom: A Literary Reexamination," *JBL* 97 (1978): 347-51.

[57] The Heb. verb הון ("be easy") occurs only in the *hiphil* and suggests that Israel regarded the conquest as a trifling thing. However, some scholars associate *hwn* with Heb. and Aram. *zmn*, "be ready." See E. Kutsch, "הון *hôn*," *TDOT* 3:365-66; P. Grelot, "Le racine *hwn* en Dt I, 41," *VT* 12 (1962): 198-201.

"did not obey"; cf. v. 26) against the Lord and presumptuously[58] went up to the hill country (v. 43). Again the narrative of Numbers is helpful in clarifying the character of their presumption, for it says that "neither Moses nor the ark of the LORD'S covenant moved from the camp" (Num 14:44). Of all the signs or prerequisites of holy war, none was more important than the presence of the ark in battle, for it and it alone symbolized the presence of the Lord among his people when its function was fully understood (cf. Josh 3:3; 6:4,6; 1 Sam 4:3-19; Pss 78:61; 132:8).[59] For Israel to essay successful conquest of Canaan on behalf of the Lord but without his powerful accompaniment was indeed the epitome of arrogance.

1:44 What Moses predicted came to pass. As soon as the Israelite troops arrived in the hill country, they were set upon by the Amorites who, like a swarm of bees, attacked them "from Seir all the way to Hormah" (v. 44). The NIV is correct here in understanding *běśēʿîr* as "from Seir," thus allowing the preposition *bě* a meaning well attested in Ugaritic and elsewhere in the Old Testament.[60] In addition, the LXX and its derivative versions support this understanding by reading *apo* or the like. The idea is that Israel penetrated the lower Judean hills somewhere east of Hormah and was defeated in an area stretching from Hormah in the west to Seir (= Edom) in the east, a distance of about fifty miles.

Hormah (from Heb. *ḥāram*, "ban, exterminate") is likely to be identified with Khirbet el-Meshash, five miles west of Arad and seven southeast of Beersheba.[61] The name of the place, ironically enough, is derived from Israel's later devastation of the forces of the Canaanite city of Arad there (Num 21:3).[62]

---

[58] Thus זיד, זוד. J. Scharbert suggests here "a presumptuous, premeditated offense against God and his religious and moral order" ("זוד *zudh,*" *TDOT* 4:48). This, of course, is in keeping with the meaning of the companion verb מָרַר, "to rebel."

[59] Cross, *Canaanite Myth,* 94-97, 106-11.

[60] D. Pardee, "The Preposition in Ugaritic," *UF* 8 (1976): 287-88, 312; Weinfeld, *Deuteronomy 1–11,* 152. For a vigorous argument against such "double opposition of meaning" in Hebrew, however, see J. Barr, *Comparative Philology and the Text of the Old Testament* (Winona Lake, Ind.: Eisenbrauns, 1987), 175-77.

[61] Aharoni, *Land of the Bible,* 201.

[62] There is some question about when the place received this name. It is first mentioned in Num 14:45 as the place where the Amalekites and Canaanites defeated rebellious Israel when the latter attempted a premature penetration of the southern hill country. However, the "naming formula" appears in Num 21:3, a passage that speaks of Israel's defeat and annihilation of the Canaanites there: "They completely destroyed [וַיַּחֲרֵם] them . . . so the place was named Hormah [חָרְמָה]." The naming in Num 14:45, then, is proleptic of the actual designation of 21:3, and Deut 1:44 refers to the prolepsis. The fact that Hormah is mentioned in the Egyptian Execration Texts of the MK period suggests that all the biblical references may be paronomastic. Cf. A. Negev, ed., *Archaeological Encyclopedia of the Holy Land* (Jerusalem: SBS, 1980, 147), s.v. "Hormah."

Reference to the Amorites here is somewhat problematic in that the Numbers version of this campaign describes Israel's enemies as "the Amalekites and Canaanites" (Num 14:43). To attribute the differing accounts to different sources of tradition is, of course, one way of solving the dilemma[63] but only if one can demonstrate the existence of different sources prior to the problem itself. That is, one cannot posit source division merely to solve a difficulty. More likely, Moses simply was using much more generic terminology in his recapitulation of past events in Deuteronomy than he was in the original rendition in Numbers. It appears that he was following the generalization that the Amorites lived in the hill country and other folk such as Amalekites and Canaanites lived in the valleys and plains. In fact, he had made this very point in Num 14:25 (cf. 13:29) and then later, in what is clearly an exception, identified Israel's hill country foes at Hormah as Amalekites and Canaanites (14:45).

Distribution of the terminology Amalekite, Canaanite, and Amorite in Numbers and Deuteronomy is most suggestive. "Amalekite" occurs (in any of its forms) six times in Numbers and only twice in Deuteronomy (both times referring to the Amalekites of the Sinai desert). "Canaanite" is attested in any of its forms (including the references to Canaan as a land) eighteen times in Numbers and only five times in Deuteronomy. "Amorites" appears thirteen times in Numbers (nine in chap. 21 alone) and fifteen in Deuteronomy (six times in chap. 1). Except for Num 13:29 all references to Amorites in that book are to the inhabitants of the Transjordan. Thus it is clear that the precision with which Moses made ethnic and national distinctions in Numbers is lacking in Deuteronomy. In the latter it is sufficient to regard all inhabitants of the hill country as Amorites (cf. 1:7).[64]

1:45 Israel's decisive defeat in this initial attempt at conquest was so devastating and demoralizing that the people could only weep in their frustration before the Lord. But the weeping was too late and too lacking in genuine repentance as is made clear from the emphatic use of two synonyms for hearing. God would not hear (*šāmaᶜ*), nor would he listen (*ʾāzān*). This hendiadys could as well be translated, "He would by no means pay attention to your weeping."[65]

1:46 Resigned to the fact that God had abandoned his role as warrior in the pursuit of holy war—at least temporarily—and that there could therefore be no hope of Canaanite conquest, the Israelites settled in at

---

[63] Thus Driver, *Deuteronomy*, 29.
[64] Weinfeld, *Deuteronomy 1–11*, 152.
[65] *IBHS* § 32.3b.

Kadesh Barnea and vicinity for many years, thirty-eight as it turned out, until at last the rebel generation had died (2:14; cf. 1:34-40). The staccato and repetitive way in which the Hebrew refers to this period, "You settled in Kadesh many days, according to the days which you settled" (v. 46), is designed to show the wearisome monotony of that lost era of Israel's history.[66] Not a word is forthcoming in Deuteronomy about those silent years, and all Numbers records by way of narrative is negative: the rebellion of Korah (Num 16:1-40), the complaint of the people (16:41–17:13), the death of Miriam (20:1), and the rebellion at Meribah (20:2-13). All that can be said about the sojourn at Kadesh is that they stayed there.

(6) The Journey from Kadesh Barnea to Moab (2:1-15)

[1]Then we turned back and set out toward the desert along the route to the Red Sea, as the LORD had directed me. For a long time we made our way around the hill country of Seir.

[2]Then the LORD said to me, [3]"You have made your way around this hill country long enough; now turn north. [4]Give the people these orders: 'You are about to pass through the territory of your brothers the descendants of Esau, who live in Seir. They will be afraid of you, but be very careful. [5]Do not provoke them to war, for I will not give you any of their land, not even enough to put your foot on. I have given Esau the hill country of Seir as his own. [6]You are to pay them in silver for the food you eat and the water you drink.'"

[7]The LORD your God has blessed you in all the work of your hands. He has watched over your journey through this vast desert. These forty years the LORD your God has been with you, and you have not lacked anything.

[8]So we went on past our brothers the descendants of Esau, who live in Seir. We turned from the Arabah road, which comes up from Elath and Ezion Geber, and traveled along the desert road of Moab.

[9]Then the LORD said to me, "Do not harass the Moabites or provoke them to war, for I will not give you any part of their land. I have given Ar to the descendants of Lot as a possession."

[10](The Emites used to live there—a people strong and numerous, and as tall as the Anakites. [11]Like the Anakites, they too were considered Rephaites, but the Moabites called them Emites. [12]Horites used to live in Seir, but the descendants of Esau drove them out. They destroyed the Horites from before them and settled in their place, just as Israel did in the land the LORD gave them as their possession.)

[13]And the LORD said, "Now get up and cross the Zered Valley." So we

---

[66] Mayes suggests that this idiom (found also in 1 Sam 23:13; 2 Sam 15:20; 2 Kgs 8:1; Zech 10:8) "is simply a means of affirming the previous statement when that statement is vague and indefinite" (Mayes, *Deuteronomy,* 133).

crossed the valley.
¹⁴Thirty-eight years passed from the time we left Kadesh Barnea until we
crossed the Zered Valley. By then, that entire generation of fighting men had
perished from the camp, as the LORD had sworn to them. ¹⁵The LORD'S hand
was against them until he had completely eliminated them from the camp.

The chronological setting of this passage seems clear and straightforward from the account of Deuteronomy alone.[67] The Israelites had settled
in Kadesh Barnea (1:46) and now, many years later, left to begin their trek
to Canaan along the Red Sea desert road (2:1). The Book of Numbers,
however, leaves Israel in defeat at Hormah (14:45), and when movement is
next recorded, they arrive at Kadesh "in the first month" (20:1). Between
these two events occur all the activity and instruction of Num 15–19. Thus
it seems that the arrival at Kadesh in Num 20:1 refers to the same movement there as is recorded in Deut 1:46.

This cannot be the case, however, for Aaron's death, which clearly followed the arrival at Kadesh by only a brief time according to the Numbers
account, occurred in the fortieth and last year of the desert sojourn (Num
33:38). This took place precisely in the fifth month of that year, a fact that
would support the view that Israel arrived at Kadesh in the first month of
that very year and that Miriam's death took place at that time (cf. Num
33:36-37).[68]

If Num 20:1 and Deut 1:46 are not referring to the same arrival at
Kadesh Barnea, what is meant by Israel's arriving there according to the
Numbers text? First, it is important to note that Numbers has already
recorded Israel's settling at Kadesh Barnea as part of the original itinerary
from Horeb (Num 12:16; 13:3,26). This, of course, was before the thirty-
eight-year judgment sojourn was imposed on them. Therefore the arrival of
Num 20:1 cannot refer to that, particularly in light of the fact that all of
Num 20 is oriented toward events of Israel's fortieth year in the desert.
Second, it is not likely that Israel remained only at Kadesh Barnea
throughout all those years. Given the enormous population, the nomadic or
seminomadic lifestyle of the people, and the vicissitudes of climate and
pasturage, there can be no doubt that the tribes of Israel ranged widely
throughout the Sinai and Negev regions (cf. Num 14:25). All that Num
20:1 is saying is that in the first month (of the fortieth year) they returned

---

[67] For the complexity of the issues involved, especially in the comparisons of the various
itineraries, see again Davies, "The Wilderness Itineraries: A Comparative Study," and Kallai,
"The Wandering Traditions from Kadesh-Barnea to Canaan"; J. T. Walsh, "From Egypt to
Moab: A Source Critical Analysis of the Wilderness Itinerary," *CBQ* 39 (1977): 20-33.

[68] Harrison, *Numbers,* 262.

to Kadesh again. And from there they proceeded to Hor (Num 20:22) as part of the journey related in much less specific terms in Deut 2:1.[69]

INSTRUCTIONS CONCERNING EDOM (2:1-8). **2:1** Finally after thirty-eight years the people of the Lord were ready to do what he had commanded them to do long before, "turn around and set out toward the desert" (Deut 1:40). Thus Moses said, "We turned back and set out toward the desert" (2:1), clearly a literary way of establishing a connection between the original instruction and its greatly postponed fulfillment.[70] The Hebrew formula is exactly the same in both passages (except for verb forms), one consisting of the juxtaposition of the verbs "turn" and "set out." Once this is recognized, the statement that Israel "turned back" (better, "turned about") makes good sense inasmuch as it imitates a command that long since should have been obeyed.

The route, however, is uncertain. The present passage suggests that the road through the desert was the Red Sea route that connected Kadesh Barnea with the Gulf of Elath, the eastern arm of the Red Sea (cf. 1:1-2,40). Numbers 20:22 reveals that Israel, having been denied access to the main highway north by the Edomites, journeyed to Mount Hor, where Aaron died (vv. 23-29). From thence they proceeded south along the Red Sea route (Num 21:4), thus agreeing with Deut 2:1 about the route and direction they ended up going.

2:2-3 The objective seems to have been to bypass Edom to the west, south, and east and eventually to reach Canaan north of Edom. Moses spoke of this circuitous trek as making "our way around the hill country of Seir" (2:1). The purpose is even clearer in Numbers, "to go around Edom" (21:4). The way was long and treacherous. From Mount Hor straight to Elath is well over one hundred miles, and there is good reason to believe that Israel moved east of Hor to the Arabah Valley before heading south (Deut 2:8). But all this had to be done inasmuch as the direct route from Hor to the plains of Moab would require transit across Edomite territory.

The narrator did not exaggerate then when he said, "For a long time we made our way around the hill country of Seir" (Deut 2:1). A most conservative estimate of the time needed to reach the Gulf of Elath from Hor is two weeks. From there the route went east, through Edom's southernmost territory, and then north parallel to Edom's eastern border (Deut 2:3). After

---

[69] For further discussion see E. H. Merrill, "Numbers," in *The Bible Knowledge Commentary,* ed. J. F. Walvoord and R. B. Zuck (Wheaton: Victor, 1985), 238.

[70] See comments on 1:40. Christensen (*Deuteronomy 1–11*) draws attention to the frame 1:19–2:1 in which arrival at and departure from Kadesh Barnea form the elements of inclusio (p. 32).

a lengthy and arduous journey through that inhospitable desert terrain, they at last reached the Zered Valley, the boundary line at that time between Edom and its northern neighbor Moab (cf. 2:13).[71]

2:4-7 In transit Moses instructed his people that they were about to cross the border of Edom (presumably in negotiating around the upper Gulf of Elath) but in doing so were not to be provocative or seek for themselves any Edomite land (vv. 4-5).[72] This had been given to them by the Lord himself. Any food or drink they consumed must be purchased in light of Edom's claims (v. 6). The historical antecedent to this benefaction to Edom is, of course, inherent in Isaac's blessing of Esau, who went on to dispossess the inhabitants of Mount Seir and create there the nation Edom (Gen 27:39-40). More clear is the statement in this very section that the descendants of Esau drove the Horites out of Seir in order that they might enter into their God-given possession just as Israel would do (v. 12).[73]

Another reason Israel did not need the hospitality of Edom was that the Lord had cared for them for all the forty years of desert dwelling and wandering and was well able and willing to do so now that the period of sojourn was nearly over (v. 7).

2:8 In summary Moses repeated that he and his people bypassed their brother nation, Edom, by leaving the Arabah Road (that is, the Red Sea route of 2:1) at Elath and Ezion Geber and then taking the desert route east of Edom that connected Moab with the Gulf of Elath and pointed south (v. 8).[74] Elath (modern Eilat or 'Aqabah) was a Red Sea port that was in and

---

[71] The route from Kadesh Barnea to Moab is notoriously difficult to reconstruct from the biblical data (cf. Num 20:14–21:30; 33:37-49; Deut 2:1-15). See Merrill, *Kingdom of Priests*, 86-89; Aharoni, *The Land of the Bible*, 55-56; Y. Aharoni and M. Avi-Yonah, *The Macmillan Bible Atlas* (New York: Macmillan, 1968, 42).

[72] W. A. Sumner, "Israel's Encounters with Edom, Moab, Ammon, Sihon, and Og according to the Deuteronomist," *VT* 18 (1968): 216-28.

[73] For biblical, historical, and archaeological sources pertaining to Edom and the Edomites, see J. R. Bartlett, "The Moabites and the Edomites," in *Peoples of Old Testament Times*, ed. D. J. Wiseman (Oxford: Clarendon, 1973), 229-58; "The Rise and Fall of the Kingdom of Edom," *PEQ* 104 (1972): 26-37; I. Beit-Arieh, "New Light on the Edomites," *BAR* 14 (1988): 28-41; S. Hart, "Some Preliminary Thoughts on Settlement in Southern Edom," *Levant* 18 (1986): 51-58; *Midian, Moab and Edom* JSOTSup 24 (Sheffield: JSOT, 1983).

[74] One of the problems of the early (1446) exodus date was evidence, adduced primarily by N. Glueck, pointing to an absence of population in the south Transjordan area, including Moab and Edom, until the thirteenth century. See Glueck, "Explorations in Eastern Palestine and the Negev," *BASOR* 55 (1934): 3-21; *BASOR* 86 (1942): 14-24. This, of course, would preclude Israelite contact with these peoples that early and would presuppose either that our Deuteronomy narrative is anachronistic or that it must fit a late exodus setting and date. Subsequent research has exposed the deficiencies of Glueck's methodology and has revealed the existence of significant population groups in LB and in the very areas in question. See G. L.

out of Edomite and later Israelite and Judahite hands depending on particular historical and political circumstances. It was a center of Uzziah's maritime industry (2 Kgs 14:22) but eventually returned to Edomite and then Nabatean control. Ezion-Geber (to be identified with Tell el-Kheleifeh) was a mile or two west of Elath.[75] It was Solomon's principal port through which he carried on worldwide trade (1 Kgs 9:26) and later was rebuilt by Jehoshaphat for the same purpose, though without success (1 Kgs 22:48).

INSTRUCTIONS CONCERNING MOAB (2:9-15).   **2:9**   The instructions relative to Edom pertain also to Moab. Their land, given to them by the Lord, was inviolable and could not be trespassed by Israel without Moabite permission.[76] The reference to this territory as Ar (v. 9) is a case of synecdoche, a figure of speech in which a part stands for the whole. That is, the city Ar (el-Misna?),[77] perhaps the capital of Late Bronze Moab, is just another way of speaking of the whole nation.

Moab, like Edom, was a "brother" nation to Israel, one whose founders could trace their roots back to the patriarchs. This explains the circumlocution "descendants of Lot" as a descriptive term. It will be recalled that when Sodom, Gomorrah, and the other cities of the Dead Sea plain were destroyed, Lot and his daughters fled to the east and lived in caves temporarily. Bereft of husbands, these daughters made themselves pregnant by their drunken father and subsequently gave birth to sons, whom they named Moab and Ben-Ammi (Gen 19:30-38). Moab became the patronym of the land and nation of Moab and Ben-Ammi of Ammon.

2:10-12   In a lengthy parenthesis the historian supplied details concerning the indigenous populations of Moab and Edom, how they were driven out, and the justification for their dispossession. Moab, he said, was originally inhabited by Emites who, like the Anakites, were a gigantic race related to the Rephaites (vv. 10-11). Apart from this passage the Emites

---

Mattingly, "The Exodus-Conquest and the Archaeology of Transjordan: New Light on an Old Problem," *GTJ* 4 (1983): 245-62; J. A Sauer, "Transjordan in the Bronze and Iron Ages: A Critique of Glueck's Synthesis," *BASOR* 263 (1986): 1-26. Sauer does point out (pp. 8-9) that LB is not as well attested in South Transjordan as it is in the north and central areas. This, of course, would not rule out the strong presence of nonsedentary peoples who would be less detectable archaeologically.

[75] G. D. Pratico, "Nelson Glueck's 1938–1940 Excavations at Tell el-Kheleifeh: A Reappraisal," *BASOR* 259 (1985): 1-32. To this point neither Elath nor Ezion Geber has yielded evidence of LB occupation, but it is possible that their sites have not yet been correctly identified. For some misgivings see Mazar, *Archaeology,* 397, 450-51.

[76] Bartlett, "The Moabites and Edomites," 232-33; J. R. Kautz, "Tracking the Ancient Moabites," *BA* 44 (1981): 27-35.

[77] H. G. May, ed., *Oxford Bible Atlas,* 3d ed. (New York: Oxford University Press, 1984), 122; J. M. Miller, "The Israelite Journey through (around) Moab and Moabite Toponymy," *JBL* 108 (1989): 590-95.

appear only in Gen 14:5, where they are among the peoples defeated by the four kings of the east who invaded Canaan and vicinity in the days of Abraham. There they are associated with a place called Shaveh Kiriathim ("the valley of Kiriathim"), to be located perhaps some eight or ten miles east of the northern end of the Dead Sea.[78]

The Emim and Anakites (cf. Deut 1:28) are here identified with the Rephaites, a people attested to both in the Old Testament and in extrabiblical literature.[79] According to the narrative of the invasion of the eastern kings (Gen 14:1-12), they lived in or around Ashteroth Karnaim (Gen 14:5), a site that cannot presently be located with certainty but most likely one to be identified with Ashtaroth in the Bashan plateau just east of the Sea of Galilee. Known today as Tel 'Ashtarah,[80] this suggested site has the advantage of being close to another named Karnaim and also would be first in the list of towns sacked by the eastern kings in what clearly is a north-to-south itinerary (Gen 14:5-6). Later, Og, king of Bashan, who is described as a Rephaite (Josh 12:4; cf. 13:12), ruled from Ashtaroth (Deut 1:4), thus linking that city with Bashan.[81]

Deuteronomy itself provides most of the biblical information about the Rephaites. They lived not only in Moab and Bashan but also in Ammon (2:20). It seems, then, that virtually all the Transjordan was their home at one time (3:13) and that their reputation as a strong, numerous, and tall people is well justified. Og, for example, was a Rephaite who required an iron bed thirteen feet long and six feet wide (3:11)! Giants who lived west of the Jordan in Canaan proper may also have sprung from the Rephaites as their linkage with the Anakites might suggest (Deut 1:28; Josh 11:21-22; 14:12,15; 15:13-14; Judg 1:20). Eventually they were driven out of Israelite territory and took up residence in Gaza, Gath, and Ashdod (Josh 11:22), the home of Philistine giants such as Goliath (1 Sam 17:4; 1 Chr 20:4-8). The famous battlefield known as the Valley of Rephaim also supports the presence of these giants (Josh 15:8; 18:16; 2 Sam 5:18-22; 23:15).

Continuing his digression, Moses identified the original settlers of the high plateau of Seir as Horites.[82] This is in agreement with the ancient

---

[78] G. J. Wenham, *Genesis 1–15,* WBC (Waco: Word, 1987), 311.

[79] A. Caquot, "Les rephaim ougaritiques," *Syria* 37 (1960): 75-93; J. Gray, "The Rephaim," *PEQ* 81 (1949): 127-39; C. L'Heureux, "The Ugaritic and Bible Rephaim," *HTR* 67 (1974): 265-74; S. Talmon, "Biblical *REPA'IM* and Ugaritic *RPU/I(M),*" *HUCA* 7 (1983): 235-49.

[80] Aharoni, *Land of the Bible,* 160.

[81] T. C. Butler, *Joshua,* WBC (Waco: Word, 1983), 136.

[82] Most scholars identify the biblical Horites with the well-known ancient Near Eastern Hurrians, an ethnic element with wide geographic distribution attested as early as the Ur III period (ca. 2150 B.C.). See H. Hoffner, "The Hurrians," in *Peoples of Old Testament Times,* 221-28.

account in Gen 36, which speaks of Seir, the patronymic of the area, as a Horite (v. 20), and of his descendants as Horite chiefs. The account of the eastern kings had also referred to the "Horites in the hill country of Seir" (Gen 14:6). Genesis 36 furthermore makes the connection between Esau and his descendants, who created the Edomite kingdom (vv. 8-19,31-43), and the indigenous Horites whom they displaced (esp. vv. 8,43).

The passage at hand amplifies previous information by spelling out the expulsion of the Horites by the Esauites not only as a historical datum but also a matter of theological import (v. 12). The Bible is clear in its witness to the universal sovereignty of God and to his allocation to the nations of their territorial jurisdictions (cf. Deut 32:8; Acts 17:26), but nowhere is the point more clearly made than here, especially with regard to the allotments to Israel's "brother" nations (Deut 2:5,9,19).[83] Esau and the Edomites therefore had as much right to expel the Horites from Seir as Israel did to expel the Canaanites, Amorites, and others from the land of promise, a point that is at least implied in the comparison "just as Israel did in the land the LORD gave them as their possession" (v. 12).

Before leaving this matter, it might be well to look briefly at the problem of the alleged anachronism of v. 12, which indicates that Israel had already entered Canaan and displaced its inheritance. Many scholars cite this passage as a "clear indication" that the "final composition" of Deuteronomy was post-Mosaic.[84] This, however, is unwarranted in light of several reasonable explanations. First, it is possible that the narrator here was employing the so-called "perfective of confidence," used to speak of a future event that is as good as done inasmuch as it is promised by the Lord.[85] Second, the statement could be a later addition to the text by an authorized individual understood to be directed by the Lord. Such an addition or additions would not need to be much later than Moses nor extensive enough to warrant speaking of a later "final composition."[86] Third, the text may have been authored by Moses himself, who was speaking of the occupation of the Transjordan that had already occurred (Deut 3:12-17).[87]

2:13 The parenthetical remarks having come to an end, the narrator picks up the itinerary where he had left off in v. 8, namely, "along the desert road of Moab." The account in Numbers is a little more specific in

---

[83] J. R. Bartlett, "The Land of Seir and the Brotherhood of Edom," *JTS* 20 (1969): 5-8; E. H. Merrill, "A Theology of the Pentateuch," in *A Biblical Theology of the Old Testament,* ed. R. B. Zuck (Chicago: Moody, 1991), 75.

[84] E.g., Christensen, *Deuteronomy 1–11,* 42.

[85] For examples of this so-called "accidental perfective," see *IBHS* § 30.5.1e.

[86] J. S. Deere, "Deuteronomy," in *The Bible Knowledge Commentary,* 266.

[87] Thompson, *Deuteronomy,* 92.

that it mentions Oboth and Iye Abarim, places evidently on the eastern border of Moab (Num 21:10-11; 33:44). By then Israel had reached the upper Zered river valley (v. 13), the frontier between Edom to the south and Moab to the north.[88]

2:14-15 Once more the résumé of the journey is briefly interrupted, this time by the information that thirty-eight years had passed from the beginning of the sojourn at Kadesh Barnea to the crossing of the Zered and that all the rebellious generation of fighting men had died. The intent of the passage is not (as in NIV) to suggest that the present phase of the journey, that from Kadesh Barnea (cf. 2:1), had lasted thirty-eight years. This is an impossible meaning in light of the fact that the promise of years of wandering had been given when Israel first arrived at Kadesh Barnea and they were there in the fortieth year just before the present journey had begun (Num 20:1; cf. Deut 1:46; 2:1). Moreover, the Hebrew text reads, literally, "The days we traveled, from Kadesh Barnea until we crossed the Wadi Zered, were thirty-eight years" (2:14). The key to the interpretation is the nuance of the preposition ("left," lit., "from") prefixed to Kadesh Barnea. In a temporal sense (as here) it can include the beginning point or not.[89] In light of other requirements, the former usage is clearly to be preferred here.[90]

The reference to the demise of all the fighting men accomplishes at least two purposes: (1) it brings that whole era of desert sojourning to an end, and (2) it emphasizes more than ever that the impending victories of Israel in both the Transjordan and Canaan must be attributed not to Israel but to the Lord alone. With the heart of military capacity gone, there can be no doubt that victory is achievable only as he, the Warrior of Israel, leads them to triumph in holy war.[91]

(7) Conflict with Transjordanian Enemies (2:16–3:11)

Deuteronomy 2:16 marks a major turning point in the book thus far in

---

[88] The Zered (Wadi el-Ḥesa), at least forty miles long, arises in the Arabian desert east of Edom and Moab, well east of the route through Oboth and Iye Abarim. See Aharoni, *Land of the Bible,* 206 (and the map, p. 203).

[89] *IBHS* § 11.2.11c.

[90] Thus Craigie, *Deuteronomy,* 112, n. 5: "Perhaps the first departure from Kadesh and the unsuccessful campaign against the Amorites mark the beginning of the time span. In this case, many of the thirty-eight years would have been spent in the vicinity of Kadesh-barnea (see 1:46)."

[91] Moran puts more of a negative cast on it, viewing it as tantamount to a reverse exodus (W. L. Moran, "The End of the Unholy War and the Anti-exodus," *Bib* 44 [1963]: 333-42).

several different respects.[92] It divides between desert sojourn and permanent settlement, between the old rebel generation and the new, obedient one, and between defensive warfare and noninvolvement and a policy of aggressive conquest led by the Lord against hostile powers destined to defeat and displacement. The line of demarcation is particularly evident in the emphatic repetition of vv. 14 and 16, "that entire generation of fighting men had perished from the camp" and "when the last of these fighting men among the people had died." This is an unmistakable sign that something new and better is about to begin.

[16]Now when the last of these fighting men among the people had died, [17]the LORD said to me, [18]"Today you are to pass by the region of Moab at Ar. [19]When you come to the Ammonites, do not harass them or provoke them to war, for I will not give you possession of any land belonging to the Ammonites. I have given it as a possession to the descendants of Lot."

[20](That too was considered a land of the Rephaites, who used to live there; but the Ammonites called them Zamzummites. [21]They were a people strong and numerous, and as tall as the Anakites. The LORD destroyed them from before the Ammonites, who drove them out and settled in their place. [22]The LORD had done the same for the descendants of Esau, who lived in Seir, when he destroyed the Horites from before them. They drove them out and have lived in their place to this day. [23]And as for the Avvites who lived in villages as far as Gaza, the Caphtorites coming out from Caphtor destroyed them and settled in their place.)

[24]"Set out now and cross the Arnon Gorge. See, I have given into your hand Sihon the Amorite, king of Heshbon, and his country. Begin to take possession of it and engage him in battle. [25]This very day I will begin to put the terror and fear of you on all the nations under heaven. They will hear reports of you and will tremble and be in anguish because of you."

INSTRUCTIONS CONCERNING AMMON (2:16-25). **2:16-22** Before hostility against the enemies of the Lord could begin, Israel had to pass through or by the territory of one more "brother" people, namely, the Ammonites (vv. 16-19).[93] They lay ahead, just north of the land of Moab.

---

[92] Contra Christensen, who, on the basis of rhythmic units, sees the new section beginning with v. 17 (*Deuteronomy 1–11,* 42). This may be accepted in terms of rhetorical analysis but not necessarily in terms of narrative development. Weinfeld draws attention to the verb וַיְדַבֵּר ("said," v. 17) as an "opening formula," one to be explained "by the turning point that comes to expression here: the rebellious generation has perished, and the words of God are now addressed to the generation that is about to enter the promised land" (*Deuteronomy 1–11,* 164). For strong support of this understanding, see Mayes, *Deuteronomy,* 138-39.

[93] See G. M. Landes, "The Material Civilization of the Ammonites," *BA* 24 (1961): 65-86; Sumner, "Israel's Encounters with Edom, Moab, Ammon, Sihon, and Og according to the Deuteronomist" (pp. 216-28).

To reach Ammon, Israel could not pass "by the region of Moab at Ar" (thus NIV) because Ar was not on the border of Moab.[94] The construction of the syntax here makes it possible (and necessary) that Ar be seen not as the city but as synonymous with Moab as a whole (as argued earlier; cf. v. 9): "You are about to pass by today the territory of Moab, that is, Ar." This allows "pass by" and "Ar" to remain without being mutually exclusive.[95]

Because Ammon was related to Israel precisely as Moab was (cf. v. 9), its territory too was off limits to the Israelite armies. It was a possession from the Lord that could not be misappropriated even by God's covenant people (v. 19). Once again Moses interrupted his narration to provide information on the original inhabitants of the land. Like Moab, Ammon had once been occupied by Rephaites; but whereas the Moabites called them Emites (v. 11), the Ammonites preferred the term Zamzummites (v. 20), a name that occurs only here in this form (but see Zuzites in Gen 14:5). Finally, the Ammonites were like the Moabites in that the Lord drove out those whom they found in the land and allowed the descendants of Lot to take their places (v. 21). To be all-inclusive, the narrator went on to repeat what he had already stated (v. 12): the Lord had also expelled the Horites from Seir so that Esau could inherit it as his own possession (v. 22).

2:23 At this point Moses introduced new peoples, the Avvites and the Caphtorites,[96] the former having been displaced by the latter (v. 23). The Avvites came to mind no doubt because they too were a Rephaite tribe as the phrase "as far as Gaza" would seem to suggest. Gaza, with Gath and Ashdod, appears in Josh 11:22 as a city inhabited by Anakites who, of course, were Rephaites (cf. Josh 13:3). It seems, then, that while he was at it the historian decided to include all the Rephaite peoples who had been dispossessed at some time or other in the past.

The Caphtorites are unusually interesting in that they are prominent not only in the Old Testament but in ancient Near Eastern texts as well.[97] In the latter they are attested to as Egyptian Keftiu,[98] Ugaritic *kptr*,[99] and

---

[94] Miller ("The Israelite Journey through (around) Moab and Moabite Toponymy," 593-94) identifies Ar with Khirbet Balu, on a southeastern tributary of the Arnon and some five miles south.

[95] So Mayes, *Deuteronomy,* 139.

[96] The LXX (followed by Syr, Tg(s), Vg) reads "Cappadocians," an obvious misspelling of כפתרים by כפתכים (thus Weinfeld, *Deuteronomy 1–11,* 165).

[97] See J. Prignaud, "Caftorim et Keretim," *RB* 71 (1964): 215-29; J. E. Jennings, "The Problem of the Caphtorim," *Grace Journal* 12 (1971): 23-45; J. Strange, *Caphtor/Keftiu: A New Investigation* (Leiden: Brill, 1980); K. A. Kitchen, "The Philistines," in *Peoples of Old Testament Times,* 53-78.

[98] *AEL,* 2.37-38 ("The Poetical Stela of Thutmose III").

[99] *ANET,* 138 (V ABF = CTA 3 vi 18).

Akkadian[100] and in documents from as early as 2200 B.C. and as late as 1200. These unmistakably point to Crete as the place of origin of these peoples so that Caphtor and Crete are one and the same. The Old Testament does not contradict this evidence and, in fact, adds to it. In the table of nations of Gen 10 the Caphtorites are listed after the Casluhites "from whom the Philistines came" (10:14; cf. 1 Chr 1:12). The prophet Amos appears to have equated the Casluhites and Caphtorites when he pointed out that the Philistines came from Caphtor (Amos 9:7). That is, the Philistines were descendants of the Casluhites who came from Caphtor. Jeremiah added the information that the Philistines were "the remnant from the coasts of Caphtor" (Jer 47:4).

All this is of interest not only to the matter of the supplanting of the indigenous Avvites from Canaan's coastal plain but also to the whole question of Philistines in preconquest Israelite history. Most scholars equate the Philistines exclusively with the Sea Peoples of various ancient texts, a people who did not appear in Canaan until 1200 B.C. or later. References to Philistines in patriarchal or other earlier times are either considered anachronistic or are relegated to the realm of legend or etiological sagas.[101] If, however, Caphtorites and Philistines are one and the same and the former are attested as early as Abraham, at least as Keftiu or Kaptara, no reason remains to doubt the genuineness of pre-Mosaic and Mosaic references to these Philistines.[102] Identification of the Sea Peoples and Philistines (which is not denied) means only that there was a later migration of Philistines hundreds of years after those known to the patriarchs (cf. Gen 21:32,34; 26:1,8; Exod 13:17; 23:31).

The perspective from which the past is viewed in Deuteronomy is clearly that of remote times. Moses reached way back to describe the native peoples of the various lands he mentioned and then spoke of the ethnic, cultural, and political changes that took place long before his time thanks to the coming of these newer elements. It is not unrealistic at all that here he reflected back on the coming of the Caphtorites, known to the patriarchs as Philistines, who eventually expelled and replaced the Avvites.

2:24-25 Resuming the travel narrative again, the historian recalls the command of the Lord to the people that they press on to their destination. They had by then arrived at the Arnon River, a deep ravine that formed the traditional border between Moab and the land of the Amorites to the north

---

[100] C. J. Gadd, "The Reign of Sargon," in *CAH*, vol. I, part 2, 428-30.

[101] R. de Vaux, *Early History of Israel*, 503-4; R. Rendtorff, *The Old Testament: An Introduction* (Philadelphia: Fortress, 1986), 86-87.

[102] K. A. Kitchen, *Ancient Orient and Old Testament* (London: Tyndale, 1966), 80-81.

(cf. Num 21:13). This time the instructions were altogether different, for the Amorites, far from being a "brother" people, were inveterate foes of the Lord and his people, a nation of hopelessly unrepentant squatters who had to be removed from the lands promised to Israel's forefathers (cf. Gen 15:16; Exod 3:8; 13:5; 23:23; 33:2; 34:11).[103] Thus the command was to engage Sihon, king of the Amorites, in battle and liberate the land that he illegitimately occupied (Deut 2:24). In all this there are the clear overtones of holy war.[104] Yahweh said that he had already delivered the Amorites over to Israel and that he had already instilled in them and other antitheocratic nations terror and fear. When they learned of Israel's exploits, they would tremble and writhe with uncontrollable anguish, a state of affairs frequently associated with holy war contexts (cf. Exod 15:14-16; Josh 2:8-11).

[26]From the desert of Kedemoth I sent messengers to Sihon king of Heshbon offering peace and saying, [27]"Let us pass through your country. We will stay on the main road; we will not turn aside to the right or to the left. [28]Sell us food to eat and water to drink for their price in silver. Only let us pass through on foot— [29]as the descendants of Esau, who live in Seir, and the Moabites, who live in Ar, did for us—until we cross the Jordan into the land the LORD our God is giving us." [30]But Sihon king of Heshbon refused to let us pass through. For the LORD your God had made his spirit stubborn and his heart obstinate in order to give him into your hands, as he has now done.

[31]The LORD said to me, "See, I have begun to deliver Sihon and his country over to you. Now begin to conquer and possess his land."

[32]When Sihon and all his army came out to meet us in battle at Jahaz, [33]the LORD our God delivered him over to us and we struck him down, together with his sons and his whole army. [34]At that time we took all his towns and completely destroyed them—men, women and children. We left no survivors. [35]But the livestock and the plunder from the towns we had captured we carried off for ourselves. [36]From Aroer on the rim of the Arnon Gorge, and from the town in the gorge, even as far as Gilead, not one town was too strong for us. The LORD our God gave us all of them. [37]But in accordance with the command of the LORD our God, you did not encroach on any of the land of the Ammonites, neither the land along the course of the Jabbok nor that around the towns in the hills.

---

[103] For literature describing the Amorites, especially those of Syria-Palestine, see C. H. J. de Geus, "The Amorites in the Archaeology of Palestine," *UF* 3 (1971): 41-60; A. Haldar, *Who Were the Amorites?* (Leiden: Brill, 1971); K. M. Kenyon, *Amorites and Canaanites* (London: Oxford University Press, 1966); M. Liverani, "The Amorites," in *Peoples of Old Testament Times*, 100-133; J. Van Seters, "The Terms 'Amorite' and 'Hittite' in the OT," *VT* 22 (1972): 64-81.

[104] Moran, "End of the Unholy War," 333-42.

DEFEAT OF SIHON, KING OF HESHBON (2:26-37).[105] **2:26** Having crossed the Arnon and having arrived in the desert of Kedemoth, Moses sent terms of peace to Sihon. In return for safe passage through his territory to the Jordan River, Israel would promise to remain on the main road and would desist from taking property or produce without paying for it (vv. 26-29). Kedemoth (*ʿAleiyân*) lies about eight miles north of the Arnon on the route between Dibon and Mattanah.[106] A reconstruction of sites along Israel's march as provided by the accounts in Num 21 and 33 shows that the first campsite named after crossing the Arnon is Dibon Gad (*Dhîbān*), a place well attested biblically (Num 21:30; 32:3,34; 33:45-46; Josh 13:9,17; Isa 15:2; Jer 48:18,22; Neh 11:25) and archaeologically as a major population center.[107] Next is Mattanah (Khirbet el-Medeiyineh?),[108] ten miles northeast of Dibon. Kedemoth, not mentioned in Numbers (but see Josh 13:18; 21:37; 1 Chr 6:79), lies between these two cities as suggested earlier.

Moses apparently used Kedemoth as a base of operations, for it was from there that he sent his envoys to Sihon's capital city, Heshbon, twenty miles north. Like Dibon, Heshbon occupies a place of prominence in the Old Testament (Num 21:25-34; 32:3,37; Deut 29:7; Josh 12:2,5; 13:10-27) and in extrabiblical literature as well as in archaeology.[109] It was one of the forty-eight Levitical cities (1 Chr 6:81), claimed first by Reuben (Num 32:37) and later by Gad (Josh 13:26). Prior to Sihon's rise to power Heshbon and everything south had belonged to Moab. The energetic Amorite had then destroyed Heshbon, made the site his own capital, and pushed Moab's border all the way to the Arnon (Num 21:26-30).[110] The Israelites under Moses were therefore asking to traverse territory that had recently fallen to Sihon's control. This may in part explain his sensitivity about

---

[105] For various views concerning literary and historical aspects of the Transjordan conquest, see J. R. Bartlett, "The Conquest of Sihon's Kingdom: A Literary Re-examination," *JBL* 97 (1978): 347-51; Z. Kallai, "Conquest and Settlement of Transjordan: A Historiographical Study," *ZDPV* 99 (1983): 110-18; Sumner, "Israel's Encounters with Edom, Moab, Ammon, Sihon and Og according to the Deuteronomist," 216-28; J. Van Seters, "The Conquest of Sihon's Kingdom: A Literary Examination," *JBL* 91 (1972): 182-97; "Once Again—the Conquest of Sihon's Kingdom," *JBL* 99 (1980): 117-19.

[106] Aharoni, *Land of the Bible*, 202-3.

[107] A. D. Tushingham, *The Excavations at Dibon (Dhîbān) in Moab, The Third Campaign 1952–53*, AASOR 40 (1972).

[108] May, *Oxford Bible Atlas*, 135.

[109] R. D. Ibach, *Archaeological Survey of the Hesban Region*, Hesban 5 (Berrien Springs, Mich.: Andrews University Press, 1987).

[110] Harrison, *Numbers*, 284-86; cf. J. R. Bartlett, "The Historical Reference of Numbers 21:27-30," *PEQ* 101 (1969): 94-100.

allowing this to happen (v. 30).

2:27-29   The basis of Moses' appeal to Sihon was that the Edomites and Moabites had permitted Israel to pass through their lands on condition that they stick to the thoroughfares and pay for all they ate and drank (v. 29). The Amorites therefore ought to be at least as considerate. But evidence that Edom and Moab had indeed made such concessions is scanty. In fact, when Moses solicited such permission from the king of Edom, the answer was resoundingly negative, so much so that "Israel turned away from them" (Num 20:21). As for Moab, the record is otherwise silent about any such overture at all. Moses clearly appeared to be exaggerating the level of cooperation he received from these neighbors of Sihon to the south. This way of looking at Moses' communication with the Amorites is not contradicted by previous statements to the effect that Israel was to pay Edom (and by implication Moab) for supplies they might obtain from them (2:6). This would be done, obviously, only if and when Israel passed through these countries and requested these commodities, something for which there is no evidence. Indeed, later in this very book Moses condemned the Ammonites and Moabites for not having provided Israel with bread and water on their way to the promised land (Deut 23:4).[111]

The ethical dilemma posed by this suggestion of duplicity (if such duplicity actually exists) on the part of Moses is troublesome, but one must remember in cases like this that humans, not God, are culpable and that the biblical record is an accurate and unbiased account of human behavior as it really is. For Moses to have stretched the truth (if, in fact, he did) is indefensible, but at the same time it is understandable given the exigencies of the situation and the nature of the negotiations in which he was involved.

2:30   In any event, Sihon was not impressed and resolutely forbade Israel access to the territories under his control (v. 30). His defiance might ordinarily be attributed to a spirit of arrogance or a sense of military supremacy, but here Moses made clear that his obstinacy was something that the Lord brought upon him precisely in order to provide an occasion for his destruction at Israel's hands (cf. v. 24). Literally Moses said that the Lord "caused his spirit to be hard" and "hardened his heart." The former verb ($q\bar{a}\check{s}\hat{a}$) occurs in the same stem in Exod 7:3 to speak of the Lord hardening Pharaoh's heart to prepare him for judgment. The second verb

---

[111] Ridderbos suggests that Deut 2:29 and 23:4 are not contradictory but that 23:4 "indicates a lack of spontaneous support, which would have gone well beyond what is stated in verse 29" (*Deuteronomy,* 72). It is possible, of course, that the full account is not related and that Israel did indeed pass through Edom and Moab and trade with them just as Moses reported to Sihon.

(ʾāmaṣ) usually occurs in a positive sense with the meaning "to encourage," but here (and in 2 Chr 36:13) it connotes the same meaning as qāšâ, "to make obstinate."[112] The highly deterministic significance of the passage is appropriate to the spirit of holy war in which Yahweh, the Commander, employed whatever weapons of his arsenal he chose to. What Israel might not have been able to accomplish through ordinary diplomatic channels Yahweh could do through the extraordinary.

2:31-35 The hardness of Sihon's spirit and heart was the beginning of his downfall. In that sense, then, the Lord could say, "I have begun to deliver Sihon and his country over to you" (v. 31). All that is needed on Israel's part is the willingness to rise up and follow the Lord into battle. Having done this, they encountered Sihon and the Amorites at Jahaz,[113] just a mile or two from Mattanah, where Israel had last encamped (cf. v. 26). The outcome was decisively in Israel's favor as was always the case when it was faithful to the conditions of waging war on Yahweh's behalf. Sihon, his sons, and his army were devastated; and the populations of his cities and towns were placed under ḥerem, that is, completely annihilated (v. 34). Only livestock and other spoils of war were spared and taken by the victorious armies of Israel (v. 35).

Nothing is more integral to the waging of holy war than the placing of conquered lands and their peoples under ḥerem. This noun, derived from the verb ḥāram, "to exterminate," refers to a condition in which persons and things became the personal possession of the Lord by virtue of his inherent sovereignty and his appropriation of them by conquest.[114] They could either be left alive and intact (Lev 27:21,28; Josh 6:19) or eradicated (as here; cf. Num 21:2-3; Josh 6:21). In the passage at hand, it seems that the physical structures of the cities themselves were spared and that only the populations were decimated. The Hebrew text supports this understanding: "We placed under the ban each city of males,[115] along with

---

[112] J. Schreiner, "אמץ ʾāmats," etc., *TDOT* 1:326.

[113] Aharoni (*Land of the Bible,* 437) tentatively identifies Jahaz with Khirbet el-Medeiyineh as does J. A. Dearman, "The Levitical Cities of Reuben and Moabite Toponymy," *BASOR* 276 (1984): 55-57. May, though proposing that Mattanah may be Kh. el Medeiyineh (see n. 41), also allows for the possibility that Jahaz is thus identified (*Oxford Bible Atlas,* 132).

[114] For a full lexical discussion, see N. Lohfink, "חָרַם ḥāram; חֵרֶם ḥerem," *TDOT* 5:180-99, and the literature cited there. See also A. Malamat, "The Ban in Mari and the Bible," in *Mari and the Bible: A Collection of Studies* (Jerusalem: n.p., 1984), 52-61 (reprinted from *Biblical Essays: Proceedings of "Die Ou-Testamentiese Werkgemeenskap in Suid-Afrika"* [University of Stellenbosch, 1966], 40-49).

[115] The Heb. עִיר מְתֹם ("city of males") means, as Driver (*Deuteronomy,* 44) points out, "city male-population."

women and children; we did not spare a survivor." A smoother rendering might be, "We placed under the ban the men, women, and children of each city." In any case, there is no hint here that walls and buildings also were involved.

This outcome is, of course, in line with Moses' own policy outlined later in Deuteronomy, a code of conduct that specified that cities, houses, wells, vineyards, and olive groves—all would become Israel's without their expending any labor at all in their construction (Deut 6:10-11; cf. 19:1).[116] Following the conquest, Joshua was able to report that the Lord had given Israel "a land on which you did not toil and cities you did not build, and you live in them and eat from vineyards and olive groves that you did not plant" (Josh 24:13). In the absence of evidence to the contrary, one must assume that this included the cities of the Transjordan as well. Their populations were exterminated according to the canons of holy war, but the physical facilities themselves remained intact for later Israelite occupation. Subsequent allotment of these areas to the two and a half eastern tribes includes reference to their having received the cities and towns scattered throughout (cf. Josh 13:8-33), a rather meaningless prize if the urban structures no longer existed.

2:36-37 The extent of Israel's victory over Sihon and the Amorites is sketched out in the phrase "from Aroer . . . as far as Gilead" (v. 36), that is, from the Arnon River to the Jabbok. Aroer lies on the northern edge of the Arnon valley, just three miles from Dibon.[117] It marked the southernmost outpost of Amorite (and, later, Reubenite) territory and so gave rise to the geographical formula "from Aroer to" (cf. Deut 3:12; 4:48; Josh 12:2; 13:9,16,25; Judg 11:33; 2 Kgs 10:33; 1 Chr 5:8). As for "the town in the gorge," some scholars argue that it was none other than Ar, the capital of Moab (cf. Num 21:15).[118] While this is attractive in some respects, it is difficult to explain why the city is not simply called Ar here (and elsewhere where it is associated with Aroer; cf. Josh 13:9,16; 2 Sam 24:5). Also Ar was at least five miles south of the Arnon and so could hardly be said to have been "in the gorge." Finally, there is no evidence that Amorite (or Reubenite) territory was ever thought to extend as far south as Ar. For all these reasons, it seems best to understand the construction of the verse epexegetically, that is, to see "the town in the gorge" as an explanation of

---

[116] For a full discussion of this policy and its implications for archaeological evidence of the conquest, see E. H. Merrill, "Palestinian Archaeology and the Date of the Conquest: Do Tells Tell Tales?" *GTJ* 3 (1982): 107-21.

[117] E. Olávarri, "Sondages à ʿArôʿer sur l'Arnon," *RB* 72 (1965): 91.

[118] Thus, e.g., Driver, *Deuteronomy,* 45.

Aroer and its precise location: "From Aroer on the rim of the Arnon Gorge, namely, the town in the gorge, even as far as Gilead."[119] Very possibly there was a question about the exact location of the city at that time, or there might, indeed, have been another city by that name from which this must be further distinguished.

The northern boundary of Amorite territory is here described simply as Gilead (v. 36). The Book of Numbers, with greater specificity, refers to it as the Jabbok River, the great tributary of the Jordan that feeds it from the plateaus of the central Transjordan (Num 21:24). Simply put, Sihon's kingdom at the time of Israelite conquest extended from the Arnon to the Jabbok, a distance of about fifty-five miles, and from the Jordan River and Dead Sea on the west to the Ammonite kingdom on the east, roughly twenty to twenty-five miles.[120]

With the defeat at Jahaz (v. 32), Sihon and his forces soon capitulated; and all his lands and cities fell to Israel, a turn of events attributed, as always in holy war, to divine intervention (v. 36). But the territorial integrity of Ammon was left intact (v. 37), for the command had already been issued that Ammon, a "brother" people, must be left undisturbed (cf. 2:19). Its boundaries ran "along the course of the Jabbok" where that river flows north and then west and "around the towns in the hills." Most likely this is a way of referring to Ammon's western frontier which then, of course, would be the eastern boundary of Sihon's kingdom.[121]

[1]**Next we turned and went up along the road toward Bashan, and Og king of Bashan with his whole army marched out to meet us in battle at Edrei.** [2]**The LORD said to me, "Do not be afraid of him, for I have handed him over to you with his whole army and his land. Do to him what you did to Sihon king of the Amorites, who reigned in Heshbon."**

[3]**So the LORD our God also gave into our hands Og king of Bashan and all his army. We struck them down, leaving no survivors.** [4]**At that time we took all his cities. There was not one of the sixty cities that we did not take from them—the whole region of Argob, Og's kingdom in Bashan.** [5]**All these cities were fortified with high walls and with gates and bars, and there were also a great many unwalled villages.** [6]**We completely destroyed them, as we had done with Sihon king of Heshbon, destroying every city—men, women and chil-**

---

[119] Most scholars do indeed identify the "town in the gorge" with Aroer. Christensen (*Deuteronomy 1–11,* 49), in his prosodic analysis of v. 36, makes the equation as follows:
     From Aroer / which is on the edge of the Arnon Valley /
       Yea, the city which / is in the valley / indeed as far as Gilead /, etc.
[120] For interaction with the complexity of the biblical traditions concerning the extent of Sihon's realm, see Kallai, "Conquest and Settlement of Trans-Jordan," 112-13.
[121] De Vaux, *Early History of Israel,* 558-59.

dren. [7]But all the livestock and the plunder from their cities we carried off for ourselves.

[8]So at that time we took from these two kings of the Amorites the territory east of the Jordan, from the Arnon Gorge as far as Mount Hermon. [9](Hermon is called Sirion by the Sidonians; the Amorites call it Senir.) [10]We took all the towns on the plateau, and all Gilead, and all Bashan as far as Salecah and Edrei, towns of Og's kingdom in Bashan. [11](Only Og king of Bashan was left of the remnant of the Rephaites. His bed was made of iron and was more than thirteen feet long and six feet wide. It is still in Rabbah of the Ammonites.)

DEFEAT OF OG, KING OF BASHAN (3:1-11). **3:1** The campaign of offensive holy war continued with Israel's penetration of Gilead, the territory to the north of the Jabbok River, all the way to the land of Bashan. This heavily forested and productive high plateau was famous in ancient times for its oaks (Isa 2:13) and livestock (Deut 32:14; Amos 4:1). It lay north of Gilead, whose southern border was the Jabbok and with whom it shared a common border, the Yarmuk River. The narrative says nothing of the route that was taken, though Numbers indicates that the point of origin was Jazer (Khirbet Jazzir)[122] and, with Deut 3:1, agrees that its destination was Edrei (*Der'a*), thirty miles southeast of the Sea of Galilee (Num 21:32-33).[123] This would have been a fifty-mile march from the southwest to northeast through the Gilead tablelands.

3:2 Arriving at Edrei, the armies of Israel encountered Og, a king of Bashan (who is later identified as a Rephaite [v. 11], one of the last survivors of the indigenous giant population).[124] He was also king of an Amorite nation (v. 8) and so was subject to the same policy of extermination as was Sihon. Moses therefore had no need to fear him, for the Lord fought on Israel's behalf and would deliver Og and his land and people over to destruction (v. 2). All Israel had to do was to rise up and become the Lord's instrument of judgment as it was in the conquest of Sihon.

3:3-7 The result was exactly as predicted and planned: the Amorite population of Bashan was annihilated, and sixty cities fell to Israel's control. These cities, the historian notes, were in Argob, the technical name for a region of Og's kingdom in Bashan (v. 4).[125] They were well fortified and

---

[122] May, *Oxford Bible Atlas,* 132.

[123] R. Hill, "Aetheria XII 9 and the Site of Biblical Edrei," *VT* 16 (1966): 412-20.

[124] J. R. Bartlett, "Sihon and Og, Kings of the Amorites," *VT* 20 (1970): 257-77.

[125] Mayes dismisses the reference to the sixty cities as an "inaccurate gloss" based on 1 Kgs 4:13 (*Deuteronomy,* 143). This, of course, presupposes the dependence of Deuteronomy on Kings (in this instance at least), for which there is no solid evidence. Given what is known of population density in the northern Transjordan in Late Bronze, there is no reason to question the assertion that sixty cities fell to Israel. See Sauer, "Transjordan in the Bronze and Iron Ages," 6-8. For Argob see Aharoni, *Land of the Bible,* who speaks of it as "evidently the rich and fertile region north of the Yarmuk River" (p. 314).

yet could not resist the hosts of the Lord, a tribute and testimony to the fact that this was not ordinary war but war led and fought by the Lord himself. This is confirmed by the use once more of the technical term *ḥērem* in v. 6, "We completely destroyed (*naḥărēm*) them, as we had done with Sihon" (cf. 2:34). The formula continues with the reference to the destruction of all the men, women, and children. But, as was the case with the overthrow of Sihon, there is no hint that the city structures were demolished. In fact, they, along with livestock and plunder, were preserved for Israel's own use (v. 7).

3:8-11 The story of the Transjordanian conquest concludes with a summary of the defeat of Sihon and Og. They are both identified as Amorites, thus subject to *ḥērem* and all its consequences, and are said to have ruled over all the vast territory from the Arnon River in the south to Mount Hermon in the north, a distance of some 140 miles. All the towns of the highlands (*mîšōr*, "level place"), that is, the plateau including Gilead and Bashan, were taken. The verb used here, *lāqaḥ*, means "to capture," not "destroy," so it is clear once again that the *ḥērem* did not include the annihilation of the physical cities themselves, at least not in this holy war operation.[126]

The towns included were as far north and east as Salecah (Salkhad)[127] and Edrei (Der'a), deep in the Hauran desert. These places were part of Og's kingdom, Argob (v. 4), a Bashanite principality. This information led Moses (or more likely a later commentator) to provide further information about Og, who clearly was an object of much curious reflection. He was the last of the Rephaites, the giants who had inhabited the Transjordan from time immemorial (cf. Deut 2:11). So large was he that he required a bed of iron thirteen feet long and six feet wide![128] Its unusual construction and size made it a museum piece, one, the historian said, that was still on exhibit in the Ammonite city Rabbah in his own time.[129]

---

[126] Merrill, "Palestinian Archaeology," 109-12.

[127] Aharoni, *Land of the Bible,* 441.

[128] A. R. Millard, "King Og's Bed and Other Ancient Ironmongery," in *Ascribe to the Lord,* ed. L. Eslinger and G. Taylor, JSOTSup 67 (Sheffield: JSOT, 1988), 481-92; id., "King Og's Iron Bed—Fact or Fancy?" *BARev* 6 (1990): 16-21, 44. The term translated "bed" (עֶרֶשׂ) is thought by many scholars to refer to a sarcophagus made of basalt, a volcanic stone that resembles iron in color and texture. It was a "bed" then in the sense of a final resting place. See Mayes, *Deuteronomy,* 144.

[129] It is generally recognized that such a statement presupposes a post-Mosaic gloss, one perhaps as late as the time of David when Rabbah was the capital city of Ammon and the place where such antiquaries as the coffin of Og were likely to be collected. Thus Ridderbos, *Deuteronomy,* 75-76.

(8) Distribution of the Transjordanian Allotments (3:12-17)

[12]Of the land that we took over at that time, I gave the Reubenites and the Gadites the territory north of Aroer by the Arnon Gorge, including half the hill country of Gilead, together with its towns. [13]The rest of Gilead and also all of Bashan, the kingdom of Og, I gave to the half tribe of Manasseh. (The whole region of Argob in Bashan used to be known as a land of the Rephaites. [14]Jair, a descendant of Manasseh, took the whole region of Argob as far as the border of the Geshurites and the Maacathites; it was named after him, so that to this day Bashan is called Havvoth Jair.) [15]And I gave Gilead to Makir. [16]But to the Reubenites and the Gadites I gave the territory extending from Gilead down to the Arnon Gorge (the middle of the gorge being the border) and out to the Jabbok River, which is the border of the Ammonites. [17]Its western border was the Jordan in the Arabah, from Kinnereth to the Sea of the Arabah (the Salt Sea), below the slopes of Pisgah.

In a request that is not reported here in the Deuteronomy historical review but is elaborated in the original account in Num 32:1-5, representatives of the tribes of Reuben and Gad had approached Moses about possession and occupation of the recently conquered Transjordanian lands. Their unusual interest in this region of plains and plateaus was that they had large herds and flocks, and the territory they wanted was eminently suitable to that industry (Num 32:4).

After much hesitation and long deliberation, Moses was satisfied with the motives of the two tribes in settling there and with their pledge to assist the remaining tribes in their conquest of Canaan before they tended to their own interests (Num 32:5-32). In the Deuteronomy version the distribution of the allotments is first addressed, and then come the instructions to Reuben and Gad concerning their role in the conquest of Canaan (vv. 18-22).[130]

3:12   The Reubenites and Gadites, descendants of Jacob's eldest sons by Leah and her slave girl Zilpah, respectively, received as their inheritance all the territory that had belonged to Sihon and more, a tract extending from Aroer on the Arnon (cf. 2:36) to the middle of Gilead. The boundary between these two tribes, if in fact there was one, was very flexible indeed as the various descriptions of their areas of settlement attest. The earliest record of the division—that of Num 32:33-38—locates Gad around Dibon, Ataroth, Aroer, Atroth Shophan (all toward the south, near the Arnon), Jazer, Jogbehah, Beth Nimrah, and Beth Haran (all to the northeast of the Dead Sea and west of Rabbah). Reuben is concentrated

---

[130] For a traditio-historical analysis of the conquest and occupation of the eastern tribes, see Kallai, "Conquest and Settlement," 110-18.

around Heshbon, Elealah, Kiriathaim, Nebo, Baal Meon, and Sibmah (all just east of the north end of the Dead Sea).[131] This suggests that the Reubenites lived amongst the Gadites, in effect splitting the latter into southern and northern contingents.[132]

The most detailed description, however, occurs in the postconquest account of Josh 13:8-33. This seems very much at odds with the distribution of Num 32, so much so that critical scholars argue for differing and conflicting traditions upon which the data are based.[133] It is likely, however, that the differences lie either in the proposed allotment by Moses versus that which actually took place under Joshua or in the extremely flexible adjustments in territory that took place from one generation to the next. In any case, Joshua placed Reuben in the region from Aroer to Heshbon, including "all the towns on the plateau and the entire realm of Sihon" (Josh 13:21). Gad he located north of Reuben, concentrated especially around Jazer, Rabbah, Betonim, Mahonaim, Beth Haram, Beth Nimrah, Succoth, and Zaphon (Josh 13:25-28). This is in line with the Numbers perspective, at least in placing this part of Gad north of Reuben. As for Gad in the south, near the Arnon, very likely this was ceded over to Reuben at some point of the actual conquest, and Gad consolidated itself exclusively in the north.[134]

3:13-14 All this is of little concern to the Deuteronomic review of events (which, of course, preceded Joshua's allotment scheme anyway), so the historian went on to speak of the distribution of the remainder of Gilead and all of Bashan to the half tribe of Manasseh (v. 13). The reference to Manassehites here does not reflect the degree of confusion with which they are introduced in the other sources. Numbers 32 does not include them in the dialogue with Moses over tribal settlement in the Transjordan. It was only after he gave Reuben and Gad permission to do so that Manasseh appeared as a fellow beneficiary of that decision (Num 32–33). Meanwhile, it appears from that rendition of things that the actual conquest was by descendants of Manasseh called Makirites, notably by Jair and Nobah (32:39-42).[135] Makir was clearly a prominent clan of

---

[131] For suggestions about the identification and location of these places, see Aharoni, *Land of the Bible,* 89, 429-43; Sauer, "Transjordan in the Bronze and Iron Ages," 1-26; P. J. Budd, *Numbers,* WBC (Waco: Word, 1984), 344-45.

[132] R. de Vaux, *Early History of Israel,* 576.

[133] J. A. Soggin, *Joshua,* OTL (Philadelphia: Westminster, 1972), 154-57.

[134] M. Noth suggests that some of the southern Gadites might actually have called themselves Reubenites at a later time (*The History of Israel* [New York: Harper & Row, 1958], 63-65.

[135] Kallai, "Conquest and Settlement," 114.

Manasseh (cf. Num 26:29; 27:1; 36:1; Josh 13:31; 17:1,3; 1 Chr 2:23) but only a part. The rest of the tribe crossed the Jordan with Joshua and settled there (Josh 17:1-13).

According to Josh 13:29-31, eastern Manasseh was allocated the former holdings of Og, everything from Mahanaim on the Jabbok north. This included Og's royal cities Ashtaroth and Edrei (cf. Deut 1:4). Deuteronomy concurs, using the more specific term Argob to designate Og's realm (v. 13; cf. v. 4). Moreover, the conquest is here (as in Numbers) attributed to Jair, the Manassehite, who occupies Argob to its limits, all the way to the Bashanite kingdoms of Geshur to the west and south and Maacah to the northwest (v. 14).[136] Jair then changed the name of his kingdom to Havvoth Jair ("villages of Jair"), a name that probably replaced only Argob at first but then was extended to Bashan as a whole (v. 14). The new name appears to have been short-lived, for it never occurs in late literature.

3:15-17 Makir, Moses said, received Gilead as an inheritance (v. 15). The relationship between Makir and Jair is not altogether clear, but the genealogy of 1 Chr 2:21-23 suggests that Jair was a grandson (or some descendant) of Makir, who was, of course, a Manassehite (cf. Num 26:29).[137] In short, half of Gilead and all of Bashan became the property of east Manasseh. By recapitulation Moses went on to complete the picture of occupation. Reuben and Gad, he said, settled from Gilead south to the Arnon and east to the Jabbok, which, one should note, flows from south to north before it makes a sharp bend west to empty into the Jordan (v. 16). The western border (certainly, of all the Transjordanian inheritance) was the Jordan River from Kinnereth (that is, the Sea of Galilee) to the Dead Sea, specifically to Mount Pisgah, its most prominent elevated landmark (v. 17).

(9) Instructions to the Transjordanian Tribes (3:18-22)

[18]I commanded you at that time: "The LORD your God has given you this land to take possession of it. But all your able-bodied men, armed for battle, must cross over ahead of your brother Israelites. [19]However, your wives, your children and your livestock (I know you have much livestock) may stay in the towns I have given you, [20]until the LORD gives rest to your brothers as he has to you, and they too have taken over the land that the LORD your God is giving them, across the Jordan. After that, each of you may go back to the possession I have given you."

[21]At that time I commanded Joshua: "You have seen with your own eyes all

[136] B. Mazar, "Geshur and Maacah,' *JBL* 80 (1961): 16-28.
[137] R. Braun, *1 Chronicles,* WBC 14 (Waco: Word, 1986), 40.

that the LORD your God has done to these two kings. The LORD will do the same to all the kingdoms over there where you are going. ²²Do not be afraid of them; the LORD your God himself will fight for you."

3:18 Harking back again to the events of the past, but now (and since Deut 2:1) to just a few months or even weeks ago (cf. Num 20:1; Josh 5:6,10),[138] Moses restated his response to the two and a half tribes that had requested their inheritance to be in the Transjordan. This could be done, he said, if the men of war were willing to lead their brother tribes in the conquest of Canaan (v. 18). This apparently harsh condition would test the level of their commitment to remain in the land where they were and also make clear the fact that they were still part of the twelve-tribe confederation and as such must participate in the conquest action of the whole. This they could show best by leading the way (cf. Num 32:28-32).

3:19-20 To further measure their resolve, the fighting men must leave their wives, children, and livestock in the Transjordan (v. 19). Only after the task of conquest in the west was over could they return (v. 20). As it turned out, this appears to have taken at least seven long years (Josh 14:6-15; cf. 22:1-4), far longer, no doubt, than the most pessimistic would have thought. As to the matter of the security and maintenance of the families left behind, one must assume that the youth and the men over the normal maximum age for military service could more than meet these needs. Of course, it would also have been possible for troops from the west to recross the Jordan to take up arms on behalf of their loved ones should the need arise, particularly in light of the fact that Gilgal, just five miles west of the Jordan, was Joshua's headquarters during the early years of the conquest (Josh 4:19; 10:6-7,15,43; 14:6).

3:21-22 Moses now turned to the subject of Joshua, his theocratic successor, and reviewed the words of encouragement he had shared with him (v. 21). The Lord had defeated "these two kings," that is, Sihon and Og, and what he had done as commander of the hosts in the east he would do also in the west. Once more in the language of holy war he said, "Do not be afraid," for he is the "fighting one" who wages war on their behalf (v. 22).

(10) Denial to Moses of the Promised Land (3:23-29)

²³At that time I pleaded with the LORD: ²⁴"O Sovereign LORD, you have

---

[138] The phrase "at that time" (הַהוּא בָּעֵת; cf. 1:9,16,18; 2:34; 3:4,8,12,21,23; 4:14; 9:20; 10:1,8), though usually referring to a rather remote past, can also recall events of the immediate past. See Driver, *Deuteronomy*, 15; S. E. Loewenstamm, "The Formula *bāʿēt hahîʾ* in Deuteronomy," *Tarbiz* 38 (1968): 99-104 (Heb.).

begun to show to your servant your greatness and your strong hand. For what god is there in heaven or on earth who can do the deeds and mighty works you do? [25]Let me go over and see the good land beyond the Jordan—that fine hill country and Lebanon."

[26]But because of you the LORD was angry with me and would not listen to me. "That is enough," the LORD said. "Do not speak to me anymore about this matter. [27]Go up to the top of Pisgah and look west and north and south and east. Look at the land with your own eyes, since you are not going to cross this Jordan. [28]But commission Joshua, and encourage and strengthen him, for he will lead this people across and will cause them to inherit the land that you will see." [29]So we stayed in the valley near Beth Peor.

3:23-25   For a second time in Deuteronomy, Moses reflected back on the act of rebellion that had closed the door to his access to the land of promise (cf. 1:37). In neither the earlier passage nor the original setting in Num 20:9-12 is there a hint of reaction from Moses to the word of divine judgment—no repentance, complaint, or appeal. Here, however, he filled out the account by speaking of his fervent plea[139] to the Lord. He had already witnessed God's mighty acts of salvation and provision, but these were only preliminary to what God had in view for the nation in the future. Plaintively, Moses argued, "You have begun to show to your servant" (v. 24). The implication, of course, is that what God had begun for Moses he ought also to complete.[140]

That God *can* do so is, of course, not the matter in dispute. He is absolutely incomparable over against the gods of the nations. Such a confession on Moses' part is not to be understood as equivocation regarding monotheism. His subsequent teaching in Deuteronomy alone is sufficient to show his commitment to absolute monotheism (see, e.g., 4:35,39; 6:4). Rather, he was comparing his God to those conceived by the pagan world, and in comparison to them, God excels in every respect. The issue at hand, however, is what God *will* do. Thus Moses appealed to his purposes rather than his power, "Let me go over and see the good land" (3:25). His inclusion of Lebanon with the hill country as a definition of that land is, of course, in line with the ancient land promises to the patriarchs (cf. Deut 1:7; 11:24). This is not to suggest that Lebanon was part of the covenant grant but that it stood at its northern and western borders.

3:26   The lawgiver's urgent appeal was to no avail, however, for the Lord was angry with Moses "because of" (*lĕmaʿan*; cf. 1:37) the people.

---

[139] The *hithpael* stem of the verb חָנַן ("show favor, be gracious") plus the preposition אֶל suggests a seeking of God's favor in a pointed, specific way. Cf. D. N. Freedman and J. R. Lundbom, "חָנַן *hānan*," etc., *TDOT* 5:31.

[140] Cairns, *Word and Presence,* 50.

He does not (and cannot) shirk responsibility for his intemperate smiting of the rock in the desert (Num 20:9-11), but he was insistent that what he did was motivated by their incessant complaining and by his desire to meet their demands for water. In sharp words of rebuke ("enough of this!"), the Lord forbade further discussion (v. 26). The matter was settled.[141]

3:27 But true to his nature as a God of grace, the Lord commanded Moses ascend Pisgah from whose heights he might at least be able to view the land from a distance (v. 27). This eminence, whose modern name, most likely, is Ras es-Siyaghah,[142] lies just north of Mount Nebo and about ten miles east of the Jordan River where it flows into the Dead Sea. From this elevation and vantage point it is possible to take in all of Canaan from Hermon in the north to Beersheba in the south and all the way west to the Mediterranean. Moses waited to ascend the mountain until the time came for him to die (Deut 34:1-5), thus making this view of the land of promise the last act of his long life.

3:28-29 Joshua had already been appointed to succeed Moses as covenant mediator and theocratic administrator (cf. 1:38), so the command here to "commission" (lit., "to command") Joshua was merely a reaffirmation of his new role. Moses would see the land, but his younger colleague and protégé would enjoy the inestimable privilege of entering it and bringing it under the sovereign sway of the Lord and his people (v. 28). The finality of these decisions is seen in Moses' laconic statement, "So we stayed in the valley near Beth Peor" (v. 29).

This place, later to be the burial ground of Moses (Deut 34:6), lay just north of Pisgah.[143] It is more commonly known as Baal Peor (4:3; Hos 9:10) or simply Peor (Num 23:28; 25:3,5,18; 31:16; Josh 22:17; Ps 106:28). Apparently the center of a Transjordanian Baal cult, Peor was the scene of Balaam's frustrated efforts to curse Israel at the request of the Moabite king Balak (Num 23:27–24:25) and also of Israel's syncretistic apostasy, which resulted in the near decimation of the tribe of Simeon (Num 25:1-18; cf. 2:13; 26:14). Interestingly enough, neither episode receives significant attention in Moses' résumé of the past here in Deuteronomy, that concerning Balaam, in fact, not being mentioned at all. The omission clearly is to be explained on the basis of theological and not historiographical considerations.

---

[141] T. W. Mann, "Theological Reflections on the Denial of Moses," *JBL* 98 (1979): 490-92.

[142] M. Noth, *The Old Testament World* (Philadelphia: Fortress, 1966), 62. See discussion on Deut 34:1.

[143] Aharoni and Avi-Yonah, *Macmillan Bible Atlas,* map #53.

2. The Exhortation of Moses (4:1-40)

The end of the historical review proper leaves Moses and Israel at Pisgah and Peor, the setting for the delivery of Deuteronomy as a Mosaic address and its composition in essentially its present form. It also marks a major literary turning point, a transition from itinerary or historical narrative to parenesis. Having traced the course of Israel's forty years in the desert, Moses then drew conclusions from that experience and urged a course of action for the present and future.

Scholars have long recognized the parenetic character of the section 4:1-40 (or 44) and now since the recovery of Late Bronze treaty texts have seen how it forms a fitting conclusion to the entire division 1:6–4:40, a division that corresponds to the historical review section of those kinds of documents. Strictly speaking, that review ends, as we have seen, at 3:29; so the following parenesis is not inherently and technically part of a normal covenant pattern. But Deuteronomy as a whole does not conform to such a pattern, for it is a specially composed treatise whose overall form is that of a treaty text but one that is constantly interspersed with narrative, exhortation, and other noncovenant genres. Viewed from that perspective, the passage at hand is interruptive of the covenant structure, but it is at the same time essential and appropriate as a comment on the historical review and as an anticipation of the stipulation sections to follow.[144]

(1) The Privileges of the Covenant (4:1-8)

[1]Hear now, O Israel, the decrees and laws I am about to teach you. Follow them so that you may live and may go in and take possession of the land that the LORD, the God of your fathers, is giving you. [2]Do not add to what I command you and do not subtract from it, but keep the commands of the LORD your God that I give you.

[3]You saw with your own eyes what the LORD did at Baal Peor. The LORD

---

[144] For the problems attendant to the unique character of Deut 4 and its integration into the rest of the book, see C. Begg, "The Literary Criticism of Deut 4:1-40: Contributions to a Continuing Discussion," *ETL* 56 (1980): 10-55; G. Braulik, "Literarkritik und Archäologische Stratigraphie: Zu 5. Mittmanns Analyse von Deuteronomium 4, 1-40," *Bib* 59 (1978): 351-83; id., *Die Mittel deuteronomischer Rhetorik: erhoben aus Deuteronomium 4:1-40* (Rome: Biblical Institute Press, 1978); D. Knapp, *Deuteronomium 4: Literarische Analyse und Theologische Interpretation* (Göttingen: Vandenhoeck & Ruprecht, 1987); A. D. H. Mayes, "Deuteronomy 4 and the Literary Criticism of Deuteronomy," *JBL* 100 (1981): 23-51; S. Mittmann, *Deuteronomium 1:1–6:3: Literarkritisch und Traditionsgeschichtlich Untersucht, BZAW* 139 (Berlin: de Gruyter, 1975); A. C. Welch, "The Purpose of Deuteronomy, Chapter iv," *ExpTim* 42 (1930-31): 227-31.

your God destroyed from among you everyone who followed the Baal of Peor, [4]but all of you who held fast to the LORD your God are still alive today.

[5]See, I have taught you decrees and laws as the LORD my God commanded me, so that you may follow them in the land you are entering to take possession of it. [6]Observe them carefully, for this will show your wisdom and understanding to the nations, who will hear about all these decrees and say, "Surely this great nation is a wise and understanding people." [7]What other nation is so great as to have their gods near them the way the LORD our God is near us whenever we pray to him? [8]And what other nation is so great as to have such righteous decrees and laws as this body of laws I am setting before you today?

4:1   The connection between 4:1-40 and what precedes it is clear from the introductory formula *wĕʿattâ* (lit., "and now"), a use of the logical particle or adverb that builds the argument of the present passage on what has gone before.[145] That is, the exhortation is not delivered in a vacuum but finds its orientation in the historical review. What has already transpired is gone forever, but the lessons of history must not be forgotten and, in fact, must serve as the springboard for future thought and action.

What was imperative was that Israel "hear" (*šĕmaʿ*) the "decrees and laws" about to be promulgated. The imminency of Moses' impartation of these is seen in the use of the participle "learn" (*mĕlammēd*), a use that suggests that the process of instruction had already begun.[146] The field of reference is that of covenant as the technical terms *ḥuqqîm* ("decrees") and *mišpāṭîm* ("laws") make clear. Recent covenant studies have demonstrated that this kind of vocabulary is pervasive in covenant literature, invariably denoting the stipulations of such documents. That is, they are the specific items or elements of the covenant texts that are incumbent on their signatories, especially on the vassals of suzerainty treaties as is the case here in Deuteronomy.[147]

The combination *ḥuqqîm* and *mišpāṭîm* is so common as almost to be taken as a frozen form, perhaps a hendiadys (two nouns expressing a single idea), but they do occur separately as well and in combination with other

---

[145] *IBHS* § 39.3.4f. Cf. Driver, *Deuteronomy,* 62, "Introducing the practical conclusion which the writer desires to be drawn from the preceding retrospect."

[146] The *piel* participle of לָמַד ("learn") and other forms of the *piel* occur four times in Deut 4 (vv. 1,5,10,14), thus revealing the highly hortatory nature of the passage. For this nuance of the participle see *GKC* § 116p.

[147] For discussion of these and other technical covenantal and legal terms see Z. W. Falk, "Hebrew Legal Terms," *JSS* 5 (1960): 350-54; id., "Hebrew Legal Terms: II," *JSS* 11-12 (1966-67): 241-44; "Hebrew Legal Terms: III," *JSS* 14 (1969): 39-44; N. Lohfink, "Die *ḥuqqîm ûmišpāṭîm* im buch Deuteronomium und ihre Neubegrenzungdurch Dtn 12," *Bib* 70 (1989): 1-30. Lohfink points out that these particular terms occur only in the framing of Deut 5–11 and 12–26 and never between 12:1 and 26:17.

technical terms such as *miṣwôt* ("commands," Deut 4:40) and *ʿēdôt* ("stipulations," Deut 6:17). By far the most frequent occurrence of the two together is here in Deuteronomy (cf. 4:5,8,14,45; 5:1,31; 6:1,20; 7:11; 11:1; 12:1), a fact that is hardly surprising given Deuteronomy's character as a covenant document.[148] They also are attested in Exodus (18:16,20), though strangely not in the "Book of the Covenant" (Exod 20:1–23:33), and abundantly in Leviticus (18:5,26; 19:37; 20:22; 25:18; 26:3,15,43,46). Moses thus was appealing to a well-understood covenant tradition and in language that needed no explanation.

What was demanded was that the people do all that was embodied in these stipulations. In fact, Moses said, this was essential if they hoped to go on living and to enter and possess the land (v. 1). There was clearly a conditional aspect to the covenant promises here, but the relationship between them and the Lord, who called them into covenant, was strictly and exclusively at his initiative and by his grace (cf. vv. 20,23,31). Consistent with the whole Old Testament covenant theology, the call to covenant and its effective response was unconditional, but blessing upon its recipients and within its framework was conditioned upon faithful obedience to its precepts.[149]

4:2 The divine origination of and responsibility for the covenant is underscored here also by the solemn admonition that nothing can be added to or subtracted from it (v. 2; cf. 12:32; Rev 22:18-19).[150] In a unilateral arrangement of this type the sovereign and he alone set its terms.[151] The vassal could only accept them as given and then make every effort to keep them. These are summarized here by the term *miṣwôt* ("commands"), a term that in context is synonymous with the combination *ḥuqqîm* ("decrees") and *mišpāṭîm* ("laws").

4:3 In order to impress his hearers with what it meant to obey the Lord and thus to live, Moses reminded them of the incident at Baal Peor, a place to which he had already made passing reference (v. 3; cf. 3:29). There just a few weeks earlier the Israelites had engaged in the grossly

---

[148] For the data on occurrences, see H. Ringgren, "חָקַק *ḥāqaq*," *TDOT* 5:143, 145.

[149] W. Van Gemeren, *The Progress of Redemption* (Grand Rapids: Zondervan, 1988), 124-25.

[150] Such prohibitions are well known in ancient Near Eastern law and covenant texts. See the Lipit-Ishtar Lawcode epilogue in Pritchard, *ANET,* 161; and D. J. Wiseman, *The Vassal-Treaties of Esarhaddon* (London: British School of Archaeology, 1958), 60, ll. 410-13: "(You swear that) you will not alter (it) [the covenant text], you will not consign (it) to the fire nor throw (it) into the water, nor [bury (it)] in the earth nor destroy it by any cunning device, nor make [(it) disappear], nor sweep (it) away."

[151] Mendenhall, "Law and Covenant in Israel and the Ancient Near East," 29.

sensual rites of Canaanite paganism with the result that many of them had perished (Num 25:1-9). Though the technical vocabulary of covenant is lacking in the account of this sordid episode, the violation of covenant statute is crystal clear.[152] The Lord's people had indulged in sexual immorality with Moabite women, they had sacrificed to their gods, and they had celebrated the religious festivals that accompanied their worship—all of which was clearly proscribed by previous covenant stipulation (cf. Exod 34:15-16; 20:3; 22:20; 23:24,32).

4:4 As for those who refused to violate the high standards of covenant conduct, they were still alive, Moses said (v. 4; cf. Num 25:4). Thus his point is made: Just as obedience to the Lord in the past resulted in life, so obedience in time to come would guarantee ongoing life. Obviously the converse was equally true. Those who fell short of the Lord's expectations of them would die (cf. 8:1; 30:19).

4:5 What Moses implied about preexisting covenant regulation in v. 3 he made explicit in v. 5. Once again employing the twin nouns *ḥuqqîm* and *mišpāṭîm*, he referred to them as subjects of his teaching in bygone days, obviously for all the nearly forty years since the covenant encampment at Sinai.[153] These are still relevant and binding, and what he was about to teach them would only reinforce and expand upon them. This, of course, is what Deuteronomy as a covenant renewal document achieves. It is not a radically new statement about the relationship between the Lord and Israel but an updating of an old one appropriate to new times and different circumstances. There will clearly be differences in the text, but not in principle. This is why the decrees and laws of Exod 20–23 are sufficient guidelines for entry into and occupation of the land.

4:6 These statutes (and those about to be promulgated, v. 8) would do more than merely provide guidelines for successful life in the land. By obeying them, God's people would also display before the nations what it means to be the people of the Lord and to have him in their midst (vv. 6-7).[154] In a clear linkage with wisdom thought, Moses argued that keeping and doing the commandments of the Lord is in itself a definition of wisdom (*ḥokmâ*) and understanding (*bînâ*). That is, the very essence of wisdom is conformity with the will of God.[155] Even the pagan nations—by whom

---

[152] Harrison, *Numbers,* 337.

[153] These terms for covenant stipulations do not occur together in the Book of the Covenant (Exod 20:1–23:33) (in fact, חֹק is totally lacking), but מִשְׁפָּט is used once to speak of the covenant stipulations as a whole (Exod 21:1).

[154] C. Wiéner, "Valeur inestimable de la Loi du Seigneur (Dt 4, 1-2, 6-8)," *AS* 53 (1970): 34-38.

[155] G. Braulik, "Weisheit, Gottesnähe und Gesetz: zum Kerygma von Deuteronomium 4:5-8," in *Studien zum Pentateuch,* ed. G. Braulik (Vienna: Herder, 1977), 165-95.

wisdom was prized and highly sought after—would see in Israel's covenant provisions a wisdom of a higher order, one to be eagerly emulated. This, of course, was part of the attraction of Israel by which they were to become a means of blessing the whole earth (cf. 1 Kgs 10:4,7,23-24).

4:7-8 The other side of the coin of obedience—and, indeed, the divine response to it—is the presence of God among his people (v. 7).[156] The theology of the nations at large taught that the supreme gods were remote and inaccessible. Though they were perceived in highly anthropomorphic terms, they also were thought to be so busy and preoccupied with their own affairs that they could scarcely take notice of their devotees except when they needed them.[157] It was in contrast to these notions, then, that Moses drew attention to the Lord, God of Israel, who, though utterly transcendent and wholly different from humankind, paradoxically lives and moves among them. The idea of the immanence of God is ancient, indeed, finding its first expression in the Eden narratives where God "walked about" in the presence of his people (Gen 3:8). Thereafter he came in epiphany and theophany throughout patriarchal times until finally, at the burning bush and at Sinai, he disclosed his nearness to Moses and Israel. It was to these experiences within living memory that Moses here made special reference.

That this was what was in view is clear from the context with its references to "decrees and laws" (vv. 5,8), for it was in the dramatic setting of the granting of the covenant and transmission of its stipulations that God most clearly and extensively revealed himself. He said he would "come to you in a dense cloud" (Exod 19:9) and would "come down on Mount Sinai in the sight of all the people" (Exod 19:11). He then indeed "descended on it in fire" (v. 18). Following the revelation of the covenant text, the Lord said to Moses, "Come up to the LORD" (Exod 24:1), which he did. And there on the mountain Moses, Aaron, Nadab, Abihu, and the seventy elders "saw the God of Israel" (Exod 24:9-10). That is, they saw the cloud of his glory "like a consuming fire on top of the mountain" (vv. 16-17). No wonder Moses could dismiss the pagan gods as indifferent to and uninvolved with their worshipers in comparison to the Lord, Israel's God, who was always accessible as his people called upon him.

It was not Israel's God alone, however, that set them off from the other

---

[156] S. Terrien, *The Elusive Presence* (San Francisco: Harper & Row, 1978), 27-31.

[157] M. Eliade, *The Sacred and the Profane* (New York: Harper & Row, 1959), 121-25. For a counterbalance to the notion that such gods were only numinous powers or gods of nature and had no concern for history, see B. Albrektson, *History and the Gods* (Lund: CWK Gleerup, 1967), 42-52.

nations. It also was their possession of "righteous decrees and laws," which Moses was about to outline to them (v. 8).[158] Again the familiar technical terms *ḥuqqîm* and *mišpāṭîm* occur, but this time the former are called "righteous" (*ṣaddîqîm*). This obviously was a way of describing the ethical quality of God's decrees, that is, they are inherently righteous, and they suggest a righteous spirit and way of life on the part of those who obey them. But the root *ṣdq* and its various forms also have to do with adherence to standards. The decrees are righteous in the sense that they enable those who obey them to achieve a God-ordained pattern or level of expectation. Thus there is a relational dimension to the term, one that finds itself very much at home in a covenant context. A "righteous" decree, in short, is one that leads to and maintains proper covenant relationship.[159]

(2) Reminder of the Horeb Covenant (4:9-14)

⁹Only be careful, and watch yourselves closely so that you do not forget the things your eyes have seen or let them slip from your heart as long as you live. Teach them to your children and to their children after them. ¹⁰Remember the day you stood before the LORD your God at Horeb, when he said to me, "Assemble the people before me to hear my words so that they may learn to revere me as long as they live in the land and may teach them to their children." ¹¹You came near and stood at the foot of the mountain while it blazed with fire to the very heavens, with black clouds and deep darkness. ¹²Then the LORD spoke to you out of the fire. You heard the sound of words but saw no form; there was only a voice. ¹³He declared to you his covenant, the Ten Commandments, which he commanded you to follow and then wrote them on two stone tablets. ¹⁴And the LORD directed me at that time to teach you the decrees and laws you are to follow in the land that you are crossing the Jordan to possess.

4:9 It was on the basis of what Israel saw and heard forty years earlier that Moses' offer of covenant renewal could be made. Only as they remembered the past and the commitments they made could they expect to receive and abide by the covenant revelation and expectation that was about to be disclosed to them. Thus Moses urged that his people take utmost care (double use of *šāmar*, plus adv. *mĕ'ōd*) lest they forget what they had seen with the result that the whole episode and its meaning com-

---

[158] B. Lindars, "Torah in Deuteronomy," in *Words and Meanings*, ed. P. R. Ackroyd and B. Lindars (Cambridge: Cambridge University Press, 1968), 117-36. Lindars rightly connects the use of הוֹרֹת in v. 8 to the wisdom motif of vv. 5-8; i.e., it suggests instruction (p. 130).

[159] H. G. Stigers, "צָדֵק (*ṣādēq*), etc. *TWOT* 2:752-55; N. H. Snaith, *The Distinctive Ideas of the Old Testament* (London: Epworth, 1944), 72-74.

pletely escaped their memory. And this must be an ongoing reflection, one that remains part and parcel of the experience of that generation and every one to follow. What is implied is that such an experience with the living God must be rooted and grounded in a historical event, an event that must be recalled and celebrated regularly and faithfully by all who participate in it and benefit from it. There is no room in Old Testament theology for existential encounters without historical and spatial points of reference.[160]

4:10-11   Then, precisely in order to refresh their memories, Moses shared with his listeners that momentous experience of covenant making in detail. He reminded them of their assembly at Horeb (v. 10; cf. 1:2), where they had gathered to link life and destiny with the God who had already redeemed them from Egyptian bondage and who desired to make of them a specially chosen servant nation (cf. Exod 19:1,4-6). Having accepted his overtures to them to become a "kingdom of priests and a holy nation," Israel had stood before the mountain covered as it was with the blazing fire and impenetrable darkness of God's glory (v. 11; cf. Exod 19:16-19). The apparently contradictory elements of fire and cloud symbolize respectively the epiphanic self-disclosure and self-obscurity of the God who simultaneously is immanent and transcendent.[161]

4:12   The intensely epiphanic nature of the revelation is clear from the fact that the Lord spoke to the assembly from the midst of the fire. This was nothing new to Moses, for God had already spoken to him from the midst of the burning bush (Exod 3:2-4). As on that occasion Moses had seen nothing but flame and yet addressed and was addressed by the living God (Exod 3:5-6), so the people of Israel, Moses said, had seen "no form" at Horeb; they had simply heard a voice).[162] (For discussion of "form" see v. 15.)

The "voice" the people heard was likely not the articulation of words, for it was Moses alone, according to the Exodus account, who received the commandments directly from the Lord (cf. Exod 19:20-22; 20:1). The statement here, "He declared to you his covenant" (v. 13), refers to the statement of the covenant and its terms as mediated through Moses (Exod 24:3). Moreover, the narrative in Exod 19 describes the voice (*qôl*) as a trumpet (v. 19).[163] What to Moses were intelligible words were to the

---

[160] On the importance of the recall of history as a basis for present action see E. P. Blair, "An Appeal to Remembrance: The Memory Motif in Deuteronomy," *Int* 15 (1961): 41-47.

[161] W. Eichrodt, *Theology of the Old Testament* (Philadelphia: Westminster, 1967), 2:29-35.

[162] See R. P. Carroll, "The Aniconic God and the Cult of Images," *ST* 31 (1977): 51-64.

[163] Hebrew קוֹל (like Greek φωνή) fundamentally means "sound" regardless of its nature. As "voice" it can describe either articulate (Deut 1:45; 21:18; 1 Sam 2:25; Luke 4:33; 8:28; John 11:43) or inarticulate (Isa 6:4; Jer 48:34; Acts 9:7) speech. Cf. BDB, 876-77; BAGD, 870-71.

masses below a sound like a mighty trumpet or even thunder (Exod 19:16; cf. Paul's encounter with Jesus on the Damascus road; Acts 9:4-7; 22:6-9).

4:13 The content of the revelation at Horeb, Moses went on to say, was "his covenant" (*bĕrîtô*), that is, as specified here, "the ten commandments" (v. 13). This is the first explicit occurrence in Deuteronomy of *bĕrît*, the fundamental term for expressing the covenant idea and relationship. It appears over three hundred times in the Old Testament, including some twenty-eight times in Deuteronomy, and can apply generically to covenants of all kinds—conditional or unconditional, bilateral or unilateral, royal grant, or suzerain-vassal—or to just an element of covenant, as here. (For full discussion see the Introduction, pp. 24-28.)[164]

The restricted use of the term here clearly defines *bĕrît* as the "ten commandments" (lit., "ten words"), the very heart of the so-called "Book of the Covenant" (Exod 20:1–23:33) or, in its later expansion and revision, the Book of Deuteronomy. Though the covenant idea is obviously a pervasive Old Testament theme, the technical term "ten words" occurs only here and in Exod 34:28 and Deut 10:4. In each of these passages both the importance and the limited extent of these "words" are seen in the connection between them and the "two stone tablets" on which they were inscribed. In line with much modern scholarship it probably is best to see these two tablets as duplicates, with each containing all ten commandments.[165] This would reflect the custom whereby each party to the covenant would have a copy of the document for his own archives and future reference.

4:14 In addition to the "words" (or commandments) per se, the covenant text, wherever it is fully developed in the Old Testament, also consisted of the elaborative principles and cases that expound the "words" and provide guidance for their application in particular instances. These in Deuteronomy are almost always called (as here) "decrees and laws" (*ḥuqqîm* and *mišpāṭîm*, v. 14). As already noted (cf. 4:1) this combination occurs also in Exod 18:16,20 and frequently in Leviticus (esp. 26:3,15,43,46). In the Exodus account to which Moses was referring here, however, the stipulations are called *mišpāṭîm* alone (Exod 21:1; 24:3) or,

---

[164] See M. Weinfeld, "בְּרִית *bĕrîth*," *TDOT* 2:253-79; J. Begrich, "Berit," *ZAW* 60 (1944): 1-11; O. Loretz, "ברית - Band - Bund," *VT* 16 (1966): 239-41; W. L. Moran, "A Note on the Treaty Terminology of the Sefire Stelas," *JNES* 22 (1963): 173-76; M. Weinfeld, "The Covenant of Grant in the Old Testament and in the Ancient Near East," *JAOS* 90 (1970): 184-203; *JAOS* (1972): 468-69; id., "Covenant Terminology in the Ancient Near East and Its Influence on the West," *JAOS* 93 (1973): 190-99.

[165] Thus and foremost M. Kline, "The Two Tables of the Covenant," *WTJ* 22 (1959-60): 133-46; id., *The Structure of Biblical Authority* (Grand Rapids: Eerdmans, 1972), 113-22.

perhaps, *miṣwâ* (24:12). Clearly, Deuteronomy reflects a refinement and greater specialization of covenant vocabulary as one would expect given its later and more expansionist expression.

In any case these specifications of covenant behavior were given to Israel through Moses to provide guidelines for life in the land they were about to enter and possess.

(3) The Nature of Israel's God (4:15-24)

[15]You saw no form of any kind the day the LORD spoke to you at Horeb out of the fire. Therefore watch yourselves very carefully, [16]so that you do not become corrupt and make for yourselves an idol, an image of any shape, whether formed like a man or a woman, [17]or like any animal on earth or any bird that flies in the air, [18]or like any creature that moves along the ground or any fish in the waters below. [19]And when you look up to the sky and see the sun, the moon and the stars—all the heavenly array—do not be enticed into bowing down to them and worshiping things the LORD your God has apportioned to all the nations under heaven. [20]But as for you, the LORD took you and brought you out of the iron-smelting furnace, out of Egypt, to be the people of his inheritance, as you now are.

[21]The LORD was angry with me because of you, and he solemnly swore that I would not cross the Jordan and enter the good land the LORD your God is giving you as your inheritance. [22]I will die in this land; I will not cross the Jordan; but you are about to cross over and take possession of that good land. [23]Be careful not to forget the covenant of the LORD your God that he made with you; do not make for yourselves an idol in the form of anything the LORD your God has forbidden. [24]For the LORD your God is a consuming fire, a jealous God.

4:15 In this section attention turns from the covenant itself to the God of the covenant, to him who brought Israel out of Egypt in order to make them his special servant people (v. 20). Moses had already pointed out that Israel's God who met them at Horeb did so phenomenologically, by sight and sound, but that there was "no form" to his self-manifestation (v. 12). That is, the Lord is transcendently and ontologically invisible, one who exists as spirit and not materially. This, of course, is a pervasive biblical idea (Pss 51:13; 106:33; 143:10; Isa 63:10-14; Neh 9:20; Hag 2:5; Zech 4:6; John 4:24). Nowhere is the idea more fully advanced than here, however; for not only does the Lord not have form (*tĕmûnâ*), but he is conceptually set over against images and idols that do (vv. 16,23,25). That is, a major difference between the Lord and the imagined deities of the nations is precisely in the fact that they could be represented iconically whereas he cannot. For Israel to attempt to encapsulate God in any form whatsoever was to attempt to reduce him to the level of pagan imagination.[166]

4:16-18   For the Israelite to undertake to do this was, Moses said, to "become corrupt" (v. 16).[167] The reason obviously is that in so doing one confuses the Creator with the creature, a reversal in perception that betrays a twisted mind and perverted heart. Paul was certainly alluding to this idea and possibly to this passage when he declared that fallen, natural humanity had "exchanged the truth of God for a lie, and worshiped and served created things rather than the Creator" (Rom 1:25), with the result that "he [God] gave them over to a depraved mind, to do what ought not to be done" (v. 28).[168]

Creation texts are clearly in mind here, though the order of created things varies somewhat from the standard formulae of Gen 1. Thus there must not be made any idol (*pesel*) or image (*sāmel*) in the form (*tabnît*) of man, woman, "animal on earth," bird, "creature that moves along the ground" (*rōmēś*), or fish. The very same terms occur in Gen 1:26-27, the "dominion mandate" statement wherein the Creator God outlines his purposes for humankind as they relate to the remainder of the creation.[169] There humankind (*'ādām*) is told to rule over the fish, birds, livestock, and the "creatures that move along the ground." Exactly the same creatures appear in both Genesis and Deuteronomy including the "male and female" (*zākār ûnĕqēbâ*), who are the image of God (Gen 1:27) and as such cannot themselves be worshiped (Deut 4:16).[170] The clear spheres of sovereignty meticulously spelled out in the creation mandate—God over humankind over all creation—are overturned and rearranged in any system where humankind worships the creation rather than rules over it and repudiates the sovereignty of God rather than submitting to it. It is precisely this grotesque aberration that forms the essence of Moses' exhortation in this passage.

4:19   But the warning is not limited to prohibition of idols or images. God's creation included more than living things upon the earth; it also

---

[166] E. M. Curtis, "The Theological Basis for the Prohibition of Images in the Old Testament," *JETS* 28 (1985): 283-84.

[167] The Heb. verb שָׁחַת in the *hiphil* stem means "to act corruptly" (cf. Isa 1:4; 2 Chr 27:2).

[168] N. Hyldahl, "A Reminiscence of the Old Testament (Dt 4, 15-18) at Rom 1, 23," *NTS* 2 (1956): 285-88; D. Moo, *Romans 1–8*, WEC (Chicago: Moody, 1991), 104.

[169] See Merrill, "A Theology of the Pentateuch," 13-16; id., "Covenant and the Kingdom: Genesis 1–3 as Foundation for Biblical Theology," *CTR* 1 (1987): 297-302

[170] Most scholars correctly view the specific prohibitions against animal worship here to be a polemic against the zoomorphic representation of Egyptian deities with which the Israelites would have been so recently familiar (thus, e.g., Craigie, *Deuteronomy*, 135-36). For a description and discussion of these see D. P. Silverman, "Divinity and Deities in Ancient Egypt," in *Religion in Ancient Egypt*, ed. B. E. Shafer (London: Routledge, 1991), 7-87.

embraced the inanimate objects of the skies above, the sun, moon, and stars (v. 19). These too were objects of worship by the nations, if not in and of themselves then at least in terms of the deities they symbolized.[171] Idols and images were merely representations of powers otherwise inaccessible to mere humankind and in most pagan systems were not construed as the realities themselves.[172] Thus their being made in the form of animals or birds suggested only that the gods of nature manifest themselves as such creatures or in such forms. Likewise, the heavenly bodies, though not images in the strict sense, were thought to represent superterrestrial deities that affected life in each and every detail.[173]

Again, however, like all animal life these creations of God were to be subservient to him and even to humankind and in any case were not to be worshiped. The Genesis account underscores that these lights were designed "to separate the day from the night" and to "serve as signs to mark seasons and days and years" (Gen 1:14). In other words, they were for the benefit of humankind and not for their idolatrous bondage to them. To that our present passage adds the information that the heavenly spheres must not be worshiped because they are things "the LORD your God has apportioned to all the nations under heaven" (v. 19).

There have been many interpretations offered for this statement about apportionment,[174] but in the context of both the immediate passage and the

---

[171] H. G. May, "Some Aspects of Solar Worship at Jerusalem," *ZAW* 55 (1937): 269-81.
[172] For the conceptual basis for such construals, see H. Frankfort et al., *Before Philosophy* (New York: Penguin, 1949), 28-29.
[173] A. L. Oppenheim, *Ancient Mesopotamia* (Chicago: University of Chicago Press, 1964), 197-98.
[174] Most scholars hold that the passage describes the worship of the heavenly bodies, a practice, if not sanctioned by God, allowed by him at least. Craigie, for example, says that "these false forms of worship, though assigned by God to other nations (v. 19), would be antithetic to the revelation of Israel's true religion" (*Deuteronomy*, 137). Weinfeld suggests that "the heavenly bodies as objects of worship were assigned to the nations by God himself" (*Deuteronomy 1-11*, 206). Driver asserts that "the God of Israel is supreme: He assigns to every nation its objects of worship; and the veneration of the heavenly bodies by the nations (other than Israel) forms part of His providential order of the world" (*Deuteronomy*, 70). This interpretation suffers both theological and biblical deficiencies. It is impossible to harmonize the overall biblical concept of a Creator who stands above and beyond his creation with the notion that he would assign lower parts of that creation to be objects of worship by the highest part of his creation, namely, humankind. In perhaps the clearest exposition of the matter, Paul spoke of the rejection of the true God with the result that "they worshiped and served created things rather than the Creator" (Rom 1:25). It is true the apostle said that God "gave them over in the sinful desires of their hearts" (v. 24), but nowhere did he teach that God assigned the heavenly bodies (or anything else) as objects of worship.
Thompson proposes that the passage deals with the allotment of the peoples of the world

Genesis creation texts it seems best to understand the author as arguing that the sun, moon, and stars, far from being deities who control humankind, are actually at his service. They have been "apportioned" (thus *ḥālaq*) in such a way as to function for all people everywhere exactly as God intended—as separators of day from night and as signs marking the divisions of time. That is, there is a word here of polemic in the suggestion that it is the Lord who controls his creation for the benefit of humankind, who must be revered and not creation itself no matter how awesome and powerful it might appear to be.

4:20   That the Lord is sovereign is illustrated by Moses immediately by reference to the Lord's having brought his people Israel out of the "furnace" of Egypt (v. 20). If ever there was an example of lordship, it was this; for Egypt by any standard was the dominant economic and military power in the world in the Late Bronze Age. For the Lord to be able to humiliate that great empire by rescuing an impotent slave people from its grasp was ample witness to his incomparability. The effect is all the more dramatic by virtue of the image here—Egypt was a furnace. The Hebrew term used here (*kûr habbarzel*) is related to the Akkadian word for "crucible,"[175] a kiln in which metals and glass were melted down and refined. Any nation caught up in the white heat of Egyptian wrath and oppression was virtually hopeless. But the Lord had used that time of bondage as a purifying process for his people, and when the process was over, he had powerfully delivered them from it (cf. Isa 48:10; Jer 11:4). The result was that they were then qualified to be the people of the Lord, fit to enter the land he had promised to them.

4:21-22   His mention of the land reminded Moses once more that his intemperate act of smiting the rock on behalf of his people had disqualified him from entering it (v. 21). This is the third time in Deuteronomy that he made this point (cf. 1:37; 3:26), and each time it is in connection with the

---

to various areas, but this clearly is not in line with the context (*Deuteronomy,* 106). The key here is the phrase אֲשֶׁר חָלַק יְהוָה ("which Yahweh allotted"). Though חָלַק normally has the idea of dividing up or distributing (BDB, 323), it can also mean "to assign" (Job 20:29; 39:17; Jer 10:16; Hab 1:16), that is, without dividing (M. Tsevat, "חָלַק *chālaq* II," etc., *TDOT* 4:450-51). It is in this sense that God created the heavenly beings and assigned them to all the human race (Gen 1:14-19). Far from being worthy of worship, Moses here was arguing that they themselves were the common property of humankind, made to serve him (Deut 4:19a). Schroeder is correct, after all, when he says that the point here is the contrast between the heavenly creation, which was given to all humanity, and Yahweh himself, "which was the portion of Israel" (F. W. J. Schroeder, *Deuteronomy: Commentary on the Holy Scriptures by John Peter Lange* [Grand Rapids: Zondervan, 1879], 72).

[175] *The Assyrian Dictionary,* ed. A. L. Oppenheim et al. (Chicago: Oriental Institute, 1971), 8: 571, s.v. *kūru.*

"good land" they were about to possess. It is most understandable that his reflection on the good land would trigger an automatic reaction of sorrow and regret that he would be unable to enjoy its benefits firsthand. Instead, he must die in the Transjordan while his countrymen passed over the river to their reward on the other side (v. 22).

4:23-24 The pericope ends as it begins—with a solemn warning to "watch yourselves" (v. 23; cf. v. 15). And in both places the warning has to do with idolatry, a practice that v. 23 says is tantamount to forgetting the covenant. This connection is almost self-evident, for the very essence of the covenant is the truth that there is only one God, the Lord, and the recognition and worship of any other is nothing other than high treason, covenant violation of the grossest kind (cf. Deut 6:4-5). As such, it demands and deserves the judgment of divine wrath, that of a "jealous God" who is a consuming fire (v. 24).[176] The "jealousy" (or "zeal") of God speaks not of a petty, selfish envy but of his right to sole recognition and worship by virtue of his sovereignty over and election of his people in covenant.[177] This is why idolatry or any other kind of violation of covenant brings the severest judgment. Perhaps the clearest explanation of the connection between idolatry and God as jealous (ēl qannāʾ) is found in Deut 6:15, where disloyalty to the only God brings forth a holy wrath that destroys the sinner from off the earth. He himself becomes a consuming fire that accomplishes that task (cf. Lev 10:2; Num 16:35).

(4) Threat and Blessing Following Covenant Disobedience (4:25-31)

²⁵**After you have had children and grandchildren and have lived in the land a long time—if you then become corrupt and make any kind of idol, doing evil in the eyes of the LORD your God and provoking him to anger, ²⁶I call heaven and earth as witnesses against you this day that you will quickly perish from the land that you are crossing the Jordan to possess. You will not live there long but will certainly be destroyed. ²⁷The LORD will scatter you among the peoples, and only a few of you will survive among the nations to which the LORD will drive you. ²⁸There you will worship man-made gods of wood and stone, which cannot see or hear or eat or smell. ²⁹But if from there you seek the LORD your God, you will find him if you look for him with all your heart and with all your soul. ³⁰When you are in distress and all these things have happened to you, then in later days you will return to the LORD your God and obey him. ³¹For the LORD your God is a merciful God; he will not abandon or**

---

[176] The juxtaposition of the "iron-smelting furnace" of v. 20 and the "consuming fire" (אֵשׁ אֹכְלָה) of v. 24 is not without purpose. Yahweh had brought his people out of the fiery oppression of Egypt, but if they broke covenant with him, they could expect his fiery wrath.

[177] Cf. L. J. Coppes, "קָנָא (qānāʾ)," *TWOT* 2:802-3.

destroy you or forget the covenant with your forefathers, which he confirmed to them by oath.

4:25-26   The warning against idolatry already delivered to Moses' contemporaries (vv. 15-19,23) is pertinent also for generations of Israelites yet unborn. If after many generations have lived and died in Canaan the people become corrupt (v. 16) and idolatry rears its ugly head (v. 25), they could expect the inexorable wrath of God, the "consuming fire" of his judgment (v. 24). This would be inflicted as punishment for covenant disloyalty as the courtroom language of the passage makes clear. Though the full form is lacking here, the very phrase "I call heaven and earth against you this day" (v. 26) is sufficient to show that Moses was invoking, vestigially at least, the so-called "*Rîb*-pattern" as a vehicle by which to communicate the formal process of dealing with covenant violation on the part of an indicted vassal.[178]

All covenants or treaties obviously presupposed some means of enforcement of their obligations and redressing their violation.[179] The aggrieved party would press charges in the case and present his complaints before a duly authorized court of law. In addition to the contending plaintiffs and defendants there would naturally be a judge and also, if possible, witnesses for both sides. In the case of international treaties such as those between the Hittite and Egyptian rulers, the documents themselves were forsworn before the gods who therefore served as witnesses. Presumably these same witnesses would be invoked in the event one party or the other were accused of breaking the covenant and brought to account for it.

The covenant between the Lord and Israel was no different. And even though the process by which the matter of Israel's covenant disloyalty was to be adjudicated is not clear in the major covenant texts themselves (i.e., The Book of the Covenant and Deuteronomy), there are hints (as here) that there was a legal, formal mechanism by which the Lord made charges against his people and, once having found them guilty, levied appropriate punishment. Evidence for this in Deuteronomy is especially to be found in the sanctions section of the document, that is, in chaps. 27–32 (cf. 30:19;

---

[178] Among the extensive literature on the subject of the legal and literary genre "*rîb*" is the following: B. Gemser, "The Rib- or Controversy-Pattern in Hebrew Mentality," in *Wisdom in Israel and in the Ancient Near East*, ed. M. Noth and D. W. Thomas (Leiden: Brill, 1969), 120-37; J. Harvey, "Le 'Rib-pattern,' réquisitoire prophétique sur la rupture de l'alliance," *Bib* 43 (1962): 172-96; H. B. Huffmon, "The Covenant Lawsuit in the Prophets," *JBL* 78 (1959): 285-95.

[179] Mendenhall, "Law and Covenant in Israel and the Ancient Near East," 34-35; J. A. Fitzmyer, *The Aramaic Inscriptions of Sefire*, BO 19 (Rome: Pontifical Biblical Institute, 1967), 13, 32-40.

31:28; 32:1). There, as here, heaven and earth are invoked as witnesses to testify on behalf of the Lord both as to the solemnity and legality of his threatened curses upon his disobedient people and to the rightness of his judgment once that disobedience has become a historical reality.

The "*Rîb*-pattern" is much more commonly and fully employed by the canonical prophets who, while not referring directly to the covenant relationship, presuppose its existence. Isaiah, for example, appealed to heaven and earth as witnesses and then on the Lord's behalf spoke of the rebellion of Israel, a corrupt people who had forsaken and despised their Lord and as a result suffered from head to toe (Isa 1:2-7).[180] Micah developed the form even more. He viewed the mountains and hills as witnesses to the Lord's "case" (*rîb*) against his people, a case detailed by a full catalog of social and spiritual sins (Mic 6:1-8; 9–16). All these they committed against the Lord despite his covenant faithfulness in redeeming them from Egypt and leading them through the desert to the promised land (vv. 3-5).[181]

It is against this same kind of background that Moses pressed his warning of future divine judgment. If after many years in the land of promise the Israelites betrayed their solemn commitment to the Lord, he would invoke the covenant curses against them, and they would quickly and with utmost certainty perish.[182] In the strongest possible terms he repeated his message of woe: they would be absolutely decimated. The same terms occur in the sanctions section (chaps. 27–32) that outlines the calamities that follow covenant disobedience. Moses there spoke of perishing because of the sin of forsaking the Lord (28:20,22; 30:18) and of becoming decimated for the same reason (28:20,24,45,51,61).

4:27 Those who survive will be forced to leave the land, scattered among the nations and reduced in population until only a few remain to return home again (v. 27). This too was an important element in the treaty curses of the Old Testament as many passages in Deuteronomy (28:64; 29:28; 30:3; 32:26) and elsewhere (Jer 9:16; 13:24; 18:17; Ezek 11:16;

---

[180] H. Wildberger, *Isaiah 1–12, A Commentary* (Minneapolis: Fortress, 1991), 8-17. Wildberger limits the *rîb* section to 1:2-3, but his discussion is nonetheless most full and helpful.

[181] J. L. Mays, *Micah: A Commentary*, OTL (Philadelphia: Westminster, 1976), 128-36.

[182] B. Otzen points out that the total phrase תֹּאבֵדוּן מֵעַל הָאָרֶץ (or the like) suggests not perishing *in* the land but *away from* the land, i.e., perishing by the very act of deportation ("אָבַד ʾābhadh," etc., *TDOT* 1:22). This finds support in v. 27, where deportation is clearly in mind. The verb שָׁמַד, however, speaks of such violent and irreversible annihilation that it seems difficult to view it as an uprooting into exile (cf. BDB, 1029). On balance it is preferable to see the judgment as one of extermination in the land (אָבַד) and scattering (פּוּץ, v. 27) from the land. Thus Ridderbos, *Deuteronomy*, 88.

12:15; 20:23; 22:15; 36:19) attest. This—and the preceding warnings of destruction as well—came to pass regularly throughout Israel's history and climactically in the deportations of Israel and Judah by the Assyrians in 722 B.C. and Babylonians in 586 B.C., respectively.

4:28 At this point Moses predicted the irony of poetic justice: Those who would go into exile because of their idolatry would find themselves participating in it while there (v. 28). The deities involved may be different in name and even function from those they worshiped in Canaan, but their character as lifeless, man-made blocks of wood and stone would be the same. The polemic employed here in describing these idols—that they were goods manufactured by their very worshipers, senseless and insensitive—is graphic and pointed. But in comparison to the sarcasm of the later prophets Isaiah (41:6-7; 44:12-20; 46:6-7) and Jeremiah (10:3-5), they were very mild indeed.[183]

4:29 Exile need not signal the end of Israel's covenant hopes; if the captives of the days to come would seek the Lord fervently and sincerely, they would find him even on distant shores. The intensity of their longing is expressed in the cliché "with all your heart and with all your soul" (*bekol lĕbābkā ûbĕkol napšekā*), a formula, interestingly enough, that is used in covenant contexts to speak of the degree of commitment that Israel was expected to display toward the Lord (cf. Deut 6:5; 10:12).[184] To seek him in captivity, then, was to renew one's pledges of covenant loyalty.

4:30 This is fully clarified in vv. 30-31, which speak of the captivity as "distress" (*ṣar*) in the midst of which God's people may return to him and once more obey him. "To return" translates the Hebrew verb *šûb,* which means "to repent" in situations like the one described here.[185] Together with "obey" the idea is one of repudiation of the idolatry and other sins that brought about the dispersion and a total acceptance of the claims of sovereignty of the God against whom they had rebelled. Not to be overlooked here is the absence of any conditionality. The text is clear that it is not a matter of *if* Israel returns and obeys but *when.* Repentance is obviously a matter of free will, but the biblical witness is unanimous that the impetus to repent is something God himself will plant within his people in order to encourage and enable them to return to him and to the land (cf. Lev 26:40-45; Deut 30:1-10; Jer 31:27-34; Ezek 36:22-31).[186]

---

[183] E. H. Merrill, "Isaiah 40–55 as Anti-Babylonian Polemic," *GTJ* 8 (1987): 3-18.

[184] Christensen, *Deuteronomy 1–11,* 94.

[185] See the authoritative work by W. L. Holladay, *The Root šûbh in the Old Testament* (Leiden: Brill, 1958).

[186] T. E. McComiskey, *The Covenants of Promise* (Grand Rapids: Baker, 1985), 65-66, 75-76.

4:31 This divine initiative is underscored by the reminder here (v. 31) that "the LORD your God is a merciful God" and it is his compassion (*raḥûm*) that both spares them his wrath and makes it impossible for him to forget the covenant he made with the patriarchal ancestors. Once more the conditional nature of the Sinai covenant is oriented to the unconditional nature of the so-called Abrahamic. Israel as the seed of Abraham constituted an indispensable element of the promise and for that reason could never fail to exist before God. For him to forget Israel would constitute a violation of the oath he swore to the fathers (Gen 15:12-21; 17:1-8). This, of course, is theologically inconceivable. But the conditional side of the Sinai covenant also must be stressed, for Israel's success in fulfilling its mandate as a kingdom of priests and holy nation is dependent on its covenant fidelity. The biblical resolution of the tension created by the unconditionality versus conditionality of the respective covenants lies always (as here) in the grace of God, who guarantees the wherewithal by which his people can meet the terms requisite to achieving his high and holy calling for them.

(5) The Uniqueness of Israel's God (4:32-40)

[32]Ask now about the former days, long before your time, from the day God created man on the earth; ask from one end of the heavens to the other. Has anything so great as this ever happened, or has anything like it ever been heard of? [33]Has any other people heard the voice of God speaking out of fire, as you have, and lived? [34]Has any god ever tried to take for himself one nation out of another nation, by testings, by miraculous signs and wonders, by war, by a mighty hand and an outstretched arm, or by great and awesome deeds, like all the things the LORD your God did for you in Egypt before your very eyes?

[35]You were shown these things so that you might know that the LORD is God; besides him there is no other. [36]From heaven he made you hear his voice to discipline you. On earth he showed you his great fire, and you heard his words from out of the fire. [37]Because he loved your forefathers and chose their descendants after them, he brought you out of Egypt by his Presence and his great strength, [38]to drive out before you nations greater and stronger than you and to bring you into their land to give it to you for your inheritance, as it is today.

[39]Acknowledge and take to heart this day that the LORD is God in heaven above and on the earth below. There is no other. [40]Keep his decrees and commands, which I am giving you today, so that it may go well with you and your children after you and that you may live long in the land the LORD your God gives you for all time.

Having dealt with the matter of the nature of Israel's God (vv. 15-24) and what that means for Israel in terms of covenant relationship and responsibility (vv. 25-31), Moses focused on the uniqueness of the Lord, a theme suggested already in v. 28, where the contrast is made between him and the gods of wood and stone. The passage at hand is without comparison as a discourse on the doctrine of God. Here in brief scope the character, attributes, and actions of God are clearly and logically spelled out as are the implications of all this for Israel, his people.

4:32 Because of the importance here of the latter consideration—that of Israel as the recipient of the Lord's work of election and redemption—Moses' point of departure is the exodus/covenant/wilderness/conquest cluster of events. They were so unique as a display of divine grace and power that appeal to the most distant past—even to creation—and to the most remote centers of civilization would fail to turn up even one other example (v. 32). The argument here was picked up centuries later by Isaiah, who also referred to the "former days" (yāmîm riʾšōnîm) or "former things" (riʾšōnîm alone) as providing examples from history of God's unique saving work (Isa 43:9,18; 48:3) on the basis of which he would do even greater things in days to come (Isa 46:9).[187] The best argument for who God is and what he can do is the historical argument, for that is empirically testable and verifiable.[188] It also is a test, Moses said, of the alleged gods of the nations whose exploits and even very existence were shown to be devoid of historical evidence.

4:33 Most specifically, no people other than Israel have ever heard God (or a god) speak from "out of fire" (lit., "from the midst of the fire"; cf. 4:12) and lived to tell about it (v. 33). The point, of course, is not that anyone else has experienced this phenomenon and then died as a result; rather, it is the speaking that is at issue. No one has ever heard God speak from fire at all. The fact that Moses and Israel lived after hearing God speak under such remarkable circumstances simply adds to the uniqueness and miraculous character of their experience (cf. Exod 19:21; 20:18-21; 24:17). The fact is, Moses went on to say, no other people but Israel had

[187] See Albrektson, *History and the Gods,* 85; C. R. North, "The 'Former Things' and the 'New Things' in Deutero-Isaiah," in *Studies in Old Testament Prophecy Presented to Professor Theodore H. Robinson,* ed. H. H. Rowley (Edinburgh: T & T Clark, 1957), 111-26; C. Stuhlmueller, "'First and Last' and 'Yahweh-Creator' in Deutero-Isaiah," *CBQ* 29 (1967): 194-95; E. H. Merrill, "The Unfading Word: Isaiah and the Incomparability of Israel's God," in *The Church at the Dawn of the 21st Century,* ed. P. Patterson et al. (Dallas: Criswell College, 1989), 141-44.
[188] N. C. Habel, "Appeal to Ancient Tradition as a Literary Form," *ZAW* 88 (1976): 253-72.

been the recipient of revelation from their gods or even from the Lord, the true and only God.[189]

Such an argument does not imply that other peoples have never claimed such an experience. They might well have done so, especially in those religious traditions in which cosmic and nature deities played such an important role. But testimony to such encounters does not amount to proof as far as Moses was concerned. What can be proved, however, is what he and thousands of his countrymen saw and heard with their own senses as they came face to face with the Lord in the Sinai desert.

4:34 A second parade example of the Lord's mighty acts in the past that attest to his uniqueness as well as that of his people is the exodus from Egypt with all its accompanying plagues and signs and wonders (v. 34).[190] Again Moses challenged his listeners to cite a similar occurrence on behalf of any other people and through all the annals of history. The nations of the earth might indeed have their mythic and epic traditions about the intervention of their gods on behalf of their ancestors or even themselves,[191] but none of these can compare in the least to the act of delivering a disorganized, dispirited, militarily inexperienced horde of slaves from the dominion of the mightiest power on earth. Unlike the exodus release, an episode punctuated by a series of miracles that the people of Israel had seen with their very eyes (v. 34), none of the alleged events of comparable proportions adduced by pagan apologists rested on any palpable and persuasive documentary evidence. In the nature of the case they were mythical precisely because they were beyond human experience and therefore empirically unverifiable. Modern scholars might assert that the account at hand is also of the nature of myth or legend, but the canonical witness is that Moses, himself a historical figure, was appealing precisely to history and not myth or saga to make his theological point.

4:35 After arguing for the uniqueness of the Lord and his dealings with Israel in the past, the passage goes on to speak of the rationale for these acts (vv. 35-38). They were not incidental, random, or even self-justifying but rather were accomplished for pedagogical and salvific purposes. Preeminently, they came to pass so that "you might know that the LORD is God" (v. 35).[192] Until this truth could be communicated and indel-

---

[189] A. Rofé, "The Monotheistic Argumentation in Deuteronomy 4:32-40: Contents, Composition and Text," *VT* 35 (1985): 434-45.

[190] B. S. Childs, "Deuteronomic Formulae of the Exodus Traditions," in *Hebraisches Wortforschung,* ed. W. Baumgartner (Leiden: Brill, 1967), 30-39.

[191] Albrektson, *History and the Gods,* 24-41.

[192] B. Hartmann, "Es giht keinen Gott ausser Jahwe," *ZDMG* 110 (1961): 229-35; C. J. Labuschagne, *The Incomparability of Yahweh in the Old Testament* (Leiden: Brill, 1966).

ibly impressed upon his people, the Lord could not take them further down the pathway of covenant affiliation and service. His mighty acts in history, then, were designed to demonstrate the sovereignty of the Lord and to put his uniqueness beyond any doubt (cf. Exod 8:10; 9:14; Deut 33:26; Isa 45:5,14; 46:9). Upon that bedrock confession rests all hope of Israel's redemption and mission.

4:36 In language somewhat repetitive of vv. 33-34, Moses reminded his audience of the dramatic self-disclosures of the Lord from heaven (i.e., from Mount Sinai; cf. Exod 19:3,16-20; 20:18-19) and from earth (that is, the fire; cf. Exod 3:1-4; 24:16-18).[193] In a rather rigidly constructed literary parallelism, the purpose of these awesome revelations is declared: "to discipline you" (v. 36). The purpose statement—expressed by the infinitive construct form of the verb *yāsar*—lies at the fulcrum of the verse so that hearing the Lord's voice from heaven and seeing the revelatory fire on earth coincide in their function. The "discipline" here in context has nothing to do with punishment. Rather, it denotes training or education, in this case instruction in "his words." This likely should be understood in the technical sense of "words" as equivalent to the Ten Commandments.[194]

4:37 Again repeating from an observation previously made, namely, that God had delivered his people from bondage in a unique historical act (cf. v. 34), Moses added to it the reason, "He loved your forefathers and chose their descendants after them" (v. 37). In this brief motive clause occur two of the most covenantally significant words in the Old Testament, "love" and "choose."[195] As technical terms they are virtually synonymous as a great many scholars have put beyond doubt. In other words, "to love" is to choose, and "to choose" is to love.[196]

The effect of this combination of terms is to put in most emphatic language the doctrine of election, at least as far as the call and role of Old Testament Israel is concerned.[197] Deuteronomy stresses this theme over and over (cf. 7:7-8; 10:15; 33:3), but it finds its source, as the passage suggests,

---

[193] For a harmonization of the various traditions about Yahweh's Horeb appearances (Exod 19:16-20; 20:18-19; 24:16-18; Deut 4:36), see Weinfeld, *Deuteronomy 1–11,* 213. Citing *Mek.,* R. Ishmael, Weinfeld sees Deut 4:36 as a synthesis of the Exodus passages.

[194] R. D. Branson, "יָסַר *yāsar,*" *TDOT* 6:129.

[195] D. J. McCarthy, "Notes on the Love of God in Deuteronomy and the Father-Son Relationship between Israel and Yahweh," *CBQ* 27 (1965): 144-47; W. L. Moran, "The Ancient Near Eastern Background of the Love of God in Deuteronomy," *CBQ* 25 (1963): 77-87; B. E. Shafer, "Root *bḥr* and pre-Exilic Concepts of Chosenness in the Hebrew Bible," *ZAW* 89 (1977): 20-42.

[196] H. Seebass, "בָּחַר *bāchar,*" *TDOT* 2:84.

[197] See W. Van Gemeren, *The Progress of Redemption* (Grand Rapids: Zondervan, 1988), 78-80.

in the call of the patriarchs to covenant privilege and responsibility. This call is never accompanied in the patriarchal narratives themselves by either verb (*love* or *choose*), but the notion of choice is clearly there (cf. Gen 12:1; 15:1; 17:1-8; 25:23; 26:24; 28:13-14). The prophets and other later Old Testament witnesses affirmed the elective nature of the call of the patriarchs and of Israel, the seed promised to them (Pss 33:12; 105:6,43; Isa 41:8-9; 43:10,20; 44:1-2; 45:4; Jer 31:3; Amos 3:2).

What is important to note here is that the exodus deliverance was predicated on Israel's prior election by the Lord. It was precisely because of his love and choice that he acted to redeem. This, of course, is already clear from the preexodus dialogue between the Lord and Moses in which the Lord referred to Israel as "my people" (Exod 3:7,10) and, even more significantly, as "my firstborn son" (Exod 4:22-23). The exodus and even the ensuing covenant did not make Israel the people of the Lord. Rather, it was because they were his people by virtue of having been descended from the patriarchs, the objects of his love and choice, that he was moved to save them and enter into covenant with them.[198]

4:38 The work of exodus deliverance was not over, of course, until the conquest and occupation of Canaan, the land of promise, was a *fait accompli*. The land was part of the pledge made to the fathers (cf. Gen 13:14-18; 15:18-21), and on the basis of that solemn commitment to them and to their seed he would now bring possession of it to pass (v. 38). Just as the exodus was a logical and theological outgrowth of divine election, so conquest and possession would follow in its train, the "greater and stronger" nations that lived there notwithstanding.

4:39-40 The passage concludes with a strong exhortation to covenant obedience, one that insists once more on the recognition of the Lord as the universal ("in heaven above[199] and on the earth below") and only ("no other") sovereign. That is, it underscores (as has the entire section) the nature and character of Israel's God—who he is. But it also summarizes what he does and what he expects. Simply put, he demands obedience to his decrees (*ḥuqqîm*) and commands (*miṣwôt*), that is, to the covenant stipulations about to be disclosed through his servant Moses. If they do that, they can expect blessing and longevity in the land for both themselves and their descendants after them. One should observe that though there is a note of contingency ("so that") to the enjoyment of blessing, the promise

---

[198] For a much fuller discussion of the relationship between the exodus and Israel's election, see Merrill, "A Theology of the Pentateuch," 30-32.

[199] On this important divine epithet see R. A. Oden, *"Baʿal Šāmēm and ʾĒl," CBQ* 39 (1977): 457-73.

of the land itself is without qualification ("the land the LORD your God gives you for all time").[200]

The first lengthy parenesis in Deuteronomy closes, then, on a most profound theological note: Yahweh, God of Israel, is the omnipresent and only God, the sovereign one who has redeemed his people and who now was about to reveal a magnificent covenant arrangement that would, in its keeping, guarantee them long and prosperous life in the land they were about to enter.

---

[200] The grammatical and syntactical construction of v. 40 favors the view that "for all time" (כָּל־הַיָּמִים) refers to God's giving (נֹתֵן) and not to "living long" (תַּאֲרִיךְ יָמִים) in the land. That is, the "living" long is conditioned (לְמַעַן) upon obedience of the decrees and commands, but the "for all time" is an unconditional gift to Israel as a covenant entity if not to any particular members. The NIV reflects this correctly. Weinfeld (*Deuteronomy 1–11*, 214) argues cogently that "for all time" refers to the gift because to link it with "living long" would create a tautology.

III. THE PREPARATION FOR THE COVENANT TEXT (4:41-49)
   1. The Narrative concerning Cities of Refuge (4:41-43)
   2. The Setting and Introduction (4:44-49)

III. THE PREPARATION FOR THE COVENANT TEXT (4:41-49)

The question about whether this is a unified or homogeneous passage is most apropos, for 4:41-43 and 4:44-49 clearly deal with quite different matters.[1] Most scholars suggest that vv. 44-49 are part of the larger covenant material that follows (5:1–28:68), serving it as a narrative introduction,[2] but the positioning of vv. 41-43 is more problematic.[3] The issue with which these verses are concerned, namely, the cities of refuge, is greatly expanded later, in 19:2-13. This is to be explained not as a result of multiple sources or an inadvertent interpolation but as the meeting of an immediate need for such sanctuaries in the Transjordan (4:41-43) and a later anticipation of such a need in Canaan proper (19:2-13).

This still leaves the question of the location of the text unanswered. The best solution may be a simple matter of association. That is, Moses had just spoken of long life in the land (v. 40) and part of its safe and proper enjoyment was the provision for places of refuge. Furthermore, this is the first reference to Moses by name since 1:1-5, the introduction to the first address.[4] In that section the conquest of the Transjordan had been accom-

---

[1] See Introduction.

[2] J. Levenson, "Who Inserted the Book of the Torah?" *HTR* 68 (1976): 203-8. O. Eissfeldt, *The Old Testament: An Introduction*, trans. P. R. Ackroyd (New York: Harper & Row, 1965), 221; R. Rendtorff, *The Old Testament: An Introduction* (Philadelphia: Fortress, 1986), 151-52; M. Weinfeld, *Deuteronomy 1–11*, AB (New York: Doubleday, 1991), 9-10.

[3] Most view the section as a late insertion placed where it is without any clear rationale. See A. D. H. Mayes, *Deuteronomy,* NCB (Grand Rapids: Eerdmans, 1981), 47; G. von Rad, *Deuteronomy: A Commentary*, OTL (Philadelphia: Westminster, 1966), II. Von Rad (and most critics) identifies it as P material. For arguments that it is Deuteronomistic, however, see S. R. Driver, *Deuteronomy*, ICC (Edinburgh: T & T Clark, 1902), 78.

[4] Strangely enough, von Rad does not see this as a mark of the passage's originality or even its function as a framing device around 1:6–4:40 (ibid., 51-52). D. Christensen does not note this either, but he does show the propriety of the text's present location as an element matching the setting apart of the tribe of Levi (Deut 10:8-11), all within a frame he describes as "The Great Peroration" (4:1–11:25; *Deuteronomy 1–11* [Dallas: Word, 1992], 69, 97).

plished, and various parts of the land had been named. It is most appropriate, then, that 4:41-43, which parallels 1:1-5 in at least some respects, be viewed as an introduction to the lawgiver's second major address. These verses, together with vv. 44-49, constitute a kind of double introduction, therefore, one to the address as such and the other to the covenant document more specifically.

(1) The Narrative concerning Cities of Refuge (4:41-43)

[41]Then you replied, "We have sinned against the LORD. We will go up and fight, as the LORD our God commanded us." So every one of you put on his weapons, thinking it easy to go up into the hill country.
[42]But the LORD said to me, "Tell them, 'Do not go up and fight, because I will not be with you. You will be defeated by your enemies.'"
[43]So I told you, but you would not listen. You rebelled against the LORD's command and in your arrogance you marched up into the hill country.

4:41-42 The conquest of the Transjordan having been successfully achieved (cf. 3:12-17), Moses set about to fulfill the mandate of the Lord that cities of refuge be singled out as places to which perpetrators of manslaughter could flee until their cases could be fairly adjudicated (cf. Num 35:9-28).[5] Since the rationale for and specific provisos of this legislation are elaborated in Deut 19:2-13, comments here will be limited to the cities of the Transjordan that were set aside for this purpose.

4:43 The first of these, Bezer, was located in the desert plateau (or tableland) and was designated particularly for the residents of Reuben. If Bezer is the same as Bozrah (Umm el-ʿAmad) as some scholars maintain,[6] the place in view was some six miles east of Heshbon, well within the territory that had already been assigned to the tribe of Reuben (cf. 3:16-17). The second city is the well known "Ramoth in Gilead" (modern Tell Ramith) so named as to distinguish it from other places with the same name. It lay some thirty-five miles east of the Jordan River and southeast of the Sea of Galilee, high up in the Gilead plateau. It was conveniently located for the Gadites who had settled there. Finally, Golan (Saḥem el-

---

[5] A. G. Auld, "Cities of Refuge in Israelite Tradition," *JSOT* 10 (1978): 26-40; F. S. Frick, *The City in Ancient Israel* (Missoula, Mont.: Scholars Press, 1977), 137-42; M. Greenberg, "The Biblical Conception of Asylum," *JBL* 78 (1959): 125-32; J. A. Dearman, "The Levitical Cities of Reuben and Moabite Toponymy," *BASOR* 276 (1989): 55-66.

[6] This place is mentioned near the end of the Mesha Inscription as a place already in ruins by 850 B.C. See E. Ullendorff, "The Moabite Stone," in *Documents from Old Testament Times,* ed. D. W. Thomas (London: Thomas Nelson, 1958), 195-98. Ullendorff suggests identification with the Bozrah of Jer 48:24.

Jolan) was selected as the sanctuary for the Transjordanian Manassites. It was only forty miles north of Ramoth-Gilead and about the same distance due east of the Sea of Galilee.

The actual use of these cities as places of sanctuary is never documented in later Old Testament literature. Bezer and Golan, in fact, never appear again in historical narrative, and Ramoth-Gilead does so only as a place of strategic political and military importance (1 Kgs 22; 2 Kgs 9:1-13). There is no reason to doubt, however, that they actually served the purpose for which they were set aside.

(2) The Setting and Introduction (4:44-49)

[44]This is the law Moses set before the Israelites. [45]These are the stipulations, decrees and laws Moses gave them when they came out of Egypt [46]and were in the valley near Beth Peor east of the Jordan, in the land of Sihon king of the Amorites, who reigned in Heshbon and was defeated by Moses and the Israelites as they came out of Egypt. [47]They took possession of his land and the land of Og king of Bashan, the two Amorite kings east of the Jordan. [48]This land extended from Aroer on the rim of the Arnon Gorge to Mount Siyon (that is, Hermon), [49]and included all the Arabah east of the Jordan, as far as the Sea of the Arabah, below the slopes of Pisgah.

One of the important and perhaps unique aspects of biblical revelation is the fact that it took place in time and space, that is, in the context of actual historical events. It is most fitting then that the Deuteronomic covenant text should arise out of a historical experience and that it should be provided with a narrative that leads up to and, indeed, provides a setting for it. This is the function of this brief pericope, one that contains the technical language of covenant form against the backdrop of a historical and geographical environment.

4:44 What is about to be disclosed is "the law" (v. 44). The term here is *tôrâ*, a noun that, with the definite article (as here), usually refers to the entire body of Mosaic literature, that is, the Pentateuch. At this point, however, that literature was still in process as the very appearance of the noun in Deuteronomy makes obvious. Thus *tôrâ* as used here must be synonymous with the covenant text itself, the full collection of principles and stipulations about to be promulgated by Moses. This, of course, is a common usage (cf. Exod 24:12; Deut 1:5; 4:8; 17:18-20; 31:9,11).[7]

---

[7] For a full discussion of various nuances see B. Lindars, "Torah in Deuteronomy," in *Words and Meanings,* ed. P. R. Ackroyd and B. Lindars (Cambridge: University Press, 1968), 117-36.

4:45   This precise meaning of *tôrâ* is confirmed in the explanatory expansion of v. 45, which describes the law as "stipulations, decrees and laws."[8] The first of these (*'ēdôt*) refers to the particulars of covenant requirement that occur in any such text.[9] That is, they are the conditions agreed to by the contracting parties. Therefore, *'ēdût / 'ēdôt* is a generic term embodying "decrees" (*ḥuqqîm*) and "laws" (*mišpāṭîm*), which are more explicit ways of identifying stipulations. Etymologically these two words are obviously much different, the former being derived from the verb *ḥaqaq* ("to cut in, inscribe, decree") and the latter from the verb *šāpaṭ* ("to judge, govern"). Hence, many of the versions render them, respectively, as "statutes" and "judgments" or the like.

By usage the two are virtually synonymous and interchangeable, serving separately or together as terms for the covenant stipulations. Any particular nuances they communicate will be noted in the course of the continuing exposition that follows.

4:46   Lest there be any doubt about the exact corpus the narrator had in mind, he identified it as those laws that Moses delivered culminating the series of historical events that began with the exodus and ended in the encampment "in the valley near Beth Peor" (v. 46). The grammar suggests that the giving of the law is a thing of the past, so very likely these verses constitute a later reflection on the completed address. This thesis also accounts for what appears to be an unnecessary repetition of episodes already covered in rather great detail, though, admittedly, historical recapitulation seems to be a common feature in the book (1:1-5; cf. 3:1-11).

4:47-49   The settlement at Beth Peor (cf. 3:29) had come about after the defeat of the Amorite king Sihon, who controlled that area (cf. 2:30-37). Then followed the conquest and occupation of Bashan, whose king Og was the second of the two Amorite rulers mentioned here (v. 47; cf. 3:1-11). The extent of all the land thus taken is described here as extending from Aroer in the south to "Mount Siyon" in the north (v. 48). This differs from the previous description of Transjordanian territory (3:8-9) mainly in identifying Mount Hermon as "Siyon" rather than Sirion or Senir. The spelling here probably is a corruption of the original Sirion.[10] As for the remainder of the land, that of the central part of the country (v. 49), its extent is virtually identical to that described in 3:17b.

---

[8] N. Lohfink, "Die *ḥuqqîm ûmišpāṭîm* im Buch Deuteronomium und ihre Neubegrenzung," *Bib* 70 (1989): 1-30.

[9] B. Couroyer, "*'Ēdût*: Stipulation de Traité ou Enseignement?" *RB* 95 (1988): 321-81; N. Lohfink, "*'d(w)t* im Deuteronomium und in den Königsbüchern," *BZ* 35 (1991): 86-93.

[10] P. C. Craigie, *Deuteronomy,* NICOT (Grand Rapids: Eerdmans, 1976), 147.

IV. THE PRINCIPLES OF THE COVENANT (5:1–11:32)
1. The Opening Exhortation (5:1-5)
2. The Ten Commandments (5:6-21)
    (1) The Commandments Pertaining to Humankind's Relationship to God (5:6-15)
    (2) The Commandments Pertaining to Humankind's Relationship to Others (5:16-21)
3. The Narrative Relating the Sinai Revelation and Israel's Response (5:22-33)
    (1) The Rehearsal of the Theophany (5:22-27)
    (2) The Preparations for the Covenant Stipulations (5:28-33)
4. The Nature of the Principles (6:1-25)
    (1) Exhortation to Keep Them (6:1-3)
    (2) The Essence of the Principles (6:4-5)
    (3) Exhortation to Teach Them (6:6-9)
    (4) Exhortation to Give the Lord Exclusive Recognition and Worship (6:10-15)
    (5) Exhortation to Give the Lord Exclusive Obedience (6:16-19)
    (6) Exhortation to Remember the Past (6:20-25)
5. The Content of the Principles (7:1–11:32)
    (1) The Dispossession of Nonvassals (7:1-26)
    (2) The Lord as the Source of Blessing (8:1-20)
    (3) Blessing as a Product of Grace (9:1–10:11)
    (4) Love of the Lord and Love of Humankind (10:12-22)
    (5) Obedience and Disobedience and Their Rewards (11:1-32)

—— **IV. THE PRINCIPLES OF THE COVENANT (5:1–11:32)** ——

The Introduction has already addressed the matter of ancient Near Eastern covenant texts and their standard form, especially those of Hittite suzerain-vassal types, and has argued that the Book of Deuteronomy fits that pattern in its overall structure. Two of the major elements, it was noted, are lists of stipulations, the first of a general, principal nature and the second of a more specific and applicational kind. That is, the first spelled out in broad strokes the kinds of actions and reactions the Great King expected of his vassal, and the other offered examples of how these general expectations could and should be worked out in everyday life within the relationship.

While a general correspondence exists between Deuteronomy and the secular treaty texts, especially in form, there are significant differences as well. Among these are the narrative sections and the extensive parenesis, both of which are lacking in the extrabiblical models.[1] It is important to note here, moreover, that Deuteronomy, in addition to being a covenant text, is also a law code, or, more precisely, contains a law code. The general stipulation section (5:1–11:32)[2] and the specific stipulation section (12:1–26:15) function as such a law code and thus serve both in this capacity and in that of covenant stipulation. To put it more succinctly, the stipulations of the Deuteronomic covenant constitute the law code for the nation Israel that was about to enter the new conditions and expectations of life in the land of promise.[3] This is why the following principles resemble both legal statutes and covenant stipulations at one and the same time.

1. The Opening Exhortation (5:1-5)

[1]Moses summoned all Israel and said:

---

[1] For the occurrence of these elements in the general stipulation section, see F. C. Tiffany, "Parenesis and Deuteronomy 5–11 (Deut. 4:45; 5:2–11:29): A Form Critical Study," (Ph.D. diss., Claremont Graduate School, 1978).

[2] Christensen, in line with a prosodic analysis approach to Deuteronomy, does not view 5:1–11:29 as a separate, self-contained unit but as a part of what he calls "The Inner Frame: Part 1—The Great Peroration" (4:1–11:25) (*Deuteronomy 1–11*, WBC [Dallas: Word, 1991], 69). This is balanced by "The Inner Frame: Part 2" (27:1–30:20), the central core being Deut 12–26 (p. 100). While he makes his case well from a rhetorical structural standpoint, Christensen pays too little attention to more overriding covenant considerations. See F. G. Lopez, "Analyse Littéraire de Deuteronome, 5–11," *RB* 84 (1977): 481-522; *RB* 85 (1978): 5-49; N. Lohfink, *Das Hauptgebot: eine Untersuchung literarischer Einleitungsfragen zu Dtn 5–11* (Roma: Pontificio Instituto Biblico, 1963); B. Peckham, "The Composition of Deuteronomy 5–11," in *The Word of the Lord Shall Go Forth: Essays in Honor of David Noel Freedman*, ed. C. Meyers and M. O'Connor, ASOR Special Volume Series 1 (Winona Lake, Ind.: Eisenbrauns, 1983), 217-40.

[3] For the connection between law and covenant see W. Eichrodt, "Covenant and Law," *Int* 20 (1966): 302-21; E. Gerstenberger, "Covenant and Commandment," *JBL* 84 (1965): 38-51; Mendenhall, *Law and Covenant in Israel and the Ancient Near East;* C. F. Whitley, "Covenant and Commandment in Israel," *JNES* 22 (1963): 37-48. For the matter of the origin of law in Israel in general see H. Reviv, "The Traditions Concerning the Inception of the Legal System in Israel: Significance and Dating," *ZAW* 94 (1982): 566-75.

Hear, O Israel, the decrees and laws I declare in your hearing today. Learn them and be sure to follow them. [2]The LORD our God made a covenant with us at Horeb. [3]It was not with our fathers that the LORD made this covenant, but with us, with all of us who are alive here today. [4]The LORD spoke to you face to face out of the fire on the mountain. [5](At that time I stood between the LORD and you to declare to you the word of the LORD, because you were afraid of the fire and did not go up the mountain.) And he said:

5:1   At last the time arrived for Moses actually to articulate the great covenant principles by which Israel was to live in the land of Canaan as the servant people of Yahweh. He therefore convened them in the valley near Beth Peor (cf. 4:46) and, in strong hortatory language, commanded them to hear (i.e., obey) the "decrees and laws" (the *ḥuqqîm* and *mišpāṭîm*),[4] the very elements of covenant requirement he was about to deliver (*ʾānōkî dōbēr*) to them. The meaning of obedience is expanded by the second set of commands: "Learn them and be careful to do them" (v. 1).

5:2   The precise identity of the covenant Moses had in mind is immediately clarified by his referring to it as the covenant made at Horeb (v. 2; cf. 1:2,6). Thus what was about to be revealed was not something radically new and different but simply a reaffirmation or renewal of what had already been given. In line with secular covenant arrangements, each new generation of covenant partners must subscribe to the terms sworn to by their respective ancestors, though, obviously, changing times and circumstances would dictate the need for amendments or qualifications of the original stipulations. The covenant about to be stated was the old Horeb pact but, as will be seen, the old pact with new wrinkles.

5:3   Not only is the covenant referred to here the same as that at Horeb, but it is only that and not anything anterior to it. "It was not with our fathers," Moses said, "that the LORD made this covenant, but with us" (v. 3). This rules out the identification of the Deuteronomic covenant with the patriarchal and, in fact, draws a clear line of demarcation between the two.[5] This is in line with the generally recognized theological fact that the Horeb-Deuteronomy covenant is by both form and function different from the so-called Abrahamic. The latter is in the nature of an irrevocable and unconditional grant made by the Lord to the patriarchs, one containing promises of land, seed, and blessing. The former is a suzerain-vassal arrangement between the Lord and Israel designed to regulate Israel's life as the promised nation within the framework of the Abrahamic covenant.[6] The existence of Israel is unconditional, but its enjoyment of the blessing

---

[4] For the meaning of these terms cf. comments on 4:45.
[5] Weinfeld, *Deuteronomy 1–11,* 239.

of God and its successful accomplishment of the purposes of God are dependent on its faithful obedience to the covenant made at Horeb. Thus the covenant in view here is not the same as that made with the fathers (i.e., the patriarchal ancestors), but it (and that at Horeb) finds its roots there and is related to it in a subsidiary way.[7]

For Moses to say that the Horeb covenant was made "with us" does not require that all with whom it was made thirty-eight years earlier were still alive or that all who were presently hearing him were living then. This is manifestly not the case, for thousands had died in the interim (cf. 2:14,16; Num 16:49; 25:9), and many more thousands had been born since the giving of the law. This is merely the use of corporate language, the recognition that Israel as an entity was at Horeb though multiplied thousands of individual Israelites may not have been.[8]

5:4-5 In keeping with this idea of "corporate solidarity," the lawgiver went on to recount how the Lord had spoken to "you" (i.e., the nation) out of the fire (v. 4; cf. 4:33) and how Moses had mediated between the Lord and the people on that terrifying occasion (v. 5; cf. Exod 19:16,21-24; 24:1-2).[9] Specifically, Moses was on the mountain, surrounded by the theophanic glory of God, in order to serve as a conduit of divine revelation, the "word of the LORD" delivered then and about to be repeated now.

2. The Ten Commandments (5:6-21)[10]

The technical term for this collection of statutes, the "ten words," does not occur here, but they clearly are what was in mind when the formula

---

[6] M. Weinfeld, "The Covenant of Grant in the Old Testament and in the Ancient Near East," *JAOS* 90 (1970-72): 184-203, 468-69.

[7] Merrill, "Theology of the Pentateuch," 32-33.

[8] "The covenant was made not with the particular individuals who were then alive, but rather with the nation as an organic whole" (Keil and Delitzsch, *The Pentateuch,* vol. 3, 319).

[9] See E. W. Nicholson, "Decalogue as the Direct Address of God," *VT* 27 (1977): 422-33; E. Nielsen, "Moses and the Law," *VT* 32 (1982): 87-98. Nielsen rejects the historicity of the account of Moses' receiving the law, but he does admit that the Deuteronomic traditions point to Moses as the prophet who mediated the Decalogue (pp. 97-98).

[10] Of the massive literature on the Ten Commandments, some major studies are: C. M. Carmichael, *The Ten Commandments* (Oxford: Oxford Centre for Postgraduate Hebrew Studies, 1983); R. H. Charles, *The Decalogue* (Edinburgh: T & T Clark, 1923); W. Harrelson, *The Ten Commandments and Human Rights, Overtures to Biblical Theology* 8 (Philadelphia: Fortress, 1980); R. H. Kennett, *Deuteronomy and the Decalogue* (Cambridge: Cambridge University Press, 1920); E. Nielsen, *The Ten Commandments in New Perspective*, trans. D. J. Bourke, SBT 7 (London: SCM, 1968); A. Phillips, *Ancient Israel's Criminal Law: A New Approach to the Decalogue* (Oxford: Blackwell, 1970); J. Schreiner, *Die Zehn Gebote im Leben des Gottesvolkes* (Munich: Kösel, 1988); B. Segal, ed., *The Ten Commandments as Reflected in Tradition and Literature throughout the Ages* (Jerusalem: Magnes, 1985); J. J. Stamm and M. E. Andrew, *The Ten Commandments in Recent Research* (Naperville, Ill.: Allenson, 1967).

was used elsewhere (cf. Exod 34:28; Deut 4:13; 10:4). The fact that they were inscribed on two stone tablets (4:13) suggests to many scholars that some of the commandments were contained on one tablet and the rest on the second. Others, however, maintain, in line with covenant practice, that all ten were engraved on each.[11] That is, they were duplicates with each party to the covenant retaining a copy for his own archives. This appears to be a likely construal of the facts given the analogies to extrabiblical documents.

But the tradition that the list of commandments was divided into two also has some support. First, both tablets were written on both the obverse and reverse (Exod 32:15). While this proves nothing and may only mean that four surfaces in all were needed for all Ten Commandments, the view that the tablets were duplicates leaves only two surfaces for each. What was on the front and what was on the back of each remains at issue. One solution is that since the commandments relate to two dimensions—the human to God (the vertical) and the human to human (the horizontal)—the former were on one side and the latter on the other. This is attractive but lacks any ancient proof.[12]

In any case the configuration of the tablets and their contents is almost irrelevant to the analysis that suggests the vertical and horizontal dimensions suggested above. The law indeed addresses these two aspects, not only here but throughout the Mosaic corpus. In fact, the "greatest law," as Jesus defined it, was to love God with all one's heart, soul, and mind; and, he said, the second was like it—love one's neighbor as oneself. "All the law and the prophets hang on these two commandments" (Matt 22:37-40). It is most appropriate then to consider Deut 5:6-15 first and then 5:16-21.

(1) The Commandments Pertaining to Humankind's Relationship to God (5:6-15)

[6] "I am the LORD your God, who brought you out of Egypt, out of the land of slavery.

[7]"You shall have no other gods before me.

[8]"You shall not make for yourself an idol in the form of anything in heaven above or on the earth beneath or in the waters below. [9]You shall not bow down to them or worship them; for I, the LORD your God, am a jealous God, punishing the children for the sin of the fathers to the third and fourth generation of

---

[11] M. Kline, "The Two Tables of the Covenant," 133-46.

[12] Cf. M. Breur, "The Division of the Decalogue into Verses and Commandments," in *The Ten Commandments in History and Tradition*, ed. B. Z. Segal (Jerusalem: Magnes, 1990), 291-330; M. Lestienne, "Les dix 'Paroles' et le Décalogue," *RB* 79 (1972): 484-510.

those who hate me, [10]but showing love to a thousand [generations] of those who love me and keep my commandments.

[11]"You shall not misuse the name of the LORD your God, for the LORD will not hold anyone guiltless who misuses his name.

[12]"Observe the Sabbath day by keeping it holy, as the LORD your God has commanded you. [13]Six days you shall labor and do all your work, [14]but the seventh day is a Sabbath to the LORD your God. On it you shall not do any work, neither you, nor your son or daughter, nor your manservant or maidservant, nor your ox, your donkey or any of your animals, nor the alien within your gates, so that your manservant and maidservant may rest, as you do. [15]Remember that you were slaves in Egypt and that the LORD your God brought you out of there with a mighty hand and an outstretched arm. Therefore the LORD your God has commanded you to observe the Sabbath day.

In analyzing the Ten Commandments from a strictly form-critical point of view, it is necessary to recognize that at least two aspects must be considered—that of the form of the individual laws and that of the structure of the section as a whole. One of the most important and positive contributions made by form critics has been the distinction to be seen between apodictic law and casuistic law.[13] The former, characteristic especially of the Decalogue both here and in Exod 20, consists of the statement of expectations or prohibitions without specifying any particular qualifications or prescribing any kind of sanction in the event of infraction. The regular pattern in the statement of expectation ("you shall") is either the simple imperative followed by the demand (as in the fifth commandment, v. 16) or its equivalent, the infinitive absolute (as the fourth commandment, v. 12). The commandments that express prohibition do so with the negative particle *lōʾ* plus the imperfect of the verb.[14]

The casuistic law, on the other hand, deals with specific cases or potential cases. There are scores of these throughout the Pentateuch, particularly in the Book of the Covenant (Exod 20:1–23:33) and in Deut 12:1–26:19, the so-called specific stipulations of the Deuteronomic covenant. They

---

[13] A. Alt, "The Origins of Israelite Law," in *Essays on Old Testament History and Religion* (Garden City: Doubleday, 1968), 101-71; S. Amsler, "Loi orale et loi écrite dans le Deutéronome," *Das Deuteronomium. Entstehung, Gestalt und Botschatt,* BETL 68 (Leuven: University Press, 1985), 51-54; W. M. Clark, "Law," in *Old Testament Form Criticism* (San Antonio: Trinity University Press, 1974), 99-139; M. Weinfeld, "The Origin of the Apodictic Law: An Overlooked Source," *VT* 23 (1963): 63-75; R. Westbrook, "Biblical and Cuneiform Law Codes," *RB* 92 (1985): 247-64.

[14] Apodictic law outside the Decalogue is much more varied and complex. For the various formulae see Alt, "The Origins of Israelite Law," 142-54. For a full assessment of the criticism and refinement of Alt, see H. W. Gilmer, *The If-You Form in Israelite Law,* SBLDS 15 (Missoula, Mont.: Scholars Press, 1975), 11-15, 19-20.

consist usually of two main sections, a protasis and an apodosis, the former raising the contingency ("if one does thus and so") and the latter the expected result ("then here is what should happen"). More technically put, the form of such a law is a dependent clause introduced by a particle such as *kî* or *ʾim* ("if, when, given that," etc.) followed by the main clause usually introduced by the particle *waw* ("then" or the like).[15] These kinds will receive more detailed attention as they occur in subsequent discussion.

As for the relationship between the apodictic and casuistic law forms in the covenant texts, at the risk of oversimplification one might say that the apodictic serve as great, fundamental covenant principles whereas the casuistic are applications or even explications of these principles in the specific situations of everyday life.[16] Thus the apodictic "ten words" here in the Deuteronomy Decalogue function as the essence of divine standards and expectations against which every conceivable human attitude and conduct is to be measured. They are, in fact, expressive of the very character of God himself and for that reason alone are timeless and universally applicable. They may be couched in the framework of a covenant between God and a particular people at a particular time, but they cannot be limited by those or any other circumstances.[17] This is clear from the fact that Jesus and the New Testament nowhere rescind them and, in fact, always endorse and uphold them as relevant to the church and to all people.[18]

To return to the matter of the structure of the Decalogue, research on the pattern of ancient Near Eastern treaty texts reveals that the body of stipulations almost invariably is preceded by a preamble and a historical prologue. We have noted already that this is the case with Deuteronomy as a whole, and now this possibility must be applied to the heart of this document, namely, the Decalogue and the following stipulation sections. When this is done, it is clear that there is at least a vestigial or greatly abbreviated preamble in v. 6 ("I am the LORD your God") and an equally succinct historical prologue ("who brought you out of Egypt, out of the land of slavery").[19] The same is true of the Sinai rendition of the covenant text where the identical words are spoken in Exod 20:2.

---

[15] Alt, "Origins of Israelite Law," 112-14. Again there is great variety within this category including curse, jussive, participial, and if-you forms, all of which share in common a specified violation and usually an attendant punishment. Cf. Gilmer, *If-You Form*, 3-11, 17-19.

[16] S. A. Kaufman, "The Structure of the Deuteronomic Law," *Maarav* 1/2 (1978-79): 108-10; Phillips, *Ancient Israel's Criminal Law*, 17.

[17] W. J. Dumbrell, *Covenant and Creation: A Theology of Old Testament Covenants* (Nashville: Thomas Nelson, 1984), 91-92; G. Vos, *Biblical Theology* (Grand Rapids: Eerdmans, 1954), 147-48.

[18] Van Gemeren, *Progress of Redemption*, 330.

[19] Thompson, *Deuteronomy*, 114.

There are several implications of this including the impossibility of considering v. 6 as the first and a separate commandment and vv. 7-10 as the second, a view held especially in the Jewish tradition.[20] If (as seems certain in view of modern form-critical analysis) v. 6 is actually the preamble plus historical prologue, v. 7 is the first commandment and vv. 8-10 the second. Also the fact that the commandments as a collection are introduced by elements regularly connected with covenant texts places them squarely within a covenant context and precludes their being viewed simply as a block of legal material within an ordinary Mosaic address.

5:6   To turn now to the commandments themselves, they follow a preamble and prologue statement (v. 6), that is, as has been noted, identical to that found in the Sinai version of Exod 20:2.[21] The first commandment also is identical in its wording (v. 7; cf. Exod 20:3). Its position in the list and its profound simplicity and succinctness are impressive. Clearly this appeal to the exclusivity and implicit uniqueness of Yahweh forms the basis upon which Israel's faith and action must be built. The difficult phrase "before me" (*ʿal pānāy*) means literally "against my face" or "in [my] presence."[22] That is, other gods must not be brought into Yahweh's company, for he exists alone as Israel's God. The fact that "other gods" (*ĕlōhîm ʾăḥērîm*) are mentioned does not, of course, concede that they exist in reality. The nations accepted their existence, but Israel was to refuse to permit them a place alongside Yahweh even if they went so far as to admit their possibility. The command is not so much an apologetic for the sole existence of Yahweh, then, as it is a prohibition about allowing them in his same company as a theoretical rival.[23]

---

[20] Weinfeld, *Deuteronomy 1–11*, 243-45. The Roman Catholic, Lutheran, and certain other Christian traditions take the first two commandments (vv. 6-10) as one and divide the tenth (v. 21) into two, still yielding ten. See C. F. Keil and F. Delitzsch, *Biblical Commentary on the Old Testament*, vol. II, trans. J. Martin (Grand Rapids: Eerdmans, n.d.), 108-12.

[21] For the relationship between the Exodus and Deuteronomy versions of the Decalogue and suggested mutual dependences, see A. Graupner, "Zum Verhältnis der beiden Dekalogfassungen Ex 20 und Dtn 5: ein Gespräch mit Frank-Lothar Hossfeld," *ZAW* 99 (1987): 308-29; A. Lemaire, "Le Decalogue: Essai d'Histoire de la Redaction (Ex 20:2-17; Deut 5:6-21), in Melanges Biblique et Orientaux en l'Honneur de M. Henri Cazelles, ed. A. Caquot and M. Delcor, AOAT 212 (Kevelaer/Neukirchen-Vluyn: Butzon & Bercker/Neukirchener, 1981), 259-95; J. M. Vincent, "Neuere Aspekte der Dekalogforschung," *BN* 32 (1986): 83-104; S. A. White, "The All Souls Deuteronomy and the Decalogue," *JBL* 109 (1990): 193-206.

[22] KB, 767. This lexicon translates the word in both Exod 20:3 and Deut 5:7 as "in defiance of me," a translation difficult to defend etymologically but certainly appropriate in context of covenant relationships. See the exhaustive discussion of the options in Weinfeld, *Deuteronomy 1–11*, 276-77; cf. R. Knierim, "Das Erste Gebot," *ZAW* 36 (1965): 20-39.

[23] Thus U. Cassuto, *A Commentary on the Book of Exodus*, trans. I. Abrahams (Jerusalem: Magnes, 1967), 241.

5:7-8 The wording of the second commandment (vv. 8-10) is virtually a carbon copy of that in Exod 20:4-6. It builds upon and logically follows the first by specifying how people could and did represent "other gods" and why it was forbidden for Israel to do so.[24] It also deals with the issue of the invisibility of God and the impossibility of representing him in any kind of concrete form. The word for "idol" (*pesel*) describes anything that is hewn out of wood or stone (from the verb *pāsal;* cf. Exod 34:1,4; Deut 10:1,3; 1 Kgs 5:32) though even metal images could be hewn (cf. Judg 17:3-4; Isa 40:19; 44:10; Jer 10:14).[25] As is clear from the objects of this kind from archaeological and ancient artistic sources, they existed in a variety of sizes, shapes, and forms, conforming indeed to things "in heaven above" (birds), "on the earth beneath" (land creatures), and "in the waters below" (fish and other marine animals).[26] This three-tiered notion of the universe as above, on, and below the earth was, of course, common to ancient Near Eastern cosmology.[27]

Such likenesses must not be made, at least with the intention of worshiping them; for this would lead to the unthinkable position of a creature being regarded as the creator and of humans, the very image of God and sovereign of all the universe, bowing down before that over which they were commissioned to be master (cf. 4:15-19). In other words, the whole enterprise was one of egregious confusion of levels of sovereignty and one that engendered the grossest insubordination.

5:9 This is evident from the further proscription against bowing down and worshiping these idols (v. 9).[28] The verb translated "worship" is ʿābad, the more literal meaning of which is "serve." Though worship is the essence of service in the language of the cult,[29] the covenant nature of the relationship between the Lord and Israel would favor the notion of service beyond that. To bow down is to recognize the sovereignty of a god, but to serve is to express commitment to that sovereignty in a practical, tangible way.[30] Israel had been redeemed from bondage or service in Egypt in order

---

[24] W. B. Tatum, "The LXX Version of the Second Commandment (Ex 20:3-6 = Deut 5:7-10): A Polemic against Idols, Not Images," *JSJ* 17 (1986): 177-95.

[25] A. L. Oppenheim, *Ancient Mesopotamia: Portrait of a Dead Civilization* (Chicago: University of Chicago Press, 1964), 185-89; cf. B. Vawter, "A Note on 'the Waters Beneath the Earth,'" *CBQ* 22 (1960): 71-73.

[26] See, e.g., Shafer, ed., *Religion in Ancient Egypt,* 13-20.

[27] H. Frankfort et al., *Before Philosophy,* 53-56, 150-61.

[28] J. N. M. Wijngaards, "'You Shall Not Bow Down to Them or Serve Them,'" *IJT* 18 (1969): 180-90.

[29] G. von Rad, *Old Testament Theology,* vol. 1, trans. D. M. G. Stalker (New York: Harper & Row, 1962), 241.

[30] J. I. Durham, *Exodus,* WBC (Waco: Word, 1987), 286-87.

to serve Yahweh. To serve other gods, then, was to reverse the exodus and go back under bondage, thus betraying the grace and favor of Yahweh.

This explains the divine reaction in v. 9: "I, the LORD your God, am a jealous God, punishing." Because he had redeemed his people from slavery to another and had made covenant with them, the Lord deserved and demanded their exclusive allegiance. This is why he is a "jealous God" (ʾēl qannāʾ), that is, one who is zealous for his own person and position as Israel's sovereign God (cf. 4:24; 6:15). The jealousy here is not the human emotion of envy but the proper insistence by God of his uniqueness and exclusiveness. Those who fail or refuse to recognize that exclusiveness by resorting to idolatry may expect inexorable punishment for that iniquity (so Heb. ʿăwôn, from the verb ʿāwâ, "to bend, distort").[31] The repercussions are so great as to impact generations yet unborn if they continue to hate God.

5:10 The idea of "hating" God in the context of covenant is tantamount to rejecting him. Thus the hating is identical to the turning away suggested by the noun ʿăwôn. The opposite, "to love," obviously means to choose in this setting, a point made previously (cf. 1:27; 4:37). Those who hate (i.e., repudiate) God in favor of idols may expect his judgment, but those who love (ʾāhēb) him and demonstrate it by keeping his commandments will benefit from his covenant loyalty (thus Heb. ḥesed) for thousands of generations (v. 10). The term "commandments" (miṣwôt) means more than just the Ten Commandments (usually referred to as "words"), for it is a generic word encompassing the covenant as a whole.

No term is more theologically significant than ḥesed, translated in the NIV here as "love."[32] It speaks of God's unmerited favor by which he elects people to covenant relationship and on the basis of which he extends all its blessings. In fact, ḥesed and bĕrît ("covenant") are used as synonymous (Deut 7:9) and interchangeable terms (Deut 7:12). As the basis for covenant election, ḥesed is unconditional, for it is a manifestation of pure grace. Within that relationship, however, ḥesed is part of a reciprocal process, a disposition conditioned upon the love (ʾāhăbâ) and obedience of those who owe them (v. 10).[33]

---

[31] C. Schultz, עָוָה (ʿāwâ), *TWOT* 2:650. This "bending" suggests a turning away from the covenant, the very thing that most incites Yahweh's rage. Cf. W. Zimmerli, *Old Testament Theology in Outline,* trans. D. E. Green (Atlanta: John Knox, 1978), 110-11.

[32] For this richly significant covenant term see H.-J. Zobel, "חֶסֶד ḥesed," *TDOT* 5:44-64 (esp. 54, 60-61); N. Glueck, *Hesed in the Bible,* trans. A. Gottschalk (Cincinnati: Hebrew Union College, 1967); K. D. Sakenfeld, *The Meaning of Hesed in the Hebrew Bible,* HSM 17 (Chico, Cal.: Scholars Press, 1978).

[33] G. Wallis, "אָהַב ʾāhabh," etc., *TDOT* 1:115.

5:11   The third commandment also finds its source in the first—the unique and exclusive God—but more remotely than did the second. Whereas the second has to do with iconic, visible representations of God (or gods), this concerns the use of his name as an extension or even substitution for himself.[34] Deuteronomy is particularly replete with references to the divine name as an alter ego for God (cf. 12:5,11,21; 14:23-24; 16:2,6,11; 26:2) and in light of the well-known ancient Semitic belief in the knowledge or other use of one's name as a means of manipulating its owner,[35] the commandment, like the second, prohibits inappropriate approach to and prostitution of the person and power of God. This is a form of idolatry, for even though engraved images are not in mind, the divine name as a kind of talisman or *shibboleth* can serve idolatrous ends.

The prohibition says, literally, "You shall not lift up the name of Yahweh your God without reason."[36] The meaning clearly is that one must not view the name as a counterpart of Yahweh and then proceed to take it in hand (or in mouth) as a means of accomplishing some kind of ill-advised or unworthy objective. This was typical of ancient Near Eastern sorcery or incantation where the names of the gods were invoked as part of the act of conjuration or of prophylaxis.[37] Whoever violates the sanctity of the name will not be left unpunished.

5:12-15   The fourth commandment, that having to do with Sabbath observance, is one of two commandments expressed in the affirmative.[38] It also varies most from the wording of the Sinai Decalogue and not merely stylistically. It is quite apparent that the events between the giving of the law at Horeb and its renewal here near Beth Peor call for a new understanding of the meaning of the Sabbath and its proper observance. These contrasts will be pointed out in the course of the exposition.

The commandment begins with an infinitival form of the verb *šāmar* that functions here as an imperative. With the following infinitive and

---

[34] J. G. McConville, "God's 'Name' and God's 'Glory,'" *TynBul* 30 (1979): 149-63.

[35] Von Rad, *Old Testament Theology*, 2:81, 83-84.

[36] Thus לַשָּׁוְא; see KB, 951; A. J. Wagner, "An Interpretation of Exodus 20:7," *Int* 6 (1952): 228-29

[37] R. I. Caplice, *The Akkadian Namburbi Texts: An Introduction*, SANE 1/1 (Los Angeles: Undena, 1974), 12-13.

[38] For important studies see N.-E. Andreason, "Festival and Freedom: A Study of an Old Testament Theme," *Int* 28 (1974): 281-97; id., "Recent Studies of the Old Testament Sabbath," *ZAW* 86 (1974): 453-69; G. F. Hasel, "The Sabbath in the Pentateuch (Gen. 2:1-3; Ex. 20:8-11; 31:12-17; Deut. 5:12-15)," in *The Sabbath in Scripture and History* (Washington: Review & Herald, 1982), 21-43; M. Tsevat, "The Basic Meaning of the Biblical Sabbath," *ZAW* 84 (1972): 447-59; M. F. Unger, "The Significance of the Sabbath," *BSac* 123 (1966): 53-59; H. W. Wolff, "The Day of Rest in the Old Testament," *LTQ* 7 (1972): 65-76.

preposition (*lĕqaddĕšô*), it forms a common hortatory expression, "Watch carefully to keep holy." The parallel in Exod 20:8 also employs an infinitive absolute, but the verb is *zākar*, "remember," rather than *šāmar*.[39] The verbs as used here are essentially synonymous, but *šāmar* implies more of an active participation. There is more to Sabbath observance than mere recollection of the past or even determination to conform; there must be a studied effort to keep the day holy, an actual involvement in its requirements and prohibitions. The change in verb may well reflect a tendency on Israel's part to have made the requirement of Sabbath keeping a matter of mere formality or even indifference (cf. Num 15:32-36). This new expression of the commandment would then address this issue more firmly.[40] Support for this view lies in the clause "as the LORD your God has commanded you" (v. 12), a statement lacking in Exodus and one no doubt referring directly back to that first giving of the law.

The word "Sabbath" (Heb. *šabbāt*) derives from the verb *šābat*, "to stop, cease, rest." The theological and, hence, legal implications go back to the first use of the verb in Gen 2:2-3, which states that God, having created all things in six days, "rested from all his work." He then blessed the seventh day and "made it holy" (*wayqaddēš*), the same verb as occurs here. The reason it was made holy was that "on it he rested from all the work of creating that he had done."

It is important to note that *šābat* means both "to cease" and "to rest," for both meanings occur in the respective versions of the fourth commandment. In Exodus, as the motive clause makes clear, the seventh day must be set apart because God ceased his creative work on that day, and therefore human work also should cease (Exod 20:11). In Deuteronomy the motive clause bases Sabbath observance on the fact that the Israelites had been slaves in Egypt and therefore it was most appropriate to celebrate deliverance from that bondage by abstaining from labor for one day, that is, by resting (Deut 5:15).

In both cases the seventh day must be made "holy." Fundamentally, the idea of the word group "holy" is that of separation, of being set aside for some particular use.[41] That is, it has no inherent element of moral content

---

[39] J. D. W. Watts, "Infinitive Absolute as Imperative and the Interpretation of Exodus 20:8," *ZAW* 74 (1962): 141-45

[40] Weinfeld helpfully distinguishes between the two verbs as follows: "The former [*šāmar*] is used for observance of the law, while the latter [*zākar*] is reserved for historical remembrance" (*Deuteronomy 1–11*, 303).

[41] See the still authoritative treatment of the lexemes קׁדֶשׁ, קָדְשׁה, etc. by N. H. Snaith, *The Distinctive Ideas of the Old Testament* (London: Epworth, 1944), 21-50; cf. also C. Barth, *God With Us: A Theological Introduction to the Old Testament*, trans. G. W. Bromiley (Grand Rapids: Eerdmans, 1991), 140-43.

or purity. As holiness becomes associated with God, however, as the absolutely transcendent and perfect one, his attributes of sinlessness and moral and ethical perfection come to stamp holiness itself with these characteristics. Therefore for a person to be holy as the Lord himself is holy (cf. Lev 19:2) is to suggest a way of thought and life that is above reproach.[42]

Obviously, a day cannot be holy in the moral sense, so the meaning of keeping the seventh day holy is that of the normal meaning of the verb, to set it apart for a particular purpose. In this instance it is to withhold that day from profane use so that it may be used for other purposes such as reflection on the Lord and his works of creation and redemption. The form of the verb *qdš* (*piel*) when it is used in this sense of setting apart reflects a factitive nuance such as to "put the seventh day into a state of holiness."[43]

The setting apart of the seventh day having been established, the law goes on to speak of those who must observe it (v. 14). These include the head of the family, family members, slaves, animals, and foreigners. These last, who were not members of the covenant community and are therefore listed even after slaves and animals, were nonetheless responsible to live by the covenant requirements of the host people to whom they had attached themselves. They could include such elements as the "many other people" who accompanied Israel in the exodus (cf. Exod 12:38) or Midianites who joined them later (Num 10:29-33).

An interesting introduction to the so-called "motive-clause," that is, the statement of rationale for the commandment, appears at the end of v. 14, "So that your manservant and maidservant may rest, as you do."[44] This is lacking in the Exodus version (cf. Exod 20:9) for a perfectly understandable reason: the motive-clause in Exodus centers on the Sabbath as creation celebration (Exod 20:11) whereas that in Deuteronomy is concerned with the Sabbath as redemption celebration (5:15).

For many years Israel had languished in Egyptian sojourn and slavery and so knew full well the hapless plight of the slave. How appropriate then that Israel's own slaves, whether indentured fellow Israelites or otherwise, should know something of release even if for only one day a week. In fact, Israel must remember (*zākar* this time, rather than *šāmar*, v. 12) their slave days and how the Lord graciously and powerfully delivered them out of

---

[42] As Eichrodt puts it, "The man who belongs to God must possess a particular kind of nature, which by comprising at once outward and inward, ritual and moral purity will correspond to the nature of the holy God" (*Theology of the Old Testament,* 1:137).

[43] *IBHS* § 24.2e.

[44] See R. Sonsino, *Motive Clauses in Hebrew Law,* SBLDS 45 (Chico, Cal.: Scholars, 1980), 86-87, 104, 200-201.

slavery, for this was the underlying reason for Sabbath observance.[45] This stands in contrast to the motive clause in Exodus: "For in six days the LORD made the heavens and the earth, the sea, and all that is in them, but he rested on the seventh day. Therefore the LORD blessed the Sabbath day and made it holy" (Exod 20:11).

The principal theological truth to be seen here is the changing theological emphases of the unchanging God. For a people freshly delivered from Egyptian overlordship by the mighty exodus miracle, God as Creator is a central truth. Therefore it is most appropriate that the Sabbath focus on him as Creator and the cessation of that creative work, the very point of the Exodus commandment. From the perspective of the Deuteronomy legislation, some forty years later, creation pales into insignificance in comparison to the act of redemption itself. With the benefit now of historical retrospection and with the anticipation of the crossing of another watery barrier—the Jordan—and the uncertainties of conquest, Israel was to recall its plight as slaves and its glorious release from that hopeless situation. Sabbath now speaks of redemption and not creation, of rest and not cessation.[46]

All this gives theological justification for the observance by the Christian of Sunday rather than Saturday as the day set apart as holy. For the Christian the moment of greatest significance is no longer creation or the exodus—as important as these are in salvation history. Central to his faith and experience is the resurrection of the Lord Jesus Christ, a re-creating and redemptive event that eclipses all of God's mighty acts of the past. Thus by example if not by explicit command Jesus and the apostles mandated the observance of the first day of the week as commemorative of his triumphant victory over death.[47]

(2) The Commandments Pertaining to Humankind's Relationship to Others (5:16-21)

16"Honor your father and your mother, as the LORD your God has commanded you, so that you may live long and that it may go well with you in the land the LORD your God is giving you.

17"You shall not murder.

18"You shall not commit adultery.

---

[45] Cairns, *Word and Presence,* 75.

[46] There are, of course, overtones of creation in redemption. As Craigie points out, "The Exodus from Egypt marks in effect the creation of God's people as a nation" (*Deuteronomy,* 157). There is thus a mixture of motives inherent in v. 15.

[47] G. Vos, *Biblical Theology,* 157-58.

¹⁹"You shall not steal.

²⁰"You shall not give false testimony against your neighbor.

²¹"You shall not covet your neighbor's wife. You shall not set your desire on your neighbor's house or land, his manservant or maidservant, his ox or donkey, or anything that belongs to your neighbor."

In the hierarchy of human relationships, that between children and their parents ranks beneath only that of their relationship to God. This was particularly evident in the patriarchal family structures that recognized the headship of the father and even the mother in all areas of life and even beyond the immediate family.⁴⁸ This was not merely a reflection of conventional cultural mores, for the Old Testament makes clear, in Israel's case at least, that there were profoundly theological ideals involved. These will become identified in the forthcoming exposition of the specific stipulation section. For now the very fact that the next commandment after the four that speak to the matter of the human-divine relationship should address exclusively the role and rights of parents is in itself highly significant.

5:16 Like the one before it (vv. 12-15) this commandment commences with a positive injunction but this time with the simple imperative "honor" (*kabbēd*). Honor, however, is not something that can be commanded if it remains only an attitude or disposition. Therefore, and very much in line with the underlying root meaning of the verb, to honor demands action that betokens the inner spirit. Essentially *kabbēd* (the *piel* imperative of *kābēd*) carries the nuance of weighing down with honor or respect. In the particular stem used here the idea is declaring to someone or effectively conveying to something the quality of honor.⁴⁹ The command to honor therefore is a command to demonstrate in tangible, empirical ways the respect people must have for their parents.

Again note that the version of the commandment here, as opposed to that of Exod 20:12, contains the words "as the LORD your God has commanded you" (cf. v. 12). This is an unmistakable reference to the initial disclosure of the covenant at Sinai, and no doubt the warning was added because of some infraction of the statute in the interim.⁵⁰ Compliance with this mandate, on the other hand, would have two positive results: long life and prosperity in the land they were about to enter. Both of these boons

---

⁴⁸ R. de Vaux, *Ancient Israel: Social Institutions* (New York: McGraw-Hill, 1965), 19-23.

⁴⁹ Waltke and O'Connor (*IBHS* § 24.2g) speak of כבד in the *piel* as having an "estimative" nuance; i.e., "to regard as heavy." Cf. Weinfeld, *Deuteronomy 1–11*, 309-10.

⁵⁰ The added clause is also indicative of the hortatory or sermonic style of Deuteronomy as compared to Exodus (so Craigie, *The Book of Deuteronomy*, 158, n. 21).

were standard promises to those who kept covenant faith with the Lord (cf. Lev 26:3-13; Deut 7:12-16; 28:1-14).

5:17   Though there is no technical term in Hebrew for premeditated homicide, the translation of the verb *rāṣâ* as "murder" in the NIV rendition of the sixth commandment (v. 17) is most accurate. Usage elsewhere as well as overall theological context makes a clear distinction between the prohibition here and the endorsement otherwise of capital punishment, killing in warfare, the application of *ḥērem,* and the like.[51] Because life is sacred in God's eyes (hence, blood must not be spilled on the ground carelessly or eaten [Lev 17:10-16]), and that of humankind especially in that they are the image of God, the violation of a person to the point of death is an affront to the sovereignty of God, an assault upon his earthly representative (cf. Gen 9:6).[52]

5:18   If murder is a violation of life itself, adultery is a violation of its most important and sacred human relationship, that of marriage.[53] The seventh commandment deals with this matter rather specifically in that it addresses adultery and not sexual impropriety in general as the precise verb *nā'ap* makes clear.[54] Elsewhere such matters as fornication (Num 25:1), prostitution (Deut 22:21), and homosexuality (Judg 19:22; Lev 18:22; Deut 23:17-18) receive attention and are soundly condemned. Adultery, however, implies unfaithfulness, covenant breaking, and so is an apt analogue to covenant infidelity on a higher plane—the divine-human. Later revelation speaks of "going whoring" after other gods, that is, abandoning the redeeming sovereign in favor of another who has no covenant claim or legitimacy (cf. Hos 4:1-19; Jer 3:9-13).

---

[51] For a good treatment of the several words for killing and their ethical implications see W. C. Kaiser, Jr., *Toward Old Testament Ethics* (Grand Rapids: Zondervan, 1983), 90-92.

[52] G. Von Rad puts the matter well: "The establishment of the divine sovereign right over human life is expressed apodictically and unconditionally . . . not for man's sake because of some law of humanity, or 'reverence for life,' but because man is God's possession and was created in God's image" (*Genesis: A Commentary*, OTL [London: SCM, 1961], 128).

[53] Cf. R. Westbrook, "Adultery in Ancient Near Eastern Law," *RB* 97 (1990): 542-80; A. Phillips, "Another Look at Adultery," *JSOT* 20 (1981): 3-25; S. E. Loewenstamm, "The Laws of Adultery and Murder in Biblical and Mesopotamian Law," in *Comparative Studies in Biblical and Ancient Oriental Literatures,* AOAT 204 (Neukirchen-Vluyn: Neukirchener, 1980), 146-53. So egregious is adultery that in both the OT (Gen 20:9; cf. Exod 32:21,30-31; 2 Kgs 17:21) and the ancient Near East it is called "the great sin." See W. L Moran, "The Scandal of the 'Great Sin' at Ugarit," *JNES* 18 (1959): 280-81; J. J. Rabinowitz, "The 'Great Sin' in Ancient Egyptian Marriage Contracts," *JNES* 18 (1959): 73.

[54] The usual term for sexual impropriety is the root זנה, one almost always limited to female activity. Male adultery is normally described by a form of נאף. See S. Erlandsson, "זָנָה *zānāh,*" etc. *TDOT* 4:99-104; cf. F. I. Andersen and D. N. Freedman, *Hosea,* AB 24 (Garden City: Doubleday, 1980), 160-63.

5:19   The descending hierarchical order of relationships continues in the next commandment, the prohibition of theft.[55] Just as adultery is the violation of one's family, so theft is the violation of one's property. The sixth commandment, then, speaks of the theft of life, the seventh the theft of the purity and sanctity of the marriage relationship, and the eighth the theft of goods and possessions. There obviously is an inherent evil in the illegitimate appropriation of another's property, but on an even higher covenantal and theological level theft betrays an essential dissatisfaction with one's lot in life and an acquisitive desire to obtain more than the Lord, the Sovereign who dispenses to his vassals what seems best, has granted already.

5:20   The ninth commandment forbids false testimony against another. Such testimony is tantamount to character assassination and so is another form of killing or theft. The progression from murder to adultery to theft to perjury is thus clearly one of decreasing violence on the one hand and yet of a common infraction of the integrity of another human being on the other hand.[56] The verb describing false testimony (ʿānâ) is one at home in the law court with its nuance of reciprocal dialogue. The version of the commandment in Exodus describes the "testimony" or witness (ʿēd) as "false" (šeqer), that is, untrue. Here "false" translates šawʾ, meaning more precisely "empty" or "without substance." The same word describes the misuse of the divine name in v. 11. There is no basic difference, of course, for if one is accused on no valid or substantial grounds, he is accused falsely.[57] And the prohibition is not limited to slander of a fellow Israelite, for the word for "neighbor" (rēaʿ) can refer to an Israelite (Lev 19:18), an alien (that is, a gēr, Lev 19:34), or even a pagan (Exod 11:2).[58]

5:21   As has been noted repeatedly by scholars, the tenth commandment differs greatly from the other nine in that it has to do with an inner disposition more than with an outward act. That is, it has to do with the

---

[55] Though the verb here (גָּנַב) can mean "to kidnap" (cf. Exod 21:16; Deut 24:7), that is not its primary meaning even though in the context here (murder and adultery followed by lying, v. 20) that might be implied. What is often overlooked is that property in the OT is more than mere objects—it is a vital part of whoever owns it. See V. Hamp, "גנב gānabh," *TDOT* 3:39-45; R. K. Gnuse, *You Shall Not Steal: Community and Property in the Biblical Tradition* (New York: Orbis, 1985); H. Klein, "Verbot des Menschendiebstahls im Dekalog?" *VT* 26 (1976): 161-69.

[56] For similar ways of looking at the arrangement of the laws see Keil and Delitzsch, *The Pentateuch*, vol. II, 123; von Rad, *Deuteronomy*, 59; G. F. Oehler, *Theology of the Old Testament*, rev. G. E. Day (1883; reprint, Grand Rapids: Zondervan, n.d.), 188-89.

[57] Durham, *Exodus*, 296.

[58] Weinfeld broadens the term to mean anyone else but here in context an adversary (*Deuteronomy 1–11*, 316; cf. 1 Sam 15:28; 2 Sam 12:11).

desires and not the practical steps to satisfy those desires.[59] What is less frequently observed is that this is in line with the progression of violence or disruption in a descending spiral from the shedding of blood to the ruin of personal reputation. What has been manifest empirically in acts and words is now hidden in thoughts and cravings. Also of interest is the fact that this last commandment appears to be a summary of at least the previous three. To covet another's wife is tantamount to adultery, to covet another's properties is akin to theft, and to covet anything else would certainly cover such matters as a person's good standing in the community.

The verb "covet" (as in NIV), translated as such from Hebrew *ḥāmad,* is used consistently throughout the Exodus version of the commandment (Exod 20:17). But here the second verb, translated "set your desire," reflects a different Hebrew word, *ʾāwâ.* It is doubtful that any major distinction in thought exists, for each verb means "desire" whether or not of a lustful, sensual type. Very likely Deuteronomy uses *ʾāwâ* as a synonym for *ḥāmad* only for the sake of literary variety.[60]

Other differences also exist between the two accounts. Deuteronomy lists the coveted objects as wife, house, land, manservant, maidservant, ox, donkey, or anything else, whereas Exodus indicates them to be house, wife, manservant, maidservant, ox, donkey, or anything else. Thus in Deuteronomy house and wife are reversed and land is added. Again, rather than reflecting differing legal or literary traditions, as some critics maintain, the differences more likely lie in a theological development in which women's rights come increasingly into the foreground in view of the social situa-

---

[59] It was noted on p. 146 (n. 20) that some traditions divide the tenth commandment into two, (1) coveting another's house and (2) coveting his wife and his other properties. This was done apparently to allow the first two commandments to be combined into one without textual, exegetical, or even unanimous ancient traditional basis. See Keil and Delitzsch (*The Pentateuch,* II:108-13, 125) for the various views, especially the evidence that the commandment on coveting has always been regarded as one by Jewish tradition notwithstanding the accentuation and *parashoth* division of some manuscripts. Cf. C. H. Gordon, "A Note on the Tenth Commandment," *JBR* 31 (1963): 208-9; W. L. Moran, "The Conclusion of the Decalogue (Ex. 20:17 = Dt. 5:21)," *CBQ* 29 (1967): 543-54; A. Rofé, "The Tenth Commandment in the Light of Four Deuteronomic Laws," in *The Ten Commandments in History and Tradition,* 45-65.

[60] As G. Wallis ("חָמַד *chāmadh,*" etc., *TDOT* 4:453) points out, חָמַד is closely related to אָוָה and often occurs in parallel to it (Gen 3:6; Prov 6:25; Ps 68:17). G. Mayer goes so far as to suggest that they are synonymous ("אָוָה *ʾāvāh,*" etc., *TDOT* 1:135). The meaning here is likely somewhere between חָמַד, as thought necessarily leading to action (as in Josh 7:21; Mic 2:2), and אָוָה, as a casual kind of desire. Both terms speak of a longing, a "first step, liable to lead to the second—adultery, theft, and possibly even murder." Thus Cassuto, *Exodus,* 249.

tions envisioned by Moses on the eve of the conquest and occupation of Canaan.[61]

The remarkable thing about this tenth and final statute is that it raises the issue of sin and disobedience from the level of mere act to that of attitude, thought, and desire. Though coveting no doubt frequently finds expression in deed, it need not. But that does not lessen its sinfulness. It is at this very point that the Old Testament understanding of sin and culpability most approximates the teaching of Jesus himself. He said, with reference to adultery, "You have heard that it was said 'Do not commit adultery.' But I tell you that anyone who looks at a woman lustfully has already committed adultery with her in his heart" (Matt 5:27-28).[62] In this manner our Lord emphasizes that coveting, though last on the list of commandments, may after all encapsulate them all. At the same time that it is the least overtly violent and injurious, it is the commandment most at the root of covenant disobedience in that it logically precedes the rest.

3. The Narrative Relating the Sinai Revelation and Israel's Response (5:22-33)

We have noted repeatedly that one of the features that marks Deuteronomy off from standard covenant texts attested to from the ancient Near East is the regular interruption of technical covenant material by that of other genres such as narrative and parenesis.[63] This usually occurs at the end of clearly self-contained units (such as the Decalogue, just discussed) and consists either of a reflection on what has just been stated or an anticipation of or introduction to something about to be disclosed. The present passage does both, but primarily it is another of the several examples of a brief historical résumé.

(1) The Rehearsal of the Theophany (5:22-27)

22These are the commandments the LORD proclaimed in a loud voice to your whole assembly there on the mountain from out of the fire, the cloud and the deep darkness; and he added nothing more. Then he wrote them on two stone tablets and gave them to me.

---

[61] Ridderbos, *Deuteronomy,* 108-9.

[62] D. A. Carson has noted the subtle transition Jesus made from the seventh to the tenth commandment: "In effect, by labeling lust adultery, Jesus has deepened the seventh commandment in terms of the tenth, the prohibition of covetousness" (D. A. Carson, *The Sermon on the Mount* [Grand Rapids: Baker, 1978], 43-44).

[63] Tiffany, "Parenesis and Deuteronomy 5–11 (Deut 4:45; 5:2–11:29)."

[23]When you heard the voice out of the darkness, while the mountain was ablaze with fire, all the leading men of your tribes and your elders came to me. [24]And you said, "The LORD our God has shown us his glory and his majesty, and we have heard his voice from the fire. Today we have seen that a man can live even if God speaks with him. [25]But now, why should we die? This great fire will consume us, and we will die if we hear the voice of the LORD our God any longer. [26]For what mortal man has ever heard the voice of the living God speaking out of fire, as we have, and survived? [27]Go near and listen to all that the LORD our God says. Then tell us whatever the LORD our God tells you. We will listen and obey."

5:22 In order to reinforce the idea that he was simply repeating (even though not exactly) the covenant text of the Sinai revelation, Moses harked back to that time and place once more. So that there was no misunderstanding, he referred to the commandments just given as the "words" (v. 22), the same term used in Exod 20:1 and 24:3. He further defined them as having come in a loud voice from the mountain and out of fire, cloud, and darkness (v. 22; cf. Exod 19:16-19; 24:16-18; Deut 4:11-14,33,36; 5:2-5). Finally, all that is in view here is the Decalogue itself, for the Lord "added nothing more" than what was contained on the two tablets.[64] This at once identifies with precision the corpus that Moses had just reviewed and also suggests that what was on the stones, namely, the Ten Commandments, was a self-contained section of unusual importance to the larger covenant text.

5:23-27 The narrative continues to rehearse the first giving of the law, drawing attention to its immediate aftermath when Moses came down from the mountain to present the tablets and to assuage the fears of the terror-stricken assembly that had witnessed the glorious theophany from afar (cf. Exod 20:18-21).[65] Though the Deuteronomy version is much more expansive than that of Exodus, the same scene is in mind as the reference to the fear of death in both places makes clear. The people had observed that it was possible for a human being (Moses) to have audience with the glorious and powerful God and still live (v. 24; cf. Exod 20:19). But they were not sure that that privilege extended to all people, so they urged Moses to assume his mediatorial responsibility on their behalf (v. 27). In fact, history could record no other instance where a human being (lit., "any flesh") had heard the voice of God in such circumstances and had lived to tell of it

---

[64] Weinfeld, *Deuteronomy 1–11*, 323.
[65] The two passages (Exod 20:18-21; Deut 5:25-27) are explicitly linked by Driver, *Deuteronomy*, 87.

(v. 26). The encounter between the Lord and Moses was thus unique (v. 24b; cf. 4:33).[66]

(2) The Preparations for the Covenant Stipulations (5:28-33)

[28]**The LORD heard you when you spoke to me and the LORD said to me, "I have heard what this people said to you. Everything they said was good. [29]Oh, that their hearts would be inclined to fear me and keep all my commands always, so that it might go well with them and their children forever!**

[30]**"Go, tell them to return to their tents. [31]But you stay here with me so that I may give you all the commands, decrees and laws you are to teach them to follow in the land I am giving them to possess."**

[32]**So be careful to do what the LORD your God has commanded you; do not turn aside to the right or to the left. [33]Walk in all the way that the LORD your God has commanded you, so that you may live and prosper and prolong your days in the land that you will possess.**

Though the Decalogue was the foundation and heart of the covenant document, it was by no means all there was to it, for the Book of the Covenant contained, in addition, a set of specific stipulations (cf. Exod 20:22–23:33). This is analogous to the structure of Deuteronomy, though Deuteronomy contains two kinds of additional stipulations, the general and the specific, whereas Exodus makes no such distinction.

5:28 In order to prepare for the reception of the stipulations, Moses recounted how he had appealed to the former generation of Israelites at Sinai with the same objective. He reminded his hearers that the Lord had been pleased with their spirit of reverence and humility, a point made explicit in Exodus, which states that the Lord's overwhelming appearance had been manifest in order "to test you" (Exod 20:20). Having passed the test of compliance and thus having qualified themselves to receive even more revelation, the people waited for Moses to return to the Lord to receive the fullness of the covenant (Exod 20:21).

5:29-31 What the test had revealed was a fear of God and a determination to keep all his commandments (*miṣwôt,* generic for law as a whole), something the Lord wished might be true of them and their descendants forever. The very wish, however, implies a lack of confidence in its fulfillment. Nevertheless, the people were dismissed to their tents while Moses made his way up the mountain again, this time to obtain the "commands,

---

[66] It is true the people had "heard the voice" and had seen God's glory and majesty, but the Exodus version makes it plain that it was from a distance (Exod 20:18) and that God did not actually come to speak but to test (v. 20). Only Moses could enter into intimate dialogue with Yahweh. Cf. Childs, *Exodus,* 371-73.

decrees and laws" (v. 31). This collocation of technical terms (*miṣwâ, ḥuq-qîm,* and *mišpāṭîm,* respectively) is the standard way of referring to the stipulations of the covenant as opposed to the Ten Commandments or the law as a whole (cf. Deut 4:1-8).[67] A further linkage between that initial giving of the stipulations and the repetition in Deuteronomy is evident in their having been given in preparation for life in the land of promise (v. 31b).

5:32-33 As the grammar and syntax make clear, the narrative ends here and the exhortation begins.[68] That narrative had consisted of a summary of events at Sinai culminating with the connection between the covenant stipulations and life in the land. The exhortation ends the same way but stresses that the quality of life they anticipated was possible only as the people obeyed the terms of the covenant (v. 33). Blessing is never automatic but is always conditioned upon compliance with the will of God.

That compliance is described here under the metaphor of journeying. To obey the Lord is to keep to the pathway, to walk in such a way as to avoid drifting to either the right or the left (vv. 32-33). Such imagery is very common in Old Testament wisdom literature as a description of the lifestyle of the godly (cf. Prov 4:27; 8:20; 9:6).[69] In a most effective manner Moses formed a bridge between the revelation of the covenant stipulations to the preceding generation and a call now to the present generation to hear and obey them.

4. The Nature of the Principles (6:1-25)

Before the principles, that is, the general stipulations, of the covenant are spelled out, Moses devotes a great deal of attention to describing their nature and how they are to be applied and transmitted. Thus once more the strictly "legal" or technical parts of the document are set within a hortatory framework as part of a major Mosaic address.

(1) Exhortation to Keep Them (6:1-3)

¹These are the commands, decrees and laws the Lᴏʀᴅ your God directed me to teach you to observe in the land that you are crossing the Jordan to possess, ²so that you, your children and their children after them may fear the Lᴏʀᴅ your God as long as you live by keeping all his decrees and commands

---

[67] Weinfeld, *Deuteronomy 1–11,* 326.

[68] The historical résumé of vv. 22-31 provides the backdrop against which the perfect, שְׁמַרְתֶּם, takes on its imperatival force, "be careful." See Craigie, *Deuteronomy,* 166.

[69] F. J. Helfmeyer, "הָלַךְ, halakh," *TDOT* 3:396-97.

that I give you, and so that you may enjoy long life. ³Hear, O Israel, and be careful to obey so that it may go well with you and that you may increase greatly in a land flowing with milk and honey, just as the LORD, the God of your fathers, promised you.

6:1 The formula "commands, decrees and laws" as an expression of the covenant document as a whole appears here as a response to the command already given by the Lord to Moses that he should teach it to the nation (5:31).[70] In line with such "command-response" formulae elsewhere, one can observe the similarity of language between 5:31 and 6:1, especially in the connection in both places between the technical terms of the covenant and the need to observe it in the land they were about to enter as an inheritance.

6:2-3 The similarity extends beyond this initial comparison, though the precise wording of 5:32-33 differs from that of 6:2-3. Thus the exhortation not to turn to the right or to the left (5:32) becomes an injunction to fear the Lord, a fear that results in obedience to the decrees and commands for generations to come (6:2).[71] The command to walk in the ways of the Lord (5:33) is also restated, this time in the appeal to hear and obey (6:3). In both cases it is with the end in view that God's people might live (5:33) and do so with success, prosperity, and for many years. This would be in a land flowing with milk and honey as God had promised the patriarchal ancestors (6:3b) and had reaffirmed to Moses on the occasion of his call to liberate his people (Exod 3:8,17).

The phrase "milk and honey" is a hyperbolic way of describing the richness of the land of promise.[72] These two commodities, the one the product of human labor, or agriculture, and the other the product of nature, represent the fullness of blessing associated with the fulfillment of God's promises. Though obviously not to be taken literally, the description of Canaan's bounty and fertility is much in line with the reality of the situa-

---

[70] Weinfeld links 6:1-3 to 5:22-33, labeling the whole "Epilogue to the Decalogue" (*Deuteronomy 1–11*, 319). For different reasons Christensen does the same but as a subsection of 4:44–6:3 according to prosodic analysis (*Deuteronomy 1–11*, 132). He describes 5:23[not 22]–6:3 as "Conclusion of the Matter," linking it with the opening frame "Introduction: 'This Is the Torah'" (4:44-49; p. 101). While both Weinfeld and Christensen can make a case for a formal connection between 5:22-33 and 6:1-3, it is obvious that the former passage has a retrospective orientation and the latter a prospective one. Having described Israel's encounter with Yahweh at Sinai, Moses now urged his people to obedience to the covenant being renewed with them in the present generation. See Craigie, *Deuteronomy,* 167-68.

[71] V. H. Kooy, "The Fear and Love of God in Deuteronomy," in *Grace upon Grace,* ed. J. I. Cook (Grand Rapids: Eerdmans, 1975), 106-16; H. F. Fuhs, "יָרֵא yārēʾ," etc., *TDOT* 6:306-8.

[72] S. D. Waterhouse, "A Land Flowing with Milk and Honey," *AUSS* 1 (1963): 152-66.

tion in that day and time, especially in comparison to the deprivations of
the desert and even of Egypt, a land whose fields had to be irrigated by foot
(Deut 11:10; cf. Num 13:23,27; Deut 8:7-10; 11:9,11-12,14).

(2) The Essence of the Principles (6:4-5)

**⁴Hear, O Israel: The LORD our God, the LORD is one. ⁵Love the LORD your
God with all your heart and with all your soul and with all your strength.**

6:4-5 The Decalogue (or Ten Commandments) of Deut 5:6-21 (=
Exod 20:2-17) embodies the great principles of covenant relationship that
outline the nature and character of God and spell out Israel's responsibilities to him. It is thus an encapsulation or distillation of the entire corpus of
covenant text. The passage at hand is a further refinement of that great
relational truth, an adumbration of an adumbration, as it were.[73] It is the
expression of the essence of all of God's person and purposes in sixteen
words of Hebrew text. Known to Jewish tradition as the Shema (after the
first word of v. 4, the imperative of the verb *šāmaʿ*, "to hear"), this statement, like the Decalogue, is prefaced by its description as "commands,
decrees, and laws" (or the like) and by injunctions to obey them (6:1-3; cf.
4:44–5:5).[74]

The sentence itself commences with the imperative of *šāmaʿ* in the second person singular form. "To hear," in Hebrew lexicography, is tantamount to "to obey," especially in covenant contexts such as this. That is, to
hear God without putting into effect the command is not to hear him at all.
The singular form of the verb emphasizes the corporate or collective nature
of the addressee, that is, Israel. The covenant was made with the nation as
a whole and so the nation must as a unified community give heed to the
command of the Lord.

The plurality of the people is also noted here, however, in that it is
"Yahweh *our* God" who is the subject of the following clause. Despite a
variety of ways of viewing that clause ("Yahweh our God is one Yahweh,"
"Yahweh our God, Yahweh is one," and the like), the structure of the line,
almost poetic, favors the rendering "Yahweh (is) our God, Yahweh is one."

---

[73] Thus already Keil and Delitzsch, *The Pentateuch,* vol. III, 322.

[74] Cf. P. A. H. de Boer, "Some Observations on Deuteronomy 6:4,5," in *Von Kanaan bis
Kerala,* ed. W. Delsman et al., AOAT 211 (Kevelaer: Butzon & Bercker, 1982), 45-52; R.
Hammer, "A Legend Concerning the Origins of the Shema," *Judaism* 32 (1983): 51-55; P. F.
Hoeffken, "Eine Bemerkung zum religionsgeschichtlichen Hintergrund von Dtn 6:4," *BZ* 28
(1984): 88-93; J. G. Janzen, "On the Most Important Word in the Shema (Deut 6:4-5)," *VT* 37
(1987): 280-300; S. D. McBride, "The Yoke of the Kingdom: An Exposition of Deuteronomy
6:4-5," *Int* 27 (1973): 273-306.

That is, the Divine Name should be construed as a nominative in each case and the terms "our God" and "one" as parallel predicate nominatives. However, as the following discussion points out, there is sufficient ambiguity as to allow the idea of God's oneness as well as his uniqueness.

Postbiblical rabbinic exegesis understood the role of the Shema to be the heart of all the law. When Jesus was asked about the greatest of the commandments, he cited this (and its companion in Lev 19:18) as the fundamental tenet of Jewish faith, an opinion with which his hearers obviously concurred (Matt 22:34-39; Mark 12:28-31; Luke 10:25-28).[75] So much so did the centrality of this confession find root in the Jewish consciousness that to this very day the observant Jew will recite the Shema at least twice daily.[76]

It is possible to understand v. 4 in several ways, but the two most common renderings of the last clause are: (1) "The LORD our God, the LORD is one" (so NIV) or (2) "The LORD our God is one LORD." The former stresses the uniqueness or exclusivity of Yahweh as Israel's God and so may be paraphrased, "Yahweh our God is the one and only Yahweh" or the like. This takes the noun ʾeḥād ("one") in the sense of "unique" or "solitary," a meaning that is certainly well attested.[77] The latter translation focuses on the unity or wholeness of the Lord. This is not in opposition to the later Christian doctrine of the Trinity but rather functions here as a witness to the self-consistency of the Lord, who is not ambivalent and who has a single purpose or objective for creation and history.[78] The ideas clearly overlap to provide an unmistakable basis for monotheistic faith. The Lord is indeed a unity, but beyond that he is the only God. For this reason the exhortation of v. 5 has practical significance.

The confession of the Lord's unique oneness leads to the demand that Israel recognize him as such by obedience to all that that implies. In language appropriate to covenant, that obedience is construed as love; that is, to obey is to love God with every aspect and element of one's being.[79] This

---

[75] M. Wyschogrod, "The 'Shema Israel' in Judaism and the New Testament," in *The Roots of Our Common Faith* (Geneva: World Council of Churches, 1984), 23-32.

[76] I. Epstein, *Judaism* (Baltimore: Penguin, 1959), 162-63.

[77] N. Lohfink and J. Bergman, "אֶחָד ʾechādh," *TDOT* 1:200; see also H. Ben-Shammai, "Qirqisani on the Oneness of God," *JQR* 73 (1982): 105-11; R. W. L. Moberly, "'Yahweh Is One': The Translation of the Shema," in *Studies in the Pentateuch* VTSup 41 (Leiden: Brill, 1990), 209-15; M. Peter, "Dtn 6:4–ein Monotheistischer Text?" *BZ* 24 (1980): 252-62.

[78] E. H. Merrill, "Is the Doctrine of the Trinity Implied in the Genesis Creation Account?" in *The Genesis Debate,* ed. R. Youngblood (Nashville: Thomas Nelson, 1986), 123-24, 127-28.

[79] W. L. Moran, "The Ancient Near Eastern Background of the Love of God in Deuteronomy," 77-87.

equation has already been made clear in the Decalogue itself, where the Lord said, in reference to the second commandment, that he displays covenant faithfulness (*ḥesed*) to the thousands who love him and keep his commandments (Deut 5:10). In covenant terms, then, love is not so much emotive or sensual in its connotation (though it is not excluded in those respects), but it is of the nature of obligation, of legal demand. Thus because of who and what he is in regard to his people whom he elected and redeemed, the Lord rightly demands of them unqualified obedience.

The depth and breadth of that expectation is elaborated upon by the fact that it encompasses the heart, soul, and strength of God's people, here viewed collectively as a covenant partner. The heart (*lēb*) is, in Old Testament anthropology, the seat of the intellect, equivalent to the mind or rational part of humankind.[80] The "soul" (better, "being" or "essential person" in line with commonly accepted understanding of Heb. *nepeš*) refers to the invisible part of the individual, the person qua person including the will and sensibilities.[81] The strength (*mĕʾōd*) is, of course, the physical side with all its functions and capacities. The word occurs only here and in 2 Kgs 23:25 as a noun with nonadverbial nuance, and even here the notion is basically that of "muchness." That is, Israel must love God with all its essence and expression.

Jesus said that this was "the first and greatest commandment" (Matt 22:38), an observation that is profoundly correct in at least two respects. First it qualifies as such inasmuch as it constitutes the essence of the Deuteronomic covenant principle and requirement. As stated before, the Shema is to the Decalogue what the Decalogue is to the full corpus of covenant stipulations. But it also is first and greatest because it is a commentary on the very first of the Ten Commandments—"You shall have no other gods before me" (Deut 5:7).[82] This affirmation of the uniqueness and exclusiveness of Yahweh as Israel's Sovereign and Savior finds full endorsement and explication in the Shema, for to recognize Yahweh's unity and solitariness and to respond to that confession with total obedience is the strongest possible way of demonstrating adherence to the first commandment.

Jesus' use of the Shema is attested in all three Synoptic Gospels (Matt 22:37-38; Mark 12:29-30; Luke 10:27). Matthew and Mark placed it immediately after the denial by the Sadducees of a resurrection whereas Luke recorded it as a response to the lawyer's question, "What shall I do to

---

[80] H. W. Wolff, *Anthropology of the Old Testament* (Philadelphia: Fortress, 1974), 46-51.
[81] Ibid., 17, 21-22, 53.
[82] Craigie, *Deuteronomy,* 169-70.

inherit eternal life?" In fact, in Luke's account it is the lawyer who quotes the second half of the Shema (Deut 6:5) in answer to Jesus' follow-up question to him, "What is written in the law?"

What seems clear here is that the Shema was cited on two different occasions, once by Jesus in his reply to the Pharisee lawyer concerning the greatest commandment and once by the seeker who desired to know the way of life.[83] Doubtless these instances are not exhaustive of all the citations of the Shema in Jesus' public ministry; indeed, they may reflect a widespread recognition of its centrality in Jewish religious thought. It is striking, to say the least, that the "great commandment" (so Matthew) or the "first of all" (so Mark) is the very one which, if followed, leads to life (so Luke 10:28). All this must be understood against the background of the Shema in Deuteronomy, where, as noted already, it serves as the essence of the Decalogue and, indeed, of all the law. It is first and most important precisely because it encapsulates all of God's saving intentions and provisions. To love God as it commands is to place oneself within the orbit of his saving grace because the Shema, the heart and core of the Old Testament law, was designed, as Paul said, to be "put in charge to lead us to Christ that we might be justified by faith" (Gal 3:24).

It is not possible here to engage in a full discussion of the textual variants among the Synoptic renditions of the Shema,[84] but it is worth noting that only Mark cites Deut 6:4 ("Hear, Israel, the LORD our God is one LORD") and only Mark uses the Greek preposition *ek* ("with"), as does the Septuagint, in rendering "with all your heart," etc. Matthew and Luke employ *en,* clearly reflecting the Hebrew preposition *b* (*bêt*). On the other hand, Matthew alone limits the list of psychophysical terms to "heart," "soul," and "mind" (Gr. *dianoia,* almost always the translation of Heb. *lēb,* "heart," in the LXX). Matthew appears to distinguish between "heart" and "mind" by viewing "heart" (Gr. *kardia*) as synonymous with love or affection.[85] This is likely the way Mark and Luke take "heart" as well. They both, however, add to the list "strength" (Gr. *ischus*), a translation of Hebrew *mĕʾōd.* The Septuagint also translates the Hebrew noun as "strength" but by a different Greek noun (*dynamis*). A comparison of the order (heart, soul, mind in Matthew; heart, soul, mind, strength in Mark; heart, soul, strength, mind in Luke; heart, soul, strength in the MT; and

---

[83] For evidence pro and con see I. H. Marshall, *The Gospel of Luke* (Grand Rapids: Eerdmans, 1978), 440-41.

[84] For detailed discussion see W. Dittmar, *Vetus Testamentum in Novo. Die alttestamentlichen Parallelen des Neuen Testaments* (Göttingen: Vandenhoeck & Ruprecht, 1903), 50-51.

[85] BAGD, 404.

mind, soul, strength in the LXX) among the various lists suggests that Mark and Luke add "mind" to the MT/LXX formula whereas Matthew substitutes "mind" for "strength."

Again it is impossible here to enter the debate about Synoptic traditions,[86] but several observations may be made about the New Testament use of this Old Testament text and the implications for theology.[87] First, it is clear that citation is not necessarily synonymous with quotation. Second, the variety of ways in which New Testament authors cited the same Old Testament texts reveals that their concern was not with the letter of the cited passage but with its intent, its fundamental message. Third, in this case, at least, nothing was subtracted from the meaning of the Old Testament passage by the Gospel writers. In fact, Mark and Luke fleshed out the original text by dividing the Hebrew term *lēb* into its proper semantic categories of emotion (or feeling) and mind (the intellect). As for Matthew's use of "mind" for original "strength" or "might," it is possible, with many scholars, to understand mind as both the formulator and expeditor of action, that is, thought at work.[88] In any event, all three citations of the Shema agree in demanding that one love God with all his being if he is to claim to be obedient to the first and great commandment.

(3) Exhortation to Teach Them (6:6-9)

⁶These commandments that I give you today are to be upon your hearts. ⁷Impress them on your children. Talk about them when you sit at home and when you walk along the road, when you lie down and when you get up. ⁸Tie them as symbols on your hands and bind them on your foreheads. ⁹Write them on the doorframes of your houses and on your gates.

As noted already (4:9-10; 6:2), an important demand of the covenant relationship was that it be perpetuated beyond the immediate generation of those with whom the Lord made it, for its promises and provisions were for generations yet unborn (4:25,40; 5:9-10,29). In practical terms this necessitated a regular routine of instruction. Father must educate son and

---

[86] Cf. Marshall, *Gospel of Luke,* 443.

[87] For the principles of interpretation involved in the NT use of the OT in general, cf. O. P. Robertson, "Hermeneutics of Continuity," and P. D. Feinberg, "Hermeneutics of Discontinuity," both in *Continuity and Discontinuity: Perspectives on the Relationship between the Old and New Testaments,* ed. J. S. Feinberg (Westchester, Ill.: Crossway, 1988), 89-108 and 109-128,respectively.

[88] Cf. R. H. Gundry, *The Use of the Old Testament in St. Matthew's Gospel* (Leiden: Brill, 1967), 22-23.

son the grandson so that the fact and features of the covenant might never be forgotten.

6:6 The whole is here described as "these commandments" (lit., "these words"), a term that encompasses the full corpus of the covenant text as communicated by Moses but which is encapsulated especially in the Shema of vv. 4-5. This is evident in the instruction to "tie them as symbols on your hands and bind them on your foreheads" (v. 8) as well as to "write them on the doorframes of your houses and on your gates" (v. 9). In the larger sense they are to be committed to memory as the idiom "upon your hearts" (v. 6) makes clear. In the psychology of the Old Testament the heart is not the center of emotional life and response but the seat of the intellect or rational side of humankind. To "be upon the heart" is to be in one's constant, conscious reflection.[89]

6:7 So much so is this the case that the covenant recipient must impress the words of covenant faith into the thinking of his children by inscribing them there with indelible sharpness and precision (thus the *piel* of *šānan*).[90] The image is that of the engraver of a monument who takes hammer and chisel in hand and with painstaking care etches a text into the face of a solid slab of granite. The sheer labor of such a task is daunting indeed, but once done the message is there to stay. Thus it is that the generations of Israelites to come must receive and transmit the words of the Lord's everlasting covenant revelation.

In less figurative terms and yet with clear hyperbole, Moses said that the way this message is made indelible is by constant repetition. Thus whether while sitting at home or walking in the pathway, whether lying down to sleep or rising for the tasks of a new day, teacher and pupil must be preoccupied with covenant concerns and their faithful transmission (v. 7). The pairing of these sets of contrasting places and postures forms a double merism (using opposing terms to express an all-encompassing concept). Sitting suggests inactivity; and walking, of course, activity. Together they encompass all of human effort. Likewise, to retire at night and rise up in the morning speaks of the totality of time. So important is covenant truth that it must be at the very center of all one's labor and life.

In what was apparently intended to be another figurative way of expressing the centrality of the covenant to everyday life, Moses instructed

---

[89] As Wolff puts it, to be upon the heart (עַל־לְבָבֶךָ) means that hearers should "remain conscious" of what they have learned (*Anthropology of the Old Testament*, 48; cf. Prov 7:3; Jer 17:1; Dan 7:28).

[90] BDB, 1042. See J. W. McKay, "Man's Love for God in Deuteronomy and the Father/ Teacher–Son/Pupil Relationship," *VT* 22 (1972): 426-35; cf. J. L. Crenshaw, "Education in Ancient Israel," *JBL* 104 (1985): 602-3.

the people to tie the words of covenant to their hands and foreheads (v. 8). In the former instance—the binding to the hands (or forearms, as *yad* clearly means here)[91]—the purpose is that the words might be "for a sign" (*lĕʾôt*). That is, they would identify their bearer as a member of the covenant community. When attached to the forehead (thus NIV as opposed to the literal "between the eyes"), the words function as bands wrapped around the head at the level of the forehead, the purpose of which, as the Hebrew parallelism makes clear, was also to serve as symbols of covenant affiliation.[92] In postbiblical Judaism and to the present day a miniature box containing verses of the Torah (Exod 13:1-10; 13:11-16; Deut 6:4-9; and Deut 11:13-21) were placed inside the four chambers of the box, the whole being known as the *tĕpillîn* ("prayers") or phylactery (cf. Matt 23:5). A similar box with only one chamber but containing the same texts was worn on the forearm as a "hand phylactery."[93]

That this binding on arm and forehead was originally intended to be figurative (more precisely, metaphorical) is quite clear from the context of the instruction, where there can be no doubt about the nonliteral meaning ("upon the heart," v. 6; "at home," "along the road," v. 7). Moreover, the practical impossibility of wearing such objects in everyday life suggests the figurative nature of the injunction as, indeed, does the fact that they are worn only on special worship occasions in modern Judaism. Such restriction to special times is not to be found in any of the four passages where the *tĕpillîn* are discussed (see above).

The covenant words also were to be written on the doorframes of Israelite houses and on the gateposts of their villages (v. 9). Once more this should be understood metaphorically, but in postbiblical practice observant Jews placed a *mĕzûzāh* (the same word as that for "doorpost"), a small metal receptacle containing Deut 6:4-9 and Deut 11:13-21 in twenty-two lines, at the right of the doorway in obedience to Moses' instructions here.[94] The form of the commandment is in any case most significant. After ordering that the covenant commandments be worn on the person of the faithful Israelite, Moses expanded the sphere of covenant claim to the house and then to the village. In this manner the person and his entire family and community become identified as the people of the Lord.

---

[91] For ‏יָד‎ as "wrist" or "arm" see P. R. Ackroyd, "‏יָד‎ *yād*," etc., *TDOT* 5:400.

[92] See J. Gamberoni, ‏טוֹטָפֹת‎ *ṭôṭāpōt*, *TDOT* 5:319-21; E. A. Speiser, "T(W)ṬPT," *JQR* 48 (1957): 208-17; J. E. Tigay, "On the Meaning of T(W)ṬPT," *JBL* 101 (1982): 321-31.

[93] L. H. Schiffman, *From Text to Tradition: A History of Second Temple and Rabbinic Judaism* (Hoboken: KTAV, 1991), 244-45; Driver, *Deuteronomy*, 93; *Encyclopedia Judaica* (Jerusalem: Keter, 1971), 15:898-903, s.v. "Tefillin."

[94] Ibid., 11:1474-77, s.v. "Mezuzah."

(4) Exhortation to Give the Lord Exclusive Recognition and Worship (6:10-15)

[10]When the LORD your God brings you into the land he swore to your fathers, to Abraham, Isaac and Jacob, to give you—a land with large, flourishing cities you did not build, [11]houses filled with all kinds of good things you did not provide, wells you did not dig, and vineyards and olive groves you did not plant—then when you eat and are satisfied, [12]be careful that you do not forget the Lord, who brought you out of Egypt, out of the land of slavery.

[13]Fear the LORD your God, serve him only and take your oaths in his name. [14]Do not follow other gods, the gods of the peoples around you; [15]for the LORD your God, who is among you, is a jealous God and his anger will burn against you, and he will destroy you from the face of the land.

6:10 Once more establishing the linkage between the soon-coming conquest and occupation of the land of Canaan and the ancient promises to the patriarchal fathers, Moses made the remarkable statement that the conquest would be nonviolent in terms of its effect on the physical structures of the Canaanite towns, houses, cisterns, and other facilities (vv. 10b-11). Previous instructions about the disposition of the Canaanite peoples and properties had been limited to the placing under *ḥerem* of heathen altars, pillars, and other worship apparatus (Exod 3:24; Num 33:52). Nothing was said about the annihilation of the populations and their physical, material possessions.[95]

Ḥerem, an element of so-called holy war, had been employed already in the course of Israel's journey to the plains of Moab. When the king of Arad had attacked Israel, the Israelites vowed to place the offending Canaanites under *ḥerem* if the Lord would grant them victory. After he had done so, the triumphant Israelites "completely destroyed [*wayyaḥărēm*] them and their towns; so the place was called Hormah [*ḥormâ*]" (Num 21:2-3). It appears beyond doubt that *ḥerem* here included the physical structures of the towns as well as the populace.

In his rehearsal of the wilderness itinerary in Deut 1:1–3:17 Moses referred again to military exploits involving *ḥerem*. Thus he spoke of the towns of Sihon as having been taken by Israel, but this time all that was destroyed (*naḥărēm*) were the men, women, and children, that is, the populations. Nothing is said of the buildings themselves falling under *ḥerem* (Deut 2:34). In fact, the livestock and other plunder were spared destruction (Deut 2:35). In the only other instance of *ḥerem* thus far, Moses

---

[95] See commentary on Deut 2:34 and Merrill, "Palestinian Archaeology and the Date of the Conquest," 109-11.

related the defeat of Og of Bashan in terms identical to those describing the overthrow of Sihon (Deut 3:1-11). Once more there is no hint that anything was destroyed except the people (v. 6). Indeed, the livestock and other goods were kept by Israel; in fact, the various Transjordanian towns were taken by Israel (v. 10) and later distributed to the tribes who settled there (v. 12).

Clearly, then, with the possible exception of the destruction of the towns of the king of Arad (Num 21:1-3), it was not Moses' policy to apply *ḥērem* to anything but the wicked populations. And this policy was to be continued on into the conquest of Canaan proper as our present text informs us. The reason obviously was to provide ready-made facilities for Israel to live in and work with. Moses spoke of this same policy later as a matter of a *fait accompli* (Deut 19:1); and Joshua, following the conquest, pointed out to the people of his time that they indeed now lived in a "land on which you did not toil and cities you did not build" (Josh 24:13). One can only conclude that Moses' conquest instructions, in this respect at least, were followed to the letter.

The implications of all this for the nature of the conquest are immensely profound though they cannot be treated here.[96] Suffice to say that the conquest did not result in major destruction of towns and properties so therefore did not leave archaeologically definable evidence. Any attempt to date the conquest must therefore rest on some basis other than the presence or absence of evidence of destruction.

6:11-12 Of more importance to the passage at hand is Moses' warning not to forget that it was the Lord who was responsible for dropping all these good things into their laps. Their possession of all this and the sense of satiety it brought (v. 11b) might lead Israel to believe that it and not God was the source of blessing. "Do not forget," then, was Moses' injunction, one echoed frequently in Deuteronomy, usually in connection with the covenant relationship (4:9,23,31; 8:11,14,19).[97]

Confidence in Israel's ability to enter, conquer, and occupy the land lies, once more, in its being the beneficiary of the Lord's promises to the fathers and in his initiative in leading the way (v. 10). It is he who "brings you into the land," the stem of the verb underlining the fact that the work is all of God. He who had promised Abraham, Isaac, and Jacob had put himself under obligation to fulfill his pledge to them as the original covenant pas-

---

[96] For a detailed discussion of the debate and literature regarding various contemporary models of Israel's origins and the conquest, see E. H. Merrill, "The LB/EI Transition and the Emergence of Israel: An Assessment and Preliminary Proposal," *ABW* (forthcoming).

[97] E. P. Blair, "An Appeal to Remembrance: The Memory Motif in Deuteronomy," 41-47.

sages had made so clear (Gen 13:14-18; 15:18-21; 17:1-8; 26:1-4). Especially significant was the ceremony recorded in Gen 15, where the Lord swore by himself, that is, by his own name and reputation, to accomplish all he had sworn to Abraham including the bestowal of the land of Canaan (Gen 15:9-11; cf. Heb 6:13-18).

As for the details of the land promise—the cities, houses, wells, and agricultural infrastructure that would come into their hands—these were not specifically contained in the ancient promises but were added here by Moses (vv. 10b-11). Part of the providential grace of God was his intention to transfer not only the land to Israel but its developments, all those products of labor and achievement that had taken the Canaanites centuries to create.

The cities were large and flourishing (lit., "good"), the houses well stocked and furnished, the wells ready-made, and the vineyards and olive groves productive. All of these would fall to Israel intact, making it unnecessary to destroy them, clear away the rubble, and begin all over again. That this could be done (and was; cf. Josh 24:13) is testimony to the Lord's power and goodness for conquest of this kind, which destroyed peoples but not properties, and is without analogy in the history of warfare.

6:13-15 But it was this very goodness of God that would lead to Israel's sense of self-sufficiency, a feeling that all that had been done was by human hand. The inevitable result would be to forget him, the very one who not only would achieve such an unparalleled conquest but who had effected Israel's redemption from bondage in the first place (v. 12). The only remedy for such memory lapse was renewed commitment to the covenant that lay at the heart of the Lord's relationship to the nation Israel. Moses thus enjoined upon his people that they fear, serve, and swear by the Lord only (v. 13), commands that are permeated with covenant language (cf. Deut 10:12,20; 31:12-13).[98] Lingering doubt about the covenant focus here is dispelled in vv. 14-15, which recall unmistakably the first two commandments of the Decalogue (Deut 5:7-10).[99] The "do not follow other gods" of v. 14 is clearly a rephrasing of the first commandment—"You shall have no other gods before me"—and the reference to the "jealous God" who judges and punishes covenant violation (v. 15) harks back to the second commandment that describes the Lord as such and speaks of his punishment of sin. To sin in such a way as to forget the source of Israel's blessing was to invite the ultimate covenant curse, removal from the land (v. 15; cf. 28:63; Lev 26:43).

---

[98] Craigie, *Deuteronomy,* 173.

[99] Mayes, *Deuteronomy,* 179.

(5) Exhortation to Give the Lord Exclusive Obedience (6:16-19)

[16]Do not test the LORD your God as you did at Massah. [17]Be sure to keep the commands of the LORD your God and the stipulations and decrees he has given you. [18]Do what is right and good in the LORD'S sight, so that it may go well with you and you may go in and take over the good land that the LORD promised on oath to your forefathers, [19]thrusting out all your enemies before you, as the LORD said.

6:16-17 The covenant basis for Israel's behavior in the land of Canaan and thereafter is further elaborated and emphasized in this section. The command in v. 12 was followed by an exhortation to keep the first two commandments (vv. 13-15), and now Moses enjoined upon the people the command that they not test the Lord their God (v. 16). This in turn is followed by reference to the covenant stipulations as a whole, referred to here by the usual technical terms *miṣwôt* (commands), *ʿēdôt* (stipulations), and *ḥuqqîm* (decrees; v. 17). Thus both the Decalogue and its explication, the stipulations, provide the basis for relationship and behavior.

To test God (not "tempt" as in AV and other older versions) is to make upon him demands or requirements that are inappropriate either to his nature and character or to the circumstances.[100] Jesus quoted this text in responding to Satan's overtures that he cast himself from the pinnacle of the temple (Matt 4:7; Luke 4:12). The point is not that God could not have rescued him but that such an act would trivialize the power of God and his care for those he loves.[101] Moses reminded his own contemporaries of their violation of this principle, when on the way to Sinai from Egypt they had questioned whether or not God was with them (Exod 17:7). The evidence they demanded was a miraculous supply of water (Exod 17:2). Rather than trusting God to provide it in his own way, probably through natural springs and wells (cf. Exod 15:23-27), they insisted on a supernatural intervention, one designed not so much to provide physical nourishment as to satisfy spiritual curiosity. Though displeased with their carnality, God nevertheless allowed water to issue from a rock, a miracle that gave rise to the place name Massah ("testing").[102] They must never resort to such tactics in the land of promise, Moses warned.

---

[100] Driver: "Men test, or prove, Jehovah when they act as if doubting whether His promise be true, or whether He is faithful to His revealed character" (*Deuteronomy,* 95).

[101] J. A. Broadus, *Commentary on the Gospel of Matthew,* AC (Philadelphia: American Baptist Publication Society, 1886), 66.

[102] Cassuto refers to several documented instances in which water appeared from underground sources in the Sinai when rock was chipped away to allow it to issue forth. The miracle still exists in the precise location of the source and even more so in God's patient forbearance (*Commentary on Exodus,* 203).

6:18-19 The conditional aspect of the covenant is clear in the statement that the people must do "what is right and good" before the Lord *so that* the favorable results of conquest and dispossession might follow (vv. 18-19). The Hebrew particle translated in this manner (*lĕmaʿan*) introduces the apodosis that is conditioned upon doing "right" and "good" before the Lord, namely, to accomplish what God had already promised. The apparent paradox of "contingent certainty" is best resolved by recognizing two things: (1) God's promises to the fathers were, indeed, without condition and qualification (Gen 13:14-17; 15:18; 17:8; etc.), but (2) any individual or generation in succession to the patriarchs could appropriate their blessings only through faith and obedience (Gen 15:6; Exod 19:5; Deut 4:40; 5:16,29,33).[103] To put it another way, the pledge of redemption and conquest by Israel was a settled and nonnegotiable matter (the unconditional side of the covenant), but their reality in the experience of individual Israelites or even a generation of them was contingent on covenant faithfulness (the conditional side). Failure to meet the conditions would result in judgment and even defeat and deportation, but it could never cancel out the eternal purposes of God for his chosen nation (cf. Lev 26:27-45; Jer 31:31-37; 32:36-40; Ezek 36:22-31; 37:1-14).

(6) Exhortation to Remember the Past (6:20-25)

20In the future, when your son asks you, "What is the meaning of the stipulations, decrees and laws the LORD our God has commanded you?" **21**tell him: "We were slaves of Pharaoh in Egypt, but the Lord brought us out of Egypt with a mighty hand. **22**Before our eyes the LORD sent miraculous signs and wonders—great and terrible—upon Egypt and Pharaoh and his whole household. **23**But he brought us out from there to bring us in and give us the land that he promised on oath to our forefathers. **24**The LORD commanded us to obey all these decrees and to fear the LORD our God, so that we might always prosper and be kept alive, as is the case today. **25**And if we are careful to obey all this law before the LORD our God, as he has commanded us, that will be our righteousness."

6:20 Moses' reference to the covenant stipulations as a precondition to success in the land (v. 17) gives rise to his exhortation to the people to remember them in time to come and to transmit them to succeeding generations. The terms differ somewhat here in v. 20 (*ʿēdôt, ḥuqqîm, mišpāṭîm*), but the covenant reference is just as clear and compelling.

---

[103] For the twin and inseparable notions of unconditionality and responsibility see W. C. Kaiser, Jr., *Toward an Old Testament Theology* (Grand Rapids: Zondervan, 1978), 93-94, 156-57.

It is crucial with the passing of time that descendants of people who have participated in or witnessed events that have been fundamental to their origin and that explain their unique destiny should be continually reminded of those events lest they lose their sense of history and meaning. This is all the more true of ancient Israel, for no other people had been called to such a significant mission, one that enveloped within it the very salvation of humankind. Israel must therefore recall its history and pass along its facts and value to generations yet to come. The way this was to be done was through the recitation of God's saving deeds in the past, a "sacred narrative" underlying the more formal and legal embodiment in the covenant texts.[104]

When children ask about the meaning of the covenant, then, the answer will be provided in story form. It will begin with slavery in Egypt and then will rehearse the exodus, an act of redemption (v. 21). The narrative will continue by describing the contest for sovereignty between the Lord and Pharaoh, one displaying the signs (*ʾōtôt*) and wonders (*mōpĕtîm*) of the ten plagues (v. 22). Finally, it will speak of the land of promise, the place to which the redeemed of the Lord would move in fulfillment of the promise to the fathers (v. 23). As Moses put it, "He brought us out . . . to bring us in," a remarkably clear and concise summation of the narrative.

6:21-23   Many scholars, following von Rad, view vv. 21-23 (or 25) as an example of Israel's so-called credo, that succinct statement of *Heilsge-schichte* that reflects the earliest and most profoundly important traditions.[105] An even more famous rendition occurs in Deut 26:5b-9. That one adds to the sacred history the traditions about patriarchal ancestry (v. 5b) lacking in the present version except in the oblique reference in v. 23. Otherwise the two accounts are very similar, even to the extent of referring to the "signs and wonders" and the "bringing out and bringing in" that became part of the formulaic language.

Missing from both passages, however, is any reference to Sinai and the making of covenant there. Von Rad argues that this suggests that the Sinai covenant traditions were only later added to the credo because they were unknown to its earliest Israelite tradents.[106] In the context of both passages, however, the reason for the omission is crystal clear. Deuteronomy 26 does so because it is the harvest festival of *Shebuʿot* (firstfruits) that is

---

[104] L. Perlitt, "Deuteronomium 6, 20-25: Eine Ermutigung zu Bekenntnis und Lehre," in *Glaube-Bekenntnis-Kirchenrecht,* ed. G. Besier (Hannover: Lutherische Verlagshaus, 1989), 222-34.

[105] G. von Rad, "The Form-Critical Problem of the Hexateuch," in *The Problem of the Hexateuch and Other Essays,* trans. E. W. T. Dicken (London: Oliver & Boyd, 1966), 5-6.

[106] Ibid.

being celebrated, one having to do with the bounty of the new land that was their own and not that of a slave master. The emphasis therefore is on the deliverance of the nation from one land (Egypt) to another (Canaan), a fact that requires no mention of Sinai and the covenant.[107]

The passage at hand omits reference to Sinai in so many terms, but the "stipulations, decrees and laws" of v. 20, the "decrees" of v. 24, and the "law" of v. 25 put beyond doubt that the narrative includes Sinai as a fundamental element of Israel's faith.

6:24-25 Moses brought his discussion of the nature of the covenant principles to a close in a summation in which he described them by the one word "decrees" (*ḥuqqîm*) and expressed their adherence in terms of obeying and fearing God (v. 24). The combination of these commands to define what is meant by covenant keeping is common in Deuteronomy (cf. 6:1-2,13; 10:12,20; 31:12). To fear is to obey, and to obey is to fear. Only when this spirit of submission is sincerely manifest can prosperity (lit., "good") and life assuredly follow. This had been Israel's experience in the past and on up to the present, said Moses ("as is the case today," v. 24),[108] and it could be the same in the future if the people would obey "all this law" (*miṣwâ;* v. 25). Then in strongly evangelical terms Moses equated faithful compliance with the covenant to righteousness (v. 25). The word used here is *ṣĕdāqâ*, the very one applied to Abraham as a result of his having believed in the Lord (Gen 15:6).[109] Later Judaism wrongly concluded that covenant keeping was the basis for righteousness rather than an expression of faithful devotion. But true covenant keeping in the final analysis is a matter of faith, not merely of works and ritual. Thus the central feature of the covenant stipulations is their providing a vehicle by which genuine saving faith might be displayed (cf. Deut 24:13; Hab 2:4; Rom 1:17; 4:1-5; Gal 3:6-7).

5. The Content of the Principles (7:1–11:32)

Having introduced the major section of the covenant document described here as the general stipulations, Moses went on to categorize

---

[107] Craigie is not convinced that Deut 26:5b-9 is a creed in the first place and says that the passage selects those events "which most naturally highlight God's gift of a land to his people" (*Deuteronomy,* 322).

[108] Cf. B. S. Childs, "A Study of the Formula 'Until This Day,'" *JBL* 82 (1963): 279-92.

[109] G. J. Wenham, *Genesis 1–15,* WBC (Waco: Word, 1987), 330. Wenham observes that "this faith [of Abraham] leads to righteous action (e.g., 18:19), but only here [Gen 15:6] in the OT is it counted as righteousness." This is correct, but one still cannot separate righteousness as a state from its expression in life and action. Cf. Snaith, *The Distinctive Ideas of the Old Testament,* 170-73.

them under at least five rubrics: (1) the dispossession of nonvassals (7:1-26), (2) the Lord as the source of blessing (8:1-20), (3) blessing as a product of grace (9:1–10:11), (4) love of the Lord and love of humankind (10:12-22), and (5) obedience and disobedience and their rewards (11:1-32). These clearly are not laws or commandments as such but primarily series of parenetic homilies in which Moses exhorted the people to certain courses of action in light of the upcoming conquest and occupation of Canaan.[110] Within these sections, however, are specific and explicit injunctions, instructions based upon the Decalogue and anticipatory of further elaboration in the large section of detailed stipulations that follows (12:1–26:15).

(1) The Dispossession of Nonvassals (7:1-26)

[1]**When the LORD your God brings you into the land you are entering to possess and drives out before you many nations—the Hittites, Girgashites, Amorites, Canaanites, Perizzites, Hivites and Jebusites, seven nations larger and stronger than you— [2]and when the LORD your God has delivered them over to you and you have defeated them, then you must destroy them totally. Make no treaty with them, and show them no mercy. [3]Do not intermarry with them. Do not give your daughters to their sons or take their daughters for your sons, [4]for they will turn your sons away from following me to serve other gods, and the LORD'S anger will burn against you and will quickly destroy you. [5]This is what you are to do to them: Break down their altars, smash their sacred stones, cut down their Asherah poles and burn their idols in the fire. [6]For you are a people holy to the LORD your God. The LORD your God has chosen you out of all the peoples on the face of the earth to be his people, his treasured possession.**

[7]**The LORD did not set his affection on you and choose you because you were more numerous than other peoples, for you were the fewest of all peoples. [8]But it was because the LORD loved you and kept the oath he swore to your forefathers that he brought you out with a mighty hand and redeemed you from the land of slavery, from the power of Pharaoh king of Egypt. [9]Know therefore that the LORD your God is God; he is the faithful God, keeping his covenant of love to a thousand generations of those who love him and keep his commands. [10]But**

> **those who hate him he will repay to their face by destruction;**
> **he will not be slow to repay to their face those who hate him.**

---

[110] W. Crump describes Deut 7, for example, as "a covenant sermon" (W. Crump, "Deuteronomy 7: A Covenant Sermon," *ResQ* 17 [1974]: 222-35).

[11]Therefore, take care to follow the commands, decrees and laws I give you today.

7:1 The first action Israel was to undertake as a result of the conquest of Canaan and its aftermath was the systematic and total annihilation of the indigenous populations, for they were squatters in the land of promise and furthermore would lead Israel into idolatry and moral decay. The implementation of this mandate required the exercise of *ḥērem*, or the ban, a policy by which the enemies of the Lord were slain by his people in holy war and all their properties either destroyed or confiscated by him for his own use (see Deut 2:34).

The nations in view are seven in all—the Hittites, Girgashites, Amorites, Canaanites, Perizzites, Hivites, and Jebusites. Inasmuch as the number seven is commonly used to speak of totality,[111] it is possible that the peoples listed here represent all the inhabitants of the land no matter their nationality or ethnic identity. In any event, they are said to have been, either individually or collectively, "larger and stronger" than Israel (7:1). Given the census lists of Num 1:20-46 and 26:5-51, where Israel's total adult male population was 603,550 and 601,730 respectively, that of the combined nations of Canaan must have exceeded even those enormous figures. Nevertheless, their defeat and destruction was a foregone conclusion, for the Lord would have delivered them over to Israel's armies. Such divine intervention was one of the characteristics of holy war, conflict undertaken by the Lord to achieve his redeeming and kingdom purposes (cf. Deut 1:30; 3:22; 20:4).[112]

Of the nations listed, little or nothing is known of the Girgashites, Perizzites, and Hivites. The Girgashites and Hivites appear in the Table of Nations as descendants of Canaan (Gen 10:16-17).[113] The Girgashites are also in the list of nations the Lord described to Abraham as occupants of Canaan, along with the Hittites, Perizzites, Amorites, Canaanites, and Jebusites (Gen 15:20-21). Otherwise they are merely listed in the standard catalog of Canaanite nations (Josh 3:10; 24:11; Neh 9:8).

---

[111] J. J. Davis argues that the major significance of the number seven in the OT is "completeness" (*Biblical Numerology* [Grand Rapids: Baker, 1968], 119). Driver fails to note that aspect, choosing rather to stress seven as a round, sacred number. It may, indeed, be that the seven nations here represent a round number for a precise total; cf. G. R. Driver, "Sacred Numbers and Round Figures," in *Promise and Fulfillment*, ed. F. F. Bruce (Edinburgh: T & T Clark, 1963), 67.

[112] Gottwald, "Holy War in Deuteronomy: Analysis and Critique," 296-310.

[113] T. Ishida, "The Structure and Historical Implications of the Lists of Pre-Israelite Nations," *Bib* 60 (1929): 461-90; B. Oded, "The Table of Nations (Genesis 10)—A Sociocultural Approach," *ZAW* 98 (1986): 14-30.

The Perizzites are lacking in the Table of Nations but are mentioned in Gen 13:7 with the Canaanites in such a way as to suggest that they, unlike the Girgashites, were not a Canaanite tribe (cf. Gen 34:30). They do appear, however, in many lists that omit the Girgashites such as in Exod 3:17; 23:23; 33:2; 34:11; Deut 20:17. Moreover, they maintained their identity until postexilic times, long after the last references to Girgashites and Hivites (Ezra 9:1).

The Hivites are believed by some scholars to have been the same as the Hurrians (or Horites otherwise in the OT; cf. Gen 14:6; 36:20-22,29,30; Num 13:5; Deut 2:12,22).[114] If so, they appear to have been the people indigenous to Seir (later Edom) whom the Edomites supplanted. By the name Hivite they are traced to Canaan (Gen 10:17) and appear regularly in the lists of those who constituted the nations to be expelled by Israel (Exod 3:8,17; 13:5; 23:23,28; Deut 20:17). A particular community of Hivites lived at Gibeon, a city-state with whom Joshua mistakenly made terms of peace (Josh 9:1,7; 11:19). In addition, Hivites appear to have lived in Kephirah, Beeroth, and Kiriath Jearim as well (Josh 9:17), all of which were in the vicinity of Gibeon. Thus "greater Gibeon" seems to have been a center of Hivite life.[115]

Others resided on the lower slopes of Mount Hermon in the land of Mizpah, an area otherwise unattested (Josh 11:3) except in Judg 3:3, where it is further defined as lying "in the Lebanon mountains from Mount Baal Hermon to Lebo Hamath," that is, in an eighty-mile-long stretch of land east of the Beqa Valley of Lebanon. Because of geographical considerations it is tempting to identify these as Hurrians as opposed to the Hivites of Gibeon who may have been Canaanites in a more strict sense.[116]

The Jebusites are always closely associated with Jerusalem in the biblical narratives. They are designated as offspring of Canaan in the Table of Nations (Gen 10:16) and appear in the list of Israel's enemies in the land (Gen 15:21; Exod 3:8,17; 13:5; Deut 20:17). They differed from the Canaanites in respect to their dwelling place, however, for they, with the Amorites and Hittites, lived in the hill country whereas the Canaanites inhabited the coastal areas and the Jordan Valley (Num 13:29; cf. Josh 11:3). So secure was their entrenchment in Jerusalem, the city remained out of Israelite control until the kingship of David except for a brief time

---

[114] H. Eybers, "Who Were the Hivites?" *OTWSA* 2-5 (1959): 6-14.

[115] R. G. Boling, *Joshua,* AB (Garden City: Doubleday, 1982), 264-65.

[116] The LXX, in fact, reads "Horite" frequently for "Hivite," reflecting both an orthographic and ethnic confusion (cf. Gen 34:2; Josh 9:7). Such confusion also existed between "Hittite" and "Hivite," one assumed by many scholars in Judg 3:3. So G. F. Moore, *Judges,* ICC (New York: Scribners, 1895), 79, 81-82.

during Joshua's conquest (Judg 1:8). After that it was regained by the Jebusites (Josh 15:63; Judg 1:21; 19:11) for about 350 years and then taken by David as his capital city (2 Sam 5:6-9). Jebusites continued to live in Jerusalem along with the Israelites thereafter (2 Sam 24:16) and, in fact, still retained their ethnic identity into postexilic times (Ezra 9:1).

The term "Hittite" is somewhat ambiguous since it can refer to the indigenous peoples of central Anatolia (modern Turkey), known technically as Hattians; to the classical Hittite peoples of the mid- and late-second millennium B.C.; or to enclaves of peoples who lived in Syria-Palestine as late as the end of the Old Testament period. Those of the conquest period were likely from the third category, the Hittites who appear in the standard list of Israel's adversaries in Canaan (Gen 15:20; Exod 3:8,17; 23:23). They would have been Hittite "colonialists," a term that need not imply that they were genetically linked to the ethnic Hittites of Anatolia. The personal names of postpatriarchal Hittites appear always to be Semitic, thus lending force to the view that they were Hittites only in the sense of a political or military allegiance to Hatti.[117]

The Hittites of the Table of Nations (Gen 10:15) also no doubt were the same inasmuch as they were descendants of Canaan. So was Uriah the Hittite, David's mercenary soldier (2 Sam 11:3), and the Hittites with whom Solomon traded (1 Kgs 10:29) and intermarried (1 Kgs 11:1) and whom later kings of Israel employed as allies (2 Kgs 7:6). The Hittites of the patriarchal stories, however, could well have been elements of the Hattians since the date of the patriarchs precedes that of even Old Kingdom Hittite times. Especially famous was Ephron, "the Hittite" from whom Abraham bought a piece of land for a burial site (Gen 23:3-20). Esau's wives also were Hittites, daughters of Beeri and Elon (Gen 26:34), likewise, no doubt, to be viewed technically as Hattians.[118]

7:2-4 However all these peoples came to be in the land, they were trespassers in the eyes of the Lord, for he already had promised Abraham to give the land to him and his descendants (Gen 12:1,7; 13:17; 15:18). The Lord himself would therefore drive them out and deliver them over (*nātan*) to Israel, who would defeat them. But Israel must follow this up by subjecting these hopelessly unrepentant idolaters to the *ḥērem,* that is, to total and unexceptional destruction. The verb "destroy them totally" used to describe this act occurs only in the causative stem (*heḥĕrîm*) and means "to devote someone or something to the Lord by exterminating it."[119] This drastic action was taken as a form of immediate divine judg-

[117] H. A. Hoffner, "The Hittites and Hurrians," in *Peoples of Old Testament Times,* ed. D. J. Wiseman (Oxford: At the Clarendon Press, 1973), 213-14.
[118] Kitchen, *Ancient Orient and Old Testament,* 51-52, 154-56.

ment upon those who had sinned away their day of grace (cf. Gen 15:16; Lev 18:24-30). It also was to preclude their wicked influence on God's covenant people who would otherwise tend to make covenant and intermarry with them (Deut 7:3) and adopt their idolatry (v. 4), something that, in fact, did take place because of Israel's failure to obey the *ḥērem* decree. The net result was violation of the first two commandments (v. 4; cf. 5:7-10; 6:13-15).

7:5-7 Having destroyed the idolaters, Israel also was to demolish the paraphernalia of their worship (v. 5). This included their altars, their sacred stones (*maṣṣēbôt*), their Asherah poles (*ʾăšērîm*), and their idols (*pĕsîlîm*). The "sacred stones" represented the male procreative aspect of the Canaanite fertility religion; and the Asherah, the female. Asherah was also the name of the mother goddess of the Canaanite pantheon, the deity responsible for fertility and the productivity of soil, animals, and humankind. She was represented by either an evergreen tree or by a pole that also spoke of perpetual life.[120] The cult carried on in their name was of the most sensual and sordid type, one practiced in the temples and also under the open sky at high places and in groves of trees. Prominent in its services was sacred prostitution involving priests and priestesses who represented the male and female deities.[121]

There is no wonder that such a system had to be eliminated along with its devotees, for Israel was called to be a people entirely opposite in its life and faith. In words reminiscent of their call at Sinai to be a covenant nation, Israel was told again that they were a "people holy" (*ʿam qādôs*) to the Lord, one chosen (*bāḥar*) to be his from among all peoples of the earth, a "treasured possession" (*sĕgullâ*) (v. 6; cf. Exod 19:5-6).[122] To be holy was to be different from those nations out of whom Israel came.

7:8 This reminder of Israel's call is linked, first of all, to the Lord's elective grace and then to his faithfulness to his promise to the patriarchs (v. 8; cf. 6:10,23). In addition to the strongly elective verb *bāḥar* ("choose") in v. 6 stands the equally evocative covenant verb *ʾāhēb* ("love") in v. 8. In covenant contexts these verbs are synonymous, for the Lord chooses those he loves and loves those he chooses (cf. 4:37; 10:15; Pss 47:4; 78:68).[123] Those whom he hates, therefore, are those whom he

---

[119] KBL, 334; N. Lohfink, "חרם, *hāram*," etc., *TDOT* 5:184, 186-87.

[120] H. Ringgren, *Religions of the Ancient Near East* (Philadelphia: Westminster, 1973), 140-41, 158-59.

[121] Ibid., 167.

[122] See Shafer, "Root *bḥr* and pre-Exilic Concepts of Chosenness in the Hebrew Bible," 20-42; M. Greenberg, "Hebrew *segulla*: Akkadian *sikiltu*," *JAOS* 71 (1951): 172-74.

[123] McCarthy, "Notes on the Love of God in Deuteronomy and the Father-Son Relation-

had rejected as covenant partners (Mal 1:2; cf. Rom 9:13). In this sense love and hate are not emotive terms but technical language to speak of divine election for salvation and service.

7:9 Evidence of the Lord's elective love is his having redeemed Israel from Egyptian slavery (v. 8). Such a mighty act also testifies to his claim to be the only God (v. 9; cf. 4:35,39; 6:4), one who is absolutely dependable (*ne'ĕmān*) to keep covenant faith (*habbĕrît wĕhaḥesed,* lit., "the covenant and the loyalty," i.e., "loyalty to covenant").[124] As noted already (cf. 5:10), *ḥesed* is a term central to covenant vocabulary and meaning. Parties to a bilateral covenant express their mutual commitment by pledging their *ḥesed,* and so here the Lord speaks of himself as one who is covenantally loyal to those who love (*'āhēb*) him and keep his commands (*miṣwôt*), that is, his covenant and all its terms.

7:10 On the contrary, those who hate him will quickly experience his destruction. Again, "to hate," in the context of covenant terminology, means "to reject, to repudiate as a covenant partner" (cf. 5:9; 9:28). Such covenant disloyalty deserves recompense, one described here (literally) as "repay to their face." This expression occurs only here and probably means that the judgment would not be reserved for unborn generations but would fall immediately upon those who had sinned in this manner, right there and then.[125] This view finds support in the fact that God "will not be slow" to repay (lit., "will not be afterward" in doing so).

7:11 Moses concluded this section of his command to dispossess the Canaanite nations by once more appealing to the "commands, decrees and laws," meaning, of course, the covenant as a whole. By now it is clear that use of these terms not only constitutes a covenant reminder but serves to mark out significant divisions in the text (cf. 4:1,40; 5:1; 6:1,20; 8:11; 10:12-13; 11:1,32; 12:1; 26:16; 30:15-16). The exhortation resumes after this pivot point in a somewhat chiastic pattern in which vv. 12-16 reflect much of the sentiment of vv. 7-11 and vv. 17-26 match vv. 1-6.[126] The exegesis will draw attention to some of these common elements.

---

ship between Israel and Yahweh," 144-47; W. L. Moran, "The Ancient Near Eastern Background of the Love of God in Deuteronomy," *CBQ* 25 (1963): 77-87.

[124] As Weinfeld notes, the construction is a hendiadys, one he translates "a gracious covenant" (*Deuteronomy 1–11,* 370).

[125] Thus Driver, *Deuteronomy,* 102.

[126] Christensen sees v. 11 as "a summary of the larger structure of 6:4–7:11 as a whole" but does not subscribe to our view of the structure of the entire chap. 7 (*Deuteronomy 1–11,* 157). Weinfeld suggests some kind of pattern based on late editorializing in which 6:1–7:11 and 7:12–8:20 are major sections framed, respectively, by "the command, law, and judgments" (6:1; 7:11) and by promised reward for covenant obedience (7:12) and punishment for disobedience (8:20; *Deuteronomy 1–11,* 372).

¹²If you pay attention to these laws and are careful to follow them, then the
LORD your God will keep his covenant of love with you, as he swore to your
forefathers. ¹³He will love you and bless you and increase your numbers. He
will bless the fruit of your womb, the crops of your land—your grain, new
wine and oil—the calves of your herds and the lambs of your flocks in the land
that he swore to your forefathers to give you. ¹⁴You will be blessed more than
any other people; none of your men or women will be childless, nor any of
your livestock without young. ¹⁵The LORD will keep you free from every disease. He will not inflict on you the horrible diseases you knew in Egypt, but he
will inflict them on all who hate you. ¹⁶You must destroy all the peoples the
LORD your God gives over to you. Do not look on them with pity and do not
serve their gods, for that will be a snare to you.

¹⁷You may say to yourselves, "These nations are stronger than we are. How
can we drive them out?" ¹⁸But do not be afraid of them; remember well what
the LORD your God did to Pharaoh and to all Egypt. ¹⁹You saw with your own
eyes the great trials, the miraculous signs and wonders, the mighty hand and
outstretched arm, with which the LORD your God brought you out. The LORD
your God will do the same to all the peoples you now fear. ²⁰Moreover, the
LORD your God will send the hornet among them until even the survivors who
hide from you have perished. ²¹Do not be terrified by them, for the LORD your
God, who is among you, is a great and awesome God. ²²The LORD your God
will drive out those nations before you, little by little. You will not be allowed
to eliminate them all at once, or the wild animals will multiply around you.
²³But the LORD your God will deliver them over to you, throwing them into
great confusion until they are destroyed. ²⁴He will give their kings into your
hand, and you will wipe out their names from under heaven. No one will be
able to stand up against you; you will destroy them. ²⁵The images of their gods
you are to burn in the fire. Do not covet the silver and gold on them, and do
not take it for yourselves, or you will be ensnared by it, for it is detestable to
the LORD your God. ²⁶Do not bring a detestable thing into your house or you,
like it, will be set apart for destruction. Utterly abhor and detest it, for it is set
apart for destruction.

7:12-16   Having spoken of the "commands, decrees and laws" in v. 11,
Moses urged his people to obey them, for in doing so they could expect the
covenant loyalty of the Lord in return (v. 12; cf. v. 9). That loyalty (ḥesed)
would be expressed in multiplication of population, abundance of crops
and livestock, and fertility of man and beast (vv. 13-14). This promise was
in contrast to the relative weakness and smallness of the exodus generation, who were "the fewest of all peoples" (v. 7). God promises also that
covenant obedience would result in freedom from the diseases Israel had
known in Egypt. Rather, they would be inflicted on their enemies instead
(v. 15; cf. v. 8). What these diseases were is not clear. The Hebrew suggests

only generic illness, any weakness or debilitation that brings one low.[127] Whatever they were, they would be a thing of the past to God's faithful ones. In addition to the diseases the Lord would bring upon the wicked nations, Israel must also destroy them mercilessly and avoid worship of their gods (v. 16).

7:17-19 The connection between vv. 17-26 and vv. 1-6 is established in the reference to the nations that are stronger than Israel (v. 17; cf. v. 1). Moses already had promised that the Lord would overcome them, and yet Israel's fear persisted. He therefore reminded them of the past when the Lord struck Egypt with his awesome power, confounding them with the plagues (i.e., the "signs and wonders," v. 19; cf. v. 8; 6:22) and devastating them with the exodus deliverance ("the mighty hand and outstretched arm," v. 19; cf. 4:34; 5:15). This, he said, would happen again, this time to the Canaanite foes (v. 19; cf.v. 2a).

7:20-24 A major difference this time, however, was that Israel was not leaving a land but entering one and would not flee from a pursuer but would instead chase others. One of God's agents would be "the hornet" (v. 20), a terror so powerful and persistent that it would search out and destroy even those who hid themselves. Whether this should be understood as the insect, either literally or metaphorically, or as depression or discouragement, the fact remains that it was some instrument used by the Lord to assist Israel in conflict (cf. Exod 23:28; Josh 24:12).[128]

Indeed, the hornet possibly could have been the Lord himself, for Moses went on to say that the Lord would be among his people as an awesome God and that he would drive the enemy from Canaan little by little (vv. 21-22; cf. v. 1, where the same verb, *nāšal,* occurs). The command to annihilate (v. 2) must be qualified, therefore, to allow for a gradual process of expulsion, one that would not leave the land unpopulated and open to the wild animals. Yahweh as warrior continued his mighty exploits by confounding the enemy (v. 23), delivering over their kings until their very memories were forgotten (v. 24; cf. v. 2).

7:25-26 The Lord's initiative was to be followed by Israel's own action and in exactly the same way as outlined in vv. 1-6. After the nations were destroyed, their images had to follow suit (v. 25a; cf. v. 5). The gold

---

[127] KBL, 301, 496. Cf. K. Seybold, "חָלָה, *chālāh*," etc., *TDOT* 4:401. Seybold suggests that "in OT usage, of the various expressions available for referring to general conditions of bodily malaise and disease, the group of words based on חלה is drawn on by far the most frequently." "Diseases of Egypt" would include such maladies as elephantiasis, boils, and eye and bowel disorders (thus Craigie, *Deuteronomy,* 181).

[128] Cp. BDB, 864 and KBL, 817. See also E. Neufeld, "Insects as Warfare Agents in the Ancient Near East," *Or* 49 (1980): 30-57.

and silver that adorned such idols could not be saved and used by the Israelites, for it, like the people, were under *ḥērem* and thus subject to annihilation (v. 25; cf. v. 2). The reason, specifically, for their being thus categorized is that idols and their accoutrements are detestable to the Lord. This means that what they symbolized was so counter to the Lord and his purposes that they could not coexist with him (cf. 12:31; 18:9,12; 27:15; 32:16; 1 Kgs 11:5-7; Isa 41:24; 44:19).[129]

So reprehensible are these objects that they contaminate those who use them or who even bring them into their homes (v. 26). Indeed, they render them to the same judgment as was appropriate to the objects themselves, namely, total eradication. This was illustrated most tragically but clearly in the episode of Achan; following Jericho's destruction, he seized some of the detestable goods of that city, brought them into his tent, and subsequently perished along with them (Josh 7:16-26).[130] The motive for destroying these images of vv. 25-26—that they not cause God's own people to become corrupt—finds linkage also in vv. 5-6. There, however, such objects were to be placed under the ban (*ḥērem*) because Israel was a "people holy to the LORD your God." Thus on the positive side detestable things were antithetical to the nature of Israel as an elect and separated nation, and on the negative side they would inevitably obliterate that distinct uniqueness and make God's people like any other.

(2) The Lord as the Source of Blessing (8:1-20)

[1]Be careful to follow every command I am giving you today, so that you may live and increase and may enter and possess the land that the LORD promised on oath to your forefathers. [2]Remember how the LORD your God led you all the way in the desert these forty years, to humble you and to test you in order to know what was in your heart, whether or not you would keep his commands. [3]He humbled you, causing you to hunger and then feeding you with manna, which neither you nor your fathers had known, to teach you that man does not live on bread alone but on every word that comes from the mouth of the LORD. [4]Your clothes did not wear out and your feet did not swell during these forty years. [5]Know then in your heart that as a man disciplines his son, so the LORD your God disciplines you.

[6]Observe the commands of the LORD your God, walking in his ways and revering him. [7]For the LORD your God is bringing you into a good land—a

---

[129] P. Humbert, "Le substantif *toʿēbā* et le verbe *tʿb* dans l'Ancien Testament," *ZAW* 72 (1960): 217-37; J. L'Hour, "Les interdits *toʿēbā* dans le Deutéronome," *RB* 71 (1964): 481-503.

[130] See the helpful comments by T. C. Butler on the judgment of Achan for bringing the "devoted thing" (חֵרֶם) into his house (*Joshua*, WBC [Waco: Word, 1983], 86).

land with streams and pools of water, with springs flowing in the valleys and hills; [8]a land with wheat and barley, vines and fig trees, pomegranates, olive oil and honey; [9]a land where bread will not be scarce and you will lack nothing; a land where the rocks are iron and you can dig copper out of the hills.

[10]When you have eaten and are satisfied, praise the LORD your God for the good land he has given you. [11]Be careful that you do not forget the LORD your God, failing to observe his commands, his laws and his decrees that I am giving you this day. [12]Otherwise, when you eat and are satisfied, when you build fine houses and settle down, [13]and when your herds and flocks grow large and your silver and gold increase and all you have is multiplied, [14]then your heart will become proud and you will forget the LORD your God, who brought you out of Egypt, out of the land of slavery. [15]He led you through the vast and dreadful desert, that thirsty and waterless land, with its venomous snakes and scorpions. He brought you water out of hard rock. [16]He gave you manna to eat in the desert, something your fathers had never known, to humble and to test you so that in the end it might go well with you. [17]You may say to yourself, "My power and the strength of my hands have produced this wealth for me." [18]But remember the LORD your God, for it is he who gives you the ability to produce wealth, and so confirms his covenant, which he swore to your forefathers, as it is today.

[19]If you ever forget the LORD your God and follow other gods and worship and bow down to them, I testify against you today that you will surely be destroyed. [20]Like the nations the LORD destroyed before you, so you will be destroyed for not obeying the LORD your God.

8:1 In language reminiscent of Deut 6:1-3 and 4:1-8 Moses continues his exposition of the content of the covenant principles by focusing on the Lord as the source of all blessing, both past and future.[131] He begins this new section by calling attention to the need to base all belief and behavior on the covenant relationship, one reduced here to the single word "command" (*miṣwâ*, v. 1).

8:2-3 Also in line with previous literary and theological pattern, Moses recalled the past—especially from the time of covenant making at Sinai-Horeb—as a means of underscoring both the redeeming and preserving grace of God and the wicked unbelief and insufficiency of his people Israel (vv. 2-5; cf. 4:1-8; 1:6–3:29). The Lord had led them through the desert in order to humble and test them about their commitment (v. 2). He did this by allowing them to hunger and then to be fed by the miraculous supply of manna (Exod 16:1-30; Num 11:4-9), an act so clearly supernatural that the people had to recognize that it was all of God and not of them-

---

[131] R. H. O'Connell, "Deuteronomy viii 1-20: A Symmetrical Concentricity and the Rhetoric of Providence," *VT* 40 (1990): 437-52.

selves (v. 3; cf. Exod 16:32). In fact, the manna symbolized more than mere physical nourishment but the word of God itself (v. 4), for the God who could provide in such a mighty and unexpected way was well worth listening to.[132] This is the point Jesus made to the devil when he quoted this very passage while being tempted to change stones into bread (Matt 4:4). There are relative values in life, and one of them is that spiritual food is more important than physical.[133]

8:4-5 The granting of unending supply of food, of clothing that never wore out, and of physical stamina for the wilderness journey (v. 4) were all part of the process by which God instructed and prepared his people on their way to Canaan. The translation "disciplines" (v. 5) is suitable generally for the verb used here; but in light of the verbs "humble" and "test" in v. 2, it may be best to see the desert itinerary as a learning experience rather than a punishing one (cf. Exod 16:4; 20:20; Deut 8:16; 13:4 [Eng., 13:3]).[134] Thus this is discipline in the positive sense of education.

8:7-9 Even as God's past blessings flowed out of covenant obedience, so would those of the future (v. 6), those concomitant with life in the land (vv. 7-9). No more graphically beautiful landscape of Canaan exists than in the word picture Moses painted here (cf. also 11:8-12). The land, he said, is a "good land" (ʾereṣ ṭôbâ), good because of its abundant water supplies (v. 7), its rich diversity of produce in ample supply (vv. 8-9a), and of mineral wealth (v. 9b). The reference to "iron rocks" is somewhat problematic in light of the absence of iron smelting in this early, pre-Iron Age, but there is clear evidence that meteoric iron was known and processed in practical ways long before the advent of the Iron Age proper in the ancient Near East (ca. 1200 B.C.).[135] It may have been this that Moses described (cf. Num 31:22; 35:16; Deut 27:5; 28:23; 33:25). As for copper, it existed in

---

[132] F. G. Lopez, "Yahve, Fuente Ultima de Vida: Analisis de Dt 8," *Bib* 62 (1981): 21-54; R. C. Van Leeuwen, "What Comes out of God's Mouth: Theological Wordplay in Deuteronomy 8," *CBQ* 47 (1985): 55-57.

[133] L. Perlitt, "Wovon der Mensch Lebt (Dtn 8:3b)," in *Die Botschaft und die Boten. Festschrift H. W. Wolff,* ed. J. Jeremias and L. Perlitt (Neukirchen-Vluyn: Neukirchener, 1981), 403-26; A. B. Taylor, "Decisions in the Desert: The Temptation of Jesus in the Light of Deuteronomy," *Int* 14 (1960): 300-309.

[134] Thus Keil and Delitzsch, *The Pentateuch,* III:332. In referring to עִנָּה in particular, Cairns (*Word and Presence,* 96) observes that to be humbled "is to be led to an awareness of our own meager resources and hence into trustful dependence on the resources of God."

[135] W. F. Albright, *The Archaeology of Palestine* (London: Penguin, 1960), 110; *The New International Dictionary of Biblical Archaeology,* ed. E. M. Blaiklock and R. K. Harrison (Grand Rapids: Zondervan, 1983), 252, s.v. "Iron."

plentiful supply in the south Arabah; and, in fact, an important copper processing industry was developed there in later times.[136]

8:10-17   The very blessing and abundance of the land, however, would tend to lull its inhabitants into a sense of complacency and self-sufficiency. Moses therefore exhorted the people to remember that their fullness was from the hand of God just as the manna of the desert had been (v. 10; cf. v. 3). And it also is a manifestation of the special privileges they had as covenant partners with him, hence the need to adhere rigidly to all of its stipulations (the *miṣwôt, mišpāṭîm,* and *ḥuqqîm,* v. 11). Failure to do so would inevitably invite divine judgment (vv. 19-20) despite fullness of belly, construction of fine houses, and accumulation of livestock and other material things (vv. 12-13). These things, while testifying to the Lord's love and grace, would be no automatic hedge against his punishment should his people forsake him.

The chief danger was that they would become amnesiac about their history and in the pride of the present would forget the sacred story of their election and redemption. They would no longer recall that the Lord had brought them out of Egyptian slavery (v. 14; cf. 4:9; 6:12), that he had led them through the trackless and terrible deserts (v. 15; cf. 1:19; 2:7; 32:10) and had given them water and food in supernatural ways (vv. 15b-16a). They could even have forgotten the lessons he had taught them then and there, instruction designed to prepare them well for the purpose to which he had called them (v. 16b). Instead, they would claim credit for all their successes as though by their own wisdom and strength they had managed to become so prosperous (v. 17).

8:18   The connection between covenant and blessing is clearly affirmed in v. 18, where Moses commanded his hearers to remember the Lord inasmuch as the success they enjoyed was confirmation of his covenant favor and the covenant relationship was the source of their blessing. In other words, there is a reciprocal dynamic in which covenant produces blessing and blessing proves the reality of covenant.

This interpretation (favored by NIV) rests on a reading of the text supplied by Qumran, the Samaritan Pentateuch, and certain LXX manuscripts, as opposed to the Masoretic Text. The matter in question is the particle *lĕmaʿan* ("that" or "in order that"), which appears without a preceding conjunctive *waw* in the MT and so is construed as introducing a purpose clause: "It is he who gives you the ability to produce wealth *so that* he might confirm his covenant." This suggests it is by the means of prosperity

---

[136] The site was Timna, just north of Elath. See A. Mazar, *Archaeology of the Land of the Bible,* ABRL (New York: Doubleday, 1991), 285.

that the covenant of the Lord is seen to have validity or even that prosperity is essential to covenant reality. This is clearly against the whole tenor of covenant theology that allows no conditionality to covenant initiation. Rather, material (or any other kind of) success is a concomitant of covenant fellowship. It provides evidence that the covenant relationship exists, but it is by no means its prerequisite. Thus the reading with *waw* is to be preferred because it allows God's grace as the source of all wealth to be also the source of the covenant itself.[137] As already suggested, blessing and covenant are two sides of the same coin.

8:19-20 Finally, in a most stern warning Moses moved beyond the matter of Israel's merely ascribing to themselves the success to be attributed to God (as serious as that was) to the inevitable result of forgetting him, namely, turning to other gods (vv. 19-20). This would strike right at the heart of the covenant relationship, the acknowledgment of the uniqueness and exclusiveness of the Lord as expressed in the first two commandments (5:7-10; cf. 6:12-15; 7:1-5) and the Shema (6:4-5). The language of the warning is packed with covenant overtones such as "follow [lit., "walk after"] other gods" (cf. 5:7), "worship [lit., "serve"] them," "bow down to them" (5:9), and "testify against you" (cf. 4:26; 30:19; 31:28; Jer 11:7; Amos 3:13).[138] Moses stood as the representative of the Lord to swear that Israel's covenant infidelity would surely result in their total destruction. They would be just like the Canaanite nations (7:1), who, subject to the *ḥērem* of God's holy wrath, had to be rooted out (cf. 7:4). As he had warned previously (7:25-26), for Israel to participate in pagan ways was to invite the doom reserved for pagan practice.

(3) Blessing as a Product of Grace (9:1–10:11)

Moses commenced this section on a note of greatest urgency and importance by his use of the imperative *šĕmaʿ*, "listen!" He did so three other times in Deuteronomy (4:1; 5:1; 6:4), each time either introducing a major section of the book or drawing attention to something of unusual significance (as the Shema in 6:4-5). There can be no doubt then that the long passage at hand is set apart as a particularly noteworthy part of Moses' series of parenetic addresses.[139] As will be seen, its importance lies prima-

---

[137] For לְמַעַן as introducing a final or result clause, see *IBHS* 38.3c; cf. Exod 4:5; Gen 18:19; 1 Sam 15:15; Jer 27:15.

[138] Mayes points out that v. 19 especially alludes to the first commandment, sharing much common vocabulary with it (*Deuteronomy,* 194).

[139] B. Peckham, "The Composition of Deut 9:1–10:11," in *Word and Spirit: Essays in Honour of David Michael Stanley SJ* (Willowdale, Ont: Regis College Press, 1975), 3-59.

rily in its emphasis on the gracious initiative of the Lord in bringing his people to the present hour despite their contrariness. No matter their sin in the past, up to and including unbridled idolatry, Israel was the nation of promise and election, and the Lord would guarantee their ultimate salvation and sovereignty.

From a literary standpoint Deut 9:1–10:11 is a travel narrative much like Deut 1:6–3:29, with which, in fact, it shares much in common. For example, both are introduced (1:1-5; 9:1-6) and concluded (3:29; 10:11) by a setting in the plains of Moab in anticipation of the conquest of Canaan. Other shared features (as well as uniquenesses) will be pointed out in the course of the following analysis.

[1]Hear, O Israel. You are now about to cross the Jordan to go in and dispossess nations greater and stronger than you, with large cities that have walls up to the sky. [2]The people are strong and tall—Anakites! You know about them and have heard it said: "Who can stand up against the Anakites?" [3]But be assured today that the LORD your God is the one who goes across ahead of you like a devouring fire. He will destroy them; he will subdue them before you. And you will drive them out and annihilate them quickly, as the LORD has promised you.

[4]After the LORD your God has driven them out before you, do not say to yourself, "The LORD has brought me here to take possession of this land because of my righteousness." No, it is on account of the wickedness of these nations that the LORD is going to drive them out before you. [5]It is not because of your righteousness or your integrity that you are going in to take possession of their land; but on account of the wickedness of these nations, the LORD your God will drive them out before you, to accomplish what he swore to your fathers, to Abraham, Isaac and Jacob. [6]Understand, then, that it is not because of your righteousness that the LORD your God is giving you this good land to possess, for you are a stiff-necked people.

9:1-2 To heighten the sense of the impossibility of what they were about to do, Moses hyperbolically described the peoples of Canaan as more populous and stronger than Israel (cf. 7:1) and as inhabiting cities with sky-high walls (v. 1). This in fact was the essence of the report brought back to Moses from the twelve spies whom he had sent to reconnoitre the land nearly forty years earlier (Num 13:28; cf. Deut 1:28). Most fearsome of these peoples were the Anakites, a race so intimidating that a proverb arose because of them—"Who can stand up against the Anakites?"

This would be a familiar rhetorical question whenever insurmountable difficulties arose in life.[140]

9:3 But what is insurmountable to humankind is of no consequence to God, the one who like a "devouring fire" (cf. 4:24) leads the battle (v. 3).[141] It is he, the divine warrior, who would destroy the Anakites and all other foes, driving them out and bringing them to utter ruin. The same holy war imagery appears in the earlier narrative, where it is said that "he will fight for you" (1:30; cf. 3:22) and that he had delivered up the enemy to them (2:33,36; cf. 3:2-3,18,21).

9:4-5 Reflecting the warning of 8:11-18, Moses went on to urge his people to refrain from taking credit for the victory once it had been achieved, as though it were a natural corollary to their righteousness, something they deserved because of their own merit. To the contrary, it was because of the wickedness of the Canaanite nations that they would be expelled to make room for Israel. This shocking and humbling disclosure, far from placing Israel's election on any basis other than grace, emphasizes that very truth; for the whole point here is that all peoples, Israel included, are wicked and undeserving of any divine favor.[142] For one people to be chosen to salvation out of all other possible candidates is a mystery beyond human understanding.

9:6 The nations of Canaan must be driven out because of their wickedness, and were it not for God's elective grace, Israel should never have been allowed to enter in. Thus in fulfillment of the promises to the patriarchs, Israel, despite their having been a "stiff-necked people" (v. 6), would subdue and possess the land of Canaan. "Stiff-necked" is a metaphor for stubbornness, one suggesting unwillingness to submit to the yoke of God's sovereignty (cf. Exod 32:9; 33:3,5; 34:9; Isa 48:4).[143] It is indeed marvelous that such a people could inherit the land, but for them to continue to resist the Lord's covenant obligations would eventually and certainly lead to their expulsion from it (cf. 4:40; 5:33; 28:25,36,63-68).

[7]Remember this and never forget how you provoked the LORD your God to anger in the desert. From the day you left Egypt until you arrived here, you

---

[140] For the form and function of proverbs in biblical literature, see R. E. Murphy, *The Tree of Life: An Exploration of Biblical Wisdom Literature,* ABRL (New York: Doubleday, 1990), 5-13.

[141] For the divine epithet אֹכְלָה אֵשׁ ("devouring fire") see M. Ottosson, "אָכַל *ʾākhal,*" etc. *TDOT* 1:238-39.

[142] Thompson, *Deuteronomy,* 138-39.

[143] Cf. B. Couroyer, "'Avoir de nuque raide': ne pas incliner l'oreille," *RB* 88 (1981): 216-25.

have been rebellious against the LORD. [8]At Horeb you aroused the LORD'S wrath so that he was angry enough to destroy you. [9]When I went up on the mountain to receive the tablets of stone, the tablets of the covenant that the LORD had made with you, I stayed on the mountain forty days and forty nights; I ate no bread and drank no water. [10]The LORD gave me two stone tablets inscribed by the finger of God. On them were all the commandments the LORD proclaimed to you on the mountain out of the fire, on the day of the assembly.

[11]At the end of the forty days and forty nights, the LORD gave me the two stone tablets, the tablets of the covenant. [12]Then the LORD told me, "Go down from here at once, because your people whom you brought out of Egypt have become corrupt. They have turned away quickly from what I commanded them and have made a cast idol for themselves."

[13]And the LORD said to me, "I have seen this people, and they are a stiff-necked people indeed! [14]Let me alone, so that I may destroy them and blot out their name from under heaven. And I will make you into a nation stronger and more numerous than they."

[15]So I turned and went down from the mountain while it was ablaze with fire. And the two tablets of the covenant were in my hands. [16]When I looked, I saw that you had sinned against the LORD your God; you had made for yourselves an idol cast in the shape of a calf. You had turned aside quickly from the way that the LORD had commanded you. [17]So I took the two tablets and threw them out of my hands, breaking them to pieces before your eyes.

9:7 Their future propensity to do this very thing was predicated on their past record, a point Moses made over and over (cf. 4:9-14; 6:10-15; 8:1-4,11-16). And that record was a sorry one, punctuated—indeed, characterized—by resistance to the Lord and rebellion against his covenant expectations. From the time they left Egypt until they arrived in the Moabite plain, Israel had provoked (*qāṣap*) the Lord and had been rebellious (*mārâ*) against him (v. 7). The same two verbs appear in parallel in Ps 106:32-33 with particular reference to the uprising of Israel against the Lord and Moses at Meribah, where they had arrogantly demanded water to drink (Num 20:2-13).

9:8 As serious as that incident was, it could hardly compare to the classic act of Israel's covenant defection, the manufacture and worship of the golden calf at Horeb.[144] Its importance as a paradigm of provocation is clear from the fact that Moses devoted fourteen verses to recounting it (vv. 8-21). Once more he used the rare verb *qāṣap* to describe the Lord's anger,

---

[144] For a traditio-historical understanding of the pericope of the golden calf, see H. Motzki, "Ein Beitrag zum Problem des stierkultes in der Religionsgeschichte Israels," *VT* 25 (1975): 470-85.

a wrath so severe that it seemed that he would annihilate (*šāmad*) his chosen people (v. 8; cf. Exod 32:10). Though *šāmad* commonly refers to the Lord's enemies elsewhere and sometimes in connection with *ḥērem*, the ban (cf. Deut 2:21-23; 4:3; 7:24; 9:3), here the target of his anger was Israel (vv. 14,19,25; cf. 28:48,63).

In line with Moses' practice (and that of ancient Semitic narrative in general), he recounted the Horeb rebellion in some detail. The original account is in Exod 24:18; 31:18–34:28, but the arrangement of the episodes is somewhat different there.[145] This, too, is characteristic of biblical literature, for it is not always slavishly repetitious but employs freedom of arrangement in line with the purpose(s) in view.[146] Here the emphasis is on the sin of Israel and its nearly calamitous results, not on the forgiveness of the Lord and renewal of the ruptured covenant.

9:9 Moses spoke first of his having ascended Horeb (Sinai in the Exod account; Exod 19:11) to receive from the Lord the stone tablets of the covenant, that is, the Ten Commandments (v. 9a; cf. Exod 24:12,18; 31:18; Deut 4:13; 5:22). He remained there for forty days and nights without food or drink, a fact related to his second ascent of the mountain in the Exodus version (Exod 34:28). This clearly miraculous sojourn gives tangible support to Moses' own observation that "man does not live on bread alone but on every word that comes from the mouth of the LORD" (Deut 8:3). Jesus too was deprived of food for forty days (Matt 4:2), and in the midst of his temptation to create bread from stones he quoted Deut 8:3 to make that very point (Matt 4:4). One cannot help but note the reference to bread and stones in light of the experience of Moses, who received the Word of God on stone tablets even while being denied physical food and drink.[147]

9:10 Both the original stone tablets and those that replaced them were composed by the Lord, or, as Moses related it, "by the finger of God" (v. 10; cf. Exod 31:18; 32:15-16; 34:1,28). Though "finger" is clearly anthropomorphic, the figurative language should not obscure the fact that something highly unique took place when the Lord delivered the Decalogue to Moses. Nowhere else in Scripture is God said to have written anything.[148] Indeed, he consistently revealed himself to human penmen through dreams and visions (or even "face to face," Num 12:6-8), and they inscribed his

---

[145] Driver, *Deuteronomy*, 112-13.

[146] Thompson describes the account here as "a free retelling of the Exodus story" (*Deuteronomy*, 139).

[147] For other connections see C. L. Blomberg, *Matthew*, NAC (Nashville: Broadman, 1992), 83-85.

[148] See, however, John 8:6-8 and R. W. Wall, "The Finger of God: Deuteronomy 9:10 and Luke 11:20," *NTS* 33 (1987): 144-50.

words for him. The personal attention to the Ten Commandments underscores their fundamental importance to the entire covenant revelation.

9:11-12 After the forty days Moses descended from the mountain, having learned that the people had "become corrupt" (*šiḥḥēt*) in his absence. More explicitly, this corruption consisted of the casting of an idol which, the longer Exodus version says, was the object of their worship and sacrifice (vv. 11-12; cf. Exod 32:6,8). Only here, Deut 4:16, in the parallel version of Exod 32:7 (and possibly in Deut 32:5) is idolatry described by this verb and stem.[149]

It is worth noting that the Lord referred to Israel as "your people" (v. 12; Exod 32:7; 34:10), meaning Moses' people, rather than "my people," his own. The contexts of such usage make clear that Moses as covenant mediator and leader of his people was being tested. Though he was absent from this act of idolatry and therefore blameless and without fear of the divine wrath, would he be willing to identify with his people and even suffer with them? Was he willing for Israel to be known as "his" people?[150]

The answer was not long in coming, for Moses did indeed claim the people as his own and entered into urgent intercession on their behalf (Exod 32:11-14,30-33; cf. Deut 9:18-20). By being willing for them to be his people, Moses was able to restore them to fellowship with God as his people. Moses' insistence that Israel was the people of God no matter how they may have sinned makes for an interesting dialogue in the Book of Exodus (Exod 32:11-12; 33:13,16).

9:13-14 Moses continued his report of the Horeb rebellion by recalling the Lord's description of Israel as a stiff-necked people (cf. v. 9) whom he would so thoroughly destroy that their very memory would be lost to future generations (vv. 13-14). To "blot out the name" is, in the context of covenant disloyalty, tantamount to the Lord's termination of his relationship with his people.[151] Thus in the curse section of this book it is said that anyone who hears the words of the Lord's covenant requirements but disregards them will have his name blotted out from under heaven (29:18-19 [Eng., vv. 19-20]). Even more striking is the Exodus version of the Horeb incident where Moses implored the Lord to forgive Israel's sin of the golden calf. If God would not, then, said Moses, "blot me out of the book you have written" (Exod 32:32). The Lord's response was, "Whoever has

---

[149] Schroeder describes the verb form "as in the highest degree descriptive of image worship" (*Deuteronomy*, 109).

[150] In the language of anthropopathism, Yahweh also was distancing himself from these evil people, saying, in a sense, that he no longer recognized them as his own; cf. Ridderbos, *Deuteronomy*, 133.

[151] Thompson, *Deuteronomy*, 140.

sinned against me I will blot out of my book" (v. 33). The "book" here is clearly that of covenant relationship though elsewhere it refers as well to the "book of life" in which the names of all believers are recorded (cf. Ps 69:28; Dan 12:1; Mal 3:16; Rev 13:8; 17:8; 20:12,15; 21:27).[152]

The covenant ramifications of the Lord's threatened action are clear also in his promise to Moses to make of him a stronger and larger nation than even Israel was (v. 14b; cf. Exod 32:10). In other words, Moses would become another Abraham, and through his offspring all the ancient patriarchal promises presumably would be fulfilled. Though Moses' response to that overture is not reported at this point of the account (see vv. 25-29), Exodus describes his immediate insistence that for the Lord to abandon his promise to the fathers and give up on Israel would cast the very name of God into disrepute among the nations (Exod 32:11-14).

9:15-17   Once Moses was aware of what had transpired down below, he descended with the stone tablets in his hands. Only Deuteronomy points out that the mountain was "ablaze with fire," a description no doubt of the theophanic splendor of the Lord (cf. 4:33,36; 5:24-26) but also suggestive of the heat of his anger (cf. Exod 32:10; Deut 9:19). When Moses saw the idol "cast in the shape of a calf," he dashed the tablets to the ground, shattering them as a sign of Israel's having shattered the covenant (vv. 16-17).[153] The "cast calf" was manufactured by pouring molten metal into a mold (cf. Exod 32:4,8; 34:17; Lev 19:4; Judg 18:17; Isa 42:17; 44:10; Hos 13:2).[154] The "tool" (*ḥereṭ*) referred to in Exod 32:4 should, with the NIV, be understood as a file or some other implement used to "fashion" the idol once it had been cast.[155]

[18]Then once again I fell prostrate before the LORD for forty days and forty nights; I ate no bread and drank no water, because of all the sin you had committed, doing what was evil in the LORD'S sight and so provoking him to anger. [19]I feared the anger and wrath of the LORD, for he was angry enough with you to destroy you. But again the LORD listened to me. [20]And the LORD was angry enough with Aaron to destroy him, but at that time I prayed for Aaron too. [21]Also I took that sinful thing of yours, the calf you had made, and burned it in the fire. Then I crushed it and ground it to powder as fine as dust and threw the dust into a stream that flowed down the mountain.

[22]You also made the LORD angry at Taberah, at Massah and at Kibroth Hattaavah.

---

[152] W. Herrmann, "Das Buch des Lebens," *Das Altertum* 20 (1974): 3-10.

[153] For examples in Akkadian literature see *CAD* 6:171-72, s.v. *ḥepû*.

[154] L. R. Bailey, "The Golden Calf," *HUCA* 42 (1971): 97-115; S. E. Loewenstamm, "The Making and Destruction of the Golden Calf," *Bib* 48 (1967): 481-90.

[155] Durham, *Exodus*, 420.

[23]And when the LORD sent you out from Kadesh Barnea, he said, "Go up and take possession of the land I have given you." But you rebelled against the command of the LORD your God. You did not trust him or obey him. [24]You have been rebellious against the LORD ever since I have known you.

[25]I lay prostrate before the LORD those forty days and forty nights because the LORD had said he would destroy you. [26]I prayed to the LORD and said, "O Sovereign LORD, do not destroy your people, your own inheritance that you redeemed by your great power and brought out of Egypt with a mighty hand. [27]Remember your servants Abraham, Isaac and Jacob. Overlook the stubbornness of this people, their wickedness and their sin. [28]Otherwise, the country from which you brought us will say, 'Because the LORD was not able to take them into the land he had promised them, and because he hated them, he brought them out to put them to death in the desert.' [29]But they are your people, your inheritance that you brought out by your great power and your outstretched arm."

9:18-20 In line with Moses' character and his role as covenant mediator, it is not surprising that he entered into an intense forty-day regimen of prayer and fasting, an experience, he says, like one he had undergone at some previous time (v. 18). The purpose, of course, was to avert the wrath of the Lord against Israel generally and Aaron specifically, a holy anger so inflamed that it threatened to destroy the whole nation (vv. 19-20).

The forty-day session with the Lord to which Moses referred was that in which he had received the revelation of the covenant in the first place (Exod 24:18; cf. 32:11-14).[156] It was appropriate, then, that he spend forty more days in confession and repentance as he awaited the renewal of the gracious covenant of the Lord (Exod 34:28; Deut 9:9,11; 10:10). The number forty throughout Scripture symbolizes testing and/or judgment (cf. Gen 7:17; 8:6; Num 13:25; 14:33-34; 32:13; Deut 8:2; Ps 95:10; Matt 4:2). In the present account it is noteworthy that Moses fasted throughout the time of covenant reaffirmation, an act that not only expressed his brokenhearted mediation for his people but his total preoccupation with spiritual things. This, too, was the concern of Christ, who, in agonizing trial in the Judean desert, reminded the tempter that "man does not live on bread alone but on every word that comes from the mouth of God (Matt 4:4; cf. Deut 8:3).

9:21 Repentance and restoration were not complete, however, until the immediate symbol of the apostasy, the golden calf, was totally eliminated. This Moses did by reducing it to fine powder, which he cast into the nearby mountain stream (v. 21).[157] The Exodus account adds the detail that

---

[156] Weinfeld, *Deuteronomy 1-11*, 411.

[157] C. T. Begg, "The Destruction of the Calf (Exodus 32:20; Deuteronomy 9:21)," in *Das Deuteronomium*, ed. N. Lohfink, BETL 68 (Leuven: University Press, 1985), 208-51.

Moses made the people drink the water that had become the watery grave of the idol (Exod 32:20). In this manner the thing they had worshiped would become a product of their own waste, the very epitome of worthlessness and impurity.[158] It might also speak of the psychosomatic means of determining the guilt or innocence of the people, much as the drinking of the holy water of the tabernacle did in the case of wives accused by their husbands of adultery (Num 5:5-31).[159]

9:22-24 The recital of rebellion continues with a parenthetical reference to Israel's defections at various places including Taberah, Massah, Kibroth Hattaavah, and Kadesh Barnea (vv. 22-24). At the first of these places, Taberah, Israel had engaged in bitter complaint though they had traveled only three days from Sinai, the place of unparalleled blessing (Num 10:35–11:1). As a result the Lord sent fiery judgment (hence *tabⁿerâ*, "burning," from *bāⁿar,* "to burn"). Even before they reached Sinai the people had grumbled over the lack of water, a lack remedied by Moses' striking the rock and bringing water from it (Exod 17:1-6). Because they tested the Lord there, the place was called "Massah" ("testing," from *nāsâ,* "to test, try"; Exod 17:7).

The incident at Kibroth Hattaavah also centered on the complaining of the people, who, despite the miraculous supply of manna, rejected God's provision and lusted after the foods of Egypt (Num 11:4-32). While they gorged themselves on the quail he supernaturally provided, the Lord sent a plague and destroyed many of them, a disaster that gave rise to the place name "Graves of Craving" (vv. 33-34).

Finally, Moses reminded the Israelites of their shameful disbelief of the report from Joshua and Caleb who, as two of the spies sent ahead to reconnoitre the land of Canaan, related that it was a beautiful and fertile land and one well able to be taken by them if they trusted in the Lord (Num 13:30; 14:6-9; cf. Deut 1:22-33). The purpose of recalling this and the other incidents was to underscore the fact that the matter of the golden calf was not an isolated or unique event but one that was part and parcel of a history of rebellions both before and after it took place (v. 24).[160]

---

[158] B. Jacob, *The Second Book of the Bible: Exodus* (Hoboken, N.J.: KTAV, 1992), 950. ("The repulsive drink would end in the sewer.")

[159] Thus S. R. Driver, *The Book of Exodus,* CBSC (Cambridge: University Press, 1953), 353.

[160] In light of the statement of Israel's continuous rebellion against the Lord in v. 7, it is best (with the LXX) to read יְדַעְתּוֹ ("he knew you") for יְדַעְתִּי ("I have known you") in v. 24. This proposal gains strength in the fact that the verb יָדַע is a technical covenant term. Cf. H. B. Huffmon, "The Treaty Background of Hebrew *yādaⁿ," BASOR* 181 (1966): 35.

9:25-29   Resuming the narrative, Moses rehearsed the reason for the urgency of his intercessory prayer: that the Lord might not destroy Israel and thus abrogate the covenant he had made with them (vv. 25-26). To do so would be a violation of the promise made to the patriarchal ancestors (v. 27) and, moreover, would reflect badly on the Lord in the view of the Egyptians, Israel's erstwhile masters. The contest between Yahweh and the mighty gods and rulers of Egypt that had resulted in the glorious victory of the exodus deliverance (v. 26b) would be forgotten because of the Lord's impotence in not being able to take them to the land of promise (v. 28a). Even worse, Moses said, what appeared to be the love of God for his people in his act of exodus redemption would instead be seen as hatred, for the death of Israel in the desert would allow no other conclusion (v. 28b).[161] In short, the very nature of Israel as God's people, his inheritance whom he had redeemed by his own power and grace, demanded their ongoing existence and thus their forgiveness in the here and now (v. 29).

[1]**At that time the** LORD **said to me, "Chisel out two stone tablets like the first ones and come up to me on the mountain. Also make a wooden chest.** [2]**I will write on the tablets the words that were on the first tablets, which you broke. Then you are to put them in the chest."**

[3]**So I made the ark out of acacia wood and chiseled out two stone tablets like the first ones, and I went up on the mountain with the two tablets in my hands.** [4]**The** LORD **wrote on these tablets what he had written before, the Ten Commandments he had proclaimed to you on the mountain, out of the fire, on the day of the assembly. And the** LORD **gave them to me.** [5]**Then I came back down the mountain and put the tablets in the ark I had made, as the** LORD **commanded me, and they are there now.**

[6]**(The Israelites traveled from the wells of the Jaakanites to Moserah. There Aaron died and was buried, and Eleazar his son succeeded him as priest.** [7]**From there they traveled to Gudgodah and on to Jotbathah, a land with streams of water.** [8]**At that time the** LORD **set apart the tribe of Levi to carry the ark of the covenant of the** LORD**, to stand before the** LORD **to minister and to pronounce blessings in his name, as they still do today.** [9]**That is why the Levites have no share or inheritance among their brothers; the** LORD **is their inheritance, as the** LORD **your God told them.)**

[10]**Now I had stayed on the mountain forty days and nights, as I did the first time, and the** LORD **listened to me at this time also. It was not his will to destroy you.** [11]**"Go," the** LORD **said to me, "and lead the people on their way, so that they may enter and possess the land that I swore to their fathers to give them."**

---

[161] Just as God's love for his people was tantamount to his having elected them, so his hate would speak of his rejection of them. Cf. 7:8.

10:1-5   The efficacy of Moses' intercession is clear from the Lord's response: "Come up to me on the mountain" (10:1). This is an invitation to covenant renewal, to beginning all over again, as the precision of the language in vv. 1-5 makes clear. First, Moses had to prepare two stone tablets "like the first ones" (v. 1), and then the Lord would write on them "the words that were on the first tablets" (v. 2). He obeyed and made tablets "like the first ones" (v. 3) upon which the Lord wrote "what he had written before" (v. 4).

A comparison with the original account of Exod 34:1-9 reveals an additional detail here in Deuteronomy, namely, the command to make a wooden chest, that is, the ark (vv. 1,3,5).[162] The instruction to make such a vessel to contain the tablets had been given shortly after the covenant ceremony of Exod 24 (cf. Exod 25:10), but the actual construction of the ark appears to have come some time later, later, in fact, than the incident of the golden calf (Exod 37:1).[163] It is possible, of course, that the chest Moses was told to make as he was about to ascend Sinai to receive the new stone tablets was not the Ark of the Covenant but a temporary container for the Ten Commandments. However, the fact that he made it of acacia wood (v. 3; cf. Exod 25:10) and that the tablets were there as of the time of the composition of Deuteronomy ("they are there now," v. 5) would seem to rule this out. More likely, the whole pericope of Exod 32:1–34:35 is out of chronological order, the apostasy of the golden calf having occurred sometime after all the manufacture of the tabernacle and its furnishings was complete (cf. Exod 40:20).[164] The order of events in Exodus according to this view would be as follows:

The covenant ceremony (24:1-11)
Moses' ascent of the mountain (24:12–33:23)
Narrative of the ascent (24:12-18)
Instructions for the tabernacle (25:1–31:18)
The golden calf (32:1–33:23)
The construction of the parts of the tabernacle (35:1–40:16)
The reascent of the mountain (34:1-35)
The assembly of the tabernacle (40:17-38)

---

[162] See T. E. Fretheim, "The Ark in Deuteronomy," *CBQ* 30 (1968): 1-14.

[163] For similarities and differences between the two accounts, see Driver, *Deuteronomy,* 117-18. Driver says the discrepancy "does not admit of reconciliation," suggesting that when JE was compiled (after the composition of D) with P, reference to the ark was omitted "as inconsistent with the more detailed particulars, which he preferred, contained in the narrative of P." This solution, however, begs the question of such sources.

[164] See already Keil and Delitzsch, *The Pentateuch,* 3:340; Schroeder, *Deuteronomy,* 112-13.

The reversal of 34:1-35 and 35:1–40:16 permits the ark to have been constructed prior to Moses' reascent of the mountain and thus to have contained the newly inscribed tablets. The reason for the present canonical order of the accounts in Exodus was no doubt to place the reascent in direct juxtaposition to the events that necessitated it, namely, Israel's apostasy concerning the golden calf. In any event, the version here in Deuteronomy is unambiguous in asserting that the ark was made by Moses prior to his climbing the mountain to receive the tablets (10:1-3); and, in fact, upon his return he placed them within it where, according to the narrator, "they are . . . now" (v. 5).

10:6-7 Continuing his recital of Israel's disobedient ways and God's gracious response, Moses spoke of the trek from the "wells of the Jaakanites to Moserah" (v. 6), the place where Aaron died. They then went on to Gudgodah and Jotbathah (v. 7). Again, however, there are differences from the itinerary in the Book of Numbers, which traces the route from Moseroth (= Moserah?) to Bene Jaakan (Num 33:31) and then from Hor Haggidgad to Jotbathah (vv. 32-33). Also Numbers locates the death of Aaron at Mount Hor and not Moserah (Num 33:38).

The problems in the comparisons of the two accounts are exacerbated by the lack of positive identification of most of these sites. Moserah is unknown otherwise and may, in fact, be different from Moseroth. Bene Jaakan is likewise unidentifiable and may also be different from "the wells of the Jaakanites." Gudgodah may be the same as Hor Haggidgad, but there is no way to make a certain connection. Even the famous Mount Hor cannot be located with confidence, though most scholars place it northeast of Kadesh Barnea. Perhaps Mount Hor was in a region known as Moserah. The only place, in fact, that can be identified with any degree of assurance is Jotbathah, probably to be associated with Tabeh, ten miles southwest of Elath and on the Gulf of Aqaba.[165]

The most reasonable way to understand the Numbers and Deuteronomy passages is to assume that Deuteronomy, unlike Numbers, is not in the form of a technical itinerary and therefore is to be seen as a mere listing of sites of significance without any necessary attention to spatial or even chronological sequence. In other words, the purpose of the passage is not to dictate one's understanding of its geographical data.[166] Moses was content to mention places that bore out his contention that Israel's history had been one of constant covenant defection.

---

[165] Aharoni, *Land of the Bible,* 199-200, 437.
[166] Thompson, *Deuteronomy,* 145.

10:8-9   Support for this assumption lies in the following statement concerning the setting apart of the Levites to serve the Lord in a special way (vv. 8-9). Moses said it was done "at that time," that is, it seems, at the time of Aaron's death. However, the selection of Aaron's Levitical kinsmen and the description of their tasks had been articulated long before Aaron's demise (Num 3:5–4:49; 8:6-22; 18:1-7).[167] "At that time," then, is simply a formula referring to the general past that Moses was recalling.[168] The reason he stressed the functions of the Levites—carrying the ark, standing to minister, and pronouncing blessings—was to highlight all the more their allegiance to the Lord in the matter of the golden calf.[169] Their leader Aaron had failed to suppress the people's idolatry and, in fact, had taken the initiative in it (Exod 32:1-6). The Levites were noticeably absent until Moses descended from the mountain, and then they became the Lord's ministers of wrath and punishment (Exod 32:25-29). By both election and obedience they demonstrated their qualifications to be the Lord's inheritance (v. 9; cf. Num 18:20,24).

10:10-11   Moses concluded his historical résumé by referring once more to his intimate communion with the Lord on the mountain of Horeb (vv. 10-11). He was amazed perhaps that the Lord listened to him again for forty days, even after his people had so grievously sinned. In a remarkable tribute to God's covenant faithfulness he testified that "it was not his will to destroy you" (v. 10), and this in spite of his threats to do precisely that (Exod 32:7-10). Moses had come to learn that God's irrefragable promises prevail no matter what; for should they not, he himself would lose his reputation and glory among the nations and, in fact, would deny himself (Exod 32:11-14). On the basis of his very person and promises, therefore, he had commanded Moses to lead the people on to the land he had promised their fathers to give them (v. 11).

(4) Love of the Lord and Love of Humankind (10:12-22)

[12]**And now, O Israel, what does the LORD your God ask of you but to fear the LORD your God, to walk in all his ways, to love him, to serve the LORD your God with all your heart and with all your soul, [13]and to observe the LORD'S commands and decrees that I am giving you today for your own good?**

---

[167] R. Abba, "Priests and Levites in Deuteronomy," *VT* 27 (1977): 257-67; J. A. Emerton, "Priests and Levites in Deuteronomy," *VT* 12 (1962): 129-38; G. E. Wright, "The Levites in Deuteronomy," *VT* 4 (1954): 325-30

[168] S. E. Loewenstamm, "The Formula *bāʾēt hahîʾ* in Deuteronomy," *Tarbiz* 38 (1968): 99-104.

[169] Mayes, *Deuteronomy,* 206.

¹⁴To the LORD your God belong the heavens, even the highest heavens, the earth and everything in it. ¹⁵Yet the LORD set his affection on your forefathers and loved them, and he chose you, their descendants, above all the nations, as it is today. ¹⁶Circumcise your hearts, therefore, and do not be stiff-necked any longer. ¹⁷For the LORD your God is God of gods and LORD of lords, the great God, mighty and awesome, who shows no partiality and accepts no bribes. ¹⁸He defends the cause of the fatherless and the widow, and loves the alien, giving him food and clothing. ¹⁹And you are to love those who are aliens, for you yourselves were aliens in Egypt. ²⁰Fear the LORD your God and serve him. Hold fast to him and take your oaths in his name. ²¹He is your praise; he is your God, who performed for you those great and awesome wonders you saw with your own eyes. ²²Your forefathers who went down into Egypt were seventy in all, and now the LORD your God has made you as numerous as the stars in the sky.

As has been noted repeatedly, covenant relationship between the Lord and Israel had to be expressed in both a vertical and horizontal dimension. To love God is to love one's neighbor, and to serve God necessitates societal obligation.[170] The point is made here again, in perhaps its strongest statement in the entire Book of Deuteronomy, for the litany of covenant failure since Sinai as just elaborated in 9:6–10:11 calls for a fresh appeal by Moses that the sins of the past not be repeated.

The structure of the passage reveals an enveloping pattern in which injunctions to obey God (vv. 12-13; 20–22) embrace the corollary command to exhibit proper care and concern for other people, especially the socially and economically disadvantaged (vv. 14-19).[171] The motive clause and that which binds the whole together is v. 17, a confession of the sovereignty of God and of his justice.

10:12-13 The appeal to covenant recommitment is in the form of a rhetorical question packed with covenant vocabulary. What does the Lord your God ask? He asks for five things specifically, all of which have been addressed over and over in Moses' pareneses throughout the book (cf. also Mic 6:8).

---

[170] S. Amsler, "La motivation de l'ethique dans la parenese du Deutéronome," in *Beiträge zur alttestamentlichen Theologie,* ed. H. Donner et al (Göttingen: Vandenhoeck & Ruprecht, 1977), 11-22.

[171] Christensen notes that the temporal marker ועתה occurs in vv. 12 and 22, thus enveloping the passage as a whole. His further analysis is much like our own (*Deuteronomy 1–11,* 205):

A   The "Great Commandment"—fear YHWH your God (vv. 12-13)

B   YHWH owns all, but he has chosen you (vv. 14-16)

B´   YHWH is "God of gods," but he loves the sojourner (vv. 17-19)

A´   Fear YHWH, for he is your God (vv. 20-27)

1. He demands first of all that his people fear him. The verb employed (*yārēʾ*) is one that speaks of terror, indeed, but more than that. It expresses reverential awe, the kind one shows in the presence of transcendent and awesome power and that motivates one to worship and obedience (cf. Deut 5:29; 6:2,13,24; 31:12-13).[172]

2. Proper fear leads to a godly walk or lifestyle. The language of travel or pilgrimage is a favorite biblical metaphor to express adherence to principles and pathways of obedience (cf. Deut 5:33; 11:22; 19:9; 26:17; 28:9; 30:16).[173]

The sequence of fearing and walking is logical enough, for one's behavior must be predicated upon attitude. How, then, does love come next, particularly if it be viewed (as it should here) as a technical term denoting covenant reciprocation? The answer lies perhaps in viewing (1) and (2) as a matching pair and (3), (4), and (5) as a second group in which love becomes the basis for serving God and observing his covenant requirements.[174]

3. Love, though most commonly bearing emotive overtones, is much at home in covenant contexts as a synonym of election.[175] That is, God's choices are a function and expression of his love, a love that must find its response and counterpart in the commitment of the chosen one to love (i.e., choose) God in return (Deut 5:10; 6:5; 7:9,13; 11:1,13,22; 13:3; 19:9; 30:6,16,20). Such response, to be meaningful, must be manifest in deeds.

4. Thus, Israel was to serve the Lord with unreserved and unqualified devotion, one that marked them out as God's peculiar people who had been made his servant nation in achieving his redemptive purposes (Deut 6:13; 7:4; 11:13; 13:4).

5. Specifically, this service consists of observing the Lord's commands (*miṣwôt*) and decrees (*ḥuqqôt*). Service is not abstract or vacuous, then, but in covenant relational terms it speaks of strict conformity to precise stipulations (Deut 4:6; 6:1; 8:6,11; 11:8,22; 12:14; 26:16; 28:45).

10:14-15 The introduction to the horizontal demands of the covenant is couched in an appeal to recognize the absolute uniqueness and dominion of the Lord, he who is Lord of heaven and earth (v. 14) and who, therefore, has the authority to elect whom he will to salvation and service (v. 15). The

---

[172] Kooy, "The Fear and Love of God in Deuteronomy," 108-9.

[173] *TDOT* 3:396.

[174] Christensen makes the helpful observation that the command to love "stands at the very center of the rhythmic unit." This tends to cloud the issue, however, by causing prosody to override logical and theological concerns (*Deuteronomy 1–11*, 206).

[175] Moran, "The Ancient Near Eastern Background of the Love of God in Deuteronomy," 77-87.

phrase "highest heavens" does not suggest some cosmological scheme in which there are levels of heavenly realm, but it is merely a Hebrew construction indicating totality.[176] As Creator, the Lord obviously rules over all things and disposes of them as he will.

It is all the more remarkable then that he took notice of the patriarchs. He set his affection (ḥāšaq) on them, that is, he loved them, that is, he chose (bāḥar) them. In a powerful and breathtaking sequence of elective terms Moses described the grace of God in choosing only Israel out of all the options at his disposal. All three verbs are essentially synonymous as their usage elsewhere clearly shows. Thus ḥāšaq and bāḥar occur in parallel in Deut 7:7, and the two are explained by ʾāhēb in v. 8. The words bāḥar and ʾāhēb are combined in Deut 4:37, also in a synonymously parallel manner.[177]

The condescension of the Lord, Sovereign over all, to choose Israel is a theme expressed at the very beginning of the nation's covenant history, for in the desert of Sinai the Lord had invited Israel into covenant partnership on the very basis of his elective grace. "Although the whole earth is mine," he said, "you will be for me a kingdom of priests and a holy nation" (Exod 19:5-6). This sentiment is echoed in Deut 7:6-8, where Israel is reminded that they possessed no special qualifications to be God's people but became such only as he chose them among many options.

10:16 Israel therefore had no claim on God and no right to be arrogant or proud. In fact, Moses said, the people should circumcise their hearts and stop being stiff-necked (v. 16). Circumcision was the sign of outward conformity to the covenant ideal and was not only perfectly acceptable but required (Gen 17:9-14; cf. Exod 12:48).[178] However, it was not enough if it was only physical and formal. More important was an inner conformity to the requirements and purposes of God, a circumcision of the inner person (cf. Jer 4:4; Rom 2:28-29). To be stiff-necked is to be unsubmissive, like an ox that refuses to bow its head to the yoke and to turn at the command of its owner. Throughout the Old Testament "stiffnecked" is a metaphor for stubbornness and recalcitrance (cf. Job 9:4; 2 Chr 30:8; 36:13; Neh 9:16-17,29; Jer 7:26; 17:23; 19:15). In the present context it denotes a lack of compliance to the covenant requirements.

10:17 Such a spirit of indifference is incomprehensible in light of who God is, the "God of gods and Lord of lords, the great God, mighty and

---

[176] Craigie, *Deuteronomy,* 204.

[177] G. Wallis, "חשק, ḥāšaq," etc. *TDOT* 5:262.

[178] For a helpful discussion of the rite of circumcision in antiquity, especially in Israel, see the excursus by Westermann, *Genesis 12–36,* 265.

awesome" (v. 17). Such a description does not admit to the reality of other gods but simply emphasizes the absolute uniqueness and incomparability of the Lord and his exclusive right to sovereignty over his people (cf. Deut 3:24; 4:35,39). As Lord over all he cannot be enticed or coerced into any kind of partiality through influence peddling (v. 17) and, in fact, is the special advocate of defenseless persons who are so often victims of such unscrupulous behavior (v. 18).

10:18-19 What God does in the social realm his people are to imitate (cf. Exod 22:22-24).[179] They must be especially sensitive to aliens living among them, particularly since they also had been aliens in Egypt (v. 19). The word for alien here (*gēr*) is the same as appears in Lev 19:34: "The alien living with you must be treated as one of your native-born. Love him as yourself." Exactly the same sentiment (but with "neighbor," *rēʿa*) is expressed in Lev 19:18, the verse Jesus quoted when he was quizzed about the greatest of the commandments (Matt 19:19). Jesus attached this to the command to "love the LORD" with all one's being (cf. Deut 6:5), thus joining love for God with love for others. This is precisely what the present passage is teaching as the enveloping structure makes clear.

10:20 The conclusion of this section consists of the second element of the bracketed material, a repetition of the injunction to love and serve the Lord (v. 20; cf. v. 12). To this is added the command to hold fast to him and swear by his name. These, too, are covenant requirements as the usage of the respective verbs elsewhere makes clear. Thus to hold fast (*dābaq*) to the Lord appears with the verbs of walking in his ways and loving (*ʾāhēb*) him (Deut 11:22) and with loving him (*ʾāhēb*) and obeying (*šāmaʿ*) him (Deut 30:20). To hold fast to the Lord is to express covenant faithfulness to him.[180]

To take oaths in his name (or to swear by him) is also to be understood in covenant terms. This same collocation of verbs ("fear," "serve," "swear by") occurs in Deut 6:13, a passage set in a context of appeal to covenant loyalty (cf. vv. 14-15). The exact injunction occurs in Josh 23:7-8, where Joshua, referring to the Mosaic covenant (v. 6), exhorts Israel not to invoke the names of pagan gods "or swear by them."[181] This is followed by a prohibition to serve (*ʾābad*; cf. Deut 10:20) them or bow down to them.

---

[179] L. E. Toombs, "Love and Justice in Deuteronomy," *Int* 19 (1965): 399-411; F. C. Fensham, "Widow, Orphan and the Poor in Ancient Near Eastern Legal and Wisdom Literature," *JNES* 21 (1962): 129-39; R. D. Patterson, "The Widow, the Orphan, and the Poor in the Old Testament and the Extra-Biblical Literature," *BSac* 130 (1973): 223-34.

[180] G. Wallis, "דָּבַק *dābhaq*," etc., *TDOT* 3:81-83.

[181] Butler, *Joshua,* 255.

Rather, God's people must "hold fast" (*dābaq*) to him (cf. Deut 10:20). Again, to hold fast to the Lord is to express exclusive devotion to him.

10:21-22   The justification for this uncompromising allegiance was both the person and the works of God. He was their praise (v. 21; i.e., the object of their praise by metonymy), their God who redeemed them by exodus deliverance accompanied by "awesome wonders" (*nôrā²ôt*), that is, the plagues and other manifestations of his presence and power. Most remarkable of all, perhaps, was his multiplication of his people from the seventy who descended into Egypt with Jacob (cf. Gen 46:27) to the multitude so numerous as to be compared to the stars in the sky (v. 22; cf. 1:10), a direct fulfillment of the promise to the patriarchal ancestors (Gen 15:5; 22:17). A God so faithful to his promise and with sufficient resources to bring it to pass was surely worthy of his people's wholehearted commitment to the covenant he had graciously made with them.

(5) Obedience and Disobedience and Their Rewards (11:1-32)

¹Love the LORD your God and keep his requirements, his decrees, his laws and his commands always. ²Remember today that your children were not the ones who saw and experienced the discipline of the LORD your God: his majesty, his mighty hand, his outstretched arm; ³the signs he performed and the things he did in the heart of Egypt, both to Pharaoh king of Egypt and to his whole country; ⁴what he did to the Egyptian army, to its horses and chariots, how he overwhelmed them with the waters of the Red Sea as they were pursuing you, and how the LORD brought lasting ruin on them. ⁵It was not your children who saw what he did for you in the desert until you arrived at this place, ⁶and what he did to Dathan and Abiram, sons of Eliab the Reubenite, when the earth opened its mouth right in the middle of all Israel and swallowed them up with their households, their tents and every living thing that belonged to them. ⁷But it was your own eyes that saw all these great things the LORD has done.

⁸Observe therefore all the commands I am giving you today, so that you may have the strength to go in and take over the land that you are crossing the Jordan to possess, ⁹and so that you may live long in the land that the LORD swore to your forefathers to give to them and their descendants, a land flowing with milk and honey. ¹⁰The land you are entering to take over is not like the land of Egypt, from which you have come, where you planted your seed and irrigated it by foot as in a vegetable garden. ¹¹But the land you are crossing the Jordan to take possession of is a land of mountains and valleys that drinks rain from heaven. ¹²It is a land the LORD your God cares for; the eyes of the LORD your God are continually on it from the beginning of the year to its end.

The climax of this lengthy conclusion to the general stipulation section of the Deuteronomy covenant document is found in vv. 26-32, the setting forth of a statement of blessing and curse for covenant obedience and disobedience respectively. This call to commitment is, in fact, the pervasive theme of the whole chapter, a fact suggested by reference to "decrees" (*ḥuqqîm*) and "laws" (*mišpāṭîm*) in both the opening and closing verses. It was only as Israel took these to heart and obeyed them that they could expect the blessing of the Lord. It is fitting, moreover, that the general stipulation section should conclude with exhortation to covenant loyalty, for that is exactly how it began (5:1-5; cf. 4:32-40).[182]

The blessing and curse here follow in accordance to Israel's attitude toward (1) the Lord's dealings with his people in the past (vv. 1-7), (2) his promise to them of a good land (vv. 8-17), and (3) their adherence to and instruction of the covenant requirements to their offspring yet to come (vv. 18-25).

11:1-2   As is common in his parenetic addresses, Moses urged his people to love (i.e., be wholly obedient to) the Lord, the proof of which must be the keeping of his requirements (*mišmeret*) (cf. Lev 18:30; Num 9:19,23), his decrees (*ḥuqqîm*), his laws (*mišpāṭîm*), and his commands (*miṣwôt*). That is, to love God is to obey him in every respect (cf. Deut 6:5; 10:12; 11:13,22; 15:3; 30:6,16,20; Josh 22:5; 23:11). The basis for his appeal, first of all, is that these very people to whom he spoke had witnessed with their own eyes the mighty things the Lord had done for his people in the recent past (v. 7). It was they, and not their children, who had experienced his discipline (*mûsār*), an instruction produced by his greatness, his powerful hand, and his outstretched arm (cf. 8:5). The context makes clear that *mûsār* here refers not to Israel's punishment but to what they had learned as they observed God's mighty acts of deliverance (cf. Job 33:16; 36:10; Jer 32:33; 35:13; Zeph 3:2,7).

11:3-5   Another way of describing these instructive acts is as "signs" (*ʾōtōt*) accomplished by the Lord against Pharaoh, his armies, and the very heart of Egypt (v. 3).[183] These ranged from the changing of Moses' rod to

---

[182] Christensen describes 4:1–11:25 as part 1 of "The Inner Frame" of Deuteronomy (*Deuteronomy 1–11*, 69). He then matches the end of Deut 11 with the opening of Deut 4. While a prosodic analysis allows this understanding of the structure, the more common view that chaps. 5–11 form the general stipulation section of the covenant document seems to be decisive in connecting 11:26-32 with 5:1-5. Cf. Kline, *The Structure of Biblical Authority*, 137-38; S. A. Kaufman, "The Structure of the Deuteronomic Law," *Maarav* 1/2 (1978-79): 110.

[183] For the special, parenetic use of אוֹת here, see F. J. Helfmeyer, "אוֹת, *ʾôth*," *TDOT* 1:177-78.

a snake (Exod 4:8), to the plagues (Exod 7:3; 10:1), and to the mighty exodus event itself (Deut 4:34; 6:22; 7:19). These were not done in some peripheral, unpopulated area of Egypt but in its very midst, and they affected not just the poor and weak and defenseless but mighty Pharaoh (cf. Exod 12:29), his chariotry (Exod 14:26-27), and indeed the whole nation of Egypt (v. 3; cf. Exod 12:30). The result was "lasting ruin" (v. 4), literally, "The Lord destroyed them until this very day." It is a documented fact that neither Thutmose IV nor Amenhotep III, the kings of Egypt who succeeded the pharaoh of the exodus, Amenhotep II, were able to field large armies or undertake major military campaigns until after the period suggested by "until this very day," that is, about 1400 B.C.[184]

11:6-7 The second phase of the Lord's instruction was played out in the Sinai deserts, but this time it took the form of judgment upon fellow Israelites, not foreigners. The episode in view was the rebellion of the Reubenites, Dathan and Abiram. Moses commanded Dathan and Abiram to appear before him to answer to charges of insubordination to him and Aaron, and they refused to do so (Num 16:12). They had joined Korah, a Levite, in an insurrection against God's appointed leadership. Korah, it seems, wished to take over the priesthood while Dathan and Abiram aspired to political office (Num 16:1-3,13). The result was the utter annihilation of the rebels and their families by the opening up of the earth to swallow them (Num 16:31-35). The reason Korah is not mentioned here may be that the issue is sovereignty and not cultic leadership, as the previous reference to Pharaoh would suggest.[185] It is interesting to observe that this act of "instruction," like that in Egypt, occurred publicly, in the midst of (bĕqereb) Israel (v. 6; cf. v. 3).

Both of these lessons from history—the positive in Egypt and the negative in the desert sojourn—should have been fresh in the minds of Moses' audience, for it was they, and not their children (cf. vv. 2,5), who had seen them. As adult participants, therefore, they could not plead either ignorance or lack of personal accountability. What they had experienced should have provided the highest motivation to loving response and obedience.

11:8-9 It is therefore precisely on the basis of the lessons of history that Moses exhorted Israel to view the prospects of the future in a proper manner. "Observe therefore all the commands" (miṣwâ), he said, for only

---

[184] Merrill, *Kingdom of Priests*, 99.
[185] The usual explanation by source critics is that Korah is not mentioned in Deuteronomy because Deuteronomy follows the JE tradition in which the secular leadership of Moses is in question. The reference to Korah in Num 16:32 is assigned to P, the document concerned with cultic authority. Thus Weinfeld, *Deuteronomy 1–11*, 444.

in so doing would they have strength sufficient to enter and occupy the land they were about to inherit (v. 8) and, having occupied it, be able to live there for a long time to come (v. 9). This, of course, picks up exhortations and promises already verbalized by the great lawgiver (cf. 4:40; 5:16,33; 6:3; 8:1). Even though it was a land that the Lord "swore to your forefathers to give to them and their descendants" (v. 9), the nation still had the obligation to keep the covenant mandates in order that the promise might become effective.

The land in view is described in virtually paradisal terms: "flowing with milk and honey" (v. 9b). This familiar formula, though hyperbolic, speaks of the comparatively lush vegetation of Canaan that makes cattle grazing and bee production thriving industries.[186] By comparison to some parts of the world Canaan, of course, is far from verdant, but the comparison here is to Egypt from which the Israelites had just recently come. Except for the delta region of the north, Egypt was (and is) a desert land whose very survival depended on a complex system of artificial irrigation.

11:10   This is what the narrator had in mind as he spoke of Egypt as a place "where you planted your seed and irrigated it by foot" (v. 10).[187] The technique referred to is attested in ancient texts and drawings and still exists in parts of Egypt. It consists of networks of ditches, canals, and holding tanks from and into which river water could be "pumped" by means of a paddlewheel-like device called a *shadūf* in Arabic. This was powered by pedals or similar systems so that one could indeed say that the irrigation was done by foot.

11:11-12   Canaan, to the contrary, needed no such man-made inventions or human energy to make it fertile and productive, for it is a hilly land and as such captures and capitalizes on the prevailing westerly winds and clouds that deposit their burden of rain on its hills and into its valleys. It is quite true that these rains are seasonal, occurring mainly in the autumn (former rains) and spring (latter rains), but the porous limestone that forms much of Canaan's substratum allows for abundant subterranean reservoirs that can be tapped throughout the year through both artesian and man-made wells.[188] Thus it is a land that the Lord "cares for" (lit., "seeks after,"

---

[186] F. C. Fensham, "An Ancient Tradition of the Fertility of Palestine," *PEQ* 98 (1966): 166-67; S. D. Waterhouse, "A Land Flowing with Milk and Honey," *AUSS* 1 (1963): 152-66. Cf. Exod 3:8,17; 13:5; 33:3; Lev 20:24; Num 13:27; 14:8; 16:13-14; Deut 6:3; 26:9,15; 27:3; 31:20; Josh 5:6; Jer 11:5; 32:22; Ezek 20:6,15.

[187] L. Eslinger, "Watering Egypt (Deuteronomy 11:10-11)," *VT* 37 (1987): 85-90; G. E. Nicol, "Watering Egypt (Deuteronomy 11:10-11) Again," *VT* 38 (1988): 347-48; C. Aldred, *The Egyptians* (New York: Praeger, 1961), 181.

[188] G. A. Smith, *The Historical Geography of the Holy Land* (London: Hodder & Stoughton, 1900), 63-90.

v. 12), one so precious to him that he keeps it within his purview of care the entire year long. The Nile overflows its life-giving waters only once a year, and those who depend upon it for their survival have only one opportunity to get access to it and preserve it for the dry months to come. In Canaan, however, the Lord sends his showers of sustenance and survival throughout much of the year and even when it is dry makes possible treasure houses beneath the earth from which his people can draw in their times of need.

[13]So if you faithfully obey the commands I am giving you today—to love the LORD your God and to serve him with all your heart and with all your soul— [14]then I will send rain on your land in its season, both autumn and spring rains, so that you may gather in your grain, new wine and oil. [15]I will provide grass in the fields for your cattle, and you will eat and be satisfied.

[16]Be careful, or you will be enticed to turn away and worship other gods and bow down to them. [17]Then the LORD'S anger will burn against you, and he will shut the heavens so that it will not rain and the ground will yield no produce, and you will soon perish from the good land the LORD is giving you. [18]Fix these words of mine in your hearts and minds; tie them as symbols on your hands and bind them on your foreheads. [19]Teach them to your children, talking about them when you sit at home and when you walk along the road, when you lie down and when you get up. [20]Write them on the doorframes of your houses and on your gates, [21]so that your days and the days of your children may be many in the land that the LORD swore to give your forefathers, as many as the days that the heavens are above the earth.

11:13-15   The "natural" benefits of the land of promise would tend to lull the people into complacency, into a sense of independence in which the land itself and not its Creator and Sustainer would be viewed as the ultimate source of blessing. To forestall this, Moses added a conditionality to the promise of a land of plenty: Its benefits of rain and harvest would materialize only as Israel was faithful to obey the covenant terms, the "commands" (*miṣwâ*, v. 13). Chief among these, indeed their very quintessence, was to love and serve the Lord with all one's heart and soul, that is, to keep the Shema (cf. Deut 6:5). The autumn (or former) rains would then surely come to provide harvests of grain, and the spring (or latter) rains would make possible bountiful increases of new wine and olive oil (v. 14).

11:16-17   The "natural" fluctuations of the seasons with their predictable showers of rain were, moreover, at the very foundation of Canaanite religious belief and practice. It was *Baʿal* with his various consorts and through his various conflicts with and conquests of the forces of aridity and death who brought fertility to the land, or so Canaanite myth and ritual presupposed.[189] Immersed as they would have been in the nature cult of Baalism, it would be easy for Israel to share the naturalistic point of view that forces of nature must be acknowledged and appeased if productivity of animal and vegetable life were to be achieved. Thus Moses issued the most urgent warning to his people that they be careful lest they be deceived by what appeared to be cause-and-effect reality and worship the gods who represented the vital elements of nature (v. 16). Far from eliciting the desired results, such idolatrous defection from the Lord would result in his withholding the blessing of rainfall, a calamity that not only would preclude the possibility of harvest but the very possibility of remaining in the land (v. 17). Such a threat already had been spoken on more than one occasion (cf. 4:26; 7:4; 8:19-20), each time in connection with the promise of the good land and the tendency toward idolatry that its benefits would encourage if not properly assessed (cf. 4:21,25; 7:1-3; 8:7-10,14).

11:18   The third part of the present homily addresses Israel's need to remember all these lessons and warnings and to teach them to future generations so that the Lord's promises of blessing might find fulfillment in all the years to come (vv. 18-25). Once more this involves total commitment of heart and mind (or "soul," *nepeš*, as in v. 13), but this time it is a resolve to remember (lit., "set these my words upon your heart and mind," v. 18). By way of reminder the people were to attach the words of Moses to their hands and foreheads as symbols, a practice already enjoined upon them in a previous passage (cf. 6:8). Then, in words identical to those that immediately followed the pronouncement of the Shema (cf. 6:7-9), Moses insisted that his words be taught to the children in such indelible ways that they would never be forgotten.

11:19-21   The exact repetition of words between 11:19-21 and 6:7-9 is highly instructive, for the location of the latter passage in the context of the Shema underscores the significance of this confession as the very essence of covenant faith. Clearly, therefore, the words of Moses to which he referred in 11:18 were most especially the Shema. Everything else he had said in between was but commentary on or elaboration of that central covenant principle. The repetition, moreover, provides support for the view that Deut 5–11 constitutes a unified bloc of material, the so-called general stipulations of the covenant text. The command to memorize and pass on to posterity its provisions precedes those specific terms and concludes

---

[189] T. H. Gaster, *Thespis: Ritual, Myth and Drama in the Ancient Near East* (New York: Harper & Row, 1966), 124-29; W. F. Albright, *Yahweh and the Gods of Canaan* (Garden City: Doubleday, 1969), 115-40.

them as well, thus framing everything from the Decalogue and Shema to the special stipulations of Deut 12–26.[190]

> [22]If you carefully observe all these commands I am giving you to follow—to love the LORD your God, to walk in all his ways and to hold fast to him— [23]then the LORD will drive out all these nations before you, and you will dispossess nations larger and stronger than you. [24]Every place where you set your foot will be yours: Your territory will extend from the desert to Lebanon, and from the Euphrates River to the western sea. [25]No man will be able to stand against you. The LORD your God, as he promised you, will put the terror and fear of you on the whole land, wherever you go.
>
> [26]See, I am setting before you today a blessing and a curse— [27]the blessing if you obey the commands of the LORD your God that I am giving you today; [28]the curse if you disobey the commands of the LORD your God and turn from the way that I command you today by following other gods, which you have not known. [29]When the LORD your God has brought you into the land you are entering to possess, you are to proclaim on Mount Gerizim the blessings, and on Mount Ebal the curses. [30]As you know, these mountains are across the Jordan, west of the road, toward the setting sun, near the great trees of Moreh, in the territory of those Canaanites living in the Arabah in the vicinity of Gilgal. [31]You are about to cross the Jordan to enter and take possession of the land the LORD your God is giving you. When you have taken it over and are living there, [32]be sure that you obey all the decrees and laws I am setting before you today.

11:22 Just as the promise of bounty in the land was predicated on steadfast adherence to the covenant law (cf. vv. 8,13), so Israel's conquest and occupation of the land would be possible only as they were careful to observe "all these commands" (lit., "this command," *miṣwâ*, v. 22). The verb structure (infinitive absolute of *šāmar*) occurs frequently in Deuteronomy to express emphatically the need to abide by the covenant mandates[191] (cf. 5:12; 6:17; 16:1; 27:1) as does its regular imperative (4:6; 5:1,29; 7:12; 11:8,32; 29:8 [Eng. 29:9]). What it means to keep the commands in this manner is spelled out here in v. 22: to love the Lord, to walk in his ways, and to hold fast to him. Ceremony, ritual, and other professions of religion would count for nothing if this personal relationship with God were to be discounted.

---

[190] Weinfeld observes that "this section [11:18-20] seems to form an inclusio with 6:6-9, making Deut 6:4–11:21 appear to be a continuous, comprehensive sermon" (*Deuteronomy 1–11*, 448).

[191] *IBHS* § 35.5.1a: "[The inf abs] predominantly expresses divine and/or prophetic commands" [as opposed to normal human discourse]."

11:23 The result of heartfelt obedience would be the expulsion of all the Canaanite peoples from the land even though these were greater and stronger than Israel (v. 23). This does not prove in any way that they outnumbered the Israelite tribes, for the grammatical construction (possibly a hendiadys) could mean that the Canaanites and their fellow inhabitants were greatly superior to Israel in military might, a point made even by the spies years earlier (Num 13:28,31) and conceded by the Lord and Moses (Num 14:42-45; Deut 1:42). With the Lord as commander, however, that mattered little, for he would fight for them and thus assure them of victory over insuperable odds (v. 23; cf. v. 25; 7:20-24).

11:24 The extent of their conquest would be measured by the amount of territory on which they trod, specifically from the desert (i.e., the Negev) to Lebanon, the south to north extremities, and from the Euphrates River to the western (i.e., Mediterranean) sea, the east to west boundaries (v. 24). This was very much in line with the land grant promised to Abraham (Gen 15:18) and reaffirmed to Moses (Exod 23:31; Num 34:1-15; Deut 1:7-8). It is worth noting that David and Solomon created an empire that included all this (2 Sam 8:1-14; 1 Kgs 4:21-24), but it is equally significant that the Transjordan was not in the ancient promises even though it was settled by the tribes of Reuben, Gad, and half of Manasseh's tribe (cf. Num 32:33-42), even with God's blessing (Deut 3:18-23).

To tread on the land (*dārak*) was to assert dominion as many instances of the use of this verb attest.[192] For example, Caleb's land grant was that property on which he trod in faith (Deut 1:36), and in the blessing of Moses on the tribes he equated victory over Israel's enemies with treading upon their "high places" (33:29). Isaiah is especially rich in this idiom. The prophet spoke of the returning exiles as treading a previously unknown path in triumph (42:16) and of the Lord himself treading victoriously over his fallen foes (62:1-3). The imagery here is of a wine vat in which the grapes are crushed underfoot until their "blood" (i.e., their juice) spatters the robe of the wine maker. The same picture appears elsewhere in Isaiah (22:5; 26:6; 28:3) and in the Book of Revelation, where Jesus Christ, as conquering King, rules the nations with an iron scepter and treads recalcitrant sinners under his feet like grapes in a winepress (Rev 19:11-16).

11:25 Israel's conquest would be possible because the Lord himself would fight for them, but here it was not by overt act but by the sheer terror that he would cause to flood the hearts of the enemies. When they heard of Israel's coming, they would tremble with fright and thus become com-

---

[192] H. Wolf, "דָּרַךְ (*dārak*)," etc. *TWOT* 1:196-97.

pletely immobilized (cf. Deut 2:25). This, indeed, was how Rahab of Jericho described the psychological state of her own people and, in fact, of all Canaan (Josh 2:9). They had heard of the Lord's mighty exploits since the time of the exodus and now were faint with fear over the prospects of war.

11:26 Having completed his presentation of the general stipulations of the Deuteronomic covenant text (chaps. 5–11), Moses, in customary covenant practice, set before the people the blessing and curse that follow obedience and disobedience.[193] They did not take the form of lists of each according to specific acts of covenant conformity or of the lack thereof but consisted only of the broadest possible linkage of obedience and disobedience and their inevitable results (vv. 26-28). This is, in this respect, much different from the catalog of curses and blessings that follow the disclosure of the specific stipulations of chaps. 12–26. These occupy two full chapters (chaps. 27–28) in elaborate detail. The reason for the difference in the two statements of curse and blessing may lie in the principal nature of the general stipulations as opposed to the casuistic character of the specific stipulations.

On the other hand, the two promulgations of curse and blessing share much in common. For example, both emphasize that the covenant statutes were being given "this very day," that is, they were immediately binding and obligatory (compare 11:26-27,32 with 26:16-18; 27:1,9-11). Moreover, both refer to the command to assemble at Shechem in order to solemnize and formally ratify the covenant once the conquest of Canaan had been achieved (11:29,31b-32; 27:2-8,12-14).[194]

11:27-28 Moses, in briefest form, set forth the premise that blessing is the outflow of obedience. As they obeyed (*šāmaʿ*) the commands (*miṣwôt*), they could anticipate the blessing in the myriad forms that implies. What it means to obey is, in essence, to remain true to the Lord as a loyal covenant vassal. This is clear from the reverse of this, the disobedience that brings the curse, for that disobedience is spelled out as turning away from the way of the Lord and following other gods (v. 28). The commands of the Lord, then, are all expressions of the one covenant demand that he and he alone

---

[193] Christensen notes that vv. 31-32 "restate the central theme of Deuteronomy as a whole" and that vv. 26-32 provide both a conclusion to chaps. 4–11 and an introduction to chaps. 27–30 (*Deuteronomy 1–11*, 221-22). Finally, these verses form a concentric framework around the specific legislation of chaps. 12–26 with vv. 26-28 matching 28:1–29:1 (each dealing with present covenant renewal) and vv. 29-32 matching 27:1-26 (each dealing with future covenant renewal; p. 223).

[194] Clearly, then, a case can be made for the major break between chaps. 5–11 and 12–26, if for no other reason than the reference to curse and blessing and the anticipated conclave at Shechem.

be recognized as Israel's God and be worshiped and served as such. In other words, the *miṣwôt* are the Ten Commandments; and the Shema, the very essence of the covenant relationship (cf. Deut 5:10,26 [Eng. 29],28 [Eng. 31]; 6:1-2,17,25).[195]

11:29 When the covenant was first made at Sinai, a ceremony followed in which the Lord and his people pledged mutual fidelity to it and to one another (Exod 24:3-8). This was a standard element of covenant procedure and therefore had to accompany the covenant renewal of which Deuteronomy was the text. This would have taken place not in Moab but in Canaan itself inasmuch as Deuteronomy was the expression of covenant for the new political and religious entity to be established there. It was only after conquest and occupation were complete or at least well under way that it would be appropriate to sanction the new form of the Yahweh-Israel relationship articulated in Deuteronomy (vv. 29,31).

Just as the original covenant was made at a special place, namely, Mount Sinai, so the renewal could not have been undertaken at just any place in Canaan. It had to, in fact, occur at Shechem, at the base of the mountains Gerizim and Ebal (v. 29). Half the tribes would stand on one mountain and half on the other and in antiphonal chorus assent to the curses and blessings as they were shouted out by the Levites (cf. 27:11-14; Josh 8:30-35). The reason for the selection of Shechem and its vicinity was clearly the association of this holy place with the patriarchs to whom the Lord had first appeared and made covenant promises concerning the land.[196] It was there that Abraham had built his first altar (Gen 12:6-7); there Jacob had bought a piece of property (Gen 33:19), where he built an altar (Gen 33:20) and dug a well (John 4:6); and there his son Joseph was buried (Josh 24:32). From those ancient days onward Shechem was closely associated with covenant making of all kinds, both legitimate and illegitimate (cf. Josh 24:1-28; Judg 9:1-21).

11:30 Lest there be any chance that the people misunderstand the location of Gerizim and Ebal, no matter how unlikely the possibility, Moses took pains to pinpoint them as being "on the other side of the Jordan" and "to the west" (lit., "beyond the way of the going down of the sun," v. 30). More specifically, they were "near the great trees of Moreh,

---

[195] Mayes, *Deuteronomy,* 217-18.
[196] J. L'Hour, "L'alliance de Sichem," *RB* 69 (1962): 5-36, 161-84; E. Nielsen, *Shechem: A Traditio-Historical Investigation* (Copenhagen: G. E. C. Gad, 1959); B. W. Anderson, "Shechem, The 'Navel of the Land': Part II. The Place of Shechem in the Bible," *BA* 20 (1957): 18-19.

in the territory of those Canaanites living in the Arabah in the vicinity of Gilgal."

All this must be understood in the context of Moses' vantage point at Shittim. From there Shechem was about thirty-five miles northwest as the crow flies. By road the route would pass through Gilgal to Bethel, Shiloh, Arumah, and Shechem.[197] The "trees of Moreh" (probably oaks) are mentioned in connection with Shechem in the Abraham itinerary (Gen 12:6) and also appear as the burial place of the teraphim Rachel stole from her father (Gen 35:4), again in proximity to Shechem. Though very little can be known of Canaanite political or administrative districts during this period, it seems from Moses' account here that Shechem may have been part of a kingdom or city-state ruled by a Canaanite dynast located in Gilgal. On the other hand, the description may be understood simply as pointing out the road as that which passes through the Gilgal of the Arabah, the one inhabited by Canaanites as opposed to any other Gilgal.

11:31-32 In any event, once the conquest was over, the covenant could be renewed. But it must be the very covenant Moses was sharing with the people here and now. It is not surprising that Joshua was punctilious in carrying out the ceremony of renewal and ratification in precisely the place and manner prescribed by his great mentor (Josh 8:30-35).

---

[197] Thus the reference to Gilgal has nothing to do with conflation of cultic traditions as many scholars argue (thus Cairns, *Word and Presence,* 118-19), but it simply serves as a directional marker (so Driver, *Deuteronomy,* 133-34).

V. SPECIFIC STIPULATIONS OF THE COVENANT (12:1–26:15)
  1. The Exclusiveness of the Lord and His Worship (12:1–16:17)
    (1) The Central Sanctuary (12:1-14)
    (2) The Sanctity of Blood (12:15-28)
    (3) The Abomination of Pagan Gods (12:29-31)
    (4) The Evil of False Prophets (12:32–13:18)
    (5) The Distinction between Clean and Unclean Animals
        (14:1-21)
    (6) Tribute to the Sovereign (14:22–16:17)
  2. Kingdom Officials (16:18–18:22)
    (1) Judges and Other Officials (16:18–17:13)
    (2) Kings (17:14-20)
    (3) Priests and Levites (18:1-8)
    (4) Prophets (18:9-22)
  3. Civil Law (19:1–22:8)
    (1) Laws concerning Manslaughter (19:1-13)
    (2) Laws concerning Witnesses (19:14-21)
    (3) Laws concerning War (20:1-20)
    (4) Laws concerning Unsolved Murder (21:1-9)
    (5) Laws concerning Wives and Children (21:10-21)
    (6) Laws concerning Preservation of Life (21:22–22:8)
  4. Laws of Purity (22:9–23:18)
    (1) Illustrations of the Principle (22:9-12)
    (2) Purity in the Marriage Relationship (22:13-30)
    (3) Purity in Public Worship (23:1-8)
    (4) Purity in Personal Hygiene (23:9-14)
    (5) Purity in Treatment of the Disadvantaged (23:15-16)
    (6) Purity in Cultic Personnel (23:17-18)
  5. Laws of Interpersonal Relationships (23:19–25:19)
    (1) Respect for the Possessions of Another (23:19–24:7)
    (2) Respect for the Dignity of Another (24:8–25:4)
    (3) Respect for the Sanctity of Another (25:5-16)
    (4) Dealing with the Amalekites (25:17-19)
  6. Laws of Covenant Celebration and Confirmation (26:1-15)
    (1) Presentation of the Firstfruits (26:1-11)
    (2) Presentation of the Third-year Tithe (26:12-15)

―――――――――― V. SPECIFIC STIPULATIONS ――――――――――
OF THE COVENANT (12:1–26:15)

As argued in the Introduction, Deuteronomy, as a covenant text akin to others recovered from the ancient Near East, contains two sets of stipulations. The first (chaps. 5–11) is more general in nature, comprising the basic principles which are elaborated and made more specific in the second set (12:1–26:15). Even the section of general stipulations appears to provide an expansive commentary on the first two commandments of the Decalogue, as Kaufman and other scholars have proposed.[1] The specific stipulations, on the other hand, constitute an elaboration of all ten commandments, in terms, however, that reflect life in the land and a centralized, monarchial society rather than one that is tribal and familial. Furthermore, the connections between the individual commandments and their development in this section are not always readily apparent, certainly not to the extent argued by many scholars.[2] The section outline, therefore, reflects an analysis provided by the text itself but one that undeniably finds linkage with the Decalogue and in the very order in which the commandments of the Decalogue occur.

1. The Exclusiveness of the Lord and His Worship (12:1–16:17)

(1) The Central Sanctuary (12:1-14)

[1]These are the decrees and laws you must be careful to follow in the land that the LORD, the God of your fathers, has given you to possess—as long as you live in the land. [2]Destroy completely all the places on the high mountains and on the hills and under every spreading tree where the nations you are dispossessing worship their gods. [3]Break down their altars, smash their sacred

―――

[1] S. A. Kaufman, "The Structure of the Deuteronomic Law," *Maarav* 1-2 (1978-79): 110; cf. N. Lohfink, *Das Hauptgebot: eine Untersuchung literarischer Einleitungsfragen zu Dtn 5–11* (Rome: Pontifical Biblical Institute, 1963), 23.

[2] For various analyses of the laws of Deut 12–26 and their arrangement see C. M. Carmichael, "A Singular Method of Codification of Law in the Mishpatim," *ZAW* 84 (1972): 19-24; Kaufman, "The Structure of the Deuteronomic Law," 105-58; R. P. Merendino, *Das deuteronomische Gesetz: eine literarkritische, gattungs–und überlieferungsgeschichtliche Untersuchung zu Dt 12–26* (Bonn: P. Hanstein, 1969); A. Rofé, "The Arrangement of the Laws in Deuteronomy," *ETL* 64 (1988): 265-87; G. Braulik, *Die deuteronomischen Gesetze und der Dekalog Stuttgarter Bibelstudien 145* (Stuttgart: Katholisches Bibelwerk, 1991); "Die Abfolge der Gezetze in Deuteronomium 12–26 und der Dekalog," in *Das Deuteronomium,* 252-72.

stones and burn their Asherah poles in the fire; cut down the idols of their gods and wipe out their names from those places. [4]You must not worship the LORD your God in their way. [5]But you are to seek the place the LORD your God will choose from among all your tribes to put his Name there for his dwelling. To that place you must go; [6]there bring your burnt offerings and sacrifices, your tithes and special gifts, what you have vowed to give and your freewill offerings, and the firstborn of your herds and flocks. [7]There, in the presence of the LORD your God, you and your families shall eat and shall rejoice in everything you have put your hand to, because the LORD your God has blessed you.

[8]You are not to do as we do here today, everyone as he sees fit, [9]since you have not yet reached the resting place and the inheritance the LORD your God is giving you. [10]But you will cross the Jordan and settle in the land the LORD your God is giving you as an inheritance, and he will give you rest from all your enemies around you so that you will live in safety. [11]Then to the place the LORD your God will choose as a dwelling for his Name—there you are to bring everything I command you: your burnt offerings and sacrifices, your tithes and special gifts, and all the choice possessions you have vowed to the LORD. [12]And there rejoice before the LORD your God, you, your sons and daughters, your menservants and maidservants, and the Levites from your towns, who have no allotment or inheritance of their own. [13]Be careful not to sacrifice your burnt offerings anywhere you please. [14]Offer them only at the place the LORD will choose in one of your tribes, and there observe everything I command you.

12:1 The general stipulation section had been introduced by Moses' exhortation to obey the decrees (*ḥuqqîm*) and laws (*mišpāṭîm*) he had spoken to them (5:1), and the special stipulation section repeats these very words (12:1). Moreover, the previous section ended with the identical injunction (11:32), thus enveloping the whole and marking it off as a unit and, at the same time, creating a clear bridge between the general and specific stipulations. This is not surprising inasmuch as the general stipulations, as just suggested, are an amplification of the first two commandments—those having to do with the person of the Lord and his exclusive worship—and this is the theme of Deut 12:1-32 as well (and, indeed, of 12:1–16:17).[3]

12:2 The first Mosaic interpretation of the exclusivity of the Lord as revealed in the first two commandments (Deut 5:6-10) has to do with the public worship of the Lord at one central place. The first commandment (5:6-7) identified the Lord as the only God, the one who redeemed Israel and who would countenance no competing gods. The second dealt with

---

[3] Thus J. A. Thompson, *Deuteronomy,* TOTC (Downers Grove: InterVarsity, 1974), 161.

such "gods" by absolutely forbidding their worship or even their iconic representation. The order of these is reversed in Deut 12, for it obviously would be difficult if not impossible for the Lord alone to be worshiped in Canaan as long as there were pagan centers of worship.[4] Thus the idols and their shrines first had to be demolished (vv. 2-3), then a single, central place for Yahweh worship had to be established (vv. 4-7), one to which the whole covenant community would resort at stated times and for stated purposes (vv. 8-14).

The command to destroy is couched in the strongest terms,[5] for there must be no residue of paganism remaining after the conquest. And the strategy of destruction would be, first, the elimination of the "places" of worship and then their paraphernalia. "Places" (*hammeqōmôt*) is a quasi-technical term referring to sites thought to be holy because of a special visitation by deity.[6] These were usually in groves of trees (representing fertility) and on high hills, esteemed by the very height to be in closer proximity to the gods. In contrast to such "places" would be the "place" where the Lord must be worshiped. Seven times (vv. 5,11,13,14,18,21,26) this single place (*māqôm*) is mentioned in this passage in which the exclusiveness of the Lord is emphasized.

12:3 The specific objects to be destroyed—altars, sacred stones, Asherah poles—had already been singled out in Deut 7:5, a chapter that shares much in common with Deut 12. All of these are accoutrements of idol worship, so the idols themselves must be dismantled and their very names (that is, memory) obliterated (v. 3). This figure of speech in which the name represents the reality (metonymy) is most significant in this passage, for the removal of the names of the heathen gods makes possible the introduction of the name of Yahweh, that is, his very presence, a major theme in the centralization of Yahweh worship (cf. vv. 5,11,21; 14:23-24; 16:2,6,11; 26:2).[7]

12:4 Having commanded the removal of idols and their places of worship, Moses turned to the matter of where and how the Lord must be wor-

---

[4] As S. R. Driver points out, the destruction of Canaanite places of worship was "a fundamental and necessary condition for the pure and uncontaminated worship of Jehovah" (*Deuteronomy*, 139).

[5] The Hebrew phrase אַבֵּד תְּאַבְּדוּן uses an infinitive absolute, a form whose purpose is to enjoin a given behavior in unmistakable and urgent terms. For other examples of אָבַד in the *Piel* and with idolatry in view, see Num 33:52; 2 Kgs 21:3; and the discussion by B. Otzen, "אָבַד *ʾābhadh*," etc., *TDOT* 1:21-22.

[6] KBL, 560; cf. R. de Vaux, *Ancient Israel* (New York: McGraw-Hill, 1985), 2:279-80, 309.

[7] P. C. Craigie, *The Book of Deuteronomy*, NICOT (Grand Rapids: Eerdmans, 1976), 216.

shiped. Whatever else may be said, it was to be totally contrary to pagan practice (v. 4). More positively, it must be in the place to be chosen (*bāhar*) by the Lord himself, one place and one alone amongst the tribal allotments. There he would place his name, that is, there he would live (v. 5).[8] That this is tantamount to God's residence is clear from the command to literally "seek his dwelling place and go there" (v. 5b), a juxtaposition not clear in the NIV.

All of this is in line with the idea, inherent in suzerain-vassal treaties and relationships, that the great king resides in a palace in the central (capital) city to which the client princes and peoples must come periodically to assert their loyalty and present their tribute and other symbols of submission.[9] The place of the Lord's name, then, is his "palace," that is, the tabernacle or temple in which he resides among his people. Obviously, in line with human covenant analogy this could be only one place at a time, a place determined solely at the king's discretion.

It is precisely this unambiguous call to cult centralization that gave rise to the view that Deuteronomy was the impetus for Josiah's reformation in 622 B.C., a reformation that, among other things, included the destruction of pagan shrines and the renovation of Solomon's Temple as the only legitimate place of community worship (2 Kgs 23:1-25; 2 Chr 34:8-33). Since Deuteronomy specifically calls for such measures, it is assumed that this was the "book of the covenant" (2 Kgs 23:21) or "book of the law" (2 Kgs 22:8; cf. Deut 31:26) that was found in the temple and that motivated Josiah to his godly course of action.[10] It is further assumed that Deuteronomy was composed only in the seventh century, perhaps to achieve the very reformation that did indeed take place. Such hypotheses gave rise to the documentary or source-critical analysis of the Pentateuch (in which P presupposes D and D presupposes the prophets) and to the so-called "Deutero-nomistic history," an approach that views Joshua to 2 Kings as an interpretation of Israel's past based on the philosophy or theology of history embedded in

---

[8] R. de Vaux, "Le lieu que Yahvé a chois pour y établir son nom," in *Das ferne und nahe Wort. Festschrift L. Rost,* rd. I. Maass, BZAW 105 (Berlin: Töpelmann, 1967), 219-28.

[9] G. E. Mendenhall, "Covenant Forms in Israelite Tradition," *BA* 17 (1954): 50-76; now reprinted in *Law and Covenant in Israel and the Ancient Near East* (Pittsburgh: Biblical Colloquium, 1955), 33; J. A. Fitzmyer, *The Aramaic Inscriptions of Sefire,* BO 19 (Rome: Pontifical Biblical Institute, 1967), 124-25.

[10] See W. H. Irwin, "Le sanctuaire central israélite avant l'établissement de la monarchie," RB 72 (1965): 161-84; J. R. Lundbom, "The Lawbook of the Josianic Reform," *CBQ* 38 (1976): 293-302; D. W. B. Robinson, *Josiah's Reform and the Book of the Law* (London: Tyndale, 1951).

Deuteronomy. Clearly the late date of Deuteronomy is crucial to both of these interpretations.

This issue has been addressed in the Introduction, but it might be helpful to point out here that the notion of a central sanctuary was already implicit in the early prophets and that Josiah's own reformation, in which centralization was indeed an issue, had commenced before the recovery of the scroll in the temple (cf. 2 Chr 34:1-8). His reading of the scroll only confirmed the propriety of what he had already begun, and his actions before and after the scroll was found suggest he already was most familiar with the "Deuteronomic" tradition.[11] It is also worth noting that if Deuteronomy was composed late in the monarchy period, it is incredible that it makes no mention of monarchy as an existing institution.[12] There is not the slightest hint that the Davidic dynasty existed, nor is there even vague reference to Jerusalem as its capital or as the religious center prescribed by Deuteronomy.[13] In fact, Deuteronomy is oriented to the east of the Jordan (cf. 12:9-10) and looks forward to a central shrine in a place so imprecisely defined as to be "the place the LORD your God will choose" (v. 5). One can only conclude either that the command to centralization was Mosaic, as the tradition unanimously attests, or that a person or party in later times developed it as a politico-religious tactic designed to enhance its own position or point of view, even if that required the historical anachronism and fraud of attributing that command (and, indeed, all of Deuteronomy) to Moses.

12:5   Once the place of community worship had become identified, the people of Israel were to go there to present their tithes and offerings. That this is worship of the community as a whole and in one place and one time is clear not only from the comparison of this command to that of festival gatherings (cf. Lev 23:37-38; Num 29:39-40; esp. Deut 16:2,5-6,11,15-16) but also from the use of the plural pronouns throughout vv. 1-12.[14] All the people were to come to the one place at designated times, a requirement set in contrast to the worship elsewhere by individuals or assemblies on occasions that were not of a generally theocratic and community nature (cf. 1 Sam 7:5-12; 11:15; 1 Kgs 3:4).

---

[11] G. J. Wenham, "The Structure and Date of Deuteronomy" (PhD. diss., University of London, 1969), 230, 233.

[12] Thompson, *Deuteronomy,* 45.

[13] Craigie, *Deuteronomy,* 46-47; cf. J. Niehaus, "The Central Sanctuary: Where and When?" *TynBul* 43 (1992): 3-30.

[14] D. L. Christensen, "The Numeruswechsel in Deuteronomy 12," in *Proceedings of the Ninth World Congress of Jewish Studies,* ed. R. Giveon et al. (Jerusalem: World Union of Jewish Studies, 1986), 61-68.

12:6 The gifts to be presented were burnt offerings (ʿōlôt), sacrifices (zĕbāḥîm), tithes (maʿaśrōt), and "special gifts" (tĕrûmôt), all of which (except for tithes) appear together elsewhere only in Lev 7. As the beginning of Leviticus makes clear, all of these were gifts (qorbān), that is, presentations made to the Lord to effect and maintain peaceful fellowship with him (Lev 1:2; 2:1; 3:1; 4:23; 7:13-16,29,38).[15] The tithe in particular should be viewed as tribute paid to the sovereign by his grateful and dependent servant (cf. Lev 27:30-32; Num 18:26,28; Deut 14:23-25,28).[16]

12:7 The nature of these assemblies—times of covenant reaffirmation and renewal—is evident from the festivity carried out at those times and at the central sanctuary (v. 7). It consists essentially of a meal shared by all the congregants, a repast "in the presence of the LORD your God." This does not mean only that the Lord was there but that he too shared in the banqueting as the Great King among his loyal subjects. This was standard protocol at times of covenant making or renewal as a number of biblical texts attest (cf. Exod 24:11; Deut 12:18; 14:23,26; 15:20; 27:7).[17]

12:8-9 Having introduced the concept of a central sanctuary (v. 5), Moses went on to elaborate the specifics about the timing of its selection (vv. 8-10), its function as the focal point of community worship (v. 11), and the procedures to be followed there (vv. 12-14). All of this is in stark contrast to the place and manner of worship from Sinai to the present (v. 8). By everyone doing "as he sees fit" cannot mean a complete lack of rule and regimentation because guidelines for cultic behavior had been established nearly forty years earlier (Exod 25:1-9; 29:38-45; 31:12-17). What is in view is the permanency of a central site, one to be chosen by the Lord at some indeterminate point in the future.[18] Until that time the sanctuary would be portable (as it had been since Sinai), even in the immediately future period of conquest and occupation. As long as Israel was on the move and clustered about the tabernacle, that would be the central and exclusive place of convocation. In Canaan, however, a widespread distribution of the people following their occupation of the land would necessitate the erection of local altars in addition to that of the central

---

[15] J. E. Hartley, *Leviticus,* WBC 4 (Dallas: Word, 1992), 11.

[16] In most suzerain-vassal arrangements, the treaty texts specified payment of tribute, usually on an annual basis. See the "Treaty between Mursilis and Duppi-Tessub of Amurru," *ANET* 2:203: "The tribute which my father had imposed upon your father, he brought year for year; he never refused it." Cf. Mendenhall, "Law and Covenant in Israel and the Ancient Near East," 33.

[17] D. J. McCarthy, *Old Testament Covenant* (Atlanta: John Knox, 1972), 41-43; F. C. Fensham, "The Treaty between Israel and the Gibeonites," *BA* 27 (1964): 98.

[18] Craigie, *Deuteronomy,* 218.

sanctuary.[19] Moses had, in fact, already made provision for these following the original declaration of the Ten Commandments. Wherever the Lord appeared, he said, would be a suitable place for worship (Exod 20:24). The only restrictions were that the altars must be of earth or unhewed stones (20:24-25), and the dress of the priests must be modest (20:26), both injunctions being designed to counter prevailing Canaanite custom in those respects.

12:10-11 As is well known, the first permanent location of the tabernacle was Shiloh (Josh 18:1), a site chosen only after the land had been brought under control. How long after the conquest Shiloh was chosen cannot be known precisely, but it seems to have been a minimum of seven years (cf. Josh 14:7-10). In the meantime it is clear that altars of the kind authorized by the Lord in Exod 20 were built in Canaan both before (Josh 8:30) and after the selection of Shiloh as the place of national convocation (Josh 22:10-11; Judg 6:24-26; 13:20; 21:4; 1 Sam 7:17; 2 Sam 24:18-25).

The point still remains, however, that something decisive would occur with the establishment of a central shrine, something quite different from the religious practice of the desert and conquest years (Deut 12:8-9). Whereas it was permissible to do as each individual saw fit (lit., "what is right in his own eyes") in the years of wandering, this would no longer be the case when the community reached the "resting place," that is, the land of inheritance. This does not suggest that worship could be carried out in the place and manner dictated by personal whim, even in the desert, but only that no fixed and permanent site had yet been selected as the place of the Lord's dwelling. That state of affairs would be rectified once Israel had reached the safety and security of a conquered Canaan (v. 10). Then the Lord would reveal the place for his Name (Yahweh), that central shrine to which his people must come with their tokens of tribute (v. 11; cf. vv. 5-7).

12:12-14 The community nature of this injunction is clear from the all-inclusive character of the list of participants in the sacred festivals. Entire families, slaves, and even those without inheritance, such as the Levites, were to come to the central designated place, and to that place only (v. 13), and there render their worship to the Lord (v. 12). The reference to Levites confirms the view that community worship was to be undertaken by the community as a whole and in one place, for otherwise the Levites and others could officiate at services in the various towns of their allotment as both legal prescription (Deut 12:15,20-23) and historical practice (Judg 6:19-24; 13:19-20; 1 Sam 6:14-15; 7:9; 9:11-14; 11:14-15)

---

[19] For a helpful distinction between a "central" sanctuary and a "sole" sanctuary, see Wenham, *Structure and Date of Deuteronomy*, 244-57.

attest. This localizing of certain cultic activities in no way militates against the principle of a central sanctuary, for the former involved acts of a non-community nature whereas the latter pertained to the community-wide expression of submission and devotion to the Great King of the covenant.

(2) The Sanctity of Blood (12:15-28)

[15]Nevertheless, you may slaughter your animals in any of your towns and eat as much of the meat as you want, as if it were gazelle or deer, according to the blessing the LORD your God gives you. Both the ceremonially unclean and the clean may eat it. [16]But you must not eat the blood; pour it out on the ground like water. [17]You must not eat in your own towns the tithe of your grain and new wine and oil, or the firstborn of your herds and flocks, or whatever you have vowed to give, or your freewill offerings or special gifts. [18]Instead, you are to eat them in the presence of the LORD your God at the place the LORD your God will choose—you, your sons and daughters, your menservants and maidservants, and the Levites from your towns—and you are to rejoice before the LORD your God in everything you put your hand to. [19]Be careful not to neglect the Levites as long as you live in your land.

[20]When the LORD your God has enlarged your territory as he promised you, and you crave meat and say, "I would like some meat," then you may eat as much of it as you want. [21]If the place where the LORD your God chooses to put his Name is too far away from you, you may slaughter animals from the herds and flocks the LORD has given you, as I have commanded you, and in your own towns you may eat as much of them as you want. [22]Eat them as you would gazelle or deer. Both the ceremonially unclean and the clean may eat. [23]But be sure you do not eat the blood, because the blood is the life, and you must not eat the life with the meat. [24]You must not eat the blood; pour it out on the ground like water. [25]Do not eat it, so that it may go well with you and your children after you, because you will be doing what is right in the eyes of the LORD.

[26]But take your consecrated things and whatever you have vowed to give, and go to the place the LORD will choose. [27]Present your burnt offerings on the altar of the LORD your God, both the meat and the blood. The blood of your sacrifices must be poured beside the altar of the LORD your God, but you may eat the meat. [28]Be careful to obey all these regulations I am giving you, so that it may always go well with you and your children after you, because you will be doing what is good and right in the eyes of the LORD your God.

12:15 The theme of the central sanctuary finds continuing elaboration in vv. 15-28 but with special focus on the use (or misuse) of blood in animal slaughter and sacrifice, whether at a local altar or at the national one. What is clear is that blood in any case is holy inasmuch as it represents life (v. 16; cf. Lev 17:10-12), and therefore it must be properly disposed of whether shed in the process of obtaining meat for food or in the course of sacrifice offered to the Lord.[20]

Life in the land would bring widespread settlement, so much so that it would be impossible from a practical standpoint for all acts of worship, including sacrifice, to be carried out at any one central place, to say nothing of the slaughter of animals for food. Thus animals could be slain in local villages—even those normally reserved for sacrifice—to provide a food supply (vv. 15,20-22). Such animals could be considered as wild game in such circumstances, that is, they could be used for noncultic purposes. This is why both the ceremonially clean and unclean could partake of it (v. 15b).

12:16-19 Even so, the blood remained sacred and like that obtained in sacrifice had to be poured upon the ground like water (v. 16). The idea seems to be that blood, as the very essence of life, must be returned to the earth from which the Creator at the beginning had brought it forth (cf. Gen 1:24; 2:19; 3:23; 4:10-11; Deut 15:23). In a sense, then, even profane slaughter had overtones of worship and holiness and was subject to cultic regulation. This was also true of other foodstuffs. The Israelite could help himself to his heart's content except for the tithes of crops, the firstborn of animals, the subjects of vows, and freewill offerings and gifts (v. 17), all of which must be taken to the central sanctuary and there alone eaten before the Lord as a symbol of covenant oneness (v. 18). In this manner the Levite as well was to be sustained (v. 19; cf. v. 12; 26:12-13).

12:20-25 The rationale for this allowance of local animal slaughter follows in vv. 20-21. Granting that it was natural and proper for the individual to desire meat as part of his diet, Moses legislated that such could be done once the land was conquered and settled and great distances precluded easy access to the tabernacle or temple. Again he underscored the sanctity of even animal life by repeating his demand that the blood shed in

---

[20] Though most scholars view the slaughter regulations here as strictly profane and insist that the cultus was limited to the central sanctuary throughout Israel's post-Deuteronomy history, there are too many instances of legitimate places and practices apart from the central sanctuary to allow this view to be unchallenged. For support of the position espoused here, see Driver, *Deuteronomy*, 136-38; Wenham, *Structure and Date of Deuteronomy*, 244-48; de Vaux, *Ancient Israel*, 2:331-37; J. G. McConville, *Law and Theology in Deuteronomy*, JSOT-Sup 33 (Sheffield: JSOT, 1984), 28-29; von Rad, *Deuteronomy*, 115. It is important to note, however, that those scholars (including some just listed) who admit multiple places of legitimate worship in early (pre-Josianic) history do so on the basis of a late composition of Deuteronomy that eventually condemned such practices. If one holds to an early (Mosaic) date, it is almost impossible to avoid the interpretation offered here, namely, that the cultus could be and was indeed carried out in local places alongside the community central sanctuary, at least until the end of the preexilic period.

such circumstances must be properly disposed of (vv. 23-24). Adherence to the prohibition against eating it would bring about the favor and blessing of the Lord (v. 25).

12:26-28 In a highly repetitive manner, Moses went on to insist that consecrated things and things vowed to the Lord must be taken to the "place the LORD will choose" and offered to him there (v. 26; cf. vv. 17-18). There the meat could be eaten as part of certain sacrificial rituals such as the "fellowship" or "peace" offerings (cf. Lev 3:1-17), but the blood, as always, must be poured out upon the earth (v. 27). Finally, in a summary and conclusion of the matter of the central sanctuary, Moses urged his hearers to absolute obedience to the words he had spoken, for in doing so they would please the Lord and make possible his good favor upon them (v. 28; cf. 4:40; 5:16,29,33).

(3) The Abomination of Pagan Gods (12:29-31)

[29]The LORD your God will cut off before you the nations you are about to invade and dispossess. But when you have driven them out and settled in their land, [30]and after they have been destroyed before you, be careful not to be ensnared by inquiring about their gods, saying, "How do these nations serve their gods? We will do the same." [31]You must not worship the LORD your God in their way, because in worshiping their gods, they do all kinds of detestable things the LORD hates. They even burn their sons and daughters in the fire as sacrifices to their gods.

Having established the centrality and sanctity of the place of the Lord's residence among his people, Moses turned now to the uniqueness of the Lord and his demands for exclusive recognition and worship. As noted already, this injunction is an elaboration of the first commandment in which those very concepts are promulgated (Deut 5:7). As noted also, this exposition of the commandment follows that of the notion of the central sanctuary because it logically and theologically makes sense that the exclusive worship of the Lord could not be a practical reality until the pagan shrines had been eliminated and the place where the Lord chose to place his name had been set up in their stead.

12:29-30 That this was the strategy behind Moses' approach is clear from the present passage itself. It was only after the nations of Canaan were defeated and dispossessed that the worship of the Lord could be centralized and undertaken without the risk of syncretism or competition (v. 29). Ironically, however, the mere destruction of the nations would not automatically remove the temptation to worship their gods (v. 30). As strange as it might seem, the attraction of the false deities was not at all diminished by the overthrow of the peoples who worshiped them. It was as though no linkage at all existed between them and their capability, between the notion of a god and that of his role in event and history.

Subsequent events were to demonstrate the possibility of such a paradoxical outcome, however, for over and over again in Israel's history they showed their proclivity to follow after gods that were defeated and discredited in the face of the Lord's powerful displays of sovereignty. This began as early as the time of the conquest and its immediate aftermath, for no sooner had Joshua and the elders who followed him delivered the land from its indigenous, pagan populations than the people of Israel began to go after the very gods of those nations (Judg 2:7-15). More often than not this shameless devotion to nonexisting gods characterized the history of God's chosen people ever afterward.

12:31 Such deviant behavior is a direct violation of the first commandment as v. 31 makes clear. To serve other gods is tantamount to aberrant worship, for denial of the uniqueness of the Lord leaves one open to a pluralism of faith and action that knows virtually no limits. To use an extreme example, Moses cited the practice of human sacrifice, a rite exacerbated by the use of one's own children as offerings. Such unspeakable forms of religious expression were common in the ancient Near Eastern world, especially in Canaan, and tragically enough sometimes were emulated by God's own elect nation (see 2 Kgs 16:3; 17:17; 21:6).[21]

(4) The Evil of False Prophets (12:32–13:18)

[32]See that you do all I command you; do not add to it or take away from it.

[1]If a prophet, or one who foretells by dreams, appears among you and announces to you a miraculous sign or wonder, [2]and if the sign or wonder of which he has spoken takes place, and he says, "Let us follow other gods" (gods you have not known) "and let us worship them," [3]you must not listen to the words of that prophet or dreamer. The LORD your God is testing you to find out whether you love him with all your heart and with all your soul. [4]It is the LORD your God you must follow, and him you must revere. Keep his commands and obey him; serve him and hold fast to him. [5]That prophet or dreamer must be put to death, because he preached rebellion against the LORD your God, who brought you out of Egypt and redeemed you from the land of slavery; he has tried to turn you from the way the LORD your God

---

[21] For an especially egregious expression of the cultic activity suggested here see G. C. Heider, *The Cult of Molek: A Reassessment,* JSOTSup 43 (Sheffield: JSOT, 1985). Cf. R. A. Oden, "The Persistence of Canaanite Religion," *BA* 39 (1976): 36; N. Wyatt, "Of Calves and Kings: The Canaanite Dimension in the Religion of Israel," *SJOT* 6 (1992): 68-91.

commanded you to follow. You must purge the evil from among you.

[6]If your very own brother, or your son or daughter, or the wife you love, or your closest friend secretly entices you, saying, "Let us go and worship other gods" (gods that neither you nor your fathers have known, [7]gods of the peoples around you, whether near or far, from one end of the land to the other), [8]do not yield to him or listen to him. Show him no pity. Do not spare him or shield him. [9]You must certainly put him to death. Your hand must be the first in putting him to death, and then the hands of all the people. [10]Stone him to death, because he tried to turn you away from the LORD your God, who brought you out of Egypt, out of the land of slavery. [11]Then all Israel will hear and be afraid, and no one among you will do such an evil thing again.

[12]If you hear it said about one of the towns the LORD your God is giving you to live in [13]that wicked men have arisen among you and have led the people of their town astray, saying, "Let us go and worship other gods" (gods you have not known), [14]then you must inquire, probe and investigate it thoroughly. And if it is true and it has been proved that this detestable thing has been done among you, [15]you must certainly put to the sword all who live in that town. Destroy it completely, both its people and its livestock. [16]Gather all the plunder of the town into the middle of the public square and completely burn the town and all its plunder as a whole burnt offering to the LORD your God. It is to remain a ruin forever, never to be rebuilt. [17]None of those condemned things shall be found in your hands, so that the LORD will turn from his fierce anger; he will show you mercy, have compassion on you, and increase your numbers, as he promised on oath to your forefathers, [18]because you obey the LORD your God, keeping all his commands that I am giving you today and doing what is right in his eyes.

12:32   In the Hebrew Bible Deut 12:32 is the first verse in chap. 13. While the meaning is not at stake one way or the other, this arrangement is preferable, for in addition to the Hebrew tradition v. 32 appears not to be a concluding exhortation but an opening statement. In the only other place where the formula "add to" (ʾāsap) and "take away from" (gāraʿ) occurs with reference to the word of the Lord (Deut 4:2), it introduces a new section.[22] Furthermore, there is a principle of canonization here as well in that nothing is to be added to or subtracted from the word.[23] This testifies to the fact that God himself is the originator of the covenant text and only he is capable of determining its content and extent.

13:1   As for the topic introduced by this heading—false prophets and their treatment—its linkage with the second commandment is most apparent, for that commandment prohibits worship of false gods, the enticement to which is at the very heart of the message of these prophets (13:2). It is

---

[22] Driver, *Deuteronomy*, 151.

[23] C. J. Labuschagne, "Divine Speech in Deuteronomy," in *Das Deuteronomium*, 122-23.

appropriate, then, to address the matter of competing gods once that of the exclusive existence and worship of the Lord has been addressed in the preceding section (12:29-31).

The institution of prophetism appears to have been established under Samuel, but the existence of prophets long preceded the formal institution, reaching back at least as far as Abraham (cf. Gen 20:7).[24] The principal term used to describe the Old Testament prophet is *nābî'*, a word derived apparently from Akkadian *nabû* and meaning "proclaimer" or "forth-teller."[25] Its definition by usage is seen most clearly in the account of Moses' call by the Lord to return to Egypt to lead his people out. When Moses protested that he was inarticulate and therefore unable to confront Pharaoh, the Lord responded by promising to send Aaron, his brother. "You shall speak to him and put words in his mouth," said the Lord, and "he will speak to the people for you, and it will be as if he were your mouth and as if you were God to him" (Exod 4:15-16). Then, and even more specifically, Moses was told, "I have made you like God to Pharaoh, and your brother Aaron will be your prophet [*nābî'*]" (Exod 7:1). The prophet then was a spokesman for God, a messenger who represented him before other people.

This same role of the prophet is abundantly attested throughout the ancient Near Eastern world. The prophet was a kind of ambassador of the gods, one who professed to speak for them and otherwise to champion their cause. The prophet in view in the passage at hand was not from among the pagan nations, however, but from Israel itself as the phrase "appears among you" (v. 1) makes plain. This demonstrates the existence of false prophets even among the chosen people, a fact first clearly articulated here but exemplified over and over again in Israel's subsequent history (cf. Deut 18:9-14,20-22; 1 Kgs 18:19; 22:6). Thus there could be false prophets of false gods or even false prophets of the Lord, the one and only God.

One of the means by which prophets received revelation was by dreams, so here the prophet is further defined as a "dreamer of dreams" (v. 1; cf. Gen 37:1-10; Num 12:6). This epithet was later commonly associated with false prophets, however, and it may connote negative overtones already to the passage (cf. Jer 23:23-32; 27:9-10; 29:8).[26] The fact that he could per-

---

[24] For a convenient history of the OT prophetic movement see W. J. Beecher, *The Prophets and the Promise* (Grand Rapids: Baker, 1963), 36-65; E. W. Heaton, *The Old Testament Prophets* (Atlanta: John Knox, 1977).

[25] J. Blenkinsopp, *A History of Prophecy in Israel* (Philadelphia: Westminster, 1983), 36-38. Cf. *CAD* 11:31, s.v. *nabû*, "called" (adj.); or 11:37-38, s.v. *nabû*, "proclaim" (verb).

[26] R. B. Y. Scott, *The Relevance of the Prophets* (New York: Macmillan, 1957), 44-45.

form signs and wonders did not by itself legitimize him as a prophet of the Lord.

A "sign" (*ʾōt*) or "wonder" (*môpēt*) was any kind of supernatural deed or act that was done to authenticate its performer as a representative of deity.[27] The most familiar instance of their use is that of the exodus plagues that the Lord allowed Moses to inflict upon Egypt as a witness to his God-given ministry as leader and prophet (cf. Exod 4:8,21; 7:3; 11:9-10; Deut 4:34; 6:22; 7:19; 26:8). But such displays of power could also be performed by false prophets, thereby making it impossible to rely upon these alone as criteria for determining truth. This is why the sign or wonder had to be tested against the message of the prophet, for only when the message was consistent with the whole range of divine revelation could the accompanying miracles be given credibility.

13:2-4   This is at the very heart of Moses' instruction in vv. 1-5. If a prophet was able to produce miraculous works but urged defection from the Lord and adherence to other gods (v. 2), that prophet was to be rejected, for he had been granted supernatural power only to test the covenant loyalty of God's people.[28] That is, he became an instrument in the Lord's sovereign hand by which the people of Israel could be measured at precisely the point of covenant relationship. The language of v. 3, "whether you love him with all your heart and with all your soul," is that of the Shema, the epitome of the covenant faith, disobedience of which was tantamount to repudiation of the saving grace and goodness of the Lord (cf. Deut 6:4-5,13-15).[29] What is required is wholehearted commitment to the Lord and his commands, supernatural signs to the contrary notwithstanding (v. 4).

13:5   The fact that the false prophet fulfilled a God-ordained function did not deliver him from personal responsibility, however, so he was to be put to death as a leader of sedition against the dominion of the Lord (v. 5). The word for "rebellion" (*sārâ*) frequently occurs in reference to disobedient children (cf. Deut 21:18-21) but more often speaks of covenant defection and disloyalty (cf. Isa 1:23; Jer 6:28).[30] The most complete exposition of what that means follows in vv. 6-11. So serious was this offense that the guilty prophet had to be "purged" from among Israel, that is, literally, "burned out" of the community so that his pernicious ways and teachings could be eradicated and nullified (v. 5; cf. 17:7,12; 19:13,19; 21:21).

---

[27] F. J. Helfmeyer, "אוֹת *ʾôth*," *TDOT* 1:177.

[28] Thompson, *Deuteronomy,* 174.

[29] Mayes, *Deuteronomy,* 232.

[30] R. D. Patterson, "סָרַה (*sara*)," *TWOT* 2:621.

13:6-10 Any doubts that the apostate prophets were from within the community of faith are laid to rest with the further specification that they could be even from among one's family or closest friends (v. 6). Their appeal, as in v. 2, was to "worship other gods," a solicitation directly in opposition to the second commandment, which prohibited "other gods" (Deut 5:7) and their "worship" (5:9). Whether such gods were from distant places or nearby (v. 7), those who encouraged their adoption must not be heeded but, rather, must be put to death and that without exception or equivocation (v. 8). As painful as it might be, that loved one must be stoned by his own near kinsman first of all (presumably because he was first to hear of the treacherous invitation; cf. 17:7), and then by the community (v. 9).[31] The seriousness of the punishment fits the seriousness of the crime, a boldfaced act of rebellion against the sovereign who had brought his people out from other lordship and bondage in order to make them his own treasured possession (v. 10).

13:11 The purpose of implementing such drastic action was not only to satisfy the wounded honor of a holy and righteous God but to serve as a deterrent to future covenant violation (v. 11). Unfortunately, the injunction must seldom if ever have been carried out. Over and over again Israel and Judah were unfaithful to the Lord, a pattern of life that brought a series of judgments upon them, culminating in the eventual demise and deportations of the respective kingdoms (cf. 2 Kgs 17:7-23; 24:3).

Thus far Moses had dealt with false prophets of Israel who would rise up from among the people, even family members and friends, and who would brazenly encourage spiritual rebellion. These could be readily identified because they were nearby and, in fact, were known and heard by their accusers. But what about rumors of such seditionists in more distant places? How were they to be identified and dealt with? This is the subject of vv. 12-18.

13:12-13 These false prophets were also Israelites, for they too rose from "among you" (v. 13), having settled in towns allotted to Israel by the Lord (v. 12). Unlike the ones mentioned earlier, however, these were characterized as "wicked men" (lit., "sons of Belial"). This phrase, commonly used to refer to worthless persons in general, has here (and elsewhere, as in Prov 6:12; 16:27; 19:28; Nah 1:11) the notion of a misleading or deceitful one.[32] The reason these, and not the prophets first mentioned, were so described lies no doubt in the desire to make the latter appear less inher-

---

[31] Cairns, *Word and Presence,* 137.

[32] B. Otzen, "בְּלִיַּעַל *bĕliyyaʿal*," *TDOT* 2:135-36: "Those who induce Israel to commit the cardinal cultic sin, that of worshipping [sic] foreign gods."

ently wicked inasmuch as they were family and friends. They all shared in common, nonetheless, a disloyalty to the Lord that impelled them to lead their fellow citizens astray.

13:14-15 In order to certify the truth of the rumor about such distant false prophets, the leaders of the community had to research the reported case very carefully (v. 14). Having determined the truth of the allegations, they must put into effect the penalty of death as already prescribed (v. 5). But now the punishment extended beyond the culpable parties, that is, the false prophets themselves, to include the entire community in which they lived (v. 15). The reason for this presumably was (1) the failure of the citizens of that town to address the matter themselves or (2) the fact that they had succumbed to the enticements of the prophets and had followed them into idolatry. In either case the entire place was placed under *herem,* the judgment of annihilation, as though it were a Canaanite city, for this was the very judgment reserved for such recalcitrant pagans (cf. Deut 7:1-5). Clearly, those who rebel against the Lord by breaking the covenant and going after other gods are no better than the heathen and deserve the same divine punishment.

13:16 The reduction of the offending town to a ruin forever (*tēl,* "mound," "ruin-heap") is reminiscent of the fate that awaited Ai under Joshua's conquest (Josh 8:28). In a sense their lot would be even worse, for the livestock and plunder of Ai were allowed to remain unscathed as gifts to the Israelites (Josh 8:2,27), but absolutely everything had to be destroyed in an Israelite community that accommodated false prophets (Deut 13:16). This no doubt was because Israel would have sinned against greater light and therefore was held to a higher standard and a more severe judgment. An illustration of that may be seen in the experience of Achan, who stole items from Jericho that had been placed under *herem* (Josh 7:10-21). As a member of the covenant community he should have known better, so his punishment was the loss of his life along with that of his family and livestock and the utter destruction of all his goods. This outcome was even more severe than that affecting Jericho itself, the place from which he had obtained the illicit objects (cf. Josh 6:24).[33]

13:17-18 If Israel retained none of these "condemned things" (v. 17; lit., "nothing from the *herem*") but rather carried out the will of God fully, they could expect his mercy and blessing to be on them (v. 18). In other words, the keeping of his commands is the secret to covenant success. The

---

[33] M. H. Woudstra, *The Book of Joshua,* NICOT (Grand Rapids: Eerdmans, 1981), 130; cf. R. I. Vasholz, "A Legal 'Brief' on Deuteronomy 13:16-17," *Presbyterion* 16 (1990): 128-29.

use of the word *miṣwâ* ("command") in v. 18 harks back to its use in 12:32, thus providing an enveloping device that encapsulates the whole unit and validates the view that 12:32 belongs with the present pericope.

(5) *The Distinction between Clean and Unclean Animals (14:1-21)*

[1]You are the children of the LORD your God. Do not cut yourselves or shave the front of your heads for the dead, [2]for you are a people holy to the LORD your God. Out of all the peoples on the face of the earth, the LORD has chosen you to be his treasured possession.

[3]Do not eat any detestable thing. [4]These are the animals you may eat: the ox, the sheep, the goat, [5]the deer, the gazelle, the roe deer, the wild goat, the ibex, the antelope and the mountain sheep. [6]You may eat any animal that has a split hoof divided in two and that chews the cud. [7]However, of those that chew the cud or that have a split hoof completely divided you may not eat the camel, the rabbit or the coney. Although they chew the cud, they do not have a split hoof; they are ceremonially unclean for you. [8]The pig is also unclean; although it has a split hoof, it does not chew the cud. You are not to eat their meat or touch their carcasses.

[9]Of all the creatures living in the water, you may eat any that has fins and scales. [10]But anything that does not have fins and scales you may not eat; for you it is unclean.

[11]You may eat any clean bird. [12]But these you may not eat: the eagle, the vulture, the black vulture, [13]the red kite, the black kite, any kind of falcon, [14]any kind of raven, [15]the horned owl, the screech owl, the gull, any kind of hawk, [16]the little owl, the great owl, the white owl, [17]the desert owl, the osprey, the cormorant, [18]the stork, any kind of heron, the hoopoe and the bat.

[19]All flying insects that swarm are unclean to you; do not eat them. [20]But any winged creature that is clean you may eat.

[21]Do not eat anything you find already dead. You may give it to an alien living in any of your towns, and he may eat it, or you may sell it to a foreigner. But you are a people holy to the LORD your God.

Do not cook a young goat in its mother's milk.

The exclusiveness of the Lord and his worship finds expression next in guidelines relative to Israel's separation from all other peoples as the covenant agent through whom he will effect his regal and saving purposes on the earth.[34] That this is the intent of the pericope at hand is clear from the

---

[34] Kaufman suggests that Deut 14 is a continuation of the rejection of apostasy introduced in Deut 13 and that both are commentaries on the third commandment, "You shall not use the name of the LORD your God in vain." He makes the connection on the basis of v. 3 ("You shall eat no abomination"), a prohibition of a pagan practice that he links with apostasy and, in turn, the prohibition of false oaths in God's name ("The Structure of the Deuteronomic Law, 127). The connection here seems somewhat tenuous (as Kaufman himself

initial statement ("You are the children of the LORD your God," v. 1) and the cliché "You are a people holy to the LORD your God" in both vv. 2 and 21. Within this inclusio is a catalog of clean and unclean creatures and how they are to be dealt with. The purpose of this information is illustrative, that is, pedagogical, to the effect that separation between pure and impure animals is a reminder of Israel's own separation from the world of nations.

14:1 The uniqueness of Israel is first spelled out in the opening frame of the inclusio and then elaborated once more in the closing frame. Thus the prohibition "Do not cut yourselves or shave the front of your heads for the dead" (v. 1) matches formally "Do not cook a young goat in its mother's milk" (v. 21). The recognition of this function of the respective prohibitions sheds a great deal of light on the rather enigmatic character of these two taboos and also contributes to the connection between them and the material they enclose, namely, the instructions concerning the clean and the unclean.[35]

The juxtaposition between the programmatic statement that Israel is the child of the Lord and the warning against cutting or shaving themselves underscores that the latter practice was typical of pagan behavior and for that reason had to be avoided. To be God's people requires a lifestyle commensurate with that high and holy calling. While it is not altogether clear what such customs signified to the Canaanite world, they did apparently pertain to mourning and/or burial rites as v. 1b declares. The same point is made in Lev 19, where Moses instructed that the people should "not cut the hair at the sides of your head or clip off the edges of your beard" (v. 27) and "not cut your bodies for the dead" (v. 28).[36] Then in chap. 21 he addressed the priests and commanded that they "must not shave their heads or shave off the edges of their beards or cut their bodies" (v. 5), all because "they must be holy to their God" (v. 6). One is reminded also of the frenzied dancing of the prophets of Baal, who, when taunted by Elijah, "shouted louder and slashed themselves with swords and spears, as was their custom, until their blood flowed" (1 Kgs 18:28; cf. Zech 13:4-6).[37]

---

admits, p. 124), but if Deut 12–26 is indeed an elaboration of the Decalogue, Deut 14 must relate somehow to the third commandment. Cf. Braulik, *Die deuteronomischen Gesetz und der Dekalog,* 34-35; Rofé, "The Arrangement of the Laws in Deuteronomy," 279. Rofé is content with showing the linkages between Deut 13:12-18; 14:1-2,3-21, and 22-29. He implicitly rejects the view that Deut 12–26 is an elaboration of the Decalogue.

[35] Braulik, *Die deuteronomischen Gesetz und der Dekalog,* 34.

[36] G. J. Wenham puts it well: "The external appearance of the people should reflect their internal status as the chosen and holy people of God" (*The Book of Leviticus,* NICOT [Grand Rapids: Eerdmans, 1979], 272).

[37] The verb גדד in the *hithpael* ("administer incisions to oneself," KB, 169) occurs also in 1 Kgs 18:28; Jer 16:6; 41:5; Mic 4:14. In all but the last reference the context is mourning.

This may well have been done in the hope of reviving a moribund or at least a sleeping Baal.[38]

14:2 The covenant overtones of all this are immediately apparent in the clause "the LORD has chosen you to be his treasured possession" (v. 2b), for the noun "treasured possession" (*sĕgullâ*) appears in the identical form in the classic text Exod 19:4-6, where Israel was first invited into covenant participation. Also the same noun and the verb "choose" (*bāḥar*) appear in Deut 7:6 in a context of separation in which pagan practices and paraphernalia are to be abjured (vv. 1-5) and Israel is summoned to covenant obedience in light of their election (vv. 7-11).

14:3 The list of animals prohibited for human consumption is characterized by the single word "detestable," a term that suggests anything that is repulsive to and abhorred by God or even man (cf. Lev 18:22-30; Deut 7:25; 12:31; 17:1; 18:9-14; 25:13-16; Prov 6:16-19). In the context these creatures were detestable because they represented objects outside the pale of covenant allowance for the Israelite diet and not simply because they may or may not have had nutritive or hygienic deficiency.[39] That is, they were impure simply because the Lord said so and for that reason alone were detestable and to be avoided. This is precisely the principle underlying the Lord's words to a protesting Peter, who, in his vision, refused to eat animals let down from heaven: "Do not call anything impure that God has made clean" (Acts 11:9). All things are pure or impure as God himself dictates and not by inherent character or quality. Israel also, then, was pure (or

---

[38] The practice is now well attested in the Ugaritic texts and elsewhere. See J. Gray, *1 & 2 Kings*, OTL (Philadelphia: Westminster, 1970), 398-99; J. C. L. Gibson, *Canaanite Myths and Legends* (Edinburgh: T & T Clark, 1977), 120 (*CTA* 19, iv, 172-73); cf. ibid., 73 (*CTA* 5, vi, 20-21).

[39] For various views see K.-K. Chan, "You Shall Not Eat These Abominable Things: An Examination of Different Interpretations on Deuteronomy 14:3-20," *East Asia Journal of Theology* (1985): 88-106; G. J. Wenham, "The Theology of Unclean Food," *EvQ* 53 (1981): 6-15. Not to be overlooked is the novel but influential discussion of M. Douglas, *Purity and Danger* (London: Routledge & Kegan Paul, 1966). As a sociologist she seeks a basis for distinctions in the social mores of peoples. Since the Israelites were pastoralists, the animals with which they were familiar and on which they depended would have been clean. All others, then, were unclean simply because their characteristics and habits did not conform to the norm already dictated by the culture that determined such arbitrary matters (pp. 53-55). Douglas does not, however, pay sufficient attention to the theological context of the laws of separation where the whole point is that the distinction among animals is just as arbitrary and irrational as was Israel's election by Yahweh from among the nations. Von Rad is close to the truth when he says that "the individual Israelite had to give his assent to this separation of Israel by Yahweh from all other cults by means of certain abstentions as a profession of his faith" (*Deuteronomy*, 102).

holy) and the nations impure (or unholy) according to the elective purposes of God, not because of intrinsic qualities (cf. Deut 7:7-8).

14:4-8 The list begins with ten animals that are acceptable for meat, all of which share in common the fact that they are split-hoofed ruminants (vv. 4-5). These arbitrary criteria are, again, divinely directed and without apparent practical significance. Both must be in place, however, for animals such as the camel, rabbit, and coney, though they chew the cud, do not have cloven hoofs and therefore are disqualified (v. 7). Conversely, the pig may have a split hooves, but because it does not chew the cud it was also to be considered out of bounds (v. 8). All such unclean animals were not only to be precluded from table fare, but one was not even to come in contact with their carcasses (v. 8b).

14:9-10 The standard by which to judge marine creatures is even more simple and straightforward: they must possess both fins and scales (vv. 9-10). This obviously eliminated shellfish, eels, sharks, and the like, leaving only a relatively limited variety of fishes. The practical wisdom of this limitation is more readily apparent, for it was well known that many of the forbidden sea creatures contain properties and propensities that rendered them harmful to human consumption, especially in the absence of refrigeration or other means of preservation.

14:11-18 Infinitely more complex are the regulations concerning edible birds, so much so that the impure appear in a comprehensive list of twenty-one species or subspecies (vv. 11-18).[40] A few of these are difficult to identify with certainty (e.g., the "vulture," the "black vulture," the "red kite," the "black kite," the "horned owl," the "screech owl," the "white owl," and the "desert owl"), and the bat, of course, is technically not a bird. What most of these share, despite the imprecision in ornithological terms, is their carnivorous nature, nearly all, in fact, being consumers of carrion.[41] Again, while these habits did not alone or even primarily determine the uncleanness of these creatures, their predilections clearly served to highlight what it meant to be impure.

14:19-20 The fourth category of animal life addressed here is that of the insect world. Those that swarm (Heb *šereṣ hāʿôp*, lit., "swarmer, the flying thing") were strictly forbidden. All others, including birds and insects, that were clean could be eaten. This rather ambiguous information is greatly clarified in the parallel instructions of Lev 11:20-23. There the

---

[40] For a comprehensive treatment of the identity of these various birds see J. Milgrom, *Leviticus 1–16*, AB (New York: Doubleday, 1991), 661-64; cf. also W. L. Moran, "The Literary Connection between Lv. 11:13-19 and Dt. 14:12-18," *CBQ* 28 (1966): 271-77.

[41] J. E. Hartley, *Leviticus*, WBC (Dallas: Word, 1992), 159.

insects are divided between those that "walk on all fours" (the forbidden) and those, such as the locust, katydid, cricket, and grasshopper, that "have jointed legs for hopping on the ground" (the acceptable).[42] The "swarmers" of our passage must be equivalent to insects that "walk on all fours" with unarticulated legs.

14:21 Finally, God's people must refrain from eating "anything you find already dead." Such diet was perfectly acceptable for the resident alien and could even be sold to a foreigner, so there cannot have been any notion of contamination or other nutritional deficiencies lying behind the prohibition. The actual reason is clearly spelled out: "You are a people holy to the LORD your God." This suggests that the problem was one having to do with the proper slaughter of the animal and the ritually correct disposal of its blood (cf. Deut 12:23-25).[43] Animals found already dead would not be "kosher," that is, would not have been slain according to prescribed ritual.

The discussion of dietary regulation ends, as noted already, with a statement of Israel's holiness and a prohibition linked to that statement, one pertaining to some common heathen practice. At the outset of the passage (v. 1) that practice was described as self-laceration and a hair arrangement associated with mourning rites. Here, in laconic but rather abstruse terms, the injunction is against another such practice: "Do not cook a young goat in its mother's milk" (v. 21b).

Exactly what this means has been much debated, but it clearly has to do with a religious or cultic ritual so abhorrent to the Lord that it is mentioned twice previously as a summary statement of that which is illicit to Israel as a special people.[44] The first of these occurrences is in Exod 23:19, the verse that brings to a conclusion the so-called Book of the Covenant. Here it is also in the immediate context of festival keeping and proper use of blood and other materials of sacrifice (23:14-19). The second allusion to the rite appears in Exod 34:26, at the end of the "ritual decalogue" of vv. 10-26. Here it follows a statement identical to that of Exod 23:18-19 and in the same liturgical context of festival and offering.[45]

---

[42] For the criteria worked out in rabbinical tradition, see Milgrom, *Leviticus 1–16*, 665.

[43] Ridderbos, *Deuteronomy*, 175.

[44] See P. C. Craigie, "Deuteronomy and Ugaritic studies," *TynBul* 28 (1977): 155-69; E. A. Knauf, "Zur Herkunft und sozialgeschichte Israels. 'Das Bockchen in der Milch seiner Mutter,'" *Bib* 69 (1988): 153-69. Knauf suggests (incorrectly) that the prohibition arose from the extension of ancient practice to postexilic Judaism living among pagan Palestinian populations.

[45] See B. S. Childs, *The Book of Exodus* (Philadelphia: Westminster, 1974), 483-86.

It is reasonable to conclude that the boiling of a young goat in its mother's milk was part of a Canaanite festival ritual that so epitomized that depraved cultus that it came to symbolize all that was evil and detestable in it. Both uses of the prohibition against it in Exodus are in festival contexts and, indeed, this is the case here in Deuteronomy as well, though here the festival instructions follow rather than precede it (Deut 14:22-29). Its position in Deuteronomy is to allow it to serve as a framing device matching the prohibition of 14:1.[46]

(6) Tribute to the Sovereign (14:22–16:17)

A major responsibility of any king in vassalage to a Hittite ruler was the periodic presentation of tribute to him, tokens of his submission and loyalty (cf. 12:6-14). This was no less true of Israel, which, in line with the sovereign-vassal nature of the Sinaitic covenant, must bear appropriate offerings to the Lord on stated occasions. This was part and parcel of true worship, a vital aspect of what it meant to give recognition to the Lord as the only God and to respond to him accordingly. Thus tribute is an expression of obedience to the fourth commandment, that which celebrates redemption from the bondage of Egyptian slavery to the happy service of the Great King, the Lord (5:12-15).[47]

The entire section under review addresses (1) the matter of the procedure for presenting tribute (14:22-29), (2) its use in regard to other Israelites, especially the poor (15:1-11) and indentured (15:12-18), (3) special instruction concerning animal offerings (15:19-23), (4) and the three major festival times when tribute was to be taken to the Lord at the central sanctuary (16:1-17).

---

[46] G. Braulik, "Die Abfolge der Gesetze in Deuteronomium 12-26 und der Dekalog," in *Das Deuteronomium,* 262.

[47] Kaufman, though placing the law of tithes (Deut 14:22-29) under the rubric of the third commandment, is really most ambivalent about it ("The Structure of the Deuteronomic Law," 128-29). In fact, he sees it as a transition between the concern for foodstuffs (14:3-21) and that for periodic release (15:1-11). Rofé ("The Arrangement of the Laws in Deuteronomy," 279) is correct in viewing 14:3-21 as a self-contained unit and the law of tithes that is more properly connected to 15:1-11 (cf. מִקְצֵה שָׁלֹשׁ שָׁנִים, 14:28; and מִקֵּץ שֶׁבַע־שָׁנִים 15:1). Braulik takes 14:22–16:17 to be a single collection but associates it (as does Kaufman) with the third commandment (*Die deuteronomischen Gesetze und der Dekalog,* 35-38). Finally, J. Walton suggests that Deut 14:22–16:17 teaches gratitude to God as the source of one's goods (creation) and the source of one's freedom (exodus). The tithe laws therefore pertain to the fourth commandment ("Deuteronomy: An Exposition of the Spirit of the Law," *GTJ* 8 [1987]: 223-24).

²²Be sure to set aside a tenth of all that your fields produce each year. ²³Eat the tithe of your grain, new wine and oil, and the firstborn of your herds and flocks in the presence of the LORD your God at the place he will choose as a dwelling for his Name, so that you may learn to revere the LORD your God always.

²⁴But if that place is too distant and you have been blessed by the LORD your God and cannot carry your tithe (because the place where the LORD will choose to put his Name is so far away), ²⁵then exchange your tithe for silver, and take the silver with you and go to the place the LORD your God will choose.

²⁶Use the silver to buy whatever you like: cattle, sheep, wine or other fermented drink, or anything you wish. Then you and your household shall eat there in the presence of the LORD your God and rejoice.

²⁷And do not neglect the Levites living in your towns, for they have no allotment or inheritance of their own.

²⁸At the end of every three years, bring all the tithes of that year's produce and store it in your towns, ²⁹so that the Levites (who have no allotment or inheritance of their own) and the aliens, the fatherless and the widows who live in your towns may come and eat and be satisfied, and so that the LORD your God may bless you in all the work of your hands.

14:22-23 In line with long-standing precedent (cf. Gen 14:20; 28:22; Lev 27:30-32; Num 18:21-28), the tribute the Lord required was 10 percent of the individual's or family's annual produce. In a day when things were ordinarily bought and sold in kind, this would have taken the form of grain, wine, oil, livestock, and other commodities actually produced by the farmer (vv. 22-23). More specifically, these were all edibles; for the presentation of these goods, in line with covenant ratification and renewal procedures, involved a meal shared by the Lord and the people alike at the dwelling place of the Great King, the central sanctuary (cf. Exod 23:19; 24:11; 34:26; Deut 12:5-7). The "eating" by the Lord was, of course, represented by the burning of the offerings whereas that by the people was literal and actual.[48] Not to be overlooked is the fact that the underlying purpose for presenting the tithe was to instill within the Israelite a proper reverence for the Lord as the Sovereign, the one to whom he was ultimately accountable (v. 23).

14:24-25 One problem with the presentation of tribute such as cattle and other large offerings was the distance that must be covered between villages in remote parts of the land and the central sanctuary. To expedite matters the law permitted the conversion of the produce into money (lit., "silver," the most common metal of exchange), which then could be used

---

[48] Craigie, *Deuteronomy,* 217-18.

to purchase the same goods upon arrival at the house of the Lord (vv. 24-25). This practical and perfectly legitimate way of making pilgrimage manageable continued on into New Testament times and, in fact, lies behind the gospel accounts of Jesus and the moneychangers (Matt 21:12-13; cf. John 2:13-16). Like any other concession of this kind, it was subject to abuse by those who, like the moneychangers, would profit from the exchange by charging exorbitant rates.

14:26 The communal nature of the occasion of offering is clear from the concluding statement that those rendering their tribute to the Lord are to do so, in part at least, as a feast "in the presence of the LORD your God" (v. 26). This phrase strongly suggests that the Lord is more than an interested observer in what is going on. He is, in fact, a participant, for such was the nature of banquets that accompanied the making and ratification of covenant relationships.[49] The most striking example of this, perhaps, was Jesus' participation in the communion meal with his disciples at which he spoke of a new covenant (Luke 22:20; cf. 1 Cor 11:25), one that in eschatological times would be celebrated again in the "wedding supper of the Lamb" (Rev 19:6-10). Clearly, God and humankind, in covenant one with the other, celebrate that oneness, mystically at least, in the breaking of bread together.

14:27-29 A necessary adjunct to the presentation of tribute to the Great King is the generous support of those who serve him. Thus the Levite, who had no property or secular occupation by which to provide for himself, had to be sustained by the community of God's people (v. 27; cf. 12:12; 26:11-13). This was to be done by allocating the tithe of every third year to the Levites and, indeed, to all dependent members of the community such as aliens, orphans, and widows (vv. 28-29). The implications of this for the regular times of offering to the Lord are not altogether clear, but it seems that presentations of tribute over and above the third-year tithe must be taken to the central sanctuary even in those years (cf. 15:20; 16:10,17).[50]

---

[49] It is true that the phrase לִפְנֵי יְהוָה frequently refers to the Lord's presence as a witness to covenant, but the context of banqueting strongly suggests his participation as well. Cf. D. C. T. Sheriffs, "The Phrases *ina IGI DN* and *lipĕnēy yhwh* in Treaty and Covenant Contexts," *JNSL* 7 (1979): 61-65. Milgrom, while recognizing that "food" (לְחֶם) on the altar "stands for God's food," concludes that "in the cultic texts this term can be characterized as a linguistic fossil" (*Leviticus 1–16*, 213). Cf. Lev 21:6,8,17,22; 22:25; 23:17. This does not remove the imagery, however, of a shared meal.

[50] Perhaps, as de Vaux suggests, the tithe on the third year was retained totally at home and was reported to the central sanctuary to have been used for the purpose for which it was intended by the law (*Ancient Israel*, 2:380; cf. Deut 26:13).

The tithe referred to here was not the only means of support for the Levite, for Num 18 spells out other provisions for him. Inasmuch as the Levite served the Lord, he could share in the tithe offered to the Lord (Num 18:21-24). That is, not everything brought to the tabernacle or temple was consumed on the altar. Much of it, in fact, was set aside for the Levites who themselves had to offer 10 percent to the Lord as their own expression of homage (Num 18:26).[51] The purpose of the triennial tithe in the local villages was to provide for the Levites and their families in their own place of residence whereas that given to them at the sanctuary was for the purpose of using it then and there as sustenance and sacrifice for their immediate needs. As all of these dependent members of the community were blessed by its citizens, so the latter could expect the blessing of the Lord upon their lives and labors (v. 29).

The theme of the defenseless or dependent members of society is further expanded in 15:1-11, again as an aspect of service to the Lord. The issue here specifically is debt cancellation, reflective of the problem indigenous to every culture, that of borrowing and lending. Through poor judgment, wrong advice, or circumstances beyond human control, there are always persons who become destitute and who must therefore cast themselves upon the merciful beneficence of others. Such contingencies in ancient Israel could be addressed by interest-free loans that could be repaid either by goods or by labor. The latter case is legislated in vv. 12-18, so the focus here is on loans that are to be repaid in "cash." The terms under which such transactions were set up are not spelled out in the Old Testament except that the lender could charge no interest to a fellow Israelite (Exod 22:25; Lev 25:35-37). Presumably arrangements were made on a good-faith basis with adequate protection for the creditor as well as the debtor.

If, however, the debtor could not repay his loan, his debt must be canceled after seven years. One must assume that he had done everything in his power to discharge his responsibility and that such failure was rare, for otherwise it is difficult to believe that lenders would readily enter into such ventures. There was, of course, the sense of moral obligation toward a fellow Israelite that might have encouraged risk taking and a willingness to forgive indebtedness that would not ordinarily prevail in the secular world. This seems to be the sentiment behind vv. 4-5.

¹At the end of every seven years you must cancel debts. ²This is how it is to

---

⁵¹ Budd, *Numbers*, 203-4.

be done: Every creditor shall cancel the loan he has made to his fellow Israelite. He shall not require payment from his fellow Israelite or brother, because the LORD'S time for canceling debts has been proclaimed.

³You may require payment from a foreigner, but you must cancel any debt your brother owes you.

⁴However, there should be no poor among you, for in the land the LORD your God is giving you to possess as your inheritance, he will richly bless you, ⁵if only you fully obey the LORD your God and are careful to follow all these commands I am giving you today. ⁶For the LORD your God will bless you as he has promised, and you will lend to many nations but will borrow from none. You will rule over many nations but none will rule over you.

⁷If there is a poor man among your brothers in any of the towns of the land that the LORD your God is giving you, do not be hardhearted or tightfisted toward your poor brother. ⁸Rather be openhanded and freely lend him whatever he needs. ⁹Be careful not to harbor this wicked thought:

"The seventh year, the year for canceling debts, is near," so that you do not show ill will toward your needy brother and give him nothing. He may then appeal to the LORD against you, and you will be found guilty of sin. ¹⁰Give generously to him and do so without a grudging heart; then because of this the LORD your God will bless you in all your work and in everything you put your hand to. ¹¹There will always be poor people in the land. Therefore I command you to be openhanded toward your brothers and toward the poor and needy in your land.

15:1-2   In any case, however such transactions originated, there was no question about how they were to be resolved in the event of default. The lender must simply forgive the debt as a necessary consequence of God's declaration of a "time for canceling debts" (v. 2).[52] This was, as already noted, at the end of seven years, a period not necessarily commencing with the making of the loan but, as v. 9 makes clear, a universally recognized year of release (cf. Exod 23:10-11; Lev 25:2-4). To protect both lender and borrower, the loan, one assumes, was of such an amount as to reasonably be repaid in whatever time remained until the year of cancellation. That is, the size of the loan was commensurate with the time to repay it.[53]

[52] The phrase כִּי־קָרָא שְׁמִטָּה לַיהוָה ("because a šĕmiṭṭâ has been called for by yhwh") refers to the formal proclamation of a regularly recurring time of release, namely, the Sabbatical Year. This is clarified in Deut 31:10, where it is appropriately linked to the Feast of Tabernacles, that festival that celebrated release from Egyptian bondage. Cf. Driver, *Deuteronomy,* 174-75; Keil and Delitzsch, *The Pentateuch,* 3:369-70.

[53] Many scholars propose that the šĕmiṭṭâ pertains only to release from debt payment on the seventh year, the year the land must lie fallow and unproductive and therefore of no monetary benefit to the debtor. According to this view the debt must eventually be repaid, but no payment could be exacted in the year of release. See, e.g., Craigie, *Deuteronomy,* 236-37. For arguments to the contrary see Mayes, *Deuteronomy,* 247-48, and the following discussion.

15:3 This generous policy was applicable only to fellow Israelites, however. The foreigner, because he was not the recipient of God's special grace of election and covenant, could not enjoy its benefits either. Such a prerequisite must have served as an inducement to the foreigner to contemplate the privileges of covenant fellowship and to want them for himself.

15:4-6 The matter of borrowing and lending ought to be a moot point anyway, Moses argued, for poverty ought not to exist in the rich land the Lord would give them.[54] This seems to be the best understanding of v. 4 rather than the idea that there would absolutely not be any poor among them. Complete absence of poverty is squarely contradicted by v. 11, which avers that "there will always be poor people in the land." The tension between the two statements is indicative of the gulf that exists between the ideal and actual, what could be the case were God's purposes carried out and what inevitably occurs when they are not. This is the import of v. 5, which plainly states that full compliance with covenant requirements was the precondition to Israel's prosperity in the land. When this was achieved, not only would Israel be blessed but, in line with the ancient patriarchal promises, they would be the means of blessing the whole world and having dominion over the nations (v. 6; cf. Gen 12:2-3; 17:4-6; 26:3-4).[55] They would be the lender to whom all others would be in debt (cf. Deut 28:12-13).

15:7-9a Having addressed the matter of debt cancellation and the theoretical possibility of there being no poverty in the land of promise, Moses shifted the emphasis to the practical reality of poverty and how the more affluent in society must deal with it. Granted the existence of the poor, the attitude toward them must be one of softness of heart and openness of hand (vv. 7-8). That is, true charity consists of compassion at work. The real test of commitment to this principle would be the brother who asked for help at the last hour, just before the time of debt cancellation or suspension of payment came about (v. 9a). To lend to him then would likely be tantamount to making him an outright gift inasmuch as he would have little or no time left to pay back the loan.[56] In such circumstances the tendency would be not to make a loan at all and to let the needy brother go unsatisfied.

---

[54] McConville, *Law and Theology in Deuteronomy,* 96-97.

[55] The "ruling" (*māšal*) here should, in context, be limited to financial, not political, dominion. That is, Israel would be so prosperous that the nations would be in subjection to it in terms of economic dependence. Cf. Driver, *Deuteronomy,* 176.

[56] Again the question is whether the *šĕmiṭṭâ* refers to outright forgiveness of debt in the seventh year or merely a time of grace in which payment was deferred. In either case the creditor must give no thought to his own financial profiteering but only to his brother's needs. Thus Craigie, *Deuteronomy,* 237-38.

15:9b-11 Such a response, however, is not at all appropriate for a kingdom citizen. Not only might the offended and neglected brother make appeal to the Lord, who is concerned about the plight of all his people (v. 9b), but the very attitude of stinginess is unbecoming to one who claims to be a servant of the Lord. Rather, one should give freely (so the inf. abs. of the verb *nātan*, v. 10a), not grudgingly, for this is what delights the Lord and prompts him to respond in like manner with blessing and prosperity (v. 10). In the real world of fallen humanity there will always be the poor (v. 11a), but there must also always be, among God's people, a spirit of generosity to them (v. 11b). Jesus himself made note of this when he commended the woman with the precious ointment for having used it to anoint him in view of his impending death and burial (Matt 26:6-13). The poor about whom his hypocritical detractors professed to be concerned would always be with them, he said. They would have ample opportunity to unleash their compassion and largess upon them if they so desired.[57]

¹²**If a fellow Hebrew, a man or a woman, sells himself to you and serves you six years, in the seventh year you must let him go free. ¹³And when you release him, do not send him away empty-handed. ¹⁴Supply him liberally from your flock, your threshing floor and your winepress. Give to him as the LORD your God has blessed you. ¹⁵Remember that you were slaves in Egypt and the LORD your God redeemed you. That is why I give you this command today.**

¹⁶**But if your servant says to you, "I do not want to leave you," because he loves you and your family and is well off with you, ¹⁷then take an awl and push it through his ear lobe into the door, and he will become your servant for life. Do the same for your maidservant.**

¹⁸**Do not consider it a hardship to set your servant free, because his service to you these six years has been worth twice as much as that of a hired hand. And the LORD your God will bless you in everything you do.**

15:12-15 Extreme cases of poverty sometimes resulted in voluntary servitude in which a man or woman would come under the care of a benefactor who would provide for all the needs of the destitute individual until either he had paid off his obligations or served for a six-year period (v. 12).[58] Thereupon he was to be released from his economic bondage so that

---

[57] Blomberg correctly sees the need to view the whole context of Deut 15:11 as the basis for Jesus' observation (*Matthew*, 386). As he suggests, "well-to-do believers abuse this passage by citing v. 11a as grounds for social inaction." Jesus was not minimizing the plight of the poor but, to the contrary, was urging his hearers to do what Moses commanded in the Deuteronomic covenant.

[58] For the matter of slavery in Israel, esp. as regards provision for indenturehood and manumission, see H. L. Ellison, "The Hebrew Slave: A Study in Early Israelite Society," *EvQ*

once again he could be free and independent. Moreover, he was to be provided with a stake, as it were, with supplies that would make it possible for him to begin again. The rationale for this was the comparable situation in which Israel had found itself in Egypt.[59] There they had been pressed into slavery, cruelly mistreated, but at last delivered by the redemptive grace and power of God. But even the Egyptians had sent them away with provisions to tide them over until they could stand on their own feet (cf. Exod 12:35-36). If this mighty act of redemption was carried out by the Lord on Israel's behalf, how much more should the beneficiaries of that goodness be quick to exercise it on behalf of their financially oppressed brothers and sisters (Deut 15:14b-15).

15:16-17 It was altogether possible, however, that some persons who had entered into this arrangement were content to remain in it for whatever reason. The text itself suggests at least two such motives: (1) a bond of affection that had developed between the debtor and his patron and (2) his or her greatly improved standard of life under the arrangement (v. 16).[60] There could obviously be benefits to the master as well in having a loyal and loving servant who worked for him out of his own free will. Should this be the case, the relationship had to be formalized by the legal procedure of public declaration of intent, a procedure that, in such cases as these, consisted of the piercing of the ear of the man or woman with an awl pressed against the door (v. 17). This clearly was the door of the master, and the act speaks of the identification of the servant with his or her lord for life.[61]

---

45 (1973): 30-35; N. P. Lemche, "The Manumission of Slaves—the Fallow Year—the Sabbatical Year—the Jobel Year," *VT* 26 (1976): 38-59; E. Lipínski, "L'esclave hébreu," *VT* 26 (1976): 120-23; A. Phillips, "The Laws of Slavery: Exodus 21:2-11," *JSOT* 30 (1984): 51-66.

[59] Once more the appeal is to history, to remembering the past as a basis for present and future action; cf. Blair, "An Appeal to Remembrance," 41-47.

[60] At this point it is noteworthy that the Deuteronomic version of manumission differs significantly from that of the Book of the Covenant (Exod 21:2-11). Here the freed slave is provided with gifts, both males and females are included, but provisions for the wife and children of slaves are not separately dealt with. As M. Weinfeld argues, these differences most likely are attributed to a more "humanistic" code, one characterized by such sentiments as the slave's "love" for his master exclusively (v. 16; *Deuteronomy and the Deuteronomic School* [Oxford: Clarendon, 1972], 282-83). Weinfeld's explanation for the more humane nature of Deuteronomy rests, however, on the assumption of a long period of national reflection on the traditions of the Book of the Covenant, a period commensurate with the hypothesis of a Josianic *Sitz im Leben*. This is unnecessary, however, for the change in Deuteronomy can as well be accounted for by the changed socioeconomic conditions in Canaan anticipated by the Deuteronomic covenant.

[61] Durham, though equivocating about whether the doorpost was at the sanctuary or the home, agrees that "by this ceremony the 'temporary' slave became a 'permanent' slave, through devotion to his family" (*Exodus*, 321; cf. F. C. Fensham, "New Light on Exodus 21:6 and 22:7 from the Laws of Eshnunna," *JBL* 78 [1959]: 160-61).

15:18   If, on the other hand, the six years passed and the servant wished to go free, his request must willingly be granted. The benefactor, after all, had no complaint; for he had received the compensation of six years of labor, a service considered twice as good as that of a hireling since the very life of the indentured man or woman had been involved (v. 18).[62] Compliance with this petition for release and freedom would, as always, guarantee the blessing of the Lord upon the life and labor of the provider.

Certain unusual and technical terms in this passage (vv. 12-18; cf. Exod 21:2-6; Lev 25:39-43) have led some scholars to a different view from that proposed here, namely, that the persons seeking financial relief here are not fellow Israelites at all but outsiders known as *ʾibrî* (Hebrew). The transliteration "Hebrew," it is thought, disguises the real identity of these people, perhaps the *ʾapiru* (or *Habiru*) of widespread fame in ancient Near Eastern texts.[63] Arguments favoring this interpretation are as follows:

1. Israelites in the Old Testament rarely referred to themselves as Hebrews. The only exceptions, in fact, were Jonah, who, in speaking to Phoenician sailors, referred to himself as a Hebrew (Jonah 1:9), and the Lord, who described himself as the God of the Hebrews (Exod 7:16; 9:1; 10:3). This was done, no doubt, to accommodate persons who would themselves have used the term to denote them. Otherwise, "Hebrew" is a term used by others to speak of Israelites (Gen 39:14,17; Exod 1:15; 2:6), usually in a derogatory sense.

2. In one or two instances "Hebrew" describes people who clearly are not Israelites. The classic case is that of the narrative of 1 Sam 13:1–14:46, where Hebrews are explicitly distinguished from Israelites. First Samuel 14:21 is especially relevant: "Those Hebrews who had previously been with the Philistines and had gone up with them to their camp went over to the Israelites who were with Saul and Jonathan." With many scholars we suggest that "Hebrews" here refers to *ʿapiru*, remnants of which had sur-

---

[62] For discussion of the term "twice as much" מִשְׁנֶה see J. M. Lindenberger, "How Much for a Hebrew Slave? The Meaning of Misneh in Deut 15:18," *JBL* 110 (1991): 479-82. Contrary to Tsevat, Craigie, and other scholars, Lindenberger supports the traditional rendering of the NIV and not a meaning "equivalent to" or the like. Cf. Craigie, *Deuteronomy*, 239.

[63] For discussion of this problem see especially N. K. Gottwald, *The Tribes of Yahweh* (Maryknoll, N.Y.: Orbis, 1979), 769, n. 412; M. Greenberg, *The Hab/piru* (New Haven: American Oriental Society, 1955), 92-93; N. P. Lemche, "The 'Hebrew Slave'; Comments on the Slave Law Ex. xxi 2-11," *VT* 25 (1975): 129-44; E. Lipinski, "L'esclave hébreu," 120-23; id., "ʿApiru et Hebreaux," *BO* 42 (1985): 562-67; N. Naʿaman, "Ḥabiru and Hebrews: The Transfer of a Social Term to the Literary Sphere," *JNES* 45 (1986): 271-88; S. Paul, *Studies in the Book of the Covenant in the Light of Cuneiform and Biblical Law* (Leiden: Brill, 1970), 45-52.

vived from the Late Bronze era and which continued to occupy themselves in their traditional way as mercenaries.[64]

3. The identification of Hebrews as something other than Israelites would also fit the pattern of the overall passage (15:1-18) better, for there appears to be an ascending order of circumstances relative to impoverishment in society and its means of redress. In the first place (vv. 1-6) ordinary loans are in view with no particular sense of dire poverty at issue. These appear to be rather straightforward transactions between brother Israelites with the only unusual proviso being that the indebted brother be exculpated at the end of seven years. In the second place (vv. 7-11) the debtor was clearly poor, but the level of moral responsibility of the lender was even greater, for he had to look out for his disadvantaged brother even if it meant he had to suffer the loss of his investment. In the third place (vv. 12-18) the needy one was of an inferior social class in Israel and therefore could be brought into servitude if need be so that his obligation could be discharged.[65] Even here, however, an opportunity for release exists if both parties so desire it.

4. The reference to the released Hebrew as "free" may suggest a change in social status from a kind of chattel to a full-fledged citizen. The argument hinges on the Hebrew word *ḥopšî,* which may denote a social class rather than just a condition of being free. That is, the *ʿebed* (servant) becomes a *ḥopšî* (citizen or, more likely, "freedman").[66] This is exactly what transpired in the exodus when Israel was redeemed (*pādâ*) from slavery to become a nation of freed men and women (Deut 15:15). It is difficult to imagine that here in Deuteronomy, however, an Israelite had become slave to another only to become a freedman upon his emancipation from financial bondage. One can conceive of the *ʿapiru* making this transition.

All of these arguments notwithstanding, there still remains a case for identifying the Hebrew man or woman here as an Israelite.[67] First, the qualification of the Hebrew as a "brother" (*ʾāḥ*) greatly nuances the situation. Wherever *ʾāḥ* and *ʾibrî* occur elsewhere together, the context favors an Israelite identification (Exod 2:11; Jer 34:14). Second, it is possible to concede that a distinction exists in the Old Testament between Hebrew and Israelite in some settings (e.g., 1 Sam 13-14) without necessitating that that

---

[64] Gottwald, *Tribes of Yahweh,* 419-25.

[65] Lipínski, "L'esclave hébreau," 121.

[66] Lemche, "The 'Hebrew Slave,'" 136-42.

[67] For compelling reasons to identify the *ʿebed ʿibrî* as Israelites, see A. Phillips, "The Laws of Slavery," 51-66.

distinction always exists. That is, there may instead exist a difference between Hebrew (i.e., ʿibrî) and ʿapiru that the present text obscures. Third, the literary scheme and structure of the whole passage (15:1-18) stand intact whether or not Hebrew = Israelite. The point still remains that an ascending hierarchy of destitution and means of addressing it are in view whether the sufferer be an Israelite or non-Israelite. Fourth, ḥopšî, though admittedly a technical term describing a social class, carries also the regular, ordinary meaning of "free," that is, free from any kind of restraint including economic (cf. Lev 19:20; 1 Sam 17:25; Isa 58:6). There is no compelling reason why it cannot bear that meaning here. In short, the traditional understanding should prevail, that which views all three cases as intra-Israelite in character.

[19]Set apart for the LORD your God every firstborn male of your herds and flocks. Do not put the firstborn of your oxen to work, and do not shear the firstborn of your sheep. [20]Each year you and your family are to eat them in the presence of the LORD your God at the place he will choose.
[21]If an animal has a defect, is lame or blind, or has any serious flaw, you must not sacrifice it to the LORD your God. [22]You are to eat it in your own towns. Both the ceremonially unclean and the clean may eat it, as if it were gazelle or deer. [23]But you must not eat the blood; pour it out on the ground like water.

Having dealt with the issue of providing for one's brother as an aspect of rendering tribute to the Lord, Moses turned now to a more direct expression of that liege-duty, the offering of firstborn animals (vv. 19-23). The reason for addressing the matter here may be its association with the exodus event in which the firstborn of Israel were miraculously preserved while those of Egypt were slain (cf. Exod 12:12,29; 13:2,12; 22:29), an event to which reference has already been made in the immediate context (cf. 15:12-15).[68] The passage also provides a suitable conclusion to the section on tribute that began with instruction concerning the firstfruits of produce and firstborn of the flocks and herds (14:22-23).[69]

15:19-20 Just as Israel was delivered from onerous bondage in Egypt, so the firstborn of Israel's oxen and sheep were to be free of labor and of yielding their by-products (v. 19). Instead they, like Israel's firstborn sons, must be presented as offerings to the Lord. Obviously, in the case of human firstborn this meant devotion to service, an offering up of life to God as ministry. In the case of animals, however, the offering was unto

---

[68] McConville, *Law and Theology in Deuteronomy*, 93-97.
[69] Braulik, *Die deuteronomischen Gesetze und der Dekalog*, 36-37.

death, for only in their death could they serve as a means of covenant effectuation and celebration. The sacrifice in mind here is not fundamentally atoning in nature but expressive of atonement already achieved and of covenant relationship between the Lord and his people based upon it. The firstborn here were the offerings of Israel to the Lord that celebrate atonement and all the blessings of oneness and fellowship that flow from it. They constitute the repast at the table of communion around which the Lord and his elect people fellowship (v. 20). The fact that this is done each year suggests that the occasion is one of the annual festivals, most likely the Feast of Tabernacles.[70] This finds support in Exod 22:29-30, where the firstborn are mentioned in connection with cattle and sheep and in the context of a harvest festival. This is also the thrust of Deut 14:22-23, which, as we noted before, speaks of the presentation of tribute to the Sovereign on an annual basis. Finally, of all the festivals the Feast of Tabernacles is most closely identified with peace or fellowship offerings, the very kind in view in the passage (cf. Deut 16:13-15).

15:21-23 The offering of the firstborn is qualified further by the stipulation that it be as near a perfect specimen as possible (v. 21). This is not so much because God does not love and accept the flawed and failed but because the offerer must be prepared to part with what is most valuable to him. There is little sacrifice in giving up something that has little or no market value anyway (cf. Lev 22:17-25).[71] But such animals may be used for human consumption at home, by both the ceremonially clean and unclean (v. 22). This removes such animals from the realm of the cult to that of everyday life in which any clean animal could be eaten without any special preliminary purification rites on the part of the consumer (cf. 12:15-16; 14:3-21). Even in such cases, however, the blood remains sacrosanct as the very symbol of life itself, and so it must not be eaten but poured out upon the ground (cf. 12:16,23,24).

The final instruction concerning the offering of tribute to the Lord pertains to the seasons and cycles of its presentation. These were not according to the whim of the worshiper but were to conform to particular and stated festival occasions when the whole community made pilgrimage to the central sanctuary to appear before the Great King. The passage at hand outlines the specifications to be followed in regard to the three great annual festivals (16:1-17).[72]

---

[70] So, e.g., Mayes, *Deuteronomy,* 253.

[71] Craigie, *Deuteronomy,* 249.

[72] For a survey of the three great annual feasts, see de Vaux, *Ancient Israel,* 2:484-506.

¹Observe the month of Abib and celebrate the Passover of the LORD your God, because in the month of Abib he brought you out of Egypt by night. ²Sacrifice as the Passover to the LORD your God an animal from your flock or herd at the place the LORD will choose as a dwelling for his Name.

³Do not eat it with bread made with yeast, but for seven days eat unleavened bread, the bread of affliction, because you left Egypt in haste—so that all the days of your life you may remember the time of your departure from Egypt. ⁴Let no yeast be found in your possession in all your land for seven days. Do not let any of the meat you sacrifice on the evening of the first day remain until morning.

⁵You must not sacrifice the Passover in any town the LORD your God gives you ⁶except in the place he will choose as a dwelling for his Name. There you must sacrifice the Passover in the evening, when the sun goes down, on the anniversary of your departure from Egypt. ⁷Roast it and eat it at the place the LORD your God will choose. Then in the morning return to your tents.

⁸For six days eat unleavened bread and on the seventh day hold an assembly to the LORD your God and do no work.

⁹Count off seven weeks from the time you begin to put the sickle to the standing grain. ¹⁰Then celebrate the Feast of Weeks to the LORD your God by giving a freewill offering in proportion to the blessings the LORD your God has given you.

¹¹And rejoice before the LORD your God at the place he will choose as a dwelling for his Name—you, your sons and daughters, your menservants and maidservants, the Levites in your towns, and the aliens, the fatherless and the widows living among you. ¹²Remember that you were slaves in Egypt, and follow carefully these decrees.

¹³Celebrate the Feast of Tabernacles for seven days after you have gathered the produce of your threshing floor and your winepress. ¹⁴Be joyful at your Feast—you, your sons and daughters, your menservants and maidservants, and the Levites, the aliens, the fatherless and the widows who live in your towns. ¹⁵For seven days celebrate the Feast to the LORD your God at the place the LORD will choose. For the LORD your God will bless you in all your harvest and in all the work of your hands, and your joy will be complete.

¹⁶Three times a year all your men must appear before the LORD your God at the place he will choose: at the Feast of Unleavened Bread, the Feast of Weeks and the Feast of Tabernacles. No man should appear before the LORD empty-handed: ¹⁷Each of you must bring a gift in proportion to the way the LORD your God has blessed you.

16:1-2 The first of these, the Passover, must be observed in the month Abib (ca. mid-March to mid-April), otherwise known as Nisan (cf. Exod 12:2; 13:4).⁷³ Before the institution of the Passover, the year had begun in

---

⁷³ L. Bauer, "Deuteronomium 16:1-18," *NKZ* 37 (1926): 794-805; J. Halbe, "Passa-Massot im Deuteronomischen Festkalendar: Komposition, Netstehung und Programm von Dtn 16:1-8," *ZAW* 87 (1975): 147-68; J. A. Wharton, "Deuteronomy 16:1-8," *Int* 41 (1987): 287-91.

the autumn, in the month Tishri; but following God's mighty act of exodus deliverance, the religious calendar thereafter would commence on the first day of Abib. The ritual and significance of the Passover (and its attendant and related festival of Unleavened Bread; cf. Exod 12:15; 23:15; 34:18) are well known and otherwise expounded fully (Lev 23:4-8; Num 28:16-25). The special nuances of the Deuteronomic instruction are important, however, and must be given some attention here.

First of all is the reminder that the Passover animal (unspecified except as coming from the flock or herd; v. 2; cf. Exod 12:3-5) must be sacrificed "at the place the LORD will choose as a dwelling for his Name" (v. 2). This allusion to the central sanctuary as the Lord's dwelling place is, of course, unique to Deuteronomy (cf. 12:5,11,13, etc.) as is the general notion of the Passover being part of a pilgrimage by the whole community to a common place. The reason for the modification is evident. On the first occasion of the ceremony of the Passover and Unleavened Bread, the setting was in private homes in Egypt where individual families offered sacrifice and gathered around their own tables (Exod 12:1-14). Following the exodus and the formation of the tribes and clans into a covenant community, the festival was held at the tabernacle, the center of community life (Exod 23:15; 34:18-20; Lev 23:5-8). There was no need to insist on pilgrimage to a central site in such a cohesive and geographically close-knit society, for in the desert of preconquest times the entire camp was already oriented around the tabernacle (cf. Num 1:1–2:34).

16:3-4   The nature and composition of Israel as envisioned in Deuteronomy was quite another matter, however. It presupposed conquest and occupation that would result in widespread settlement. So great would be the distances from far-flung parts of the nation to any central place that long journeys would be required. This lies beneath the emphasis on a central sanctuary in the first place (Deut 12:1-5,9-11) and the special measures that must be taken about what could and could not be done in local villages as opposed to that to be done at the tabernacle or temple (cf. 12:15,20-28; 14:24-26).

Otherwise, the same Passover regulations remained in force. Only unleavened bread could be eaten during the days of festival and for the same reason as ever—as a reminder of the haste with which the Israelites left Egypt (v. 3; cf. Exod 12:11). The time required for leavened bread to rise necessitated the removal of all yeast from the home as a symbol of the urgency of immediate departure from bondage (v. 4). For the same reason, the entire sacrificial animal must be consumed on the evening of Passover. To leave any until the morning suggests time-consuming preparation for breakfast, a delay in departure that could prove fatal (v. 4b; cf. Exod 12:10-

14). Leaven and aged meat also suggest corruption and spoilage, a condition hostile to the holiness of the event expected by the Lord (cf. Lev 6:14-17; 7:15-18).[74]

16:5-7 The lawgiver went on to reinforce the idea of a central place of worship in the land of Canaan by excluding from consideration just "any town the LORD your God gives you" (v. 5). Such an arrangement would have been proper for local services (cf. Exod 20:24-26) but strictly forbidden for the great festivals and other occasions of community worship. Thus the Passover was to be at the Lord's "dwelling," and it was to be carried out according to the protocol of the original enactment, at least as far as the time of day and disposition of the sacrificial animal were concerned (vv. 6-7a). The date was always to be the fourteenth of Nisan, the anniversary of the first Passover (cf. Exod 12:6), and the victim must be slain at dusk on that day. When that, the following meal, and all else had been performed, the people were to return to their tents (v. 7b).

Reference to "morning" and "tents" presents certain problems about the duration of the Passover celebration and the setting of the entire ceremony. To deal with the second matter first, "tents" has nothing to do with a desert setting as opposed to one in Canaan in which one would expect references to houses and villages. That is, this is not a slip of the pen (or mind) of the Deuteronomist who inadvertently located the Passover in the wilderness in his attempt to archaize it.[75] Rather, it speaks of the temporary housing that must have been a necessary part of attendance at the great Israelite festivals.[76] The hundreds of thousands who attended must certainly have had to take their tents with them so they could "camp out" in those days.

To return to the tents "in the morning" need not imply daybreak of the next day, for the day began at sundown. Therefore anytime after that could be considered "in the morning." However, it is more likely that the participants in the festival did indeed remain throughout the night.[77] This is suggested by the inauguration of the Passover in Egypt, where an all-night feast clearly appears to have been in view (Exod 12:10,29-31), one to be observed thereafter by Israel as keeping "vigil" to honor the Lord (Exod 12:42). As the Lord watched over them all through the night, so the people were to spend the night hours of Passover from then on in remembrance of his mighty deliverance.

---

[74] Hartley, *Leviticus,* 100.

[75] Thus Driver, *Deuteronomy,* 194.

[76] Phillips, *Deuteronomy,* 113.

[77] As Craigie (*Deuteronomy,* 244) notes, the pilgrims would observe a "night vigil" following the sacrifice of the Passover animal.

16:8 The Passover/Feast of Unleavened Bread continued for six more days, culminating in a great assembly on the seventh, the twenty-first day of Nisan (v. 8; cf. Exod 12:18). This assembly, called a "sacred assembly" (*miqrā* *qōdeš*) in Lev 23:21,36, was a Sabbath, that is, a day of cessation or rest inasmuch as it was the seventh day.[78] Therefore any work on that day was strictly prohibited.

16:9-10 The second pilgrimage festival to be observed in the land was the Feast of Weeks (vv. 9-12). The name (*šābuʿôt* in Heb.) derives from the fact that it commenced seven weeks after the beginning of grain harvest (v. 9), the grain in view being wheat (cf. Exod 34:22). It was thus a harvest festival, the very term applied to it in Exod 23:16 (*ḥag haqqāṣîr*). In order to standardize its observance, however, the festival was also tied in to the Passover/Unleavened Bread convocation by arbitrarily marking the day of the beginning of wheat harvest as the day following the great day of assembly on the twenty-first of Nisan (Lev 23:15-16). The Feast of Weeks by this arrangement must always fall fifty days after Passover-Unleavened Bread.[79] This gave rise to the Greek name for the festival, Pentecost (*pentēkostē*, "fiftieth"). The reason it is the fiftieth day is that the festival day occurred the day after the seventh Sabbath (Lev 23:16), a detail not spelled out here in Deuteronomy. The Feast of Weeks fell, therefore, on a Sunday; hence the special significance of Pentecost to the early church as marking the Lord's Day as a kind of firstfruits, the beginning of something new (cf. Acts 2:1).

16:11-12 The focus of the festival was a joyous meal in celebration of the bountiful blessing of God in providing crops of grain. All the members of the community, regardless of their social or economic status, were invited to participate in the festivities. The most disadvantaged among them were, in fact, especially to be welcomed, for Israel must remember their own bondage in Egypt and how the Lord had freed them so that now they could enjoy such blessings (v. 12). The sign of that divine favor was the produce itself, a portion of which must be presented to the Lord and to his needy people. The amount to be offered should be in proportion to the abundance with which God had blessed in every case. It was a proportionate "freewill offering" (*missat nidbat,* v. 10),[80] but, as noted before, it must also

---

[78] Hartley, *Leviticus,* 375.

[79] de Vaux, *Ancient Israel,* 2:493-94.

[80] The hapax legomenon מִסַּת ("sufficiency," BDB, 588) is cognate to both Aramaic and Syriac terms meaning "sufficiency." The LXX translates καθότι . . . ἰσχύει "to the degree of strength." A similar idea appears in v. 17, where the phrase is כְּמַתְּנֹת יָדוֹ, "according to the gift of your strength," attested by the LXX κατὰ δύναμιν. The idea in both verses is that one must give according to what he has or is able to produce. Cf. Driver, *Deuteronomy,* 196-97.

be a tithe (cf. 14:22-27). That is, the tithe was the minimum expected, but a grateful people should gladly go above and beyond that legal requirement.

16:13-15 The third pilgrimage festival at the central sanctuary was the Feast of Tabernacles (from Heb. *sukkôt,* "huts" or "booths").[81] This seven-day celebration of grain harvest and gathering of other produce began, according to Lev 23:34, on the fifteenth day of the seventh month (Tishri), that is, in the autumn (ca. mid-September to mid-October). Whereas the Feast of Weeks marked the first of the harvest season for wheat, the Feast of Tabernacles signified its culmination. At the same time, almost all other crops of field and orchard matured by this time and were likewise gathered in (cf. Lev 23:40).

Though Deuteronomy focuses on the agricultural nature of this festival, it elsewhere is described as a most important commemoration of the Lord's acts in history on behalf of his chosen people. Leviticus 23:42-43 commands the Israelites to live in booths for seven days so that their descendants would know that "I had the Israelites live in booths when I brought them out of Egypt." The harvest festival thus has historical (and theological) roots as well.[82] The reason for Deuteronomy's emphasis is quite clear, however, for the entire section 14:22–16:17 has to do with tribute to be paid to the Lord, the Great King. One naturally thinks of this tribute in terms of the presentation of agricultural products, so much the more so in an agrarian-based economy such as Israel's. The issue therefore is not one of separate and individual traditions regarding the nature and purpose of the Feast of Tabernacles, for Leviticus ties both the agricultural and historical/redemptive together (Lev 23:39-44). The point here in Deuteronomy is that the Israelites, who were about to enter, conquer, and farm the land of Canaan, were to recognize God's hand in it all and render him proper homage as a result (v. 15b).

16:16-17 In summary of the entire section, Moses reiterated that all the males of Israel were to appear before the Lord at his dwelling, the central sanctuary, three times a year, namely, at the time of the three annual great festivals. This is the only time in Deuteronomy that males (Heb. *zĕkûr,* as opposed to the normal *zākār*) are specified, but elsewhere this is clearly spelled out (Exod 23:17; 34:23). The lack of such distinction in gender in the longer festival passages and, indeed, direct reference to

---

[81] G. W. MacRae, "The Meaning and Evolution of the Feast of Tabernacles," *CBQ* 22 (1960): 251-76.

[82] For a standard traditio-historical reconstruction of the melding of harvest and historical themes into the one festival, see de Vaux, *Ancient Israel,* 2:495-502. For a response see McConville, *Law and Theology in Deuteronomy,* 110-12.

female participation (cf. e.g., Deut 16:11,14) make clear that only the males were required to attend but that females were welcome and, indeed, encouraged to do so.[83]

All three festivals, despite their different historical and agricultural origins and purposes, share in common the fact that they were occasions of tribute presentation. At specified times and in only one authorized place the vassal people of the Lord were to appear before him with offering in hand, thus pledging their ongoing loyalty and their continuing recognition that it is he who is Lord and the source of all their blessing (v. 17). So much so is this the great central truth of 14:22–16:17 that the entire pericope, as noted already, begins and ends on this note (14:22-23; cf. 17:16-17).

2. Kingdom Officials (16:18–18:22)

(1) Judges and Other Officials (16:18–17:13)

[18]Appoint judges and officials for each of your tribes in every town the LORD your God is giving you, and they shall judge the people fairly. [19]Do not pervert justice or show partiality. Do not accept a bribe, for a bribe blinds the eyes of the wise and twists the words of the righteous. [20]Follow justice and justice alone, so that you may live and possess the land the LORD your God is giving you.

[21]Do not set up any wooden Asherah pole beside the altar you build to the LORD your God, [22]and do not erect a sacred stone, for these the LORD your God hates.

[1]Do not sacrifice to the LORD your God an ox or a sheep that has any defect or flaw in it, for that would be detestable to him.

[2]If a man or woman living among you in one of the towns the LORD gives you is found doing evil in the eyes of the LORD your God in violation of his covenant, [3]and contrary to my command has worshiped other gods, bowing down to them or to the sun or the moon or the stars of the sky, [4]and this has been brought to your attention, then you must investigate it thoroughly. If it is true and it has been proved that this detestable thing has been done in Israel, [5]take the man or woman who has done this evil deed to your city gate and stone that person to death. [6]On the testimony of two or three witnesses a man shall be put to death, but no one shall be put to death on the testimony of only one witness. [7]The hands of the witnesses must be the first in putting him to death, and then the hands of all the people. You must purge the evil from among you.

---

[83] Weinfeld, *Deuteronomy and the Deuteronomic School,* 291-92. Weinfeld attributes the inclusion of women in Deuteronomy to the more humane and enlightened spirit of that code.

⁸If cases come before your courts that are too difficult for you to judge—whether bloodshed, lawsuits or assaults—take them to the place the Lᴏʀᴅ your God will choose. ⁹Go to the priests, who are Levites, and to the judge who is in office at that time. Inquire of them and they will give you the verdict. ¹⁰You must act according to the decisions they give you at the place the Lᴏʀᴅ will choose. Be careful to do everything they direct you to do. ¹¹Act according to the law they teach you and the decisions they give you. Do not turn aside from what they tell you, to the right or to the left. ¹²The man who shows contempt for the judge or for the priest who stands ministering there to the Lᴏʀᴅ your God must be put to death. You must purge the evil from Israel. ¹³All the people will hear and be afraid, and will not be contemptuous again.

The abrupt switch from observance of festivals to recognition of duly constituted leadership and authority is in line with the proposal already suggested that the specific stipulations of Deut 12–26 are elaborations of the Ten Commandments and in the same order. Therefore the topic at hand reflects the injunction of the fifth commandment—"Honor your father and your mother"—just as the previous section had dealt with the fourth—"Observe the Sabbath day by keeping it holy."[84] As long as one is content to see only general parallels and not expect absolute correspondence and consistency, such an analysis remains most persuasive.

With the transition from a patriarchal, familial structure in Egyptian and wilderness times to that of a village-centered culture following the conquest, Israel's understanding of authority patterns also changed. While one must continue to honor his parents, there were other, more comprehensive hierarchies that also must be given due consideration. The multiplication of urban centers, the breakdown of community cohesion, the increasing division and specialization of labor—all contributed to the need for government at increasingly higher and broader levels. The result in due time would be the rise of monarchy itself.[85]

For the present, however, Moses was content to deal with judges (*šōpĕtîm*) and other leaders, described generically as "officials" (*šōṭĕrîm*). Though technically the latter term derives from a root meaning "to write" or "to arrange," it is used commonly in the Old Testament to

---

[84] Cf. Braulik, who, however, identifies this as the fourth rather than fifth commandment (*Die deuteronomischen Gesetz und der Dekalog*, 22, 46-61); Kaufman, "Structure of Deuteronomic Law," 133-34. Kaufman correctly observes that "these rules proclaim the authority figures of the nation just as the Fifth Commandment proclaims the authority of the parents within the family" (p. 133).

[85] For a comprehensive treatment from a "Deuteronomistic" perspective, see U. Rutersworden, *Von der politischen Gemeinschaft zur Gemeinde: Studien zu Dt 16,18–18,22* (Frankfort am Main: Athenaum, 1987).

pertain to persons who decide legal cases and administer justice.[86] That was clearly the case here; in fact, even the "officials" mentioned may have been judges, taking the construction as a hendiadys to be construed as "judging officials" or the like. This finds support in the fact that the only function described here is judging (vv. 18-20).

16:18-20   The sociological changes suggested above are implicit in the instruction that judges were to be installed in every town that the Lord would give to Israel (v. 18). As the Lord's own underlings they must be scrupulously fair (lit., "render righteous judgment"). In a shift of subject the judges themselves were addressed and warned not to pervert (*nāṭâ*, "thrust aside") judgment or show partiality to (*nākar*, "pay regard to") anyone. Above all, they must reject bribes (*šōḥad*), for bribes encouraged people to do the very things just forbidden.[87] Instead, they were to make it a practice to follow hard after justice (v. 20). When judge and people alike followed this standard of justice, they could expect long and prosperous life in the land (v. 20). This was precisely the promise for those who keep the fifth commandment (Deut 5:16).

Scholars have long noted the apparent interpolation of irrelevant prohibitions (16:21–17:1) between the section on the appointment of judges (16:18-20) and that describing two case laws (17:2-13), usually proposing either that 16:21–17:7 is an intrusion from elsewhere,[88] 17:2-7 originally belonged to chap. 13,[89] or that 16:18 introduces 17:8-13, with 16:19–17:7 being secondary.[90] Closer examination reveals, however, that such resorts to smoothing out the passage are unnecessary once the purpose of the prohibition section is properly understood.[91]

16:21-22   Moses had just discussed the matter of righteous judgment and the blessing that followed such a policy. Now he provided a hypothetical case or two to illustrate what he meant by untainted jurisprudence and the practices to be followed in achieving it. The violations he adduced could not be more significant, for they strike right at the heart of the covenant relationship. In fact, they challenged the uniqueness of the Lord and

---

[86] Fensham, "Judges and Ancient Israelite Jurisprudence," 15-22; Milgrom, "Office of the Judge in Deuteronomy," 129-39; A. van Selms, "The Title 'Judge,'" 41-50.

[87] M. L. Goldberg, "The Story of the Moral: Gifts or Bribes in Deuteronomy?" *Int* 38 (1984): 15-25.

[88] Driver, *Deuteronomy,* 201.

[89] Cairns, *Word and Presence,* 162: "It is possible that [the two passages] originally formed a unity."

[90] Mayes, *Deuteronomy,* 263.

[91] Kaufman sees 17:2-13 as case law instructing the judges of 16:18-20 in the instance of the violation of 16:21–17:1 ("Structure of Deuteronomic Law," 134). The whole, therefore, is mutually dependent.

the exclusiveness of his worship, on the one hand (16:21-22), thus disobeying the first two commandments; and, on the other hand, they spoke to the sin of cultic impurity in defiance of the third and fourth commandments (17:1). At stake was nothing less than who God is and how he is to be worshiped.[92] Were such sins to be committed, how must the case be investigated and prosecuted? This was the concern of the case law that follows (17:2-7).

The first prohibition concerns the erection of an Asherah pole, which, as noted previously, was a Canaanite cult object representing the forces of fertility and reproduction, forces attributed especially to the Canaanite mother goddess (cf. Deut 7:5). It is not coincidental that such an object is also mentioned in connection with the establishment of Yahweh as the one and only God precisely at the beginning of the special stipulation section (Deut 12:3). The issue there as well as here is the proper understanding of and adherence to the first commandment with its insistence on the solitariness of the Lord as God. By associating the Asherah with the altar of Yahweh (v. 21), there is implicit endorsement of the Asherah as well as the sacred stone (*maṣṣēbâ*; cf. Deut 7:5; 12:3) as legitimate paraphernalia of worship, a misconception severely condemned in the second commandment. The Lord hates these kinds of things (v. 22b), the very sentiment expressed in Deut 12:31, the summary of Moses' protracted exposition of the first two commandments.

17:1 The second prohibition proscribes the presentation to the Lord of any defective or flawed animal sacrifice. The particular case in view is a synecdoche, that is, one of a number that could be adduced to illustrate cultic impropriety. In a larger sense the issue here, as already suggested, is one of conforming to the protocol expected of those who aspire to worship the Lord and enjoy fellowship with him. This is the gist of the fourth commandment, especially, the full exposition of which appears in Deut 14:1–16:17. The specific infraction here is addressed in detail in 15:19-23. There the rejected animals are described as *mûm* ("defective") or *rāᶜ* ("flawed"), exactly the adjectives used here in Deut 17:1. Clearly the two prohibitions are intended to suggest covenant violation of the most blatant and serious kind.

Attention turns now from apodictic statements about false worship to (1) a case law that provides a specific example of such behavior and how it is to be addressed (17:2-7) and (2) legal procedure to be followed in general (vv. 8-13). The one has to do with the application of justice and the other with its administration.

---

[92] Thompson, *Deuteronomy,* 201.

17:2-3 In typical fashion the case in view is expressed by protasis-apodosis construction, in this example there being two protases (vv. 2,4) and one apodosis (v. 5).[94] The first condition relates to the allegation of wrongdoing (vv. 2-4a) and the second to an investigation of the charges that results in a finding of guilt (v. 4b). The accusation was that an Israelite had done "evil" by transgressing the covenant of the Lord. To transgress the covenant (*ʿābōr habbĕrît*, lit., "to cross over [the limitations of] the covenant") is a term commonly used to speak specifically of disloyalty to the Lord with a concomitant worship of other gods (see, e.g., Josh 23:16; Judg 2:16-20; 2 Chr 24:17-20).[95] This, of course, was the issue here as v. 3 makes clear. The accused party had broken covenant by serving (*ʿābad*) and worshiping (*hištāḥăwâ*) other gods such as the sun, moon, and stars. These very verbs (in reverse order) occur in Deut 5:9 as part of the prohibitions of the second commandment. The violation of covenant here, then, was expressly the breaking of that commandment.[96] Moreover, the astral cult suggested here had already been addressed in the prologue to the covenant text (Deut 4:15-24) and in terms filled with allusion to the second commandment.

17:4-5 The responsibility for investigating rumors of such disloyalty to the covenant rested upon the community as a whole as the singular pronoun "you" attests throughout the passage. If the community determined that an infraction (Heb. *tôʿēbâ*, "abomination"; cf. 12:31; 13:14; esp. 17:1) had occurred in Israel (i.e., among the covenant people), the perpetrator was to be conducted to an open place near the city gate and there publicly stoned to death (v. 5).[97] Again this was not private vengeance or administration of judgment but that by the community. This is consistent with the application of capital punishment throughout the Old Testament (cf. Gen 9:6; Exod 21:12,15-17; Lev 20; 24:16-17; Num 15:35; 35:16-17; Deut 13:10; 18:20; 19:12; 22:22,25). It was carried out either by the community or part of the community as a group or by an individual appointed and sanctioned by the community.

---

[94] For discussion of this so-called "juridical if-you formulation," see Gilmer, *The If-You Form in Israelite Law*, 69-78.

[95] M. Weinfeld, "בְּרִית berith," *TDOT* 2:261.

[96] Craigie, *Deuteronomy*, 250.

[97] Frick suggests, quite convincingly, that the imposition of community execution took place in a "profane" area, that is, outside the gates and not within them. See F. S. Frick, *The City in Ancient Israel*, SBLDS 36 (Missoula, Mont: Scholars Press, 1977), 126, 163n., 259. As G. R. Driver points out, the usual word for stoning (רָגַם), when applied to offenses against God, is replaced in this passage by סָקַל, a verb ordinarily used in interpersonal contexts ("Affirmation by Exclamatory Negation," *JANES* 5 [1973]: 112).

17:6-7 The implementation of the apodosis and its penalties was qualified, however, by the requirement that the prior allegation be witnessed and attested to by at least two witnesses (v. 6; cf. Num 35:30; Deut 19:15; Matt 18:16; John 7:51; 8:17-18).[98] The purpose for this contingency was to preclude personal or private vindictiveness and to assure that what was observed had actually occurred and was not the product of poor sensory perception or an overactive imagination. To forestall a conspiratorial process in which witnesses would collaborate in misrepresenting the truth, the witnesses would themselves be forced to hurl the first stones of execution (v. 7). The gravity of what they were called upon to do would be so great that it was likely that the collusion would unravel either in the judicial process itself or subsequent to the miscarriage of justice. Parties to such a cover-up knew all too well the potential for blackmail that existed in these circumstances.

The participation of the whole community in the punishment (as in 13:11) speaks to the corporate nature of the covenant people. If one member sinned, the entire fellowship felt its impact and in a very real sense was culpable. Unless and until the community addressed the evil by removing the source of its calamity, all together would continue to experience its baleful effects. This is what lies behind the insistence that "you must purge the evil [$r\bar{a}^c$, as in v. 2] from among you" (v. 7).

The subject of the application of justice in the hypothetical case just related gives rise to a more extended discussion of legal procedure (vv. 8-13). At the beginning of the section on officials, they were identified as functioning on a local level, in the several and individual towns throughout Israel (16:18). Now the focus is on centralized courts of law established for the purpose of receiving appeals from the lower courts in cases too difficult for them to adjudicate.

17:8 Though specific kinds of crimes are mentioned here (bloodshed, assault, and lawsuits), these appear to be only typical, not exhaustive. The general and inclusive nature of the matters addressed is clear from the indefinite noun "thing" (*dābār*), translated here as "cases" (plural, v. 8). Whatever they might have been, if they were too difficult for the local court, these matters were to be transferred to the high court, to "the place the LORD your God will choose" (v. 8). The idea of a chosen place at first blush appears to suggest the central sanctuary, a suggestion that finds support in the fact that the priests were also there in a judicial capacity (v. 9).[99] But the place is not referred to as that locale where the Lord had

---

[98] B. S. Jackson, "Two or Three Witnesses," in *Essays in Jewish and Comparative Legal History* (Leiden: Brill, 1975), 153-71.

[99] Thus Craigie, *Deuteronomy,* 252.

placed his name (cf. 12:5; etc.). It was simply a place chosen by him as the national center of legal appeal, the supreme court of last resort. It is, of course, possible that the center of cult and law could have been one and the same, but the present text cannot be used to prove it. In fact, there is no evidence at all before the rise of the monarchy in Israel that the two foci of national life coexisted in one place.[100]

17:9 Evidence favoring the separation of the two may lie within our present text, for the priests who officiated at these sites were not designated as high priest(s) but as "the priests, who are Levites" (v. 9). Regardless of whatever else that phrase might mean, especially in Deuteronomy,[101] it clearly was never applied to the high priest as though his Levitical ancestry had to be established. The very qualification "Levites" might suggest, indeed, that the priest in view was decidedly not the high priest.

Wherever the place of ultimate appeal may have been, the officials charged with hearing and disposing of cases were a priest and a judge. Even though Israel was a theocratic community and therefore technically knew nothing of the separation of "church" and state, there clearly were distinctions between infractions of cultic and moral law on the one hand and civil law on the other. The two categories of law would therefore necessitate the expertise of religious and secular arbiters who could both interpret and apply the law to any given situation. The role of priests in such a setting is well known. As representatives of the people before the Lord they frequently exercised their judicial role "before the LORD," that is, on his behalf and with his sanction. A famous example is that of the woman accused of adultery (Num 5:11-31). She had to appear before the priest who then would "bring her and have her stand before the LORD" (v. 16). After completing a certain ritual, the facts of the case would come out, and a proper verdict would be rendered. Other allusions to priestly jurisprudence may be found in Exod 18:19; Deut 19:17; 21:5; 2 Chr 19:8; and Hag 2:11.

The identity of the "judge" is less clear in a sense, for there is no further qualification about the procedures and criteria of his selection. There was to be only one in supreme position, it seems, and to him presumably came all cases not properly within priestly jurisdiction.[102] For the most part, however, judges were spoken of in the plural even when a central

---

[100] See Cairns, *Word and Presence,* 163-64.

[101] See Abba, "Priests and Levites in Deuteronomy," 257-67; Emerton, "Priests and Levites in Deuteronomy," 129-38; Wright, "The Levites in Deuteronomy," 325-30.

[102] Craigie, *Deuteronomy,* 252.

tribunal was in view (cf. 1 Chr 26:29). This need not contradict the present text, for all that was being asserted here was that there would be one judge at a time ("the judge who is in office at that time," as in the NIV). Obviously there would have been many over the course of time.

17:10-13 There was no court of higher appeal beyond that of the priest and judge of the central place of jurisdiction, so the verdicts rendered had to be accepted by those who had sought redress there (v. 10). The text is most insistent that the law (*tôrâ*) and decisions (*mišpāṭ*) (that is, the rulings of the court)[103] must result in unswerving compliance on the part of the litigants. Failure to do so and thus to manifest insubordination to the court (lit., "in insolence and without obeying") and, more seriously, to the Lord himself, whom both priest and judge represent, was to invoke self-destruction (v. 12). The reason for such harsh measures was to preclude any similar contempt for law in the future (v. 13). Behind it all, of course, was the inextricable linkage between law and covenant. It was absolutely incumbent on the kingdom citizen to demonstrate loyalty and obedience to the Great King, evidence of which, among other things, was strict adherence to theocratic law and its application.

(2) Kings (17:14-20)

14When you enter the land the LORD your God is giving you and have taken possession of it and settled in it, and you say, "Let us set a king over us like all the nations around us," 15be sure to appoint over you the king the LORD your God chooses. He must be from among your own brothers. Do not place a foreigner over you, one who is not a brother Israelite. 16The king, moreover, must not acquire great numbers of horses for himself or make the people return to Egypt to get more of them, for the LORD has told you, "You are not to go back that way again." 17He must not take many wives, or his heart will be led astray. He must not accumulate large amounts of silver and gold.

18When he takes the throne of his kingdom, he is to write for himself on a scroll a copy of this law, taken from that of the priests, who are Levites. 19It is to be with him, and he is to read it all the days of his life so that he may learn to revere the LORD his God and follow carefully all the words of this law and these decrees 20and not consider himself better than his brothers and turn from the law to the right or to the left. Then he and his descendants will reign a long time over his kingdom in Israel.

The present passage,[104] because of its anticipation of Israelite monarchy, is one commonly adduced in favor of a late monarchical date for

[103] Mayes, *Deuteronomy,* 269.

[104] For literature on the passage see A. Caquot, "Remarques sur la 'loi royale' du Deutéronome (17, 14-20)," *Semitica* 9 (1959): 21-33; K. Galling, "Das Konigsgesetz im

Deuteronomy and the related "Deuteronomistic History." It presupposes kingship in Israel, so the argument goes, and functions as a diatribe against it in light of its historical development.[105] Solomon particularly appears to have been the object of the polemic as the references to many horses and multiple wives would suggest (vv. 16-17).

Such a view, besides being contrary to the tradition of the Mosaic authorship of Deuteronomy, ignores many facts about the passage and about Israelite understanding of the monarchy as a divine institution.[106] First, this section of the covenant code differs from others in general in that it neither prescribes nor condemns kingship as an institution but merely seeks to regulate it as a foregone conclusion. If the motive of the "deuteronomist" was antithetical to kingship, it is difficult to understand why he did not plead his case in categorical terms. If anything, the text is promonarchic, so much so that it attempts to safeguard kingship from excesses that would cripple it.

Second, kingship was foreseen as early as patriarchal times (cf. Gen 17:6,16; 35:11), and unless one posits that such early references are also late redactions, it is clear that there was preparation for Israelite monarchy in both tradition and theology. The text cautions that the king was to be one whom the Lord chose (v. 15), a qualification that is certainly pro-monarchy and in line with the later establishment of kingship under Samuel. When the people demanded a king "such as all the other nations have" (1 Sam 8:5), the Lord did not reject outright their plea for such a ruler but only their timing and rationale.[107] Samuel responded by predicting that the king they demanded would be the very kind against whom Moses warned in our passage (1 Sam 8:10-18; cf. Deut 17:16-17). Later, however, David recognized the legitimacy of his own role as king (cf. Ps 2:7-12), a legitimacy previously sanctioned by Samuel, who informed

Deuteronomium," *TLZ* 76 (1951): 133-38; D. M. Howard, Jr., "The Case for Kingship in Deuteronomy and the Former Prophets," *WTJ* 52 (1990): 101-15 (review of G. E. Gerbrandt, *Kingship according to the Deuteronomistic History* (Atlanta: Scholars Press, 1986); D. J. McCarthy, "Compact and Kingship: Stimuli for Hebrew Covenant Thinking," in *Studies in the Period of David and Solomon and Other Essays,* ed. T. Ishida (Winona Lake, Ind.: Eisenbrauns, 1982), 75-92; E. T. Mullen, Jr., "The Divine Witness and the Davidic Royal Grant: Ps 89:37-38," *JBL* 102 (1983): 207-18.

[105] So E. W. Nicholson: "One cannot avoid the feeling that when the author of Deuteronomy drew up the law concerning monarchy (Deut. xvii. 14f.) he was dealing with an existing institution which . . . had to be reckoned with as part of the life of the people among whom he lived and for whom, presumably, he was legislating" (*Deuteronomy and Tradition* [Philadelphia: Fortress, 1967], 80-81).

[106] M. G. Kline, *Treaty of the Great King* (Grand Rapids: Eerdmans, 1963), 97-98.

[107] J. R. Vannoy, *Covenant Renewal at Gilgal* (Cherry Hill, N.J.: Mack, 1978), 229-31.

tion to kingship[108] and serves as an endorsement of the theological propriety of the institution.

Finally, monarchy was the prevalent mode of government in the Late Bronze Age throughout the eastern Mediterranean world. It is inconceivable that Israel alone would embrace some other system even as a theocracy. In fact, theocracy itself is monarchy in its purest form, one in which the deity is king. True to the ancient purposes of God for humankind that they rule over all things (Gen 1:26-28), it was inevitable that that transfer of power from the Lord to his royal nation take place once the land of promise had been conquered, occupied, and at last made ready in all respects for the Lord's rule through his chosen people.[109] In other words, Israelite monarchy, far from being inimical to the Lord's purpose and unforeseen by his people, was at the core of his redemptive and historical purposes. Instruction about its proper regulation is very much at home in the covenant text of Deuteronomy and precisely here where covenant officials of all kinds are the focus of attention.

17:14-17   The key to the limitations placed upon Israelite kingship seems to reside in the anticipated demand of the people themselves who, having settled in Canaan, would seek a king "like all the nations around us" (v. 14). On occasion such kings would be foreigners, either conquerors or appointees of conquerors, and nearly always they would attempt to amass horses, harems, wealth, and other accoutrements emblematic of royalty and power. It is in opposition to things such as these that the law speaks, for the Lord's people and their rulers were to treasure and depend on him more than anything else. Foreign kings would tend to divert Israel's loyalty from the covenant; a large contingent of horses would rekindle interest in returning to Egypt from which the best were obtained;[110] and many wives, with their diverse backgrounds in pagan religions, would induce their husbands to follow after their illicit cults. Samuel hinted that Saul would emulate some of these improprieties, at least in spirit (1 Sam 8:10-18), and, of course, Solomon embraced many of them with unbridled enthusiasm (cf. 1 Kgs 10:14–11:8). That all of this

---

[108] Thus Heb. בְּקֶשׁ אִישׁ לוֹ יְהוָה כִּלְבָבוֹ; cf. P. K. McCarter, Jr.: "The free divine selection of the heir to the throne" (*I Samuel*, AB [Garden City: Doubleday, 1980], 229).

[109] Merrill, "Covenant and the Kingdom," 295-308.

[110] D. J. Reimer, "Concerning Return to Egypt: Deuteronomy 17:16 and 28:68 Reconsidered," in *Studies in the Pentateuch*, ed. J. A. Emerton, VTSup 41 (Leiden: Brill, 1990), 217-29. There is evidence that the domesticated horse was known in Middle Kingdom Egypt, but its use, especially with the chariot, proliferated in the so-called Hyksos era (ca. 1730–1580 B.C.). See J. Van Seters, *The Hyksos* (New Haven: Yale University Press, 1966), 183-85.

came to pass does not by any means prove that the Deuteronomy text was composed after the event; nor, in fact, does it mean that it is predictive prophecy. It is simply a statement of profound insight into the human condition, one that understands the pride and predilections of those who would rule in ignorance or defiance of divine mandate.

17:18-19   The positive side of the "royal handbook" is the instruction to the king of Israel to make a copy of "this law" (v. 18). Most immediately, this is a reference to the pericope at hand, vv. 14-20, but the phrase elsewhere describes the entire covenant text of Deuteronomy (cf. 1:5; 4:44; 27:3,8,26; 29:21,29; 30:10; 31 passim).[111] The king's copy was to be made from the "official" version, that retained by the priests, presumably in or near the ark of the covenant (cf. Deut 31:9,25-26). This is most likely the "book of the law" found by Josiah's priests and scribes in the days of Judah's reformation (cf. 2 Kgs 22:8-13). By then, however (622 B.C.), the king's own copy had long since been repressed or destroyed, and the monarchy had functioned without its God-given guidelines.

Part of the protocol of royal succession in the ancient Near Eastern world was the transfer of documents that legitimized the succession and provided standards by which the new king was to administer the affairs of his regime.[112] This was the practice in Israel and Judah as well, a practice inaugurated by the Deuteronomic law (v. 18; cf. 1 Kgs 2:3; 2 Kgs 11:12; 23:3). This was more than a formality, however, for each king must, through all the years of his tenure, read the document so that he might properly revere God, the Great King, and adhere to every provision of covenant law and statute, that is, to Deuteronomy as a whole as the terms *tôrâ* and *ḥuqqîm* make clear (v. 19; cf. 4:44-45; 30:10). The king was to rule for the Lord on the earth, and therefore he was to do so in line with the holiness and righteousness of the Lord.

17:20   This did not mean that the ruler was superior to his subjects, however, especially when it came to his need to obey God (v. 20).[113] All are alike before the Great King, and all alike must be faithful to the commandment (*miṣwâ*), specifically to this code of behavior addressed in vv. 14-20. Unswerving compliance to the heavenly mandate would ensure for the king a long and happy reign and peaceful succession for generations to come (v. 20b). Obviously the converse would also be true, that those

---

[111] Thompson, *Deuteronomy,* 206.

[112] Kline, *Treaty of the Great King,* 98, "The king, therefore, is not the lord of the Torah. He is subordinate."

[113] As N. Lohfink points out, "Der König ist also nicht der Herr der Tora. Er ist ihr unterstellt," *Studien zum Deuteronomium und zur deuteronomistischen Literator I* (Stuttgart: Katholisches Bibelwerk, 1990), 318.

who forsook the Lord and disregarded the principles of godly rule would face personal disaster and lack of royal succession. The history of Israel would prove this to be all too true.

(3) Priests and Levites (18:1-8)

[1]The priests, who are Levites—indeed the whole tribe of Levi—are to have no allotment or inheritance with Israel. They shall live on the offerings made to the LORD by fire, for that is their inheritance. [2]They shall have no inheritance among their brothers; the LORD is their inheritance, as he promised them.
[3]This is the share due the priests from the people who sacrifice a bull or a sheep: the shoulder, the jowls and the inner parts. [4]You are to give them the firstfruits of your grain, new wine and oil, and the first wool from the shearing of your sheep, [5]for the LORD your God has chosen them and their descendants out of all your tribes to stand and minister in the LORD'S name always.
[6]If a Levite moves from one of your towns anywhere in Israel where he is living, and comes in all earnestness to the place the LORD will choose, [7]he may minister in the name of the LORD his God like all his fellow Levites who serve there in the presence of the LORD. [8]He is to share equally in their benefits, even though he has received money from the sale of family possessions.

This next classification of theocratic officials consists of the entire tribe of Levi with its subdivision, the priests. Again, no case can be made for an ascendancy of Levitical priests in late Old Testament times as opposed to those of the earliest period who were distinguished from the Levites by being Aaronic priests.[114] From the very establishment of the priestly order under Moses it was clear that the tribe of Levi had been set apart for special service to the Lord and that the priests were to be taken from among the Levites. The only lineal qualification for the priest in addition to his being a Levite was his descent from the first priest, Aaron.

The text here is therefore not suggesting that there were priests who were not Levites but that the whole tribe of Levi, including the priests, must conform to the stipulations being outlined. The grammatical construction favors this (lit., "to the priests the Levites, indeed, to the entire tribe of Levi," etc.; v. 1) as does the lack of precision in describing the various privileges and responsibilities of both priests and Levites in this passage.[115] The purpose of the instruction here was not to draw such fine

---

[114] For the discussion see Mayes, *Deuteronomy*, 274-76.

[115] The juxtaposition of "Levitical priests" and "the whole tribe of Levi" is not to be construed, with some scholars, as an asyndetic coordination but rather as apposition. That is, the intent is not to limit the following instructions to the priests per se but to enjoin them upon priests and Levites alike. Craigie takes vv. 1-2 to refer to all Levites, vv. 3-5 to refer to Levitical priests, and vv. 6-8 to refer to Levites who would not normally function as priests (*Deuteronomy*, 258). Cf. Abba, "Priests and Levites in Deuteronomy," 262-67.

lines but to provide an overview of the role of the Levite in Israelite leadership. The priests were mentioned first because they occupied a more prominent role in the Levitical hierarchy.

18:1-2 Having been set apart by the Lord to serve him, the priests and other Levites had no other inheritance but that sacred call (v. 1). In a practical sense their allotment was the burnt offerings presented to the altar (cf. 14:28-29), but in a more profound and incomparably blessed way the Lord himself was their portion (cf. 10:9; Num 18:20). What they lacked in territorial terms (the underlying meaning of *naḥālâ*, "inheritance") they gained by virtue of their privileged position as intercessors between the Lord and his people.

18:3-5 The matter of practical support of the Levites has already been addressed in a very general way in chap. 14 (vv. 27-29). There the community was instructed to allocate the third-year tithe to the Lord's servants, but the content of that tithe was not spelled out. Here it is defined as the shoulder, jowls, and inner parts of the bull or sheep (v. 3); the firstfruits of grain, new wine, and oil; and the wool from the first shearing of the sheep (v. 4). This list, though partially paralleled in Lev 7:32-34 and Num 18:11-12, is the most detailed of all the Old Testament. Whatever else may have been given is impossible to tell, but it is clear elsewhere that the Levites could provide part of their own sustenance from the limited plots of land they owned adjacent to their towns of residence (cf. Num 35:2-8). In the final analysis they were at the mercy of their fellow countrymen who had the responsibility as well as the privilege of caring for them. This would free them up to undertake their God-given role as the Lord's ministers (v. 5).

18:6-8 The proviso that follows in vv. 6-8 is also adduced as evidence for an increasingly enhanced role for the Levites in later Old Testament times. It is argued in some circles that a strict line of demarcation existed between the priests, who functioned at the central sanctuary alone and the Levites, most of whom were restricted to the outlying villages and towns assigned to them and who were not allowed to function in any priestly capacity. With the reformation of Josiah in 622 B.C., the local shrines throughout the countryside were destroyed, thus depriving the Levites of any further service there. Of necessity they were to be allowed to minister at Jerusalem, the central sanctuary, for that was all that was left (cf. 2 Kgs 23:4-20; 2 Chr 34:1-7).[116]

---

[116] This reconstruction found its classic expression in J. Wellhausen, *Prolegomena to the History of Ancient Israel* (Cleveland: World, 1957), 121-51. For a good response that denies any role of the Josiah reformation as background to this pericope, see R. K. Duke, "The Portion of the Levite: Another Reading of Deuteronomy 18:6-8," *JBL* 106 (1987): 195, 198-201.

This is clearly not the impression conveyed by our text, however, for there is no reference to the illegitimacy and/or destruction of Levitical towns. The movement by the Levite to the central sanctuary is based on his own choice and not by default (thus Heb. ʾawwat napšô, lit., "the desire of himself"); he is not looked down upon as inferior or as a concession (v. 7); and his coming may have involved the sale of his private holdings, something not likely to have been the case had he been forced to abandon a ruined cult center (v. 8).[117] The whole passage reflects a condition in which Levites moved freely from place to place, especially from a local shrine to the central sanctuary, with no hint of necessity or coercion or restriction one way or the other. Those Levites who decided to make such a move could join the ones already serving at the central sanctuary and there could share and share alike with them despite the fact that they might have their own patrimony[118] in addition (v. 8).

(4) Prophets (18:9-22)

[9]When you enter the land the LORD your God is giving you, do not learn to imitate the detestable ways of the nations there. [10]Let no one be found among you who sacrifices his son or daughter in the fire, who practices divination or sorcery, interprets omens, engages in witchcraft, [11]or casts spells, or who is a medium or spiritist or who consults the dead. [12]Anyone who does these things is detestable to the LORD, and because of these detestable practices the LORD your God will drive out those nations before you. [13]You must be blameless before the LORD your God.

[14]The nations you will dispossess listen to those who practice sorcery or divination. But as for you, the LORD your God has not permitted you to do so. [15]The LORD your God will raise up for you a prophet like me from among your own brothers. You must listen to him. [16]For this is what you asked of the LORD your God at Horeb on the day of the assembly when you said, "Let us not hear the voice of the LORD our God nor see this great fire anymore, or we will die."

[17]The LORD said to me: "What they say is good. [18]I will raise up for them a prophet like you from among their brothers; I will put my words in his mouth, and he will tell them everything I command him. [19]If anyone does not

---

[117] For an excellent analysis of 18:1-8 (and particularly vv. 6-8), see McConville, *Law and Theology in Deuteronomy*, 142-51.

[118] The phrase מִמְכָּרָיו עַל־הָאָבוֹת (lit., "his sellings according to the fathers") apparently refers to earnings gained by the sale of inheritances or inheritance rights. See T. E. Ranck, "Patrimony in Dt 18:8—A Possible Explanation," in *The Answers Lie Below: Essays in Honor of Lawrence Edmund Toombs*, ed. H. O. Thompson (Lanham, Md.: University Press of America, 1984), 281-85; L. S. Wright, "MKR in 2 Kings 12:5-17 and Deuteronomy 18:8," *VT* 39 (1989): 438-48.

listen to my words that the prophet speaks in my name, I myself will call him to account. [20]But a prophet who presumes to speak in my name anything I have not commanded him to say, or a prophet who speaks in the name of other gods, must be put to death."

[21]You may say to yourselves, "How can we know when a message has not been spoken by the LORD?" [22]If what a prophet proclaims in the name of the LORD does not take place or come true, that is a message the LORD has not spoken. That prophet has spoken presumptuously. Do not be afraid of him.

Of the three major institutions of ancient Israelite social and religious life—royalty, the priesthood, and prophetism—only the last was charismatic and nonsuccessive. Prophets were men and women raised up individually by God and called and empowered by him to communicate his purposes to the theocratic community. Frequently this ministry would take the form of a word of instruction or even rebuke to the leaders of the people as well as messages addressed to the present and future promises of covenant accomplishment and fulfillment.

As already noted (cf. Deut 13), prophetism was not unique to Israel. However, it assumed forms and engaged in practices among the pagan nations that were strictly forbidden to God's people. The passage under consideration speaks to these aberrant expressions of prophetism (vv. 9-13) and then turns to that of Israel for the purpose of defining its nature (vv. 14-20) and establishing criteria about the validity of its message (vv. 21-22).

18:9   The ways of the prophets of Canaan are described as "detestable" (Heb. *tôʿēbâ*), a favorite term in Deuteronomy to express all that is repulsive to a holy God (cf. 7:25-26; 12:31; 13:14; 14:3; 17:1,4). Usually the adjective refers to religious or cultic objects or activities, a fact that establishes the present discussion solidly within a religious context. More particularly it is a context in which divination and other occult means of ascertaining the will of the gods and either encouraging or averting its implications are at the forefront.

18:10-11   All this is important in seeking to understand the mysterious reference to human sacrifice in v. 10. The phrase in Hebrew *maʿăbîr bĕnô ûbittô bāʾēš* is rendered literally "whoever makes his son or daughter pass through the fire," a practice attested fairly commonly elsewhere in the Old Testament (cf. Lev 18:21; 2 Kgs 16:3; 17:17; 21:6; 23:10; Jer 32:35; Ezek 16:21; 20:26,31; 23:37).[119] At least three times the rite is associated with Molech, an Ammonite god (Lev 18:21; 2 Kgs 23:10; Jer 32:35), and twice it is linked with divination or sorcery (2 Kgs 17:17;

---

[119] Cf. V. Hamp, "אֵשׁ *ʾēsh*; אִשֶּׁה *ʾishsheh*," *TDOT* 1:424.

21:6). The fact that it is listed in our passage with terms that are exclusively divinatory in nature argues strongly for its usage in that kind of practice. The Molech connection would suggest that the rite was originally indigenous to an Ammonite cult with which Israel came in contact very early on (cf. Judg 10:6). Exactly how human sacrifice entered into the realm of divination is not at all clear.

The same mystery attends the remaining technical terms in the passage as far as the specifics of technique and ritual are concerned. Enough has been learned from innerbiblical and ancient Near Eastern texts, however, to provide at least a general understanding of what was involved.[120] In any case, the concern of the passage is that God's people must avoid any heathen means of achieving revelation and must, rather, avail themselves of those prophetic instruments whom he himself would raise up and through whom exclusively he would reveal himself.

The phrase "practicers of divination" (*qōsēm qĕsāmîm*) refers generically to the whole complex of means of gaining insight from the gods regardless of any particular technique. Sorcerers (*mĕʿônēn*, lit., "those who cause to appear") were diviners whose specialty lay in their ability to create apparitions (cf. Judg 9:36-37).[121] The interpreter of omens (*mĕnaḥēš*) divined through the use of certain revelatory objects or devices such as a cup (cf. Gen 44:5) or through the actions or words of others (1 Kgs 20:32-33). He or she who engaged in witchcraft (*mĕkaššēp*) was adept at performing signs (cf. Exod 7:11) to ward off evil (Isa 47:9,12) or to mislead God's people (Mal 3:5).[122] The "spell caster" (*ḥōbēr ḥeber*, v. 11), literally, "the binder with a band," was thought capable of invoking powerful curses that would bring their intended targets under control (cf. Ps 58:5; Isa 47:9).[123] The "medium" (*šōʾēl ʾôb*, "asker of the pit") was a necromancer, one who sought to communicate with the dead and thereby gain secret information. The best known such practitioner in the Old Testament was the witch of Endor (1 Sam 28:3,9; cf. Isa 8:19). In the same

---

[120] For a sampling of the vast literature in this area see R. I. Caplice, *The Akkadian Namburbi Texts: An Introduction,* SANE 1/1 (Los Angeles: Undena, 1974); E. V. Leichty, *The Omen Series Summa Izbu,* TCS 4 (Locust Valley, N.Y.: J. J. Augustin, 1970); A. L. Oppenheim, "A Babylonian Diviner's Manual," *JNES* 33 (1974): 197-220; E. Reiner, "Fortune-telling in Mesopotamia," *JNES* 19 (1960): 23-31; D. C. Snell, "The Mari Livers and the Omen Tradition," *JANES* 6 (1974): 117-24; I. Starr, "Notes on Some Technical Terms in Extispicy," *JCS* 27 (1975): 241-47; id., "In Search of Principles of Prognostication in Extispicy," *HUCA* 45 (1974): 17-23.

[121] R. B. Allen. "עָנַן *ʿānan*," etc. *TWOT* 2:685.

[122] For the meaning and use of the Akkadian cognate *kispū*, see *CAD* 8:454-56.

[123] H. Cazelles, "חָבַר *chābhar;* חֶבֶר *chābhēr*," *TDOT* 4:195 ("charmer of charms").

category is the spiritist (*yiddĕʿōnî*, from *yādaʿ*, "to know"). This does not appear to be a different kind of false prophet from the medium, for both are associated with necromancy and the pit (cf. Lev 20:6,27; 1 Sam 28:3,9; 2 Kgs 21:6; Isa 8:19).[124] Finally, he "who consults the dead" (*dōrēs ʾel hammētîm*) is listed, no doubt as a general and summary term for necromancy (cf. Isa 8:19; 11:10; 19:3).

18:12-13 Regardless of the precision with which the foregoing can be identified, the most important point to be made is that any means employed by the heathen to gain information from their gods or even to manipulate them to a certain course of action had to be strictly avoided by God's elect people. Such practices were detestable (*tōʿēbâ*) as were those who engaged in them. Indeed, it was because the nations of Canaan were involved in such nefarious behavior that they would be expelled from the land (v. 12). In contrast to such wicked behavior, the servants of the Lord were to be blameless (*tāmîm*, "upright") in all their relationship and association with him (v. 13).

18:14 This does not mean that Israel would have had no means of access to their God and no way to determine his purposes for them. They were not to emulate the divination of the peoples whom they would dispossess (v. 14), but in the stead of these purveyors of lies there would be an order of God's own prophets who would speak true revelation (v. 15). This order was first spoken of in the singular—"a prophet like me" and "listen to him"—but the continuing context makes it clear that the term was being used in a collective sense to refer to prophetism as an institution (cf. "a prophet" and "that prophet" in vv. 20,22).[125] There is nonetheless a lingering importance to the singular "prophet," for in late Jewish and New Testament exegesis there was the expectation of an eschatological prophet par excellence who would be either a messianic figure or the announcer of the Messiah (cf. John 1:21,25; Acts 3:22; 7:37).[126] The ambiguity of the individual and collective both being expressed in the grammatical singular is a common Old Testament device employed to afford multiple meanings or applications to prophetic texts.[127]

---

[124] Driver, *Deuteronomy,* 226.

[125] Beecher, *The Prophets and the Promise,* 350-52.

[126] For the linkage of Moses, Elijah, Jesus, and the "Prophet par excellence," see E. H. Merrill, "Deuteronomy, New Testament Faith, and the Christian Life," in *Integrity of Heart, Skillfulness of Hands: Biblical and Leadership Studies in Honor of Donald K. Campbell,* ed. R. B. Zuck and C. H. Dyer (Grand Rapids: Baker, 1994).

[127] See W. C. Kaiser, Jr., *Toward an Old Testament Theology* (Grand Rapids: Zondervan, 1978), 215-17.

18:15 The promised prophet in Israel would differ from the charlatans addressed above (and cf. chap. 13) in that he would be like Moses and would come from among his own people. Moreover, he would speak with authority and so was to be heeded by the people (v. 15). There had already been persons designated as prophets (nābî') in Israel's past, some, like Abraham, who were named (Gen 20:7) and others who were anonymous (cf. Num 11:29; 12:6-8). Moses introduced something new, however, a channel of revelation to whom the Lord spoke "face to face" and "not in riddles" (Num 12:8). The composer of Moses' epitaph went on to say, in fact, that no one up to his own time had equaled Moses as a prophet, one whom the Lord knew "face to face" and whom he used to accomplish signs and wonders (Deut 34:10-11).

18:16-17 The reason for a prophetic voice like that of Moses was (as Moses himself said) that the awesomeness of Yahweh in his epiphanic glory at Horeb terrified the people (v. 16). They could not bear to look upon his radiant presence, nor could they listen to his words because of their transcendent quality. This point had already been made most forcibly in Deut 5:23-27 (cf. Exod 20:18-19). What was needed was a mediator who could approach God for them and who then could transmit the divine revelation to them. Further, post-Mosaic generations would also need such spokesmen to bear the message of heaven. This would be particularly the case when the peculiar role of Moses (and of Joshua after him) as covenant mediator came to an end. The new situation would require some individual or institution to carry on the ministry of revelation and of covenant enforcement. This would fall to the order of prophets from then on.

18:18-20 The prophetic function is most clearly spelled out. The Moses-like spokesmen, called by God from among the people of Israel, would receive and speak only those things committed to them by the Lord (v. 18). So great would be their authority that anyone who disobeyed their word would have disobeyed the word of the Lord and accordingly would be made accountable (v. 19). Moreover, any persons who profess to speak for the Lord but in fact do not, or who speak on behalf of other gods, must be executed (v. 20). This latter contingency was already addressed in 13:1-11. There are thus at least two kinds of false prophets: (1) prophets of the Lord who proclaim a false message and (2) prophets of false gods.

18:21-22 It is obvious that there would have been occasions when it would have been difficult to judge the falsity or authenticity of a given prophet. As far as those who prophesied in the names of other gods were concerned, there would be no question (v. 20b; cf. 13:1-18). However, what would be the criteria when a man or woman issued a word in the name of the Lord? The answer in the text is very much to the point: the fulfillment of the prophesied message. Anything short of that would brand the prophet as false and unreliable. He had not spoken from God and therefore need not be feared as an envoy of the Lord (v. 22).

Such a litmus test must, of course, be somewhat nuanced. It suggests prediction, first of all, and not a word of a general moral or theological nature. Second, the time frame would have to be such that the predicted word would come to pass in the prophet's own lifetime if his authenticity were to be judged by his contemporaries. A false prophet could speak of a day in the distant future long after his own decease and thereby evade detection as false on that basis alone. It would seem likely that one who spoke only of remote times and never of the near future would be suspect in any case. The true prophet, then, would have to validate his calling by inerrantly speaking of events in both the near and distant future. Only at the end of history could he be fully vindicated, but unfailing fulfillment of his predictive word where testable would certainly give him the benefit of the doubt.[128]

3. Civil Law (19:1–22:8)

(1) Laws concerning Manslaughter (19:1-13)

[1]When the LORD your God has destroyed the nations whose land he is giving you, and when you have driven them out and settled in their towns and houses, [2]then set aside for yourselves three cities centrally located in the land the LORD your God is giving you to possess. [3]Build roads to them and divide into three parts the land the LORD your God is giving you as an inheritance, so that anyone who kills a man may flee there.

[4]This is the rule concerning the man who kills another and flees there to save his life—one who kills his neighbor unintentionally, without malice aforethought. [5]For instance, a man may go into the forest with his neighbor to cut wood, and as he swings his ax to fell a tree, the head may fly off and hit his neighbor and kill him. That man may flee to one of these cities and save his life. [6]Otherwise, the avenger of blood might pursue him in a rage, overtake him if the distance is too great, and kill him even though he is not deserving of death, since he did it to his neighbor without malice aforethought. [7]This is why I command you to set aside for yourselves three cities.

[8]If the LORD your God enlarges your territory, as he promised on oath to your forefathers, and gives you the whole land he promised them, [9]because

---

[128] For these and other criteria see C. H. Bullock, *An Introduction to the Old Testament Prophetic Books* (Chicago: Moody, 1986), 26-27.

you carefully follow all these laws I command you today—to love the LORD your God and to walk always in his ways—then you are to set aside three more cities. ¹⁰Do this so that innocent blood will not be shed in your land, which the LORD your God is giving you as your inheritance, and so that you will not be guilty of bloodshed.

¹¹But if a man hates his neighbor and lies in wait for him, assaults and kills him, and then flees to one of these cities, ¹²the elders of his town shall send for him, bring him back from the city, and hand him over to the avenger of blood to die. ¹³Show him no pity. You must purge from Israel the guilt of shedding innocent blood, so that it may go well with you.

The difficulty of establishing some kind of pattern or rationale for the organization of the material in chaps. 12–26 continues to be felt here in this section loosely referred to as "civil law." Inasmuch as a reasonable case could be made for viewing the previous section (16:18–18:22) as an enlargement and application of the fifth commandment, it is natural to seek for such a connection between the present section and the sixth commandment—"You shall not murder" (Deut 5:17). The following analysis reveals that this can be done on the whole though isolated verses here and there are somewhat intractable to a rigid, nonexceptional structure.[129]

The NIV translation "murder" for Hebrew *rāṣaḥ* in the sixth commandment may be somewhat too narrow in light of the elaborations of our present section.[130] It may be better to suggest "manslaughter" or the like and then determine the difference between manslaughter, murder, and other ways of taking human life such as capital punishment, the *ḥērem,* and casualties in war. The last three, sanctioned as they are by the Old Testament itself, cannot be the subject of the commandment. It therefore refers either to murder or manslaughter, most likely to both depending on the nature of the homicide. Those very specifications are at the heart of 19:1–22:8.

---

[129] Braulik identifies this section with the notion of preservation of life ("Leben bewahren") but does not include 22:1-8 as part of the pericope (*Die deuteronomischen Gesetze und der Dekalog,* 62-72) (*Die deuteronomischen Gesetze und der Dekalog,* 62-72). Rather, he views 22:1-12 as a transition between the sixth and seventh commandments (fifth and sixth according to his analysis, p. 72). Kaufman draws attention especially to the "priority system of socioeconomic worth" according to which the material is arranged, namely, institutions (19:1–21:9), free citizens (21:10-21), criminals (21:22-23), and animals (22:1-4,6-7; "The Structure of the Deuteronomic Law," 134-37). He notes that 22:8, a law pertaining to negligent homicide, is a fitting conclusion to the whole, particularly since it has to do with one's house, thus forming a bridge with commandment seven and its reference to the vineyard and the edges of one's garment (22:9,12).

[130] W. White, "רָצַח (*rāṣaḥ*)," etc., *TWOT* 2:860 ("applies equally to both cases of premeditated murder and killings as a result of any other circumstances").

19:1-3 The definition of manslaughter and its proper redress are the theme of 19:1-13. In anticipation of it occurring in the sedentary life of Israel in the land, Moses instructed the people to select three cities as places of refuge to which persons accused of manslaughter could flee for protection.[131] This is the second time in the book such instruction appears, the first adding the specification that these be cities to the east of the Jordan, that is, in Transjordan (Deut 4:41-43). Numbers provides an even earlier listing of cities of refuge, three on each side of the river (Num 35:6,11-15), and Josh 20:7-9 gives their names. It is likely that the three cities of the Transjordan already were recognized as places of refuge by the time the law of Deut 19 was given, so here it is necessary to speak only of the other three.[132]

The cities selected—Kedesh,[133] Shechem, and Hebron—would not need to be built from scratch but would fall to the Israelites by conquest and be unscathed (cf. 6:10-11). Each would be centrally located within one of three districts into which the land would be divided (v. 2) and each must be of ready access to anyone in the land who needed sanctuary (v. 3). Kedesh served the Galilee region, Shechem the central hill country, and Hebron the highlands of Judah.

19:4-5 The law concerning manslaughter clearly distinguished between accidental and premeditated homicide and allowed sanctuary only for perpetrators of the former crime. The one example of causes of death in such cases makes it most apparent that any objective witness would conclude that the death was accidental. It might be that an ax head might fly from its handle and strike a workman and kill him (v. 5). On the face of it one would hardly assume murder, for the likelihood of murder being carried out in such an unpredictable and inaccurate manner is nil. Moreover, there is no history of previous hostility between the accused and his victim, no "malice aforethought" (v. 4, lit., "without knowledge").

But human emotion being what it is, objectivity would frequently give way to visceral reaction, and the "avenger of blood" would seek to take matters into his own hands and render appropriate punishment for the crime, namely, the *lex talionis* of life for life (v. 6). The notion of an "avenger of blood" (Heb. *gōʾēl haddām*) is ancient, being traceable back into early patriarchal and tribal times (cf. Gen 4:24).[134] It was not only

---

[131] M. Greenberg, "The Biblical Conception of Asylum," 125-32.

[132] Auld, "Cities of Refuge in Israelite Tradition," 26-40.

[133] Of the many places by this name, the one in view here is Kedesh of Galilee (T. Qades), ca. seven miles northwest of Hazor. Cf. Aharoni, *Land of the Bible,* 222.

[134] de Vaux, *Ancient Israel,* 1:10-12.

allowed by the Lord, but Num 35 provides explicit instruction about its implementation. It was forbidden in cases of accidental homicide (as here); but if the slayer was found with a weapon in hand or had been known to harbor malice toward the deceased, he must be put to death by the avenger himself (Num 35:16-21). All of this, of course, presupposes due process, the assembly of citizens having determined the guilt or innocence of the alleged murderer (Num 35:24). If the verdict was in favor of the accused, he was to be protected by the assembly and allowed to return to the city of refuge from which he had been earlier brought for trial (v. 25).

19:6-7 These details are lacking here in Deuteronomy, but clearly the blood avenger might pursue, overtake, and kill the manslayer before the latter could find refuge even if he were innocent of murder, all in the heat of emotion. This obviously would be a miscarriage of justice, one that could result in a criminal charge against the avenger himself. All of these factors explain the need for multiple places of sanctuary, for in practical terms the shorter the distance one must travel to reach such a place, the greater the likelihood that justice would prevail. This apparently is the meaning of the conditional clause "if the distance is too great" (v. 6).

19:8-10 In somewhat of a parenthesis, Moses went on to speak of the possibility of there being more than three cities of refuge once the land had been enlarged and secured according to the promise of the Lord (v. 8). This blessing of increased territory would, of course, come to pass as a result of Israel's commitment to covenant obedience, expressed here in terms reminiscent of the very heart of the covenant requirement, namely, "to love the LORD your God and to walk always in his ways" (v. 9; cf. 6:5). Then and only then would the need arise for even more places of sanctuary for the manslayer. At last the reason for such places is clearly spelled out—to spare an innocent party from miscarriage of justice and to prevent the avenger (and, indeed, the whole community as represented by him) from the guilt of shedding innocent blood (v. 10).

The allusion to three more cities of refuge (v. 9) is somewhat problematic in that only here is this proviso stated, and at no time in subsequent history were other cities singled out for this purpose as far as the record is concerned. In the only reference to such places later on, the Israelites under Joshua set apart three cities west of the Jordan and three to the east (Josh 20:7-9). No additional ones are even anticipated here. What is likely is that Moses made allowance for such additional sites, but their selection either never took place or was unrecorded.[135]

---

[135] The protasis-apodosis construction (וְ . . . כִּי, "if . . . then") makes the addition of three cities conditional on full obedience, something that obviously did not subsequently occur; cf. Craigie, *Deuteronomy,* 267-68.

19:11-12   Having concluded this brief digression regarding additional cities, the lawgiver returns to the regulations concerning homicide. He prescribed community response to accidental or unintended death (vv. 4-7) and then addressed murder itself. The act, first of all, is a response to or at least linked to an attitude. Homicide following hatred gives a presumption of intention to kill. This is in line with the observation of Jesus that anger toward one's brother is tantamount to murder (Matt 5:21). But the case was made ironclad if there was evidence that the perpetrator had killed his victim after lying in wait for him for that very purpose (v. 11). Even if this occurred, the malefactor had the protection of the law and could flee to a city of refuge while his case was adjudicated. Such proceedings are only implicit here, but the full discussion of manslaughter cases in Num 35 suggests that a murderer was to be executed by the family avenger (vv. 19-21) if and when at least two witnesses implicated him (v. 30). This could be done whether or not the accused found sanctuary in a city of refuge. He was to be retrieved from wherever he had fled and brought back to the scene of the crime to suffer his fate (Deut 19:12).

19:13   So heinous was murder its penalty was to be inflicted without pity or compassion of any kind. The reason is that humankind is the image of God (cf. Gen 1:27; 9:6) and therefore murder was deemed to be an assault on God himself, an ultimate act of insubordination and rebellion (Gen 9:5-6).[136] The shedding of innocent blood polluted the very ground (Gen 4:10-11) and brought upon the community as a whole a culpability that could be atoned for only by the administration of talionic justice (v. 13). For the covenant community to tolerate such egregious sin by one of its members was to assume for itself the guilt of his deed. Only by excising the errant member could the community be restored to full covenant fellowship. Again, Num 35 states clearly the theology of the stipulation: "Do not pollute the land where you are. Bloodshed pollutes the land, and atonement cannot be made for the land on which blood has been shed, except by the blood of the one who shed it" (v. 33).

(2) Laws concerning Witnesses (19:14-21)

[14]Do not move your neighbor's boundary stone set up by your predecessors in the inheritance you receive in the land the LORD your God is giving you to possess.

[15]One witness is not enough to convict a man accused of any crime or offense he may have committed. A matter must be established by the testimony

---

[136] C. Westermann, *Genesis 1–11* (Minneapolis: Augsburg, 1984), 468 ("the murderer by his action despoils God").

of two or three witnesses.

[16]If a malicious witness takes the stand to accuse a man of a crime, [17]the two men involved in the dispute must stand in the presence of the LORD before the priests and the judges who are in office at the time. [18]The judges must make a thorough investigation, and if the witness proves to be a liar, giving false testimony against his brother, [19]then do to him as he intended to do to his brother. You must purge the evil from among you. [20]The rest of the people will hear of this and be afraid, and never again will such an evil thing be done among you. [21]Show no pity: life for life, eye for eye, tooth for tooth, hand for hand, foot for foot.

The need for witnesses in legal proceedings having already been alluded to by implication, it is logical that a full discussion of their role should follow, especially in light of the homicide cases just described. Clearly such matters were so serious both in their commission and their adjudication that a well thought out policy of witness to and testimony about them was mandatory.

19:14 At first glance v. 14 appears to be irrelevant to either its preceding or following context, for it speaks of moving a neighbor's boundary stone (or, better, encroaching upon a neighbor's property, as Heb. *nāsag* in the *hiphil* suggests; cf. Prov 23:10). However, it is well known that a common cause of hostility between persons is a failure to agree upon common boundaries and to respect property rights.[137] A major way of avoiding strife and even homicide among landowners would be to observe scrupulously the sanctity of personal landholdings and to desist from unlawful use or appropriation of one another's territory. An example of failure in this regard is Ahab's seizing of Naboth's vineyard by perjury and murder, a transgression that eventually cost him his own life (1 Kgs 21:1-26; 22:37-38).[138] The reason Ahab's crime was so serious was that he was trying to rob Naboth not just of land but of his patrimony (1 Kgs 21:3), the inheritance originally allocated to his ancestors by the Lord himself. This is also what was at stake here in Deuteronomy as reference to "inheritance" (*nahǎlâ*) makes clear (cf. Lev 25:23; Num 36:7).

19:15 Turning to the matter of witnesses, Moses repeated an injunction already articulated in Num 35:30 and Deut 17:6, both of which passages deal with capital offenses. It is obvious that in life-and-death issues one would want to rest his case on sound evidence and reliable testimony. In the nature of the case one witness would be insufficient, for it would

---

[137] Kaufman, "The Structure of the Deuteronomic Law," 137.

[138] For the linkage between the present statute and the Naboth incident, see C. C. Carmichael, *Law and Narrative in the Bible* (Ithaca: Cornell University, 1985), 117-22.

then become a matter of one word against another. Even Jezebel knew that she had to hire more than one witness to testify against Naboth if her case were to have any merit (1 Kgs 21:10,13). Nor was such a stipulation required, for only serious allegations such as murder for the law here speaks of "any crime or offense" (v. 15).

19:16-19   In the event there were only one witness, however, and he wished to prosecute the case, he could do so; but he himself would undergo as close a scrutiny as the person he had accused. Such a witness might be reliable, a contingency not addressed here, but more often than not he would be motivated by malice (Heb. *ḥāmās*), that is, with intent to do violent harm to an innocent party.[139] In any case, where a single witness was involved, both he and the one against whom he was pressing charges must appear "in the presence of" the Lord (v. 17). What this means (as in 17:8-12) becomes apparent in the appositional phrase "in the presence of the priests and the judges." These representatives of the Lord (cf. 16:18-20; 17:8-9) acted judicially on his behalf in investigating (lit., "seek thoroughly") and prosecuting the case brought before them. If the result showed the witness to be a liar, he was to suffer the punishment that would have been dealt to the one whom he had implicated (v. 19a). Only in this way could the evil (*rāʿ*) be purged (*bîʿar*) from the community (v. 19b; cf. 13:6; 17:7,12; 19:13; 21:21; 22:21-22,24; 24:7 for other occurrences of this technical phrase in Deuteronomy). Such severe measures would also instill so great a fear among the people that they would be unlikely ever again to perjure themselves or tolerate those who did.

19:20-21   To guard against a tendency to recoil from carrying out the prescribed penalty, Moses issued an oft-repeated warning—"Show no pity" (cf. Deut 7:16; 13:9; Isa 13:18; Ezek 7:4; 20:17). Heinous crimes called for equally stern response, one elaborated here and elsewhere (cf. Exod 21:23-25; Lev 24:19-20) as a measure for measure of *lex talionis* application of justice.[140] Whether this was to be administered literally or

---

[139] The עֵד חָמָס ("malicious witness") here was clearly a plaintiff in a case and not a mere observer. His intent was to do violence to the accused for some gain that might accrue to him thereby (cf. Exod 20:16; Ps 35:11). H. Haag, חָמָס, "*chāmās*," *TDOT* 4:484. E. Jenni makes a case for understanding the crime of which the defendant was accused that of lying (thus Heb. סָרָה; "Dtn 19:16: Sara 'Falschheit' [Deut 19:16]," in *Melanges Bibliques et Orientaux en l'honneur de M. Henri Cazelles,* ed. A. Caquot et M. Delcor [Kevelaer: Butzon & Bercker, 1981], 201-11).

[140] Cf. C. M. Carmichael, "Biblical Laws of Talion," *HAR* 9 (1985): 107-26; T. Frymer-Kensky, "Tit for Tat: The Principle of Equal Retribution in Near Eastern and Biblical Law," *BA* 43 (1980): 230-34; J. K. Mikliszanski, "The Law of Retaliation and the Pentateuch," *JBL* 66 (1947): 295-303; R. Westbrook, "Lex Talionis and Exodus 21, 22-25," *RB* 93 (1986): 52-69.

could be addressed by the payment of fines or other compensation is not clear in all cases. Numbers 35:31 seems to suggest that ransom (*kōper*, i.e., "the price of a life") could sometimes be paid as a substitute for one's life but never in a case of murder. On the other hand, Exod 22:21 prescribes a fine (*ʿōneš*) in certain kinds of physical assault, thus opening up the possibility that they could otherwise be levied in lieu of corporal punishment.

(3) Laws concerning War (20:1-20)

[1]When you go to war against your enemies and see horses and chariots and an army greater than yours, do not be afraid of them, because the LORD your God, who brought you up out of Egypt, will be with you. [2]When you are about to go into battle, the priest shall come forward and address the army. [3]He shall say: "Hear, O Israel, today you are going into battle against your enemies. Do not be fainthearted or afraid; do not be terrified or give way to panic before them. [4]For the LORD your God is the one who goes with you to fight for you against your enemies to give you victory."

[5]The officers shall say to the army: "Has anyone built a new house and not dedicated it? Let him go home, or he may die in battle and someone else may dedicate it. [6]Has anyone planted a vineyard and not begun to enjoy it? Let him go home, or he may die in battle and someone else enjoy it. [7]Has anyone become pledged to a woman and not married her? Let him go home, or he may die in battle and someone else marry her." [8]Then the officers shall add, "Is any man afraid or fainthearted? Let him go home so that his brothers will not become disheartened too." [9]When the officers have finished speaking to the army, they shall appoint commanders over it.

[10]When you march up to attack a city, make its people an offer of peace. [11]If they accept and open their gates, all the people in it shall be subject to forced labor and shall work for you. [12]If they refuse to make peace and they engage you in battle, lay siege to that city. [13]When the LORD your God delivers it into your hand, put to the sword all the men in it. [14]As for the women, the children, the livestock and everything else in the city, you may take these as plunder for yourselves. And you may use the plunder the LORD your God gives you from your enemies. [15]This is how you are to treat all the cities that are at a distance from you and do not belong to the nations nearby.

[16]However, in the cities of the nations the LORD your God is giving you as an inheritance, do not leave alive anything that breathes. [17]Completely destroy them—the Hittites, Amorites, Canaanites, Perizzites, Hivites and Jebusites—as the LORD your God has commanded you. [18]Otherwise, they will teach you to follow all the detestable things they do in worshiping their gods, and you will sin against the LORD your God.

[19]When you lay siege to a city for a long time, fighting against it to capture it, do not destroy its trees by putting an ax to them, because you can eat their

fruit. Do not cut them down. Are the trees of the field people, that you should besiege them? ²⁰However, you may cut down trees that you know are not fruit trees and use them to build siege works until the city at war with you falls.

Obviously relevant to the subject of death and thus to the sixth commandment is the matter of warfare and its prosecution.[141] War in the Old Testament was always viewed as a necessary evil in the defense of God's people from those who would seek their harm but also as an offensive measure in advancing their territorial interests. As the Creator and Sovereign over all things, the Lord had the right to bring them under his dominion, by force if necessary. And this he chose to do through the human instrument of his elect people. All war by Israel under divine protection is therefore "holy war" (or "Yahweh war") and as such was not only permitted by the Lord but initiated and carried out by him and his heavenly and earthly hosts.[142] The wicked nations as a whole were viewed as under hostile and even demonic leadership and so they had to either capitulate to Yahweh's lordship or face his wrathful judgment. The peoples of Canaan in particular were to be eradicated, for they occupied the land of Israel's inheritance and, furthermore, constituted a never-ending threat to Israel's purity and separateness as a kingdom of priests. The biblical witness is univocal that the Canaanites were beyond hope of redemption and had to be placed under the merciless *ḥērem* of the Lord.

The passage at hand provided a "manual of war" for Israel, a handbook addressing in a comprehensive if brief way the proper attitude of God's people toward enemy forces and the approach to be used in undertaking war against them. After an introductory statement identifying such conflict as the Lord's (vv. 1-4), the text provided provisions whereby exemption from military service could be allowed (vv. 5-9), strategy to be followed in offensive war against distant cities (vv. 10-15), and the invocation of *ḥērem* with respect to the nations of the land of promise (vv. 16-18). There is finally an appendix pertaining to the sparing of trees, a most ironic twist in a document devoted to the destruction of human life (vv. 19-20).

Many scholars maintain that apart from holy war the Old Testament never sanctions offensive warfare but only defensive.[143] This view not

---

[141] See, in general, A. Rofé, "The Laws of Warfare in the Book of Deuteronomy: Their Origins, Intent and Positivity," *JSOT* 32 (1985): 23-44; H. E. von Waldow, "The Concept of War in the Old Testament," *HBT* 6 (1984): 27-48.

[142] See the discussion of "Yahweh war" earlier in 7:1-5.

[143] The argument goes that once the conquest was completed, Israel's wars in the period

only is often based on a flawed theology, motivated perhaps from pacifistic concerns, but also a misreading of the biblical texts. Admittedly, the passage at hand is somewhat ambiguous on the matter, but v. 1 allows at least the likelihood of offensive military operation by Israel in the words, "When you go to war against," and so forth. Only special pleading can see this action as defense against an already initiated campaign by an enemy invader.

20:1-3 Divine authorization for this kind of war permeates the "manual." When Israel was about to engage in battle, they were not to fear superior numbers and armaments; for the Lord, the Warrior who defeated Egypt and led his slave people in the triumph of exodus, would be with them (v. 1; cf. 3:22; 7:18-24; 31:6,8; Exod 14:14-18; 15:3-10). Moreover, he would lead the armies himself as the reference to the priest attests (v. 2). Not only did the priest address the army on the Lord's behalf (v. 3), but his presence suggests also the presence of the ark of the covenant, the symbol of the Lord's visitation in war at the forefront of his hosts (Num 10:35; Josh 3:1-6; 6:1-14; 1 Sam 4:3-8).

20:4 Especially significant is the "do not fear" language of the pericope, whether in the imperfect (*lō³ tîrâ³;* v. 1) or jussive (*³al tîr³û;* v. 3) forms.[144] This formula is endemic to "holy war" texts elsewhere in the Old Testament (Num 14:9; Deut 1:29; 3:2,22; 7:18; Josh 10:8; Isa 43:1). The exodus motif is likewise pervasive in such contexts (cf. 4:34-38; 6:20-23; 7:8; 11:3-7; 26:8; Isa 11:11-16; Jer 32:16-23).

The concessions and exemptions that follow (vv. 5-9) are not so much prompted by compassion (though that is not altogether lacking) as by the desire for singlemindedness on the part of those who bear arms.[145] It is a well-attested fact that fear or preoccupation in the midst of conflict can endanger the life not only of the person afflicted by it but also the person's compatriots. Far better for a few who are wholly committed than for sheer multitudes of hangers-on where the well-being of the community is involved. But there may also be an undercurrent here of that same spirit

---

of the judges and Saul were defensive. Resumption of conquest under David and the later kings were, it is argued, offensive but without divine authorization. Texts that appear to suggest that wars of conquest (i.e., holy war or Yahweh war) were undertaken later are explained either as misreadings of the texts (as here in Deut 20) or as archaizings designed to legitimate expansionism. See for the various views Wenham, *The Structure and Date of Deuteronomy,* 258-68. Weinfeld argues that Deut 20 lacks the essential elements of holy war ritual and therefore cannot be construed as sanctioned aggression of the kind prescribed in holy war (*Deuteronomy and the Deuteronomic School,* 238-39).

[144] H. F. Fuhs, "יָרֵא yare," etc. *TDOT* 6:304-5.

[145] S. B. Gurewicz, "The Deuteronomic Provision for Exemption from Military Service," *AusBR* 6 (1958): 111-21.

that later was manifest in the paring down of Gideon's army from thirty-two thousand to three hundred men. This was done so that Israel might not boast "that her own strength has saved her" (Judg 7:2). In line with holy war, once more, it was to be clear to all observers that battles were won because of the power and presence of the Lord and not because of human prowess.

20:5 The first of the listed occasions for exemption from service is the permission for one who had built but not dedicated a new house to return to his home to do so. If he did not, he might die in battle and lose his property to another. The verb used here to speak of dedication (*ḥānak*) occurs elsewhere with this meaning only in 1 Kgs 8:63 (= 2 Chr 7:5), a passage describing Solomon's dedication of the temple of the Lord. The noun (*ḥānukkâ*) speaks of the consecration of the altar of the same temple (2 Chr 7:9) and also of the wall of Jerusalem in postexilic times (Neh 12:27). In all cases there are strong religious overtones, suggesting that what was being done was a sacred ceremony before the Lord.

20:6-7 In the present context the purpose of the dedication appears to have been the public solidification of legitimate claims of ownership and occupation of the property. Were this attestation not declared before the community, there would have been no commonly recognized ownership by the builder of the house and no way to guard his successors against unjust appropriation of their estate. The same concern is reflected in the second example of disqualification, the need to benefit from the produce of the vineyard (v. 6). Were one to lose his life in conflict, his labors in planting and tending the grapevines would go unrewarded, for another would enjoy their fruits instead. Indeed, for this very reason a man engaged to be married was to be excused from military service (v. 7).[146] Should he die before taking a wife, she would doubtless become the bride of another man. Moreover, the original husband-to-be would leave no posterity and thus his name would die out forever. In each of these instances death in war resulted in the dispossession of blessing and its appropriation by someone else who otherwise had no just claim to it. Mixed with the demand for compulsory military service, then, was a leaven of compassion that made possible to all men the enjoyment of that which constitutes life in its fullest—home, sustenance, and family love.

20:8-9 The fourth provision for exemption is different from the other three in that the interest of the army and not the individual is in view. It is common knowledge that a frightened soldier is an enemy, not an ally, for his timidity is contagious and can put a whole army in retreat. Therefore

---

[146] H. Palmer, "Just Married, Cannot Come," *NovT* 18 (1976): 241-57.

those of Israel who were afraid or "weak of heart" (*rak hallēbāb*) were to return to their homes and thus avoid undermining the morale of their companions. This principle was put into practice in the instructions of the Lord to Gideon that "anyone who trembles with fear" should turn back, an offer accepted by two-thirds of Gideon's army (Judg 7:3).

20:10 Military policy is the subject of vv. 10-15, specifically that pertaining to war against "distant" cities. In the context this refers to any places outside the parameters of the land the Lord had promised to Israel as an inheritance (cf. v. 16). These peoples were not subject to *ḥerem*, but many of them would constitute a threat to Israel from time to time and so had to be preemptively or defensively attacked; in addition, all were hostile to the purposes of God and so were subject to his punitive wrath.[147] Nevertheless, the Lord's policy toward them was merciful and redemptive. If they surrendered to him and submitted to his sovereignty, they could be spared. Such leniency was impossible toward the hopelessly unrepentant Canaanites.

The first step in undertaking war of this kind was the offer of terms of peace. The formula here, "If you call out to it with respect to peace," followed by the words "if they reply peace to you" (v. 11), expresses the technical language of making treaty (cf. Judg 21:13).[148] The idea was not that of a simple nonaggression pact in which both parties agreed to live in peace but a demand for capitulation. Only under such terms could the threatened city expect survival. To make peace was therefore tantamount to making covenant, the kind in which the city under attack placed itself in subservience to the peoples demanding the terms of peace.

20:11 All this is clear from the fact stated here that cities that comply do not go free but, rather, are reduced to forced labor (v. 11). The status reflected by the term *lāmas* ("to forced labor") occurs elsewhere with reference both to peoples pressed into civil service by their own governments, especially Israel by Solomon (1 Kgs 5:27; 9:15,21; 12:18) and conquered populations (as here; cf. also Josh 16:10; 17:13; Judg 1:28,30-35; Isa 31:8; Lam 1:1). The most celebrated case in the Old Testament is that of the Gibeonites who, having deceived Joshua into making a treaty with them, were forced into compulsory labor on Israel's behalf.[149] The

---

[147] It is common to separate vv. 10-15 from 16-18 on the basis not of simultaneous policy affecting distant and near places but as reflecting either more ancient or modern traditions. Thus Cairns proposes that "Deut 20:15-18 may be from a later and more radical Deuteronomic hand, seeking to tighten up the 'overly tolerant' stance of vv. 10-14" (*Word and Presence*, 185).

[148] Thompson, *Deuteronomy*, 222.

[149] J. M. Grintz, "The Treaty of Joshua with the Gibeonites," *JAOS* 86 (1966): 113-26.

term *mas* does not appear in the narrative (Josh 9:3-27), but it is clear that the Gibeonites were being dealt with as the Deuteronomic legislation here mandated, that is, as "distant" peoples, for that, indeed, was what they professed to be (Josh 9:6).

20:12-15   For a "distant" city to reject overtures of peaceful subservience was to invite stern measures of retribution. Such a place was to be placed under siege (v. 12) until the Lord had delivered it over to Israel (v. 13a). Then all the men were to be slain (v. 13b), but the women, children, livestock, and all other assets of the city could be taken as plunder and used in any way deemed appropriate by the victorious Israelites (v. 14).

This response occupies a medial place between the terms of peace articulated in vv. 10-11 and the harsh demands of *ḥerem* in vv. 16-18. A distant city under such circumstances could not go altogether unpunished for its refusal to capitulate, but inasmuch as there was hope for repentance by the comparatively innocent women and children, they could be spared. The death of the men was not only to induce other cities to a more ready submission to Israel but to prevent future uprising in the city that had just been taken. These drastic measures seem harsh indeed, but one must never forget that the sovereign purposes of God are not up for negotiation. Those who attempt to thwart them lay themselves open to swift and sure retribution.

20:16   The principle of *ḥērem* to which reference has repeatedly been made finds full definition in the next section of the "Manual of War" (vv. 16-18). Inasmuch as this principle and its underlying theology have been dealt with before (cf. 7:1-5), it is necessary here only to see how the principle was to be fleshed out in the context of offensive warfare.

The object of this action was the cities the Lord had promised to Israel as an inheritance (v. 16). The land they occupied had in the distant past been entrusted to Abraham, Isaac, Jacob, and their descendants and was therefore rightfully Israel's. The Canaanite nations were squatters who had no right to be there and who were to be evicted from it. Moreover, they had so irrevocably and implacably set themselves against the lordship of the Lord and were such a moral and spiritual risk to his people Israel that there was no other course of action than to annihilate them, men, women, and children (v. 16). The verb describing this type of all-consuming destruction of life is the familiar term *ḥāram,* almost always in the causative (*hiphil*) stem *heḥărîm* (cf. Deut 7:2,16; 12:2; 13:15).

20:17-18   The list of Palestinian peoples here (v. 17) is identical to that of Deut 7:1 except for the omission here of Girgashites.[150] The rea-

---

[150] The LXX and SP include the Girgashites, no doubt in order to bring the respective lists into conformity.

son for their inclusion in the earlier passage is that seven nations are mentioned, so a seventh one had to be added in order to make up that total. Seven, of course, symbolizes completeness, and Israel's conquest of the land was to be complete. The motive for destroying them (as in 7:4) was to eliminate a source of temptation to emulate their pernicious idolatry and thus to sin against the Lord, the only true God (v. 18).

20:19-20 The "War Manual" ends with a most curious and, at first blush, irrelevant paragraph about the treatment of trees in a time of siege. It does provide practical information about the preservation of fruit trees for their nutritional value and allows the use of others to build siege works (*māṣôr*, lit., "enclosure," perhaps encircling trenches or staging). The real thrust of the passage, however, is to contrast the tree with humankind (v. 19b). It is only humans, ironically the image of God and the crowning glory of creation, who sin against the Creator in such egregious ways as to call upon themselves divine judgment. The innocent tree, tainted as it is by the fall of humankind, is nevertheless not culpable and should therefore be spared. No more graphic depiction of the awful calamity brought by sin could be imagined.

(4) Laws concerning Unsolved Murder (21:1-9)

¹If a man is found slain, lying in a field in the land the LORD your God is giving you to possess, and it is not known who killed him, ²your elders and judges shall go out and measure the distance from the body to the neighboring towns. ³Then the elders of the town nearest the body shall take a heifer that has never been worked and has never worn a yoke ⁴and lead her down to a valley that has not been plowed or planted and where there is a flowing stream. There in the valley they are to break the heifer's neck. ⁵The priests, the sons of Levi, shall step forward, for the LORD your God has chosen them to minister and to pronounce blessings in the name of the LORD and to decide all cases of dispute and assault. ⁶Then all the elders of the town nearest the body shall wash their hands over the heifer whose neck was broken in the valley, ⁷and they shall declare: "Our hands did not shed this blood, nor did our eyes see it done. ⁸Accept this atonement for your people Israel, whom you have redeemed, O LORD, and do not hold your people guilty of the blood of an innocent man." And the bloodshed will be atoned for. ⁹So you will purge from yourselves the guilt of shedding innocent blood, since you have done what is right in the eyes of the LORD.

Laws pertaining to homicide up to this point have involved the presence of witnesses. Commonly, however, corpses are discovered bearing evidence of foul play but with no witnesses to the act or none willing to testify. How could such dilemmas be resolved in Israel in such a way as to exculpate the community, which otherwise must bear corporate responsibility and guilt? The answer lay in a ritual, the details of which comprise the present section.[151]

21:1   The situation is that of the discovery of a person who clearly had not died naturally but was a victim of a fatal wound. This is brought out by the use of an adjective (*ḥālāl*) meaning "a pierced one," thus, in general, a victim of homicide (cf. Num 19:16; 23:24; Jer 51:52; Ezek 26:15; 30:24; 31:17-18).[152] The person was found in an open field somewhere in the land of promise. The latter qualification was to underscore the fact that the crime had occurred in the holy land, on sacred soil as it were, and therefore was more than "ordinary" homicide. It became a sin against the Lord as well as against the victim, for it had taken place on the Lord's own estate, on common ground.[153]

21:2-4   Under ordinary circumstances one would presume that the perpetrator lived nearby, so the citizens of the town nearest the scene of the crime had to lead in the ritual of atonement. Having determined the nearest town by measurement (v. 2), the elders and judges of the district (perhaps the same as the "judges and officials" of Deut 16:18) would instruct the elders of that town to undertake the prescribed ceremony. This consisted of the selection of a heifer that had never been broken (v. 3) and the leading of that heifer to a stream in an uncultivated wadi bed (thus Heb. *naḥal*), where its neck was broken (v. 4). The fact that the animal and field had never been worked suggests that they were undefiled, never having been ritually contaminated by humans. The beast and place were ideally suited for an act of expiation.[154]

The mode of death—one in which the heifer's blood was not shed—reveals this to be no regular sin or trespass offering, however, for those invariably demanded the presentation of blood (cf. Lev 17:11). Rather, the ritual here was similar to that of Exod 13:13, where the firstborn of a donkey was either redeemed by a slain lamb or presented directly to the

---

[151] See especially P. E. Dion, "Deuteronome 21, 1-9: Miroir du Developpement Legal et Religieux d'Israel," *Studies in Religion/Sciences Religieuses* 11 (1982): 13-22; "The Greek Version of Deut 21:1-9 and Its Variants: A Record of Early Exegesis," in *De Septuaginta: Studies in Honour of John William Wevers*, ed. A. Pietersma and C. Cox (Mississauga, Ont.: Benben, 1984), 151-60; D. P. Wright, "Deuteronomy 21:1-9 as a Rite of Elimination," *CBQ* 49 (1987): 387-403; Z. Zevit, "The ʿeglâ Ritual of Deuteronomy 21:1-9," *JBL* 95 (1976): 377-90.

[152] W. Dommershausen, "חָלַל *chālal* II,' *TDOT* 4:419.

[153] Craigie, *Deuteronomy,* 277-78.

[154] Carmichael, *Law and Narrative,* 138 ("Both the heifer and the piece of land where it is slaughtered are characterized by their untapped vitality").

Lord by breaking its neck. The relevance here perhaps was that the heifer, like the donkey, was disqualified as a blood sacrifice, the latter because it was an unclean animal and the former because it was unbroken. Another (and possibly more likely) explanation is that blood sacrifices always had to be offered on altars at recognized cult centers, and towns most proximate to scenes of homicide often would fail to meet that criterion.[155]

21:5 The ritual of the heifer nonetheless remained squarely within the realm of the cult. Once the heifer was slain, the priests, chosen by the Lord not only to offer sacrifices and pronounce blessings but also to function in judicial capacities (cf. 17:9; 19:17), assumed a role in the proceedings (v. 5). The nature of that role is unclear, but in some undisclosed manner they determined guilt or innocence in the case. Inasmuch as the murderer was unknown, it was the guilt or innocence of the community at large that was at stake.

21:6-9 In light of this uncertainty the town elders, on behalf of all the people, were to symbolize the innocence of the community by washing their hands over the carcase of the heifer (v. 6), then state their collective innocence of the deed or even of being witness to it (v. 7), and plead with the Lord to accept their act of exculpation and absolve them of any blame for the death of the victim (v. 8). Once this was carried out sincerely and properly, the removal of guilt effected by it would be proclaimed, presumably by the priests who must somehow become instruments of this declaration.

The act of washing hands as a sign of exculpation is known elsewhere in the Old Testament (cf. Pss 26:6; 73:13) and, of course, was done even by the unbeliever Pontius Pilate as a gesture of his innocence in the death of Jesus (Matt 27:24). Atonement was not to be achieved by this, however, but by the implicit swearing of an oath before the Lord over the body of a slain animal sacrifice. Only this could "purge away innocent blood" (*tĕbaᶜēr haddām hannāqî*; cf. 19:13), that is, remove from the community any responsibility for the homicide. One may suppose that if the felon himself were later apprehended he would be dealt with according to the prescription of Deut 19:11-13 whether or not he was a member of the exonerated community.

(5) Laws concerning Wives and Children (21:10-21)

10When you go to war against your enemies and the LORD your God delivers them into your hands and you take captives, **11**if you notice among the

---

[155] Zevit, "The ᶜeglâ Ritual of Deuteronomy 21:1-9," 383-84.

captives a beautiful woman and are attracted to her, you may take her as your wife. [12]Bring her into your home and have her shave her head, trim her nails [13]and put aside the clothes she was wearing when captured. After she has lived in your house and mourned her father and mother for a full month, then you may go to her and be her husband and she shall be your wife. [14]If you are not pleased with her, let her go wherever she wishes. You must not sell her or treat her as a slave, since you have dishonored her.

[15]If a man has two wives, and he loves one but not the other, and both bear him sons but the firstborn is the son of the wife he does not love, [16]when he wills his property to his sons, he must not give the rights of the firstborn to the son of the wife he loves in preference to his actual firstborn, the son of the wife he does not love. [17]He must acknowledge the son of his unloved wife as the firstborn by giving him a double share of all he has. That son is the first sign of his father's strength. The right of the firstborn belongs to him.

[18]If a man has a stubborn and rebellious son who does not obey his father and mother and will not listen to them when they discipline him, [19]his father and mother shall take hold of him and bring him to the elders at the gate of his town. [20]They shall say to the elders, "This son of ours is stubborn and rebellious. He will not obey us. He is a profligate and a drunkard." [21]Then all the men of his town shall stone him to death. You must purge the evil from among you. All Israel will hear of it and be afraid.

The associative nature of biblical legal texts (and of Hebrew literature in general) is well exemplified in this passage that loosely organizes itself around the theme of the treatment of wives and children. Its place in the larger context of laws having to do with unnatural death (i.e., exposition of the sixth commandment) appears elusive at first glance, but the set of laws ends with explicit reference to the capital punishment of irremedially unmanageable children (v. 21). This clearly links it to the larger concern of 19:1–22:8. As for the section on wives (vv. 10-17), the first part (vv. 10-14) deals with wives obtained as prisoners of war, a theme that is allusive of the "War Manual" of chap. 20. Having raised the issue of such wives, the lawgiver went on to expatiate on problems that could arise were a married man to take such a wife in addition to his own. Though vv. 15-17 would seem to be out of place in a strict sense, their appearance here is understandable in light of the association of the issue of multiple wives with that of wives gained through war.[156]

---

[156] Kaufman suggests that vv. 10-14 serve as a bridge between the rules of war (chap. 20) and homicide (21:1-9), on the one hand, and the laws concerning wives and children (21:15-21, on the other ("The Structure of the Deuteronomic Law," 136). Deuteronomy 21:15-17 in turn links the unloved wife of 21:10-14 and the unloving son of 21:18-21, whose authorized death was in line with death in warfare. Braulik, though linking 21:1-9 with 21:22-23 sees within 21:10-22 associations that justify its inclusion here as a comment on the sixth commandment (*Die deuteronomischen Gesetze und der Dekalog,* 71-72).

21:10-11 The enemies referred to in v. 10 are obviously those of "distant" cities since only they (and specifically the women and children) could be spared the *ḥērem* (cf. 20:10-15). Women taken prisoner as a result of conquest could be taken as wives by Israelites, another indication that they were not from among the Canaanite nations (v. 11; cf. Exod 34:16; Deut 7:3). The issue here was not polygamy, so nothing was said about the propriety or impropriety of a married man taking a captive girl as his wife. One should assume that this was not sanctioned by the Lord and the community (cf. the observations of Jesus in Mark 10:1-12) even though polygamous relationships abounded throughout the Old Testament. The allowance here then would have been the undertaking of a first marriage by an Israelite soldier. The fact that multiple wives are referred to in vv. 15-17 does not demonstrate divine tolerance of polygamy but only guidelines about its proper regulation given its existence.

21:12-13 A woman taken in such a case was to shave her head, trim her nails, discard her native clothing, and fulfill a month of mourning for her parents before becoming a wife of an Israelite. The idea behind all these procedures seems to be that of cutting off all ties to the former life in order to enter fully and unreservedly into the new one.[157] This presupposes a degree of willingness on the part of the maiden to forsake the past and to embrace a new and different way of life, for one can hardly conceive of all this taking place coercively.

21:14 It is apparent that not all such relationships would be successful, for the differences in culture and ideology would have been difficult to overcome. The husband could therefore terminate the marriage by simply releasing his bride to go wherever she wished. In no case could he sell her as property or regard her as a slave (lit., "deal tyrannically" with her). She had already been shamefully humiliated by having been taken prisoner and made a sexual partner to begin with (v. 14). There is, as usual, no reference here to any initiation of divorce by the wife.

It must be stressed that the allowance of divorce (the meaning of *šillaḥtâ*, "let her go," in v. 14)[158] is not a blanket endorsement of it.[159] This and other references to such termination of marriages in the Old Testament (cf. Lev 22:13; Num 30:9; Deut 24:1-4) must be balanced against others that either show it in a negative light or bar it altogether (Lev 21:7,14; Deut 22:19,29; Mal 2:16; cf. Matt 5:31-32; 19:3-9; 1 Cor 7:10-

---

[157] Mayes, *Deuteronomy,* 303.

[158] Craigie, *Deuteronomy,* 282.

[159] W. C. Kaiser, Jr., *Toward Old Testament Ethics* (Grand Rapids: Zondervan, 1983), 200-204.

16). In the pristine days of Israel's election to be a covenant people, the Lord tolerated many of their "subbiblical" ways, slowly but surely educating them to the moral perfections that he gradually revealed to them. Forbearance toward improper behavior and affirmation of it are altogether different responses.

Were one to keep his second wife, on the other hand, she was to be treated as favorably as his first wife, no better and no worse. The fact that this principle follows the guidelines concerning the acquisition of a wife from among prisoners of war need not imply that the principle obtains only under such rather restricted conditions. It is likely that the particular set of circumstances that gave rise to multiple marriages provides a framework in which to legislate such arrangements generally.[160]

The Old Testament record presents a dismal history of the problems inherent in polygamous marriages or such other variations as surrogate motherhood and the like.[161] One can recall the well-known examples of Abraham, Sarah, and Hagar (Gen 16:1-6); Jacob, Leah, Rachel, and the concubines (Gen 29:21–30:24); and Elkanah, Hannah, and Peninnah (1 Sam 1:1-8). Invariably there would arise favoritism, envy, discrimination, and other manifestations of family and social breakdown; in the intimacy of married life there can be no successful division of affection and favor.

21:15-16   The case in point involves a bigamous relationship in which the husband rejected his firstborn son because he was the offspring of a wife he did not love (v. 15). Instead, he favored a son of a second wife whom he did love. If the case presented here flows from the preceding legislation about wives taken by conquest, the wife who was loved would appear to have been one of these. The text itself does not demand that understanding, however, and deliberately remains ambiguous about the chronological priority of the two wives. What is important here is that a husband's attitude toward his wife cannot affect his legal responsibilities to her and her children.

The matter of law that is pertinent here is the proper bestowal of inheritance rights. On the basis of what appears to be long-standing custom, the eldest son was to receive a double portion (v. 17) of his father's estate, a stipulation first recorded here in biblical law.[162] The custom is implied

[160] See A. Rofé, "Family and Sex Laws in Deuteronomy and the Book of the Covenant," *Henoch* 9 (1987): 131-59.

[161] de Vaux, *Ancient Israel,* 1:24-26.

[162] B. J. Beitzel, "The Right of the Firstborn (*pî šnayim*) in the Old Testament (Deut 21:15-17)," in *A Tribute to Gleason Archer,* ed. W. C. Kaiser, Jr. and R. F. Youngblood (Chicago: Moody, 1986), 179-90; E. W. Davies, "The Meaning of *pi snayim* in Deuteronomy 21:17," *VT* 36 (1986): 341-47; I. Mendelsohn, "On the Preferential Status of the Eldest Son," *BASOR* 156 (1959): 38-40.

in the story of Jacob's surreptitious acquisition of Esau's birthright (Heb. *bĕkōrâ*; Gen 25:31-34) and in Jacob's blessing of Ephraim, Joseph's younger son, rather than Manasseh, the older one (Gen 48:8-22). In neither case (nor anywhere else), however, is a double portion specifically denoted. Later on Elisha requested a double share of Elijah's spirit (2 Kgs 2:9), and Elkanah gave his favorite wife, Hannah, twice what he gave Peninnah (1 Sam 1:5).

21:17   The technical term "rights of the firstborn" is a translation of the Hebrew *lĕbakkēr,* a verb that in the factitive (or *piel*) stem means to "make as firstborn."[163] The law here affirms that a son who was not in reality the firstborn could not be made so simply by a declaration of the father to that effect (v. 16). To the contrary, he had to regard the true firstborn as such and certify that recognition by bestowing a double portion of his inheritance on him (v. 17). The motive for this is clearly articulated: The firstborn "is the first sign of his father's strength." The meaning of this phrase (*rēʾšîtʾōnôʾ*) is that a man first gives indication of his virility and capacity to sire succeeding generations when his first son is born (cf. Gen 49:3; Ps 105:36).[164] It is altogether fitting and proper that that son who gave the father such recognition be recognized himself for what he symbolized.

Exceptions to this principle are attested in the Old Testament but usually are regarded as improper deviations from custom (so Jacob and Esau; Gen 27:1-40), a punishment for some infraction of law or custom (Gen 49:4; cf. 35:22), or are dictated by divine mandate (so possibly Ephraim and Manasseh; Gen 48:8-20).

These special protections for unloved wives and firstborn sons provide occasion for a related concern, that of recalcitrant sons (and doubtlessly daughters as well) who manifest blatant disrespect to their parents by refusing to obey them (vv. 18-21).[165] These children certainly were not minors as their behavior (v. 20) and punishment (v. 21) made clear, but they also could not have been fully mature and independent adults who were out from direct parental supervision and heads of their own households. Rather, they were adolescents, dependents who were under the care of their fathers and mothers but fully responsible for their actions and resulting consequences.

---

[163] M. Tsevat, "בְּכוֹר *bĕkhôr*," etc., *TDOT* 2:122, 125-26.

[164] G. Fohrer, "Twofold Aspects of Hebrew Words," in *Words and Meanings,* 99 ("a man's 'procreative power'").

[165] E. Bellefontaine, "Deuteronomy 21:18-21: Reviewing the Case of the Rebellious Son," *JSOT* 13 (1979): 13-31; P. R. Callaway, "Deut 21:18-21: Proverbial Wisdom and Law," *JBL* 103 (1984): 341-52.

The behavior that occasioned the particular legislation of the passage would seem to have been best addressed in connection with the fifth commandment ("Honor your father and your mother," Deut 5:16), but since it might result in death for the rebellious child, it appeared here in the elaboration of the sixth commandment. Yet the description of the attitudes and actions of the unruly offspring graphically depicts what it means to dishonor one's parents.[166]

21:18 Specifically the charge was that the child was "stubborn" and "rebellious" against his father and mother, disobedient and unresponsive to discipline (v. 18). "Stubbornness" here means more than just willfulness. With its companion word, "rebellious," it possibly constitutes a hendiadys suggesting outright rebellion against constituted parental authority. That is, he was rebelliously stubborn, first with respect to his parents and then, by extension, with respect to God, whose sovereignty is transmitted through family headship.[167] The same construction, in fact, occurs elsewhere to speak of insubordination to the Lord himself (Jer 5:23; Ps 78:8).

21:19 That the child in question was not fully adult is supported by the instruction that his father and mother must "take hold" (Heb. *tāpaś*) of him and "bring" (Heb. *hôṣiʾ*) him to the elders (v. 19). The former verb connotes a physical grasping with the hands (cf. Gen 39:12; Deut 22:28; 1 Kgs 11:30; Jer 37:14; Ezek 29:7), and the latter appears in the causative stem, implying that the son was being forced to appear. The place of the hearing was the gate, that is, the broad plaza just outside the gate where matters of public interest were conducted (cf. 22:15,24; 25:7; Ruth 4:1,11; Ps 69:12; Prov 31:23,31; Jer 17:19). The tribunal before which the case is presented consisted of elders, not those of a district or the whole nation (as in 21:2) but the rulers of the local village (cf. 19:12; 21:3,6; 25:7-8; Judg 8:14,16; Ruth 4:2; 1 Sam 11:3). It was they who had to hear the evidence, pronounce a verdict, and prescribe appropriate punishment.

21:20 Having arrived at the gate, the parents leveled their charges against their recalcitrant child, adding to the accusation of rebellious stubbornness those of profligacy and drunkenness (v. 20). The former speaks usually of immoderate consumption of food (i.e., gluttony) and the latter of insobriety. The two vices occur together elsewhere (cf. Prov 23:20-21) and apparently serve as a cliché for self-indulgence and lack of

---

[166] Rofé points out that 21:15-17 and 21:18-21 share in common a feeling of hatred and a similar opening phrase, thus partially explaining their juxtaposition ("The Arrangement of the Laws in Deuteronomy," 272).

[167] Craigie, *Deuteronomy,* 284.

constructive activity.[168] The sin was not so much incontinence as it was the laziness or indolence that followed in its train, a deficiency of character severely condemned in the Old Testament (cf. Prov 10:4; 12:27; 26:15; Eccl 10:18).

21:21 Once the case was heard and the elders judged the child to be guilty as charged, the townsmen would execute the felon by stoning. Only by this drastic means could the "evil be purged" (cf. 13:5; 17:7,12; 19:19; 21:9; 22:21,24; 24:7) from the community. Youth who heard of the outcome would not be likely to replicate such behavior in the future. The severity of the punishment appears to outweigh the crime, but we must recognize that parental sovereignty was at stake. Were insubordination of children toward their parents to have been tolerated, there would have been but a short step toward the insubordination of all of the Lord's servant people to him, the King of kings.[169] This, of course, would have resulted in the breakdown and eventual dissolution of Israel as a chosen vessel.

(6) Laws concerning Preservation of Life (21:22–22:8)

[22]If a man guilty of a capital offense is put to death and his body is hung on a tree, [23]you must not leave his body on the tree overnight. Be sure to bury him that same day, because anyone who is hung on a tree is under God's curse. You must not desecrate the land the LORD your God is giving you as an inheritance.

[1]If you see your brother's ox or sheep straying, do not ignore it but be sure to take it back to him. [2]If the brother does not live near you or if you do not know who he is, take it home with you and keep it until he comes looking for it. Then give it back to him. [3]Do the same if you find your brother's donkey or his cloak or anything he loses. Do not ignore it.

[4]If you see your brother's donkey or his ox fallen on the road, do not ignore it. Help him get it to its feet.

[5]A woman must not wear men's clothing, nor a man wear women's clothing, for the LORD your God detests anyone who does this.

[6]If you come across a bird's nest beside the road, either in a tree or on the ground, and the mother is sitting on the young or on the eggs, do not take the mother with the young. [7]You may take the young, but be sure to let the mother go, so that it may go well with you and you may have a long life.

[8]When you build a new house, make a parapet around your roof so that you may not bring the guilt of bloodshed on your house if someone falls from the roof.

[168] Weinfeld, *Deuteronomy and the Deuteronomic School,* 303-4.
[169] Cairns, *Word and Presence,* 191.

The reverse side of taking life is preserving it, an appropriate and positive aspect with which to conclude this lengthy discussion of death as both a violation of covenant statute and a justified expedient in war and punishment. The rationale for including this section under the general rubric "You shall not murder" is the opening and closing statements, the one having to do with the disposition of the body of an executed felon (21:22) and the other with the measures to be taken to prevent accidental death (22:8).[170] One may assume that the intervening material, though appearing to have little to do with death, does indeed belong where it is and makes its own contribution to the issue be it ever so indirect.

21:22-23   Having just addressed a case that resulted in capital punishment (21:18-21), Moses turned to the policy to be followed in retrieving and properly disposing of the corpses of those thus dealt with. The focus is specifically on criminals whose bodies had been hanged from a tree (or wood). One may assume that those executed by stoning or other means would have been dealt with in a similar manner, but the peculiar nature of hanging and its aftermath called for particular attention.

Hanging in a public place was practiced widely by both the Israelites and their neighbors either as a means of execution (Josh 8:23,29; Esth 2:23; 5:14; 7:10; 8:7) or as a public display after death (Gen 40:19,22; Josh 10:26; 2 Sam 4:12; 21:12).[171] The latter was in view in our text, for the act of hanging follows the person's having been put to death. The passage reads literally, "If there should be with regard to a man a sin deserving of death, then he must die; and if you hang him on a tree," etc. The purpose of such a post-mortem display was doubtless to provide a sober warning to the community of the serious consequences of the crime committed.

In any event, the corpse was to be brought down and buried before sunset because the curse applied to the criminal would otherwise accrue to the community and the land as a whole.[172] Why an individual who was put on such display was considered especially cursed is not clear. Nowhere else in the Old Testament is the linkage made; and in Gal 3:13, where crucifixion and the divine curse are related, Paul was simply quot-

---

[170] Braulik notes that the reference to land as a gift to Israel frames Deut 21 (vv. 1,23) and also that the Stichwort "tree" links 20:22-23 with 21:22-23 (*Die deuteronomischen Gesetze und der Dekalog,* 71). Notwithstanding this, Kaufman makes a good case for associating 22:1-8 with what precedes: institutions (19:1–21:9), free citizens (21:10-21), criminals (21:22-23), and animals (22:1-4,6-8; "The Structure of the Deuteronomic Law," 134-37).

[171] J. A. Fitzmyer, "Crucifixion in Ancient Palestine, Qumran Literature, and the New Testament," *CBQ* 40 (1978): 493-513.

[172] M. J. Bernstein, "*ky qllt ʾlhyn tlwy* (Deut 21:23): A Study in Early Jewish Exegesis," *JQR* 74 (1983): 21-45.

ing the Deuteronomy passage.[173] The answer lies, perhaps, in the Hebrew abhorrence of death and the desire to provide for burial as quickly and unobtrusively as possible, especially where the wicked were concerned. To expose the body, therefore, would be to hold it up to public shame and ridicule. A greater curse than this could hardly be imagined.

22:1-3 Prevention of curse because of improper disposition of hanged corpses is followed in the passage by prevention of death to animals and people through various preventative measures (22:1-8). In the first instance if one happened upon a neighbor's straying animal, he was to return it to him if the owner was known (v. 1). The implication is that animals left to roam would eventually become prey to harm or death by the elements or at the hand of unscrupulous thieves. Besides this, the animals in question were a valuable resource whose loss would bring hardship and even impoverishment to the man who lost them. So much so was this the case that the one who found them had to keep them at his own expense until the owner, whether from a distance or not immediately identified, should come and claim them (v. 2). In fact, this principle applied to anything lost and found (v. 3).

22:4 A related case had to do with a neighbor's work animal that had fallen on the road (v. 4). Unlike the straying ox or sheep, which would not normally have been on the public roadways and would have been subject to rustlers, the donkey was commonly found in transit. One may assume that in this case the animal had not wandered away on its own but was in the company of its owner when the mishap occurred. Love for one's neighbor alone should dictate that the fallen creature be assisted, but in the context here the focus is on the animal's well-being. If allowed to remain in that condition, it could well have suffered loss of life.

22:5 Next follows a restriction on transvestism, a regulation that seems most intrusive in the overall passage (v. 5). Kaufman offers the suggestion that the theme of separation in this law (men's and women's clothing) finds parallels in the separation between a mother bird and its young in the next law (vv. 6-7).[174] Inasmuch as the latter at least indirectly touches on the subject of death ("You may take the young"), the law on transvestism may also do so by association. In fact, anyone who so blurs these divinely ordered distinctions is a *tôʿăbat* the Lord, "an abomination of the Lord," one who can expect most serious consequences for

---

[173] A. Caneday, "'Redeemed from the Curse of the Law': The Use of Deut 21:22-23 in Gal 3:13," *TrinJ* 10 (1989): 185-209; M. Wilcox, "'Upon the Tree'—Deut 21:22-23 in the New Testament," *JBL* 96 (1977): 86-99.

[174] Kaufman, "The Structure of the Deuteronomic Law," 136.

his deeds. Another linkage between the verse and its context is the chiasm connecting vv. 5-8 with 9-12: dress (v. 5), animals (vv. 6-7), house (v. 8), field (v. 9), animals (v. 10), dress (vv. 11-12). There is thus a strong tie-in between death and mixtures, that is, between the expositions of the sixth and seventh commandments. The sin in improper mixtures is brought out in the laws of purity that follow (22:9–23:18).

22:6-7 Preservation of life, mixed, ironically, with permission to take it, is the subject of the stipulation concerning the mother bird and its young.[175] In a culture dependent on agriculture and hunting for its food, death of animals was obviously not only allowed but positively sanctioned (cf. Gen 9:2-3). However, there were to be wise policies in the procurement of life's necessities, for they were finite and conceivably could be depleted to the point of nonexistence. Therefore in the case of game birds one could take the eggs or even chicks for food but not the mother.[176] Her life was to be preserved so that she could continue to produce offspring for human consumption. To kill the mother would effectively have cut off any prospects of her providing much-needed food in the future.

One notices here a descending order of value or significance in the animals listed. First was the ox or sheep (v. 1), clean animals useful for food or sacrifice. Then follows the donkey or ox (vv. 3-4), one of which (the donkey) was unclean but essential to one's livelihood as a work animal. Finally there was the undomesticated bird (vv. 6-7), of little intrinsic value since it was not owned but of great worth as a source of food supply. Even within the last category the mother bird was more valuable than her eggs or chicks, for they were more vulnerable to accident or premature death then she.

22:8 The prescriptions concerning preservation of life (21:22–22:8) and, indeed, the entire section on life and death (19:1–22:8) conclude with the instruction to home builders to build a guard rail around the perimeter of the rooftop to prevent persons from accidentally falling off.[177] Such a requirement is most understandable and practical given the flat-roofed architecture of ancient Israelite buildings and the extensive use of the roof as a place for relaxation, work, and even additional shelter. As for the literary construction of the whole passage, another transition is

---

[175] R. M. Johnston, "'The Least of the Commandments': Deuteronomy 22:6-7 in Rabbinic Judaism and Early Christianity," *AUSS* 20 (1982): 205-15.

[176] E. Segal, "Justice, Mercy and a Bird's Nest," *JJS* 42 (1991): 176-95.

[177] The security suggested here is immediately relevant to the fallenness of the bird's nest in vv. 6-7 and even that of the stumbling ox and donkey of v. 4. Cf. Carmichael, *Law and Narrative in the Bible,* 177-78.

observable, from active homicide, whether or not intentional (19:1–21:23), to the failure to preserve life (22:1-4), to carelessness resulting in loss of life (22:5-8). All relate to the covenant stipulation of Deut 5:17: "You shall not kill."

4. Laws of Purity (22:9–23:18)

(1) Illustrations of the Principle (22:9-12)

**[9]Do not plant two kinds of seed in your vineyard; if you do, not only the crops you plant but also the fruit of the vineyard will be defiled.
[10]Do not plow with an ox and a donkey yoked together.
[11]Do not wear clothes of wool and linen woven together.
[12]Make tassels on the four corners of the cloak you wear.**

Though adultery is clearly alluded to only once in this entire section on purity (22:22), there can be no doubt that the laws here on the whole are elaborations of the seventh commandment of Deut 5:18: "You shall not commit adultery."[178] Known elsewhere in the ancient Near East as the "Great Sin,"[179] adultery epitomizes all that impurity means, whether in family, social, political, or religious life. As noted repeatedly already, Israel's idolatry and covenant violation is frequently described as adultery, for the covenant between the Lord and Israel was akin to a marriage relationship. Unfaithfulness to its terms was nothing less than spiritual infidelity (cf. Isa 57:3-10; Jer 3:6-10; 9:2; 23:9-15; Ezek 16:30-43; 23:30-42; Hos 1:1–4:19).

If adultery is the metaphor for illicit relationships in general, the antithesis is separation from such mixed behavior. To drive home the importance of separation from sexual (and, indeed, covenant) impurity, the passage provides a number of instances in which separation must be practiced for its pedagogical value alone.[180] Apart from whatever other benefits may be derived from these behavioral requirements, their very observance would impress indelibly upon God's people the need to be separated from the contaminating influences of Canaanite social and religious life and to be wholly faithful in their commitment to him alone.

---

[178] Kaufman, "The Structure of the Deuteronomic Law," 138-39. Braulik (*Die deuteronomischen Gesetze und der Dekalog*, 79-89) limits this section to 22:13–23:15 (Eng. 23:14), having taken 22:1-12 to be a transition between commandments six and seven (p. 72) and 23:16–24:7 as a redactional bridge between the seventh and eighth (p. 89).

[179] See comments on Deut 5:18.

[180] C. M. Carmichael, "Forbidden Mixtures," *VT* 32 (1982): 394-415; C. Houtman, "Another Look at Forbidden Mixtures," *VT* 34 (1984): 226-28.

22:9 There is first a prohibition against planting mixed seed in one's vineyard (v. 9). The implication is that a crop in addition to grapes may be in view. While this might be possible in the world of actual agriculture, it was not to be undertaken in Israel because it symbolized an admixture of spiritual elements that is abhorrent to the Lord. The result would be a defiling (Heb. *tiqdăs,* "it will be consecrated") of both crops, that is, a rendering of them impure and unfit for sacred use.[181] Elsewhere Israel is referred to as a vineyard (cf. Ps 80:8-19; Isa 5:1-7; Jer 2:10), so the imagery here is clear and deliberate: Israel, the vineyard, must not be contaminated by being oversown with alien seed. Every time the Israelite farmer refrained from planting wheat or barley in his vineyard, he reflected this important principle.

22:10 The same lesson is taught by the command to yoke only the same species of animal together (v. 10). Paul the apostle understood this text in the way just suggested by quoting it to underscore his point that believers should not be yoked together with unbelievers (2 Cor 6:14-18).[182] To do so is to undermine the purity of God's people and to tarnish their status as ones set apart for his service (cf. Lev 26:12). As some scholars have noted, such a mixture of animals would not be advisable anyway because of their differing strength, gaits, and temperaments, but this is not the issue here.[183] A mixed yoke speaks of unwholesome partnership, an attempt to find common ground when none in fact exists. The temptation of religious syncretism would be especially appealing in Canaan but was to be resisted at all cost (cf. Deut 7:2-5).

22:11 Clothing of mixed fabric was also taboo, for that too would symbolize a breakdown of the standards of holiness the Lord demanded of his people (v. 11). The clearest connection between the mingling of clothing materials and the principle of holiness is found in Lev 19, where the phrase "I am the LORD" occurs over and over (vv. 2-37), commencing with the affirmation, "You shall be holy" (v. 2). In the midst of this refrain on holiness stands the injunction "Do not wear clothing woven of two

---

[181] Rofé observes that a linkage may be found between 22:8 and 22:9 in that a person's fatal fall from a roof would bring defilement through bloodshed (דָּמִים דָּמִים) whereas mixing seed produces crops that are "sanctified" (תִּקְדָּשׁ), terms that are opposites (Rofé, "The Arrangement of the Laws in Deuteronomy," 272-73).

[182] J. D. M. Derrett, "2 Cor 6:14: A Midrash on Dt 22:10," *Bib* 59 (1978): 231-50.

[183] Schroeder, *Deuteronomy,* 164. Carmichael proposes a figurative meaning for the (literal) ox plowing a donkey and vice-versa, namely, that the law prohibits sexual union between two different species. This finds support in the parallel passage Lev 19:19 and lends itself to a closer connection to the law prohibiting sowing with mixed seed (Carmichael, *Law and Narrative in the Bible,* 195-97).

kinds of material" (v. 19). Again, therefore, an apparently innocuous act becomes filled with spiritual significance as a paradigm of behavior.

22:12   Reference to clothing continues in v. 12, but this time the command is positive: "Make tassels on the four corners of the cloak you wear." The purpose of such ornamentation (Heb. *gidilîm,* "twisted threads") is not clear from this text; but in an apparently related passage where a different Hebrew word (*ṣîṣit*) is used (Num 15:37-41), the tassels are to serve as reminders of the Lord's covenant commands.[184] Specifically, they would call to mind the prohibition against idolatry, to "not prostitute yourselves by going after the lusts of your own hearts and eyes" (v. 39). The impulse toward purity and separation here is inescapable. Thus all four statutes of Deut 22:9-12 underscore the emphasis epitomized in the seventh commandment and elaborated in this major section.

(7) Purity in the Marriage Relationship (22:13-30)

¹³**If a man takes a wife and, after lying with her, dislikes her ¹⁴and slanders her and gives her a bad name, saying, "I married this woman, but when I approached her, I did not find proof of her virginity," ¹⁵then the girl's father and mother shall bring proof that she was a virgin to the town elders at the gate. ¹⁶The girl's father will say to the elders, "I gave my daughter in marriage to this man, but he dislikes her. ¹⁷Now he has slandered her and said, 'I did not find your daughter to be a virgin.' But here is the proof of my daughter's virginity." Then her parents shall display the cloth before the elders of the town, ¹⁸and the elders shall take the man and punish him. ¹⁹They shall fine him a hundred shekels of silver and give them to the girl's father, because this man has given an Israelite virgin a bad name. She shall continue to be his wife; he must not divorce her as long as he lives.**

²⁰**If, however, the charge is true and no proof of the girl's virginity can be found, ²¹she shall be brought to the door of her father's house and there the men of her town shall stone her to death. She has done a disgraceful thing in Israel by being promiscuous while still in her father's house. You must purge the evil from among you.**

²²**If a man is found sleeping with another man's wife, both the man who slept with her and the woman must die. You must purge the evil from Israel.**

²³**If a man happens to meet in a town a virgin pledged to be married and he sleeps with her, ²⁴you shall take both of them to the gate of that town and stone them to death—the girl because she was in a town and did not scream for help, and the man because he violated another man's wife. You must purge the evil from among you.**

²⁵**But if out in the country a man happens to meet a girl pledged to be**

---

[184] Harrison, *Numbers,* 229-30.

married and rapes her, only the man who has done this shall die. [26]Do nothing to the girl; she has committed no sin deserving death. This case is like that of someone who attacks and murders his neighbor, [27]for the man found the girl out in the country, and though the betrothed girl screamed, there was no one to rescue her.

[28]If a man happens to meet a virgin who is not pledged to be married and rapes her and they are discovered, [29]he shall pay the girl's father fifty shekels of silver. He must marry the girl, for he has violated her. He can never divorce her as long as he lives.

[30]A man is not to marry his father's wife; he must not dishonor his father's bed.

It is commonplace in the Old Testament to find the Lord's covenant with Israel compared to the marriage relationship between husband and wife. The following section should be understood against that theological background, though obviously the instructions here had practical and immediate relevance to Israel's family life as well. As for the structure of the pericope, it follows an order of ascending or increasing degree of impropriety. There first is a section dealing with the undertaking and dissolving of marriage (vv. 13-21),[185] followed by statutes concerning improper sexual relations with a married woman (v. 22), one who is betrothed (vv. 23-27), and a virgin who is neither married nor betrothed (vv. 28-29). The unit closes with a prohibition against marrying one's stepmother (v. 30). The degree of seriousness lies not always in the deeds themselves but to some extent in the amount of complicity by the offended parties. For example, the adultery of v. 22 is deemed not as offensive as the violation of the engaged girl in vv. 23-27 because in the former case the act was by mutual consent whereas in the latter there may be a question of force, especially as far as rape within a village was concerned (vv. 23-24). Marriage with a stepmother was worst of all because it degraded the father who, under God, retained dignity and sovereignty even after his death.

22:13-16   The first case pertains to a marriage in which a man, having consummated the relationship, rejects (so Heb. *śānēʾ* here) his wife publicly by accusing her of not being a virgin at the time of the marriage (vv. 13-14). The "proof of her virginity" (lit., "I did not find virginity [*bětû-lîm*] with respect to her") would be the bloodstained sheets resulting from

---

[185] For the pericope dealing with marriage alone (22:13-21) see C. Locher, *Die Ehre einer Frau in Israel. Exegetische und rechtsvergleichende Studien zu Deuteronomium 22, 13-21* (Freiburg: Universitätsverlag, 1986). Locher particularly draws attention to parallels from ancient Near Eastern law, though he concludes that there is more in this law that is unique to Israel than what it shares in common with other cultures (pp. 381-87).

a ruptured hymen (cf. v. 17). Evidently the bride retained the telltale cloth (described as a *śimlâ*, "covering," in v. 17), for her parents could present it to the town elders to contest the husband's allegations (v. 15). If the cloth indeed bore proof of the girl's virginity, her parents had good basis for their claim that the husband had rejected her for reasons other than those he professed.[186] He had come to despise (*śānēʾ*, as in v. 13) her and tried to shift the onus onto her in order to be more gracefully free of the relationship.

22:17-19 Once the incriminating evidence had been presented and accepted as such by the elders, they would administer appropriate punishment to the lying husband. This consisted of a fine of a hundred shekels of silver to be paid to the bride's father as compensation for sullying the name (i.e., reputation) of the maiden and, by implication, that of her family. Moreover, the husband had to maintain the marriage as long as he lived (v. 19).

The amount of the fine was considerable relative to that economy. David, for example, later bought Araunah's threshing floor and oxen for only fifty silver shekels (2 Sam 24:24). Such an enormous penalty would clearly deter young husbands from such frivolous and fallacious allegations. The reason the money was given to the bride's father and not to her is obvious, for to give to her would, in effect, result in the husband's retaining it for himself. The payment to the father was not compensation for actual loss but for damages, that is, for the dishonor that accompanied such charges against his daughter, as baseless as they might be. An even more severe punishment in such cases was the talionic justice implicit in the husband's inability ever to free himself of his wife. He had tried to rid himself of her by duplicity but now must forever remain in union with her. One must wonder about the misery of a woman in such circumstances, but at least she would mother a line of descendants. Moreover, it is quite possible that she could have initiated divorce herself if the situation deemed it necessary or desirable.

22:20-21 Occasionally, of course, the husband's accusations would have substance and the evidence of virginity would not be forthcoming (v. 20). Should this occur, the woman must be stoned to death and at the door of her father's house at that! Just as an unfounded accusation brought

---

[186] Wenham suggests that the stained cloth, already in the possession of the girl's parents, would be evidence not of her virginity on the night of her marriage but of menstruation just prior to marriage, thus showing her not to be pregnant. He supports this by pointing out the uses of *bĕtûlîm* with the meaning "of marriageable age" or the like. The issue here, then, would be whether or not the girl was a suitable candidate for marriage. G. J. Wenham, "*Bĕtûlāh*—A Girl of Marriageable Age," *VT* 22 (1972): 331-32.

undeserved dishonor to the father's name, one that could be proved brought justified dishonor. The reason is that the girl had clearly had sexual intercourse before her marriage, an act described here as "being promiscuous." This translates the Hebrew ʿāśĕtâ nĕbālâ, literally, "She has done a disgraceful thing" in Israel. This formula occurs frequently to speak of a moral or spiritual breakdown of such proportions as to impact the whole covenant community negatively (cf. Gen 34:7; Judg 19:23; 20:6,10; Jer 29:23).[187] Only her death at the hands of the community could remove the disgrace brought about by her deed (cf. Deut 17:12; 19:13; 21:21; 22:24; Judg 20:13).

22:22 More serious than the sin of fornication and marriage under false pretenses was that of adultery, for then the woman concerned had not even professed virginity. She was "another man's wife" and as such was off bounds to any other man be he married or single. Should such a pair be caught in the act of adultery, both were to be executed for the good of the community. There is no hint here of coercion, so one must assume that the sin was one of common consent. The marital state of the man had nothing to do with the fact of adultery. In ancient Israel the wife was considered as belonging to her husband in a way that was not true of the converse.[188] Thus it was always the woman who was being abused (along with her husband) and not the man, whether or not he was married.

22:23-24 The next case—the rape of betrothed maidens—was even more heinous because it involved assault or at least its possibility (vv. 23-27). The latter contingency is dealt with first. The parties in view were a man (married or not) and an engaged woman (naʿărā bĕtûlâ mĕʾōrāśâ lĕʾîš, "a young woman, a virgin betrothed to a man"). The setting was in a town, a place where rape could not ordinarily occur without being noticed. Should a sexual encounter take place, therefore, the presumption would have been that the woman was a willing partner unless and until she cried out for help (v. 24). This, of course, presupposes her ability to scream or otherwise to draw attention to her plight. Inasmuch as this normally could not have been established absent any witnesses, both the man and the woman would have been judged guilty and would have been publicly stoned to death. The woman was to die for her consent by silence;

---

187 A. Phillips, "nebalah—A Term for Serious Disorderly and Unruly Conduct," *VT* 25 (1975): 237-42.

188 The phrase בְּעֻלַת־בַּעַל (lit., "mastered by a master") suggests, etymologically at least, the extent to which a wife "belonged" to her husband. Cf. de Vaux, *Ancient Israel*, 1:26.

the man, for having violated another man's fiancée, described here as elsewhere in the Bible as his wife (*'iššâ*; cf. Deut 28:30).[189]

22:25 In a related situation but one that has a greatly different locale, the judgment is also quite different. This time a man confronted an engaged woman in a desolate, uninhabited area, a place where his crime was likely to go undetected. Now he did not merely lie with her (as *šākab* suggests in v. 23, language that leaves open the possibility of her cooperation), but he seized her (*ḥāzaq*) and raped her, as the NIV correctly translates. In such an event only he was judged guilty and only he had to die, for the presumption was that she must have screamed for help but to no avail (v. 27).[190] Again solid evidence would be lacking were there no witnesses, but circumstantial evidence would weigh in favor of the girl here just as it weighed against her in the previous contingency.

22:26-27 Legal justification for rendering such a verdict finds support in the analogous case of unwitnessed murder. There is no statute in the biblical law that deals with such kind of homicide specifically, but the case of one being slain by another who had previously disclosed animosity toward his victim might be apropos (cf. Deut 19:11-13). Were a rapist known to have signaled evil intentions toward a girl before a sexual assault, one must assume that such a deed, even if done in secret, was forced upon her.

22:28-29 At first glance the next example, the rape of an unbetrothed girl, might appear to have been a lesser offense than those already described, but this was not the case at all. First, he seized (Heb. *tāpaś*, "lay hold of") her and then lay down (*šākab*) with her, a clear case of violent, coercive behavior. Moreover, the assailant had forever marred the purity of the woman, making it nearly impossible ever to enjoy a normal, happy marriage. This had negative repercussions on her father as well, for he stood to lose the bride price (Heb. *môhār*) that a prospective husband would have paid him (cf. Gen 34:12; Exod 22:16; 1 Sam 18:25).[191] In fact, the compensation for this loss was the fifty shekels of silver assessed as a penalty by the court (v. 29). This was half the amount demanded of the man who misrepresented his wife's virginity (v. 19), for she already was married and would never have command any additional bride price whereas the girl in the present situation not only would have afforded her

---

[189] For the range of meanings and uses, see N. P. Bratsiotsis, "שׁ֫יאִ *'ish*; הָשִּׁאִ *'ishshah*," *TDOT* 1:224-25.

[190] Carmichael also correctly observes that the young woman must protect herself against the charge almost certainly to be leveled against her later by her husband that she was not a virgin at the time of their marriage (*Law and Narrative in the Bible*, 217-18).

[191] For the *môhār* and its Akkadian parallel *tirḫatu*, see de Vaux, *Ancient Israel*, 1:26-29.

father fifty shekels of compensation for her humiliation but most certainly the normal bride price in addition.[192]

In any event, the perpetrator of the act must marry the girl (assuming her willingness) and could never divorce her. Again the deterrent effect of such an outcome is most evident (cf. v. 19).

22:30   The final case was particularly abhorrent because it involved the honor and dignity of one's father (v. 30). Here it is supposed that the father had died, leaving a widow, the stepmother of a son, whom he himself took as wife. Though there are some resemblances between this kind of relationship and levirate marriages, in which a man could marry his brother's widow (cf. Gen 38:1-11; Deut 25:5-10; Ruth 4:5-12), the role of a brother was quite different from that of a father. For a man to have sexual intercourse with a woman who had enjoyed such intimacy with his own father was tantamount to the son having exposed his father's nakedness. This is clearly the meaning of the Hebrew clause *lōʾ yĕgalleh kĕnap ʾābîw*, "he must not uncover his father's garment."[193] The same euphemism occurs elsewhere to refer to dishonorable attitudes or actions, especially of a sexual nature (Deut 27:20; Ruth 3:9; cf. Gen 9:20-24). The act smacks of filial insubordination, of a direct challenge to the commandment that one honor his father and his mother.

(8) Purity in Public Worship (23:1-8)

¹No one who has been emasculated by crushing or cutting may enter the assembly of the LORD.

²No one born of a forbidden marriage nor any of his descendants may enter the assembly of the LORD, even down to the tenth generation.

³No Ammonite or Moabite or any of his descendants may enter the assembly of the LORD, even down to the tenth generation. ⁴For they did not come to meet you with bread and water on your way when you came out of Egypt, and they hired Balaam son of Beor from Pethor in Aram Naharaim to pronounce a curse on you. ⁵However, the LORD your God would not listen to Balaam but turned the curse into a blessing for you, because the LORD your God loves you. ⁶Do not seek a treaty of friendship with them as long as you live.

⁷Do not abhor an Edomite, for he is your brother. Do not abhor an Egyptian, because you lived as an alien in his country. ⁸The third generation of children born to them may enter the assembly of the LORD.

---

[192] Mayes, *Deuteronomy,* 311-12.

[193] A. Phillips, "Uncovering the Father's Skirt," *VT* 10 (1980): 38-43; cf. H.-J. Zobel, "גָּלָה, galah," etc., *TDOT* 2:477.

23:1 A corollary to the holiness of Israel as the special, elect people of the Lord is the manifestation of that holiness both in terms of their ethnic identity and the recognition of that identity in physical ways. In the present passage the latter received attention first by reference to emasculation, an act associated with paganism and perhaps intended here, by synecdoche, to represent any and all outward signs of ethnic and cultic impurity (v. 1).[194] The emasculation, described here as a "wounding by crushing" (*pĕṣûaᶜ dakkâ*) or a "cutting off of the male organ" (*kĕrût šapkâ*), may, presumably, be genetic, accidental, or intentional; but that is irrelevant because the end result is the same—the male thus deformed could have no access to the assembly of the Lord.

The "assembly" (*qāhāl*) refers here to the formal gathering of the Lord's people as a community at festival occasions and other times of public worship and not to the nation of Israel as such. This is clear from the occurrence of the verb "enter" (*bōʾ*) throughout the passage (vv. 1-3,8), a verb that suggests participation with the assembly and not initial introduction or conversion to it. Furthermore, Israelites with such handicaps are elsewhere assumed to have been full members of the community with the only restriction being their ineligibility for the priesthood (Lev 21:20).[195] Our text, then, more fully clarifies the extent to which deformed Israelites could participate in the cultus and does not speak to the issue of whether or not they belonged to the covenant community. It is everywhere assumed that they did. Their exclusion from the worship assembly, as discriminatory as such a policy might seem, was to underscore the principle of separation from paganism, where such deformities were not only acceptable but frequently central to the practice of the cult. A well-known example was the *assinnu* of the Babylonian cult who took part as an actor, perhaps in female dress, in religious performances.[196]

23:2 This principle underlies the next prohibition as well, that which forbids any of illegitimate birth from the assembly (v. 2). The word used here (*mamzēr*) occurs only one other time, in late Hebrew, to describe

---

[194] Keil and Delitzsch: "[Such mutilation reflects] the mutilation of the nature of man as created by God, which was irreconcilable with the character of the people of God" (*The Pentateuch,* 3:413).

[195] Craigie correctly understands קְהַל יְהוָה here (and in vv. 2-3,8) to have a narrower definition than the nation of Israel as a whole (*Deuteronomy,* 296). As he points out, "There would be resident aliens and others who, though a part of the community, were nevertheless not full members of it." This would surely pertain to the individuals precluded by the criteria of this passage.

[196] H. W. F. Saggs, *The Greatness That was Babylon* (New York: The New American Library, 1962), 332.

children of mixed marriages or even of incest (cf. Zech 9:6).[197] Again, denial to the assembly could not mean exclusion from the community as such but only from the formal times and places of community worship. It would have been a simple matter to issue a command that such a one be excommunicated from the community (i.e., be "cut off" and the like; cf. Exod 12:15,19) if that were the intent here. To invoke such a penalty against an innocent product of illicit sexual relationships would obviously put conditions on covenant inclusion that exist nowhere else. One was an Israelite and therefore a member of the covenant community by birth. Only by some act of his own will could he lose that privilege. On the other hand, Israelite birth did not automatically qualify one for full participation in community worship, the very point of vv. 1-2.

23:3 The exclusion of a *mamzēr* was "down to the tenth generation," that is, forever.[198] He and all his descendants were to be precluded from the assembly, for they represented in a most graphic way a violation of the principle of holiness and purity that must characterize Israel in its status as a chosen people. An illustration of what it meant to be a *mamzēr* follows in vv. 3-6. According to Gen 19:30-38, the Ammonites and Moabites were descendants of Lot through his incestuous relationship with his daughters. For this reason they could never enter the assembly of the Lord though there is no reason to think they were denied affiliation with Israel as such (cf. Deut 2:9,19; Ruth 4:10; 1 Sam 22:3-4). They and any other peoples could qualify as proselytes to Yahwism (cf. Exod 12:38) though this did not give them automatic access to the worshiping assembly.

23:4-6 The emphasis here, however, is not on the ancestry of the Ammonites and Moabites but on their hostile behavior toward Israel in the transit from Egypt to Canaan. They had refused the normal Eastern courtesies of hospitality (a matter not referred to elsewhere in the tradition) and, indeed, had hired Balaam to curse Israel (v. 4; cf. Num 22:5-6). This was to no avail as it turned out, for the Lord turned the curse into a blessing because of his love (i.e., his covenant favor) for Israel (v. 5; cf. Num 23:5-12,26; 24:13). Nevertheless, because of this attitude of hatred and belligerence by the Ammonites and Moabites toward Israel, they were to forever be precluded from the assembly (v. 3) and as nations were never to receive kind treatment at Israel's hands (v. 6). Subsequent history

---

[197] M. Fishbane, *Biblical Interpretation in Ancient Israel* (Oxford: Clarendon, 1985), 120-21. Fishbane notes that the context (22:30 and 23:3) is that of incestuous relationships.
[198] Keil and Delitzsch, *The Pentateuch,* 3:414: "Ten is the number of complete exclusion."

reveals how careful Israel was to keep this in mind (cf. Judg 10:7–11:33; 2 Sam 10:1-19; 2 Kgs 1:1; 3:4-27).

23:7-8 The list of those forbidden access to the assembly concludes with the Edomites and Egyptians, both of whom could enter it after only three generations.[199] There is clearly a pattern of progression in the list from the deformed individual who could never participate in corporate worship (v. 1); to the relatively innocent victim of incest or other improper sexual relationships and his descendants, who likewise were permanently barred (v. 2); to the Ammonite and Moabite, who, as individuals, could never enter though they could enjoy proselyte status (vv. 3-6); to the Edomite and Egyptian, whose period of "probation" was long but nonetheless finite (vv. 7-8). What is evident is increasing amelioration and acceptance.

Disbarment from the assembly was not synonymous with exclusion from the covenant community itself as the one example of Ruth the Moabite makes clear. Having determined to return with her Israelite mother-in-law to Bethlehem, she vowed: "Where you go I will go, and where you stay I will stay. Your people will be my people and your God my God" (Ruth 1:16). This was more than mere wishful thinking or personal resolve, for Ruth went on to marry a leading citizen of Bethlehem (4:13), and she eventually became a great-grandmother of King David (4:21). There can be no doubt that Ruth was welcomed among the people of the Lord as one of their own though presumably never with access to the assembly.

(9) Purity in Personal Hygiene (23:9-14)

[9]**When you are encamped against your enemies, keep away from everything impure. [10]If one of your men is unclean because of a nocturnal emission, he is to go outside the camp and stay there. [11]But as evening approaches he is to wash himself, and at sunset he may return to the camp.**

[12]**Designate a place outside the camp where you can go to relieve yourself. [13]As part of your equipment have something to dig with, and when you relieve yourself, dig a hole and cover up your excrement. [14]For the LORD your God moves about in your camp to protect you and to deliver your enemies to you. Your camp must be holy, so that he will not see among you anything indecent and turn away from you.**

---

[199] The Edomites were, of course, descended from Esau (Gen 36:9) and were therefore "full brothers" of Israel. The Egyptians, while hostile to Israel in the years just prior to the exodus, had provided safe and prosperous haven for Israel for centuries prior to that. Cf. Carmichael, *Law and Narrative in the Bible,* 231-34.

The topic of this stipulation rises, no doubt, from reference to both sexual deformity (v. 1) and interethnic hostility (vv. 4-6) in the previous section. The two are interwoven in the injunction to be pure in the camp when undertaking military activity. To illustrate what is meant, the text offers two examples.

23:9-11 First, there is the general injunction to guard against anything that is impure (lit., "evil," thus Heb. *rāʿ*, v. 9). Specific cases then follow, the one dealing with involuntary, unconscious circumstances and the other with more deliberate choices. The former presents the situation of a nocturnal seminal emission, which, though accidental and unplanned, still renders the man unclean. As such he must leave the encampment for the entire following day and return only after bathing himself by sundown (vv. 10-11).

The uncleanness is not fundamentally physical in nature but ritual, as the parallel teaching of Lev 15:16-18 makes clear.[200] There not only is the man himself rendered impure (Heb. *ṭāmēʾ*, synonymous with *lōʾ ṭāhōr* of Deut 23:10), but so are his clothes and any woman with whom he has come in sexual contact. The verb used (*ṭāmēʾ*) invariably refers to ritual disqualification whereas the adjective *ṭāhôr* (and its cognate verb *ṭāhēr*), used here in Deuteronomy, is an exact antonym made synonymous by the negative particle. The verb *ṭāhēr* occurs also in Lev 22:4 to speak of priests who, because of any kind of genital emission (*zôb*), become unclean. In all such cases ritual bathing is a necessary prerequisite to reentry into the community.

23:12-13 The second kind of contingency has to do with defecation, another form of emission. Inasmuch as there is usually forewarning in such circumstances, it must be done in a designated and prepared place outside the camp (v. 12). In fact, the soldier should include a digging tool with his regular field equipment so that he might bury the excrement (v. 13). There is no reference here to ritual bathing, for there is no ritual defilement if the procedure has been followed properly. Were the defecation to have taken place within the camp, proper cleansing would certainly have been required.

23:14 The rationale for the legislation in both kinds of impure practices lies in the fact that the Lord was there in the camp with his army, "moving about" (*mithallēk*) as its commander to bring deliverance and victory. This stem of the verb speaks of the Lord's intimacy with his people, his face-to-face encounter with them (cf. Gen 3:8) and desire to have

---

[200] See the enlightening and exhaustive discussion of the matter by Milgrom, *Leviticus 1–16*, 926-34.

fellowship with them (cf. Lev 26:12).[201] But even more than this, he is a holy God, one who demands holiness of his people (cf. Lev 19:1-2). Bodily emissions of the kind described here are of the most private and personal nature and must not be witnessed by others or cause them to become contaminated. In the language of the text they are "indecent" (v. 14), even for the eyes of the Lord.

The term "indecent" (Heb. *ʿerwat dābār*, lit., "nakedness of a thing") is a euphemistic periphrasis for the sexual organs themselves and, by extension, behavior involving the sexual organs. When Ham entered his drunken father Noah's tent, he saw his nakedness (*ʿerwat ʾabîw*), that is, his private parts (Gen 9:22-23).[202] The priests of Israel were warned not to ascend the altar by steps lest their nakedness (*ʿerwatkā*) be revealed (Exod 20:26). Especially shameful was the "uncovering of the nakedness" of any family member, an indecency correctly translated by the NIV as having "sexual relations" (cf. Lev 18:6-12,16-19; 20:11,17-21).

In conclusion, though the passage in no way suggests that bodily emissions (whether or not of a quasi-sexual kind) are in themselves inherently evil or even cultically impure, it does underscore the importance of a proper time and place for such things. The principle therefore seems to be in line with other stipulations concerning purity, namely, that God himself determines arbitrarily the very definition of what is acceptable and what is not. What is fundamentally important is that no "indecency" be done by the covenant people, for the Lord is offended by it and will turn himself away from them if they persist in its practice.

(10) Purity in Treatment of the Disadvantaged (23:15-16)

15If a slave has taken refuge with you, do not hand him over to his master. 16Let him live among you wherever he likes and in whatever town he chooses. Do not oppress him.

23:15-16 The location of this legislation in its present context has given rise to various opinions about its original placement. It appears, at first blush, to have little or nothing to do with the overall theme of 22:9–23:18—laws of purity—but by the principle of literary or topical association one can make a good case for the logic of its present position.[203]

---

[201] F. J. Helfmeyer, "הָלַךְ, halakh," *TDOT* 3:402.

[202] Driver, *Deuteronomy,* 264.

[203] Rofé suggests a verbal association between בְּשִׁבְתְּךָ חוּץ ("when you sit outside," v. 13) and יֵשֵׁב בְּקִרְבְּךָ ("he will sit in your midst," v. 16; "Arrangement of Laws in Deuteronomy," 273).

First, the previous pericope (vv. 9-14) deals with camp life in the pursuit of military affairs, a situation that could easily give rise to slaves escaping from the enemy. Second, this law and the next (vv. 17-18) provide a transition to the exposition of the commandment "You shall not steal" which follows next (23:19–24:7). As Kaufman points out, kidnapping was regarded as a most grave offense in ancient Near Eastern law in general, but failure to return a slave to his owner was not to be included under the rubric of theft in the covenant law of Deuteronomy.[204]

It is likely that this unusual treatment of escaped slaves belongs in a discussion of purity precisely because God's people, as a holy and distinct nation, must, as always, demonstrate that apartness in tangible ways. If it is customary for the heathen to repatriate slaves, Israel must not do so as an expression of the mercy and grace of its God.[205] Israel, after all, had been a slave nation whom the Lord had delivered from bondage, never to be returned to their Egyptian overlord. How appropriate that slaves of enemy nations be allowed free access to and refuge among the Lord's covenant people. In strongest terms the text insists, "Do not oppress him" (v. 16). The verb used here (*yānâ*) occurs elsewhere to speak of the merciful treatment of strangers (Exod 22:21) who must, in fact, be loved as one would love himself (Lev 19:34).[206]

(11) Purity in Cultic Personnel (23:17-18)

[17]No Israelite man or woman is to become a shrine prostitute. [18]You must not bring the earnings of a female prostitute or of a male prostitute into the house of the LORD your God to pay any vow, because the LORD your God detests them both.

23:17-18   The final law concerning purity not only graphically brings the whole collection of such legislation to a conclusion but provides a transition to the next section, that having to do with theft (23:21–24:7). This is implicit in the reference to paying vows to the Lord with illegitimate earnings (v. 18) and explicit in the connection between *keleb* ("dog"; "male prostitute") in v. 18 and *nāšak* (lit., "bite"; "charge interest") in v. 19.[207] The placement of this stipulation where it is gives every evidence

---

[204] Kaufman, "The Structure of the Deuteronomic Law," 138.

[205] The manumission of escaped slaves was a common and expected practice in the ancient Near Eastern world. The law here, then, was in stark contrast to that policy. See Weinfeld, *Deuteronomy and the Deuteronomic School,* 272-73.

[206] In context, יָנָה (here in the *hiphil*) suggests returning an escapee to his master and therefore to the state of bondage; thus H. Ringgren, "יָנָה *yānâ*," *TDOT* 6:105.

[207] Kaufman, "The Structure of the Deuteronomic Law," 139.

of careful literary and thematic design, contrary to those scholars who view this and other entries as consisting of miscellanea thrown together in a more or less hodgepodge manner.[208]

Though prostitution of any kind was regarded with contempt in ancient Israelite society and therefore as antithetical to covenant law and behavior (cf. Lev 19:29; 21:9; Deut 22:21), such practice in the name of religion was particularly reprehensible. So-called cultic prostitution was widespread among the fertility cults of the ancient Near Eastern world that saw in its employment a means of achieving productivity of plant, animal, and even human life.[209] Whole guilds of male and female temple personnel participated in grossly sexual rituals designed to induce the various gods and goddesses to release their procreative powers on the earth. Nowhere was this more commonly practiced than among the peoples of Syria and Canaan, hence the special need to warn Israel against it.

The technical terms used to describe such personnel set them and their activities off from "regular," noncultic prostitution. Here (and elsewhere; cf. Gen 38:21-22; 1 Kgs 14:24; 15:12; 22:47; 2 Kgs 23:7; Hos 4:14) they are called *qĕdēšâ* and *qādēš*, describing the female and male respectively.[210] No Israelite is permitted to become engaged in such abhorrent behavior (v. 17), nor may any earnings of prostitution in general be presented as an offering to the Lord (v. 18). In the latter category are the female prostitute (Heb. *zônâ*) and the male sodomite, disparagingly described here as a "dog" (Heb. *keleb*; NIV "male prostitute").[211] Though the vocabulary is not always mutually exclusive (that is, *zônâ* and its cognates may also refer to cultic prostitution; cf. Exod 34:15-16; Lev 17:7; 20:5), here there is a distinction between the prostitution of v. 17 and that

---

[208] Though Braulik dissociates Deut 23:15-25 from commandment seven, regarding it instead as the introduction to commandment eight, he does show the artistry of the composition, an artistry that can also be seen as providing a transition between the two commandments (*Die deuteronomischen Gesetze und der Dekalog*, 95-96):

  A   23:15-16 Human claims (with regard to the slave)
    B 23:17-18 Divine claims (fulfillment of a vow)
  A   23:19-20 Human claims (with regard to the brother and the stranger)
    B 23:21-23 Divine claims (fulfillment of a vow)
  A   23:24-25 Human claims (with regard to the neighbor).

[209] H. Ringgren, *Religions of the Ancient Near East* (Philadelphia: Westminster, 1973), 25-30, 163-65.

[210] W. F. Albright, *Archaeology and the Religion of Israel* (Garden City: Doubleday, 1969), 153-54.

[211] Driver, *Deuteronomy*, 265. For the view that "dog" may also be descriptive of the faithful follower of a deity, see D. W. Thomas, "*Kelebh*, 'Dog': Its Origin and Some Usages of It in the Old Testament," *VT* 10 (1960): 423-26.

of v. 18 as the phrase "both of them" (v. 18) makes clear.[212] The Lord considers both to be an abomination no matter how allegedly lofty the purpose for which it is being done.

4. Laws of Interpersonal Relationships (23:19–25:19)

(1) Respect for the Possessions of Another (23:19–24:7)

[19]Do not charge your brother interest, whether on money or food or anything else that may earn interest. [20]You may charge a foreigner interest, but not a brother Israelite, so that the LORD your God may bless you in everything you put your hand to in the land you are entering to possess.
[21]If you make a vow to the LORD your God, do not be slow to pay it, for the LORD your God will certainly demand it of you and you will be guilty of sin. [22]But if you refrain from making a vow, you will not be guilty. [23]Whatever your lips utter you must be sure to do, because you made your vow freely to the LORD your God with your own mouth.
[24]If you enter your neighbor's vineyard, you may eat all the grapes you want, but do not put any in your basket. [25]If you enter your neighbor's grainfield, you may pick kernels with your hands, but you must not put a sickle to his standing grain.

[1]If a man marries a woman who becomes displeasing to him because he finds something indecent about her, and he writes her a certificate of divorce, gives it to her and sends her from his house, [2]and if after she leaves his house she becomes the wife of another man, [3]and her second husband dislikes her and writes her a certificate of divorce, gives it to her and sends her from his house, or if he dies, [4]then her first husband, who divorced her, is not allowed to marry her again after she has been defiled. That would be detestable in the eyes of the LORD. Do not bring sin upon the land the LORD your God is giving you as an inheritance.
[5]If a man has recently married, he must not be sent to war or have any other duty laid on him. For one year he is to be free to stay at home and bring happiness to the wife he has married.
[6]Do not take a pair of millstones—not even the upper one—as security for a debt, because that would be taking a man's livelihood as security.
[7]If a man is caught kidnapping one of his brother Israelites and treats him as a slave or sells him, the kidnapper must die. You must purge the evil from among you.

There can be little doubt that this unit provides an extended commentary on the eighth commandment, "You shall not steal" (Deut 5:19). First

---

[212] Mayes, *Deuteronomy,* 320.

of all, 23:19-25 prohibits theft of property of any kind, whether it belongs to a kinsman (vv. 19-20), to the Lord (vv. 21-23), or to a neighbor (vv. 24-25). Then 24:6-7 forbids the stealing of another's "life," that is, his person (v. 7) or even his means of earning a living (v. 6). The apparently intrusive 24:1-5 is, as Kaufman argues, very much at home here inasmuch as the separation of the two millstones of v. 6 provides a most appropriate imagery for the separation of marriage partners by war or other duty (v. 5). The previous injunctions concerning divorce and remarriage (vv. 1-4) are also at home here since the phrase introducing them is identical in Hebrew to that introducing the regulation of v. 5: "If a man takes a [new] wife." Moreover, the idea of divorce may conceptually relate to the preceding prohibition against stealing the grain of one's neighbor (23:25), particularly in light of a husband's finding "something indecent" about his new bride (24:1).[213]

23:19-20 Theft of a fellow Israelite's property is limited here to requiring him to pay interest on whatever he might borrow, money or otherwise (v. 19). Such arrangements are acceptable where the foreigner is concerned (v. 20), but to exact penalties of a brother is to put the "bite" (so Heb. *nešek*, "interest," or *nāšak*, "pay interest") on him.[214] Proper treatment of a brother in such matters would ensure the blessing of God in the land of promise (v. 20). God himself gives freely and graciously, so why should his people profit from the misfortune of one another (cf. Lev 25:35-38)?

23:21-23 An example of stealing from the Lord is to make a vow to him and then to fail to pay it (v. 21). Such pledges were strictly voluntary (v. 22) but once made were obligatory (v. 23). The vow (*neder*) here was limited to the presentation of goods or property as the context makes clear, but vows could also be pledges of service (Gen 28:30; 31:13; Num 6:2,5,21; 1 Sam 1:11) or, more technically, part of the regular worship services of the tabernacle or temple (Num 15:8; 29:39; Deut 12:6,17; 1 Sam 1:21; Ps 66:13). A lesson to be learned here surely is that one must be careful not to make rash or unthinking promises to God (cf. Jephthah's

---

[213] Kaufman, "The Structure of the Deuteronomic Law," 140. Rofé offers still more associations binding the section together, especially the sexual innuendoes of "grinding" (24:6) in the context of the "divorce law" (vv. 1-4) and the law allowing the military recruit deferment so that he might "bring happiness to the wife he has married" ("The Arrangement of the Laws in Deuteronomy," 274-75).

[214] Cf. H. Gamoran, "The Biblical Law against Loans on Interest," *JNES* 30 (1971): 127-34; E. Neufeld, "The Prohibitions against Loans at Interest in Ancient Hebrew Law," *HUCA* 26 (1955): 355-412.

vow in Judg 11), but having made them he must be committed to carrying them out. To fail to do so is to be guilty of theft (cf. Matt 5:33).[215]

23:24-25 Finally, the property of the neighbor is also inviolable but with a most interesting qualification. If one merely passed through his neighbor's vineyards or fields (presumably as a shortcut or for similar casual reasons), he could help himself to the produce short of harvesting it in any manner. If he entered with a harvest basket or a sickle, his intentions obviously were to steal and so he stood condemned for theft. The allowance for the passerby was, no doubt, to create an atmosphere of general grace and hospitality and to provide practical aid for the traveler who, in those ancient days, might not be able to carry sufficient food supplies for a long journey and who would have no way of preserving certain foodstuffs from spoilage. The practice prevailed on into New Testament times as is seen in the incident of Jesus' disciples who passed through a certain grainfield and helped themselves to some stalks (Matt 12:1-8; cf. Mark 2:23-28; Luke 6:1-5). The Pharisees became most upset at the disciples but not because of the act itself. What troubled them was that Jesus and his friends were walking through the fields on the Sabbath and, furthermore, were working on the holy day by crushing the heads of grain in their hands![216]

24:1-4 The law turns next to matters of divorce and remarriage (24:1-4), a topic much at home in the larger context of respect for property and personal rights.[217] The issue here specifically is that of a man who, having married, becomes displeased with his wife (lit., "she finds no favor in his sight") because "he finds something indecent about her" (v. 1). Under such circumstances he may divorce her, thus freeing her to marry again; but if her second husband also divorces her, she may not come back and remarry the first husband. She would have become "defiled" (Heb. *huṭṭammāʾâ*) in the process and such remarriage would be "detestable" to the Lord (v. 4).

The legislation here neither commands nor condones divorce in general but only regulates its practice for ancient Israel. Jesus, in fact, cited

---

[215] For illustrations of this principle in the vows of Jacob and Jephthah, see Carmichael, *Law and Narrative in the Bible,* 246-50; cf. L. J. Coppes, "נָדַר (*nadar*) make a vow," *TWOT* 2:557-58.

[216] Reaping was "one of thirty-nine activities specifically forbidden on the Sabbath [according to the Mishna]" (Blomberg, *Matthew,* 196).

[217] The syntax of vv.1-4 is clear: in vv. 1-3 is the protasis, hence a hypothetical scenario, and in v. 4 is the apodosis, the command or prohibition. For an excellent, comprehensive review of biblical teaching on the matter of divorce and remarriage see W. A. Heth and G. J. Wenham, *Jesus and Divorce* (Nashville: Thomas Nelson, 1985).

this text and restricted its application to divorce only for reasons of "marital unfaithfulness" (Gr. *porneia;*[218] Matt 5:31-32; 19:7-9). It is important to note also that the "exception clause" in Matt 19 follows Jesus' teaching that the ideal is no divorce at all, for "what God has joined together, let man not separate" (Matt 19:6).

This use of our text by Jesus suggests that in his view the "something indecent" had to do with marital unfaithfulness, specifically adultery, for this is the only exception Jesus allowed and, apparently, the only one he addressed in his use of the Deuteronomy stipulation.[219] The same issue is at stake in Deut 22:13-21 (cf. Num 5), though there the unfaithfulness is alleged of a woman who sinned when she had not yet fully married. In ancient Israel this little mattered because betrothal was in itself tantamount to marriage.

The major difficulty in the passage at hand is that the point of contention is described not explicitly as adultery but as *ʿerwat dābār* ("something indecent about her"; lit., "the nakedness of a thing"). The noun *ʿerwa* bears the meaning of both "nakedness" or "pudenda" (i.e., the sexual organs), meanings no doubt to be combined here to suggest the improper uncovering of the private parts. Clearly this circumlocution is to be understood as a euphemism that may or may not include adultery (cf. Lev 18:6-18; 20:11,17,20-21; Ezek 22:10; 23:29; Hos 2:10), but not in this case.[220]

Once the facts of the case had been ascertained and guilt established, the husband was free to pursue divorce proceedings. These consisted of his writing, with respect to his wife, a "certificate of divorce" (Heb. *sēper kĕrîtut*, lit., "a writing of cutting off"), placing it in her hand as a public symbolic witness to the dissolution of the relationship, and sending her "from his house" (i.e., from the family circle and all that that entails). She had thus been cut off and driven away from home and family, a punishment laden with indescribable shame and incalculable economic and social loss in that ancient Israelite world. The regular nominative term for

---

[218] BAGD, 693: "Of every kind of unlawful sexual intercourse," but specifically in Matt 19:9, "Of the sexual unfaithfulness of a married woman."

[219] Blomberg, *Matthew,* 292. See also C. L. Blomberg, "Marriage, Divorce and Celibacy: An Exegesis of Matthew 19:3-12," *TrinJ* n.s. 11 (1990): 161-96.

[220] Thus Driver, who, with most scholars, argues that something "short of actual unchastity" must be in mind since the latter required the death penalty (cf. Deut 22:22; 23:14; *Deuteronomy,* 271). It is difficult to limit the עֶרְוַת דָּבָר to anything less than adultery, however, in Jesus' use of the term *porneia* and, indeed, of the very passage here as a basis for allowing divorce. It is likely that עֶרְוַת דָּבָר is a phrase broad enough to include adultery but not synonymous with it.

"divorce" (*šallaḥ*, piel inf. cst. of *šālaḥ*) does not occur here (cf. Mal 2:16), though the cognate verb (*šālaḥ*) does, translated here "sends" (cf. Deut 22:19,29). The intensity of the husband's action here is seen in the combination of the verb for divorce and the certificate that attests to it, a juxtaposition of terms that occurs elsewhere only in Isa 50:1 and Jer 3:8.[221]

The hypothetical case of a man divorcing his wife for infidelity continues with a hypothetical remarriage of that wife to another man (v. 2). The grammatical evidence from the sequence of clauses (*ki* + *waw* conjunctive) does not demand that remarriage here be necessarily sanctioned just because divorce was allowed in the first place. That is, the entire stipulation of vv. 1-4 pertains to the regulation of the marriage relationship given the realities of sinful human behavior. Divorce for finding "something indecent" in one's wife is permitted (cf. Matt 5:32; 19:9), but it does not follow that remarriage of either partner is allowed. In fact, even this passage explicitly forbids remarriage between the divorced parties, and Jesus categorically precluded marriage by anyone to the woman who had been divorced because of adultery (Matt 5:32b).[222]

The Deuteronomic legislation does not rise to this high level inasmuch as it does not categorically prohibit the remarriage of the divorced woman, but neither does it condone such a thing. It is content to regulate what was clearly a widespread practice, yet within certain narrow parameters. Thus if the disgraced woman married again and her second husband "dislike[d] her" and publicly divorced her or died (v. 3), she could not remarry her original husband (v. 4) for she had now become "defiled" (*huṭṭammāʾâ*) and would be "detestable" (*tôʿēbâ*) to the Lord. Why the remarriage of the original partners was thus described while the divorcée's marriage to a second husband was not is not clear. Most likely it is because the original divorce was not for adultery (otherwise the death penalty would apply) whereas remarriage after an intervening marriage and divorce would be construed as adultery because of the woman's moving from one man to the next and back again.[223] She had thus become an adulteress, and for this reason it was she (and not the act) who was referred to as detestable (*tôʿēbâ hîw*, v. 4).

---

[221] T. R. Hobbs, "Jeremiah 3:1-5 and Deuteronomy 24:1-4," *ZAW* 86 (1974): 23-29.

[222] Heth and Wenham, *Jesus and Divorce,* 113-20; D. A. Carson, *The Sermon on the Mount: An Evangelical Exposition of Matthew 5–7* (Grand Rapids: Baker, 1978), 46.

[223] Craigie, *Deuteronomy,* 305. See G. J. Wenham, "The Restoration of Marriage Reconsidered," *JJS* 30 (1979): 36-40.

24:5 The next stipulation, that having to do with the newlywed (v. 5), is linked to the previous one, as already noted, by the identical opening protasis, "If a man marries a woman" (cf. v. 1). The law here has to do with the exemption of a husband, recently married, from military service or other compulsory duty. In line with the overall pericope of 23:19–24:7, this gracious provision was to safeguard possessions, in this case the "possession" of a husband by his wife.[224] Were he to go to war and lose his life, he obviously would have been "stolen" from her; indeed, even a protracted absence from one another could have been construed as theft, especially in the beginning days of marriage. Time together was a precious thing, too precious to be taken by government even in times of war.

A similar restriction appears in the "War Manual" of Deut 20, the difference there being that the couple had not yet married but only undertaken betrothal (v. 7). There the fear was that the man's death would preclude his raising up offspring in his name whereas here the happiness (*śimḥâ*) of his wife was at stake. Also the period of exemption for the newlyweds was one year whereas that of the betrothed was not stated. A one-year stay at home would afford joy to the couple in their new relationship and would also normally be sufficient time for a child to be conceived and born before the husband went off to serve.

24:6-7 Finally, the law turns to the matter of stealing life itself, in terms either of the means of sustaining it (v. 6) or of kidnapping for slavery or sale (v. 7). As for the former, the theft consisted of the taking of a pair of millstones—or even one, the upper—as security on a loan even if there is the intention to restore them. The reason is that such equipment was absolutely essential to survival itself.[225] This did not preclude the taking of any kind of deposit, for elsewhere such provision was made (cf. Exod 22:25-27; Deut 24:10-13; Ezek 18:16; Amos 2:8), but it did limit the kinds of objects that could be demanded in pledge.

Even worse, of course, was kidnapping for the purpose of enslavement or selling into slavery, especially when the victim is a fellow Israelite. Such practices were widespread in the ancient Near East and possibly even in Israel.[226] At the very least prisoners of war could be enslaved against their will (cf. Deut 20:11; 21:10-14), though nowhere is there regulation about their being bought or sold. Exodus 21:16 would appear to prohibit kidnapping of anyone for the purpose of selling him, but the con-

---

[224] Braulik, *Die deuteronomischen Gesetze und der Dekalog*, 98.

[225] Carmichael, *Law and Narrative in the Bible*, 259.

[226] S. Paul, *Studies in the Book of the Covenant in the Light of Cuneiform and Biblical Law* (Leiden: Brill, 1970), 65-66.

text would favor the limitation of this to fellow Israelites as here in Deuteronomy.

In any case, such theft of persons was so dastardly a violation of covenant that the perpetrator had to pay with his own life. As with murder or any such assault upon another, the heinousness of the deed lay in its victimizing of one who was the very image of God (cf. Gen 9:6; Deut 5:17). To steal a fellow member of the covenant community was, in effect, to rob God of his most precious possession, a human life. Respect for possessions of another thus reaches its climax in respect for another's life and independence before God.

(2) Respect for the Dignity of Another (24:8–25:4)

[8]In cases of leprous diseases be very careful to do exactly as the priests, who are Levites, instruct you. You must follow carefully what I have commanded them. [9]Remember what the LORD your God did to Miriam along the way after you came out of Egypt.

[10]When you make a loan of any kind to your neighbor, do not go into his house to get what he is offering as a pledge. [11]Stay outside and let the man to whom you are making the loan bring the pledge out to you. [12]If the man is poor, do not go to sleep with his pledge in your possession. [13]Return his cloak to him by sunset so that he may sleep in it. Then he will thank you, and it will be regarded as a righteous act in the sight of the LORD your God.

[14]Do not take advantage of a hired man who is poor and needy, whether he is a brother Israelite or an alien living in one of your towns. [15]Pay him his wages each day before sunset, because he is poor and is counting on it. Otherwise he may cry to the LORD against you, and you will be guilty of sin.

[16]Fathers shall not be put to death for their children, nor children put to death for their fathers; each is to die for his own sin.

[17]Do not deprive the alien or the fatherless of justice, or take the cloak of the widow as a pledge. [18]Remember that you were slaves in Egypt and the LORD your God redeemed you from there. That is why I command you to do this.

[19]When you are harvesting in your field and you overlook a sheaf, do not go back to get it. Leave it for the alien, the fatherless and the widow, so that the LORD your God may bless you in all the work of your hands. [20]When you beat the olives from your trees, do not go over the branches a second time. Leave what remains for the alien, the fatherless and the widow. [21]When you harvest the grapes in your vineyard, do not go over the vines again. Leave what remains for the alien, the fatherless and the widow. [22]Remember that you were slaves in Egypt. That is why I command you to do this.

[1]When men have a dispute, they are to take it to court and the judges will decide the case, acquitting the innocent and condemning the guilty. [2]If the

guilty man deserves to be beaten, the judge shall make him lie down and have him flogged in his presence with the number of lashes his crime deserves, ³but he must not give him more than forty lashes. If he is flogged more than that, your brother will be degraded in your eyes.

⁴Do not muzzle an ox while it is treading out the grain.

According to the analysis of the stipulation section of Deuteronomy that views it as an extended commentary on the several commandments, this section provides an explication and application of the ninth commandment, that which prohibits false testimony against one's neighbor (Deut 5:20). Kaufman again is most helpful in establishing the connections between the commandment and this series of case laws based on it. He sees a descending order of hierarchy in the list of offended parties with Moses, as paradigmatic leader, listed first (24:8-9), followed by the nonpoor debtor (24:10-13), the poor debtor (24:14-15), the indigent (24:17-22), the criminal (25:1-3), and even the animal (25:4). Verse 16 serves as both the focal point of the whole section and as the introduction to the legislation regarding justice in punishment (24:17–25:3).[227]

24:8-9 The unexpected reference to leprosy (v. 8) is clarified by the allusion to Miriam, Moses' sister, who, when she misrepresented and slandered her brother, was struck with leprosy (Num 12:1-15).[228] The instruction here then serves a double purpose: (1) to prescribe treatment of those who contracted leprosy by placing them under the care of the Levites (cf. Lev 13:1-14) and (2) to warn against usurpation of divinely authorized leadership, particularly by bearing false witness. Moses was unmistakably in view here as the theocratic administrator, but he represented any leader of the community, including the Levitical priests to whom the leper submitted himself for treatment. To speak evil against such leadership was to challenge the sovereignty of God himself and thus to invite his swift and sure retribution.

24:10-13 The elasticity of the application of covenant mandate is apparent in the connection between the commandment forbidding false testimony and the case here of the borrower whose pledge may not have been forcibly exacted from him. The matter of loans and pledges has already been addressed (23:19-20; 24:6; cf. Exod 22:25-26; Lev 25:35-37), but the issue here was the integrity and dignity of the person who had

---

[227] Kaufman, "The Structure of the Deuteronomic Law," 141-42.

[228] Rofé explains the present location of the leprosy law by thematic association, namely, the exclusion of both the creditor (v. 10) and the leper from one's house ("The Arrangement of the Laws in Deuteronomy," 275). Though this makes a case for a loose linkage, Kaufman's analysis is more convincing in terms of the larger context.

been forced by circumstances to borrow from his neighbor. Out of respect for the debtor, the creditor was not to go into the debtor's house to demand the item being offered as a pledge of payment. Rather, he was to honor him enough to allow him to take the initiative to render the pledge (v. 11). If the debtor was so poor that he had to pledge his cloak, it was to be returned to him at night so he would have something to cover himself with against the cold (v. 12; cf. Exod 22:26-27). To do such a thing would be regarded as a "righteous act" (Heb. *ṣĕdāqâ*) before the Lord; that is, it was a deed that conformed with covenant expectations and norms.[229]

24:14-15 The "neighbor" of this section was clearly a fellow Israelite as the context and parallel passages (cf. Exod 22:25; Lev 25:35) attest, but the subject of the next case—that of the poor hired man—may have been an Israelite or a foreigner (Deut 24:14-15).[230] His plight was so serious that he lived from hand to mouth or from day to day. He therefore was to be paid his wages daily so that he could put food on the table. The fact that he was "only a hireling" (Heb. *śākîr*), a person of a lower socio-economic status, was no excuse to deny him his rights.[231] In fact, he enjoyed such status with God that he could and might cry out to the Lord against the stingy, dishonest employer and thus invoke God's verdict of guilt (v. 15). Again the matter of the poverty stricken has previously been addressed in the context of rendering tribute to the Lord (cf. Deut 15:7-18),[232] but here the focus is on human dignity, even of the poorest of the people. To view the poor as inferior or as easy victims of oppressive manipulation is to slander them, for they, like anyone else, are created as the image of God.

24:16 The supreme worth of the individual (as well as his responsibility before God) is seen in his accountability as a sinner (v. 16). The notion of Israel as a community, as almost a corporate personality, was pervasive throughout the Old Testament but never at the expense of the

---

[229] At this point Braulik observes a further linkage of technical terminology that suggests a unity of vv. 13-17 (*Die deuteronomischen Gesetze und der Dekalog*, 103):

A   צְדָקָה, "righteousness before yhwh" (v. 13) —divine law

  B   חֵטְא, "sin" (v. 15) — divine law

  B′ חֵטְא, "crime" (v. 16) — human law

A′ מִשְׁפָּט, "justice" (v. 17) — human law.

[230] Carmichael, *Law and Narrative in the Bible*, 269-70. The illustrative narrative to which Carmichael appeals is that of Laban and Jacob. "The shrewd Laban," he observes, "ostensibly paying [Jacob] wages as a mark of filial kindness (Gen 29:15), is in effect treating him as a hired servant." Moreover, "in his position as an employer he cheated him in the paying of his hire."

[231] For this social class see de Vaux, *Ancient Israel*, 1:7b.

[232] Hamilton, *Social Justice and Deuteronomy*, 127-31.

solitary person. Admittedly, the emphasis on the individual's personal standing before God is more highly developed in later Old Testament revelation (cf. Jer 31:29-30; Ezek 18:20), so much so that its appearance in Deuteronomy was often cited as a mark of Deuteronomy's lateness.[233] But there is no reason to deny such a concept in Mosaic times. In fact, the use of the singular pronoun throughout the Deuteronomic covenant text suggests the highly personal and individualized application of the covenant requirements. Moreover, this very precept was appealed to in later times to justify the sparing of the innocent when judgment was being meted out to their guilty relatives (cf. 2 Kgs 14:5-6; 2 Chr 25:3-4). In terms of the ninth commandment, the point to be made here is that the punishment of the innocent along with the guilty would constitute false witnessing of the most horrendous kind.

24:17-18 Continuing on a descending scale, the law next addresses the worth of the most helpless of Israel's society, the aliens, orphans, and widows (vv. 17-22). Just as the innocent in general were to be protected from miscarriage of justice (v. 16), even more so were these especially needy ones. The alien (*gēr*), as a non-Israelite, would tend to be barred from many of the privileges of Israelite community and worship life by social custom, but the law everywhere accorded him full participation provided he became part of the community by circumcision and other rites of membership (Exod 12:48-49; cf. 22:21; 23:9; Lev 17:8-16; 24:22; Num 15:14-16). As such a member he was to be accorded evenhanded justice along with the orphan, for neither enjoyed the protection of normal family or tribal affiliation. The widow also was especially vulnerable, prone no doubt to constant indebtedness. In such circumstances not even her clothing could be taken as a pledge, suggesting, perhaps, that loans to her were to be made without collateral of any kind.[234] This would, in effect, have become more a gift than a loan because her opportunities for repayment would have been extremely limited depending on her age and physical capacity and the like. The mercy to be extended to her as well as to the alien and orphan was a reflex of the mercy of God, who in a mighty act of redemptive and protective grace brought helpless Israel out from Egyptian bondage (v. 18; cf. 5:15; 6:12,21; 8:14; 10:19; 15:15). Memory of the Lord's goodness to them should have evoked corresponding blessings from them to the weakest members of the community.

---

[233] Thus, e.g., W. O. E. Oesterley and T. H. Robinson, *An Introduction to the Books of the Old Testament* (London: Society for Promoting Christian Knowledge, 1934), 43-45.

[234] Carmichael cites the example of Judah, who took advantage of his widowed daughter-in-law, Tamar (Gen 38:14-26; *Law and Narrative in the Bible,* 281-82).

24:19-22   Practical ways of doing this and at the same time protecting the dignity of the persons involved are outlined in vv. 19-22. When harvest time came, care was to be taken not to pick the fields, orchards, or vineyards clean but to leave behind any residue that might at first have been overlooked (v. 19). The alien, orphan, and widow then were to be allowed to gather up what remained as a means of sustaining themselves by their own labors. The largess was thus not an outright gift but a benefit to be gained by the initiative and industry of the needy person as well as the benefactor. This permitted the recipient to salvage his own honor while at the same time delivering the landowner from any sense of arrogant control over the lives of those dependent on him. In a loose manner, at least, the ninth commandment was thereby adhered to because the reputation of the disadvantaged was left intact by those who otherwise might have undermined it by any overly patronizing manner.

The story of Boaz and Ruth provides a later application of this principle.[235] Ruth was fully aware of her right as an alien and a widow to glean from the fields of anyone with whom she found favor (Ruth 2:2). This suggests that not everyone in Bethlehem would have been inclined to allow her to do so, certainly not without permission at least. Boaz not only gave such permission to Ruth (and to many others, v. 4) but commanded his reapers to leave even the sheaves behind so that Ruth could have more than leftovers (vv. 15-16). The narrative thus provides an example of the actual application of covenant prescription to life in the land. Ruth was a Moabite, a foreigner in Israel, just as Israel had been a foreigner in Egypt. So as never to forget the Lord's gracious deliverance of his people from enslavement, they in turn were to deliver the weakest among them from social and economic bondage.

25:1-3   A remarkable feature of Old Testament society was the protection of even the criminal.[236] His guilt must first be determined by the evidence and in a court of law and then the appropriate punishment administered. In the case in view here—surely just an example out of many that could have been adduced—men who had a dispute (*rîb*) had to take the matter to court for adjudication. If the nature of the offense was such as to require flogging (that is, the man was *bin hakkôt,* "worthy of flogging"), the convicted person was to be laid prostrate on the ground and beaten with as many strokes as his particular offense deserved (*kĕdê riš*ⁿ*ātô,* lit., "according to the sufficiency of his wickedness"). This sug-

---

[235] E. F. Campbell, Jr., *Ruth,* AB (Garden City: Doubleday, 1975), 111-12.

[236] Phillips notes that the ordinary penalty for breach of criminal law was death but that "discretionary powers" were also given to judges to allow flogging (*Deuteronomy,* 166-67).

gests the principle of the punishment fitting the crime.[237] In any event the beating was not to exceed forty strokes (v. 3).[238] Any infraction of the law punishable by flogging was not serious enough to warrant more than this limit of retribution. Thus the justice of law was tempered by mercy.

To exceed forty blows would have shown dishonor or contempt for one's brother, to hold him in little esteem. Again in a broad sense this was an infraction of the ninth commandment, for to bring a brother into unwarranted shame or ignominy was to testify (falsely) against him by making him appear to be something less than he really was, namely, a fellow citizen of the covenant community. His sinful conduct against a brother was not sufficient cause to rob him of his full dignity.[239]

25:4 Finally, the very lowest creatures on the "social" scale, the animals themselves, fell under the protection of the Lord and the covenant.[240] Man had been created to have dominion over all things (Gen 1:26-28; Ps 8), but even after his fall and the consequent alienation that had developed between him and all creation, including the animal world (Gen 9:2), he was not to exploit nature but live in harmony with it (Gen 9:3-10). The prohibition here (Deut 25:4) about muzzling the working ox reflects the spirit of mercy that pervades all of God's dealings with his creation, human or otherwise.[241] The purpose clearly was not only to provide for the ox itself but to make the point by *a fortiori* argument that if a mere animal was worthy of humane treatment, how much more so was a human being created as the image of God. Paul, in fact, cited this very

---

[237] Driver, *Deuteronomy,* 279.

[238] By NT times the maximum blows were thirty-nine, a total designed, no doubt, to ensure that the OT law would not be exceeded by mistake (cf. 2 Cor 11:24). The Mishna (*Mak.* 3:10) supports the NT tradition by taking the phrase בְּמִסְפָּר אַרְבָּעִים ("by number forty," vv. 2b-3a) to mean "close to forty," a view shared by Josephus (*Ant.* 4.8.23) and Maimonides. See H. L. Strack, *Introduction to the Talmud and Midrash* (New York: Atheneum, 1976), 51, 261.

[239] As Thompson suggests, "Excessive beating would humiliate a man to the level of a beast and thus his dignity would be offended" (*Deuteronomy,* 249).

[240] Cf. G. Lisowsky, "Dtn 25, 4" in *Das ferne und nahe Worte. Festschrift Leonhard Rost,* ed. F. Maass, BZAW 105 (Berlin: A. Topelmann, 1967), 144-52; J. T. Noonan, "The Muzzled Ox," *JQR* 70 (1980): 172-75.

[241] Carmichael offers the intriguing idea that a figurative sense is intended since it would be impossible for an ox to work while unmuzzled. His connection with this to the "lost sheaf" of 24:19 and, in turn, with the levirate practice of Gen 38 seems a little far-fetched, however. Then, on the basis of this supposition, he suggests that whipping would be needed to keep the animal to its task, an act falling far short of humaneness (*Law and Narrative in the Bible,* 292-94).

text twice in making a plea for the support of those involved in Christian ministry (1 Cor 9:9-14; 1 Tim 5:17-18).[242]

Such concern for animals should not be construed as adherence to some kind of notion of pantheism, "world soul," evolutionism, or the like. The animal is nowhere "brother to the man" in Scripture but always sharply distinguished from humans. Nevertheless, the animal world, like all nature, is part of the divine creation entrusted to humankind as a stewardship. To abuse animal life is to fail to discharge that stewardship, and to fail to show mercy to God's lowest creatures is to open the door to disregard of human life as well.

(3) Respect for the Sanctity of Another (25:5-16)

⁵If brothers are living together and one of them dies without a son, his widow must not marry outside the family. Her husband's brother shall take her and marry her and fulfill the duty of a brother-in-law to her. ⁶The first son she bears shall carry on the name of the dead brother so that his name will not be blotted out from Israel.

⁷However, if a man does not want to marry his brother's wife, she shall go to the elders at the town gate and say, "My husband's brother refuses to carry on his brother's name in Israel. He will not fulfill the duty of a brother-in-law to me." ⁸Then the elders of his town shall summon him and talk to him. If he persists in saying, "I do not want to marry her," ⁹his brother's widow shall go up to him in the presence of the elders, take off one of his sandals, spit in his face and say, "This is what is done to the man who will not build up his brother's family line." ¹⁰That man's line shall be known in Israel as The Family of the Unsandaled.

¹¹If two men are fighting and the wife of one of them comes to rescue her husband from his assailant, and she reaches out and seizes him by his private parts, ¹²you shall cut off her hand. Show her no pity.

¹³Do not have two differing weights in your bag—one heavy, one light. ¹⁴Do not have two differing measures in your house—one large, one small. ¹⁵You must have accurate and honest weights and measures, so that you may live long in the land the LORD your God is giving you. ¹⁶For the LORD your God detests anyone who does these things, anyone who deals dishonestly.

Continuing the analysis pursued throughout this section, the present pericope is construed as a comment on the tenth commandment, that prohibiting coveting (Deut 5:21).[243] This assumes the unity of the last commandment and the division of Deut 5:7-10 into two commandments (the

---

[242] W. C. Kaiser, Jr. "The Current Crisis in Exegesis and the Apostolic Use of Deuteronomy 25:4 in I Corinthians 9:8-10," *JETS* 21 (1978): 3-18 (esp. pp. 11-16).
[243] Kaufman, "The Structure of the Deuteronomic Law," 142-44.

assertion of the sole worship of the Lord, v. 7, and the prohibition of idolatry, vv. 8-10), a point argued earlier. Moreover, "comment" must not be pressed too rigidly, for the subject matter of these verses is not so much an exposition of the tenth commandment as it is a set of stipulations springing from it.[244]

The passage consists of three topics—(1) the implementation of the "levirate" law (vv. 5-10), (2) improper defense of a man by his wife (vv. 11-12), and (3) the possession of dishonest weights and measures (vv. 13-16). While it is difficult to see how all (or any) of these fall under the category of coveting, they do share in common the matter of "interior behavior," that is, the life of desire or intention as opposed to deed.

25:5-6 The first part of the tenth commandment—"You shall not covet your neighbor's wife"—gives rise here to the matter of a man who had died without male offspring to carry on the family name. The case was qualified by describing the man as living among brothers (*'aḥîm*), not neighbors in general as in the commandment. Furthermore, the issue was not coveting another's wife but, to the contrary, the establishment of an exception to the law that one could not have his neighbor's wife, in this instance the widow of his very own brother.

Modern scholarship refers to the practice in view as "levirate [from Latin *levir*, "brother-in-law"] marriage," for it not only allowed but prescribed that a widow whose deceased husband had died without male heir marry one of his brothers, presumably the next eldest one who was himself unmarried.[245] The first son born of that relationship would take the name of the first husband, thus assuring the latter of an ongoing remembrance by the community. For this reason the widow was to marry within the family (lit., "not to the outside, to a stranger").

Though this is the only place in the Old Testament where the levirate custom was mandated,[246] the story of Ruth provides a narrative account of it in the view of many scholars.[247] They point out that Ruth had been

---

[244] Walton, "Deuteronomy: An Exposition of the Spirit of the Law," 225.

[245] E. W. Davies, "Inheritance Rights and the Hebrew Levirate Marriage," *VT* 31 (1981): 257-68; D. W. Manor, "A Brief History of Levirate Marriage as It Relates to the Bible," *Near East Archaeological Society Bulletin* (NS) 20 (1982): 33-52.

[246] It was known, however, throughout the ancient Near East; see especially S. Belkin, "Levirate and Agnate Marriage in Rabbinic and Cognate Literature," *JQR* 60 (1970): 284-87, 321-22; M. Ichisar, "Un Contrat de Mariage et la Question du Lévirat à l'Époque Cappadocienne," *RA* 7 6 (1982): 168-73; A. Puukko, "Die Leviratsche in den Altorientalischen Gesetzen," *ArOr* 17 (1949): 296-99.

[247] See especially E. F. Campbell, Jr., *Ruth*, AB (Garden City: Doubleday, 1975) 132-33; E. W. Davies, "Inheritance Rights and the Hebrew Levirate Marriage," *VT* 31 (1982): 257-68;

widowed (1:5) and, having gone to Bethlehem with her mother-in-law, Naomi, met there a kinsman of her dead husband, Boaz by name, who brought her under his protection (2:8). For the sake both of material provision and of perpetuating the name of her husband, Ruth, with Naomi's guidance, approached Boaz about his responsibility as a *levir* only to learn that there was another man more closely related and thus more eligible to discharge this duty (3:12). This one declined (4:6), and thus Boaz was free to take Ruth as wife. The child born to them, Obed, grandfather of David (4:17), presumably carried on the name of Ruth's first husband, Chilion.

This story accords with many of the specifications of the present stipulation. In many other respects it is greatly different, however. R. Gordis has noted that Deuteronomy speaks of brothers living together, whereas Boaz was a distant relative; that Deuteronomy makes no reference to the transfer of property; that there is stigma in Deuteronomy if the *levir* failed to discharge his responsibility (lacking in Ruth); and that the role of the woman in the ritual of the removal of the sandal was different in the two accounts. In addition to the major differences he lists many others of a less persuasive nature.[248]

25:7-10   The Deuteronomic law was moreover more comprehensive in its viewpoint in that it did not allow for mitigating circumstances that might preclude ordinary implementation of the levirate law. Instead, it declared that a widow whose brother-in-law refused to fulfill his fraternal duty was to be publicly accused of such (v. 7), and if he persisted in his refusal despite the counsel of the town elders, the widow was to take his sandal in her hand, spit in his face, and curse him with the opprobrium of an unfaithful brother, one whose own offspring would be known as "The Family of the Unsandaled" (vv. 8-9).[249]

The sandal, again, represented forfeiture by the derelict brother of any claims he might have had to his departed brother's estate. The act of spitting displays the utmost disdain or contempt.[250] In the only other instance

---

P. Joüon, *Ruth: Commentatire philologique et exégétique* (Rome: Pontifical Biblical Institute, 1953), 9; D. A. Leggett, *The Levirate and Goel Institutions in the Old Testament with Special Attention to the Book of Ruth* (Cherry Hill, N.J.: Mack, 1974), 289-91.

[248] R. Gordis, "Love, Marriage, and Business in the Book of Ruth," in *A Light unto My Path*, ed. H. N. Bream et al. (Philadelphia: Temple University Press, 1974), 246-52. See also J. Sasson, "The Issue of Geʾullah in Ruth," *JSOT* 5 (1978): 52-64; R. L. Hubbard, Jr., *The Book of Ruth*, NICOT (Grand Rapids: Eerdmans, 1988), 56-62.

[249] For the practice and its meaning see C. M. Carmichael, "A Ceremonial Crux: Removing a Man's Sandal as a Female Gesture of Contempt," *JBL* 96 (1977): 321-36; E. A. Speiser, "Of Shoes and Shekels," *BASOR* 77 (1940): 15-20.

[250] D. Kellermann, "יָרַק yāraq" etc., *TDOT* 6:362-63.

in her face (Num 12:14). If so, how much worse that she had contracted leprosy because of her insolence toward Moses. The same sense of disgust is communicated by the terms *tûp* (Job 17:6) and *rōq* (Job 30:10; Isa 50:6). The levirate duty might not have been mandatory, but it certainly was expected.

25:11-12 Commentators are generally at a loss to account for the placement of the next case in its present juxtaposition. The clue seems to lie in the reference to two men and one woman in both this and the previous section (vv. 5-10) as well as in the matter of progeny and anything that might threaten it.[251] The situation was that of two men in a brawl, the wife of one of whom comes to her husband's assistance by attacking his foe in his "private parts" (*mĕbušayw ʿbôš*, "be ashamed").[252] Besides the shame of this, especially in the ancient Eastern world,[253] there was the real possibility that the woman could effectively have emasculated her victim so as to remove any hope of his siring children. This, of course, would have rendered his plight nearly as serious as that of the brother mentioned above who died with no male heir.[254] That this was the implication is supported by the fact that the guilty woman had to lose her offending hand as punishment (v. 12).

25:13-16 The internal aspect of Old Testament law is best reflected in the tenth commandment with its focus on coveting, for coveting is not an act but an attitude. As such it clearly is most difficult to regulate, for who but God can even know it exists in another unless the coveting gives way to active deed? The present case law does, however, bridge the gap between intention and performance to some extent by dealing with temptation as the means of access to improper behavior. That is, coveting may be unavoidable, but its likelihood of finding expression in theft or other outward manifestation is lessened if the means of such expression is itself minimized.

---

[251] Thus Kaufman, "The Structure of the Deuteronomic Law," 143. Rofé observes that vv. 5 and 11 begin with similar formulae: כִּי־יֵשְׁבוּ אַחִים יַחְדָּו and כִּי־יִנָּצוּ אֲנָשִׁים יַחְדָּו respectively ("The Arrangement of the Laws in Deuteronomy," 276). For other linkage see Braulik, *Die deuteronomischen Gesetze und der Dekalog,* 108-9.

[252] L. M. Eslinger, "The Case of an Immodest Lady Wrestler in Deuteronomy 25:11-12," *VT* 31 (1981): 269-81.

[253] C. H. Gordon, "A New Akkadian Parallel to Deuteronomy 25,11-12," *JPOS* 15 (1935): 29-34; S. M. Paul, "Biblical Analogues to Middle Assyrian Law," in *Religion and Law,* ed. E. B. Firmage, B. G. Weiss, and J. W. Welch (Winona Lake, Ind.: Eisenbrauns, 1990), 333-50.

[254] Thus Cairns, *Deuteronomy,* 218.

As an example of this principle, the Israelite was warned against having two different weights for transacting sales, one heavy and one light. (Note again reference to two things, as in vv. 5 and 11.) The heavy weight would be used when he bought commodities and the light when he sold. Likewise, he was not to have two sets of measures for dry and liquid products in order to cheat those with whom he traded (vv. 13-14). There obviously was no sin in possessing these things per se, but their very possession would inevitably lead to their use in unscrupulous transactions.[255] "Innocent" objects could form the linkage between intention (coveting) and fulfillment, so their eschewal would guard the person against giving vent to his temptation. As always, dishonest dealings with one's fellow man are detestable to the Lord (v. 16), so displeasing to him that they would jeopardize long life in the land of promise (v. 15).

(4) Dealing with the Amalekites (25:17-19)

[17]**Remember what the Amalekites did to you along the way when you came out of Egypt. [18]When you were weary and worn out, they met you on your journey and cut off all who were lagging behind; they had no fear of God. [19]When the LORD your God gives you rest from all the enemies around you in the land he is giving you to possess as an inheritance, you shall blot out the memory of Amalek from under heaven. Do not forget!**

Though this closing paragraph may loosely be associated with the idea of interpersonal relationships elaborated throughout the lengthy section 23:19–25:19, its radically different subject matter (foreigners rather than fellow Israelites) and its apparent lack of reference to the Decalogue pose major problems about its present text location. Most scholars therefore either lump it under miscellaneous statutes or perceive it as having been misplaced in the text, perhaps from chap. 23.[256] It seems best, however, to view it as a transitional piece between the past and the future, between the experience of Israel in the desert, where attack by Amalek was rather paradigmatic of the years of wandering, and the hope of life in the land of promise, where God's people would enjoy peace and prosperity (26:1-19).[257]

---

[255] Kaufman, "The Structure of the Deuteronomic Law," 143-44.

[256] So Mayes, *Deuteronomy,* 330.

[257] Craigie sees it as a piece of "unfinished business" between the past and future (*Deuteronomy,* 317-18). Amalek's attack on Israel in the desert had to be avenged in the land of promise. Carmichael makes the helpful observation that the immediately preceding laws (vv. 5-10,11-12, and even 13-16) had to do with strife between brothers, and inasmuch as Amalek descended from Esau (Gen 36:12), this "law of the Amalekites" is most fitting where it is (*Law and Narrative in the Bible,* 305).

25:17-19   The Amalekites, whom the Old Testament traces back to Eliphaz, son of Esau, and his concubine Timna (Gen 36:12), lived in the Arabian deserts east and south of the Dead Sea (Gen 36:16; Num 13:29; 14:25).[258] They were a fierce nomadic people, hostile to Israel as their flagrant attack on the weak and elderly of the Exodus wanderers makes clear (Exod 17:8-16). Because of this cowardly act, the Lord placed them under his judgment (Exod 17:14), promising to bring them to utter ruin (Num 24:20). Eventually this came to pass but long after Israel's settlement in Canaan. Saul was first commissioned to do so (1 Sam 15:1-3); but when he failed, the task fell to David, who appears to have been at least largely successful in achieving the long-sought objective (2 Sam 8:12). At the best, however, Israel failed to do what the law here commanded—to "blot out" (māḥâ) Amalek's very memory "from under heaven" (v. 19).

6. Laws of Covenant Celebration and Confirmation (26:1-15)

One of the expectations by a great king of the ancient Near Eastern world was that his vassals with whom he had entered into covenant relationship acknowledge his sovereignty by paying him homage.[259] This generally took the form of taxation or other material tribute to be presented to the king's court at the capital city on stated occasions, perhaps annually. Failure to do so was to violate the covenant terms and thus to invite the God's displeasure.

This was clearly the case in the relationship between the Lord and Israel, an obligation spelled out in the initial covenant revelation at Sinai (Exod 23:14-17; 34:22-24; Lev 23:4-44; Num 28:16–29:38), and elaborated already in Deuteronomy in anticipation of life in the land (Deut 16:1-17). The purpose of the reiteration here was to connect one of the festivals—that of Firstfruits (Heb. šēbûʿōt)—with a ceremony of covenant renewal.[260] According to later Jewish tradition, the law was given to Israel at Sinai precisely on the date established for Firstfruits, so it was only natural to link the two occasions together.[261] From that time forward a part of the celebration of the first of the wheat harvest would center on covenant renewal; indeed, the ritual described here would be a major element of the day's activities.

---

[258] G. L. Mattingly, "Amalek," in *ABD* 1:169-71.
[259] Kline, *Treaty of the Great King,* 92.
[260] W. J. Dumbrell, *Covenant and Creation* (Nashville: Thomas Nelson, 1984), 116.
[261] This apparently is first attested in the pseudepigraphical Book of Jubilees (second century B.C.). Cf. L. H. Schiffman, *From Text to Tradition* (Hoboken, N.J.: KTAV, 1991), 252-53.

(1) Presentation of the Firstfruits (26:1-11)

¹When you have entered the land the LORD your God is giving you as an inheritance and have taken possession of it and settled in it, ²take some of the firstfruits of all that you produce from the soil of the land the LORD your God is giving you and put them in a basket. Then go to the place the LORD your God will choose as a dwelling for his Name ³and say to the priest in office at the time, "I declare today to the LORD your God that I have come to the land the LORD swore to our forefathers to give us." ⁴The priest shall take the basket from your hands and set it down in front of the altar of the LORD your God. ⁵Then you shall declare before the LORD your God: "My father was a wandering Aramean, and he went down into Egypt with a few people and lived there and became a great nation, powerful and numerous. ⁶But the Egyptians mistreated us and made us suffer, putting us to hard labor. ⁷Then we cried out to the LORD, the God of our fathers, and the LORD heard our voice and saw our misery, toil and oppression. ⁸So the LORD brought us out of Egypt with a mighty hand and an outstretched arm, with great terror and with miraculous signs and wonders. ⁹He brought us to this place and gave us this land, a land flowing with milk and honey; ¹⁰and now I bring the firstfruits of the soil that you, O Lord, have given me." Place the basket before the LORD your God and bow down before him. ¹¹And you and the Levites and the aliens among you shall rejoice in all the good things the Lord your God has given to you and your household.

As with all such ritual, there must be both act and word, the act consisting here of the offering of the produce (vv. 1-3a,4-5a,10b-11) and the word a statement of the present occasion (v. 3b), a recitation of Israel's "sacred history" (vv. 5b-9), and an explanation of what the offerer had done (v. 10a). It may be helpful to discuss the passage according to this analysis.

26:1-5a   The proleptic character of the Deuteronomy covenant is again underscored by the fact that the ritual outlined here was to be undertaken not in the present but only after the promised land had been appropriated and settled (v. 1). Then, in the socioeconomic life of agrarianism in which patterns of sowing, cultivation, and harvesting had been adopted, the first ($rē'šît$, perhaps qualitatively, "best," as well as temporally)[262] of the field crops (lit., "fruit of the ground") must be placed in a basket and taken to the "place the LORD your God will choose as a dwelling for his Name," namely, the tabernacle or central sanctuary (cf. Deut 12:5-14). According to the agricultural and cultic calendars, this would be in early summer, on the sixth of Sivan (= May/June), the time of the

---

[262] Mayes, *Deuteronomy,* 277, 334.

beginning of the wheat harvest (cf. Lev 23:15-16).[263] Having arrived at the sanctuary, the worshiper presented the basket to the officiating priest (v. 3a) and then, having recited the liturgy, laid his gift before the Lord, presenting himself also in prostration (v. 10b).

The prescribed litany is an adumbration of all of God's mighty elective and redemptive works on Israel's behalf. Von Rad, in fact, viewed the confession here as Israel's credo, that corpus of irreducible dogma that expresses the very essence of Israel's identity and purpose before God.[264] The same confession, von Rad argued, is to be found in less full form in Deut 6:20-24 and in a much expanded version in Joshua 24:2-13. Von Rad's traditio-historical assumptions and method aside, there is a great deal of truth to the idea that ancient Israel, like the later church, encapsulated its most significant truths in summary form and that the faithful periodically recited them in a cultic setting.

One of the problems noted by von Rad is the omission of reference in the credo to the Sinai covenant itself.[265] This led him to postulate that the Sinai tradition was originally limited to only a local community centered in and around Shechem and never found its way into the standard versions of the credo.[266] The problem with this (among other difficulties) is that it is inconceivable that the Sinai tradition would not have found its way into the Deuteronomic material if Deuteronomy is to be dated as late as most scholars suggest.[267] It is far more likely that the Sinai reference is missing because (1) the focus is on the linkage between the patriarchal promises (implied in v. 5) and their fulfillment in the land of Canaan (vv. 9-10a) and (2) the fact that the Feast of Firstfruits also marked the anniversary of the cutting of the Sinai covenant (if the tradition was indeed that ancient) and would make it superfluous to mention that covenant in the creed.[268] Moreover, the centrality of the Sinai encounter has already been asserted over and over again in Deut (cf. 1:6; 4:9-19; 5:2-5; 9:8-21;

---

[263] Schiffman, *From Text to Tradition,* 252.

[264] G. von Rad, "The Form-Critical Problem of the Hexateuch," in *The Problem of the Hexateuch and Other Essays* (London: SCM, 1966), 3-8.

[265] Ibid., 7.

[266] Ibid., 36-39.

[267] For this and other reactions and criticisms, see C. M. Carmichael, "A New View of the Origin of the Deuteronomic Credo," *VT* 19 (1969): 273-89; D. R. Daniels, "The Creed of Deuteronomy xxvi Revisited," in *Studies in the Pentateuch* (Leiden: Brill, 1990), 231-42; H. B. Huffmon, "The Exodus, Sinai and the Credo," *CBQ* 27 (1965): 101-13.

[268] Craigie argues, in fact, that the omission of reference to Sinai/Horeb undermines von Rad's interpretation of the passage as a creed and, rather, draws attention to the connection of the promise of land to the patriarchs and its impending fulfillment to the people (*Deuteronomy,* 322).

18:16; 29:1). The Deuteronomic tradition in its canonical form was very much aware of the importance of the Sinai covenant to Israel's confession.

26:5b-10   The confession begins with Jacob, the "wandering Aramean" (v. 5b), so-named because his mother was an Aramean (Gen 24:10; 25:20,26) and he himself spent at least twenty years in Aram (Gen 31:41-42). The wandering speaks of the pastoral lifestyle he pursued, living in temporary quarters much of the time and moving from place to place (Gen 25:27).[269] Canaan was his by promise (28:4,15; 35:12; 46:4) but not by possession. Only after the descent to Egypt (Deut 26:5), enslavement there (v. 6), and the supernatural deliverance by the Lord's grace (vv. 7-8) were Jacob's descendants able to come now to Canaan and bring it under control and thus fulfill the promise (v. 9). The peace and stability that would permit the inauguration of regular agricultural patterns would be irrefutable evidence that the Lord had indeed accomplished his word to the fathers. In recognition of this and in tribute to the Lord's electing and saving grace, the farmer would come to proffer the firstfruits of his fields (v. 10a).

26:11   The result of faithful obedience to this rite would be untold blessing, both spiritual ("you shall rejoice") and material. The latter is implied in the inclusion of the Levite and alien (*gēr*) along with the offerer himself, for both were disadvantaged and dependent on the largess of the people (Deut 12:10-12,18; 14:28-29). As the community as a whole was true to the Lord and therefore blessed by him, so even the poorest elements of Israel's society would benefit as well (v. 11).

(2) Presentation of the Third-year Tithe (26:12-15)

[12]**When you have finished setting aside a tenth of all your produce in the third year, the year of the tithe, you shall give it to the Levite, the alien, the fatherless and the widow, so that they may eat in your towns and be satisfied. [13]Then say to the LORD your God: "I have removed from my house the sacred portion and have given it to the Levite, the alien, the fatherless and the widow, according to all you commanded. I have not turned aside from your commands nor have I forgotten any of them. [14]I have not eaten any of the**

---

[269] Some scholars construe the participle אָבַד ("wandering") as "perishing" or the like, a meaning of אָבַד, which, indeed, is commonly attested (KB, 2-3). However, the context as a whole contrasts the sojourning impermanence of Israel's lifestyle to this point with the sedentariness and stability implied in the agricultural festival of which this confession was a major element; thus B. Otzen, "אָבַד, ʾābhadh," etc., *TDOT* 1:20. For further discussion see M. A. Beek, "Das Problem des aramaïschen Stammvaters (Deut xxvi 5)," *OTS* 8 (1950): 193-212; A. R. Millard, "A Wandering Aramean," *JNES* 39 (1980): 153-55.

sacred portion while I was in mourning, nor have I removed any of it while I was unclean, nor have I offered any of it to the dead. I have obeyed the LORD my God; I have done everything you commanded me. ¹⁵Look down from heaven, your holy dwelling place, and bless your people Israel and the land you have given us as you promised on oath to our forefathers, a land flowing with milk and honey."

Related to the ceremony of covenant renewal at the Feast of Firstfruits, both by subject matter and juxtaposition, is the ordinance concerning the third-year tithe. It mandated the setting aside of the tithe of the harvest of every third year for the purpose of meeting the material needs of the dependent of Israel including the Levite, the alien, the orphan, and the widow (v. 12). This very incumbency was dealt with earlier in Deuteronomy in the extended legislation about tithing (Deut 14:28-29), but it is reiterated here to reinforce the idea that the benevolence of God's people was to operate in two dimensions, the vertical and the horizontal. Thus the offering of firstfruits to the Lord (26:1-11) could not be separated from the beneficence to be shown to fellow kingdom citizens (vv. 12-15).

26:12-14 As suggested previously, it is not entirely clear what was meant by the "third year" tithe. Most likely, what normally went to the Lord at the central sanctuary (Deut 14:22-27) was to go to the needy, including the levites, every third year (Deut 14:28-29). One would still be giving to God by giving to his people (cf. Matt 10:42; 25:40), so the significance of the tithe as tribute was in no wise diminished. This understanding is reinforced by the reference to the tithe here as "the sacred portion" (v. 13; Heb. *haqqōdeš*, "the holy thing"), a term that suggests its exclusive ownership by the Lord (cf. Lev 5:15-16; 19:24; 27:28).[270] Furthermore, the offerer was to say, "I have removed from my house the sacred portion," the verb (*bāʿar*) referring here in this cultic context to the presentation to the Lord of consecrated things that belong to him. The literal meaning is "to exterminate," that is, to totally separate what is God's from one's house so that it might (as here) be given to others.[271]

The pronouncement of words as part of the presentation of the third-year tithe shows this also to have been a ritual and hence another linkage to what has preceded. The recitation, having commenced with the statement that the holy thing had been removed from one's house and given to others (v. 13a), continues with the assertion that all this had been done in compliance with the Lord's commandments (*miṣwôt*, i.e., covenant stipulations; v. 13b). Examples of these follow. First of all, the worshiper

---

[270] McConville, *Law and Theology in Deuteronomy*, 72.
[271] Driver, *Deuteronomy*, 290.

denied having used any of the consecrated tithe for himself while in "mourning" (v. 14). The best understanding here is that he had not participated in use of the tithe while engaged in pagan rites of fertility or sympathetic magic.[272] Such rites were characteristic of Canaanite worship as a means of inducing the underworld deities to fertilize the soil and guarantee a bountiful harvest. They would include the presentation of offerings and a sacred drama in which weeping and lamentation would play a part (cf. Ezek 8:14).

The noun translated "mourning" (ʾōneh) is derived not from the verb ʾāwan ("be strong, mighty") but from ʾānâ ("mourn"). It occurs only one other time in Hos 9:4 in the context of pagan rituals in which grain and wine were consumed and offered as sacrifices (Hos 9:1-5). Israelite mourning, to the contrary, was to include fasting as Ezek 24:15-24 makes clear. Ordinary mourning occasioned by death was not in view here, however, for the offerer was to disclaim having made any offering to the dead. This no doubt is to be understood in terms of Canaanite ritual in which deities such as Baal who had been consigned to the Netherworld were sustained by food offerings until they could revive and return to their procreative function on the earth.[273]

26:15 Having completed his twofold confession, the positive (vv. 13a,14b) and negative (vv. 13b-14a), the worshiper at the time of the third-year tithe would invoke the blessing of the Lord on the people and the land (v. 15). Contrary to the frail, ineffectual gods of the nations who could even die and lie beneath the earth, Israel's God reigned from heaven above. But his transcendence did not nullify his interest in and involvement with his covenant nation. He had made solemn promises to their fathers to give them the land of Canaan, one that flowed with milk and honey, not because of fructifying forces attributed to nature gods but because of his providential grace (cf. Deut 11:8-12).

---

[272] H. Cazelles, "Sur un rituel du Deutéronome (Deut. xxvi 14)," *RB* 55 (1948): 54-71.

[273] F. I. Andersen and D. N. Freedman understand the use of אוֹנִים in Hos 9:4 precisely in this way, "idol feeding" (*Hosea*, AB 24 [Garden City: Doubleday, 1980], 526.

VI. EXHORTATION AND NARRATIVE INTERLUDE (26:16-19)

As noted in the Introduction, one of the literary features of Deuteronomy that sets it apart from being a covenant text in a strict or limited sense is the frequent appearance of parenesis in which Moses interrupts (or, perhaps, stitches together) covenant sections by appeals to action. His interest was not only in the content of the covenant message but in Israel's unqualified obedience to all its requirements. The present pericope thus summarizes and completes the great stipulation sections of the covenant document and urges compliance with its mandates.

[16]The LORD your God commands you this day to follow these decrees and laws; carefully observe them with all your heart and with all your soul. [17]You have declared this day that the LORD is your God and that you will walk in his ways, that you will keep his decrees, commands and laws, and that you will obey him. [18]And the LORD has declared this day that you are his people, his treasured possession as he promised, and that you are to keep all his commands. [19]He has declared that he will set you in praise, fame and honor high above all the nations he has made and that you will be a people holy to the LORD your God, as he promised.

26:16-19 The recapitulative nature of this passage is clear from the repeated use of the technical covenant terms "decrees" (*ḥuqqîm,* vv. 16-17), "laws" (*mišpāṭîm,* vv. 16-17), and "commands" (*miṣwôt,* vv. 17-18) and the reference to Israel as a "holy people" (v. 19), the Lord's "treasured possession" (*ʿam sĕgullâ,* v. 18). The stipulation section had begun with an appeal to obey the "decrees and laws" that were about to be promulgated (Deut 5:1); and in declaring the heart of the covenant revelation, Moses had, in the Shema, commanded the people to love the Lord "with all your heart and with all your soul" (Deut 6:5), the very words of our text (v. 16). Then, having instructed them to uproot the wicked nations of Canaan, he spoke of Israel as God's "treasured possession" (Deut 7:6; *sĕgullâ,* as here). This same technical term appears in Deut 14:2 as an appellation of the covenant people, a people also called "a people holy to the LORD your God" (*ʿam qādôš . . . lădônai ʾĕlōheykâ*), exactly as here in v. 19. The connections between this passage and the entire thrust of chaps. 5 through 26 could not be clearer.[1]

---

[1] See N. Lohfink, "Dt 26, 17-19 und die 'Bunderformel,'" *ZKT* 91 (1969): 517-53.

Somewhat problematic is the reference to Israel's having declared "this day" that Yahweh was their God (v. 17) and the corresponding affirmation by Yahweh "this day" that Israel was his people (v. 18). The text of Deuteronomy is silent about any such mutual pledge. The most likely explanations are that (1) the record is not necessarily complete and there may have been such a dialogue;[2] (2) Deuteronomy as a covenant renewal document (as opposed to a first-time arrangement) did not require a formal statement of covenant alliance;[3] or (3) "this day" is to be taken in the sense of an entire generation, perhaps as "these days." This could include everything from the initiation of the original Sinai covenant to the very moment of Moses' exhortation.

The net result of covenant obedience was to be Israel's exaltation above all nations, an exaltation that would render them "praise, fame and honor" (v. 19). This collocation of words (*tĕhillâ, šēm, tip'eret*) forms a cliché to express renown of the highest form (cf. Jer 13:11 and 33:9, where the first two words are reversed). It is true that Israel's selection as a "kingdom of priests" and a "holy nation" carried with it a heavy responsibility. Their faithful discharge of that responsibility would, however, result in the greatest privilege and honor.

---

[2] A. D. H. Mayes, *Deuteronomy,* NCBC (Grand Rapids: Eerdmans, 1979), 338. Though Mayes implicitly rejects Smend's notion that the ceremony was that of Josiah in 2 Kgs 23:1-3, he does agree that "some cultic ceremony of covenant conclusion" is presupposed.

[3] I. Cairns, *Word and Presence: A Commentary on the Book of Deuteronomy,* ITC (Grand Rapids: Eerdmans, 1992), 227.

VII. THE CURSES AND BLESSINGS (27:1–29:1 [Heb. 28:69])
1. The Gathering at Shechem (27:1-13)
2. The Curses That Follow Disobedience of Specific Stipulations (27:14-26)
3. The Blessings That Follow Obedience (28:1-14)
4. The Curses That Follow Disobedience of General Stipulations (28:15-68)
   (1) Curses as Reversal of Blessings (28:15-19)
   (2) Curses by Disease and Drought (28:20-24)
   (3) Curses by Defeat and Deportation (28:25-37)
   (4) The Curse of Reversed Status (28:38-46)
   (5) The Curse of Military Siege (28:47-57)
   (6) The Curse of Covenant Jeopardy (28:58-68)
5. Narrative Interlude (29:1 [Heb. 28:69])

VII. THE CURSES AND BLESSINGS (27:1–29:1 [HEB. 28:69])

An indispensable part of ancient Near Eastern treaty texts was a body of sanctions that spelled out the results of obedience and disobedience of the various stipulations agreed to by the contracting parties. In the case of sovereign-vassal relationships, the sanctions fell upon the inferior party exclusively except as the sovereign might pledge himself to any degree of accountability to that inferior. Even then, of course, the great king's obligations, being self-imposed, were subject to revision or even cancellation. Only his own integrity and, perhaps, his sworn pledge to the gods, would keep him true to his word.[1]

The Introduction has already set forth the case for Deuteronomy as a sovereign-vassal treaty text and for this section as the curses and blessings element. The peculiar fact that there are two sections of curses and only one of blessings was there explained as a literary device in which the latter

---

[1] G. E. Mendenhall, *Law and Covenant in Israel and the Ancient Near East* (Pittsburgh: Biblical Colloquium, 1955), 30, 34.

is sandwiched between the former. The curses appear to relate to the specific stipulations and general stipulations respectively, whereas the blessings do double duty, referring to both bodies.[2] The reason for the brevity of the list of blessings is not apparent though one will recall that the later Neo-Assyrian treaty texts contained no blessings section at all. It might be that the blessings section in Deuteronomy is, in effect, the self-imposed obligations of the Lord to his people and, as such, there is no need to spell those out in great detail. A good and gracious God need do no more than pledge himself to the well-being of his chosen ones as they submit to his dominion over them.[3]

1. The Gathering at Shechem (27:1-13)

[1]Moses and the elders of Israel commanded the people: "Keep all these commands that I give you today. [2]When you have crossed the Jordan into the land the LORD your God is giving you, set up some large stones and coat them with plaster. [3]Write on them all the words of this law when you have crossed over to enter the land the LORD your God is giving you, a land flowing with milk and honey, just as the LORD, the God of your fathers, promised you. [4]And when you have crossed the Jordan, set up these stones on Mount Ebal, as I command you today, and coat them with plaster. [5]Build there an altar to the LORD your God, an altar of stones. Do not use any iron tool upon them. [6]Build the altar of the LORD your God with fieldstones and offer burnt offerings on it to the LORD your God. [7]Sacrifice fellowship offerings there, eating them and rejoicing in the presence of the LORD your God. [8]And you shall write very clearly all the words of this law on these stones you have set up."

[9]Then Moses and the priests, who are Levites, said to all Israel, "Be silent, O Israel, and listen! You have now become the people of the LORD your God. [10]Obey the LORD your God and follow his commands and decrees that I give you today."

[11]On the same day Moses commanded the people:

[12]When you have crossed the Jordan, these tribes shall stand on Mount Gerizim to bless the people: Simeon, Levi, Judah, Issachar, Joseph and Benjamin. [13]And these tribes shall stand on Mount Ebal to pronounce curses: Reuben, Gad, Asher, Zebulun, Dan and Naphtali.

---

[2] I. Levy, "The Puzzle of Dt. 27: Blessings Announced but Curses Noted," *VT* 12 (1962): 207-11.

[3] Thompson draws attention to the fact that over 250 out of 674 lines of the Esarhaddon treaty text are curses and suggests that "the threat of a severe judgment on the covenant breaker seems to act as a stronger stimulus to correct behaviour than any promise of blessing" (J. A. Thompson, *Deuteronomy: An Introduction and Commentary*, TOTC [Leicester: InterVarsity, 1974], 268).

The nature of Deuteronomy as a covenant renewal document designed especially for life in the promised land is evident from this set of instructions given by Moses to the people. They had received the covenant in the here and now of the plains of Moab, but they had to wait until they arrived in Canaan to formalize its implementation by a mass ceremony of commitment. This would include the erection of a monument containing the fundamental principles of the Lord-Israel relationship, a covenant meal signifying the harmony of that relationship, and a catalog of curses and blessings appropriate to the maintenance and/or disruption of that relationship.

The passage is divided into three parts: (1) the instruction to assemble at Mount Ebal (i.e., at Shechem) (vv. 1-8), (2) an exhortation to obey the covenant requirements (vv. 9-10), and (3) preparation for the solemn ceremony at Gerizim and Ebal in which the covenant sanctions would be invoked (vv. 11-13).[4] Scholars have long noted the awkwardness of arrangement of chaps. 27–28 as a whole and the abruptness with which Moses is introduced in the third person in 27:1. Some have suggested, therefore, that chap. 28 should immediately follow chap. 26 (note the similarity of 26:19 and 28:1), and chap. 27 should follow chap. 28.[5] In favor of this last point is the smoother transition into the reference to Moses in 29:1 [Heb. 28:69], a verse that concludes all the previous covenant material.

The problem with these suggestions, however, is that 29:1, if it is indeed conclusive (and it is), cannot be followed by chap. 27, for chap. 27 is an integral part of the sanctions section. Moreover, it is inconceivable that a blessings list (28:1-14) should be followed by a curses list (28:15-68) before a sanctions ceremony has even been prescribed (27:1-13). Finally, the result would be a blessing list followed by two curses lists (28:15-68 and 27:15-26) with the covenant ceremony dividing the latter two.[6]

The so-called abruptness of the reference to Moses by name in 27:1 loses its force when it is recognized that the great stipulation section of chaps. 5–26 is enveloped not only by the introduction to and conclusion of that section that shares technical terms and other common devices (Deut

---

[4] For a discussion of this passage and its relationship to Josh 8:30-32, see M. Anbar, "The Story about the Building of an Altar on Mount Ebal and the History of Its Composition and the Question of the Centralization of the Cult," in *Das Deuteronomium,* ed. N. Lohfink, BETL 68 (Leuven: University Press, 1985), 304-9.

[5] See S. R. Driver, *A Critical and Exegetical Commentary on Deuteronomy* (Edinburgh: T & T Clark, 1902), 294-95.

[6] For these and other arguments for the integrity of the existing text, see G. J. Wenham, "The Structure and Date of Deuteronomy" (Ph.D. diss., University of London, 1969), 206-10.

5:1-5; cf. 26:16-19) but by the very name Moses itself. Thus Deut 5:1 (the last time the name was mentioned) has Moses commanding obedience to the "decrees and laws" of the covenant, and here (27:1) he instructs that they keep all the covenant "commands." The linkage seems quite apparent.

27:1-4,8   As is frequently the case, the command to do something specific is preceded by a statement of general covenant exhortation (v. 1). This suggests that the meaning of details must be understood against the backdrop of the whole. Everything Israel did was within the context of the covenant relationship. The specific instruction here was to set up a large stone monument once Canaan had been reached, a stele coated with plaster on which "all the words of this law" could be inscribed (v. 3). Such techniques are well attested in the ancient world.[7] The monumental form and size were to provide ready public access, a rallying point around which the community could gather to more easily recall its commitment as a people.

The sheer length of the complete covenant text of Deuteronomy seems to preclude its having been in view in the terms "all the words of this law." What more likely was meant was the Decalogue alone, the very core and foundation of all the law. Such a view is favored by the fact that only the Ten Commandments were engraved on stone by the Lord (cf. Exod 24:4,12; 32:15-16; 34:1,4), and only they were laid up in the ark of the covenant for preservation as a witness (Exod 25:16).[8]

The place selected for the ceremony of covenant renewal was also significant, for it marked the site of Abraham's first altar in Canaan and the Lord's promise there to give his descendants the land as an inheritance (Gen 12:6-7). It was also the location of Jacob's well (Gen 33:19; cf. John 4:5) and later the tomb of Joseph (Josh 24:32).[9] The area as a whole was Shechem, two features of which were the twin mountains, Ebal and Gerizim. Moses had already described these mountains as the locales of covenant curse and blessing respectively (cf. Deut 11:29), but only Ebal appears here, probably as a *pars pro toto* ("part [taken] for the whole"; cf.

---

[7] For Egyptian models especially, see Driver, *Deuteronomy,* 296.

[8] P. C. Craigie suggests that it may include as much as the "law of the covenant," i.e., the revelation at Horeb (*The Book of Deuteronomy* [Grand Rapids: Eerdmans, 1976]: 328). Moreover, given the nature of the stele and its writing surface, it is possible that all of the nonnarrative and nonparenetic sections of Deuteronomy could have been written there. The Code of Hammurapi (which was engraved, not "written") is an instructive example; so I. Cairns, *Word and Presence: A Commentary on the Book of Deuteronomy,* ITC (Grand Rapids: Eerdmans, 1992), 231.

[9] For the significance of Shechem in OT covenant tradition see B. W. Anderson, "The Place of Shechem in the Bible," *BA* 20 (1957): 10-19. Cf. A. E. Hill, "The Ebal Ceremony as Hebrew Land Grant?" *JETS* 31 (1988): 399-406.

Josh 8:30) and also because of the greater length of the curse section with which Ebal was associated.[10] Indeed, the Samaritan Pentateuch has Gerizim for Ebal in the text, but this obviously reflects a Samaritan ideological preference and not the original reading.

27:5-7 The instruction about the memorial stele is interrupted by a further command, namely, to build an altar also (vv. 5-7). This appears so intrusive to many scholars that they posit two originally independent sources, one having to do with the covenant inscription (vv. 2-4,8) and the other with the altar (vv. 5-7).[11] Such a view founders on the fact that v. 8 would hardly have been severed from vv. 2-4 by the intrusive altar pericope, and it shows insensitivity to the literary artistry of the entire section. The repetition of the words "all the words of this law" (vv. 3,8) suggests an enveloping of the whole but an enveloping which, without the altar prescriptions, would be obviously (and needlessly) redundant. Furthermore, the presentation of the covenant by the Lord to Moses and Israel for the first time at Sinai also consisted of the writing of words and the building of an altar (Exod 24:4), the two together being necessary to the covenant ceremony (Exod 24:7-8).

The covenant context of the altar instructions is further established by the specifications that the altar be made of stones (i.e., rough field stones; cf. Josh 8:31) and with no tools (Deut 27:5-6). These are precisely the qualifications given to Moses in the Book of the Covenant concerning altars to be built in the land apart from that of the central sanctuary (Exod 20:22-26). Such stipulations were intended to set Israelite altars apart from Canaanite ones that ordinarily were built of dressed stone. The allowance to build an altar at Shechem was not at variance with earlier prohibition against multiple sanctuaries (cf. Deut 12:1-7), for the issue there was that of a central sanctuary, one place above all others where the Lord would place his name. This did not rule out the possibility of local sacrifices even after the central place of worship was established.[12] The very existence of the present command to build an altar at Shechem in a text that otherwise enjoins community worship at a single sanctuary shows the difference between the cultic and theological ideas that each expresses. In addition, of course, the central sanctuary had not even been located at Shiloh by the time Joshua fulfilled the covenant ceremony outlined here in Deuteron-

---

[10] H. Seebass, "Garizim und Ebal als Symbole von Segen und Fluch," *Bib* 63 (1982): 22-31.

[11] Thus R. P. Merendino, "Dt 27:1-8: Eine literarkritische und überlieferungsgeschichtliche Untersuchung," *BZ* 24 (1980): 194-207.

[12] Thompson, *Deuteronomy,* 263.

omy, so in this instance, at least, the matter of a central sanctuary is moot.[13]

27:9-10 Having provided instruction about the location and physical arrangements of the covenant renewal ceremony, Moses and the priests reminded the assembled throng that they were the people of the Lord and that it was for this reason that their obedience was so crucial (vv. 9-10). As noted previously (cf. 18:1), the reference to "the priests, who are Levites" (v. 9a) does not suggest two classes of priests, Levitical and otherwise; but, to the contrary, it insists that all priests are Levites as, indeed, was Moses himself. The point here is that there were no privileged persons who stand above or outside the covenant mandates. The fact that the tribe of Levi had to stand on Mount Gerizim with the other tribes makes this most clear (v. 12).

A striking point of Moses' charge to his hearers is that they had "now become" the people of the Lord (v. 9b), a fitting translation of the niphal perfect of the verb *hāyah* with the following preposition *lĕ*. But in what sense had they just become such? It is obvious that this cannot mean that Israel had to this point not been the Lord's chosen ones, for the whole history of the covenant relationship up until then said otherwise (cf. Deut 4:20; 7:6-7; 9:26,29; 10:15; 14:2; 21:8; 26:15,18-19). What is suggested is that affirmation of that special relationship must be made over and over again, particularly at strategic moments such as that of covenant renewal.[14] On the eve of conquest and in anticipation of the covenant ceremony Moses was outlining, he reminded them that once more they had become God's people by confession of that reality. In other words, existential awareness of election and redemption must periodically be invoked so as to make the historical facts behind it personal and ongoing. On the basis of that confession as God's people, they now had to obey his commands and decrees, that is, the covenant stipulations that Moses had been imparting (v. 10).

27:11-13 After the covenant text had been inscribed and appropriate sacrifices offered, the people were to divide themselves into two groups of

---

[13] This point is embarrassing to the view that Deuteronomy was composed late, for how, in that case, could there be allowance for a sanctuary to be built after a central shrine had already been designated? Surely if Deuteronomy's ideology presupposes only Jerusalem as cult center, it is difficult to account for altar building at Shechem. A typical response is that of A. D. H. Mayes, who suggests that "the verses [5-7] are a secondary insertion into this context from the hand of someone familiar with deuteronomic and deuteronomistic terminology, who thought that the setting up of stones inscribed with the law implied the presence of a sanctuary and an altar" (*Deuteronomy,* NCBC (Grand Rapids: Eerdmans, 1981), 342.

[14] Craigie, *Deuteronomy,* 329.

tribes with six standing on Mount Gerizim and six on Mount Ebal (vv. 11-13). Though the instructions here do not say so, the Joshua narrative indicates that the ark of the covenant, with its Levitical bearers, remained in the valley between the mountains as representative of the presence of the Lord and as the receptacle containing the Ten Commandments (Josh 8:33). Thus the Lord and his covenant statutes would be in plain view of the tribes as they listened and responded to the blessings and curses they invoked upon themselves in anticipation of their obedience and disobedience respectively.

It is difficult to determine any pattern or rationale for the distribution of the tribes here.[15] What is clear is that Ephraim and Manasseh were combined to constitute the tribe of Joseph, a necessary measure if Levi is to be included among the twelve. This, of course, has nothing to do with some stage of tradition development that knows nothing yet of the separation of Ephraim and Manasseh. Such a distinction existed already in the desert encampment (Num 1:10; cf. vv. 32-35) and would be reflected in the later allocation of tribal territories (Josh 14:4).

The scene, as described once before (cf. 11:26-32), would have been that of an antiphony in which the tribes (or more likely their representatives) would affirm the curses and blessings read to them by the officiating Levites (v. 14). This they would do by simply responding ʾāmēn to each as they heard it. In this manner they were not only pledging themselves to obedience but expressing their willingness to accept whatever judgment might accrue to their disobedience. Thus the representatives did indeed bless and curse their own people as they assented to the covenant requirements (v. 12).

2. The Curses That Follow Disobedience of Specific Stipulations (27:14-26)

[14]The Levites shall recite to all the people of Israel in a loud voice:

**[15]"Cursed is the man who carves an image or casts an idol—a thing detestable to the LORD, the work of the craftsman's hands—and sets it up in secret."
Then all the people shall say, "Amen!"
[16]"Cursed is the man who dishonors his father or his mother."**

---

[15] Driver offers the observation that the sons of Jacob's legitimate wives, Leah and Rachel, were chosen for blessing; and the sons of the concubines plus Reuben and Zebulun, for cursing (*Deuteronomy,* 298). Reuben and Zebulun were Leah's oldest and youngest sons respectively. Cairns notes that "the grouping of the tribes . . . is based not on eponymous ancestry but on the location of their territories" (*Word and Presence,* 235). This seems to be more likely.

Then all the people shall say, "Amen!"

[17]"Cursed is the man who moves his neighbor's boundary stone."

Then all the people shall say, "Amen!"

[18]"Cursed is the man who leads the blind astray on the road."

Then all the people shall say, "Amen!"

[19]"Cursed is the man who withholds justice from the alien, the fatherless or the widow."

Then all the people shall say, "Amen!"

[20]"Cursed is the man who sleeps with his father's wife, for he dishonors his father's bed."

Then all the people shall say, "Amen!"

[21]"Cursed is the man who has sexual relations with any animal."

Then all the people shall say, "Amen!"

[22]"Cursed is the man who sleeps with his sister, the daughter of his father or the daughter of his mother."

Then all the people shall say, "Amen!"

[23]"Cursed is the man who sleeps with his mother-in-law."

Then all the people shall say, "Amen!"

[24]"Cursed is the man who kills his neighbor secretly."

Then all the people shall say, "Amen!"

[25]"Cursed is the man who accepts a bribe to kill an innocent person."

Then all the people shall say, "Amen!"

[26]"Cursed is the man who does not uphold the words of this law by carrying them out."

Then all the people shall say, "Amen!"

It was proposed in the Introduction that Deut 27:15-26 consists of a list of curses that follow violation of specific covenant stipulations, that 28:15-68 contains curses for violation of covenant principles in general, and that 28:1-14 provides a catalog of blessings that also concern themselves with broad covenant expectations. This means that only 27:15-26 addresses particular infractions, a situation that has given rise to some speculation that a corresponding list of blessings must have existed at one time.[16]

What must be recognized, however, is that 27:15-26 is not a list of curses in the strict sense but a list of statutes whose violation brings a curse.[17] What that curse is is never stated. In both the blessings of 28:1-14

---

[16] Driver, *Deuteronomy*, 300.

[17] Because of the unique nature of this list, many scholars have viewed it as curse based on prohibition, specifically prohibition of covenant violation. See E. Bellefontaine, "The Curses of Deuteronomy 27: Their Relationship to the Prohibitions," in *No Famine in the Land: Studies in Honor of John L. McKenzie,* ed. J. W. Flanagan and A. W. Robinson (Missoula, Mont: Scholars Press, 1975), 49-61; cf. P. Buis, "Deutéronome xxvii 15-26: malédictions ou exigences de l'alliance," *VT* 17 (1967): 478-79.

and the curses of 28:15-68, on the other hand, the true formula exists in which the blessing and/or curse is specified. Form-critically, then, the latter two passages go together as blessing and curse sections whereas 27:15-26 stands alone in the present context. It is the very context, however, that also explains the purpose of the list and its relationship to the covenant as a whole.

Scholars have long described this unit as the "Dodecalogue," the "Twelve Commandments," because of the number of the curses.[18] Sensitive to its being a counterpart to the Decalogue or Ten Commandments, some have argued that vv. 15 and 26 are later additions to the text and that there were, indeed, ten curses in the original list.[19] While v. 15, with its unusual length, and v. 26, with its clearly summarizing purpose, do appear to differ from the other ten elements, there is no good textual or other evidence to support these as late additions. One might, in fact, explain the number twelve on the basis of there being twelve tribes on the opposing mountains.[20] It is not altogether unreasonable to suppose that each tribe at a time responded to the curses as they were read. Thus when the text reads in each case, "All the people shall say" (as in v. 15), the intent is to speak of all the people of each tribe.

Be that as it may, the notion that the twelve curses correspond in some way to the Ten Commandments is most attractive.[21] The ark of the covenant, which contains the stone tablets of the commandments, lies in the valley between Gerizim and Ebal. Their content was well known to all and hardly needed to be repeated. That is, their very presence was tantamount to a list of blessings, for there was indeed blessing in keeping them (cf. Deut 5:32-33; 6:3; 7:12-16; 11:8-17), a point made over and over in Deuteronomy. If the ark and obedience to the words of its contents spoke of blessing, the violation of the commandments, represented by the list of judgments here, spoke of curses.

27:14 Moses obviously would not have been involved in the Shechem ceremony of covenant renewal, having been barred from entering the land (cf. Deut 1:37), and even Joshua, Moses' successor as theocratic leader, would not preside in the reading of the present list of curses. Rather, this was left to the Levites who had been selected to bear the ark on this momentous occasion (v. 14; cf. Josh 8:33). This is striking in light of the

---

[18] G. von Rad, *Deuteronomy: A Commentary* (Philadelphia: Westminster, 1966), 167.

[19] Mayes, *Deuteronomy,* 346, citing V. Wagner, *Rechtssätze in gebundener Sprache und Rechtssatzreihen im israelitischen Recht, BZAW* 127 (1972): 33.

[20] J. Ridderbos, *Deuteronomy,* BSC (Grand Rapids: Zondervan, 1984), 253.

[21] Cairns, *Word and Presence,* 237.

fact that Joshua did build the altar and erect the stele there and, in fact, read all the lists of blessings and curses (Josh 8:30-35). Perhaps his reading of them was done in preparation for their later pronouncement by the Levites in order to familiarize the people with their content before they actually swore to them.[22]

27:15 Once Joshua took his place among his own tribe of Joseph on Mount Gerizim, the Levites in the valley below would recite the twelve curses, awaiting, in turn, the affirmation of the twelve tribes. The first of the infractions inviting divine displeasure was, fittingly enough, that of idolatry (v. 15). Such an act was in direct contradiction to the first two commandments, those having to do with the uniqueness of the Lord and the demand that only he be worshiped and then not in any plastic form (Deut 5:7-10). The form these idols took—whether carved (thus Heb. *pesel,* "image") or cast (Heb. *massēkâ,* "idol")—was beside the point. Moreover, their wickedness was not diluted by their being worshiped in secret. In any shape and in any place, idolatry is detestable (*to'ēbâ*) to the Lord.

As noted already, some scholars view this first prohibition as an addition to the text, one providing an introduction to the following list of ten just as v. 26 provides a conclusion. Besides lacking textual support, such a conjecture results in a loss of any reference to the vertical dimension of Israel's covenant responsibility, that having to do with their relationship to the Lord. It is hard to imagine that this aspect would have been lacking, particularly since it is so prominent in the following lists of blessings (28:1,9-10,14) and curses (28:15,20,36,45,47,58). In addition, if the present list is a counterpart to the blessings inherent in the Decalogue, the absence of v. 15 would result in no counterpart to the first two (or even first four) commandments.

27:16 Once the tribes (or perhaps only the first of the tribes) had affirmed the first of the twelve pronouncements of judgment, the second was read by the Levites. This has to do with dishonoring (Heb. *maqleh,* lit., "making light of") one's parents (v. 16), a violation of the fifth commandment (Deut 5:16). The verb used here (*qālâ*) is the antonym of that in the Decalogue (*kabbēd*), thus establishing a clear connection.[23] A synonymous verb occurs in Exod 21:17 but with the effect of the curse spelled out:

---

[22] Keil and Delitzsch harmonize Deut 27:14 and Josh 8:34 by suggesting that Joshua "had the law proclaimed aloud by the persons entrusted with the proclamation of the law, namely, the Levitical priests." C. F. Keil and F. Delitzsch, *Biblical Commentary on the Old Testament: Joshua, Judges, Ruth,* trans. J. Martin (Grand Rapids: Eerdmans, n.d.), 92.

[23] Bellefontaine, "The Curses of Deuteronomy," 52.

"Anyone who curses (*mĕqallēl,* from *qālal,* "be light") his father or mother must be put to death."

27:17 The third curse pertains to property as opposed to persons (v. 17). This suggests that all three elements of the Decalogue are covered— that pertaining to proper reverence of the Lord (cf. Deut 5:7-11), that having to do with one's fellow man (Deut 5:17-18,20), and that involving possessions and properties (Deut 5:19,21). These are introduced here in vv. 15-17 and then elaborated in vv. 18-25. Here the category of property is represented by the removal of boundary stones, a law not expressly articulated in the Decalogue but dealt with earlier in Deuteronomy (19:14). One always moves boundary lines to one's own advantage, an act of "theft" of immovable goods.

27:18-19 The fourth and fifth curses match the tenth and eleventh (vv. 24-25) in that both sets speak to the issue of taking advantage of others in society, in the former case the handicapped and in the latter the unwary and innocent. They also serve to envelop numbers six through ten, all of which deal with sexual improprieties (vv. 20-23). Altogether, then, curses four through eleven provide specific examples of infraction of proper covenantal interpersonal relationships, a proportion of emphasis commensurate with covenant stipulation as a whole in which more space is allocated to the human-human dimension than to the human-divine.

The handicaps of vv. 18-19 are physical and socioeconomic respectively. One invokes a curse upon himself if he misleads the blind (here representative of all who are physically disadvantaged; cf. Lev 19:14, where the deaf are included as well). But the alien, orphan, and widow were also handicapped, especially in the ancient Near Eastern world where economic well-being depended so much on the father and husband. They were constantly susceptible to unscrupulous creditors or outright extortioners who victimized them, and more often than not their appeals for justice (*mišpaṭ,* v. 19) fell on deaf ears. The covenant text had already addressed such miscarriages of justice (Deut 24:17), but their seriousness warranted special mention here in the curse list.

27:20-23 Sexual promiscuity and perversion have characterized human behavior from the beginning but nowhere and at no time in grosser form than in ancient Canaan. Apart from its occurrence in everyday social life, sexual aberration was part and parcel of the Canaanite ideology and cultus and was therefore not only tolerated but sanctioned. Against this background it is easy to see why four of the twelve curses should be devoted to this particular theme. Again there appears to be somewhat of a literary structure in that vv. 20 and 23 speak of sexual relationships with one's stepmother and mother-in-law, bracketing the heinous sins of bestiality (v. 21) and incest (v. 22).

Since it was so apparent that incest involving one's own mother was unspeakably evil, the curse does not address that possibility. The reference here to "his father's wife" (v. 20) means stepmother or, less likely, a second wife in addition to the mother. Such a distinction is, however, clearly made in Lev 18:7-8, where it is prohibited to have sexual relations with either one's mother or his father's wife (cf. Lev 20:11; Deut 22:30).[24] As in Leviticus, the sin was in not only violating the woman but in bringing shame to the father. This was an egregious display of dishonor of one's parents, an act already raised as a matter of curse (v. 16).

If one sins by violating the honor of his superior, what is to be said of bestiality, a sin violating the relationship with a lower order of creation? The Book of the Covenant regards such abhorrent behavior as worthy of death, one of the few sins with such harsh sanctions (Exod 22:19; cf. Lev 18:23; 20:15-16). This was not only because of such perversion in Canaanite and other cultures[25] but because of the reversal of roles implied, the equating of the animal world with human, the image of God, who was created to have dominion over that world, not cohabit with it (cf. Gen 1:26-28).

The third taboo in sexual behavior was the improper intercourse with one's sister, defined here as "the daughter of his father or the daughter of his mother" (v. 22). Again this refers not to a blood kin, or certainly not to a full sister, but to a foster sibling or half-sister. Such relations between full brothers and sisters are not explicitly proscribed here or elsewhere in the law, but if they are forbidden between less closely related siblings, then *a fortiori* they would be all the more intolerable within more closely defined kinships. In any case, such sin borders on incest, a most abominable practice in the Lord's eyes (cf. Lev 18:6-18) but one widely carried on in Israel's cultural environment, especially in Egyptian royal circles.[26]

The fourth breach of sexual propriety addressed here is the violation of one's mother-in-law (*ḥōtanâ*, lit., "wife's mother"). Leviticus speaks of this relationship in terms of the marriage by a man of "both a woman and her mother" and spells out the resulting consequence: death (Lev 20:14). Thus sexual transgression involving one's stepmother (v. 20) and his

---

[24] G. J. Wenham, *The Book of Leviticus,* NICOT (Grand Rapids: Eerdmans, 1979), 254-55.

[25] A. Phillips, *Deuteronomy,* CBC (Cambridge: The University Press, 1973), 182.

[26] Wenham, *Leviticus,* 251-52, 255-57.

mother-in-law (v. 23) frames this section on perverse sexual behavior with its attendant curse.

27:24-25 Curses ten and eleven, as already pointed out, comprise the closing member of the structure that embraces laws having to do with specific instances of interpersonal relationship (vv. 18-25). Numbers four and five (vv. 18-19) deal with persons disadvantaged by handicaps, and ten and eleven (vv. 24-25) concern mistreatment of the unwary and innocent. In the former case the crime is the slaying of a neighbor (Heb *rēa^c*, "friend or companion") in secret, that is, either outside public view or in a manner totally unexpected by the victim. Previous legislation (cf. Exod 21:12-14; Lev 24:17) suggests that murder, not manslaughter, is in view here, the former being defined as predetermined taking of life.[27] The fact that the curse in the present situation is visited upon one who kills "secretly" (Heb *bassāter*) supports the view that the crime here is indeed murder, for that qualification implies a prior arrangement by the perpetrator to isolate his victim. As for the killing of the innocent (v. 25), the particular facts of the case focus on the receiving of bribes as inducement to carry out the nefarious deed. Though one might expect the curse to fall on one who accomplished the task, the text is clear in asserting that culpability of murder falls on him who even accepts a bribe to do it whether or not he succeeds.[28] Life of the innocent is so precious that even threats against it cannot be taken lightly.

27:26 The present curse section ends, finally, with a general malediction against anyone who fails to uphold (Heb. *hēqîm*, "carry out, give effect to"[29]) "the words of this law," namely, the entire covenant text (cf. Deut 17:19; 27:3,8; 28:58; 29:29; 31:12; 32:46). This warning both covers any and all possible covenant infractions not spelled out in the preceding list and serves as a fitting conclusion to this series that began with an admonition to recognize and serve the Lord alone as God (v. 15). The best way one can acknowledge the Lord's sovereignty is to carry out fully his covenant expectations.

3. The Blessings That Follow Obedience (28:1-14)

---

[27] Phillips, *Deuteronomy*, 183.

[28] As Bellefontaine points out: "The acceptance of the bribe is the sole motivation for the murderer's act, for he holds no personal case against his victim. . . . The prohibitive foundation is not the prohibition against murder (Exod 20:13) but the prohibition against the acceptance of bribes which leads to the violation of justice (Exod 23:8; cf. Deut 16:19)" ("The Curses of Deuteronomy," 56).

[29] BDB, 879.

¹If you fully obey the LORD your God and carefully follow all his commands I give you today, the LORD your God will set you high above all the nations on earth. ²All these blessings will come upon you and accompany you if you obey the LORD your God:

³You will be blessed in the city and blessed in the country.

⁴The fruit of your womb will be blessed, and the crops of your land and the young of your livestock—the calves of your herds and the lambs of your flocks.

⁵Your basket and your kneading trough will be blessed.

⁶You will be blessed when you come in and blessed when you go out.

⁷The LORD will grant that the enemies who rise up against you will be defeated before you. They will come at you from one direction but flee from you in seven.

⁸The LORD will send a blessing on your barns and on everything you put your hand to. The LORD your God will bless you in the land he is giving you.

⁹The LORD will establish you as his holy people, as he promised you on oath, if you keep the commands of the LORD your God and walk in his ways. ¹⁰Then all the peoples on earth will see that you are called by the name of the LORD, and they will fear you. ¹¹The LORD will grant you abundant prosperity—in the fruit of your womb, the young of your livestock and the crops of your ground—in the land he swore to your forefathers to give you.

¹²The LORD will open the heavens, the storehouse of his bounty, to send rain on your land in season and to bless all the work of your hands. You will lend to many nations but will borrow from none. ¹³The LORD will make you the head, not the tail. If you pay attention to the commands of the LORD your God that I give you this day and carefully follow them, you will always be at the top, never at the bottom. ¹⁴Do not turn aside from any of the commands I give you today, to the right or to the left, following other gods and serving them.

Neither the instructions for the Shechem covenant convocation here nor the account of its fulfillment in Josh 8:30-35 provides insight about how the blessings section was to function on that occasion. Presumably the tribes remained on their respective mountainsides; the Levites with the ark stayed in the valley between, and there was some form of tribal affirmation as the blessings were recited. Whether or not this be so, it is clear that the blessing list belongs where it does in the text; for the summarizing statement of the curses section enjoins implicit obedience by the assembly of "the words of this law" (27:26), and the opening challenge of the blessing section is to "fully obey" (*šāmôaᶜ tišmaᶜ*) the Lord and "carefully follow" (*lišmōr laᶜăśôt*) "all his commands" (*miṣwôt*; 28:1). In other words, the negative command is recast into a positive form, but the message is the same.

The structure and form of the passage differ greatly from the previous list of curses, however, a point also made earlier. In the strict sense the latter list was not an assembly of curses at all but rather a series of covenant violations that would result in (unspecified) curses.[30] Here, however, both the condition for blessing (the protasis) and the nature of the resulting blessing (the apodosis) are spelled out.[31] Moreover, the blessings do not appear seriatim in response to a formal list of stipulations but instead arise out of one basic demand: full and unqualified obedience of the Lord.

28:1-2 There are three statements of this demand in the text, that is, 28:1a,2b,9b, and 13b-14. The first of these is in the form of an inclusio in which the opening phrase of v. 1 ("if you fully obey the LORD your God") is virtually identical to the closing phrase of v. 2 ("if you obey the LORD your God"). Between lies the blessing that the Lord would set Israel "high above all the nations on earth" (v. 1b) and the promise that the blessings that follow would come to pass (v. 2a). The blessing of being exalted above all other nations had already been articulated; in fact, it is the very last promise of the stipulation section of the book (26:19)[32] and is in line with the elective purposes of God, who chose Israel out "from among" all nations to be his special possession (7:6; 14:2; cf. Exod 19:6). Ultimately, however, the promise must find fulfillment in an eschatological setting in which Israel (or Zion) would enjoy unrivaled preeminence among the nations as the object of God's gracious favor (cf. Num 24:7; Ps 89:28; Isa 2:2).

28:3-5 What it means to be set high above all the nations is answered in part by the string of blessings that follow in vv. 3-8. Inasmuch as Israel's economy rested on an agrarian base, most of the blessing is associated with abundance in field and flock, but other aspects of safe and wholesome life are not ignored. The whole is introduced by a merism of space or locality in which city and country (lit., "field") stand for all the places of Israel's existence (v. 3). Wherever they lived, the people would know fertility of

---

[30] M. G. Kline distinguishes between Deut 27:15-26 and Deut 28 by noting that in the former the sins and not the curses are differentiated whereas in the latter both blessings and curses are precisely specified for obedience to or disobedience of the covenant principles. The former (27:15-26) he describes as the covenant oath and the latter (28:1-68) as the covenant sanctions (*Treaty of the Great King* [Grand Rapids: Eerdmans, 1963], 124).

[31] For the form and uses in Deut 28 see H. W. Gilmer, *The If-You Form in Israelite Law,* SBLDS 15 (Missoula, Mont.: Scholars Press, 1975), 78-80.

[32] This, in fact, is one reason some scholars view Deut 27 to be intrusive (so Driver, *Deuteronomy,* 294). Unless one views 28:1 as a late editorial join designed to accommodate Deut 27 as an insertion, it is apparent that it and 26:19 are too repetitive to have stood in original juxtaposition.

human offspring as well as of crops and animals (v. 4). Abundant produce would, of course, result in abundant food supplies. Harvest baskets would overflow, and bakers would have more than enough wheat with which to bake their bread (v. 5).

28:6-7   To blessing of economy would be added blessing of safety and protection (vv. 6-7). Again employing a merism, the lawgiver spoke of such blessing in all activities, coming in and going out representing life with all its movement and occupation (v. 6).[33] More particularly, God's people could rest in his watchcare in times of enemy threat (v. 7). The foes of Israel would suffer inglorious defeat. Even if they banded together to form one mighty, united force, they would be dispersed in seven directions, that is, scattered to the four winds.

28:8   Verse 8 forms a conclusion to this first set of blessings by summarizing the blessings according to the categories of what Israel would have and what Israel would do (the "barns" and "hand" respectively). All of this is linked to their occupation and development of the land of promise that lay just ahead (v. 8b; cf. 8:7-10; 11:8-17). That is, blessing lay in a vital connection with the inheritance the Lord had guaranteed to the fathers (Gen 12:7; 13:14-18; 26:3-4; Exod 3:6-8).

28:9-10   The second statement of condition for blessing also focuses on keeping the Lord's commands (*miṣwôt*, as in v. 1) and walking "in his ways" (v. 9b). In the first instance Israel was told that they would be set "high above all the nations" (v. 1b). Here the promise was that covenant fidelity would result in Israel's being established (*hēqîm*) as the Lord's holy people (v. 9a). This would cause the nations to look upon Israel with amazement and fear, for they would see that they were "called by the name of the LORD" (v. 10). This mark of identification (like being set high above all nations, v. 1b) must be understood in a context of covenant in which Israel was elected by the Lord from among all nations (Exod 19:6) and thus brought into a relationship of son to father (Exod 4:22-23; 2 Chr 7:14; Isa 63:19; Jer 14:9). The reason for fear is therefore most apparent: That nation called by Almighty God to be his own son falls under his protection and can freely call upon his omnipotent resources. To mistreat God's people is to invite divine intervention and retribution.[34]

28:11-14   A further cause for fear, however (perhaps now strictly in the sense of awe), would be the evidence of God's abundant provision for

---

[33] As Phillips puts it, "In all you undertake, your daily round" (*Deuteronomy*, 190). Cf. Ps 121:8; Isa 37:28.

[34] There is also the nuance of יָרֵא ("fear") that suggests awe or reverence. That would also be appropriate here. See H. F. Fuhs, " יָרֵא‎ *yareʾ* ," etc., *TDOT* 6:303.

his people in all the ways described under the first set of blessings (v. 11; cf. vv. 3-6). The heathen of Canaan depended upon their ability to palliate and manipulate Baal, Asherah, and the other deities of fertility to grant them rain, richness of soil, and all the other forces of nature that made survival on the land possible. When they saw that the Lord, God of Israel, was Creator and Sovereign over all things, including climate and cultivation, and that he could not be coerced or tricked into sharing his life-giving potency, but, to the contrary, bestowed it out of sheer grace and love of his people, they would be awestruck. Elijah's contest with the prophets of Baal illustrates these conflicting ideologies and the amazement that followed Yahweh's triumph over the gods of Canaan and those who worshiped them (1 Kgs 18:38-40).

The third condition of divine favor consists of two parts: (1) a protasis ("if you pay attention to the commands," etc., v. 13b) and (2) a command ("do not turn aside from any of the commands . . ., following other gods and serving them," v. 14). The blessing proper appears in vv. 12-13a,c. As in the previous two cases (vv. 1-8,9-11), the blessing is predicated upon obeying the commands (*miṣwôt*) of the Lord (cf. vv. 1a,9b). This refers to the total covenant text, especially Deut 5–26. Lest there be any misapprehension about this, the section closes with the conditions expressed as a command: "Do not turn aside [*sûr*] from any of the commands" (*miṣwôt*), a defection epitomized by going after other gods (v. 14). This last injunction reflects the sentiment of the first two commandments of the Decalogue, with which the stipulations section of Deuteronomy begins (Deut 5:7-10), and also corresponds to the first of the curses in the previous list of curses (27:15).

The blessings of this third unit are also the same as those of the other two. Fundamentally, they have to do with bountiful harvest and with success in every human pursuit (v. 12a; cf. vv. 3-8,11). This time, however, the exaltation of Israel above all nations (cf. vv. 1b, 9a) is described in terms of animal imagery (v. 13a) as well as elevation (v. 13b). Obedience to the Lord would guarantee that his people would be "the head [*rōʾš*], not the tail [*zānāb*]." Isaiah used the same metaphor to describe the ordinary people as opposed to the leaders (Isa 9:14 [Heb. 9:13]), that is, those who bring up the rear.[35] In the future, particularly in eschatological days, the Lord would so promote Israel that it would lead the procession of nations as their head (cf. Jer 31:7).

---

[35] For various other suggestions for this metaphor, especially from Egyptian sources, see H. Wildberger, *Isaiah 1–12* (Minneapolis: Fortress, 1991), 234-35.

4. The Curses That Follow Disobedience of General Stipulations (28:15-68)

It is immediately apparent that this long section corresponds in both form and content to the preceding blessings unit, and therefore its present place in the text cannot be disputed. The first subsection (vv. 15-19) answers point by point to vv. 1-14, the juxtaposition highlighting the curses as direct opposites to the blessings.[36] The remaining subsections correspond less directly but nonetheless reflect the great principles that underlie the covenant relationship and the severe penalties that follow their violation. As in the preceding blessings unit, the condition for blessing and/or curse was Israel's attitude toward the Lord and "the words of this law." The conditional element (usually in protasis form) occurs repeatedly throughout the section and in basically identical terms (cf. vv. 15,20b,45b,47,58,62b). The curses themselves, highly repetitive in places, are outlined in great detail and in a manner similar to the statement of blessing in vv. 7-14.

Many scholars have drawn attention to the remarkable parallels between the structure and content of this curse section and certain Neo-Assyrian treaty texts, especially the so-called vassal treaties of Esarhaddon. These parallels have then been adduced to argue for the dependence of the Deuteronomic material on the Assyrian models and, hence, the late, non-Mosaic composition of the biblical text.[37] While the parallels to some extent cannot be denied, other scholars have pointed out that they are not as pervasive as some have claimed, nor is their existence proof of dependence one way or the other. Most likely there was a common fund of covenant and treaty ideology and even language in the ancient Near East, a fund drawn upon by both biblical and secular composers of such texts.[38]

Also striking is the sheer length of the curse material as compared to the blessing section (forty-four and four verses respectively). Though at first blush this also seems to suggest Neo-Assyrian affinities inasmuch as these latter contained long curse sections, the Neo-Assyrian examples contain no blessings at all![39] If anything, this omission points totally away from Neo-Assyrian parallels to other, earlier kinds such as the Hittite, which always contained both blessings and curses. Moreover, extant copies of treaty

---

[36] Craigie, *Deuteronomy,* 338.

[37] See especially M. Weinfeld, *Deuteronomy and the Deuteronomic School* (Oxford; Clarendon, 1972), 116-26.

[38] Thompson points out contacts with pre-Mosaic Hittite covenant texts, especially in vv. 47-57 (*Deuteronomy,* 271; cf. Craigie, *Deuteronomy,* 339-40).

[39] K. A. Kitchen, *Ancient Orient and Old Testament* (London: Tyndale, 1966), 96.

texts from all over the ancient Near East witness consistently to the fact
that the lists of curses invariably are longer than those of blessings, frequently two or three times as long.[40] The reason presumably (as here in
Deuteronomy) was to underscore the seriousness of covenant violation
by describing its consequences in long and graphic detail.

(1) Curses as Reversal of Blessings (28:15-19)

**[15]However, if you do not obey the LORD your God and do not carefully fol-
low all his commands and decrees I am giving you today, all these curses will
come upon you and overtake you:**

[16]You will be cursed in the city and cursed in the country.

[17]Your basket and your kneading trough will be cursed.

**[18]The fruit of your womb will be cursed, and the crops of your land, and
the calves of your herds and the lambs of your flocks.**

[19]You will be cursed when you come in and cursed when you go out.

28:15-19   This subsection is unique in that it clearly has in mind a previous passage, namely, vv. 3-6, and it responds to that passage point by
point.[41] Furthermore, the conditional clause introducing the curses is
almost identical to that introducing the blessings, the major difference, of
course, being the particle of negation here ("if you do not obey"; cf. v. 1).
Especially noteworthy is the fact that curses were predicated basically on
defection from the great covenant principles that underlie the Lord's relationship to his people, just as the blessings followed conformity to those
same principles (cf. vv. 1a,2b,9b,13b-14).

Though all four curses correspond to the blessings of vv. 3-6, it is curious that numbers two and three are reversed and number three (v. 18) lacks
the phrase "the young of your livestock" in the matching blessing of v. 4.
To appeal to some kind of redactionary process whereby originally separate and independent traditions are joined is nonsense, for such a process
would more likely than not eliminate these distinctions so as to harmonize
them.[42] More credible is the supposition that the author has creatively rearranged the material precisely to break the monotony, doing so by juxtapos-
ing vv. 16 and 17 to form a chiastic pattern. The basket in which the
harvest was carried relates to the country (or field); and the kneading
trough, to the city where the baking of bread took place. As for the missing
phrase, it is missing also in the LXX of v. 4. Whether or not originally

---

[40] G. J. Wenham, *Structure and Date of Deuteronomy,* 161.

[41] Thompson, *Deuteronomy,* 271.

[42] Mayes, *Deuteronomy,* 352.

lacking, there was no need to repeat it here since the author apparently saw no need to be slavishly imitative at the expense of literary creativity and other interests.

(2) Curses by Disease and Drought (28:20-24)

²⁰The LORD will send on you curses, confusion and rebuke in everything you put your hand to, until you are destroyed and come to sudden ruin because of the evil you have done in forsaking him. ²¹The LORD will plague you with diseases until he has destroyed you from the land you are entering to possess. ²²The LORD will strike you with wasting disease, with fever and inflammation, with scorching heat and drought, with blight and mildew, which will plague you until you perish. ²³The sky over your head will be bronze, the ground beneath you iron. ²⁴The LORD will turn the rain of your country into dust and powder; it will come down from the skies until you are destroyed.

28:20-21 This pericope, though lacking the obvious verbal similarities to previous material noted in vv. 15-19, speaks primarily of agricultural disasters due to covenant disobedience, disasters that counter the blessings described in vv. 8,11-12. The anticipated judgment would take the form of curses in general (here *mĕʾērâ*, from *ʾārar*,[43] the verb for "curse" used throughout vv. 15-26), two manifestations of which are "confusion" (*mĕhûmâ*; cf. 7:23) and "rebuke" (*migʿeret*).[44] Both terms (or their cognates) occur commonly in contexts of military oppression (1 Sam 14:20; Isa 22:5) or crop failure (Mal 2:3; 3:11), both of which are in evidence throughout the entire curse section.

Most immediately, however, destruction and ruin would come through disease, blight, and unremitting drought. The nature of the sickness is unclear since the generic term *deber* is used (v. 21).[45] Whatever it is, it will be chronic, as the verb form indicates (*hidbîq*, "cause to cling to"). There will be no relief until the Lord has "finished you off" (lit., "destroyed you," v. 21) in the land. This no doubt refers to physical disease that would ravage the land from time to time (cf. 2 Sam 24:13; 1 Kgs 8:37; Ezek 5:12; Amos 4:10), but in its finality it speaks metaphorically of the affliction of deportation (Lev 26:25) or disinheritance (Num 14:12).

---

[43] For the verb אָרַר in its various forms and theological significance, see J. Scharbert, "אָרַר *ʾrr*," etc., *TDOT* 1:405-18. See also H. C. Brichto, *The Problem of "Curse" in the Hebrew Bible,* SBLMS 13 (Philadelphia: Scholars Press, 1963).

[44] See A. A. Macintosh, "A Consideration of Hebrew *gr,*" *VT* 19 (1969): 471-79.

[45] The LXX regularly translates דֶּבֶר by θανατος ("death"), suggesting its intensity and finality; cf. G. Mayer, "דֶּבֶר *debher*," *TDOT* 3:125-27.

28:22-24 Symptomatic of the illnesses would be "wasting" (lit., "consumption"), "fever," and "inflammation," a malady of body matched by the scorching heat of drought (Heb. *ḥereb*; read rather *ḥōreb*).[46] Since the last two words can both be translated "heat," it is possible to view this as a hendiadys to be rendered "terrible heat," or the like, and to connect it with the diseases already referred to. On the other hand, there are seven afflictions in all if these two are separated, a factor that favors their distinction in light of the symbolic use of *seven* to communicate fullness or finality. If this be the case, the first three curses relate to illness and the last four to adverse climatic and agricultural conditions.[47]

There can be no doubt about the nature of the last two—"blight" (*šiddāpôn*) and "mildew" (*yērāqôn*, lit., "paleness")—for both usually occur together in clearly agricultural contexts (cf. 1 Kgs 8:37 = 2 Chr 6:28; Amos 4:9; Hag 2:17).[48] The result of forsaking the Lord, then, was sickness of both people and land, a sickness that would lead to death and devastation (v. 22b). The seriousness of the drought demands hyperbole for a proper description. Thus the sky would become bronze, said the lawgiver, and the earth iron (v. 23).[49] Leviticus 26:19 employs the same imagery except that there the earth is bronze and the sky iron. The effect is the same in both. As impervious as these metals are to water and tools, so both the heavens and the earth would be in the day of calamity. The rains would not leak through the skies, nor would the earth be able to be broken up to receive the farmer's seed. Instead, the heavens would rain down dust, which would only exacerbate an already hopeless situation on the earth (v. 24; cf. 11:17).

(3) Curses by Defeat and Deportation (28:25-37)

[25]The LORD will cause you to be defeated before your enemies. You will come at them from one direction but flee from them in seven, and you will become a thing of horror to all the kingdoms on earth. [26]Your carcasses will be

---

[46] חֶרֶב ("sword") is out of place in this list and should be read חֹרֶב ("drought"); cf. Driver, *Deuteronomy*, 308.

[47] Keil and Delitzsch, while recognizing the symbolic significance of the seven curses, read "sword" (with the MT) and question the three-fourth division suggested here (*Deuteronomy*, 438).

[48] D. Kellermann, "יָרַק, *yāraq*," etc., *TDOT* 6:365-66.

[49] For an interesting stereotypical parallel see the vassal treaties of Esarhaddon: "May they make your ground (hard) like iron so that [none] of you may f[lourish]. / Just as rain does not fall from a brazen heaven so may ruin and dew not come upon your fields and your meadows; may it rain burning coals instead of dew on your land" (col. vii, lines 528-33 in D. J. Wiseman, *The Vassal-Treaties of Esarhaddon* [London: British School of Archaeology in Iraq, 1958], 70).

food for all the birds of the air and the beasts of the earth, and there will be no one to frighten them away. [27]The LORD will afflict you with the boils of Egypt and with tumors, festering sores and the itch, from which you cannot be cured. [28]The LORD will afflict you with madness, blindness and confusion of mind. [29]At midday you will grope about like a blind man in the dark. You will be unsuccessful in everything you do; day after day you will be oppressed and robbed, with no one to rescue you.

[30]You will be pledged to be married to a woman, but another will take her and ravish her. You will build a house, but you will not live in it. You will plant a vineyard, but you will not even begin to enjoy its fruit. [31]Your ox will be slaughtered before your eyes, but you will eat none of it. Your donkey will be forcibly taken from you and will not be returned. Your sheep will be given to your enemies, and no one will rescue them. [32]Your sons and daughters will be given to another nation, and you will wear out your eyes watching for them day after day, powerless to lift a hand. [33]A people that you do not know will eat what your land and labor produce, and you will have nothing but cruel oppression all your days. [34]The sights you see will drive you mad. [35]The LORD will afflict your knees and legs with painful boils that cannot be cured, spreading from the soles of your feet to the top of your head.

[36]The LORD will drive you and the king you set over you to a nation unknown to you or your fathers. There you will worship other gods, gods of wood and stone. [37]You will become a thing of horror and an object of scorn and ridicule to all the nations where the LORD will drive you.

The curses of this section (repeated with variation in vv. 47-57,63b-68) are the reverse of the blessing of victory promised in v. 7. As was the case there, so here there is no explicit protasis explaining the reason for these calamities. That of v. 15 is sufficient for the whole catalog, and, indeed, no one would have to guess why the divine judgment had come.

28:25-26   When Israel launched an offensive military operation (as opposed to being on the defensive in v. 7), it would suffer ignominious defeat, its solidity being fractured into seven pieces (i.e., totally shattered and beyond repair; v. 25).[50] Whereas it could have been the cause for nations to fear (v. 10), it would become an object of trembling, that is, a people so dismembered as to elicit revulsion and horror on the part of those who saw Israel (v. 25b; cf. Jer 15:4; 29:18; 34:17). Israel would, in fact, become a field of corpses, a banquet for winged and four-footed scavengers that would be free to eat their fill (v. 26). The irony of the contrast between Israel's feeding off the land (vv. 4-5,8,11) and being itself a food supply for carnivorous beasts is inescapable.

---

[50] This, of course, compares to the seven curses of vv. 20-24; so Cairns, *Word and Presence,* 243.

28:27 In a switch in imagery, the scene changes and evokes memories of life in Egypt (v. 27). In a kind of reverse exodus, Israel would return figuratively to Egypt and there experience the plagues that had afflicted Pharaoh and his countrymen in those former days. Just as the exodus epitomized the elective and salvific grace of God, so a return to Egypt, if only metaphorical, came to typify his judgment (cf. Deut 28:60-61,68; Hos 8:13; 9:3). Among the ailments would be boils (*šĕḥîn;* cf. Exod 9:9-11), tumors (*ʿŏpālîm;* perhaps hemorrhoids as in 1 Sam 5:6,9,12), sores (*gārāb,* "itch, scab"; cf. Lev 21:20; 22:22), and the itch (*ḥeres,* a hapax). All of these would be incurable.[51]

28:28-29 The curses move now from exodus imagery to an assortment of ailments. These would include madness (*šiggāʿôn;* cf. v. 34; 1 Sam 21:16; Zech 12:4), blindness, and mental instability (*timĕhon lēbāb,* lit., "bewilderment of heart"). The inclusion of blindness between two states of emotional or psychological disorder suggests that this loss of vision was not physical but metaphorical (cf. Ps 146:8; Isa 29:18; 35:5; 42:7,16; 43:8; 56:10).[52] The groping about in midday like a blind man (v. 29a) is a simile qualified in the next line, "You will be unsuccessful in everything you do." The blindness, then, was the incapacity to think clearly or form intelligent judgments. It would lay the ones under the curse open to all kinds of exploitation including oppression (*ʿāšûq;* here, in parallelism with *gāzûl,* connoting extortion; cf. Lev 6:4 [Heb. 5:23]; Ezek 18:18; Mal 3:5) and robbery (v. 29b). Having broken fellowship with the Lord, they would have no one to deliver them from their insanity and its consequences.

28:30-35 Nor would their problems end with their own mental and emotional derangement. It would also adversely affect family life and property (vv. 30-35). The disobedient of Israel could anticipate interrupted marriage arrangements (v. 30a), unfulfilled plans to live in newly built houses (v. 30b), the loss of produce (v. 30c) and livestock (v. 31), the capture of children and their loss (v. 32), the appropriation of lands and crops by foreigners (v. 33), incurable physical afflictions (v. 35), and eventual deportation to distant lands (vv. 36-37).

The first two of these judgments were so unthinkable that young men conscripted for military service could become exempt if they were betrothed (Deut 20:7; cf. 24:5) or had built a new house but had not dedicated it (Deut 20:5). The curse of lost possessions, moveable or immovable, had already been threatened (vv. 17-18) as a reversal of promised

---

[51] For these technical terms see Driver, *Deuteronomy,* 309-10; and for comparisons to the Neo-Assyrian treaty texts, Weinfeld, *Deuteronomy and the Deuteronomic School,* 117,121.

[52] Keil and Delitzsch, *Deuteronomy,* 439.

blessing (vv. 3-5,8,11-12). Scourge by disease had also loomed on the horizon as a sign of divine wrath (vv. 22,27), again as antithesis to blessing of body and mind promised to the faithful (vv. 4,6).

28:36-37   What is new here in the catalog of curses is the threat of conquest and deportation (vv. 36-37). There had been some hint of this, perhaps, in the reference to the plagues of Egypt (v. 27), but even there the point was only that Israel would suffer at the Lord's hands what Egypt had suffered at the time of the exodus. There is certainly no suggestion that Israel would literally return to Egypt. Deportation does, however, imply submission, a condition contrary to the exaltation of Israel described in the list of blessings. Rather than being a nation set "high above all the nations" (v. 1), God's people would lose their children to another nation (v. 32) and would themselves go off into ignominious captivity (v. 36). Rather than being "the head, not the tail" (v. 13), Israel would elicit horror (cf. v. 25) and would become "an object of scorn [māšāl, lit., "a proverb"] and ridicule" (lit., "cutting word"; cf. 1 Kgs 9:7 = 2 Chr 7:20; Jer 24:9).

The explicit references to deportation[53] and, especially, to the expulsion of a king (v. 36) have given support to those scholars who view Deuteronomy (or at least its greater part) as a seventh-century product. Monarchy, it is argued, did not rise until two hundred years after even a late date for Moses, and the Assyrian deportation of the Northern Kingdom of Israel took place, of course, in 722 B.C. The present text, then, must be a reflex of those (already historical) events.[54]

Such a view begs the question, however, for monarchy as an institution was long promised to Israel (Gen 17:6,16; 35:11; 36:31; 49:10) and provided for even in Deuteronomy (17:14-20). As for the need to posit the deportation as a *vaticinium ex eventu,* such need exists only if one finds the possibility of predictive prophecy intolerable. This becomes, then, not a historical or literary question but a theological one. Obviously those who champion a seventh-century Deuteronomy are not disposed to accepting the witness of Leviticus, which, according to traditio-historical analysis, is even later than Deuteronomy for the most part (ca. 450 B.C.). Nevertheless, Leviticus also speaks of deportation of God's people as a result of their covenant disloyalty (Lev 26:33-45).

(4) The Curse of Reversed Status (28:38-46)

---

[53] As Craigie shows, deportation was an ancient and common practice in military conquest, one that need not require a late date for its mention here (*Deuteronomy*, 346, n. 25).

[54] Von Rad, *Deuteronomy*, 25-28.

³⁸You will sow much seed in the field but you will harvest little, because locusts will devour it. ³⁹You will plant vineyards and cultivate them but you will
not drink the wine or gather the grapes, because worms will eat them. ⁴⁰You
will have olive trees throughout your country but you will not use the oil, because the olives will drop off. ⁴¹You will have sons and daughters but you will
not keep them, because they will go into captivity. ⁴²Swarms of locusts will
take over all your trees and the crops of your land.

⁴³The alien who lives among you will rise above you higher and higher, but
you will sink lower and lower. ⁴⁴He will lend to you, but you will not lend to
him. He will be the head, but you will be the tail.

⁴⁵All these curses will come upon you. They will pursue you and overtake
you until you are destroyed, because you did not obey the LORD your God and
observe the commands and decrees he gave you. ⁴⁶They will be a sign and a
wonder to you and your descendants forever.

This section is marked off from the others by the prevalence of the
adversative conjunction "but" (seven times in vv. 38-44), a translation
mandated by the obviously sharp contrasts between the independent
clauses in each case. It is important to note this reason for the inclusion of
the material, for otherwise the content is greatly repetitious of curses
already articulated.

One should note first the conditional clause (the protasis) of v. 45b
("because you did not obey," etc.) because this provides the rationale for
the curses contained in the passage. Here, as throughout the entire lengthy
curse section (except for vv. 25-37), the protasis points out that Israel's disobedience of the "commands" (*miṣwôt*) and "decrees" (*ḥuqqôt*) had
brought about (or would do so) the several afflictions. God's judgments are
never whimsical or purely arbitrary; they always come about in response to
sin. Covenant violation is a sure and certain invitation to covenant curses.

28:38-40 The order of the curses here is essentially that of the order of
blessings in vv. 1-14. The first three pertain to agricultural disaster (vv. 38-
40), the devastation of locust, worm, and premature casting of olives forming a counterpart to the blessing of field, orchard, and livestock of vv. 3b-5.
At first the next curse (v. 41) appears to be misplaced, for it is followed by
still another (v. 42) that describes a decimating locust plague. A closer
reading suggests, however, that the unit vv. 38-42 is in an enveloping
structure, one that focuses on the pernicious work of locusts (these are the
only two references to locusts in the whole book). The author here clearly
was more interested in style than in strict adherence to a formal list.

28:41-44 The fourth curse (v. 41) finds no corresponding blessing (but
cf. v. 7), but it does repeat the judgment of deportation spelled out in vv.
36-37. The sixth, however, speaking of the rise of the alien (*gēr*) at Israel's

expense, is set against the blessing of Israel's exaltation in vv. 1b and 13. The principal difference is that in the blessing section Israel excelled the nations, not the aliens, whereas in the present passage the nations found no mention. Moreover, the alien would lend to Israel and not vice-versa and would be the head while Israel would be the tail. Both ways of speaking of dominion and subservience occur in the blessings section (and in the same order, vv. 12b,13a), but again the change is made from the nations there to the alien here (v. 44). Very likely the shift from dominion by a foreigner to dominion by a resident alien is to heighten the sense of humiliation and chagrin Israel would experience in the day of judgment.[55]

28:45-46 Like a relentless predator these curses would pursue (*radap*) and overtake (*nāśag*) God's people until they were destroyed (v. 45). This combination of verbs is commonly used to describe tireless pursuit that invariably ends with the capture of the hunted game (cf. Deut 19:6; 28:2,15; Exod 15:9; 1 Sam 30:8; Ps 7:5).[56] So awesome would God's judgment be that the curses from then on would be "a sign and a wonder" forever (v. 46). This common cliché (*'ōt ûmôpĕt*) frequently refers to anything that attests to the presence and power of God (cf. Deut 4:34; 7:19; 26:8; 29:2 [Heb. 29:3]; Jer 32:21). The inevitable calamities that befall the disobedient nation would be indelibly engraved in their memories and forever after would witness to the truth that the Lord and his covenant will cannot be flaunted.

(5) The Curse of Military Siege (28:47-57)

[47]Because you did not serve the LORD your God joyfully and gladly in the time of prosperity, [48]therefore in hunger and thirst, in nakedness and dire poverty, you will serve the enemies the LORD sends against you. He will put an iron yoke on your neck until he has destroyed you.

[49]The Lord will bring a nation against you from far away, from the ends of the earth, like an eagle swooping down, a nation whose language you will not understand, [50]a fierce-looking nation without respect for the old or pity for the young. [51]They will devour the young of your livestock and the crops of your land until you are destroyed. They will leave you no grain, new wine or oil, nor any calves of your herds or lambs of your flocks until you are ruined. [52]They will lay siege to all the cities throughout your land until the high fortified walls in which you trust fall down. They will besiege all the cities throughout the land the LORD your God is giving you.

[53]Because of the suffering that your enemy will inflict on you during the

---

[55] Ridderbos, *Deuteronomy,* 259.

[56] M. C. Fisher, "נָשַׂג (*nāsag*)," *TWOT* 2:602-3.

siege, you will eat the fruit of the womb, the flesh of the sons and daughters the LORD your God has given you. [54]Even the most gentle and sensitive man among you will have no compassion on his own brother or the wife he loves or his surviving children, [55]and he will not give to one of them any of the flesh of his children that he is eating. It will be all he has left because of the suffering your enemy will inflict on you during the siege of all your cities. [56]The most gentle and sensitive woman among you—so sensitive and gentle that she would not venture to touch the ground with the sole of her foot—will begrudge the husband she loves and her own son or daughter [57]the afterbirth from her womb and the children she bears. For she intends to eat them secretly during the siege and in the distress that your enemy will inflict on you in your cities.

28:47-48   The protasis for this long subsection of curses appears in v. 47: "Because you did not serve the LORD your God joyfully and gladly in the time of prosperity." The failure here was to serve God, the Hebrew verb ʿābad suggesting a central idea in suzerain-vassal treaty texts. Above all else, the Great King demanded that subservient allies serve him; in so doing they would manifest most clearly the very essence of obedience. To fail to serve would result in Israel's being given over to another sovereign whom they would serve until they were utterly decimated (v. 48). The service this time would not be marked by joy (śimḥâ) and gladness (bĕṭûb lēbāb, lit., "with goodness of heart") but with their very opposite, destitution and deprivation. It would be onerous slavery like that of prisoners of war led about with iron yokes upon their necks.

Once more this calls to mind the motif of a reverse exodus.[57] Israel had endured slavery in Egypt under Pharaoh and his taskmasters (Exod 1:11-14; 5:6-19), a bondage so severe and hopeless that only the Lord could deliver them from it (Exod 6:6-7; Lev 26:13). This he did so that they could be his servant people and thus fulfill the purposes for which he had elected them through their patriarchal ancestors (Exod 3:6-12; 4:22-23; 8:1,20; 9:1,13). Now they were threatened by a return to Egypt, as it were, to a renewal of the cruel bondage from which they had so recently been redeemed (cf. Lev 26:17). Jeremiah especially seized on this imagery of Deuteronomy to describe the Babylonian captivity of Judah that was impending in his own time. It would be a captivity marked by the yoke of oppression and slavery (Jer 27:7-8) but one that also would end with the breaking of that yoke and the release and return of God's people to the land of promise (Jer 28:14; 30:8; cf. Ezek 34:27). In effect, it would be a second

---

[57] Thus Craigie, *Deuteronomy*, 348-49. For the use of the exodus motif in Deuteronomy, see B. S. Childs, "Deuteronomic Formulae of the Exodus Tradition," VTSup 16 (1967): 30-39.

exodus, another opportunity for Israel to take up the privileges and opportunities of servanthood (cf. Isa 43:1-7; 52:3-6).

28:49-50   The agent of the Lord's curse is not specifically identified in the passage at hand except as a faraway and fierce nation of an unknown language (vv. 49-50). Those who maintain a seventh-century date for Deuteronomy argue that the Babylonians were in view, an identification supported by Jeremiah, who, as noted, appears to link the Babylonians with the imagery of this curse section of Deuteronomy.[58] This latter point is no argument for an exclusive fulfillment by Babylon, however, nor is it proof of a late date for Deuteronomy. It is commonly recognized that predictive prophecy may allow for multiple applications (if not fulfillments in the strict sense) so that the nation here could be any one of many possible candidates from the standpoint of the setting of the text. As time passed, the historical situations would clarify the specific applications so that Jeremiah, for example, who witnessed the rise of the Neo-Babylonian Empire, would understand the prophecy to refer to Babylon.

Closer to the time of the traditional date of the text's composition was the Assyrian conquest of Samaria and the Northern Kingdom and the subsequent deportation of the ten tribes of Israel in 722 B.C. (2 Kgs 17:1-6). This took place, according to the record, because Israel "rejected his [the Lord's] decrees and the covenant he had made with their fathers" (2 Kgs 17:15), and "they forsook all the commands of the LORD their God" (v. 16). The language is clearly that of the apodoses of the Deuteronomy curses (Deut 28:15,45) and the principles of Deut 27, suggesting that the historian judged Israel's history against the standards of the covenant document of Deuteronomy.[59]

Further evidence that Assyria is predominantly in mind in this curse of siege is the description of the nation as one of incomprehensible language (v. 49) and "fierce-looking" (v. 50). The same pair of ideas is found in Isa 33:19, where the prophet speaks of Assyria (though not by name; cf. 28:11).[60] Furthermore, it is clear from the account of Sennacherib's siege of Jerusalem in 701 B.C. that the Assyrians spoke a language unknown to the Hebrew population at large (2 Kgs 18:26-28 = Isa 36:11-13). Finally, no nation of antiquity was more ruthless in its prosecution of war than

---

[58] Von Rad, *Deuteronomy,* 175-76. As Mayes points out, however, "The expressions used to describe the enemy in these verses are in many cases stereotyped; they could be used of any conqueror" (*Deuteronomy,* 356).

[59] J. Gray, *I & II Kings,* 2d ed., OTL (Philadelphia: Westminster, 1970), 647-48.

[60] Thompson, *Deuteronomy,* 276.

Assyria. With good cause the text speaks of them prophetically as "without respect for the old or pity for the young" (v. 50; cf. Nah 2:11-3:1; Isa 7:20).

28:51-52 The invasion by this distant enemy would result in the utter consumption of Israel's produce and livestock (v. 51) and the siege of all its cities (vv. 52-53). This kind of scorched-earth policy is well attested in Assyrian texts as well as in the Old Testament. Shalmaneser V besieged Samaria for three years before it fell (2 Kgs 17:5), and Sennacherib surrounded Jerusalem twenty years later and would have taken it had the Lord not intervened in a miraculous act of deliverance (2 Kgs 19:35-36).[61]

28:53-57 The most horrible effect of the siege would not be what Assyria did to Israel or Judah, however, but what the people would do to one another as a result of their dire predicament. In unspeakably gruesome language, the lawgiver described in detail the acts of cannibalism to which the Lord's people would resort (vv. 53-57). Though the prediction was no doubt laced with hyperbole, the desperation of those under siege for years could not have fallen very much short of the measures taken here. In fact, the Old Testament records at least one example of cannibalism in Israel, at a time when Samaria was besieged by the Arameans under Benhadad II (ca. 850 B.C., cf. 2 Kgs 6:24-31). On that occasion two women had agreed to slay their sons and preserve themselves by eating their flesh, an act that proved to be unnecessary as it turned out.[62] There is no record of such extreme exigencies in the biblical narratives of siege by the Assyrians, though Jeremiah predicted its occurrence in the Babylonian conquest of Judah (Jer 19:9; cf. Lam 4:10; Ezek 5:10). True to the unfolding nature of biblical prophecy, the present curse looks specifically to the Assyrian scourge but encompasses within it more remote, even eschatological, fulfillments.

The intensity of the distress is emphasized by the fact that parents would eat their children, their only hope of earthly remembrance and posterity (v. 53). And not just the most crass or barbaric among them would do so. The gentlest soul[63] would abandon all restraint and loyalty and in his hour of self-preservation would feed upon his own precious loved ones (v. 54), not retaining a shred of generosity toward others in similar plight (v.

---

[61] Sargon II appears to have taken credit for Shalmaneser's conquest of Samaria; for the texts see J. B. Pritchard, ed. *Ancient Near Eastern Texts Relating to the Old Testament,* 2d ed. (Princeton: Princeton University Press, 1955), 284, 287-88.

[62] Such a consequence of covenant violation occurs also in the Esarhaddon treaty texts. See Wiseman, *Vassal-Treaties of Esarhaddon,* 62 (col. vi, lines 448-50).

[63] The phrase is הָאִישׁ הָרַךְ ("the coddled man," KB, 890). The idea is that of a delicate person who normally would abhor the very thought of cannibalism, especially where his own family was at stake.

55). The basest human (or animal?) instincts would prevail when choice had to be made between one's own life and another's.

Lest it be thought that the maternal side of womanhood might preclude such abhorrent behavior, the text goes on to reveal, in terms that stagger the imagination, that women so refined and genteel as to avoid touching the ground with unshod feet would not hesitate to consume their own offspring (vv. 56-57a). In fact, they would keep for themselves their newborn infants and even the afterbirth even if it meant that their husbands and other children had to do without and starve. These they would hoard and eat secretly to preserve themselves in that day of unspeakable horror.

(6) The Curse of Covenant Jeopardy (28:58-68)

[58]If you do not carefully follow all the words of this law, which are written in this book, and do not revere this glorious and awesome name—the LORD your God— [59]the LORD will send fearful plagues on you and your descendants, harsh and prolonged disasters, and severe and lingering illnesses. [60]He will bring upon you all the diseases of Egypt that you dreaded, and they will cling to you. [61]The LORD will also bring on you every kind of sickness and disaster not recorded in this Book of the Law, until you are destroyed. [62]You who were as numerous as the stars in the sky will be left but few in number, because you did not obey the LORD your God. [63]Just as it pleased the LORD to make you prosper and increase in number, so it will please him to ruin and destroy you. You will be uprooted from the land you are entering to possess.

[64]Then the LORD will scatter you among all nations, from one end of the earth to the other. There you will worship other gods—gods of wood and stone, which neither you nor your fathers have known. [65]Among those nations you will find no repose, no resting place for the sole of your foot. There the LORD will give you an anxious mind, eyes weary with longing, and a despairing heart. [66]You will live in constant suspense, filled with dread both night and day, never sure of your life. [67]In the morning you will say, "If only it were evening!" and in the evening, "If only it were morning!"—because of the terror that will fill your hearts and the sights that your eyes will see. [68]The LORD will send you back in ships to Egypt on a journey I said you should never make again. There you will offer yourselves for sale to your enemies as male and female slaves, but no one will buy you.

This last section of curses, true to the form and content of the previous ones, contains a protasis clause (v. 58) followed by an extensive list of apodoses detailing the judgments that attend covenant disobedience. These in turn may be grouped in two divisions: those involving disease and other disasters in the land (vv. 59-63) and those involving deportation from the land (vv. 64-68). But the two kinds of judgment share in common the character of an "exodus reversal" (cf. v. 27); that is, the calamities in Canaan would be like the plagues Yahweh visited on Egypt (v. 60), and the exile, though universal in scope (v. 64), would be tantamount to a return to Egyptian bondage (v. 68).

28:58 The protasis appears here in a more expanded form than usual. The injunctions to be followed are "all the words of this law" (cf. 17:19; 27:3,8,26), a reference to the entire covenant text of Deuteronomy (cf. 1:1; 11:18; 31:12,24; 32:45-46). But as though to render the meaning with absolutely no ambiguity, Moses added the qualifier "which are written in this book," a phrase used here for the first time in Deuteronomy (cf. v. 61; 29:20-21,27; 30:10; 31:24,26). Similar terminology in the account of Josiah's reformation and the recovery of a scroll in the temple lies at the center of the identification of that scroll with Deuteronomy (2 Kgs 22:8, 11; 23:2,21).[64]

In addition to obeying the covenant text, Israel was to "revere this glorious and awesome name," that is, the name "Yahweh your God." This emphasis on the name is, of course, typical of Deuteronomic theology (cf. 12:5,11,21; 14:23-24; 16:2,6,11), but pervasively throughout the Old Testament the name of God is synonymous with God himself (Gen 4:26; 12:8; Exod 3:13-15; 23:21; Lev 24:16; Pss 7:17; 9:2; 18:49) and for this reason must be revered (Exod 20:7; Lev 18:21; 19:12; 22:32; Pss 61:5; 86:9,11; 96:8). This respect for Yahweh's name can best be manifested by obedience to his sovereignty, that is, by keeping the terms of his covenant with Israel. The two parts of the protasis are therefore complementary.

28:59 The sicknesses that would befall disobedient Israel are described as "fearful plagues" (v. 59). Literally the line reads, "Yahweh will make your smitings wonderful," the point being that God's judgment on his people would elicit amazement from those who witness it. The smitings (better "blows," or "wounds") refer not to plagues in general, such as those that befell Egypt, but to illness or disease. The words "plagues" and "disasters" here are both translations of the single Hebrew word *makkôt*, a term nuanced by the following noun *ḥŏlāyim* ("sickness"; cf. Deut 7:15; 1 Kgs 17:17; 2 Kgs 1:2; 8:8-9; 13:14; Isa 53:3-4), nearly always to be understood literally as a disease or wound. The judgment here then is primarily some kind of epidemic that would largely depopulate the nation.[65]

---

[64] Mayes, *Deuteronomy,* 85-103.
[65] Seybold points out that "the group of words deriving from חלה appears with particular frequency in the parenetic strand of tradition defined by [passages such as Dt. 7:15; 28:59,61; 29:21(22)]" and that common to these passages is the setting forth of the alternatives of blessing and cursing (K. Seybold, "חָלָה *chalah,*" etc., *TDOT* 4:405).

28:60   This is confirmed in v. 60 by the reference to the "diseases of Egypt," for the word here (*madwēh*) conveys also the idea of physical weakness or ailment. Furthermore, the combination *makkâ* and *ḥolî* in v. 61 ("sickness and disaster"), as in their plural forms in v. 59, connotes plagues of a physical, bodily type, a disease of some kind. In fact, the Hebrew construction in v. 61 allows the sickness to be viewed as a divinely ordained instrument of judgment, not just an illness of happenstance or of no apparent purpose.

28:61   The diseases will be of two kinds—those the Israelites knew in Egypt (v. 60) and those not hitherto even mentioned in "this Book of the Law" (i.e., Deuteronomy; v. 61). As for the former, they must have been the diseases of Yahweh's judgment on the Egyptians, namely, the plagues, for it is not said here that they afflicted Israel but only brought dread to them (cf. Exod 15:26). Among the plagues, those that could properly be categorized as sickness or disease were the so-called "murrain" (Heb. *deber*) that afflicted cattle (Exod 9:1-7) and the boils that painfully debilitated the people of Egypt (Exod 9:8-12; cf. Deut 28:27).

As suggested already, these afflictions were no doubt to be taken literally, though the Old Testament does not provide detailed accounts of such maladies as contributory to Israel's demise. The spiritual sickness of the nation is also in view, however, and became a favorite way of describing their malaise as disobedient vassals awaiting divine judgment. Isaiah graphically described Israel as sick "from the sole of your foot to the top of your head," a people in whom "there is no soundness—only wounds and welts" (Isa 1:6).[66] This is an assessment shared by other prophets contemporaneous with the last years of Israel's and Judah's national life (cf. Jer 6:7; 30:12-15; 46:11; Hos 5:13).

28:62-63   The result would be a greatly reduced population. The nation that was "as numerous as the stars in the sky" (v. 62) would end up with a comparative handful of people. This was clearly a judgment on covenant violation as the repetition of the conditional protasis clause ("because you did not obey the LORD your God") puts beyond doubt. Moreover, the reduction of numbers from the uncountable stars to the remnant is a deliberate harking back to the covenant promise made to Abraham that his offspring would be as multitudinous as the stars (Gen 15:5; 22:17; cf. Deut 1:10; 10:22). If increased population is a sign of the blessing of covenant fidelity, population decline is a sign of covenant unfaithfulness.

---

[66] O. Kaiser argues that the sickness described by Isaiah is metaphorical of devastation already wreaked by the Assyrians, a point underscored by v. 7 that speaks of the fact of that conquest (*Isaiah 1–12*, OTL [Philadelphia: Westminster, 1972], 9).

The contrast is further defined by v. 63: just as the Lord had increased Israel's numbers and prosperity, he would, in judgment, decrease them in the day of his wrath. No less tragic and stark would be the reversal of the covenant promise concerning the land. Whereas God at one time had sworn to give the land of Canaan to the patriarchs and their offspring (Gen 15:7,18-21; 17:8), he would in a future day remove them from it because of their disobedience (v. 63). Thus decrease in population and eviction from the land answer point by point (and in the same order) the matching blessings of number and land in the original promise passages (Gen 15:5-7; 17:4-8).

28:64 The reversal continues with the scattering of Israel to the ends of the earth (v. 64a). The fathers had come from distant Ur and Haran to Canaan, the land of promise (Gen 11:27-12:4; cf. Deut 26:5). Now, ironically, their descendants would return there and to a host of other places besides (Lev 26:33; cf. 2 Kgs 17:6; 18:11; 25:6-7,21). In Mesopotamia the ancestors worshiped gods other than Yahweh, icons of wood and stone (cf. Josh 24:14). In the exile to come they would do the same thing (v. 64b; cf. 4:28). Prior to their entering Canaan, Abraham and his family had been a wandering clan, one without a fixed and settled way of life (Gen 13:1-18; Deut 26:5). Having attained stability in the land of promise, they would be uprooted from it and cast once more into the turbulence of homelessness (vv. 65-67). In every way that Canaan represented blessing and fulfillment of promise, exile from the land would represent its opposite. Blessing would be turned into curse.

28:65a The restlessness of life outside the land is strikingly portrayed in a staccato-like series of realities and reactions. There would be no opportunity to settle down ("repose," *rāgaᶜ*) or to find rest (or "a resting-place"; *mānôaḥ*). The allusion to "the sole of your foot" is also reminiscent of the overturn of blessing, for the occupation and conquest of Canaan is elsewhere seen as the placing of the sole (*kap*) on the earth (cf. Deut 11:24; Josh 1:3; cf. Ezek 43:7; Mal 4:3). This image of dominion would have no relevance to the captives, for they themselves would be dominated by others.

28:65b-67 External transience would be matched by internal, emotional upheaval. The mind would be anxious (lit., "there will be a quaking heart"), the eyes would fail because of longing (cf. 28:32), and the heart (*nepeš*; i.e., the inner being as a whole) would become faint. The very lives of the people would be hung up before them, that is, would be in suspense (as in NIV). This is because they would never know what a day or a night might bring forth (v. 66). Those who rose from sleep would wish it were time to retire, and those who were ready for bed would wish the night had already passed (v. 67a). All this was because of both internal and external fears, those of the spirit and those of the outer world of experience (v. 67b).

28:68   The clearest sign that the curse was to be the exact opposite to the intended blessings is the threat that the Lord would send his people back to Egypt (v. 68).[67] Amazingly, however, the return would not be by retracing their steps through the Sinai deserts and across the Red Sea. Rather, it would be "in ships." The reference to ships has long been troublesome, but the main point is clear.[68] Israel's exodus and wandering had been a miracle from beginning to end, a journey made possible only by the Lord's providential grace. Israel's deportation, however, would be at the hands of men and by normal means of transportation. Once in Egypt, God's people once more would be slaves but this time free of charge. So little esteemed would they be that no one would offer money in exchange for them (v. 68b).

Egyptian texts are replete with accounts of slave trade, particularly with the import of Semitics for the purpose of servitude.[69] In the time of judgment for covenant violation the Lord would make his own elect nation available for the auction block of bondage, an ironic twist to the exodus in which Israel was freed from that very condition. Whether the return to Egypt is to be understood literally or it is better to see Egypt here only as a type of exile to all the nations is unclear. It is true that many Jews eventually settled in Egypt, some perhaps as slaves, and the exile probably embodied slavery at times, if not always of the body, certainly of the spirit (cf. Jer 42:13-17; 44:11-14,24-30; cf. Neh 9:36).

5. Narrative Interlude (29:1 [Heb. 28:69])

¹These are the terms of the covenant the LORD commanded Moses to make with the Israelites in Moab, in addition to the covenant he had made with them at Horeb.

All scholars recognize the transitional nature of this verse as a brief narrative interlude between the preceding blessings and curses section (27:1–28:68) and the following historical review (29:2–30:20), but there is difference of opinion about whether it concludes the preceding material or intro-

---

[67] See D. J. Reimer, "Concerning Return to Egypt: Deuteronomy 17:16 and 28:68 Reconsidered," in *Studies in the Pentateuch,* ed. J. Emerton, VTSup 41 (Leiden: Brill, 1990), 217-29.

[68] See, for example, D. G. Schley, Jr., "'Yahweh Will Cause You to Return to Egypt in Ships' (Deuteronomy 28:68)," *VT* 35 (1985): 369-72.

[69] C. Aldred, *The Egyptians* (New York: Frederik A. Praeger, 1961), 183-84.

duces the succeeding.[70] The division of the Hebrew text would favor the former and that of the English text the latter.[71]

On balance the stronger arguments favor the view that the verse forms an inclusio with the preamble section of Deut 1:1-5. Both passages begin with the phrase "these are the words . . . which Moses," both locate the setting in Moab, and both make reference to Horeb and the earlier covenant. Thus the covenant text proper may be said to have been brought to a conclusion in 29:1. Less obvious similarities exist also between Deut 4:44-49, the setting and introduction to the stipulations section, and the present verse. Such an analysis would view 29:1 as the summation of the actual heart of the covenant text, namely, the stipulations and curses and blessings.

Against the position that 29:1 introduces the succeeding material is the fact that v. 2 also provides such an introduction in its own right. The only other time the verb "summoned" (*wayyiqrāʾ*) appears in Deuteronomy in this sense is in 5:1, the opening of the general stipulation section. Both verses commence with the words, "Moses summoned all the Israelites and said to them," and both go on in the following passages to refer to the covenant terms and the need to obey them (5:1-2; cf. 29:9). It seems quite clear, then, that a major break occurs between 29:1 and 29:2, with the former bringing all the previous material to a close and the latter introducing at least the epilogic historical review.[72]

---

[70] H. F. VanRooy, "Deuteronomy 28, 69—Superscript or Subscript?" *JNSL* 14 (1988): 215-22.

[71] N. Lohfink, "Der Bundesschluss im Land Moab—Redaktiongeschichtliches zu Deut. 28:69-34:47," *BZ* 6 (1962): 32-56; A. Rofé, "The Covenant in the Land of Moab (Dt 28, 69-30, 20): Historico-Literary, Comparative, and Form-critical Considerations," in *Das Deuteronomium*, ed. N. Lohfink, BETL 68 (Leuven: University Press, 1985), 310-20.

[72] See also Craigie, *Deuteronomy,* 353; Driver, *Deuteronomy,* 319.

VIII. EPILOGUE: HISTORICAL REVIEW (29:2–30:20 [Heb. 29:1–30:20])

VIII. EPILOGUE: HISTORICAL REVIEW (29:2–30:20 [HEB. 29:1–30:20])

There is general consensus that chaps. 29 and 30 of Deuteronomy (as well as 31:1-8) are not strictly part of the covenant document as such documents were ordinarily crafted.[1] This does not mean, of course, that this section does not serve a covenant function in Moses' own unique creation of the book as a covenant instrument.[2] But even if it doesn't, it is very much at home here as a parenesis that looks to the past, present, and future of the elect nation. It provides a summation of God's past dealings with Israel, restates the present occasion of covenant offer and acceptance, and addresses the options of covenant disobedience and obedience respectively. Finally, it exhorts the assembled throng to covenant commitment. It is most fitting that these summaries and exhortations follow the body of the covenant text and precede the formalizing of the agreement by the Lord and his chosen vassal.[3]

1. Exodus, Wandering, and Conquest (29:2-8 [1-7])

²Moses summoned all the Israelites and said to them:

Your eyes have seen all that the LORD did in Egypt to Pharaoh, to all his

---

[1] A. D. H. Mayes, *Deuteronomy,* NCBC (Grand Rapids: Eerdmans, 1979), 358-59.

[2] G. J. Wenham, "The Structure and Date of Deuteronomy" (Ph.D. diss., University of London, 1969), 208-10.

[3] See F. duT. Laubscher, "Notes on the Literary Structure of IQS 2:11-18 and Its Biblical Parallel in Deut. 29," *JNSL* 8 (1980): 49-55. Laubscher draws attention especially to the unity of vv. 9-27 as demonstrated by a chiastic pattern (pp. 53-55).

officials and to all his land. [3]With your own eyes you saw those great trials, those miraculous signs and great wonders. [4]But to this day the LORD has not given you a mind that understands or eyes that see or ears that hear. [5]During the forty years that I led you through the desert, your clothes did not wear out, nor did the sandals on your feet. [6]You ate no bread and drank no wine or other fermented drink. I did this so that you might know that I am the LORD your God.

[7]When you reached this place, Sihon king of Heshbon and Og king of Bashan came out to fight against us, but we defeated them. [8]We took their land and gave it as an inheritance to the Reubenites, the Gadites and the half-tribe of Manasseh.

29:2-4 [1-3]   Just as the covenant text as a whole is introduced by a historical prologue (Deut 1:6–4:40), so this appeal to covenant commitment begins with a brief account of Israel's history from Egyptian bondage to the present moment. The story commences with a reminder of the Lord's mighty acts against the Egyptian oppressors, acts described here as elsewhere as "miraculous signs and great wonders" (v. 3 [2]; cf. Deut 4:34; 6:22; 7:19; 26:8; Exod 7:3).[4] The reference, of course, is primarily to the plagues and to other divine interventions that effected Israel's deliverance. Despite all this, Moses said, the people to that very day had not comprehended fully the meaning of their redemption and the Lord's role in it (v. 4 [3]). Their rebellion and unbelief had caused them to miss many of the blessings that should have attended their salvation. Isaiah reflected on the condition of Israel in his own day in the same terms (Isa 6:9-10), and Paul quoted this very text to speak of the hardness and blindness of his fellow Jews (Rom 11:8).[5] Even this, however, could not negate the covenant faithfulness of God; for though the nation as a whole might reject his overtures of grace, a remnant would believe, and that would be the nucleus of his salvific purposes (Isa 10:20-23; Rom 9:27-28; 11:1-7).

29:5-6 [4-5]   This was true also of the unbelieving exodus generation, and for this reason most of them wandered for forty years in the desert until they died there without having come to the promised land (v. 5a [4a]; cf. Deut 1:26; Num 14:26-35). Nevertheless, the Lord provided for them there, giving them clothes that would not wear out (v. 5b [4b]) and manna from heaven in place of the earthly food of bread and wine (v. 6a [5a]; cf. Deut 8:2-4).[6] All this he did to manifest his providential care and thus, in the face of their total dependence on him, to prove to them that he

---

[4] F. J. Helfmeyer, "אוֹת *'oth*," *TDOT* 1:168, 171, 176.

[5] P. C. Craigie, *The Book of Deuteronomy,* NICOT (Grand Rapids: Eerdmans, 1976), 356.

[6] C. T. Begg, " 'Bread, Wine, and Strong Drink' in Deut 29:5a," *BFT* 41 (1980): 266-75.

was the Lord their God (v. 6b [5b]; cf. 4:35). The notion that the Lord can and does prove himself to be God by his mighty works of deliverance and provision is a major biblical and theological motif (cf. Exod 6:7; 7:5,17; 8:10,22; 9:14; 10:2; 14:4; Ezek 6:7,10,13-14; and passim in Ezekiel).[7]

29:7-8 [6-7]   Further evidence of this fact in Israel's history was their ability to defeat Sihon of Heshbon and Og of Bashan, both powerful rulers of the Transjordanian kingdoms of the Amorites and Rephaim respectively (v. 7 [6]; cf. Deut 2:26–3:17). Having accomplished this, Moses divided the conquered lands among the tribes of Reuben, Gad, and Manasseh as they had petitioned him to do (v. 8 [7]). This could not have been done by Israel alone but only as Yahweh the Warrior led his people to conquest and occupation. From beginning to end, Israel's covenant history had been a record of miracle, and for this reason alone the present plea for covenant commitment was most reasonable indeed.

2. The Present Covenant Setting (29:9-15 [8-14])

[9]Carefully follow the terms of this covenant, so that you may prosper in everything you do. [10]All of you are standing today in the presence of the LORD your God—your leaders and chief men, your elders and officials, and all the other men of Israel, [11]together with your children and your wives, and the aliens living in your camps who chop your wood and carry your water. [12]You are standing here in order to enter into a covenant with the LORD your God, a covenant the LORD is making with you this day and sealing with an oath, [13]to confirm you this day as his people, that he may be your God as he promised you and as he swore to your fathers, Abraham, Isaac and Jacob. [14]I am making this covenant, with its oath, not only with you [15]who are standing here with us today in the presence of the LORD our God but also with those who are not here today.

The paragraph structure of the Masoretic tradition assigns v. 9 [8] to the previous section as a closing exhortation to the historical review. That is, it becomes an enjoinder to keep covenant in light of God's past dealings with his people Israel and may therefore be viewed as a result clause: "Therefore, carefully follow" and so forth.[8]

While this has much to commend it, the use of the word "covenant" (*bĕrît*) in both v. 9 [8] and vv. 14-15 [13-14] argues for the delineation of vv. 9-15 [8-14] as a separate pericope.[9] Further support for the unitary nature of the material is the references to "standing" in vv. 10 and 15 [9

[7] W. Zimmerli, *I Am Yahweh* (Atlanta: John Knox, 1982), 1-28.

[8] So Mayes, *Deuteronomy,* 362.

[9] J. Ridderbos, *Deuteronomy,* BSC (Grand Rapids: Zondervan, 1984), 264-65.

and 14], both of which relate to the making of covenant. In fact, standing to make covenant is found only here.[10]

29:9 [8]   The setting here is the same as that described in the preamble to the Book of Deuteronomy (1:1-5; cf. 4:44-49), the land of Moab. All that has changed is that the earlier passages anticipate the revelation of the covenant text and the present one views it as having already been given. The previous injunctions had been to follow (*šāmar*) the stipulations of the covenant about to be delivered (cf. 4:1; 5:1) or in the process of being articulated (7:11-12; 8:1; 12:1), but now the command is to act upon the finished corpus of instruction. As always the blessing of God is dependent upon scrupulous adherence to his covenant terms (v. 9b [8b]; cf. 5:33; 6:3; 7:13-16).

29:10-11 [9-10]   The assembly gathered here is described with unusual fullness—the leaders, the ordinary citizens, wives and children, and resident aliens. That is, the entire believing community was invited to enter into covenant relationship with the Lord without reference to social, economic, gender, or age differences. The individualizing or personalizing of the appeal is emphasized by the use of singular pronouns or pronominal suffixes throughout the passage (twelve times in vv. 11-12). The covenant was made with all Israel as a collective, to be sure, but it was also made with each and every member of the body.

The nature of the leaders here is complicated by difficulties in the text. For "your leaders and chief men" (v. 10 [9]), the Hebrew reads, literally, "your heads, your tribes," an obviously confusing pairing in a list containing technical terms for public officials (cf. the following "elders" [*zĕqēnîm*] and "officials" [*šōṭĕrîm*]). Both ancient versions (LXX, Syr) and modern scholars[11] suggest either "heads of your tribes," making "heads" construct rather than absolute (*rā'šê* for *rā'šêkem*), or "your judges," reading *šōpṭêkem* for *šibṭêkem*. The latter is much to be preferred because it leaves two sets of officials in each group—heads and judges, on the one hand, and elders and officials on the other. This is consistent with Hebrew style and also with other lists of theocratic leaders (cf. Deut 16:18; 21:2; Josh 8:33). Most important are Josh 23:2 and 24:1, where the dignitaries are "elders, heads, judges, and officials" in both places and in that order. Such lists tended to become stereotyped, a fact that also supports the reading adopted here.

---

[10] The verbs are different (נצב in v. 10 [9] and עמד in v. 15 [14]), but the concept is the same (S. R. Driver, *Deuteronomy*, ICC [Edinburgh: T & T Clark, 1902], 322-23).

[11] Driver, *Deuteronomy*, 322. Cf. C. Begg, "The Reading *sbty(km)* in Deut 29:9 and 2 Sam 7:7," *ETL* 58 (1982): 87-105.

The aliens (Heb. *gērîm*) constitute non-Israelites whose tasks consisted of menial labor from cutting wood to drawing water. The Hebrew
construction (lit., "from the cutter of wood to the drawer of water")
implies that these were only two of the occupations of this class, the two
no doubt representing a broad range of labor usually associated with servants or, in the case of drawing water, with women (cf. Gen 24:11-13;
Exod 2:16-19). The servility of such employment may be seen in the
account of Israel's covenant with the Gibeonites (Josh 9:22-27). When
Joshua discovered the Gibeonites' deception in bringing this about, he
sentenced them to the lowly and onerous service of being "cutters of
wood and drawers of water" for Israel (Josh 9:27).[12]

29:12 [11]   The purpose of the assembly, as noted already, was to
respond to the covenant overtures initiated by the Lord. That this was
indeed the direction of the relationship is clear from the fact that it was
the Lord who was making (lit., "cutting") the covenant and the people
who were invited to enter it (lit., "cross over to it") and its oath. The idea
is not so much that the Lord made an oath to keep the covenant (so NIV)
but that "covenant" and "oath" are a hendiadys expressing the relationship as a whole.[13] It was a covenant sealed by an oath, indeed, but it was
the oath of the people that was in view, their solemn pledge to keep its
terms. This is the very use of the term "oath" (*ʾālâ*) in Gen 24:41, where
Abraham told his servant that if he made his best effort to find a wife for
Isaac and still failed, he would be free from the oath of Abraham, that is,
the oath he had sworn to Abraham (vv. 8-9; cf. 26:28).

29:13 [12]   It is important to remember that this was not so much a
ceremony of covenant making as it was one of covenant affirmation or
renewal. The original covenant had been made at Horeb, so what was in
view here was the Lord's offer of the same covenant (albeit, with necessary amendments) to the next generation of Israelites. Arrangements
agreed to by their parents were not sufficient for them. They also had to
go on record as committing themselves to the Lord and his theocratic pro-
gram. Thus Moses said that the purpose of the occasion was for the Lord
"to confirm you this day as his people" (v. 13a [12a]). The verb form here
(*hiphil* of *qûm*) occurs regularly to speak of ratifying an already existing
agreement such as a covenant (cf. Gen 6:18; 9:9,11; 17:19,21; Exod 6:4;

---

[12] A. D. H. Mayes, "Deuteronomy 29, Joshua 9, and the Place of the Gibeonites in Israel," in *Das Deuteronomium,* ed. N. Lohfink, BETL 68 (Leuven: University Press, 1985),
321-25.

[13] J. Scharbert, "אָלָה *ʾālāh*," etc., *TDOT* 1:264. Cf. J. A. Thompson, *Deuteronomy,*
TOTC (Downers Grove: InterVarsity, 1974) 281.

Deut 8:18; 9:5).[14] Furthermore, the present covenant rises out of the ancient promises of the Lord to the patriarchal ancestors of the nation (v. 13b [12b]). He who had promised to be the God of the fathers (cf. Gen 17:7; Lev 11:45; 26:12) once more gave opportunity to the descendants to seize upon that great privilege and responsibility of being his people.

29:14 [13]   The existential moment of decision is again emphasized by the language of v. 14 [13]: "I am making this covenant" (*kōrēt*). It was Israel's right to accept or reject. But if accepted, the covenant brought with it an oath. The word for "oath" here is the same as in v. 12, but the meaning shifts to "curse," for the oath was now one of self-imprecation, as the following context makes clear (vv. 14-21 [13-20]).[15] That is, the people, if they agreed to the proffered covenant, agreed also to the curses that accompanied its disobedience, curses elaborated already in chaps. 27–28.

29:15 [14]   Finally, the covenant was not only retrospective as well as current, but it had a forward view. It was made with the present generation, but its benefits would extend to generations of the Lord's people yet unborn (cf. 4:9). However, just as the Horeb commitment was good only for those who made it then and there, so future offspring of Israel must over and over again pledge themselves in covenant renewal to be his kingdom of priests and holy nation.

3. The Results of Covenant Disobedience (29:16-29 [15-28])

[16]**You yourselves know how we lived in Egypt and how we passed through the countries on the way here.** [17]**You saw among them their detestable images and idols of wood and stone, of silver and gold.** [18]**Make sure there is no man or woman, clan or tribe among you today whose heart turns away from the LORD our God to go and worship the gods of those nations; make sure there is no root among you that produces such bitter poison.**

[19]**When such a person hears the words of this oath, he invokes a blessing on himself and therefore thinks, "I will be safe, even though I persist in going my own way." This will bring disaster on the watered land as well as the dry.** [20]**The LORD will never be willing to forgive him; his wrath and zeal will burn against that man. All the curses written in this book will fall upon him, and the LORD will blot out his name from under heaven.** [21]**The LORD will single him out from all the tribes of Israel for disaster, according to all the curses of the covenant written in this Book of the Law.**

[22]**Your children who follow you in later generations and foreigners who**

---

[14] W. J. Dumbrell, *Covenant and Creation* (Nashville: Thomas Nelson, 1984), 25-26.
[15] *TDOT* 1:264.

come from distant lands will see the calamities that have fallen on the land and the diseases with which the LORD has afflicted it. ²³The whole land will be a burning waste of salt and sulfur—nothing planted, nothing sprouting, no vegetation growing on it. It will be like the destruction of Sodom and Gomorrah, Admah and Zeboiim, which the LORD overthrew in fierce anger. ²⁴All the nations will ask: "Why has the LORD done this to this land? Why this fierce, burning anger?"

²⁵And the answer will be: "It is because this people abandoned the covenant of the LORD, the God of their fathers, the covenant he made with them when he brought them out of Egypt. ²⁶They went off and worshiped other gods and bowed down to them, gods they did not know, gods he had not given them. ²⁷Therefore the LORD'S anger burned against this land, so that he brought on it all the curses written in this book. ²⁸In furious anger and in great wrath the LORD uprooted them from their land and thrust them into another land, as it is now."

²⁹The secret things belong to the LORD our God, but the things revealed belong to us and to our children forever, that we may follow all the words of this law.

Having reviewed the story of Israel's marvelous deliverance from Egypt and having pressed the assembly at Moab to enter into covenant renewal with the Lord, Moses now picked up on the curses that accompanied covenant disobedience, the note with which he had brought the preceding section to an end (v. 12). The possibility that his hearers might prove to be disloyal in the future is driven home here by Moses' recital of their temptations to idolatry and defection in the past, temptations, he seems to suggest, to which they had fallen victim.

29:16-18 [15-17]   The backward glance begins with Egypt and the journey from there to the plains of Moab (v. 16 [15]). All along the way Israel had encountered other nations and their gods. The detestable nature of these objects of pagan worship is clearly brought out in the terms Moses used to describe them—*šiqqûṣîm* ("detested things") and *gillûlîm*[16] ("idols"; i.e., made of blocks)—rather than more generic words such as *pesel* ("idol"). The Pentateuchal narratives of Israel's desert wanderings do not explicitly mention these things, but it obviously follows that if Israel confronted pagan peoples they also confronted their gods (cf. Num 25:1-5). Moreover, they went so far as to manufacture their own idol, the golden calf before which the people bowed in reverence while Moses was absent on the mountain (Exod 32:1-14; cf. Deut 9:6-21). Perhaps this form of idolatry is included in Moses' injunction that those

---

[16] H. D. Preuss, "גִּלֻּלִים *gillûlîm*," etc. *TDOT* 3:1-5. Preuss suggests a root *gel*, "dung," and thus the most uncomplimentary appellation of these idols as "dung things" (p. 2).

before him "today" (as opposed to the past?) must refrain from turning from the Lord in order to worship other gods (v. 18 [17]). Though made by Israelite craftsmen as a representation of the Lord or of his pedestal, the golden calf ultimately was inspired by Egyptian idolatry and thus was a god of a foreign nation. This perhaps explains the enigmatic "root among you that produces such bitter poison" (v. 18b [17b]).[17] The people had carried the notion of idolatry (the root) with them out of Egypt, and when they concretized that notion as the golden calf (the poison), they suffered the tragic consequences of their sin.

29:19-20 [18-19]   Those who harbored such tendencies to idolatry (or any other form of covenant violation) sought for any means possible to justify their behavior or to avert its consequences. They might go so far, Moses said, as to invoke the blessings of the covenant upon themselves when they should be prepared for its curses. By doing this, the words of blessing became in their thinking a mere mouthing of magical words designed to bring protection automatically (v. 19b [18b]). How foolish it was to imagine that God was moved or deceived by such sleight of hand. Flagrant repudiation of covenant mandates brought inexorable application of covenant curses no matter the devices of the unfaithful to turn them aside.

To drive home his point, Moses appears to have cited a proverb to the effect that the wet (land?) and the dry alike were unable to escape the scorching heat of God's wrath (v. 19c [18c]). That is, even if one was a member of the covenant community and sought to protect himself by verbalizing covenant blessings, he would be no safer in his sin than the unbeliever who made no pretense and stood beneath no such contrived shelter.[18] The appropriateness of the proverb is evident in the statements of the burning wrath and zeal of the Lord that follow (v. 20 [19]).

The combination of words "watered" (Heb. *rāweh*) and "dry" (*ṣāmēʾ*) forms a merism, a figure of speech denoting totality. All, wet and dry, would be consumed in fiery judgment. Nor could there be opportunity for repentance by those who consciously and high-handedly committed treason against the Lord, particularly when they hypocritically tried to cover it up (v. 20a [19a]). Rather, God's wrath and zeal (or, as a hendiadys, his zealous wrath) would consume them, blotting out their very names from

---

[17] For רֹאשׁ ("poison") and its various possibilities, see Driver, *Deuteronomy,* 324-25.

[18] For several interpretive options see I. Cairns, *Word and Presence,* ITC (Grand Rapids: Eerdmans, 1992), 259-60. Cairns suggests that "moist" and "dry" refer to watered and unwatered plants that are wiped out alike in time of blight. That is, the sin of any member of a community affects them all.

human remembrance (v. 20b [19b]). Instead of the hoped-for blessing would come the dreaded "curses of this book," namely, the curses that all together were the lot of covenant violators.[19]

29:21 [20]   It is important to note the singular or individual character of this subsection. Indeed, clans or even whole tribes might defect from the Lord (or, for that matter, the entire nation as in the Sinai deserts; v. 18 [17]), but the emphasis here was decidedly on the individual and on personal responsibility for covenant obedience. It was the "person" who, seeking to avert curses by invoking blessings, would remain unforgiven, the object of the very curses he had sought to evade (v. 20 [19]). It was that single sinner out of all Israel whose name would be blotted out, the very epitome of what it means to suffer the curse of God's judgment (v. 21 [20]).

This observation is important precisely because of the tension between Israel perceived as a collective or "corporate" personality and Israel as a nation made up of thousands of identifiable and personally accountable individuals. The tension is obvious in the alternating uses of singular and plural pronouns throughout Deuteronomy, especially in the parenetic sections.[20] That is, Moses saw Israel in both the corporate and the individual sense, sometimes emphasizing the one and sometimes the other. Critical scholars have attempted to adduce different sources according to the use of plural or singular terms but without convincing results. It is far more satisfactory to let the tension remain and to ascribe the differences to a theological holism that understands the covenant people to be a single, undivided entity on the one hand and a collection of individual persons on the other. The nation as a whole was called into a redemptive relationship and mission, a call without repentance or abrogation. Individuals within the community could and would be called into account for their own adherence to covenant principles or the lack thereof.[21] Obedience would bring blessing (as in the cases of Caleb and Joshua; cf. Num 14:30), but disobedience would guarantee cursing, even to the point of the extirpation of the very memory of the guilty one (v. 20 [19]; cf. Ps 9:5). Inherent in this would be the cutting off of progeny, for one was remembered through future generations by means of his offspring.

---

[19] M. Harl, "Le péché irrémissible de l'idolâtre arrogant: Dt 29, 19-20 dans la Septant et chez d'autres témoins," in *Melanges Dominique Barthelemy,* ed. P. Casetti et al. (Göttingen: Vandenhoeck & Ruprecht, 1981), 63-78.

[20] See the Introduction and C. T. Begg, "The Significance of the *Numeruswechsel* in Deuteronomy: The 'Prehistory' of the Question," *ETL* 55 (1979): 116-24; G. Minette de Tillesse, "Sections 'tu' et sections 'vous' dans le Deutéronome," *VT* 12 (1962): 29-87.

[21] Craigie, *Deuteronomy,* 358-59.

29:22-24 [21-23]   Returning to the plural pronoun and thus to the nation as such, Moses looked to the future and the results of divine judgment that would accompany disloyalty to the Lord and the covenant. Future generations of Israelites and foreigners (*nokrî*) alike would bear witness to the horrible scene of devastation and abandonment, ruin described literally as "plagues" (*makkâ*; cf. this term in the previous curses list, 28:59,61) and "diseases" (*ḥălū̉îm*). These would afflict the people, but the very land and soil itself would be ravaged. The only fitting comparison that came to the prophet's mind was the destruction of the cities of the plain in Abraham's day (v. 23 [22]; cf. Gen 19:23-28). As they were totally decimated in the Lord's fiery wrath, so Israel would become a barren place of burning sulphur (thus *goprît*)[22] and salt. Crops would no more grow there than along the moonscape-like shores of the Dead Sea (cf. Ezek 47:11).

29:24 [23]   This curse, like that upon the people, is spelled out in detail in the lists of covenant curses (28:16-18,24,38-40). Nothing could be more ironic than for the land of Canaan, a land "flowing with milk and honey" (Exod 3:8; 33:3; Lev 20:24; Num 13:27; Deut 6:3; 11:9; 26:9,15; 27:3; 31:20), to become one divested of any sign of fertility and productivity. In the face of such incredible reversal of blessing to curse, the nations in the day of wrath would ask in amazement why the Lord had done such things.

29:25-28 [24-27]   The answer to this question would be unequivocal and unambiguous: because of Israel's abandonment of covenant pledged by solemn oath to the Lord. The covenant in view was not just the one presently being offered, namely, the covenant renewal document, but that single one promised to the forefathers and revealed at Horeb (v. 25 [24]) of which the Deuteronomy text was (to Israel) the current expression. The forsaking of that covenant, though taking many forms, was crystallized in the act of idolatry, for idolatry was a violation of the very core of the covenant relationship (v. 26 [25]). This is clear from the positioning of the commandments against polytheism and idolatry at the very beginning of the Decalogue (Deut 5:6-10) and the centrality of the Shema to all Old Testament faith and belief (Deut 6:4-5). Such practice was treasonous, a rebellion against the Lord, the one and only God, and attachment to his enemies, the deities of pagan imagination.

This had begun within months of the exodus deliverance in the worship of the golden calf (cf. vv. 17-18 [16, 17]; 9:16-21), was continued in

---

[22] For the Akk cognate *kibrītu/kubrītu,* meaning "sulphur" as an incendiary agent, see *CAD* 8:333.

the idolatrous affair at Baal Peor (Num 25:1-9), and would become a hallmark of Israel's history thereafter. In fact, the historian who recounted the fall of Samaria to the Assyrians in 722 attributed it to Israel's covenant infidelity throughout the whole time and in language remarkably similar to that found here (cf. 2 Kgs 17:7-18). With prophetic foresight Moses looked to the time when the "curses written in this book" (v. 27 [26]; cf. 28:58-61; 29:20-21) would come into effect, curses that culminated in the deportation of the nation from its land (v. 28; cf. Deut 28:63-68; 2 Kgs 17:6). "As it is now" (v. 28 [27]) must be understood, of course, as the words of awestruck observers of the distant future day when all of this would have come to pass.[23]

29:29 [28] The section describing the results of covenant disobedience comes to a rather enigmatic conclusion in v. 29. The main difficulty lies in the identification of "the secret things" and "the things revealed" and how these phrases (and the whole verse) relate to the overall context.

The best solution, perhaps, is to view the main clause as a proverbial evaluation of the conundrum produced by the fact of the exile of the people of the Lord to whom were given unconditional promises of ongoing existence as his servants. That is, how could Israel, the recipient of the everlasting promises to the forefathers, be destroyed and deported? The ongoing of Israel and their apparent termination seem to be mutually exclusive concepts. This perception, however, was that of the nations only, the unbelievers to whom the Lord's ultimate purposes had not been revealed. It was they who had asked incredulously how God could bring such judgment on his own chosen ones (v. 24 [23]). From an empirical standpoint all was at an end, and there was no hope of recovery. God's own people knew better, however, for he had revealed to them the end as well as the beginning (cf. 30:11-14).[24] The dry bones of Israel in exile would be infused with divine breath that would resuscitate the nation to its role as servant of the Lord and mediator of his saving grace (cf. Ezek 37:1-28). It was this knowledge and hope that should have inspired obedience to "all the words of this law" (v. 29).

---

[23] Most scholars view this verse as a postexilic addition to the text inasmuch as it appears to presuppose the Babylonian deportation (thus, e.g., Mayes, *Deuteronomy,* 367). Craigie suggests that "these words [of v. 28 (27)] may be part of the answer . . . given to the question posed in v. 23, implying that at the future point envisaged in these verses, the Hebrews would be exiled from their land" (*Deuteronomy,* 360).

[24] Cairns points out that 29:29 and 30:11-14 provide a frame for 30:1-10 with its hope of restoration. In this manner 30:11-14 becomes "a useful clue to the interpretation of 29:29" (*Word and Presence,* 262).

4. The Results of Covenant Reaffirmation (30:1-10)

[1]When all these blessings and curses I have set before you come upon you and you take them to heart wherever the LORD your God disperses you among the nations, [2]and when you and your children return to the LORD your God and obey him with all your heart and with all your soul according to everything I command you today, [3]then the LORD your God will restore your fortunes and have compassion on you and gather you again from all the nations where he scattered you. [4]Even if you have been banished to the most distant land under the heavens, from there the LORD your God will gather you and bring you back. [5]He will bring you to the land that belonged to your fathers, and you will take possession of it. He will make you more prosperous and numerous than your fathers. [6]The LORD your God will circumcise your hearts and the hearts of your descendants, so that you may love him with all your heart and with all your soul, and live. [7]The LORD your God will put all these curses on your enemies who hate and persecute you. [8]You will again obey the LORD and follow all his commands I am giving you today. [9]Then the LORD your God will make you most prosperous in all the work of your hands and in the fruit of your womb, the young of your livestock and the crops of your land. The LORD will again delight in you and make you prosperous, just as he delighted in your fathers, [10]if you obey the LORD your God and keep his commands and decrees that are written in this Book of the Law and turn to the LORD your God with all your heart and with all your soul.

The boundaries of this pericope are well defined by the enveloping structure of vv. 1-2 at the beginning and v. 10 at the end. In both places are conditions given for Israel's restoration, and both share formulae expressive of repentance. In v. 1 the conditional particle occurs (to be translated "when" as in the NIV) followed by three necessary responses if forgiveness is to be offered—"take [the blessings and curses] to heart" (v. 1), "return [*šabtâ*] to the LORD your God," and "obey [*šāmaʿtâ*] him" (v. 2). The same conditional particle appears twice in v. 10 ("if" as in NIV, or even "when" as in v. 1)—"if you obey [*tišmaʿ*]" and "if you turn [*tāšûb*]" to him. Two of the three verbs are repeated (*šāmaʿ* and *šûb*) but in reverse order and in different form.[25] The intensity of the repentance is expressed in exactly the same terminology in vv. 2 and 10, "with all your heart and with all your soul."

---

[25] A. Rofé describes this passage as "a majestic fugue on the theme of *šûb*, for this verb occurs here seven times" (vv. 1,2,3(2x),8,9,10). "All is change," he notes, "inversion of the course of history and restoration of the happy past. The passage does not merely tell it; it expresses it with its special choice of words" ("The Covenant in the Land of Moab [Dt 28, 69–30, 20]," *Das Deuteronomium,* 311).

The previous passage (29:16-29 [15-28]) ended with the proverbial aphorism about the secret things of the Lord (v. 29 [28]), a secret about to be clarified in the present text. How Israel could be deported from the land and the very earth itself left desiccated and barren, on the one hand, and how the promises of God for Israel's eternal ongoing could continue in effect, on the other hand, now finds resolution. It lies in Israel's repentance and restoration. It was in this sense that "the things revealed belong to us and to our children forever" (29:29 [28]). What the nations could not understand on the basis of empirical historical evidence Israel could understand on the basis of God's covenant promises.

30:1 In the day of Israel's exile, a day that would be inevitable apart from their full and preemptive repentance (29:28 [27]), Israel would reflect upon the blessings and curses of the covenant articulated in chaps. 27–28 (i.e., "these blessings and curses I have set before you," v. 1).[26] They would then take them to heart, return to the Lord, and obey him totally and unreservedly. The grammatical pattern suggests a lack of any true conditionality here. When the exile came to pass, so would these acts of repentance and restoration. The reason is that the Lord, who promised Israel to make them his people forever, would bring about a spirit of repentance and obedience among them (cf. Lev 26:40-45; Jer 30:3,18-22; 31:23-24,31-34; Ezek 34:11-16; 36:22-36). It was that prompting that would cause Israel to think upon their evil ways, to repent, and to enter once more upon faithful covenant compliance.[27] Such conjunction of divine sovereignty and human free will is, of course, beyond the scope of rational harmonization; rather it is a matter that can be comprehended only as God sees fit to reveal his secrets (see 29:29 [28]).

30:2-4 Israel thus would think upon their plight in captivity and would return to the Lord and obey him (vv. 1-2). This done, the Lord would undertake his work of restoration because of his great compassion. From the ends of the earth he would bring back those whom he had banished in judgment (v. 3; cf. 4:27-31). No distance would be so great as to cause him to overlook them or to prevent their return (v. 4; cf. Isa 43:6; 48:20; 62:11).

30:5-6 The judgment of devastation and deportation would produce its desired salutary effects, for the people would come back to the land of

---

[26] Craigie draws several parallels (or responses) between the curses of Deut 28 and the restoration promised here: 30:1, cf. 4:29; 30:2, cf. 4:30; 30:3, cf. 28:64; 30:5, cf. 28:62-63; 30:6, cf. 10:16; 30:7, cf. 28:60; 30:8, cf. 28:1; 30:9, cf. 28:4; 30:10, cf. 28:58 (*Deuteronomy*, 363).

[27] Cairns, *Word and Presence*, 263-64.

promise again (v. 5a), they would prosper more than ever before (v. 5b), and they would be so transformed by the Lord as to be able to love him with all their being (v. 6). While the repossession of the land can be said to some extent to have been fulfilled by the return of the Jews following the Babylonian exile (cf. Jer 29:10-14; 30:3), the greater prosperity and population was not achieved in Old Testament times. In fact, it still awaits realization in any literal sense (cf. Hag 2:6-9; Zech 8:1-8; 10:8-12). As for the radical work of regeneration described here as circumcision of the heart, that clearly awaits a day yet to come as far as the covenant nation as a whole is concerned.

Just as circumcision of the flesh symbolized outward identification with the Lord and the covenant community (cf. Gen 17:10,23; Lev 12:3; Josh 5:2), so circumcision of the heart (a phrase found only here and in Deut 10:16 and Jer 4:4 in the OT) speaks of internal identification with him in what might be called regeneration in Christian theology.[28] Paul equated circumcision of the heart with spiritual renewal, especially in the Epistle to the Romans. He argued that circumcision has value for the Jew who obeys the law (i.e., who keeps covenant), but as a mere outward, physical sign it has no value at all to the disobedient (Rom 2:25-27). What is required, he said, is inward circumcision, that of the heart and spirit that attests to genuine faith (vv. 28-29).[29] The classic example he cited is that of Abraham, whose faith and not his circumcision rendered him just and righteous before God. In effect, said the apostle, Abraham was circumcised in the heart before he ever was in the flesh, and it was that inner work that set him apart as a covenant son (Rom 4:1-12).

This renewal of the heart by faith is common to all—Jew and Gentile alike—who avail themselves of God's mercy. But in terms of Israel as an elect people in a collective, national sense, the circumcision described here by both Moses and Paul lies in the future.[30] Under a slightly different figure Israel's restoration to full covenant blessing was described by Jeremiah and Ezekiel as the engraving of the covenant stipulations upon the fleshy tablets of the heart. In the last days, Jeremiah said, the Lord will make a "new covenant with the house of Israel and with the house of Judah," one whose statutes will be put "in their minds" and written "on their hearts." The result will be that he will be their God and they will be

---

[28] See R. LeDéaut, "La Thème de la circoncision du coeur (Dt. 30:6; Jer. 4:4) dans les versions anciennes (LXX et Targum) et à Qumrân," VTSup 32 (Leiden: Brill, 1981), 178-205.

[29] D. Moo, *Romans 1–8*, WEC (Chicago: Moody, 1991), 170-73.

[30] Thompson, *Deuteronomy*, 284-85; C. F. Keil and F. Delitzsch, *Biblical Commentary on the Old Testament: The Pentateuch* (Grand Rapids: Eerdmans, n.d.), 3:453.

his people (Jer 31:31-33). Ezekiel spoke of this hope as the giving of a new heart and spirit following the return to the land, a return to be marked by prosperity and abundance for the nation (Ezek 36:24-30).

The miraculous, totally regenerating nature of the circumcision of the heart would be manifest by Israel's ability to love the Lord "with all your heart and with all your soul" (Deut 30:6). This is an obvious reference to the demand of the Shema (Deut 6:4-5), adherence to which was at the very core of covenant commitment. This impossible standard was always understood as the ideal of covenant behavior, one to be sought but never fully achieved (c.f. Matt 22:40; Mark 12:33). Here, however, Moses did not command or even exhort his audience to obedience. He promised it as a natural by-product of the renewal of the heart.[31] People can love God with all their heart only after the heart itself has been radically changed to a Godward direction. When that happens, not only is obedience possible but so is life (v. 6). Here more than physical life on the land is in view. There is a glimpse of life that does not end, life that comes to birth with the supernatural work of grace that alone is sufficient to account for all of these aspects of Israel's future restoration (cf. Lev 18:5; Ezek 20:11-13; Luke 10:28; Rom 10:5-10).

30:7-9   The remainder of the passage (vv. 7-10) is highly repetitive of the first part, especially of vv. 1-3a. The curses (qĕlālâ in v. 1, ʾalôt in v. 7) that had fallen on Israel would afflict Israel's enemies; Israel would again obey the Lord and follow his commands (v. 8; cf. v. 2); and the land would enjoy prosperity and fertility of soil and livestock (v. 9; cf. v. 3a). The differences, however, are also apparent and important. As noted already, the conditional clauses of vv. 1-6 require a nuance not of contingency but of time. The issue was not whether Israel and/or the Lord would do thus and so but when. Such lack of qualification requires that all of the blessings of restoration promised to Israel be seen as acts of divine initiative and grace, ones reserved for eschatological times and embracing the nation as such.

30:10   The syntax of v. 10 is different, however, for the dependent clause is highly conditional. The question here is not *when* Israel would obey and turn to the Lord but *if*.[32] That is, the issue here (as opposed to vv. 1-6) is not the eternality of the covenant relationship itself—a matter

---

[31] Thus von Rad: "Our text can no longer be called an exhortation; it contains no admonitions, but, with regard to Israel's future, simply affirmative propositions, that is, it is clothed altogether in the style of prophetic predictions" (G. von Rad, *Deuteronomy*, OTL (Philadelphia: Westminster, 1966), 183.

[32] Craigie, *Deuteronomy*, 364; cf. R. J. Williams, *Hebrew Syntax: An Outline* (Toronto: University of Toronto, 1967), 86.

never denied in Scripture—but the benefits and blessings attached to covenant obedience in the present. If Israel historically did all that the Lord required by way of covenant observance (v. 10), they could expect all the results listed earlier (vv. 7-9). *When* Israel did eschatologically all that the Lord made possible by way of covenant observance (vv. 1-2), they could expect all the results that followed (vv. 3-6).[33]

5. The Appeals for Covenant Obedience (30:11-20)

[11]Now what I am commanding you today is not too difficult for you or beyond your reach. [12]It is not up in heaven, so that you have to ask, "Who will ascend into heaven to get it and proclaim it to us so we may obey it?" [13]Nor is it beyond the sea, so that you have to ask, "Who will cross the sea to get it and proclaim it to us so we may obey it?" [14]No, the word is very near you; it is in your mouth and in your heart so you may obey it.

[15]See, I set before you today life and prosperity, death and destruction. [16]For I command you today to love the LORD your God, to walk in his ways, and to keep his commands, decrees and laws; then you will live and increase, and the LORD your God will bless you in the land you are entering to possess.

[17]But if your heart turns away and you are not obedient, and if you are drawn away to bow down to other gods and worship them, [18]I declare to you this day that you will certainly be destroyed. You will not live long in the land you are crossing the Jordan to enter and possess.

[19]This day I call heaven and earth as witnesses against you that I have set before you life and death, blessings and curses. Now choose life, so that you and your children may live [20]and that you may love the LORD your God, listen to his voice, and hold fast to him. For the LORD is your life, and he will give you many years in the land he swore to give to your fathers, Abraham, Isaac and Jacob.

Having set forth the results of covenant disobedience (29:16-29) and the blessings of covenant reaffirmation even in the midst of judgment and exile (30:1-10), Moses returned to the reality of the present situation and pleaded for Israel's obedience to the Lord. If God's people were faithful to him and to their responsibilities as a servant nation, they need have no fear of judgment and therefore no need for whatever measures of grace would be necessary to call them back to himself. The secret lay in accepting the terms of the covenant being offered to them then and there and resolving to commit themselves to unswerving allegiance to them.

---

[33] For the complexity of the whole passage and especially its relationship to vv. 11-14, see J. G. McConville, *Grace in the End: A Study in Deuteronomic Theology* (Grand Rapids: Zondervan, 1993), 134-39.

30:11-14 In order to make clear the possibility of knowing and doing the will of God in this respect, Moses spoke of the accessibility of the Lord's requirements (vv. 11-14). These were not remote, abstract, esoteric principles but a word that was among and within them. The "word" (v. 14) is the commandment (*miṣwâ*) of the Lord, that whole body of stipulation that Moses was commanding that very day (v. 11). This single word "commandment" occurs regularly in Deuteronomy as a term denoting the entire covenant text (cf. 4:2; 5:29; 7:9; 8:2,6; 11:8,13,22,27; 13:4,18; 15:5; 26:13,18; 27:1; 28:1,9,13; 30:8).[34]

The point at issue here was not the ease or even possibility of keeping the word of the Lord (though theoretically the latter is so) but of even knowing what it was. Contrary to the inscrutable and enigmatic ways of the pagan gods, the Lord's purposes and will for his people are crystal clear. They are not "too difficult" (*lōʾ niplēʾt*, lit., "not too wonderful," i.e., beyond comprehension) or beyond reach (v. 11).[35] That is, they can be understood by the human mind despite its limitations.

Though originating in the transcendent glory of heaven, the word of the Lord need not be pursued there by a messenger sent to inquire of God's covenant expectations (v. 12). Nor need such an envoy be sent to some distant place on earth to learn of God's revelation (v. 13). Instead, Moses said, the word is "very near you" (v. 14a), so near, in fact, that it was in their mouth and heart (v. 14b). This conjunction of mouth and heart calls to mind the injunction to Israel following the exposition of the Shema: "These commandments that I give you today are to be upon your hearts. Impress them on your children. Talk about them" (Deut 6:6-7a).[36] All that God wants for his people to know is contained in his covenant revelation, a "word" that is disclosed to their hearts (i.e., minds) and that is to be communicated to others by their mouths.

Paul cited this passage to speak of the accessibility of Christ and the gospel (Rom 10:6-8).[37] There is no need, he said, to go to heaven to bring Christ down or to descend to the deep (i.e., the netherworld, the "great deep" [*tĕhôm*] of the sea) to bring him back from the dead. The incarnation and resurrection have already occurred and need not be repeated. Instead, there is the powerful, life-changing message of the gospel, the

---

[34] Thompson, *Deuteronomy,* 286.

[35] For the phrases "too wonderful" and "not too wonderful" and the OT and ancient Near Eastern wisdom tradition, see M. Weinfeld, *Deuteronomy and the Deuteronomic School* (Oxford: Clarendon, 1972), 258-60.

[36] Noted also by Driver, *Deuteronomy,* 331.

[37] For Paul's special use of the passage and the hermeneutics involved, see E. F. Harrison, "Romans," EBC, ed. E. Gaebelein (Grand Rapids: Zondervan, 1976), 10:111-12.

word of faith that is to be believed in the heart and confessed with the mouth (Rom 10:9). Just as the gospel message represents the very presence and purpose of Jesus Christ, so the word of covenant, Moses said, is as close and authoritative as the Lord himself is.

30:15-16 That word, again, was the one being offered to the Moab assembly, a command to be acted upon here and now (vv. 15-16). The options are most clear. Acceptance and obedience would bring life and prosperity (lit., "good"), but rejection and/or disobedience would result in death and destruction (lit., "bad" or "harm"). In this succinct manner Moses challenged the nation to both the blessings inherent in undertaking the privileges and responsibilities of the covenant relationship and the curses that must inevitably follow should that gracious offer be rejected. The challenge presented here is precisely the same as that given to the first generation of Israelites at Sinai (Exod 19:5-8) and is typical of the choices offered to those whom the Lord would call to salvation and service (cf. Josh 24:14-18; 1 Sam 12:19-25; 1 Kgs 18:21,39; Matt 16:24; Mark 8:34; Luke 18:22).

The linkage between this passage and the Shema and its context, already noted earlier (v. 14), is confirmed by the appeal to "love the LORD your God," a command that lies at the very center of the covenant relationship (Deut 6:5; cf. 5:10; 7:9; 10:12; 11:1,13,22; 13:3; 19:9; 30:6,20; Josh 22:5; 23:11). What this means, as always, is to "walk in his ways and to keep his commands [*miṣwôt*], decrees [*ḥuqqôt*], and laws [*mišpāṭîm*]" (v. 16), that is, the covenant in all of its particulars (for the same three terms, cf. 6:1; 7:11; 8:11; 11:1). The result of such fastidious compliance with the divine mandate would be life and increase in the land of promise, circumstances that together are described as the blessing of the Lord. This is suggested in v. 15, where "life and prosperity," by way of metonymy, represent blessing in its most significant forms—quantity and quality of life (cf. 4:1; 5:33; 8:1; 16:20; 30:6,19-20).

30:17-18 The opposite choice, that of turning away from and disobeying the covenant stipulations—especially those, again, that lie at the core of covenant faith, namely, recognition and worship of the Lord alone (v. 17b)—would bring destruction most sure and certain (v. 18a). This is in sharp contrast to the blessing of prosperity or increase. Even worse, the nation shortly would be evicted from the land given as its possession (v. 18b), a curse that reverses the blessing of long life there (vv. 15-16).

30:19-20 Once more Moses announced that there and then he was offering the covenant to Israel, doing so as the agent of the Lord and in his name (vv. 19-20). This time, however, the offer was couched in the formal terms of a legal setting in which witnesses were invoked to bear testimony in the future to the response of Israel to the Lord's gracious overtures. In similar ancient Near Eastern legal transactions the witnesses usually were the gods of the respective litigants, but the monotheism of Israel's faith dictated that such appeal be to creation, to heaven and earth, for only it would endure into future ages. Such appeal to creation is attested elsewhere in the Old Testament when the Lord enters into some kind of formal legal encounter with his people (cf. Deut 4:26; 31:28; 32:1; Isa 1:2; Mic 1:2).[38]

Witnesses were always a part of the ceremony of covenant enactment (cf. Gen 31:44-49; Deut 31:19; Josh 24:27). But it was particularly important that they be present to hear the oaths of those who pledged themselves to covenant commitment, for in articulating such pledges they invoked upon themselves the blessings and curses that attended obedience and disobedience respectively.[39] Legally speaking, the superior party to the pact would have no grounds for dispensing either reward or punishment if there were no witnesses to the oaths of fealty that encompassed these results. Even the Lord, therefore, called his people to swear before witnesses that they were inviting divine beneficence or displeasure upon themselves, depending on the extent of their loyalty to him.

In light of the formal solemnity of covenant transaction, then, Moses set before Israel "life and death," that is, the blessings or curses that follow covenant obedience or disobedience. Obedience brings life in all its fullness whereas disobedience causes the greatest curse of all, death now and forever (v. 19). The appeal, therefore, was to choose life so that life might result. Underlying this rather cryptic way of expressing the matter is the expanded idea of choosing to obey God, for doing that brings the greatest of all blessings, life itself. One cannot choose life (or even death), but he can choose a path that will lead to one or the other (cf. Matt 7:13).

To Moses, choosing life meant choosing to enter into the covenant with the Lord and to be true to its principles. Such a choice also would enable Israel to love the Lord, to obey him (not "listen" as in NIV), and to hold fast to him (v. 20a).[40] It is striking that these are not prerequisites to

---

[38] Thompson, *Deuteronomy,* 287; Weinfeld, *Deuteronomy and the Deuteronomic School,* 62; cf. D. J. Wiseman, *The Vassal-Treaties of Esarhaddon* (London: British School of Archaeology, 1958), 22-23, 30, i:13-40; J. A. Fitzmyer, *The Aramaic Inscriptions of Sefire,* BO 19 (Rome: Pontifical Biblical Institute, 1967), 13.

[39] M. G. Kline, *Treaty of the Great King* (Grand Rapids: Eerdmans, 1963), 22-23.

[40] Cairns observes that elsewhere (with one exception) the verb "choose" always has Yahweh as subject. "Here," he points out, "the stress is on the necessity for human response" (*Word and Presence,* 266). He further notes that "life" is "virtually a title for Yahweh" so that to choose Yahweh and the covenant is to choose life.

becoming God's people but the results of having become such. This, of course, is in line with the whole notion of Israel's election by God to be his people long before he formalized the relationship by covenant (cf. Exod 4:22-23; 6:2-9; 19:4-6). It is clear, however, that had Israel refused to accept the Lord's offer of covenant, all blessings of such a privileged status would never have come to pass. Even here at Moab the second generation, like the first, had to heed the divine invitation to servanthood if it was to enter into the intimacies as well as burdens of that relationship.

The nub of the matter is at the end of the passage—"the LORD is your life" (v. 20), in terms both of mere existence and of longevity in the land. He is the life of his people because he has created and redeemed them, but he is also their life insofar as they capitulate to his sovereignty and live out their lives in compliance with his gracious covenant mandates.

IX. DEPOSIT OF THE TEXT AND PROVISION FOR ITS FUTURE IMPLEMENTATION (31:1-29)

1. The Succession by Joshua (31:1-8)
2. The Deposit of the Text (31:9-13)
3. The Commissioning of Joshua (31:14-23)
4. The Anticipation of the Leaders' Defection (31:24-29)

IX. DEPOSIT OF THE TEXT AND PROVISION FOR ITS FUTURE IMPLEMENTATION (31:1-29)

There is a strong sense of transition at this juncture in Deuteronomy, signs that the era of Moses' leadership is ending and that of his successors beginning. Moreover, the covenant text has been fully revealed, its stipulations offered to and accepted by the assembly, and its blessings and curses invoked as testimony to their pledge to obey it. Finally, the time has come for the community that is about to leave its encampment on the way to conquest to embrace the covenant as its guiding principle. This must be personal and interior, to be sure, but symbol and custom also dictated that the text of the covenant be publicly placed on deposit as a witness to its abiding relevance and authority. Israel was not to be a nation of anarchists or even of strong human leaders. It was a theocratic community with the Lord as King and with his covenant revelation as fundamental constitution and law. The theme of this section is the enshrinement of that law, the proper role of Mosaic succession, and the ultimate authority of covenant mandate over human institutions.[1]

1. The Succession by Joshua (31:1-8)

¹Then Moses went out and spoke these words to all Israel: ²"I am now a hundred and twenty years old and I am no longer able to lead you. The LORD

---

[1] All of these, of course, were standard elements in ancient Near Eastern covenant making. See M. G. Kline, *Treaty of the Great King* (Grand Rapids: Eerdmans, 1963) 19-20, 35-37, 135-38; G. E. Mendenhall, *Law and Covenant in Israel and the Ancient Near East* (Pittsburgh: Biblical Colloquium, 1955), 34, 40-41; D. J. Wiseman, *The Vassal-Treaties of Esarhaddon* (London: British School of Archaeology in Iraq, 1958), 5-9, 32-50.

has said to me, 'You shall not cross the Jordan.' [3]The LORD your God himself
will cross over ahead of you. He will destroy these nations before you, and you
will take possession of their land. Joshua also will cross over ahead of you, as
the LORD said. [4]And the LORD will do to them what he did to Sihon and Og,
the kings of the Amorites, whom he destroyed along with their land. [5]The
LORD will deliver them to you, and you must do to them all that I have commanded you. [6]Be strong and courageous. Do not be afraid or terrified because
of them, for the LORD your God goes with you; he will never leave you nor forsake you."

[7]Then Moses summoned Joshua and said to him in the presence of all Israel, "Be strong and courageous, for you must go with this people into the land
that the LORD swore to their forefathers to give them, and you must divide it
among them as their inheritance. [8]The LORD himself goes before you and will
be with you; he will never leave you nor forsake you. Do not be afraid; do not
be discouraged."

31:1-2 The admonishment of chaps. 29–30 gives way here to a lengthy
narrative akin to that of chaps. 1–3. In fact, both sections commence with
essentially the same language: "These are the words Moses spoke to all
Israel" (1:1); "Then Moses went out and spoke these words to all Israel"
(31:1). Clearly the two narrative sections envelop the great central part of
the Book of Deuteronomy, the covenant text proper with its appropriate
parenetic introductions (4:1-49) and conclusions (29:2–30:20).[2]

The great concern of Moses here was his advanced years and the debili-
tating impact that was having on his leadership capacity. Furthermore, the
conquest of Canaan was imminent, and even were his age not a consideration, his having been precluded from crossing the Jordan obviously was
about to disqualify him from any future role as theocratic administrator. A
linkage between the narratives of chaps. 1–3 and this passage, already suggested by their respective introductory formulae, is confirmed further by
noting that Moses' concern at the end of the earlier narrative (3:23-39) was
precisely the same as that at the beginning of this one—his inability to lead
his people over the Jordan to the land of promise (v. 2). The selection of
Joshua as the next leader also looms large in each passage (3:28; cf. 1:38;
31:3,7,23). Without the intervening covenant material one could view
chaps. 1–3 and 31 as a continuous narrative.[3]

---

[2] G. J. Wenham, "The Structure and Date of Deuteronomy" (Ph.D. diss., University of
London, 1969), 213-16.

[3] D. L. Christensen views Deut 1–3 as "the outer frame part 1" and 31–34 as "the outer
frame part 2" of the intervening covenant material. The former is "a look backwards" and the
latter "a look forward" ("Form and Structure in Deuteronomy 1–11," in *Das Deuteronomium,*

With his admission that he was a hundred and twenty years old, Moses was tacitly preparing the people for his death. He was forty when he fled Egypt to find refuge in Midian (Acts 7:23), eighty at the time of the exodus (i.e., forty years earlier than the present time; cf. Deut 2:7; 29:5), and now three times forty. There was no mistaking the meaning of this periodizing of Moses' life. The first two eras culminated in escapes from mortal danger into the deserts. This time, however, there was no escape, for his sin in the desert had effectively closed that door (cf. Num 20:12; 27:12-14). The urgent need for orderly succession was most apparent.

31:3 The problem was not with ultimate leadership, of course, for the Lord was King and mighty Warrior, a point repeatedly made already throughout Deuteronomy (cf. 1:30; 3:18-21; 7:1-2,17-24; 9:3-4; 20:1-4). Hitherto, however, God had worked through human leadership, Moses specifically; so naturally there was concern about the void to be left by Moses' absence. Once more, then, Moses reminded the assembly that Joshua was God's choice to succeed him, a choice that appeared evident from many years past (Exod 17:8-16; 24:13; Num 11:28) and one that was solidified by repeated verbal affirmation (Num 27:15-23; Deut 1:38; 3:23-29).

31:4-6 God's vindication of Joshua would be apparent in Israel's victories over the nations of Canaan, conquests as remarkable as those already accomplished against the Amorites of Transjordan (v. 4; cf. Deut 2:26–3:11). As he had delivered them under Moses' leadership, so the foes of future campaigns would fall to Joshua. In light of God's constancy and promise of future success, Moses could adjure the entire assembly to be strong and unafraid (v. 6).

31:7 The same combination of verbs (*ḥāzaq* and *ʾāmaṣ*) occurs in v. 7, where Moses turned to Joshua alone to offer him personal encouragement (for other examples of the verb combination, cf. 31:23; Josh 1:6-9,18; 10:25; 1 Chr 22:13; 28:20; 2 Chr 32:7).[4] The reason for addressing Joshua in these terms before all the people was to provide Moses an opportunity to endorse publicly his younger protégé. Not only Joshua but the whole community needed to hear again that the Lord had made provision for them and that his provision was a matter of public record. The challenge was that they go into the land promised to the forefathers and that they divide it according to allotment of inheritance (v. 7). It would be Joshua's special task to see that this was done expeditiously and equitably (cf. Deut 1:38; 3:28; Josh 1:6).

---

ed. N. Lohfink, BETL 68 [Leuven: University Press, 1985], 138). J. D. Levenson uses similar language in describing the connection between Deut 3 and 31. In his view chap. 31 is "the continuation [of] chap. 3," both being part of Dtr as opposed to Dt ("Who Inserted the Book of the Torah?" *HTR* 68 [1976]: 209).

[4] F. Hesse, "קְזַח *ḥāzaq*," etc., *TDOT* 4:307.

ing Israel into the inheritance, wished God's blessing on the one selected to take his place. He who had been terrified at the prospect of serving the Lord in the days of the exodus (Exod 3:11; 4:10-17) shared from his experience of God's faithfulness the truth that God was always there (v. 8).

2. The Deposit of the Text (31:9-13)

⁹**So Moses wrote down this law and gave it to the priests, the sons of Levi, who carried the ark of the covenant of the LORD, and to all the elders of Israel. ¹⁰Then Moses commanded them: "At the end of every seven years, in the year for canceling debts, during the Feast of Tabernacles, ¹¹when all Israel comes to appear before the LORD your God at the place he will choose, you shall read this law before them in their hearing. ¹²Assemble the people—men, women and children, and the aliens living in your towns—so they can listen and learn to fear the LORD your God and follow carefully all the words of this law. ¹³Their children, who do not know this law, must hear it and learn to fear the LORD your God as long as you live in the land you are crossing the Jordan to possess."**

31:9   The narrative of transition continues with the account of Moses' writing down "this law" and presenting it to the priests and elders with instructions about its future use. The term for "law" (here *tôrâ*) normally refers to the Mosaic writings generally, but in the context of Deuteronomy it must be limited to that book alone and, in fact, to just the covenant text of chaps. 5–26 (plus the blessings and curses of chaps. 27 and 28).[5] This delimitation is most clearly seen when "law" is qualified by such terms as "stipulations," "decrees," and "laws," that is, when these are understood as its constituent parts. This technically precludes such sections as the preamble, historical prologue, provisions for deposit of the text, and (perhaps) the lists of sanctions. Though all of these are elements of standard treaty (or covenant) texts, the "law" part is limited to the general and special stipulations (cf. 4:44-45; 27:26[?]; 28:58[?]; 29:21,29; 30:10; 32:46).

In an earlier instruction concerning kings Moses had pointed out that the *tôrâ* they must regularly consult would be "a copy of this law, taken from that of the priests, who are Levites" (Deut 17:18). This implies that the priests had official custody of "this law," that is, of the covenant text. This was in keeping with the obvious need for parties in covenant relationship to preserve copies of the document to which they had mutually made commitment. This was the practice in ancient Near Eastern cultures where such arrangements are attested, so it is not surprising that both the Lord

---

[5] J. A. Thompson, *Deuteronomy,* TOTC (Leicester: InterVarsity, 1974), 291, n. 1.

and Israel would follow suit.[6] "The LORD'S copy" would be the one placed in the custody of his special representatives, the priests.[7] This is elaborated more fully in vv. 24-29. That same document (or a copy of it) would, in the nature of a divine-human pact, suffice as the covenant text for the people as well.

The specific repository for the "law" was the place already set apart for the ark of the covenant as the reference to the ark in v. 9 makes clear. This symbol of the regal presence of the Lord among his people served not only as his throne (Exod 24:21-22) but as the container for the tablets of stone on which were inscribed the Ten Commandments (Exod 24:16,21). There is no hint anywhere that those tablets were ever removed from the ark in the interim, so one may infer that the scroll of the *tôrâ* was placed alongside the ark in the holy of holies as a supplement to them.[8] The Ten Commandments were perhaps viewed as the distillation of the first (Horeb) covenant text and the *tôrâ*-scroll here as the version given by Moses to the second generation nearly forty years later. The holy of holies thus became a kind of sacred archives housing the documents that attested to the Lord's relationship to his people throughout the years.

31:10 In practical terms the law scroll was to be read publicly to the assembly of all Israel once every seven years (vv. 10-13). Specifically, this was to be part of the celebration of the Feast of Tabernacles in the years of release or remission, that is, at every seventh observance of that feast. The "year of release" (*šĕnat haššĕmiṭṭâ*) refers to the covenant stipulation, already described (Deut 15:1-3), that required all debts of fellow Israelites to be canceled (as NIV, v. 10). It was appropriate that this be done at the time of the Feast of Tabernacles, for that festival above all others called to mind the Lord's great act of exodus deliverance and election to covenant responsibility (cf. Lev 23:43; Deut 16:13-15).

31:11-13 The purpose of the assembly was to provide a forum for a regular and formal renewal of the covenant before the Lord.[9] It took place "before the LORD your God" and "at the place he will choose" (v. 11), that is, in the place of the residence of the great king to whom they were

---

[6] Kline, *Treaty of the Great King,* 19.

[7] Thompson, *Deuteronomy,* 291.

[8] C. F. Keil and F. Delitzsch, *Biblical Commentary on the Old Testament,* trans. J. Martin (Grand Rapids: Eerdmans, n.d.), 3:457.

[9] P. C. Craigie, with some justification, describes the septennial ceremony as a commemoration of the covenant rather than a renewal, one with educational objectives (*The Book of Deuteronomy,* NICOT [Grand Rapids: Eerdmans, 1976], 371). See also W. L. Holladay, "A Proposal for Reflections in the Book of Jeremiah of the Seven-Year Recitation of the Law in Deuteronomy," *Das Deuteronomium,* 326-28.

accountable (cf. Deut 12:5,11). While there "this law" (here certainly the covenant text of Deut 5–26 [or 28]) was to be read so that the whole community could hear it afresh and pledge itself over and over again to recommitment (v. 12). As long as Israel was in the promised land, this was to be done because as generations died and were replaced by new ones, there would be recurring need for instruction and pledges to loyalty. The agreements of the fathers would never obviate the personal appropriations of covenant responsibility by the sons (v. 13).

An unusually full account of this being done in later times (and perhaps an almost unique instance) is that of Neh 8:13–9:38.[10] Having brought at least a measure of political and religious stability to the postexilic Jewish community, Ezra and Nehemiah convened a great throng for the Feast of Tabernacles and, in connection with it, read from the "Book of the Law of God" (Neh 8:18). There can be little doubt that this was the covenant text of the Book of Deuteronomy (cf. 8:1,14). Once the reading was over, the people confessed and repented of their sins as a community (9:1-3) whereupon the Levites, as their forebears had done on the occasion of the invocation of blessing and curses at the beginning (Deut 27:9-14), led the assembly in a ceremony of covenant renewal (Neh 9:5-37). Having heard the address, the people, leaders and all, made a "binding agreement," put it in writing, and affixed their seals to it (v. 38). Thus one generation at least took the instruction about covenant renewal seriously though the record of history is silent about other times when this might have occurred in precisely this way (see, however, 2 Kgs 23:1-3 = 2 Chr 34:29-33).

3. The Commissioning of Joshua (31:14-23)

[14]The Lord said to Moses, "Now the day of your death is near. Call Joshua and present yourselves at the Tent of Meeting, where I will commission him." So Moses and Joshua came and presented themselves at the Tent of Meeting.

[15]Then the Lord appeared at the Tent in a pillar of cloud, and the cloud stood over the entrance to the Tent. [16]And the Lord said to Moses: "You are going to rest with your fathers, and these people will soon prostitute themselves to the foreign gods of the land they are entering. They will forsake me and break the covenant I made with them. [17]On that day I will become angry with them and forsake them; I will hide my face from them, and they will be destroyed. Many disasters and difficulties will come upon them, and on that day they will ask, 'Have not these disasters come upon us because our God is

---

[10] This presupposes that the occasion coincided with the šĕmiṭṭâ, something that cannot be fully demonstrated but that has been strongly supported by many scholars. See J. Blenkinsopp, *Ezra-Nehemiah: A Commentary*, OTL (Philadelphia: Westminster, 1988), 293; F. C. Fensham, *The Books of Ezra and Nehemiah*, NICOT (Grand Rapids: Eerdmans, 1982), 221.

not with us?' [18]And I will certainly hide my face on that day because of all their wickedness in turning to other gods.

[19]"Now write down for yourselves this song and teach it to the Israelites and have them sing it, so that it may be a witness for me against them. [20]When I have brought them into the land flowing with milk and honey, the land I promised on oath to their forefathers, and when they eat their fill and thrive, they will turn to other gods and worship them, rejecting me and breaking my covenant. [21]And when many disasters and difficulties come upon them, this song will testify against them, because it will not be forgotten by their descendants. I know what they are disposed to do, even before I bring them into the land I promised them on oath." [22]So Moses wrote down this song that day and taught it to the Israelites.

[23]The LORD gave this command to Joshua son of Nun: "Be strong and courageous, for you will bring the Israelites into the land I promised them on oath, and I myself will be with you."

31:14 Moses had already become consciously aware of his great age and the certainty of his impending death (v. 2). Now any lingering question about it was removed by the Lord's precise revelation that his death was near (v. 14). Moses also had made preliminary plans for Joshua to succeed him as theocratic administrator (vv. 3,7), and now that decision was affirmed by the Lord's instruction to Moses and Joshua to appear at the Tent of Meeting for a formal commissioning (v. 14).

This "Tent of Meeting" (*ʾōhel môʿēd*) was not the same as the tabernacle (*miškān*), the portable sanctuary whose construction and purpose are elaborated in detail in Exodus (esp. chaps. 25–40).[11] That was the place where the Lord "dwelled" (*šākan*) among his people and to which they came for public worship. The tent of meeting, on the other hand, was outside the encampment. It was a special place for encounter with the Lord, especially frequented by Moses and other leaders who sought counsel from him (Exod 33:7-11; cf. 18:7-16; Num 11:16,24,26; 12:4). It appears to have existed prior to the building of the tabernacle (Exod 33:7-11) and to have served a function complementary to it, one more private than public in nature.[12]

---

[11] Cf. M. Haran, "The *ʾŌHEL MOʿĒD* in Pentateuchal Sources," *JSS* 5 (1960): 50-65.

[12] U. Cassuto offers the suggestion made already by the LXX and Ibn Ezra, that the "tent of meeting" was Moses' personal tent that he took outside the camp in order to avoid the defilement there occasioned by Israel's idolatry (*A Commentary on the Book of Exodus* [Jerusalem: Magnes, 1967], 429-30). The major problem with this view is the ongoing existence of the tent as a place of divine manifestation after the tabernacle had been built and the idolatry dealt with. While conceding somewhat to source-critical approaches to the view that the "tent of meeting" reflected ancient E material and the tabernacle later P ideology, B. S. Childs argues that the "tent of meeting" functions in contexts of impurity, that is, in settings in which the people had proved themselves unfit for Yahweh to dwell in their midst. The linkage of Deut 31:16 and the idolatry of Exod 32 appears to support Childs' understanding (*The Book of Exodus,* OTL [Philadelphia: Westminster, 1974], 590-93).

31:15-16   God was present in both places, however, as the pillar of cloud over the tent's entrance testifies (v. 15; cf. Exod 33:9; Num 12:5). He then spoke to Moses and Joshua, but not at first with a word of charge or commission. Rather, he spoke of the apostasy of Israel that would set in following Moses' death, a falling away that would result in severe judgment (vv. 16-18). In advance of this and as an everlasting witness to Israel of its covenant disloyalty, Moses and Joshua were instructed to compose a song the singing of which would come back to haunt them, as it were, and to remind them of God's spurned goodnesses and how much they would have lost by their open and unrepentant defiance of his purposes for them (vv. 19-21).

The possibility of Israel's falling away after Moses' death had already been anticipated (cf. 4:25-31; 7:1-4), but here it is presented as a foregone conclusion. With Moses' departure the Lord said, "These people will soon prostitute themselves to the foreign gods of the land they are entering" (v. 16). The imagery of prostitution (*zānâ*) conveys the very essence of covenant violation, namely, to forsake the Lord and embrace other gods (cf. Exod 34:15-16; Lev 20:5; Judg 2:17; 8:27; Ezek 6:9; 20:30; Jer 3:1; Hos 2:7; 4:15). Nothing could more clearly communicate disloyalty.

31:17-18   The result of such behavior would be the invocation of the covenant curses. Yahweh would become angry and would reciprocate by forsaking his people (cf. the verb *ʿāzab* in vv. 16b and 17a) until they were brought to utter ruin. Great harm and distress would overwhelm them, a calamity they would recognize as God's judgment because of their sin (v. 17). They would have experienced the promised curses of covenant violation and would have seen the absolute justice of it. Because Israel had turned (*pānâ*) from God, he would hide his face (*pānay*) from them (v. 18).

31:19-22   Addressing himself now to the whole assembly, the Lord commanded them to compose "this song," that is, the song of 32:1-43 (v. 19).[13] In point of fact it was Moses who literally penned the words (v. 22), but he did so as the representative of the people. In that sense they were its authors as well as its recipients and singers. Its purpose was to serve as a witness (*ʿēd*) against the nation in the generations to come. As they sang it, its words would remind them of the covenant pledges they had made and the judgments they freely and voluntarily invoked upon themselves. In other words, the song itself was a reiteration of the essence of the covenant history and text, a statement of faith they affirmed and to which they

---

[13] So most scholars. See A. Phillips, *Deuteronomy*, CBC (Cambridge: University Press, 1973), 208. Phillips translates "song" as "rule of life."

recommitted themselves every time they sang it.[14] When (not if; cf. v. 16) Israel entered the promised land, enjoyed its benefits, and then broke the covenant by rejecting the Lord and going after other gods (v. 20; cf. v. 16b), great harm and distress would befall them (v. 21a; cf. v. 17). Then they and their descendants would sing this song of witness as a testimony to their own disloyalty and of the Lord's threatened judgments. Knowing the waywardness of the human heart and Israel's constant predilection to covenant disobedience,[15] the Lord had made provision ahead of time for their judgment, the distillation of all that is contained in the song to be sung when those unhappy days came to pass (v. 22).

31:23 The intervening warning about covenant failure and the instruction to compose a song of witness having been concluded, the Lord returned to the matter of Joshua's commissioning (v. 23). At the beginning of the pericope, however, he had addressed Moses concerning Joshua (v. 14). Now he addressed Joshua himself, commanding him to "be strong and courageous." The command here is the same as the one Moses had urged upon his younger colleague already (v. 7) and the same as Joshua would hear from the Lord following Moses' death when he alone would be called upon to wear the mantle of theocratic administrator (Josh 1:6-7).

4. The Anticipation of the Leaders' Defection (31:24-29)

[24]After Moses finished writing in a book the words of this law from beginning to end, [25]he gave this command to the Levites who carried the ark of the covenant of the LORD: [26]"Take this Book of the Law and place it beside the ark of the covenant of the LORD your God. There it will remain as a witness against you. [27]For I know how rebellious and stiff-necked you are. If you have been rebellious against the LORD while I am still alive and with you, how much more will you rebel after I die! [28]Assemble before me all the elders of your tribes and all your officials, so that I can speak these words in their hearing and call heaven and earth to testify against them. [29]For I know that after my

---

[14] G. von Rad argues, in fact, that שִׁירָה ("song") is not original to the text but should be read תּוֹרָה ("law") as in v. 24. While this is unnecessary (and without basis in the text), von Rad's point that "write," "teach," and "put in their mouths" (v. 16) is vocabulary applicable to a legal document is worth noting. This is no ordinary song, then, but one of intense legal and covenantal implications (*Deuteronomy: A Commentary,* OTL [Philadelphia: Westminster, 1966], 190).

[15] "I know what they are disposed to do" (v. 21) reflects a literal rendering, "I know his tendency which he is doing today." The Heb. term יֵצֶר (*yēṣer,* "tendency") occurs in postbiblical literature to speak of almost an inexorable impulse, something beyond one's control. See B. Otzen, "יָצַר *yāṣar,*" etc., *TDOT* 6:265; E. H. Merrill, *Qumran and Predestination: A Theological Study of the Thanksgiving Hymns,* STDJ 8 (Leiden: Brill, 1975), 18-19.

death you are sure to become utterly corrupt and to turn from the way I have commanded you. In days to come, disaster will fall upon you because you will do evil in the sight of the LORD and provoke him to anger by what your hands have made."

31:24 The narrative concerning Moses' having written "this law" and having delivered it over to the Levites for safekeeping (vv. 9-13) continues here with greater specification and with more clearly spelled out motives. The expression "the words of this law," as noted repeatedly (cf. v. 9), is technical language referring specifically to Deut 5–26 (plus chap. 27 and probably 28). That is the central covenant text to which chaps. 1–4 provide prologue and 29–34 epilogue. This does not suggest that Deuteronomy in its entirety was not included in the phrase "Book of the Law" once the whole was completed, for surely the scroll as it currently exists must have been in view in the time of Josiah's reformation and other instances where the title occurs (2 Kgs 22:8,11; cf. Deut 28:61; 29:21; 30:10; Josh 1:8; 8:34; 24:26; 2 Kgs 14:6; Neh 8:1,3,8; 9:3). More important is the function of the document, for, like the song to be sung by Israel, it was to serve as a witness (ʾēd; cf. v. 19) against the people (v. 26). That is, its words of promise and of obligation to which they had sworn would be everlasting witnesses to their obedience or disobedience. The song and the scroll, then, would be two witnesses, all that the law required in legal testimony (cf. Deut 17:6; 19:15).[16]

31:25-28 The ark of the covenant, which contained the stone tablets of the Ten Commandments, resided in the holy of holies of the tabernacle, that sacred place that marked the focal point of the Lord's residence among his people (cf. v. 9; Exod 25:16; 26:33). It was fitting that the central text of the Horeb covenant be housed there and fitting likewise that "this Book of the Law" be delivered over to the Levites and placed beside the ark, for this was a covenant renewal document, one appropriate to the new generation and to life in the land of promise to which they were headed.

Moses already had instructed that the Levites read the covenant text every seventh year in a ceremony of reaffirmation (v. 10), but now he himself commanded that the leaders of the community assemble so that he could read it to them (v. 28a). The purpose of the assembly is most clear. It was that he might "call heaven and earth to testify against them" (v. 28b). What this means in context is that Moses was setting forth before the elders and other officials the options of covenant acceptance or repudiation (cf. 30:19). This was a legal setting, one in which the Lord and Israel's

---

[16] Contra von Rad, who, as noted (n. 14), emends שִׁירָה ("song," v. 19) to תֹּורָה ("law") in order to avoid what otherwise looks like a doublet.

leaders confronted one another.[17] Central to the proceedings are the sanctions of covenant agreement, the invocation by the people of the blessings and curses that followed covenant compliance or the lack thereof. What appears to be in view is a miniature preenactment of the ceremony that the whole nation was to engage in at Ebal and Gerizim once Canaan had been overcome and occupied (cf. 27:1-14).

31:29 It was important that this be done, for Moses knew that those who had been rebellious against the Lord while Moses was alive would be all the more so after his death (cf. v. 27; 9:6-24). In fact, Moses said, he was certain of Israel's defection and especially of the utter corruption of its leaders (*hašḥēt tašḥîtûn*). This would result in inevitable judgment, in the curse of God which the present assembly had met to invoke (v. 29). It might seem fruitless to call people to covenant allegiance knowing full well, as Moses did, that it would all come to naught. What is important to note, however, is that Israel's leaders did have full freedom to choose obedience and blessing. Any failure would be theirs and any punishment justly meted out, for they had formally and publicly pledged themselves to whatever outcome might result.

---

[17] The language and context here are that of the so-called "controversy (רִיב) pattern," suggesting the legal nature of the proceedings and particularly of the song itself. See J. Harvey, "Le 'Rîb-Pattern,' Réquisitore Prophétique sur la Rupture de L'Alliance," *Bib* 43 (1962): 177-79, 184-85.

X. THE SONG OF MOSES (31:30–32:44)
1. Introduction to the Song (31:30)
2. Invocation of Witnesses (32:1-4)
3. Indictment of the People (32:5-6)
4. Review of Past Blessings (32:7-14)
5. Israel's Rebellion (32:15-18)
6. God's Promise of Judgment (32:19-25)
7. The Powerlessness of Other Gods (32:26-38)
8. The Vindication of the Lord (32:39-43)
9. Conclusion to the Song (32:44)

X. THE SONG OF MOSES (31:30–32:44)

One of the major components of ancient Near Eastern treaty texts was appeal to witnesses to covenant transactions, witnesses invariably identified as the deities of the respective treaty partners. In order for Deuteronomy to bear the hallmark of such a legal form, it too must incorporate a section on witnesses. The theological problems raised by such a component are immediately apparent, for how could the Lord and Israel appeal to deities when, in fact, a major thrust of Deuteronomy's own message is the exclusive existence and recognition of the Lord as God?

The answer lay in invoking the presence of the heavens and earth, that is, of all creation (cf. Deut 30:19).[1] This gives not even tacit acknowledgment of the divinity of the created order but simply provides a formal element necessary to the language of covenant engagement. What the Lord and Israel were agreeing to was out there for all the world to see. But in addition to the heavens and earth, the scroll of "this book of the law" (31:26) would also be a witness, hence the need to lay up a copy beside the ark of the covenant in the holy of holies. Its very presence there would remind both the Lord and Israel of their mutual commitments. Finally, the song of Moses was a witness in its own right, a fact made clear to him by the Lord (31:19). In all the years to come Israel would sing this song and in

---

[1] G. E. Mendenhall, *Law and Covenant in Israel and the Ancient Near East* (Pittsburgh: Biblical Colloquium, 1955), 34, 40.

so doing would be reminded of the Lord's gracious sovereignty and of their need to remain loyal to his covenant demands. The positioning of the song in this part of the text is therefore most understandable.

1. Introduction to the Song (31:30)

³⁰**And Moses recited the words of this song from beginning to end in the hearing of the whole assembly of Israel:**

31:30   It is commonplace in modern scholarship to view the song of Moses as a late addition to this context and this verse as a necessary introduction to the song given its intrusive nature.[2] Furthermore, since the song is mentioned in 31:16-22, this section also has been seen as a late interpolation.[3] The order of the material would thus be the commissioning of Joshua (31:14-15,23), the deposit of the law scroll (31:24-29), and a concluding exhortation (32:45-47). A thesis that requires the excision of one text to account for the presence of another, however, leaves little to commend itself. Previous references to the song are quite understandable where they are, and the present introduction, though somewhat repetitive of 31:22, is for that reason alone likely to be original to the text. Besides, the order is perfectly logical and progressive: (1) instruction to write the song (31:19), (2) writing of the song (31:22), and (3) recitation of the song (31:30).

2. Invocation of Witnesses (32:1-4)

¹**Listen, O heavens, and I will speak;**
  hear, O earth, the words of my mouth.
²**Let my teaching fall like rain**
  and my words descend like dew,
 like showers on new grass,
  like abundant rain on tender plants.

³**I will proclaim the name of the LORD.**
  Oh, praise the greatness of our God!
⁴**He is the Rock, his works are perfect,**
  and all his ways are just.
 A faithful God who does no wrong,

---

[2] C. J. Labuschagne, for example, refers to v. 30 as a "redactional note about the reciting of the Song" ("The Song of Moses: Its Framework and Structure," *De Fructu Oris Sui: Essays in Honour of Adrianus van Selms,* ed. I. H. Eybers et al. [Leiden: Brill, 1971], 91.

[3] G. von Rad, *Deuteronomy: A Commentary,* OTL (Philadelphia: Westminster, 1966), 189-90.

upright and just is he.

32:1-2 Scholars are in general agreement that the song of Moses is in the form of a *rîb,* that is, a "lawsuit" address in which the Lord outlined the controversy he had entered into with Israel because of Israel's covenant disloyalty.[4] This analysis is supported by vv. 1-4 in which an appeal is made to witnesses to observe the proceedings so as to put their legality beyond doubt. Such an appeal is invariably part of *rîb*-texts and, in the Old Testament, occurs in the context of the Lord's complaints about the rebellion of his vassal people (cf. Deut 4:25-31; 30:19; 31:28; Isa 1:2; Jer 6:19; 22:29; Mic 1:2).[5] This does not nullify the idea that the song is a witness (Deut 31:21), for form and function are two different things. The song is a witness against Israel, one composed in the form of a *rîb.*

The invocation of witnesses consists of two parts, the actual appeal by Moses on the Lord's behalf (vv. 1-2) and his testimony about the Lord's character and conduct (vv. 3-4). So closely is Moses linked to the Lord as his spokesman that the first person pronouns, though usually associated with the Lord throughout the song, frequently (as here) allude to Moses. Even so, however, Moses usually spoke only as the conduit of divine address (cf. Exod 4:15-16; 7:2; Num 12:8; Deut 34:10). Thus the invocation of the heavens and earth was by the Lord (v. 1) as was the intention to disclose himself by words of instruction that would be as refreshing as moisture on dry ground (v. 2).[6] In line with usual court proceedings, the Lord, the aggrieved party or plaintiff, would offer testimony on his own behalf about his character and conduct. This testimony would prove to be most compelling and restorative.

---

[4] For an early and detailed study of the song from that assumption, see G. E. Wright, "The Lawsuit of God: A Form-Critical Study of Deuteronomy 32," *Israel's Prophetic Heritage: Essays in Honor of James Muilenburg,* ed. B. W. Anderson and W. Harrelson (New York: Harper & Brothers, 1962), 26-67. Of the vast literature before and since, see for now B. Gemser, "The *Rîb-* or Controversy-Pattern in Hebrew Mentality," VTSup 3 (Leiden: Brill, 1955), 120-37; H. B. Huffmon, "The Covenant Lawsuit in the Prophets," *JBL* 78 (1959): 285-95; J. Harvey, "Le '*Rîb*-Pattern,' Réquisitoire Prophétique sur la Rupture de L'Alliance," *Bib* 43 (1962): 172-96; J. Limburg, "The Root רִיב and the Prophetic Lawsuit Speeches," *JBL* 88 (1969): 291-304.

[5] Huffmon, "The Covenant Lawsuit in the Prophets," 288-89.

[6] J. R. Boston suggests that v. 2 is a wisdom statement and that vv. 1-3 are not a rîb unit at all but rather the "invocation of the teacher" ("The Wisdom Influence upon the Song of Moses," *JBL* 87 [1968]: 198). He cites wisdom overtones throughout the song (vv. 1-2,5,7,10,15,20,29,32-33,36) but ignores the fact that literary forms are never so rigid as to preclude a certain degree of mixture of "extraneous" elements. Deuteronomy 32 is, after all, not just a *rîb* but a song designed to teach the covenant and the need to obey it.

32:3-4   There clearly is a subject shift in v. 3, where Moses appears as a character witness on the Lord's behalf. Also addressing the heavens and the earth, he extols the Lord's greatness, especially by the public proclamation of his name, that is, of his reputation (v. 3; cf. Exod 33:19; 34:5-6).[7] The expected result was that all who heard should ascribe greatness ("praise") to God. Knowledge of God can lead to no other response than to acknowledge his might. Specific expressions of his power are his identification as "the Rock" (*haṣṣûr*; cf. vv. 15,18,30; Hab 1:12),[8] the foundation and fortress (cf. Pss 31:3; 62:7; 71:3; 89:26; 95:1; Isa 30:29) whose works are upright (thus *tāmîm*, "having integrity") and whose ways are characterized by justice (*mišpāṭ*, "rectitude"; cf. Gen 18:25; Job 40:8; Pss 111:7; 119:149). In the context of self-defense these attributes speak most particularly to the Lord's own character. Thus he is also faithful in the sense that he is dependable (*ʾĕmûnâ*; cf. Pss 88:11; 89:2-3,6,9; Isa 25:1; Hos 2:19), devoid of any hint of injustice (*ʾên ʿāwel*), a God who is righteous and just in all he does (v. 4b). These descriptions are especially apropos in a legal setting in which the reputation of the Lord may be under attack as he himself proceeds to level charges of impropriety against his covenant partner Israel.

3. Indictment of the People (32:5-6)

> [5] They have acted corruptly toward him;
>   to their shame they are no longer his children,
>   but a warped and crooked generation.
> [6] Is this the way you repay the LORD,
>   O foolish and unwise people?
>   Is he not your Father, your Creator,
>   who made you and formed you?

32:5-6   Yahweh's charges against Israel were that they had become so disobedient that they no longer acted like his children but, to the contrary, had repudiated him as their Father and Creator. The disobedience, already a part of Israel's past and an anticipated course of life in the future, is expressed here in the strong language of perversion (*piel* of *šāḥat*). What is perverted is the relationship established by election and covenant, namely, that of kinship with the Lord. Israel as the child of God is a common Old Testament motif (cf. Exod 4:22-23; Isa 1:2; 63:16; 64:8; Hos 11:1), one

---

[7] I. Cairns, *Word and Presence,* ITC (Grand Rapids: Eerdmans, 1992), 281.

[8] M. P. Knowles, "'The Rock, His Work Is Perfect': Unusual Imagery for God in Deuteronomy 32," *VT* 39 (1989): 307-22.

developed especially by Hosea. Indubitably drawing upon the imagery here in Deuteronomy (and elsewhere), the prophet spoke of Israel as "children of unfaithfulness" (Hos 1:2) who, because of their unfaithful mother (also Israel), would no longer prosper in the land and be objects of the Lord's gracious forgiveness but, to the contrary, would become "not my people" (Lo-Ammi, Hos 1:9). As the song here puts it, they had become a "warped" (*'iqqēš*, "twisted, perverted") and "crooked" (*pĕtaltōl*, "tortuous,")[9] generation, a grotesque mockery of what God created them to be.

Such behavior, the accusation reads, is an incomprehensible response to the loving beneficence of God their Father and Creator (v. 6). It bears all the marks of an obtuse and irrational people, a people willing to abandon sonship in favor of their own selfish ways. The thought of any people rejecting their god was almost beyond belief, but the Lord is more than "just God." He is Father and Creator,[10] the one who made and established his people. The personal interest and intimacy surrounding such a concept staggers the imagination and makes all the more incredible the possibility that any people could reject the God who initiated it. But this is precisely what Israel did and was expected to do in the future.

4. Review of Past Blessings (32:7-14)

[7]Remember the days of old;
   consider the generations long past.
Ask your father and he will tell you,
   your elders, and they will explain to you.
[8]When the Most High gave the nations their inheritance,
   when he divided all mankind,
he set up boundaries for the peoples
   according to the number of the sons of Israel.
[9]For the LORD'S portion is his people,
   Jacob his allotted inheritance.

[10]In a desert land he found him,
   in a barren and howling waste.
He shielded him and cared for him;

---

[9] This word occurs only here. S. R. Driver observes that a cognate verb form occurs in Job 5:13 and (with עִקֵּשׁ) in Ps 18:27; Prov 8:8 (*A Critical and Exegetical Commentary on Deuteronomy,* ICC [Edinburgh: T & T Clark, 1902], 353).

[10] The Heb. literally reads, "He created you," the verb for create (קָנֶךָ) being the same as that in the song of exodus deliverance (Exod 15:16). The idea is not so much, then, of Israel's having been created *ex nihilo* (for which בָּרָא would be expected) but having been brought into sonship by the Lord (P. C. Craigie, *The Book of Deuteronomy,* NICOT [Grand Rapids: Eerdmans, 1976], 379).

   he guarded him as the apple of his eye,
[11]like an eagle that stirs up its nest
   and hovers over its young,
 that spreads its wings to catch them
   and carries them on its pinions.
[12]The LORD alone led him;
   no foreign god was with him.

[13]He made him ride on the heights of the land
   and fed him with the fruit of the fields.
 He nourished him with honey from the rock,
   and with oil from the flinty crag,
[14]with curds and milk from herd and flock
   and with fattened lambs and goats,
 with choice rams of Bashan
   and the finest kernels of wheat.
 You drank the foaming blood of the grape.

Israel's actual and projected defection from the Lord and the covenant is particularly heinous in light of the Lord's past acts of election, redemption, and provision on their behalf. This section of the song is a recital of those mighty deeds, a reminder of the debt of gratitude owed by Israel to their God. In this sense it is a kind of credo (cf. Deut 26:5b-9) or confession of the most significant milestones of Israel's sacred history, especially that phase from the allocation of Israel's territorial inheritance to the time of Moses.

32:7 It is said that those who forget their history are doomed to repeat it, and with that sentiment in mind Moses urged the people to remember bygone days in order to be informed and inspired by them (v. 7).[11] It is impossible to know whether Genesis or any other Mosaic writings existed by the time of this poem and therefore whether or what kind of records may have been available for review. The injunction to ask the fathers and other old men about the past may, indeed, be taken literally and may suggest that most knowledge of the past was transmitted orally. On the other hand, to ask such persons may merely mean to inquire of the past no matter how that could be done. The important thing is that that generation understand its origin and the process by which it had arrived at that hour.

32:8 The point of departure was when the Most High (ʿelyôn) divided humankind into nations and assigned to them their geographical and historical allotments (v. 8a). This act of universal sovereignty supplies clear

---

[11] E. P. Blair, "An Appeal to Remembrance: The Memory Motif in Deuteronomy," *Int* 15 (1961): 41-47.

evidence of the Lord's concern for the whole world, his special selection of Israel notwithstanding.[12] Deuteronomy has already addressed this concern on a more limited level (cf. 2:9-23), but the more obvious background to the notion of dividing peoples into various racial and political entities is the so-called Table of Nations of Gen 10.[13] This sets forth the distribution of the human race following the debacle of the Tower of Babel (cf. Gen 11:8-9; 10:2-31), the most reasonable occasion for the division spoken of in our poem. The verb translated "divided" (*pārad*) occurs likewise in Gen 10:5 to speak of the separation of the race into lands, languages, clans, and nations, and it also occurs in Gen 10:32 in a statement summarizing the divine distribution of peoples throughout the earth.

Even in those ancient days Israel, as yet nonexistent in historical actuality, was central to the purposes of the Lord. This was clearly the intent of the observation that he established (cf. Ps 74:17) boundaries for all peoples according to his predetermined plan for Israel.[14] That is, God from the beginning carved out a geographical inheritance for his elect people and arranged the allotments of all other nations, especially those of Canaan, to accommodate that purpose. Not only was Canaan itself, then, set apart from the beginning to be the land of promise, but its very extent was established on the basis of Israel's "number," that is, their population and other requirements (v. 8b).[15]

32:9 To underscore this centrality of Israel in the salvific purposes of God, Moses described them as the Lord's own portion (v. 9a), his special inheritance (v. 9b). As though his provision of a land allotment for Israel among all nations was not enough, he counted Israel, from among all nations, his own precious possession. This kind of language appears also on the occasion of the Lord's making covenant with Israel where they are described as "my treasured possession," a people selected "out of all the nations" (Exod 19:5; cf. Deut 7:6; 14:2,21).

---

[12] See J. Luyten, "Primeval and Eschatological Overtones in the Song of Moses (Dt 32, 1-43)," *Das Deuteronomium,* ed. N. Lohfink, BETL 68 (Leuven: University Press, 1985), 342-43.

[13] W. F. Albright, "Some Remarks on the Song of Moses in Deuteronomy XXXII," *Essays in Honour of Millar Burrows* (Leiden: Brill, 1959), 343-44.

[14] Albright suggests emending בְּנֵי יִשְׂרָאֵל of v. 8 to בְּנֵי אֱלֹהִים on the basis of a Qumran fragment (4QDt) (ibid., 343). This would indeed create a better parallelism ("the peoples" // "children of God"), but it diminishes the role of Israel in God's redemptive plan. See, however, D. I. Block, *The Gods of the Nations* (Jackson, Miss.: Evangelical Theological Society, 1988), 13-22.

[15] Driver, *Deuteronomy,* 355-56.

32:10   Israel's lack of initiation of and total dependence in the covenant relationship is seen in their description as a foundling, an infant abandoned in a desert place and left to die. This does not mean that Israel was indigenous to the desert or even that it was there that the Lord first came to know them. The Old Testament tradition traces their origin back to Abraham, and from those ancient patriarchal times Israel had been the focus of the Lord's redemptive design (cf. Deut 26:5b-9; Josh 24:2-13). What was in view here was Israel's postexodus experience in the Sinai deserts, the "barren and howling waste" where the Lord made covenant with them and through which he guided them to the present moment.[16]

The description of the Lord's solicitous care is in most tender terms. He shielded (*sābab*, lit., "encompassed" or "surrounded") Israel and cared for (*poel* of *bîn*; "attentively considered") them. So central was Israel to the Lord's concern that they were, as it were, the "apple of his eye" (v. 10b). This meaning of the Hebrew noun *ʾîšôn* is poetic for the pupil of the eye, that is, its very center (cf. Prov 7:2; Ps 17:8). The same simile occurs in Zech 2:8 [Heb. 2:12], where, however, *bābâ* is used rather than *ʾîšôn*.[17] This term, perhaps to be understood literally as "gate" (cf. Aram. *bābāʾ*, "gate," in *Tg. Esth* 5:14), also refers to the opening of the eye, that is, to the pupil. Inasmuch as vision is dependent on an open and undamaged pupil, it is easy to see how precious that part of the eye is.

32:11-12   The poet now switches to the imagery of an eagle and its young. When the time comes for the eaglet to fly, its mother will stir up the nest, that is, she will agitate her offspring and thus prepare it for the next phase of its development. But she will do so protectingly and not prematurely. At the same time she is encouraging it to fly, she is hovering over it with comfort and assurance. Even when the eaglet ventures forth for its first flight, its parent is there to fly beneath and, if necessary, to catch the neophyte on its own outspread wings.[18] In this manner the Lord had carefully and tenderly sheltered his own offspring, Israel; and even after Israel had begun to be mobile, he was there to protect and preserve.

Hosea used comparable imagery to describe the Lord's exodus deliverance of his people. The prophet, however, viewed Israel as a "child" (11:1), one whom God called out of Egypt and whom he taught to walk,

---

[16] A. Phillips, *Deuteronomy* (Cambridge: The University Press, 1973), 217: "The Song is simply seeking to stress Israel's ingratitude by contrasting the poverty of life in the desert with its richness in Canaan."

[17] C. L. Meyers and E. M. Meyers, *Haggai, Zechariah 1–8,* AB (Garden City: Doubleday, 1987), 166. See also S. A. B. Mercer, " 'The Little Man of His Eye' (Deut. 26:5)," *ATR* 3 (1920-21): 151-52. Cf. BDB, 36,93.

[18] For a modern observation of this see Driver, *Deuteronomy,* 358.

"taking them by the arms" (v. 3). He had "led them with cords of human kindness, with ties of love" and had "lifted the yoke from their neck and bent down to feed them" (v. 4). In both cases Israel is perceived as a helpless infant, one incapable of making his own way in the howling desert of past history. But God was more than sufficient by himself to guide the objects of his love. There was therefore no foreign god needed, a fact that Israel apparently had forgotten when they resorted to the golden calf (cf. Exod 32:1-6; Deut 9:16).

32:13 Yahweh's leading, furthermore, was not with difficulty or impediment but one of triumphant success. Like the Lord himself, who rides as sovereign upon the clouds of heaven (Deut 33:26; cf. Pss 68:33; 104:3), Israel was able to scale the heights (lit., "ride the backs") of the desert land (v. 13a).[19] This connotes Israel's dominion as well, for elsewhere they are described as walking "on the heights" (*bāmôt,* as here), a figure of speech suggesting strength and triumph (Hab 3:19; cf. Deut 33:29). A result of such victorious transit is the abundant provision of sustenance along the way. There was the produce of field, honey from the rock, and oil from the flint rock (v. 13). This last refers no doubt either to olive presses carved from solid stone where olive oil was extracted from the fruit or, more likely, to olive trees growing in such inhospitable soils as flinty rock.[20]

32:14 By now the scene is changing from the deserts of Sinai to the more fertile lands of the Transjordan. Thus the fare is now curds and milk as well as lambs, goats, rams, and wheat and wine (v. 14). The area of Bashan was especially famed for its vast stands of oaks (Isa 2:13; Ezek 27:6), its lush grazing lands (Jer 50:19), and its sleek cattle (Ps 22:12; Ezek 39:18; Amos 4:1).[21] There is no wonder that the tribes of Reuben, Gad, and Manasseh had asked permission of Moses to settle there and in the land of Gilead (Num 32:1-5). Like Canaan across the river, the Transjordan was a land "flowing with milk and honey."

5. Israel's Rebellion (32:15-18)

[15]**Jeshurun grew fat and kicked;**
　filled with food, he became heavy and sleek.
He abandoned the God who made him

---

[19] J. L. Crenshaw, "*Wĕdōrek ʿal-bāmŏtê ʾāreṣ,*" *CBQ* 34 (1972): 39-53; J. M. Grintz, "Some Observations on the 'High-Place' in the History of Israel," *VT* 27 (1977): 112.

[20] For olive oil culture and production see E. W. Heaton, *Everyday Life in Old Testament Times* (New York: Macmillan, 1988), 106-8.

[21] D. Baly, *The Geography of the Bible* (New York: Harper & Brothers, 1957), 219-26.

and rejected the Rock his Savior.
¹⁶They made him jealous with their foreign gods
and angered him with their detestable idols.
¹⁷They sacrificed to demons, which are not God—
gods they had not known,
gods that recently appeared,
gods your fathers did not fear.
¹⁸You deserted the Rock, who fathered you;
you forgot the God who gave you birth.

32:15-18 The Lord's gracious goodness notwithstanding, Israel had rebelled against him at every turn and had trampled his covenant underfoot. The arrangement of the text makes this crystal clear by matching every beneficence of the Lord by a corresponding negative response by Israel. Their fatness (v. 15a), made possible by the abundance of the Lord's provision (vv. 13-14), led to their abandonment of their God, the one who had made them and delivered them from bondage and want (v. 15b). God, the one who alone exists and who lovingly and carefully brought his people through the desert places (vv. 10-12), was rejected by them in favor of foreign gods and idols (vv. 16-17).²² Finally, Yahweh, the Rock and Father of the nation (vv. 4-5) who created them and elected them to be his special possession (vv. 6-9), was deserted and forgotten by them (v. 18). The chiastic structure by which vv. 4-14 match vv. 15-18 in reverse suggests the reversal of Israel's pledges of covenant commitment to the Lord.

Israel's rebellion to that point did not bode well for the future. It was all the more urgent, then, that this recital of past failure be recalled regularly in the singing of the song so that the hard lessons of judgment that followed sin might act as a deterrent to future disobedience.

6. God's Promise of Judgment (32:19-25)

¹⁹The LORD saw this and rejected them
because he was angered by his sons and daughters.
²⁰"I will hide my face from them," he said,
"and see what their end will be;
for they are a perverse generation,
children who are unfaithful.
²¹They made me jealous by what is no god

---

²² The "demons" (שֵׁדִים) of v. 17 were technically not deities but spirits that served especially to guard persons and places from harm. They are well attested in ancient Mesopotamian texts as *šedu*. Cf. H. W. F. Saggs, *The Greatness That Was Babylon* (New York: The New American Library, 1962), 301, 303.

and angered me with their worthless idols.
I will make them envious by those who are not a people;
I will make them angry by a nation that has no understanding.
²²For a fire has been kindled by my wrath,
one that burns to the realm of death below.
It will devour the earth and its harvests
and set afire the foundations of the mountains.

²³"I will heap calamities upon them
and spend my arrows against them.
²⁴I will send wasting famine against them,
consuming pestilence and deadly plague;
I will send against them the fangs of wild beasts,
the venom of vipers that glide in the dust.
²⁵In the street the sword will make them childless;
in their homes terror will reign.
Young men and young women will perish,
infants and gray-haired men.

32:19-21a The specific act of rebellion by Israel against the Lord that commences the review in vv. 15-18 must be identified as the worship of the golden calf, for the reaction described here in vv. 19-21a points unmistakably to that incident (cf. Exod 32:1-6; Deut 9:6-21).[23] Having seen what the people did while Moses was on the mountain, the Lord became angry (32:19; cf. Exod 32:10) and threatened to hide his face from them (Deut 32:20). This speaks of the removal of his favor, a response that in effect would terminate the covenant relationship. This is what was at stake in Exod 32 where the Lord told Moses to stand aside so that he might destroy Israel and make Moses the founder of another nation (v. 10). Thus he would "see what their end will be" (v. 20a).

The reason for such holy wrath was the disloyalty of Israel (v. 20b), the very essence of which was the worship of other gods (v. 21a). This, of course, was at the heart of the golden calf episode. The people had made the Lord "jealous" by worshiping what, in reality, was a nonentity, a figment of their perverted imaginations. The word "jealous" brings to mind the Decalogue itself, for the second commandment states that the reason idolatry is forbidden is that the Lord is "a jealous God," one who will brook no rivals nor tolerate any divided affection (Deut 5:9; cf. Ps 78:58). Moreover, immediately after the enunciation of the Shema, in which Israel

---

[23] Obviously that event alone is not in view, for vv. 13-15 imply a setting in the Transjordan and, perhaps, even a prophetic look at life in Canaan. It was the incident at Horeb that inaugurated the whole sorry history of Israel's apostasy, however, and that which best suits the language of vv. 19-21a.

confessed that the Lord is one and is to be exclusively worshiped (Deut 6:4-5), the Lord again asserted that he was jealous and that he would destroy his people if they turned to idolatry (Deut 6:15).

32:21b   The catalog of judgment that follows such covenant defection is awesome in its prospect. It begins with the irony of Israel being made envious (again, *qānā᾿,* "jealous," as in v. 21a), just as the Lord had been, and by a "nonpeople," again as the Lord had been made jealous by a "nongod." The identity of the "nonpeople" is first suggested by the prophet Hosea, who was told that one of his sons, representing Israel, was to be named Lo-ammi ("not my people") because of his anticipated unfaithfulness (Hos 1:9). Amazingly, however, in the day of the Lord's eschatological redemption, "not my people" would become "my people" (Hos 2:23).

While this indeed speaks of Israel's spiritual renewal and restoration, the "not-a-people" concept here in the song of Moses agrees with Paul's assessment that the phrase also includes the Gentiles. Quoting Hosea, the apostle said, "I will call them 'my people' who are not my people; and I will call her 'my loved one' who is not my loved one" (Rom 9:25). The people all together he defined as "not only from the Jews but also from the Gentiles" (v. 24). Clearly it would be through the Gentiles that God would make his chosen people Israel envious, an envy that at first was retributive but that would at last move them back to covenant fellowship with their God (Rom 10:19; cf. 11:11).[24]

The irony continues with the threat that the Lord would make his people angry by a nation of no understanding (v. 21b; lit., "a foolish nation"). Again this "nation" must be the Gentiles and the time frame primarily eschatological.[25] Israel had enraged the Lord by bowing down to "worthless idols" (v. 21b; *hebel,* lit., "breath" or "nothingness"), so the time would come when nations empty or devoid of natural sensitivity to spiritual things would be quickened and become a means of provoking Israel to anger (cf. Rom 10:19).

32:22   Yahweh's anger with his disloyal subjects would know no boundaries. In poetic and highly graphic language he described its universality as extending into the very bowels of the earth, into Sheol itself (v. 22a). In Old Testament understanding this would have no reference to the fires of hell, a concept of much later origin, but to the netherworld as a place far removed from ordinary human life, namely, the realm of the dead

---

[24] E. F. Harrison, "Romans," EBC (Grand Rapids: Zondervan, 1976), 10:115.

[25] Scholars have proposed all kinds of historical candidates from the Philistines to the Babylonians, but the very imprecision of the reference lends preference to the eschatological aspect. For a host of opinions see Driver, *Deuteronomy,* 365-66.

(cf. Pss 9:17; 16:10; 139:8; Isa 14:9,15; Amos 9:2). Moses here was not addressing the matter of the afterlife and the condition of the righteous and wicked dead but had in mind the cosmological distinction, so common in the Old Testament, of things on the earth, below the earth, and above the earth, that is, all things everywhere (cf. Ps 139:7-10).[26] Yahweh's anger would be so intense and pervasive that it would permeate the most inaccessible regions of the created universe. Everything on the earth and under it would feel its devastating effect.

32:23-25 Turning from the imagery of fire, the Lord described the outpouring of his wrath in terms of battle, pestilence, and wild animals. To preclude any interpretation that Israel's suffering would be by happenstance or purely at the hands of natural and human forces, he commenced the list of judgments by asserting that it is he who would heap (lit., "multiply") troubles upon them and shoot the arrows of his retribution against them. These arrows would include hunger, pestilence, and plague, all of which elsewhere appear in lists of curses for covenant violation (cf. Deut 28:20-22,48).[27] The animal world would also become vicious instruments of divine wrath, biting and poisoning their hapless victims (32:24b). Though the curses of Deuteronomy do not include this, the list of Lev 26 does (Lev 26:22; cf. 2 Kgs 17:26).

The arrows of the Lord would take the more literal and concrete form of the battle sword wielded by Israel's enemies. No place would be safe ("in the street" and "in their homes" form a merism meaning "everywhere"), nor would any class or age. From stalwart young man to maiden and from infant to the eldest—all would suffer the Lord's wrath. Divine visitation by war as a punishment for covenant defection is a common motif in the curse sections (cf. Deut 28:25,36,48-57). Clearly the entire section here speaks of the calamity that would befall Israel if and when they rebelled against the Lord their God, judgment appropriate to covenant disloyalty.

7. The Powerlessness of Other Gods (32:26-38)

> [26]I said I would scatter them
>   and blot out their memory from mankind,
> [27]but I dreaded the taunt of the enemy,

---

[26] Cf. C. F. Keil and F. Delitzsch, *Biblical Commentary on the Old Testament: The Pentateuch* (Grand Rapids: Eerdmans, n.d.), 3:480-81.

[27] J. C. Greenfield, "Smitten by Famine, Battered by Plague (Deuteronomy 32:24)," *Love and Death in the Ancient Near East: Essays in Honor of Marvin H. Pope*, ed. J. H. Marks and R. M. Good (Guilford, Conn.: Four Quarters, 1986), 151-52. Greenfield suggests that רֶשֶׁף, identified as the god of pestilence, takes on a militaristic role in line with the context.

lest the adversary misunderstand
and say, 'Our hand has triumphed;
the LORD has not done all this.'"

[28]They are a nation without sense,
there is no discernment in them.
[29]If only they were wise and would understand this
and discern what their end will be!
[30]How could one man chase a thousand,
or two put ten thousand to flight,
unless their Rock had sold them,
unless the LORD had given them up?
[31]For their rock is not like our Rock,
as even our enemies concede.
[32]Their vine comes from the vine of Sodom
and from the fields of Gomorrah.
Their grapes are filled with poison,
and their clusters with bitterness.
[33]Their wine is the venom of serpents,
the deadly poison of cobras.

[34]"Have I not kept this in reserve
and sealed it in my vaults?
[35]It is mine to avenge; I will repay.
In due time their foot will slip;
their day of disaster is near
and their doom rushes upon them."

[36]The LORD will judge his people
and have compassion on his servants
when he sees their strength is gone
and no one is left, slave or free.
[37]He will say: "Now where are their gods,
the rock they took refuge in,
[38]the gods who ate the fat of their sacrifices
and drank the wine of their drink offerings?
Let them rise up to help you!
Let them give you shelter!

As fearsome and final as the Lord's judgment on recalcitrant Israel might appear to have been, however, there would be a limit to it for at least two reasons: his compassion and the misapprehension of Israel's (and the Lord's) enemies. The song turns to the latter of these first (vv. 26-27).

32:26-27 In highly anthropomorphic terms the Lord said that his intention was to annihilate his people from the earth because of their sin (v. 26). However, on second thought he realized that such a course of action would open him up to the charge that Israel's demise was not the result of his own action but the triumph of human armies. Thus the desired effect of showing divine retribution as a necessary corollary to human sin would be lost on those who should learn from it. Such musings on God's part should not, of course, suggest indecisiveness or deliberation in his mind and thoughts. There are no such conundrums in the divine purpose.[28] All that is being expressed here is the outward perception of God's design in light of the unfolding of events.

This coordination of divine and human purpose is best illustrated in the event most in the foreground here, namely, Moses' dialogue with the Lord at Horeb (Exod 32:11-14). After Israel had worshiped the golden calf, the Lord threatened to destroy them and begin again with Moses (Exod 32:10). Moses, however, counseled against such harsh measures, arguing that the Egyptians would never understand. They would think the Lord had rescued them from Egypt with the express purpose in mind of exterminating them. Moreover, he said, the Lord had made an inviolable promise to the patriarchs that they would enter Canaan and inherit it forever. Only then did the Lord relent, outwardly because of the force of Moses' arguments but inwardly and more fundamentally because of his own immutable promises. His judgment, then, would be remedial, designed to show both Israel and the nations that he and only he is God.

32:28-30 The identification of the subject throughout the passage is a matter of some difficulty, but the overall argument suggests that Israel was in view in vv. 28-30.[29] It was Israel that lacked sense (lit., "counsel") and any faculty for understanding basic truth (*těbûnâ*; cf. Prov 2:6,11; 28:16; Isa 44:19). It was God's people on behalf of whom the poet longed for wisdom and discernment about the outcome of their actions (v. 29). Their life of covenant rebellion would lead to bitter consequences that they appeared unable to foresee. And yet they had already experienced defeat by much inferior forces such as those of the Amalekites and Canaanites at Hormah (Num 14:39-45). Careful thought should have led them to understand that such a humiliating setback came about not because of the strength of these pagan peoples (for they were outnumbered by Israel by a thousand to one) or even their gods but only because the Lord their Rock had given them over to defeat (v. 30; cf. vv. 4,18).

32:31-33 The subject now shifts to the enemy nations and especially to their gods (vv. 31-33). Even their worshipers were forced to concede

---

[28] For a helpful theological analysis, see von Rad, *Deuteronomy*, 198-99.
[29] Thus Craigie, *Deuteronomy*, 386; for the case that it was the pagan nations see A. D. H. Mayes, *Deuteronomy*, NCBC (Grand Rapids: Eerdmans, 1979), 389-90.

that their gods ("their rock") were vastly inferior to the God ("our Rock") of Israel not only in power but in quality. The idea here is not so much that the nations blatantly confessed the weakness of their gods but that they were forced to face the facts when confronted by the awesomeness of Israel's God. Empirical evidence speaks for itself (cf. Exod 14:4,25). Then, in the language of irony, Moses referred to the gods of the nations metaphorically as vines, grapes, and wine.[30] The figure may also be that of metonymy in which the effect is put for the cause. That is, these elements of viticulture represented the gods who made them possible.

As far as the poet was concerned, false gods found their source in Sodom and Gomorrah, that is, in the gross perversion and unnatural affection these places epitomize (cf. Gen 18:20; 19:4-28; Isa 1:10; 3:9; Jer 23:14; Lam 4:6; Ezek 16:44-52; Matt 10:15; 11:23-24).[31] This vine of paganism with its roots in Sodom produced noxious (cf. Deut 29:18; Lam 3:5; Hos 10:4) and bitter grapes. This is a way of saying that the fruit of the worship of these detestable gods was far short of satisfying. In fact, it left a bad taste in the mouth, so to speak. But more serious than that was the final result of worshiping them—certain and agonizing death. The wine of the bitter fruit of paganism was as deadly as the venom of the most virulent snake (v. 33). Far from being merely harmless options to the worship of the Lord, devotion to the gods of paganism had fatal consequences. Israel had to understand this lest they credit these gods with what the Lord had done and thus bring most painful judgment upon themselves.

32:34-36 The mystery of God's judgment enacted through "natural" or human means is laid bare in vv. 34-35. These verses, the subject of much discussion and disagreement, appear to refer to the resolution of the question of ultimate responsibility for the punishment of covenant unfaithfulness. God had kept this (i.e., the vengeance of v. 35) within his own purview and according to his own schedule. Though the disasters of vv. 19-25 would appear to have come from forces outside of God (cf. v. 27), it must be understood that they were only instruments of God's own discipline (v.

---

[30] C. J. Labuschagne identifies Yahweh as the speaker in vv. 32-35 (for other "divine speeches" in the song see vv. 20-27 and 37-42), a unit he describes as "performative speech" or "interior monologue." What sets it apart from other divine speech in the OT is the lack of an introductory formula. The free interchange between Yahweh's direct address and that of Moses as his spokesman makes it difficult to be precise about the subject in these cases, however ("Divine Speech in Deuteronomy," *Das Deuteronomium,* 111-26).

[31] For the phrase "fields of Gomorrah" (v. 32), see M. R. Lehmann, "A New Interpretation of the Term *šdmwt*," *VT* 3 (1953): 361-71. Lehmann views the term as a combination of words (שׂדי, "field," and מות, Mot, god of death), pointing to a Canaanite cultic provenience.

30). It was he who stored up wrath until the time came to expend it on those who deserved it.

The Lord, then, had the sole prerogative to avenge, no matter the means that was used, for it was he who was offended by sin (v. 35a). It was he, therefore, who brought judgment when and as he pleased (v. 35b-d). But it also was he who acted with compassion even in the midst of judgment (v. 36). When he saw that they had turned to gods that could give no help or hope and that they were therefore completely debilitated, he still responded with pity for, as suggested already, his people were "a nation without sense," a people lacking in discernment (v. 28).[32]

32:37-38 Compassion does not negate accountability, however, and in Israel's day of judgment the question must have been raised about who really is God. The Lord himself would challenge his people to produce the gods to whom they had turned for protection and whom they worshiped in their days of apostate unbelief. The answer to the query, "Where are their gods?" is self-evident. They were not to be found because they, in fact, did not exist. In scorn the Lord would exhort Israel in the day of their calamity to invoke the gods whom they had chosen in lieu of him (v. 38c,d). Vainly they would implore these figments of imagination to help them and to provide them security.

8. The Vindication of the Lord (32:39-43)

> [39]"See now that I myself am He!
>   There is no god besides me.
> I put to death and I bring to life,
>   I have wounded and I will heal,
>   and no one can deliver out of my hand.
> [40]I lift my hand to heaven and declare:
>   As surely as I live forever,
> [41]when I sharpen my flashing sword
>   and my hand grasps it in judgment,
> I will take vengeance on my adversaries
>   and repay those who hate me.
> [42]I will make my arrows drunk with blood,
>   while my sword devours flesh:
> the blood of the slain and the captives,
>   the heads of the enemy leaders."
>
> [43]Rejoice, O nations, with his people,

---

[32] For this understanding of the passage and its use in the NT (Rom 12:19; Heb 10:30), see J. A. Thompson, *Deuteronomy,* TOTC (Leicester: InterVarsity, 1974), 302-3.

> for he will avenge the blood of his servants;
> he will take vengeance on his enemies
> and make atonement for his land and people.

32:39 In marked contrast to the weak, incompetent, and, in fact, non-existent gods of the pagans was the Lord, the one who alone exists. This self-asseveration is inherent throughout the covenant text of Deuteronomy (cf. 4:35,39; 5:7; 32:12) and argued at length elsewhere, especially in Isaiah (cf. 41:4; 43:10-12; 45:5-6).[33] He was the ultimate cause of death and the source of all life, the wounder and healer, the one from whom no one could escape (v. 39b). The order of these abilities or attributes appears to be the reverse of matching elements in vv. 26-38, where the powerlessness of pagan gods is the issue. Thus the Lord's grasp from which no one could be delivered (v. 39) opposes vv. 26-30, where Israel is said to have believed that their calamities must be attributed to the gods of the nations. Also the Lord as sovereign of life and death and of harm and health (v. 39b) was so unlike those gods whose roots and fruits were poisonous in their source and effect (vv. 31-33). Finally, his uniqueness and solitariness (v. 39a) contrasts with the imagined existence and plurality of these deities (vv. 34-38).

32:40 In an act consistent with the song as a sworn testimony (cf. vv. 1-4), the Lord raised his hand to heaven in oath to affirm his intention to punish the hostile nations of earth (vv. 40-42) and to avenge ultimately and vindicate his own people Israel (v. 43). The seriousness and irrevocability of God's pledge is seen in the oath formula "as surely as I live forever" (v. 40). Variations of this phrase occur regularly in the Old Testament to express the Lord's solemn avowal to be or do this thing or the other (cf. Num 14:21,28; Isa 49:18; Jer 22:24; 46:18; Ezek 5:11; 14:16,18,20; 16:48; 17:16,19; 18:3; Zeph 2:9).[34] The Word of God by itself is sure, but when he swears by his own life and reputation, there can be no doubt about the fulfillment of his intentions.

32:41 With sharpened sword the Lord would exercise vengeance against his enemies, that is, those who hated him. In the covenant context of Deuteronomy especially, hating God was tantamount to rejecting him. Thus just as loving him speaks of faithful covenant obedience to him (cf. Deut 5:10; 6:5; 7:9; 10:12; 11:1,13,22; 13:3; 19:9; 30:6,16,20), so hating him is descriptive of those who have no covenant relationship with him and/or who live in rebellion against him (cf. 5:9; 7:10; 2 Chr 19:2; Pss

---

[33] For the use of this polemical language in Isaiah, see E. H. Merrill, "Literary Genres in Isaiah 40–55," *BSac* 144 (1987): 148-53.

[34] For the OT oath formula see M. R. Lehmann, "Biblical Oaths," *ZAW* 81 (1969): 74-92.

81:15; 139:20-21).[35] The only remedy for those who persist in this state of alienation from God (thus the participle *limśanʾay*, "to the one hating me") is destruction.

32:42 In highly figurative and graphic language the Lord spoke of intoxicating his arrows with the blood of his enemies and eating up (*ʾākal*) their flesh with his sword. Switching the imagery, he identified the blood with the ordinary victims of his wrath, that is, with all but the leaders, and equated the flesh with the leaders. The parallelism between v. 42a and v. 42c on the one hand and between v. 42b and v. 42d on the other hand favors this view. The thrust of the whole is complete devastation of all God's enemies from the lowliest to the most exalted.

32:43 In response to this divine act of righteous judgment, the nations in general, along with God's own servant people Israel, were exhorted to rejoice (v. 43). This was not an invitation to look with glee upon the gruesome scene of carnage just described but to celebrate with Israel the vengeance of the Lord that finally resolved the moral and ethical inequities of life and history. By offering their ringing cry (thus *rānan*; "rejoice") of endorsement, all peoples would finally come to realize that the judge of all the earth would do right (cf. Gen 18:25). Though evil appeared to prevail and by its very strength to justify itself, in the day of the Lord's triumph and Israel's vindication it would be clear that the Lord and his eternal purposes for creation were brought to fruition in accordance with the standards of his own perfect holiness. The most sublime expression of this would be the atonement he made for his land and people, an atonement, as a full biblical revelation shows, that finds its foundation and fullness in Jesus Christ (cf. Ezek 16:60-63; Rom 3:25; Heb 2:17). The meaning here is that of reconciliation. God's wayward people (vv. 15-18), set for judgment (vv. 19-25) and unable to find deliverance through powerless pagan gods (vv. 26-38), would at last be purged of their sin, vindicated in the face of their enemies, and restored to perfect covenant relationship with the Lord (vv. 39-43).

9. Conclusion to the Song (32:44)

⁴⁴Moses came with Joshua son of Nun and spoke all the words of this song in the hearing of the people.

32:44 As argued already (cf. 31:30), this verse forms the closing frame of the song of Moses. The opening frame (31:30) states that Moses

---

[35] J. A. Thompson, "Israel's Haters," *VT* 29 (1979): 203.

recited the words of the song, and that is the message here. Unless one understands that the song is spoken all over again, a view that has little to commend it, it seems best to see the present verse as a rounding off of the pericope in which the song is embedded.

XI. NARRATIVE INTERLUDE (32:45-52)
1. Moses' Exhortation to Obedience (32:45-47)
2. Instructions Surrounding Moses' Death (32:48-52)

XI. NARRATIVE INTERLUDE (32:45-52)

As noted repeatedly, one of the unique characteristics of Deuteronomy as a suzerain-vassal treaty text is its parenetic interruptions in which Israel is exhorted to a course of action as a result of having been called by Yahweh into the covenant relationship. Another unusual feature is the extensive use of narrative even apart from the preamble (1:1-5) and historical prologue (1:6–4:40), which are, of course, normal elements of such documents. These narratives, interspersed throughout Deuteronomy (cf. 4:41-43; 5:22-33; 26:16-19; 28:69; 29:2–30:20; 34:1-12), do not invalidate the book as a covenant text (or as containing such a text) but merely demonstrate Moses' flexibility in adapting covenant form to an extended narrative describing events on the plains of Moab. This brief narrative, in line with that overall function of narrative in the book, provides an account of Moses' exhortation in light of the song just spoken (vv. 45-47) and an instruction to him to ascend Mount Nebo in order to view the promised land before he died (vv. 48-52).

1. Moses' Exhortation to Obedience (32:45-47)

[45]When Moses finished reciting all these words to all Israel, [46]he said to them, "Take to heart all the words I have solemnly declared to you this day, so that you may command your children to obey carefully all the words of this law. [47]They are not just idle words for you—they are your life. By them you will live long in the land you are crossing the Jordan to possess."

32:45-47 The narrative suggests that Moses addressed the assembly of Israel immediately after he had composed and spoken to them the words of the foregoing song.[1] His charge to them was that they "take to

---

[1] The boundaries of the pericope are pretty much a matter of consensus. A. D. H. Mayes, for example, suggests that this section is "the deuteronomistic continuation of 31:29," the song of 31:30–32:44 being interruptive of the longer exhortation (*Deuteronomy*, NCBC [Grand Rapids: Eerdmans, 1979], 394).

heart" all the words of the song, but not only these words. They also were to heed "all the words of this law" (v. 46), a technical phrase used consistently to refer to the entire covenant text of Deuteronomy (cf. 17:19; 27:3,8,26; 28:58; 29:29; 31:12,24). Not only were his hearers to pledge themselves to its stipulations, but they were to command their descendants to do the same. Over and over again the people of Israel were reminded that the faith and commitment of any one generation were not sufficient for all the generations to come. Each must have its own time of covenant renewal (cf. Deut 4:9-10; 5:29; 6:2,7; 11:19,21; 12:25,28; 30:19).

The seriousness of Israel's obligation can be seen in the emphatic words of the charge in v. 46. "Take to heart" (Heb. *śîmû lĕbabkem*) is a command of strongest force (cf. Deut 30:1; 2 Sam 13:20; Isa 42:25; 46:8; Ezek 3:10), one that leaves no room for equivocation. Moreover, the use of the personal pronoun "I" (*ʾānōkî*) with the participle of *ʿûd* (rendered as "I have solemnly declared" in the NIV) intensifies the sense of personal interest on the Lord's part. It was he, the sovereign God, who had laid these mandates on them. Finally, Moses pointed out that the words of covenant requirement were not "idle" words, flippant or offhanded matters of opinion (v. 47). Rather than being empty and worthless words they were, in fact, words that led to life. The same sentiment appears earlier in Deuteronomy, where the point is made that "man does not live on bread alone but on every word that comes from the mouth of the LORD" (Deut 8:3; cf. 30:20). By feeding on them, that is, by obeying them explicitly, Israel could face the prospect of long life in the land of promise (cf. Deut 4:40).

2. Instructions Surrounding Moses' Death (32:48-52)

[48]On that same day the LORD told Moses, [49]"Go up into the Abarim Range to Mount Nebo in Moab, across from Jericho, and view Canaan, the land I am giving the Israelites as their own possession. [50]There on the mountain that you have climbed you will die and be gathered to your people, just as your brother Aaron died on Mount Hor and was gathered to his people. [51]This is because both of you broke faith with me in the presence of the Israelites at the waters of Meribah Kadesh in the Desert of Zin and because you did not uphold my holiness among the Israelites. [52]Therefore, you will see the land only from a distance; you will not enter the land I am giving to the people of Israel."

32:48-52 Ironically, after Moses had exhorted the assembly to obey "all the words of this law" in anticipation of their crossing the Jordan and occupying the promised land, he was reminded once more that he himself would not be able to accompany them (cf. Num 20:12; 27:14; Deut 1:37; 3:26-27). He had done two things to disqualify himself: (1) he had "broken faith" with the Lord at Meribah Kadesh, and (2) he had failed to "uphold the Lord's holiness" (v. 51).[2]

The former term (Heb. *māʿal*) has the basic idea of treachery or unfaithfulness, suggesting here that Moses, as covenant mediator, had proved to be disloyal to that covenant commitment in a time of unusual trial. The verb occurs in numerous other places where the issue of covenant is central (cf. Lev 26:40; Num 31:16; 1 Chr 5:25; Ezek 17:15-19; 20:25-27).[3] Whatever else may have happened at Meribah Kadesh, the place where Moses struck the rock in anger (Num 20:11), the whole episode is summarized as an act of rebellion (*mārâ*) against God (Num 20:24; cf. 27:14; 1 Sam 12:15). Such an act by the very leader of the covenant community was unthinkable, so, tragically enough, Moses was barred access to the land to which he had led the people.

Failure to "uphold holiness" (*lōʾ qiddaštem ʾôtî*) with respect to the Lord (also associated with the Meribah Kadesh incident; cf. Num 20:12; 27:14) was failure to give proper consideration to who he is. That is, it was a denial of his transcendent uniqueness and lordship and an attempt, conscious or not, to reduce him to a human level. Again the covenant implications are clear, especially in Moses' act of rebellion. The Lord had told him to speak to the rock (Num 20:8), the mere act of speaking being designed to demonstrate the power of God who creates by the spoken word. To strike the rock was to introduce an interruptive element and thus to diminish the significance of the powerful word. By doing this, Moses betrayed not only anger and disobedience but he correspondingly reflected on the God whom he served by implying that God could not bring forth water by the divine word alone.

Even God's discipline is mitigated by his grace, however, so Moses was allowed to see the land of Canaan from a distance (v. 52; thus *minneged*; cf. Num 2:2; 2 Kgs 2:15; 3:22; 4:25). More specifically, he could ascend Mount Nebo, opposite Jericho, and there take in the panorama of the land before he died on the mountain (vv. 49-50). The "Abarim Range" refers to the high plateau area east of the Jordan River and Dead Sea, the

---

[2] See R. Lux, "Der Tod des Mose als 'besprochene und erzählte Welte': literatur-wissenschaftliche und theologische Interpretation von Deut. 32:48-52 und 34," *ZTK* 84 (1987): 395-425. Lux sees the death accounts as providing a framework for other Mosaic narratives leading up to them. Cf. G. W. Coats, "Legendary Motifs in the Moses Death Reports," *CBQ* 39 (1977): 34-44.

[3] V. P. Hamilton, "מָעַל (*māʿal*)," etc., *TWOT* 1:519-20.

highest peak of which was Pisgah, a part of Mount Nebo (cf. Deut 34:1).[4] This peak, with an elevation of over 2,600 feet, is about twenty miles from Jericho as the crow flies and affords an unobstructed view of nearly all the promised land (cf. Deut 34:1-3).

Aaron too had died on a mountain, Mount Hor, some ten miles northeast of Kadesh Barnea (cf. Num 20:22-29). The significance of death and burial on a mountain may lie in the notion, even in the Bible, that the mountain peak symbolizes nearness to heaven, that is, to God himself. The "high places" associated with pagan worship certainly conveyed this concept, but the Lord himself sanctions the idea that he meets in a special way with those who worship him on designated mountains (cf. Gen 22:14; Exod 3:1,12; 19:11; 24:16; Josh 8:30; Pss 43:3; 48:1; 68:16; Isa 2:2). It is fitting that Aaron and Moses, despite their rebellion, be buried "near God" on a prominent mountain top.

---

[4] *Baker Encyclopedia of the Bible*, ed. W. A. Elwell (Grand Rapids: Baker, 1988), 1:4, s.v. "Abarim."

XII. THE BLESSING OF MOSES (33:1-29)

The purpose of this section, composed, like the song of Moses, in poetic form, was to pronounce prophetic blessings on the twelve tribes of Israel.[1] In its form it very much resembles Jacob's paternal blessing of his sons (cf. Gen 49:1-27), but its function is quite different.[2] Jacob's dying words, though described as a blessing (Gen 49:28), were also unabashedly predictive. "Gather around," he said, "so I can tell you what will happen to you in days to come" (49:1). Then with divinely inspired prescience, he outlined the future for each of his sons.

Moses' speech was more strictly in the technical form and language of blessing. The passage begins with the words, "This is the blessing that Moses . . . pronounced" (33:1), and each subsection commences with the optative "let" thus and so take place (vv. 6,12) or "may" it happen (v. 13)

---

[1] There is a vast literature on the composition. See in general F. M. Cross, Jr., and D. N. Freedman, *Studies in Ancient Yahwistic Poetry,* SBLDS 21 (Missoula, Mont.: Scholars Press, 1975), 97-122; P. C. Craigie, "The Conquest and Early Hebrew Poetry," *TynBul* 20 (1969): 76-94 (esp. pp. 81-82).

[2] J. D. Heck, "A History of Interpretation of Genesis 49 and Deuteronomy 33," *BSac* 147 (1990): 16-31.

or such terms occur internally, either explicitly or implicitly.[3] Rather than being formally predictive, then, Moses' utterances concerning the tribes were in the nature of prayerful intercession. They express what he fervently desired for his people and what he confidently expected that God would do.

In the context of Deuteronomy as a covenant document the passage may also outline the manner of anticipated blessing for all Israel and for each tribe specifically, blessing predicated upon faithful adherence to the covenant stipulations as set forth especially in chaps. 5–26.[4] In other words, this list of tribal blessings may complement that of the formal blessing section of Deut 28:1-14 and at the same time redress the problem of the brevity of that section. In support of this connection, perhaps, are the narratives that precede chaps. 27–28 and chap. 33. Both of them refer to mountains, the one where the tribes were to gather in Canaan to invoke curses and blessings (27:1-13) and the other where Moses was to retire after he had recited the list of blessings (32:48-52).

The blessing of Moses consisted of an introduction (33:1), a historical review (vv. 2-5), the blessings of the individual tribes (vv. 6-25), and a praise and blessing of Israel generally (vv. 26-29).

1. Introduction to the Blessing (33:1-2a)

[1]This is the blessing that Moses the man of God pronounced on the Israelites before his death. [2]He said:

33:1-2a   Just as Jacob gathered his sons about him to bestow his blessings upon them before he died (Gen 49:1; cf. 48:21), so Moses, anticipating his own death (Deut 32:50), gathered the tribes who bore the names of Jacob's sons for the purpose of invoking God's blessings on them as they contemplated conquest and occupation of Canaan. As their theocratic leader and, indeed, almost as their father, Moses interceded for his people with prophetic vision, beseeching God's favor and confident in its bestowal.

---

[3] For "blessing" as a literary form, see C. Westermann, *Blessing in the Bible and the Life of the Church,* trans. K. R. Crim (Philadelphia: Fortress, 1978), 45-49.

[4] P. C. Craigie, *The Book of Deuteronomy,* NICOT (Grand Rapids: Eerdmans, 1976), 390-91.

2. Historical Review (33:2b-5)[5]

"The LORD came from Sinai
  and dawned over them from Seir;
  he shone forth from Mount Paran.
He came with myriads of holy ones
  from the south, from his mountain slopes.
[3]Surely it is you who love the people;
  all the holy ones are in your hand.
At your feet they all bow down,
  and from you receive instruction,
[4]the law that Moses gave us,
  the possession of the assembly of Jacob.
[5]He was king over Jeshurun
  when the leaders of the people assembled,
  along with the tribes of Israel.

33:2b-e   One of the characteristics of Deuteronomy is the recital of Israel's sacred history in anticipation of the Lord's undertaking of covenant with his people (cf. Deut 1:6–4:40; 9:6–10:11) or bestowal of blessing upon them (Deut 26:5b-9; 29:2-9; 32:7-43). Ordinarily the account is in the nature of a travelogue or itinerary, cast in rather prosaic, documentary language. Here, however, is a poetic rendition describing the Lord's past dealings with Israel in terms of epiphany. He appeared as a conquering hero to Israel, the sovereign Lord of the heavens who made covenant with them and who was able, on that basis, to dispense the blessings that followed.

As most scholars have noted, the imagery here is that of the Divine Warrior marching at the head of his armies on behalf of those whom he had chosen for protection and blessing.[6] The same motifs appear elsewhere, especially in the Song of the Sea following the exodus (Exod 15:1b-18); the Song of Deborah (Judg 5:2-5); Ps 68 (esp. vv. 7-10); and

---

[5] Freedman views vv. 2-5 and vv. 26-29 as the framework to the tribal blessing proper. For his helpful prosodic analysis of and comments on vv. 2-5 (which he calls the "Proem"), see D. N. Freedman, "The Poetic Structure of the Framework of Deuteronomy 33," in *The Bible World: Essays in Honor of Cyrus H. Gordon*, ed. G. Rendsburg et al. (New York: KTAV, 1980), 32-34, 38-44. See also D. L. Christensen, "Two Stanzas of a Hymn in Deuteronomy 33," *Bib* 65 (1984): 382-89.

[6] N. K. Gottwald, "Holy War in Deuteronomy: Analysis and Critique," *RevExp* 61 (1964): 296-310; G. H. Jones, "Holy War or Yahweh War?" *VT* 25 (1975): 642-58; P. D. Miller, "God the Warrior," *Int* 19 (1965): 39-46.

the prayer of Habakkuk (Hab 3:2-15). Particularly noteworthy are the allusions to Sinai (Deut 33:2; Judg 5:5; Ps 68:8); Seir (Deut 33:2; Judg 5:4) or Edom (Exod 15:15; Judg 5:4); Paran (Deut 33:2; Hab 3:3); and mountains (Exod 15:17; Deut 33:2; Judg 5:5; Ps 68:15-16; Hab 3:6,10).

What all these descriptions share in common in addition to the literary motifs just listed is an explicit or implicit (as here in Deut 33) polemic against all hostile forces that seek to frustrate the Lord's purposes for creation and especially for his elect people Israel. In historical terms that purpose was to bring them out of Egyptian bondage, deliver them from the Red Sea, engage them in covenant at Sinai, transport them safely through the desert, and at last lead them to a successful conquest and occupation of the promised land. To achieve this Yahweh must act as a warrior in command of a heavenly host. As such, nothing could withstand his forward march, nor could any foe prevent his people from achieving the success and prosperity he had promised them (cf. Deut 4:32-40; 7:17-24; 20:1-20).

The stylized or formulaic nature of such historical résumés allows them to depart from normal patterns of narration in which strict adherence to chronological and geographical sequence is expected. Thus the Lord could come from Sinai and appear from Seir and Paran at the same time, or at least without reference to actual historical movement which, of course, would necessitate the order Sinai, Paran, and Seir (cf. Num 10:12; 13:3,26; 20:14; 21:4; Deut 1:19; 2:4).[7] The real point here in v. 2 is that the Lord manifested himself gloriously to his people from his earthly dwelling places or at least his usual places of self-disclosure, namely, mountaintops. Whether at Sinai, Seir, or Paran, he was available to them to reveal, sustain, and deliver (cf. Exod 19:16-24; Num 10:12; Deut 2:4). The coming (*bōʾ*), dawning (*zāraḥ*), and shining (*yāpaʿ*) all refer to the Lord's theophanic glory and majestic power.[8]

The holy war imagery continues with Yahweh's coming with his myriads of holy ones (v. 2d). The phrase *ribabôt qōdeš* elsewhere refers to innumerable holy beings, angelic or human (cf. Num 10:36; Ps 3:6; Deut 33:17; Dan 11:12). Its form here, however (*mērîbĕbōt qōdeš*), might better be understood (with slight repointing) as "from Meribath Kadesh" (i.e., Kadesh Barnea)[9] or, with slightly more alteration (*ʾet rîbĕbōt*

---

[7] The chiastic literary pattern of v. 2 also lends to the breakup of a technically accurate itinerary; and if Freedman's syllable count analysis is to be accepted, there is a good reason for reversing "Seir" and "Mount Paran." Freedman, "The Poetic Structure of Deuteronomy 33," 36, 38-41.

[8] A. D. H. Mayes, *Deuteronomy,* NCBC (Grand Rapids: Eerdmans, 1981), 398.

[9] B. Margulis, "Gen. xlix 10/Deut. xxxiii 2-3," *VT* 19 (1969): 205-6.

qādēš), "with the myriads of Kadesh," that is, with his people Israel whom he led from Kadesh Barnea.[10] This is most compatible with the following line, which speaks of the Lord coming "from the south," an apt description of Kadesh Barnea from the standpoint of the Transjordan site of the blessing text. The rendering "from his mountain slopes" (v. 2e), however, is most problematic. The parallelism with v. 2d supports the Septuagint in reading "messengers [or "angels"] with him" (cf. Acts 7:53; Gal 3:19; Heb 2:2).[11] Thus, "He came with multitudes from Kadesh, from the south mighty ones came with him."

33:3-5 The multitudes who follow the Lord are called here simply "the people" (v. 3a), a generic term qualified in the next line, however, as "all his holy ones." That these refer to Israel is beyond any doubt.[12] Only Israel was said to be loved (here *ḥābab,* hapax) by God, and only they were "in his hand" in the special sense of belonging to him and enjoying his protection (cf. Deut 7:6; 14:2,21). It was they who bowed down in submission to him and at the same time were lifted up by his words, that is, his covenant revelation (v. 3c,d). This revelation is the Torah (v. 4a), a special and precious gift bestowed upon Israel ("the assembly of Jacob") alone. This idea of the Torah as a possession unique to Israel brings to mind the whole notion of Israel as the people of Yahweh's special possession (cf. Exod 19:5; Deut 4:32-40; 7:6).

The basis and culmination of this privileged relationship was the Lord's sovereignty (v. 5). He was king over Jeshurun, a pet name for Israel (cf. Deut 32:15; 33:26; Isa 44:2), suggesting its uprightness (Heb. *yāšar,* "be right"), at least as an ideal.[13] It was because he was king that he had the power and authority to convene the leaders and people of the tribes together at the time of covenant making (cf. Exod 19:7-8; 34:31-32; Deut 29:10), and likewise it was his sovereignty that gave efficacy to the promised benefits about to be articulated to the tribes.

---

[10] I. Cairns, *Word and Presence,* ITC (Grand Rapids: Eerdmans, 1992), 295.

[11] Cross and Freedman, *Studies in Ancient Yahwistic Poetry,* 106-7. This is admittedly indirect and depends on a hypothetical Vorlage אֵלִים אֲשֵׁרוּ for MT אֵשְׁדָּת לָמוֹ. G. Rendsburg, on the basis of a Ugaritic text (UT 8) proposes rendering "with radiant splendor" or the like ("Hebrew *ʾšdt* and Ugaritic *išdym,*" *JNSL* 8 [1980]: 83). Morphological and grammatical problems, however, make this somewhat unlikely.

[12] See T. H. Gaster, "An Ancient Eulogy of Israel," *JBL* 66 (1947): 57. S. R. Driver agrees that Israel is in view but emends "peoples" to "his people" (with the LXX) to avoid the otherwise unique reference to Israel as "peoples" (*A Critical and Exegetical Commentary on Deuteronomy,* ICC (Edinburgh: T & T Clark, 1902), 393.

[13] L. Alonso-Schökel, "יָשַׁר *yašar,*" etc., *TDOT* 6:471.

3. Blessing on Reuben (33:6)[14]

**6 "Let Reuben live and not die,
    nor his men be few."**

33:6 The first blessing, bestowed on Reuben, Jacob's firstborn son
(cf. Gen 29:32; 49:3), is in the form of a wish or prayer (Heb. *yeḥî*, "may
he live").[15] Contrary to the quasi curse of Gen 49:3-4 in which Reuben's
rights as firstborn were to be stripped away because of his sin (cf. Gen
35:22), the pronouncement here appears to be positive on the whole,
though the last clause may be rendered (as in the NIV footnote) "but let
his men be few."[16] This would bring the verse more in line with the Genesis version and would also prepare the way for Reuben's future loss of
population and even disappearance as a tribal entity (cf. 2 Kgs 10:33).[17]

4. Blessing on Judah (33:7)

**7And this he said about Judah:
"Hear, O LORD, the cry of Judah;
    bring him to his people.
With his own hands he defends his cause.
Oh, be his help against his foes!"**

33:7 In urgent appeal for Judah, the tribe singled out in Jacob's
blessing as the messianic people (cf. Gen 49:8-12), Moses prayed that
Judah might be brought "to his people" (v. 7). This enigmatic petition
must find its meaning in the following lines, where Judah is viewed as
contending (Heb. *rāb*) for himself and therefore in desperate need of the
Lord's help. This help could, of course, come directly from the Lord or it
could come from Judah's strong bonding with "his people," namely, the
other tribes. If this interpretation is correct, there is already an anticipa-

---

[14] For the tribal list as presented here as a whole see C. J. Labuschagne, "The Tribes in
the Blessing of Moses," in *Language and Meaning: Studies in Hebrew Language and Biblical Exegesis,* OTS 19 (Leiden: Brill, 1974), 97-112; H. Seebass, "Die Stämmeliste von Dtn.
XXXIII," *VT* 27 (1977): 158-69.

[15] This is all the more the case if one accepts the view of Cross and Freedman that the
jussive יְחִי (v. 6b) be vocalized as an imperfect plural יִחְיוּ "although [his men)] be
[few]." See their *Studies in Ancient Yahwistic Poetry,* 111.

[16] Labuschagne ("The Tribes in the Blessing of Moses," 106-7) argues that after a jussive יְחִי always expresses an additional wish, but if Cross and Freedman are correct, the
form is not יְחִי anyway.

[17] Mayes, *Deuteronomy,* 401.

tion of the rupture of the tribal confederation into the two kingdoms of Israel and Judah that occurred following Solomon's death in 931 B.C.[18]

The tribe of Judah immediately follows Reuben in this list whereas the tribes of Simeon and Levi intervene between them in Jacob's blessing. The reason, of course, is that Jacob listed his sons in the order of birth whereas Moses followed another (and unclear) principle. Moreover, Jacob's statement requires five verses and Moses' only one. Finally, the messianic role of Judah, which was central in the Jacob blessing, is missing entirely here. No amount of positing late "deuteronomistic" ideology or the like can account for all these differences. It is best to understand that Moses (who, after all, composed both lists) assumed the priority of the Genesis material and its familiarity to his own and later readers and, therefore, viewed his present composition as complementary and/or elucidative.

5. Blessing on Levi (33:8-11)

[8]About Levi he said:
"Your Thummim and Urim belong
  to the man you favored.
You tested him at Massah;
  you contended with him at the waters of Meribah.
[9]He said of his father and mother,
  'I have no regard for them.'
He did not recognize his brothers
  or acknowledge his own children,
but he watched over your word
  and guarded your covenant.
[10]He teaches your precepts to Jacob
  and your law to Israel.
He offers incense before you
  and whole burnt offerings on your altar.
[11]Bless all his skills, O LORD,
  and be pleased with the work of his hands.
Smite the loins of those who rise up against him;
  strike his foes till they rise no more."

In Jacob's blessing Simeon and Levi, the second and third sons of the patriarch by his wife Leah (Gen 29:33-34), are addressed together and not

---

[18] As J. A. Thompson points out, there is nothing here to compel a post-Mosaic composition, for the petition is so general as to be timely for any possible threat to Judah (*Deuteronomy,* TOTC [Leicester: InterVarsity, 1974], 309-10).

favorably (Gen 49:5-7). The whole focus of their father's remarks is on the bloody vengeance they had taken against the Shechemites because their sister Dinah had been violated by the young ruler of Shechem (Gen 34:1-29). There could be no blessing for this, so Jacob cursed his two sons by predicting their dispersion throughout Israel. The effect of this is evident even here in the blessing of Moses because Simeon is lacking entirely in the list, and Levi appears without reference to territory of its own. Moreover, Simeon had already become involved in idolatry at Baal Peor (cf. Num 25:6-15), a sin that brought such devastating population loss that the whole tribe eventually became assimilated into Judah (cf. Josh 19:1-9).[19]

Loss of tribal allotment to Levi did not mean loss of blessing as a whole, however, for what the tribe sacrificed by the intemperate behavior of its father was more than compensated by its election to priestly privilege.[20] Shortly after the Sinai convocation, Moses selected the tribe of Levi for special service in Israel's cultic life (Num 3:5-10). The priesthood would derive from Levi (cf. Exod 6:16-25) as would their assistants, the remainder of the tribe of Levi.

33:8 Moses had this "Levitical covenant" (cf. Mal 2:4,8; Num 25:13) in view in describing Levi as "the man you favored" (Deut 33:8).[21] This is another way of speaking of election (lit., "the man brought into your [covenant] loyalty"). The "Thummim and Urim" were the precious stones of the breastpiece of the chief priest, the purpose of which was to serve as sacred lots by which the will of God could be ascertained (Exod 28:15-30). By synecdoche Moses mentioned this part of the priestly attire as representative of the entire office and function of the priesthood.

Election of the tribe of Levi to special service carried with it, as always, special responsibility and sacrifice. Thus Levi the tribe was tested (*nāsâ*) at Massah (*massâ*, the place of "testing" or "trial"), and the Lord entered into controversy with them at Meribah (*mĕrîbâ*, "the place of

---

[19] Remnants of the tribe of Simeon are mentioned as late as Hezekiah's time (1 Chr 4:34-43), so no appeal to late dating of the list can account for the omission of Simeon here. See C. F. Keil and F. Delitzsch, *Biblical Commentary on the Old Testament: The Pentateuch* (Grand Rapids: Eerdmans, n.d.), 3:500-501.

[20] For arguments asserting the early existence of "Levitical priests," that is, the identification of Israel's priests as Levites, see J. G. McConville, *Law and Theology in Deuteronomy*, JSOTSup 33 (Sheffield: JSOT, 1984), 124-53 (esp. pp. 135-39).

[21] The MT has חֲסִידֶךָ, "your devout (man)." KB (319) suggests reading חַסְדֶּךָ "[the man of] your loyalty," that is, "the man to whom you show [covenant] loyalty." There is, however, no textual warrant for this. Nevertheless, the covenant overtones of the blessing of Levi are most clear (cf. Deut 18:1-8).

contention"). There is some difficulty in meaning here because both Massah (cf. Exod 17:7; Deut 6:16; 9:22; Ps 95:8-9) and Meribah (cf. Num 20:13,24; Ps 106:32) were places in the Sinai desert where Israel tested the Lord and not vice versa. The present text is clear, however, in asserting that the Lord had tested Levi (v. 8c,d). The resolution of this apparent difference in perspective may lie in an implied identification of Levi with Moses, who indeed was at the center of the testing at both Massah and Meribah. That is, the testing of the Lord was shared by Moses and Levi as spokesmen for the Lord.[22] That something like this was in view may be inferred from Ps 81:7, where Israel (or a part thereof) and not the Lord is said to have been tested.

33:9 Another linkage between Levi's testing and the wilderness wandering is hinted at in v. 9, where the incident of the golden calf provides the point of reference. On that occasion Moses had asked "whoever is for the LORD" (Exod 32:26) to come forward and punish the Israelite idolaters even to the extent of "brother and friend and neighbor" (v. 27). Levi volunteered and proceeded to slay their own "sons and brothers" (v. 29). Levi passed the test of obedience and commitment to the Lord by "guarding the covenant" (Deut 33:9c) at the expense of normal filial, fraternal, and paternal affection and obligation.[23] This kind of test is akin to the demand Jesus made of those who would follow him, that they must reject parents, wife, children, brothers, and sisters if necessary in order to be his disciples (cf. Luke 14:26).

33:10 The responsibilities of the Levites would lie primarily in two areas—teaching Torah and offering incense and burnt offerings (v. 10). The latter duty is abundantly attested in the law (cf. Lev 1–7; 9; Num 4; etc.) but that of instruction less so. The technical terms that are used (*mišpāṭim*, "precepts"; *tôrâ*, "law") suggest that the subject matter of the teaching was fundamentally to be the covenant text itself.[24] This is supported by the edict given to Aaron and his sons at the commencement of their priestly ministry that they "teach the Israelites all the decrees (*huqqîm*) the LORD [had] given them through Moses" (Lev 10:11; cf. Deut 31:9-13). This was followed to a greater or lesser extent in subsequent history (cf. 2 Chr 15:3; 17:9; Mic 3:11; Hag 2:11; Mal 2:7), especially in

---

[22] Craigie, *Deuteronomy,* 396.

[23] Driver, *Deuteronomy,* 400-401.

[24] Many scholars either limit this to the interpretation of the Urim and Thummim (so Cairns, *Word and Presence,* 297) or suggest that the text is referring to present practice (i.e., Josianic) rather than what is anticipated (so Mayes, *Deuteronomy,* 403). This is in line with the hypothesis that the ministry of teaching was late in the development of the office of Levite, a hypothesis lacking objective verification.

post-Old Testament times when teaching of Torah became the very center of Judaism.

33:11 The blessing of Levi ends with a prayer that the Lord might enhance Levi's skills (lit., "strength"). The parallel line favors the view that it was Levi's accomplishments as teacher and cultic mediator that concerned Moses and not just his abilities. In order for these to come to fruition, obstacles, including enemies who hated and rose up against God's servants, had to be overcome (v. 11b).[25] To "smite the loins" most likely refers to rendering one impotent, unable to produce progeny, and certainly to undermine his strength (cf. 1 Kgs 12:10; Prov 31:17; Nah 2:2).

6. Blessing on Benjamin (33:12)

[12]**About Benjamin he said:**
"Let the beloved of the LORD rest secure in him,
for he shields him all day long,
and the one the LORD loves rests between his shoulders."

33:12 As the youngest of Jacob's sons, Benjamin appears last in the patriarch's order of blessing (Gen 49:27). Furthermore, like Simeon and Levi he is cast in a negative light, a "ravenous wolf" that devours and plunders. Here he is called the "beloved" of the Lord, a term of endearment (*yādid*) particularly appropriate to Benjamin given the special place the eponymous ancestor enjoyed in the eyes of his father Jacob (cf. Gen 42:38; 43:14). His hope was to rest (or dwell; Heb. *šākan*) on the Lord, the one who shelters (ptc. *ḥāpap,* hapax) him. In fact, Benjamin would rest (or dwell, again, as in v. la) between Yahweh's shoulders. The anthropomorphism here is suggestive of the most tender compassion and solid security at the same time. The phrase speaks not of carrying on the back but of being held close to the breast or bosom.[26] The Hebrew noun *ḥêq* expresses the idea more explicitly, frequently occurring as a picture of parental love and protection (cf. Num 11:12; Ruth 4:16; 2 Sam 12:3; Isa 40:11). The most touching example of all, however, is that of John, who

---

[25] See D. L. Christensen, "Dtn 33, 11—A Curse in the 'Blessing of Moses?'" *ZAW* 101 (1989): 278-82.

[26] Cross and Freedman draw attention to the Ug. parallelism *ktp // bn ydm* ("bosom" // "between the arms"; CTA 2iv 14-22) and the similar idea here. Ug. *ktp* is cognate to Heb. כָּתֵף, both terms referring in context to the lap (Cross and Freedman, *Studies in Ancient Yahwistic Poetry,* 114-15).

reclined on Jesus' bosom (Gr. *kolmos*), a sign of the closest fellowship (John 13:23).

7. Blessing on Joseph (33:13-17)

[13]About Joseph he said:
"May the LORD bless his land
  with the precious dew from heaven above
  and with the deep waters that lie below;
[14]with the best the sun brings forth
  and the finest the moon can yield;
[15]with the choicest gifts of the ancient mountains
  and the fruitfulness of the everlasting hills;
[16]with the best gifts of the earth and its fullness
  and the favor of him who dwelt in the burning bush.
Let all these rest on the head of Joseph,
  on the brow of the prince among his brothers.
[17]In majesty he is like a firstborn bull;
  his horns are the horns of a wild ox.
With them he will gore the nations,
  even those at the ends of the earth.
Such are the ten thousands of Ephraim;
  such are the thousands of Manasseh."

Jacob's blessing of Joseph, not surprisingly, just precedes the blessing of Benjamin (Gen 49:22-26) whereas here it immediately follows. Also not surprising is the consistently affirmative tone of both passages, one that views Joseph as "a prince among his brothers" (Gen 49:20; cf. Deut 33:16) and the recipient of untold blessings from the Lord. The resemblances between the two texts are so close, in fact, that there can be no doubt that Moses "borrowed" lavishly from his own previous composition in Genesis.

33:13-14   The petition Moses made for Joseph (actually, of course, the two tribes of Ephraim and Manasseh) is divided between a wish for the fertility and productivity of land (vv. 13-16) and another for strength by which Joseph might be the means of the Lord's judgment of the nations (v. 17). In the aridity of the Palestinian littoral, rain was in short supply, so a need existed for heavy deposits of dew (cf. Gen 27:28; 2 Sam 1:21; 1 Kgs 17:1; Prov 3:20; 19:12; Isa 18:4; Hos 14:5) and for springs and wells that tapped into the underground reservoirs of water typical of limestone formation (thus the Heb. *těhôm* here (cf. Gen 49:25; Ps 33:7; Prov 8:28).[27] The result of ample moisture was abundant crops, the best (or most precious; Heb. *meged*) the sun and moon could produce (v. 14).

The participation of the moon is only to provide a literary parallel to the sun in this poetic couplet (cf. Josh 10:12-13; Ps 121:6).

33:15-16 The "choicest gifts" (lit., "the best of"; Heb. *rōʾš*) of the mountains and hills may be either the agricultural produce just referred to or mineral reserves extracted from the earth (v. 15).[28] The latter is more likely because (1) mountains and hills are not normally associated with agriculture; (2) iron, copper, and other minerals appear elsewhere as a bounty of the land of Canaan (cf. Deut 8:9); and (3) "the best gifts of the earth" (v. 15a) would needlessly repeat the promise of agricultural blessing. Regardless, all the aforementioned proceed from him who dwelt in the bush (Heb. *sĕneh*), that is, in the burning bush at Sinai (cf. Exod 3:2-4).[29] It was he, Yahweh, who first revealed himself to Moses at that place by the covenant name "I AM" (Exod 3:14). By that name he would bless Joseph as a token of his covenant faithfulness.

In most arresting imagery Moses implored God to make all of these blessings a crown on Joseph's head, a diadem attesting to his preeminence among the tribes (v. 16c,d). This role already was apparent to Jacob (Gen 49:26), who no doubt remembered well the dream in which Joseph saw his entire family bow low before him (Gen 37:5-11). Subsequent events revealed the fulfillment of the dream, both in terms of Joseph's personal rise to power (Gen 42:6-9) and the importance of the tribes of Ephraim and Manasseh in the era of Israel's monarchy.

Not only would Joseph's brother tribes recognize this importance, but it would be clear also to the nations at large. Like a firstborn bull (thus DSS, LXX, SP, Syr, Vg) or a wild ox, he would rise to ascendancy and exercise dominion (thus thrusting with a horn; cf. Heb. *nāgaḥ* in 1 Kgs 22:11; Ps 44:5; Ezek 34:21; Dan 8:4; 11:40). The broad dimensions of this promise (to "the ends of the earth," Heb. *ʾapsê ʾāreṣ*) suggests an

---

[27] The verb describing the positioning of the deep is רָבַץ, usually rendered "to couch [like an animal]." There may indeed be mythopoeic overtones of a primeval monster (Sumero-Babylonian Ti'amat = Heb. תְּהוֹם, "the deep") ready to spring, but those allusions recede into the background here. Only the subterranean wells are in view. See Driver, *Deuteronomy,* 406; cf. Cross and Freedman, *Studies in Ancient Yahwistic Poetry,* 115, for the opinion that תְּהוֹם is personified here.

[28] N. M. Waldman, "The Wealth of Mountain and Sea: The Background of a Biblical Image," *JQR* 71 (1982): 176-80; cf. N. A. vanUchelen, "The Targumic Versions of Deuteronomy 33:15: Some Remarks on the Origin of a Traditional Exegesis," *JJS* 31 (1980): 199-209.

[29] Some scholars, because of the unexpected reference to the bush (only here in the OT apart from Exod 3), emend סְנֶה ("bush") to סִינַי ("Sinai"), a suggestion with no manuscript or versional support. See M. A. Beek, "Der Dornbusch als Wohnsitz Gottes (Deut. xxxiii 16)," *OTS* 14 (Leiden: Brill, 1965), 155-61.

eschatological rather than historical fulfillment, a time when God's kingdom would rise above and rule over the kingdoms of the earth (cf. 1 Sam 2:10; Pss 2:8; 59:13; 72:8; Mic 5:4). Such were the prospects of the innumerable hosts of Ephraim and Manasseh, the blessed offspring of Joseph (cf. Gen 48:19-20).

8. Blessing on Zebulun and Issachar (33:18-19)

¹⁸About Zebulun he said:
"Rejoice, Zebulun, in your going out,
and you, Issachar, in your tents.
¹⁹They will summon peoples to the mountain
and there offer sacrifices of righteousness;
they will feast on the abundance of the seas,
on the treasures hidden in the sand."

33:18-19 Zebulun and Issachar, the sixth and fifth sons of Jacob by Leah (Gen 30:18,20), appear in that order in both the blessing of Jacob (Gen 49:13-15) and here. Otherwise where the two sons or tribes are mentioned together in the same list, Issachar precedes Zebulun. The reason for the reversal of the names in both blessing lists is not clear, but it does offer support for the idea of dependence of one passage on the other (presumably Deuteronomy on Genesis) and for common authorship.

As the last two sons of Leah, Issachar and Zebulun no doubt were closely linked within the family, a linkage that continued as tribes in Canaan as witnessed by their common border in the northern part of the land. Issachar was just north of Manasseh; and Zebulun, between Issachar to the south and Asher and Naphtali to the north. Their close juxtaposition prompted Moses to pronounce a common blessing on them but with comments especially pertinent to each one individually.

Both were exhorted to rejoice, Zebulun in going out and Issachar remaining still (i.e., "in your tents"). This figure, a merism, includes all possible activities and modes of life.[30] Moses thus was invoking upon both tribes a joy and satisfaction in all they undertook to do. With Issachar specifically in mind, the blessing spoke of assembling peoples to the hill country where they would offer proper sacrifices (or, as NIV, "sacrifices of righteousness"; for ṣedeq as "right" or "normal," cf. Lev 19:36; Deut 25:15; Job 31:6; Ezek 45:10). This is most likely a reference to the

---

[30] Thus Driver, *Deuteronomy,* 408.

Yahweh shrine at Mount Tabor, which, though later condemned (Hos 5:1), may have served as a local place of worship in pretemple times.[31]

Feasting on (better "drawing out from"; Heb. *yānaq*) the seas and from the sands (v. 19b) conjures up imagery of a maritime industry, a way of life appropriate to Zebulun, whose western border was, from time to time, the Mediterranean Sea. Jacob blessed his son Zebulun by promising that he would "live by the seashore and become a haven for ships" (Gen 49:13). While this cannot be documented as having taken place in biblical times, the promise has found startling fulfillment in the modern state of Israel, whose major port is Haifa, located in the area of ancient Zebulun.

9. Blessing on Gad (33:20-21)

20About Gad he said:
 "Blessed is he who enlarges Gad's domain!
 Gad lives there like a lion,
  tearing at arm or head.
21He chose the best land for himself;
  the leader's portion was kept for him.
 When the heads of the people assembled,
  he carried out the LORD'S righteous will,
  and his judgments concerning Israel."

33:20-21 The blessing of Gad by both Jacob (Gen 49:19) and Moses centers on Gad's militancy, in the former defensively and here more offensively. Moses celebrated the goodness of the Lord who had enlarged Gad (i.e., its territory, as in NIV; cf. Exod 34:24; Deut 12:20; 19:8; Isa 54:2; Amos 1:13) and equipped him to live (there) in strength and security (v. 20). With the ferocity of a lion he defended himself, tearing (*ṭārap*) to shreds any who dared to encroach upon him (cf. Num 23:24; Pss 7:2; 17:12; Isa 38:13; Jer 49:19; Ezek 22:25; Hos 13:7-8).

Gad's choosing the best (land) for himself (Deut 33:21a) calls to mind the circumstances by which that tribe, as well as Reuben and half the tribe of Mannaseh, received its territorial allotment. Having seen (thus Heb. *rāʾâ* for NIV "chose") the lush and desirable lands of the Transjordan, these tribes had requested Moses to allow them to settle there, a request to which the lawgiver somewhat grudgingly acceded (Num 32:1-5). Reuben occupied the southern part, Gad the central, roughly between the Dead Sea and the Sea of Chinnereth (or Galilee), and Manasseh the northern

---

[31] G. von Rad, *Deuteronomy,* OTL (Philadelphia: Westminster, 1966), 207; cf. Z. Weisman, "Connecting Link in an Old Hymn: Deuteronomy 33:19a, 21b," *VT* 28 (1978): 365-68.

part. Gad's area was by far the largest and best, conforming well to its description as "the leader's portion"[32] (lit., "the portion of the inscriber of laws"; thus the *po'el* ptc. of *ḥāqaq*).

10. Blessing on Dan (33:22)

[22] About Dan he said:
"Dan is a lion's cub,
  springing out of Bashan."

33:22 This very brief statement about the tribe of Dan shares with Jacob's blessing (Gen 49:16-17) not only brevity but animal metaphors. The Genesis text views Dan as a snake by the roadside that bites horses' heels, causing them to fall with their riders. Here Dan is the offspring of a lion (Heb. *ʾaryê*; cf. *lābîʾ*, v. 20), the role of which is unstated. All that is known is that Dan would leap forth (*zānaq*) from Bashan.[33] Though highly speculative, one might associate this with the conquest of Laish by the Danites (cf. Judg 18:27-28), a conquest that could have sprung ultimately from Bashan, just to the east of Laish.

11. Blessing on Naphtali (33:23)

[23] About Naphtali he said:
"Naphtali is abounding with the favor of the LORD
  and is full of his blessing;
  he will inherit southward to the lake."

33:23 The last two tribes of the blessing of Moses—Naphtali and Asher—share in common the fact that they were descendants of the last two sons of Jacob by the concubines Bilhah and Zilpah respectively (cf. Gen 30:7-8,12-13). After the conquest of Canaan they also enjoyed geographical contiguity with Asher being located along the Mediterranean north of Zebulun and Naphtali east of Asher and north and west of the Sea of Chinnereth.

Naphtali appears as a highly favored people, "a doe set free that bears beautiful fawns" in the colorful language of Jacob's prediction (Gen 49:21). Here the tribe is seen as one satiated (so Heb. *śĕbaʿ*) with the Lord's good pleasure (*rāṣôn*), filled up (so *mālēʾ*) with his blessing. A

---

[32] H. Ringgren, "חקק *ḥaqaq*," etc. *TDOT* 5:141 ("commander").

[33] Cross and Freedman propose *bašan*, a serpent or viper, on the basis of Ug. *btn* and Arab. *btn* (*Studies in Ancient Yahwistic Poetry*, 119). They note that Dan is called a snake also in Gen 49:17.

token of this special grace was Naphtali's favorable location, one that extended "southward to the lake." This difficult phrase (lit., "take possession of sea and south") probably is to be construed as in the NIV, "southward to the lake" (the Heb. construction being epexegetical). This in any case eliminates the Mediterranean and suits Chinnereth very well. The Galilee region embraced by Naphtali did indeed enjoy many temporal and material riches (cf. Josh 20:7; 2 Chr 16:4; Isa 9:1), but by far the most abundant blessing was the fact that the Messiah spent most of his life and exercised much of his ministry there or in nearby Zebulun (cf. Matt 4:12-17). One can scarcely imagine greater evidence of divine favor.

12. Blessing on Asher (33:24-25)

[24]About Asher he said:
"Most blessed of sons is Asher;
  let him be favored by his brothers,
  and let him bathe his feet in oil.
[25]The bolts of your gates will be iron and bronze,
  and your strength will equal your days.

33:24-25 Jacob had prophesied that Asher would be the source of "delicacies fit for a king" (Gen 49:20), a sentiment shared here by Moses. In fact, the very name Asher (Heb. *ʾāšēr*) is based on a root meaning "happiness" or "blessedness" (Heb. *ʾešer*). It is not surprising then that Moses spoke of this tribe as blessed above all others, one especially favored by his brother tribes. The full extent of this blessing is expressed in the hyperbole of bathing (lit., "dipping"; *ṭābal*) one's foot in oil. While one may understand this in terms of literal oil, such as that of the olive groves so famous in the region, it is preferable in light of the poetic character of the text to take oil (*šemen*) as a metaphor for prosperity in general, a meaning well attested throughout Scripture (cf. Deut 32:13; Job 29:6).[34]

This interpretation finds support in v. 25, where the iron and bronze gate bolts of Asher's fortifications are compared to his strength (thus Heb. *dōbeʾ* on basis of the LXX). That is, these unbreakable bolts are figurative expressions for Asher's invincibility. As long as the tribe lived, it would enjoy the Lord's blessing of protection (lit., "as your days, so your strength").

13. A General Praise and Blessing on Israel (33:26-29)

---

[34] Craigie, *Deuteronomy*, 401-2.

²⁶"There is no one like the God of Jeshurun,
  who rides on the heavens to help you
  and on the clouds in his majesty.
²⁷The eternal God is your refuge,
  and underneath are the everlasting arms.
He will drive out your enemy before you,
  saying, 'Destroy him!'
²⁸So Israel will live in safety alone;
  Jacob's spring is secure
in a land of grain and new wine,
  where the heavens drop dew.
²⁹Blessed are you, O Israel!
  Who is like you,
  a people saved by the LORD?
He is your shield and helper
  and your glorious sword.
Your enemies will cower before you,
  and you will trample down their high places."

33:26 Moses' blessing of the twelve tribes separately reached its climax in his blessing of the nation collectively. The incomparable "God of Jeshurun" (cf. 32:15; 33:5; Isa 44:2), who rides on the heavens as kings going to war ride on their mighty chargers, was Israel's helper (v. 26). The image of Yahweh riding on the heavens and clouds (*šāmayîm* and *šĕḥā-qîm*) is mythopoeic anthropomorphism adapted, no doubt, from pagan epic sources but with intensely polemic overtones against the depravity of pagan religious conception.[35] The point was that it was not really Baal (or any other god) who rode in triumph in the heavens above, but it was the Lord alone who did so, he who is unique and solitary (cf. Pss 18:10; 68:33; 104:3).

33:27-28 God the helper (*ʿēzer*) is also God the refuge (*maʿôn*; cf. Pss 90:1; 91:9) who eternally exists to bear up his people (Deut 33:27a). A tender expression of this loving care occurs in Isa 40:11:

> He tends his flock like a shepherd:
>   He gathers the lambs in his arms
> and carries them close to his heart;
>   he gently leads those that have young.

---

[35] F. M. Cross and D. N. Freedman, "A Note on Deuteronomy 33:26," *BASOR* 108 (1947): 6-7.

In a more aggressive manner the arm of the Lord was stretched out against his (and Israel's) foes, an arm that punished evil and yet provided security to his own (cf. Deut 4:34; 5:15; 7:19; 9:29; 11:2; 26:8).

It is this aspect of the Lord's power that accompanied his role of Divine Warrior, the one who drove out Israel's enemies and gave Israel the authority to destroy them (v. 27b; cf. Exod 34:11; Deut 4:38; 7:22; 9:3-5; 11:23; 18:12; 28:36-37). It is clear by now that a subtle history of salvation emerges from this final blessing. The driving out of v. 27 gives way to peaceful and secure occupation of the promised land (v. 28). In isolation (thus Heb. *bādād*; cf. Num 23:9; Ps 4:8; Jer 49:31; Mic 7:14) Israel would live in safety. This suggests that God's people would never need fear being crowded out by other occupants of the land. They would be alone in that respect but obviously not entirely, for the Lord would be with them.

The rather puzzling "Jacob's spring" (v. 28b) does not pertain to springs of water in the land but, as the parallelism makes plain, is a synonym for Israel itself.[36] It is a figurative way of describing Jacob's offspring, the descendants of his sons who came to comprise the nation Israel.[37] They would live in a land of abundance of crops and of life-giving moisture, a land described elsewhere as one "flowing with milk and honey" (cf. Gen 27:28; Exod 3:8,17; Lev 20:24; Num 13:27; Deut 6:3; 11:9; 26:9,15; 27:3; 31:20; 32:13).

33:29 The blessing of all Israel ends with a note of triumphant hope for the nation, a people unique in all the earth for having been delivered from bondage by the Lord (v. 29a; cf. Deut 4:32-40). Salvation in the past provides confidence for the present, for the God who redeemed is the Shield, Helper (cf. v. 26), and Sword of Israel. He not only provides these things but in himself he embodies them (cf. Ps 115:9-11). The future was, therefore, bright as well. On the eve of conquest it was assuring to know that Yahweh, the Divine Warrior (cf. v. 27), would lead his elect nation to victory. Their enemies would submit to them, and they would tread upon the high places of their foes (v. 29b,c).

This last figure is that of a conqueror who places his foot upon his vanquished and fallen adversary as a sign of absolute dominion (cf. Gen 49:8; Josh 10:24). The verb "trample" (Heb. *dārak*) occurs frequently to speak of the exercise of sovereignty over peoples and lands or even over nature itself (Deut 1:36; 11:24-25; Josh 1:3; 14:9; Amos 4:13; Mic 1:3;

---

[36] See D. N. Freedman, "The Original Name of Jacob," *IEJ* 13 (1963): 125-26.

[37] J. Ridderbos, *Deuteronomy,* BSC (Grand Rapids: Zondervan, 1984), 312.

5:4; Hab 3:15; cf. Job 1:7; 2:2).[38] In light of the combination of conquest and dominion, it is better to understand *bāmôt* not as "high places" but as "backs," a rendering supported by comparative Semitic lexicography (cf. Ug. *bmt*, Akk. *bāmtu*; KB, 132).[39] The mythopoeic language of the passage as a whole (cf. v. 26) favors this view as does the parallelism of cringing ("cower"; Heb. *kāḥaš*) and trampling on the back. The couplet may perhaps be rendered:

> Your enemies will be forced to prostrate before you;
> You will then trample upon their backs.

In any case, Israel's prospects, despite their historical shortcomings, were optimistic indeed, for the Lord would assure ultimate triumph.

---

[38] J. L. Crenshaw, "*Wĕdōrēk al-bāmŏtê ʾāreṣ*," *CBQ* 34 (1972): 39-53 (esp. 46).
[39] K.-D. Schunck, "בָּמָה *bamah*," *TDOT* 2:140.

XIII. NARRATIVE EPILOGUE (34:1-12)
    1. The Death of Moses (34:1-8)
    2. The Epitaph of Moses (34:9-12)

XIII. NARRATIVE EPILOGUE (34:1-12)

1. The Death of Moses (34:1-8)

[1]Then Moses climbed Mount Nebo from the plains of Moab to the top of Pisgah, across from Jericho. There the LORD showed him the whole land— from Gilead to Dan, [2]all of Naphtali, the territory of Ephraim and Manasseh, all the land of Judah as far as the western sea, [3]the Negev and the whole region from the Valley of Jericho, the City of Palms, as far as Zoar. [4]Then the LORD said to him, "This is the land I promised on oath to Abraham, Isaac and Jacob when I said, 'I will give it to your descendants.' I have let you see it with your eyes, but you will not cross over into it."

[5]And Moses the servant of the LORD died there in Moab, as the LORD had said. [6]He buried him in Moab, in the valley opposite Beth Peor, but to this day no one knows where his grave is. [7]Moses was a hundred and twenty years old when he died, yet his eyes were not weak nor his strength gone. [8]The Israelites grieved for Moses in the plains of Moab thirty days, until the time of weeping and mourning was over.

34:1-3 In a previous narrative section (32:48-52) Moses was commanded to ascend Mount Nebo to view the promised land before he died. The epilogue to the Book of Deuteronomy relates the fulfillment of that command.[1] Most ironically, Moses had begun his ministry of covenant mediator at a mountain—Mount Sinai (or Horeb)—and now he ended that ministry on another. The mountain in question was a part of a range of mountains east of the Dead Sea and Jordan, the so-called Abarim (Deut 32:49; cf. Num 27:12; 33:47-48). Pisgah apparently was the north and west part of this mountainous area, perhaps the part sloping west (thus

---

[1] For the literary and historical issues involved, see R. Lux, "Der Tod des Mose als 'besprochene und erzählte Welte': literaturwissenschaftliche und theologische Interpretation von Deut. 32:48-52 und 34," *ZTK* 84 (1987): 395-425; G. W. Coats, "Legendary Motifs in the Moses Death Reports," *CBQ* 39 (1977): 34-44.

ʾašdôt happisgâ, "the slopes of Pisgah"; Josh 13:20). Nebo, then, would have been a prominent peak at the top of the Pisgah slope, one from which the entire Cis-Jordan could be viewed. It is identified as Jebel Es-Siyâgha today, some five miles southwest of Tel Hesban and about fifteen miles east of Jericho.[2]

From there Moses could see the whole land.[3] The vista before him is described in a counterclockwise direction (vv. 1b-3)—Gilead, just to the north; Dan, a hundred miles to the north; Naphtali, eighty to a hundred miles to the northwest; Ephraim and Manasseh, to the northwest; Judah to the west and southwest as far as the western (that is, Mediterranean) sea; the Negev desert to the southwest; and everything from Jericho to Zoar (that is, the entire length of the Dead Sea), to the immediate southwest and south. It is obvious that some of these place names are latter additions to the text (e.g., Dan, Naphtali, Ephraim, Manasseh, Judah) inasmuch as they would not have been assigned to these sites until after the conquest, some years following Moses' death.

34:4 All that Moses could see in the panorama before him was promised by covenant oath to the patriarchs (v. 4a). It was Yahweh's pledge based on the royal grant he had first made with Abraham, an unconditional act of grace as sure of fulfillment as the very character of God himself (cf. Gen 12:1,7; 13:15; 15:18; 26:3; 28:13; Deut 1:8,21,25). In line with the original geographical parameters of the land as described to Abraham—"from the river of Egypt [i.e., the Wadi el-Arish] to the great river, the Euphrates" (Gen 15:18)—the reaffirmation to Moses included a territory of more than four hundred miles from southwest to northeast and on both sides of the Jordan. The only time in Old Testament history that this ideal ever reached realization was in the heyday of the United Monarchy under David and Solomon (cf. 2 Sam 10:19; 1 Kgs 4:24). Ezekiel's eschatological vision also anticipated a day when the promise to Abraham would find a geographical fulfillment of such a vast extent (Ezek 47:13-48:29).

Tragically, Moses was once more to hear the words of Yahweh denying him access to all he saw before him (v. 4b; cf. Num 20:12; 27:14; Deut 1:37; 3:26-27). The prohibition here was very simple—"You will not

---

[2] M. Piccirillo, "Les découvertes du Nebo: Aout 1976," *Bible et Terre Sainte* 188 (1977): 6-19; J. E. Jennings, "Nebo," *The New International Dictionary of Biblical Archaeology,* ed. E. M. Blaiklock and R. K. Harrison (Grand Rapids: Zondervan, 1983), 331-32.

[3] M. Weinfeld, "The Extent of the Promised Land—The Status of Transjordan," in *Das Land Israel in biblischer Zeit,* ed. G. Strecker (Göttingen: Vandenhoeck & Ruprecht, 1983), 67-70.

cross over into it"—but there no reason was stated. This, of course, was not necessary since Moses had heard it many times (cf. Deut 32:51). Moreover, this final narrative of the book is overwhelmingly commendatory of Moses; there was no point to underscoring the sin that precluded his entry into Canaan, for this would work against the otherwise positive portrayal. On the other hand, it was impossible to ignore the fact that he died east of the promised land, unable to do more than look longingly upon it.

34:5-8 The account of Moses' death and burial is both succinct and mysterious (vv. 5-8). In mitigating terms he is called "the servant of the LORD" (v. 5), a designation few others were privileged to bear (cf. Josh 24:29; Judg 2:8; 2 Sam 3:18; 7:5,8; 1 Kgs 11:13; 14:8; 2 Kgs 18:12; 19:34; 21:8; Job 1:8; 42:8; Isa 20:3; 41:8-9; 42:1; 44:1; 52:13; 53:11).[4] He might be barred from Canaan and even sentenced to death on Nebo, but he was Yahweh's servant nonetheless. He was buried (lit., "he [i.e., Yahweh] buried him) in an unmarked grave in "the valley opposite Beth Peor" (v. 6), that is, just north of Pisgah.

Later Jewish tradition speaks of the peculiar circumstances surrounding Moses' burial as does the New Testament.[5] Jude relates a confrontation between the archangel Michael and the devil over Moses' body (Jude 9), a dispute apparently having to do with Yahweh's purpose for burying Moses in a secret place to begin with.[6] Most likely the sepulchre remained hidden precisely to prevent the Israelites from taking Moses' body with them to Canaan, thus violating the divine command to disallow Moses entry there. His subsequent appearances to witnesses do little to alleviate the enigmatic character of his death and interment, but they do reveal in a most magnificent manner the reality of the ongoing existence of God's saints and of his everlasting grace toward them (cf. Matt 17:3; Mark 9:4; Luke 9:30; Rev 11:1-13[?]).

That Moses' death was premature, even though he was 120 years old, is clear from the assessment that "his eyes were not weak nor his strength

---

[4] P. D. Miller, Jr., "Moses My Servant: The Deuteronomic Portrait of Moses," *Int* 41 (1987): 245-55.

[5] S. Schwertner, "Erwagungen zu Moses Tod und Grab in Dtn 34:5, 6," *ZAW* 84 (1972): 25-45; E. Starobinski–Safran, "La Mort et la Survie de Moise d'apres la Tradition Rabbinique," *La Figure de Moise,* ed. R. Martin–Achard et al. (Genève: Éditions Labor et Fides, 1978), 31-45.

[6] For the legendary and midrashic texts to which Jude may have been appealing, see B. Reicke, *The Epistles of James, Peter, and Jude,* AB 37 (Garden City: Doubleday, 1964), 202-3.

gone" (v. 7).[7] In other words, he did not fail to enter Canaan because he died, but he died because he failed to enter Canaan. Regardless, the people of Israel rightly viewed him for what he was—a mighty champion for Yahweh—and so they accorded him all the rites and ceremonies appropriate to the demise of such a leader (v. 8; cf. Num 20:29).

2. The Epitaph of Moses (34:9-12)

⁹Now Joshua son of Nun was filled with the spirit of wisdom because Moses had laid his hands on him. So the Israelites listened to him and did what the LORD had commanded Moses.

¹⁰Since then, no prophet has risen in Israel like Moses, whom the LORD knew face to face, ¹¹who did all those miraculous signs and wonders the LORD sent him to do in Egypt—to Pharaoh and to all his officials and to his whole land. ¹²For no one has ever shown the mighty power or performed the awesome deeds that Moses did in the sight of all Israel.

For many years it had been apparent that Joshua son of Nun would someday succeed Moses as covenant mediator and leader of his people. He first appeared as a commander of Israel's fighting men, leading them to victory over the Amalekites under Moses' direction (Exod 17:8-16). After the giving of the covenant at Sinai, Joshua, designated as the "aide" (*na'ar*) of Moses, began to assert a greater spiritual role by partially ascending the holy mountain with Moses to receive the stone tablets of the Decalogue (Exod 24:12-13). Thereafter he continued this close covenant association (Exod 32:17; 33:11), always concerned to maintain Moses' leadership and to carry out his bidding (Num 11:28; 13:16; 14:6-10). When it was disclosed that Moses could not enter the land of Canaan, the mantel of leadership fell on Joshua, who, from that day forward, prepared himself with that responsibility in view (Num 20:12; 26:65; 27:15-23; 34:17; Deut 1:38; 3:28; 31:3-8,14-23).

34:9 The formal act by which the community understood that Joshua was Moses' successor was the ceremony of "laying on of hands," a rite that symbolized the transference of covenant authority and responsibility from the one to the other. This physical demonstration either accompanied the impartation of the divine Spirit or marked the recipient as one already endowed by that Spirit (v. 9). Thus after Moses had been told that he could not lead the people into the promised land, he was told to "take

---

[7] W. F. Albright, "The 'Natural Force' of Moses in the Light of Ugaritic," *BASOR* 94 (1944): 32-35.

Joshua son of Nun, a man in whom is the spirit, and lay your hand on him" (Num 27:18; cf. Num 11:16-30; 1 Sam 10:1,10; 16:13).

The principal gift of the Spirit here was wisdom, a necessary endowment if Joshua was to be able to take Moses' place and successfully complete the conquest and occupation of Canaan. The "spirit of wisdom" (i.e., the spirit that bestows wisdom) appears elsewhere in the Scriptures to meet similar needs (Exod 28:3; 31:3-6; 1 Kgs 4:29; 5:12; 7:14; 2 Chr 1:10-12; Isa 11:2; Acts 6:3; Eph 1:17). However that ministry of the Spirit might manifest itself in general, it was clear to Israel that Joshua was now properly certified and equipped to stand in Moses' place as leader of the community (v. 9b; cf. Josh 1:17).

34:10-12 The words of praise and adulation of Moses that complete this section (vv. 10-12) have, with the previous reference to his death (vv. 5-8), convinced nearly all thoughtful students that Moses himself could not have written this last part of Deuteronomy. As noted in the Introduction, the Mosaic authorship of the book as a whole is not thereby jeopardized, for there is no reason to deny the rest of it to him and, indeed, Deut 34:5-12 could well be a post-Mosaic addendum to the book which, until the addition, was entirely of Mosaic authorship.

Whoever may have penned vv. 10-12 reflected back on Moses as a prophet without compare, one whom Yahweh knew "face to face" (v. 10). This intimacy is reminiscent of the challenge to Moses' preeminence as a prophet by his sister and brother, who accused Moses of arrogating prophetic privilege only to himself (Num 12:2). Part of Yahweh's response to this challenge was that there were, indeed, other prophets (Miriam and Aaron included); but only to Moses did Yahweh speak "face to face" (Num 12:8).[8]

Moreover, no other prophet had till then performed such signs and wonders (ʾōtôt and môp̌ĕtîm; cf. Exod 7:3; Deut 4:34; 6:22; 7:19; 26:8; 29:3; Neh 9:10; Ps 78:43; 105:27), awesome displays to Pharaoh and all Egypt that Yahweh alone is God (v. 11). Nor was their effect intended only for the pagan world. Israel also needed to be reminded over and over again of the power and protection of Yahweh manifested through his humble and faithful servant Moses (v. 12). It is no less true today that the unbelieving world as well as the church depends to a great extent upon faithful servants of the Lord to make him known in his saving and sovereign purposes.

---

[8] S. R. Driver, *A Critical and Exegetical Commentary on Deuteronomy*, ICC (Edinburgh: T & T Clark, 1902), 425.

Selected Subject Index

Person Index

Scripture Index